THE REPUBLICAN
PARTY OF TEXAS

A Political History

WAYNE THORBURN

UNIVERSITY OF TEXAS PRESS
Austin

Publication of this work was made possible in part by support
from the J. E. Smothers, Sr., Memorial Foundation and the
National Endowment for the Humanities.

Requests for permission to reproduce material from this work should be sent to:
Permissions
University of Texas Press
P.O. Box 7819
Austin, TX 78713-7819
utpress.utexas.edu/rp-form

∞ The paper used in this book meets the minimum requirements of
ANSI/NISO Z39.48-1992 (R1997) (Permanence of Paper).

Library of Congress Cataloging-in-Publication Data
Names: Thorburn, Wayne J. (Wayne Jacob), 1944– author.
Title: The Republican Party of Texas : a political history / Wayne Thorburn.
Description: First edition. | Austin : University of Texas Press, 2021. | Includes index.
Identifiers: LCCN 2020033422
ISBN 978-1-4773-2251-2 (cloth)
ISBN 978-1-4773-2252-9 (library ebook)
ISBN 978-1-4773-2253-6 (non-library ebook)
Subjects: LCSH: Republican Party (Tex.)—History. | Texas—Politics and government.
Classification: LCC JK2358.T49 T48 2021 | DDC 324.2764/0409—dc23
LC record available at https://lccn.loc.gov/2020033422

doi:10.7560/322512

CONTENTS

CONTENTS

PREFACE

Political histories tend to focus on the important leader, frequently an elected official whose performance in office set the stage for a period. For Texas, there is a wealth of strong leaders who left their mark on the state and, in many instances, the nation. From Sam Houston, to John Tower and Bill Clements, to Bush father and son, and on to Rick Perry, there is no question but that each of these individuals had an impact on Texas politics, the economy, and society. Yet the reality is that none of them would have attained public office without the existence of a foundation of support, a lasting and permanent political party dependent on the time, talent, and treasure of thousands of citizen volunteers. Any history of Lone Star Republicans must recognize several key elected officials and candidates, but it must also acknowledge those who built and maintained the party organization at the precinct, county, and state levels through disappointment as well as success.

For the first one hundred years of the Texas Republican Party, elected officials were few and far between. Those who kept the party alive during these dark days as candidates, contributors, and party officials did so mainly out of a commitment to philosophical principle, family loyalties, and a concern for good government. True, some were motivated by the appeal of federal patronage but this existed only when the Republicans controlled the White House. Most Republicans knew that they were fighting on principle and realized, despite the infrequent surges of optimism, that their chances for electoral success in Texas were slight. Only by the middle of the twentieth century did Republicans begin to see the possibility of electoral success.

Throughout this work I have attempted to take note of the important contributions of these dedicated volunteers who made sure that there would be a permanent party organization in Texas, preparing the foundation for the day when Republicans might win county, state, and national office. While many dedicated individuals could be cited, two outstanding volunteers in particular served as mentors and provided me with the opportunity to help create a Texas Republican Party that would become the dominant force in state politics by the end of the twentieth century. Ray A. Barnhart worked tirelessly to involve more citizens in the party and to show that there was only one home for Texas conservatives. Barnhart was state chairman from 1977 to 1979, at the time when the first Republican governor in 104 years was elected. Chester R. Upham Jr. followed as state chairman from 1979 to 1983 during the first term of Governor William P. Clements Jr. and the election of Ronald Reagan as president. With differing personalities and backgrounds, they both contributed greatly to the unveiling of a competitive conservative Republican Party in Texas. This work is dedicated to the memory of two kind, considerate, and politically astute volunteer leaders whose friendship and support meant much to me. I would be amiss if I didn't recognize also the efforts of Ernest Angelo Jr., Republican national committeeman from 1976 to 1996 and a key ally and supporter of responsible conservative forces within the party both here in Texas and nationally. These three individuals are representative of the many thousands of volunteers who labored in the field to build the Republican Party of Texas over many years.

NINETEENTH-CENTURY REPUBLICANISM

Oⁿ a typically hot summer day in Houston, well before air conditioning, a few hundred men gathered at the Harris County courthouse. It was July 4, 1867, the disastrous war had only recently ended, and they assembled not solely to give thanks for the peace or to look farther back and celebrate the founding of the American republic, but more specifically to create a political entity that would reflect their many hopes and dreams for their nation and their state. On that momentous day these men from various parts of the relatively young state would organize the Republican Party of Texas and affiliate their new political organization with the national party dedicated to promoting free soil, free labor, and free men.

The Republican Party was formed at Ripon, Wisconsin, in 1854, and it was not until some thirteen years later that the party would come into existence in Texas. This is not surprising, in that this new party was firmly against slavery and in favor of preserving the Union. Although there were a number of political leaders opposed to secession, not the least of whom was Governor Sam Houston, none were willing to associate with what was perceived as a small, new, northern party prior to the end of the Civil War.[1] With secession and the coming of war, those who had been opposed to leaving the Union took differing paths. Some allowed their loyalty to the state to lead them to join the Confederate forces, while others fought on the Union side. Many left the state, while those who stayed either remained quiet or were viewed as traitors to the southern cause. When the Confederacy fell and the Union was preserved, these Unionists were to temporarily play important roles in the reconstruction of civil government in Texas and in the creation of the Republican Party of Texas.

The process of rejoining the Union and reestablishing state government took many turns and twists throughout the ten years from 1865 to 1875. As the war ended in 1865, federal officials appointed A. J. "Jack" Hamilton as governor of the provisional government of Texas. By early 1866 delegates were elected to a constitutional convention formed as a condition of reunification with the Union. Hamilton asked the convention to deny the right of the state to secede, repudiate the debt and statutes of the Confederate state government, and grant basic civil rights to the newly freed former slaves. The convention adopted a document promising basic rights of person and property to freedmen but denied to them the right to vote, hold office, or attend public schools. What became apparent during the convention was that the forces formerly allied as Unionists were now divided between those willing to accept the need for change and those wishing to restore the preexisting order.

Under this new constitution an election was called to select a new governor. The more conservative Unionists allied with former secessionists behind James W. Throckmorton, who overwhelmingly defeated the radical Unionists, led by former governor Elisha Pease. Throckmorton was an interesting choice to lead this coalition of more conservative forces. Of the 174 delegates to the 1861 convention on secession, Throckmorton had been one of only eight to oppose the action. When the war broke out, he joined the Confederate army.[2]

Throckmorton garnered 49,314 votes, while Pease could rally support from only 12,694 voters. As one historian of the times explains, "The failure to restore the old Unionist coalition was complete and Throckmorton's candidacy helped make it impossible. With the latter on the Conservative Unionist ticket, Texans did not face the problem of deciding between a Unionist and Secessionist. Rather, they had to choose between the views on Reconstruction held by two well-known Unionists."[3] Allied together, the conservative Unionists and secessionists attempted to bring the state back into the Union with as few changes as possible, limiting the rights of the newly freed former slaves.[4] Like most of his supporters, Throckmorton was opposed to allowing African-Americans to vote and to allocating public funds to educate African-American children.[5]

The conservative forces behind Throckmorton had overwhelming control of the Texas legislature and enacted policies diametrically opposed to the objectives of the more radical Unionists. With few dissenters, the legislature voted against ratifying the Fourteenth Amendment to the US Constitution and passed legislation to restrict the rights of the newly freed former slaves. African-Americans could operate their own schools but only with taxes "collected from Africans or persons of African descent." All labor contracts were to cover an entire family, and laborers could not leave their workplace without approval of their employer. Laborers had a duty to be "especially civil and polite to their employer, his family and guests." Meanwhile, African-Americans would not be counted in the determination of legislative districts.[6]

As Throckmorton and his supporters consolidated their control of state government, the radical Unionists felt isolated and concluded that they could not succeed in the future without African-Americans allowed to vote. This led them to oppose President Andrew Johnson's policies for readmitting the former Confederate states and to ally with the Radical Republicans in Congress and the Union League. In a speech given in Boston, former governor Jack Hamilton claimed that "if the freedmen are excluded" from the electorate, then the state governments of the South will be "in the hands of the late rebels, . . . who dread nothing so much as the cultivation in the South of a spirit of sincere attachment to the Union."[7]

By 1867, the Radical Republican majority in the US Congress was convinced that the postwar policies of President Johnson were insufficient to ensure an effective reconstruction of southern state governments in a manner that would protect the rights of all citizens, including those freed by the Emancipation Proclamation. Congress then passed a series of four Reconstruction acts that required the adoption of a new state constitution, ratification of the Fourteenth Amendment, and the election of new members of Congress from any state wishing to rejoin the Union. Until this was completed, military administration was established in each southern state, with General Philip Sheridan placed in charge of Texas and Louisiana. Under these federal acts the franchise was extended to all adult males who had not been leaders in the Confederate cause, thus preventing participation by some white males while ensuring the right to vote of former slaves. This action would have a significant impact on the election of delegates to the new constitutional convention and the subsequent election of a governor and state legislature.

JULY 4, 1867: A NEW PARTY IS CREATED

Throughout early 1867 the Union Loyal League (or Union League), made up mainly of newly enfranchised former slaves and a small number of white Unionists, held mass meetings across the state. Many of these individuals joined with Texans who had opposed secession (scalawags) and recent immigrants from the Union states (carpetbaggers) to establish a state unit of the Republican Party. On July 4, 1867, these activists met in Houston for the first Republican state convention.[8]

Presiding at the meeting was Pease, the radical Unionist candidate who had lost to Throckmorton in the governor's contest one year earlier. Closely associated with the Union and the abolition of slavery, the party's initial membership was predominantly African-American but with mainly white leaders, a large proportion of whom were German-Americans and people who had been opposed to secession and the state's membership in the Confederacy. The new party had to maintain a balancing act of appealing to the newly freed former slaves while still attracting the support of white Unionists. The convention adopted a platform promising support for free schools for all children, regardless of race or color; extension of state aid to railroads; and a homestead law offering public land, without regard to race or color, to encourage migration and allow more citizens to acquire land.[9]

While it is difficult to attribute any clear ideological position to the new party during its early years, the Republican Party's position in Texas was consistent with the national posture of the party. Its supporters were clearly Unionist and in support of "free soil, free labor, and free men."[10] The party advocated a more active state government that promoted a statewide education system open to all regardless of race. Once in office, Republicans created a statewide police force whose responsibilities included protection of settlements in the western areas of the state. This emphasis on centralized state government activities, especially education and police, was contrary to the dominant southern Democratic view of the nineteenth century and to the mid-twentieth-century view of conservative Republicans.

Later in July 1867, General Sheridan removed Throckmorton, viewing him as an impediment to the efforts at Reconstruction, and replaced him as provisional governor with Pease. As a leader of the newly formed Republican Party, Pease would serve in this capacity until the state adopted a new constitution and elected new officials under the terms of that document.

By January 1868 Texas had an electorate of approximately sixty thousand whites and nearly fifty thousand African-Americans. On February 10 these voters were asked to decide whether to hold another constitutional convention and to elect delegates to such a conclave. This election "solidified the union between blacks and the Republican party, an alliance that continued through the rest of the century."[11] When the votes were counted, those eligible to vote supported holding the convention and elected ninety individuals as delegates, seventy-eight of whom affiliated with the newly formed Republican Party.

The Republican delegation to the constitutional convention of 1868 included fifty-seven native southern-born whites, twelve immigrants from the North, and nine African-Americans.[12] While claiming affiliation with the newly formed Republican Party, these delegates split into four camps as the constitutional convention undertook its deliberations. One group of moderates included supporters of Governor Pease and former governor Jack Hamilton. A second faction, mainly East Texans, was led by James Flanagan of Rusk County. The third group consisted of prewar Unionists from western counties

4

led by Edmund J. Davis, Edward Degener, and Morgan Hamilton (a brother of Jack Hamilton). The fourth faction included the African-American delegates led by George T. Ruby of Galveston, a leader of the Union League. Each in their own way, all of these factional leaders would play roles in the Texas Republican Party over the remainder of the nineteenth century.

By the time of its second state convention in the summer of 1868, the newly formed Republican Party had split between what were viewed as more conservative Republicans, led by Governor Pease, who was in control of the party machinery, and a rump group of Radical Republicans, led by Davis and Ruby. Among those who bolted and aligned with the Radical faction were Degener, Morgan Hamilton, and George W. Whitmore, each of whom would eventually serve in Congress as Republicans. This resulted in the existence of two Republican parties, each with its own executive committee and state organization.[13]

THE DAVIS YEARS

The Texas Constitution adopted in 1868 called for state elections to be held in 1869 for both statewide offices and the legislature. The Pease forces in control of the regular party machinery nominated former provisional governor Jack Hamilton. Prior to the war Hamilton won election to Congress from the Western district, where he opposed secession and reopening of the slave trade. In 1861 he was elected in a special election to the Texas Senate, but his Unionist sentiments forced him to flee the state. He returned in the summer of 1865 as provisional governor, appointed by President Andrew Johnson. As with many others, his views on Reconstruction shifted over time, and by 1869 he was aligned with the conservative Republican faction, which favored a policy of simply readmitting the former Confederate states to the Union. In the campaign for governor, he acquired the support of many Democrats who realized that their candidate had little chance of winning.[14]

Opposing Hamilton was Davis, who had been an active community leader and attorney in Laredo, where he served as district judge from 1855 to 1861. In the 1859 election Davis had backed Governor Houston and shared his views in support of the Union. When secession came, Davis followed Houston's lead and would not swear allegiance to the Confederacy. From 1862 to 1865 he served in the Union Army as commander of the First Texas Cavalry. After war's end, Davis was elected as a delegate to the 1866 constitutional convention and aligned himself with Governor Hamilton and other Unionists.[15]

In the bitter and contentious election Davis received 39,901 votes to Hamilton's total of 39,092. Davis's election could largely be credited to support from the now eligible freedmen. According to one analysis of the election returns, "in the 31 counties in which more blacks voted than whites, Davis won easily in all but three. A strong statistical correlation existed between the Davis vote and the black population."[16] Republican candidates were elected to a majority of both Texas House and Senate seats, and the party won three of the four congressional districts. Subsequently, the new state legislature selected two Republicans to represent the state in the US Senate once Texas was readmitted to the Union.

As the winner of the 1869 election, Davis was appointed to replace Pease as provisional governor on January 8, 1870. Military rule did not end, however, until April, and it was on April 28, 1870, that Davis was inaugurated as the elected governor.[17] Once in office, Davis moved to restore law and order through the creation of a militia and state police as well as support for building county jails. Restoring order was a vital priority at the time. As Randolph Campbell noted,

> Bands of outlaws operated most notoriously in the Big Thicket and the swamps and woodlands of northeastern Texas. Led by killers such as Cullen Baker and Bob Lee, these gangs often attacked U.S. troops and freedmen, thereby gaining a measure of support from some whites. . . . Groups with names such as the Knights of the White Camelia and Knights of the Rising Sun carried out Klan-type activities—night riding, threats, whippings, and murder—especially in eastern counties.[18]

In addition to attacks by outlaws and violence against former slaves, Texans were threatened by Indian raids in western counties, where "raiders traveled hundreds of miles to murder and steal from people against whom no grievance could exist."[19]

Davis was a strong advocate of public education as a means of both individual achievement and overall economic development. By 1871, the Republican-majority legislature had passed a public school law with a centralized state board of education responsible for appointing local education officials. One year later, some 125,000 students of all races were enrolled. Many white Texans, however, were opposed to providing public education for African-American children, to the higher taxes needed to pay for public education, and to the centralized nature of the educational system put in place. It was the same Republican majority legislature under Davis's leadership that passed a bill creating Texas Agricultural and Mechanical College and providing funds to build the school.[20]

The Republican governor was one of the first public officials in the state to work toward ensuring equal treatment before the law for all citizens. He was quoted as declaring, "I do not want to see white or black named in any law whatsoever."[21] Three African-American Republicans served in the Texas Senate during Davis's term of office, including Ruby of Galveston, who acted as the chief spokesperson in the Senate for the Davis administration. Senator Ruby also was president of the Union League and had used that position to rally support for Davis in the 1869 election.

From the end of the war through much of the twentieth century, many historians viewed the Reconstruction era generally, and the Davis administration more specifically, as a time of corruption, incompetence, and carpetbagger rule. One frequently cited history of Texas claims, "the years of Carpetbagger rule were gaudy, violent, sometimes comic in retrospect, but always tragic at the time."[22] More recent interpretations, however, view this period in a more favorable light and maintain that most of those who led the state during the Davis administration were native Southern Unionists and not carpetbaggers from the North.[23] Most of those associated with the Davis administration had been active as Unionists in Texas before the war. Summarizing the accomplishments of Governor Davis, one Texas historian noted that he "championed the rights of African-Americans, sought to create Texas' first meaningful system of public education, and tried to restore law and order and bring economic development to the war-ravaged state."[24]

In November 1871 elections were held once again for the four Texas seats in the US House of Representatives. For the first time since 1866, Democrats were organized and motivated to recapture their previous position of dominance in state politics. When the votes were counted, the three Republican members of Congress had been defeated after serving one term.

The election of 1871 had uncovered several weaknesses of Texas Republicanism. No matter what benefits might exist as a result of their progress, the majority of Texans found them too expensive, and the Democrats had managed to use the issue of taxes to achieve victory for themselves. Without some changes in the party's programs, the Republicans couldn't hope to attract the white votes necessary to regain a majority position. When party leaders attempted to reorganize to bring in more whites, however, they opened themselves to accusations that they were abandoning their chief source of strength, the black voters.[25]

It would be more than twenty years before another Republican was elected to Congress. After the 1894 election, George H. Noonan served one term from a district centered on San Antonio before being defeated for re-election. Two years later Robert B. Hawley was elected to the first of two terms representing a district that included Galveston, but he did not seek a third term. The two remaining Republican US senators, James Flanagan and Morgan Hamilton, continued in office until 1875 and 1877, respectively, at which point the party's representation in the Senate ended until John Tower's election some eighty-four years later.

With the approaching national and state elections of 1872, Republicans were once again divided. Reflecting the loose and confusing terminology of the time, the so-called conservative Republicans associated with Pease and Jack Hamilton backed the Liberal Republican movement, which developed in opposition to the Reconstruction policies and perceived corruption of the administration of President Ulysses S. Grant. Pease and Hamilton led a delegation of Texans who took part in a Cincinnati Liberal Republican convention that, after six ballots, nominated Horace Greeley, editor of the *New-York Tribune*, as its candidate for president.[26] Adding to the confusion, the Liberal Republican candidate Greeley was then endorsed by the national Democratic Party, and he ran for president under their label. Those Democrats who refused to accept Greeley as the nominee, referred to as Straight-Out Democrats, met in Austin and endorsed Charles O'Conor, a states' rights Democrat from New York who had been defense counsel for Jefferson Davis in his trial for treason.[27]

Meanwhile, the Radical Republicans associated with Governor Davis sent a delegation to the Republican National Convention in Philadelphia, which renominated President Grant. Among the delegates were several who played important roles in the nineteenth-century party, including state senators Webster Flanagan and George T. Ruby, Secretary of State James P. Newcomb, and Norris Wright Cuney.[28] Governor Davis took an active role in promoting President Grant's campaign and defending his own administration. "To blacks, Davis argued that their only choice for a party was the Republican Party because they had crushed the rebellion, ensured their liberation and now protected them. Poor whites had no other home either, for the Democratic Party offered no voice for those not part of the state's landed elites."[29] Davis's efforts were in vain as Greeley carried the state by a sizeable margin of twenty thousand votes over President Grant, with the Straight-Out Democrat candidate O'Conor receiving less than three thousand votes.

Despite failing to carry Texas, the Republicans under Davis's leadership could take satisfaction in the re-election of President Grant. Any celebration of the national results was short-lived, however. Back home the election was an unmitigated disaster. All four congressional seats were won by Democrats. In the Texas House, the Republicans dropped from a fifty-seat majority to a small minority. In the Texas Senate, where only one-third of the seats were up, the party lost four of its seventeen seats.[30] As Paul Casdorph concludes, "The outcome of the election meant defeat for the regular Republicans and was an omen that Texas Republicans were soon to be relegated to the secondary party in the state."[31]

With the Republicans having lost their majority in the Texas legislature, Governor Davis's programs were soon under attack. The Democratic majority was determined to reverse many of the policies put in place by the Republican governor. While Davis attempted to use his veto power, the legislature repealed the law authorizing a state police and use of a militia, restricted the governor's ability to make appointments, decentralized the state's educational system, and limited the taxing authority of local school boards. All of this legislation passed over Davis's veto.[32]

The net effect of these actions was to limit the ability of the state to protect those western areas under Indian attack, as well as prohibit violence against freedmen in other areas of the state. While Davis and the Republicans favored a homestead act that would provide land to immigrants and others as a means of populating the state and encouraging economic development, the legislature distributed the land in a different manner. To this end, "the Democrats freely gave away the public lands, authorizing grants of sixteen sections for each mile of completed railroad to sixteen different companies."[33] With the elimination of state direction, no longer would there be a true state school system guaranteeing access regardless of race or color; this set the path for a policy of unequal educational opportunities and eventually a so-called separate but equal system of segregated schools. According to Carl Moneyhon, "By the end of their session the legislature had undone almost completely the Republican legislative program."[34]

Not satisfied with changing the immediate direction of state policy, the Democratic majority in the legislature established an election for December 2, 1873, to select state and local officials. Unlike the previous instances, this would be a one-day, rather than a four-day, election, and polling would take place at the various precincts in each county rather than at the county seat. Republicans feared that spreading the polling places to disbursed areas of the county would make it more difficult to prevent harassing tactics against African-American voters and make is easier to undertake "constructive counting" of those ballots allegedly cast.[35]

The odds against continued Republican control of the governor's office seemed so overwhelming that some party officials advocated not running any candidates at all. That was not Davis's position, however, and he sought and won renomination. To some commentators, "He had thousands of appointed officeholders, the Negro vote, and Federal influence. But the Democratic

Party approached the December election as a great crusade."[36] Having lost the war, they would take this opportunity to reclaim control of state government.

Concentrating on appealing to supporters of secession as well as conservative Republicans who were opposed to Davis, the Democrats nominated Richard Coke. A native of Virginia who had moved to Texas in 1850, Coke had been a delegate to the secession convention of 1861 and had voted for secession, and later served as a captain in the Confederate forces. At the Democratic convention in Austin that nominated Coke, "Many of the old leaders of the State were in attendance, including numerous ex-Confederate army officers."[37] The lines were drawn by the Democrats, as "throughout the campaign they reinforced Coke's theme that all white men with property had a community of interest that should keep them together against the Republican evil."[38]

The Republican campaign centered on defending what they viewed as the accomplishments of the Davis administration. As they traveled, the state Republicans "pointed out that the Thirteenth Legislature, controlled by Democrats, had increased taxes, added to the state debt, given eighty thousand acres of public lands to railroads, and destroyed the school system."[39] Both sides fought the campaign, mindful of its significance as to the future direction of the state and the fate of the two political parties.

As one historian has commented on the campaign, "Democrat politicos bluntly indicated that power would be won depending on who outfrauded whom. No practice was ignored.... Democrats rode into Negro settlements and gun on hip ordered blacks to stay away from the polls. There was terror, intimidation, and some murders on both sides. White men in some counties pulled guns on Davis officials conducting the polls. Unregistered whites and boys years under the legal age were voted. Desperadoes, thieves, planters, sweaty farmers, and ministers of the gospel damned black Republican rule and voted Democrat."[40] When the votes were finally tallied, the Democrats were clearly back in control of all elements of Texas state government. In what ended up as a landslide, Coke won by a margin of roughly two to one. Davis carried only twenty-six of the state's 130 counties, mostly located along the gulf coast and around Harris County.[41]

The election of 1873 was the end of a brief period of Republican Party control of state government. Controversy remained as to whether Davis's term of office ended four years after he was appointed provisional governor (January 8, 1870) or after he was inaugurated as the elected governor of the state (April 28, 1870). Moreover, some Republicans mounted a legal challenge of the election over the fact it was held on one day, rather than the four specified in the state constitution. When the Texas Supreme Court ruled that constitutional violations had occurred and called for a new election, Davis appealed for support from the Grant administration. No such support was forthcoming, and without federal backing, the court's ruling could not be enforced. Davis accepted the fact that he had been defeated and was prepared to leave office at the end of what he viewed as his four-year elected term. The Democrats, however, demanded that he resign on January 8. After much mounting of forces, both legal and physical, the Democratic-controlled legislature inaugurated Coke on January 15.[42] "Faced with Democrats who refused to give in and a federal administration that would not back him, Davis resigned on the morning of January 19th."[43] As one recent historical work noted, "Richard Coke's inauguration in 1874 brought an end to Radical Reconstruction in Texas and released a river of reaction that left the Republican Party in shambles and the public reputations of the Radicals besmirched almost beyond salvage."[44]

The year 1874 was in some ways the beginning of a new era, in other ways the restoration of an old order that was now led by "redeemers" who had saved the state from Radical Republicanism. "Under Coke's leadership, the Democrats of Texas, united behind the cause of white supremacy, regained power in the state government, imposed strict racial segregation, and created the one-party system by which the Democrats ruled the state until the Civil Rights Revolution in the 1950s and 1960s."[45] No Republican would be elected to statewide office for more than ninety years, and the party would not control the governor's office again until 1978.

Once in power the Democrats set about to change the Constitution, which had allowed the Republicans to gain office. In August 1875 voters approved another constitutional convention and elected delegates: seventy-five Democrats and only fifteen Republicans, six of whom were African-American.[46] The Constitution of 1876 was ratified by the voters in February, "sweeping away the last remaining vestiges of congressional directives, military rule, and Republican government."[47] Beginning with the Texas legislature elected in 1876 and on through the end of the nineteenth century, Republicans never held as many as ten seats in the House or more than three in the Senate. For all intents and purposes they had become irrelevant to state government.

The party's base of voter support through most of the remainder of the nineteenth century came from those African-Americans able to vote. Where they were a majority of the population, Republicans continued to have a base of support until the late 1880s. As the Democrats adopted a variety of policies to discourage African-Americans' voter participation, they became a decreasing proportion of the state's electorate. According to Carl Moneyhon, "The collapse of the Republican county officials before violence in Fort Bend

County in 1888 marked the fall of one of the last local party strongholds in the state. The trends set in motion by the return of the Democrats to power could be seen by the end of the century, when of some 650,000 potential black voters only 25,000 qualified."[48] Nevertheless, according to the party's official history, some forty-four African-Americans served in the Texas legislature as Republicans during the latter part of the nineteenth century.[49]

The downside for the Republican Party was that, as in many other parts of the South, it was perceived solely as the party of the North and of black people. According to Casdorph, "The Republicans did not threaten the Bourbon Democrats after Reconstruction because 'the party of Lincoln' had become indelibly stamped on the southern mind as pro-Negro. Indeed, for a southern white to question the supremacy of the Democratic party was tantamount to being branded as 'a renegade to race, to God, and to Southern womenhood.'"[50] Roscoe Martin stressed this same theme when writing in the 1930s to describe post-Reconstruction politics. He claimed that "the Democratic Party was looked upon, rightly or wrongly, as the defender of all that was dearest to the hearts of Texans, and those not members of that party were regarded virtually as traitors to the State."[51]

Defeat in 1873 was not the end for Davis, however. He would continue to be a leader in the Republican Party of Texas until his death ten years later. Conflict and division, often with changing alliances and coalitions, would be the nature of the party for years to come. Most of those who had supported the Liberal Republican effort in 1872 slowly returned to the party, but by 1875 a dispute developed between Davis and a group of Federal officeholders, some of whom Davis had attempted to have removed from office. It was claimed that "few of these men had any connection with Davis, for President Grant's appointments in Texas reflected little of the needs of the state party."[52] With his influence in party affairs under challenge, Davis sought election as chairman of the state executive committee in 1875. Prior to the voting, the candidates backed by the federal officeholders withdrew, and Davis was elected, along with Norris Wright Cuney as party secretary. Cuney, from Galveston and a protégé of Senator Ruby, was on his way to an even more important place in Texas Republican politics for the remainder of the nineteenth century.[53]

In his various battles within the party, Davis maintained the strong backing of African-American leaders such as Ruby and Cuney, and he remained committed to African-American involvement in party affairs. African-Americans continued to play an important and prominent role in Texas Republican politics, including among the small minority elected to the Texas legislature in the 1880s and 1890s.[54] As one of his biographers has noted, "He never abandoned them, and they, in the end, never abandoned him. As a result, he successfully maintained control over the Texas Republican Party through the rest of his life and continued trying to change the dynamics of life within the state."[55] Davis would make two more runs for public office. He was nominated for governor again in 1880 and then ran for Congress in 1882 before stepping down as party chairman.

THE CUNEY ERA

After Davis's death, Cuney became the leader of the party and controlled federal patronage in Texas. Cuney was undisputedly one of the most prominent African-American leaders of his time. He was well connected in the national party, served as both state chairman and national committeeman at various times, and opposed efforts to make the Republican Party a "Lily White" organization.[56]

Cuney soon confronted another split in the party when, in 1884, Republicans in Texas divided between the "straight-outs" (whites who wanted to nominate a Republican candidate for governor) and the regular party officials led by Cuney (mainly African-Americans who wished to endorse the Greenback Party candidate for governor, former member of Congress George W. Jones). After losing at the Republican state convention, the straight-outs held their own gathering and nominated A. B. Norton. This division only reinforced the weakness of any opposition to the Democrats, as Jones received 29.4 percent and Norton 7.0 percent of the votes in the 1884 election. A similar split occurred in 1892 as the Lily Whites held a separate convention and nominated A. J. Houston (son of Sam) for governor. Houston received only 1,322 votes, but this did not prevent a similar division two years later, in 1894, when the Black and Tan candidate obtained 54,520 votes to 5,036 for the Lily White candidate. Needless to say, none of these candidates posed a serious challenge to continued Democratic dominance.[57]

With the loss of their elected officials the party turned more and more to an emphasis on federal patronage at a time when local postmasters, customs agents, tax collectors, and holders of various judicial positions were political appointees of the national administration in control of the White House. "Since the national Republican Party remained in power for many years, what grew up in Texas slowly was a Federal patronage machine. Texas Republican leaders were more interested in holding such patronage control than in reviving the horse that Davis killed."[58] In a few areas of the state, including Galveston and the Rio Grande Valley, the party did continue a local presence, centered mainly on control of patronage positions, such as that of customs collector. Such was the case along much of the Mexican border as "from 1884 through 1896, James O. Luby and Robert B. Rentfro dominated Republican politics, . . . and both men served as Brownsville collectors."[59] Rentfro was one of a handful of Republicans to serve in the Texas legislature during this period, representing Cameron County for one term, 1889–1891. From 1888 to 1910, the Republican Party ran relatively competitive but losing campaigns for the congressional district that comprised the Rio Grande Valley, which was represented for much of this time by Democrats Rudolph Kleberg and John Nance Garner.

With fewer opportunities to elect public officials or even carry the state for the Republican presidential candidate, party leaders began to play primarily national convention politics, seeking to support the proper candidates for the presidential nomination so state patronage would be granted to them. Cuney was particularly adept at backing the correct presidential candidates to ensure his control of Texas appointments when the Republican Party held the White House.[60]

Patronage appointments became the carrot to attract individuals for involvement in the party organization. In a detailed study of Texas involvement in nineteenth-century Republican national conventions, Casdorph discovered that "of two hundred and forty-six delegates and alternates from the state to national Republican conventions, 1868–1896, seventy-three are known to have been postmasters, federal judges, collectors of internal revenue, or holders of other federal offices in Texas." Among the delegations to national conventions during this time, at least thirty African-Americans were included, contrasted with the solely white delegations sent to Democratic national conventions of the nineteenth century. As Casdorph concluded, "besides the fact that the Republican Party in Texas during the last quarter of the nineteenth century was one of Negroes and federal officeholders, one gets the impression that it was almost a closed club, with most of the party leaders being intimates and personally known to each other."[61]

Despite Texas Republican leaders' ability to control federal patronage in the state throughout most of the remainder of the nineteenth century, their ability to gain voter support and elect candidates to office was sorely lacking. From 1882 to 1900, Republicans ran candidates in slightly more than half of all congressional district elections; in few of these, however, did they win more than 25 percent of the vote. Support for Republican presidential candidates during this period ranged from a low of 17.3 percent for President Harrison in 1892 to a high of 30.9 percent for President McKinley in 1900. The number of Republican state legislators declined from eight in 1881 to none at the beginning of the twentieth century. Three times during this period the Republicans fielded no candidate for governor; never did they pose a challenge to the election of a Democrat to the state's highest office. As one Texas writer noted, in the 1890s "whole counties ... boasted not a single white Republican."[62]

By the 1896 state convention, the conflict over presidential nominations led to the downfall of Cuney as leader of the Texas Republicans. In a fatal decision, Cuney backed his friend Senator William Allison of Iowa for the presidential nomination, while another faction rallied behind the candidacy of Governor William McKinley of Ohio, and a third group, including future member of Congress Robert B. Hawley, supported Speaker Thomas B. Reed. The Allison and Reed forces aligned to stop McKinley's drive and were able to elect Cuney as state convention presiding officer. Conflict over the choice of delegates to the national convention led to physical assaults, and the Austin city police were called in to protect Cuney. After the convention adjourned, the McKinley forces held their own convention and selected a rival slate of delegates.[63]

Cuney's delegation was not the only one to appear at the 1896 national convention; both the McKinley forces and a Lily White group also attempted to be seated. In a close vote before the credentials committee, Cuney and the regular Republicans lost out to the McKinley supporters led by John Grant. After the convention Grant replaced Cuney as national committeeman. As historian Douglas Hales notes, "Cuney lost his hold on leadership, not at the hands of the Lily Whites, but because he backed the wrong presidential candidate."[64]

The subsequent governor's convention saw Cuney defeated in his effort to serve as temporary presiding officer. In what turned out to be his last speech at a Republican state convention, Cuney spelled out his overriding philosophy of life:

> Reputation is one thing, but character is pure gold, and on that you must judge a man, and that is the basis and the standard of what is right in life. ... A man has no more right to trifle with his integrity than a woman has the right to trifle with her virtue. The best principle to lay down to people is to tell them to speak the truth, tell the people to be honest. Teach honesty and integrity to the people, and on that basis will this great American republic go on as she has been going, and continue to be the foremost nation on earth, and this we can do in our day and generation. And our children will learn to honor and respect it.[65]

Despite his defeat as leader of the Texas party, Cuney traveled the state throughout the fall, campaigning for McKinley. It would be his last campaign, for in March 1898 Cuney passed away at the age of fifty-one. Karl Rove writes in his study of the McKinley election, "For nearly thirty years, the attractive, wealthy, and well-spoken Cuney had been a major power in the state and national GOP. He kept the Texas GOP a biracial party, having not only the backing of the state's black Republicans but also the support of many white Republicans."[66] As Casdorph observes, with Cuney's death "a powerful figure in Texas politics was no more, but an era did not really close with him because the contest between the Negroes and 'Lily Whites' was destined to continue well into the next century."[67]

Indeed, the new state chairman, E. H. R. Green, son of the supposedly richest woman in America at the time, Hetty Green, relied heavily on the support of William M. "Gooseneck Bill" McDonald, a leader of the Black and Tan faction. Green and his supporters were in conflict with backers of Congressman Hawley, the party's only elected federal official, who was aligned with Henry Ferguson, the African-American leader of Fort Bend County Republicans. Because he was present in Washington as the only Republican member of Congress from Texas, Hawley became the dominant force in patronage decisions rather than national committeeman Grant.[68] This was ironic as Grant had been a leader of the McKinley forces in 1896 while Hawley had supported Reed's presidential aspirations. As the nineteenth century came to a close, Texas Republicans were experiencing a familiar situation—little if any success on Election Day but continuing battles among various factions for control of what patronage was forthcoming from a Republican administration in Washington. The new century would only bring more of the same.

TWO

THE EARLY-TWENTIETH-CENTURY REPUBLICANS

Throughout the first thirty-two years of the twentieth century, Texas was clearly part of the "Solid South" save for the 1928 election, when Herbert Hoover carried the state over Al Smith. In all the other presidential elections, only once did another Republican candidate obtain as much as one-fourth of the total vote; that occurring in 1900 when President William McKinley received 30.9 percent of the total Texas vote. After carrying the state in 1928, President Hoover was abandoned four years later by all but 11.2 percent of Texas voters. This was not the lowest level of support for a Republican president seeking re-election, however. In a four-way contest in 1912, William Howard Taft's 9.4 percent of the vote barely squeezed out Teddy Roosevelt's 8.9 percent and Socialist Party candidate Eugene V. Debs's 8.3 percent of the Texas vote.

The tiny Republican base was divided further with Roosevelt's campaign against a sitting Republican president and would be split again in 1920 when a Black and Tan faction ran its own slate of electors, polling 5.6 percent of the vote, and to a lesser extent in 1924 with Senator Robert La Follette's Progressive Party campaign.[1] It would not be until 1952—and then only with the backing of the major Democratic elected officials in the state—that a Republican presidential candidate would duplicate Hoover's 1928 performance.

Excluding the 1928 Hoover victory, the number of Texas counties carried by the Republican presidential candidate over the first thirty-two years of the twentieth century ranged from a low of three in 1912 (Kinney, Webb, and Zapata counties along the Mexican border) to a high of twenty-six in 1920.[2] Prior to the Hoover-Smith contest, the GOP candidate carried one of the state's six largest counties only once, when Warren Harding received more votes than James Cox in Bexar County in 1920. In that election, Harding won 35.2 percent of the vote from these six largest counties, only slightly better than William Howard Taft's 28.7 percent of the vote in 1908. The unique fac-

TABLE 2.1. REPUBLICAN PRESIDENTIAL CANDIDATE
PERFORMANCE IN TEXAS, 1900–1932

Year	1900	1904	1908	1912	1916	1920	1924	1928	1932
Number of counties carried	19	13	10	3	9	26	14	140	0
Percent of total presidential vote	30.9	22.0	22.4	9.4	17.4	23.5	19.8	51.7	11.2

tors of rum, Romanism, and rebellion in 1928 can account for Hoover carrying 140 of Texas's 254 counties (table 2.1).

What support there was for Republican presidential candidates in isolated areas of the state basically died out with the coming of the Depression in 1929. Even in the traditionally Republican counties of the Hill Country and South Central Texas, Franklin D. Roosevelt and New Deal politics dominated for the next twenty-plus years. Over the thirteen presidential elections from 1900 to 1948, only three German-influenced counties supported the Republican candidate with any regularity. Gillespie and Kendall counties provided a GOP majority in eleven of the thirteen contests, while Guadalupe did so in nine. None of the three went for Taft in 1912 or Hoover in 1932. Clearly over this fifty-year period, setting aside 1928, Democratic presidential candidates could take it for granted that they would receive the Electoral College votes of Texas.

With a few exceptions in isolated parts of the state, Texas Republicans never offered serious competition for public office as Democratic candidates won nearly every election from 1900 to 1950. During this time a handful of Republican candidates won office in the traditionally German counties, including state senator Julius Real and member of Congress Harry Wurzbach, the only Republicans in the Texas Senate and its congressional delegation. Real, from Kerr County, was elected in 1908 and 1912, then served again from 1925 to 1929. His district comprised much of the historically German areas of Bexar, Bandera, Kendall, Kerr, and Gillespie counties. Wurzbach represented San Antonio and surrounding areas almost continually from 1921 to 1931.

The party was also competitive in some counties along the Mexican border in the early twentieth century, especially Cameron, Duval, Starr, Val Verde, Webb, and Zapata counties.[3] When Republican presidential candidates were averaging less than 25 percent of the statewide vote, voters in Zapata County backed the GOP in every presidential election from 1900 to 1920 and its gubernatorial candidate seven times during this period. In Starr County, the Democrats were known as Reds and the Republicans were the Blues at a time when illiteracy was widespread and the color distinction was a way of identifying each party. The Republicans were headed by Don Lino Hinojosa, a wealthy landowner who was a Republican candidate for sheriff. While the Democrats would meet at what is now the courthouse, Republicans gathered at one of Hinojosa's properties, referred to as "Lino's corales."[4]

Several of the Republican leaders in the Rio Grande Valley, such as Hinojosa, were descendants of families who settled the area prior to Texas independence. Casimiro Perez Alvarez was a rancher, educator, and lawman who grew up on land originally granted to his family by the king of Spain in 1767. He was deputy US marshal under three Republican presidents, served as Starr County Republican chairman in the 1920s, and was appointed by two other presidents as postmaster from 1928 to 1933. In a letter to another party official, Alvarez made known his commitment to the party by declaring "I will always be, am now, and will be, a Republican by choice of principles."[5] In Jim Hogg County the Salinas family has been prominent supporters of the Republican Party. Sixto Garcia was the GOP county chairman for many years and in charge of federal appointments in his area. His grandson Tony Salinas carries on the tradition to the present day. A close associate of the Bush family, Salinas has been a delegate to Republican national conventions and has been county chairman for several years.

It is in the context of losing nearly all elective offices that the Republican Party of Texas was consumed with national convention politics, internal disputes and divisions, and the competition for federal patronage. Although the party's presidential candidate had little likelihood of carrying the state, Texas provided a sizeable bloc of delegate votes at the Republican National Convention. Backing the winning candidate at that convention became the essential requirement for controlling federal patronage when a Republican administration was in place. The state's delegates to the national convention were dearly sought as candidates vied for the presidential nomination. The resultant efforts to back a winning candidate contributed to a series of internal conflicts, with the state often having two or even three delegations petitioning for recognition at the national convention.

Many of these disputes and efforts to control the party machinery took place between the Black and Tan Republicans, who were supported by most black voters, and the Lily White faction of Republicans, who attempted to win over conservative Democrats with little if any success. This rivalry over approach and principles resulted in conflict for control of the party machinery. The dispute began as Reconstruction came to an end, and it continued with different leaders and major players through the first thirty years of the twentieth century until the Lily White forces finally won out.

Especially harmful to the Black and Tan forces were the Democratic-imposed election laws, including a poll tax enacted in 1903 and the Terrell Election Law of 1905. According to Chandler Davidson, the Terrell Act "encouraged the use of the all-white primary at the county level, increased the difficulty of third-party competition, and established a poll-tax payment period that ended six months before the primaries and nine months before the general elections."[6] Moreover, a party was allowed to nominate its state-wide candidates by convention, and a primary was required only when a party's gubernatorial candidate won more than 100,000 votes—a threshold seldom passed by Republican nominees. From a combination of factors, including violence and threats of violence, black participation in Texas elections fell off precipitously, resulting in fewer reliable Republican votes and making the Black and Tan faction's task even more difficult. According to Carl Moneyhon, of approximately 650,000 potential black voters in 1900, only 25,000 qualified once the new limitations on voting were in place.[7]

Once the Lily Whites solidified control of the Republican Party and the Democrats imposed white-only primaries, it was clear that neither party appealed to the small proportion of blacks still eligible, willing, and able to pay the poll tax required. It would not be until 1944, when the Supreme Court, in *Smith v. Allwright*, struck down the white primary, that sizeable numbers of blacks would return to the Texas electorate.[8]

Control of the party organization was important not for conducting and winning elections but rather for determining who would be in charge of federal patronage appointments made in and from Texas. In this context, a history of the Republican Party of Texas from 1900 to the coming of the New Deal in 1933 is mainly about a battle for control over dispensing jobs, favors, and honorary appointments. With the exception of the years of Woodrow Wilson's presidency from 1913 to 1921, Republicans controlled the White House up to the inauguration of Franklin D. Roosevelt in 1933. During this time, federal patronage was all that kept the party alive and gave it a purpose for existence. Many party leaders became US attorneys, customs officials, prohibition agents, tax collectors, and postmasters throughout the state. The connection between appointment as a postmaster and involvement in the Republican Party was fairly clear-cut. A survey in 1928 showed that thirty-six county chairmen were postmasters and another thirty-two were married to postmasters.[9] Thus keeping the party small and discouraging the addition of new participants was useful for retaining control of patronage. The fewer the

Republicans, the less the competition for the spoils dispensed by a national Republican administration.

Ever since the end of Reconstruction, Texas Republican politics had been anything but unified. In the 1896 presidential nominating contest, Norris Wright Cuney and his Black and Tan forces supported Senator William Allison of Iowa for the nomination while another faction backed Governor McKinley of Ohio. As the 1900 presidential campaign developed, Texas Republicans were once again divided and sent two competing delegations to the national convention in Philadelphia. The forces allied with Congressman Robert B. Hawley and Henry Ferguson, a prominent black leader of Fort Bend County, were seated over the slate backed by state chairman E. H. R. Green and William "Gooseneck Bill" McDonald. After the national convention two rival state conventions were held as "each party or faction got a building for convention purposes in San Antonio a mile apart and with a river between them."[10]

CECIL LYON, LILY WHITES, AND PROGRESSIVES

Although Texas was not an essential state for presidential victory, continued division was of concern to the national party. To lessen the impact of internal divisions, President Theodore Roosevelt intervened to bring about an accommodation among his ally Cecil Lyon, Hawley, and Green. Thus, in 1902 a temporary truce was in place as Green agreed to step aside and acknowledge Lyon as state chairman and Hawley as the party's national committeeman.[11]

Lyon was born in Georgia but moved to Sherman, Texas, with his family at a young age, subsequently attending both Austin College and A&M College (now known as Texas A&M University). Lyon became the most prominent leader of the Lily White forces in the party and continued in political leadership until his death in 1916 at the age of forty-six.[12] Even with intraparty harmony, however, "as usual there was no campaign and no real effort exerted to capture state office. With a national Republican administration the Texas leaders were secure in their control of the state's patronage."[13]

By 1904 unity prevailed again and Lyon was recognized as the clear leader of the white Republicans. He remained party chairman from 1902 to 1912 and was national committeeman from 1904 to 1912. Viewed as a friend of Teddy Roosevelt, he accompanied the president on a hunting trip in Texas in 1905 and later supported the former president in his efforts to gain renomination by the Republican National Convention and then as the Progressive ("Bull Moose") Party's candidate for the presidency in 1912.

Unity within the Texas Republican ranks was too pure a commodity to last for long. Once again in 1906 Republicans were sufficiently divided in a nonpresidential election year that they ran two candidates for governor, who together received less than sixteen percent of the total vote. That division was topped in 1908 when three separate state conventions were held, each backing different presidential candidates and choosing rival delegations for the Republican National Convention in Chicago. In the end the delegation led by Lyon was recognized and cast all thirty-six votes for Secretary of War William Howard Taft, the party's eventual nominee and winner of the presidential election.

After his inauguration in 1909, President Taft toured Texas and visited El Paso, Del Rio, San Antonio, and Corpus Christi. In addition, he addressed the student body at Prairie View College (now Prairie View A&M University), a segregated black state institution.[14] Meanwhile, former president Roosevelt was becoming more upset with what he viewed as the conservative direction of the Taft administration and its perceived reversal of Roosevelt's progressive policies. Returning from a trip to Africa, Roosevelt declared in February 1911 that he would accept nomination for another term as president if it were offered. As Paul Casdorph notes, "While the nation watched with disbelief, the two giants of the Grand Old Party succeeded in dividing Republicans North and South into hostile camps during the eighteen-month interval from June 1910 until January 1912, when Roosevelt resolved to make another bid for the White House."[15]

Later in 1911 Roosevelt undertook his own tour of Texas, once again accompanied by Lyon, who was both Republican state chairman and national committeeman at the time. Roosevelt retained a broad swath of support throughout the state. A young volunteer at the Bull Moose campaign headquarters in San Antonio, Hobart Huson, would recall many years later, "Teddy Roosevelt was one president who had many 'personal friends' among the common people. His ex–Rough Riders idolized him and exerted themselves for him in the campaign of 1912."[16]

Most of the Texas Republicans moving to support Roosevelt in his challenge to the incumbent president were from the Lily White faction led by Lyon. Lyon had developed a national reputation as one of the most prominent politicians attempting to exclude blacks from participation in the Republican Party. Emmett Scott, personal secretary to prominent black Republican leader Booker T. Washington, made evident the views of many politically active blacks of the time when he said, "the most flagrant representative of 'Lily Whiteism' in the South is the man, Cecil Lyon of Texas, and the colored people of the United States have his name engraved on their memories as the most consistent representative of this odious type of Republicanism."[17] By aligning himself with Lyon, Roosevelt had made a conscious decision for exclusion, a policy that would subsequently be affirmed by his newly created Progressive Party.

McDonald and businessperson Henry F. MacGregor of Houston headed up the faction loyal to President Taft. Together these two Taft leaders "held the whip over the federal officeholders and controlled the allegiance of the Negroes."[18] At a luncheon with Republican leaders in San Antonio, MacGregor maintained that Texas would send a solid Taft delegation to the national convention. When asked about the support of federal appointees, MacGregor emphasized that "commissions will expire from time to time. We are not going to try to compel anybody to be for Mr. Taft, but where there are several capable and efficient Taft men wanting a place under this Administration, I know of no reason that a Roosevelt man should be appointed."[19]

Lyon, however, still held the loyalty of many postmasters who had obtained their patronage positions only due to his support. Every county, with few exceptions, had only one delegate vote at the state convention, and in many cases that vote was controlled by the local postmaster. The level of participation in the county conventions was meager, perhaps best exemplified by a report on the Menard County convention: "the Republican convention met on the sidewalk Saturday and threatened to be a hot encounter, but the Taft follower was called to the telephone and during his absence the other Republican instructed for Roosevelt."[20] County delegates then met by congressional district to select most of the delegates to the national convention.

By the time of the Republican state convention in May 1912, rival delegations had been named in nearly every congressional district. With proxies from many postmasters in rural areas of the state, Lyon was clearly in control of the regular convention. MacGregor and the Taft forces decided to hold their own convention a few miles away but also in Fort Worth. The end result was that the entire party became divided into Taft and Roosevelt camps as the two Republican leaders attempted to gain the presidential nomination at the 1912 Republican National Convention in Chicago.[21] At the national convention, the Taft forces prevailed and seated delegates loyal to him, and MacGregor was named national committeeman to replace Lyon in this critical patronage-dispensing role.[22]

After Taft defeated Roosevelt for the Republican nomination, "Lyon and his lily white allies looked upon rejection of his delegation by the GOP in Chicago as naked theft and fraud; he was still chief of the state's Republican apparatus, and he saw no difficulty in using the party machinery for the Bull Moose campaign."[23] The Roosevelt forces called an August national convention, where the former president was nominated along with Senator Hiram Johnson of California for vice president. With the concurrence of Roosevelt, the national Progressive Party barred southern blacks from participation in the convention and the party. Lyon remained loyal to him and attempted to bring along as many Texas Republicans as he could.[24]

Following the Republican National Convention and the August Progressive Party gathering, two rival Republican state conventions were held. At the Lyon-controlled convention, the delegates voted to change the name of the party to Progressive and endorsed the Roosevelt candidacy. A resolution was passed approving Roosevelt's exclusion of blacks from the party.[25] Meanwhile, those Texas Republicans loyal to President Taft selected C. K. McDowell of Del Rio as state chairman. McDowell came from one of the few areas where Republicans could win local office, having served two terms as county attorney followed by three terms as Val Verde County judge.[26]

Both nationally and in Texas, the division of forces between Taft and Roosevelt was a disaster. Neither candidate received as much as 10 percent of the total vote in Texas, and the party lost its control of the White House. For the next eight years under President Wilson there would be no federal patronage to sustain the Texas Republican Party.

The so-called Progressive forces under Lyon did not go away after the presidential election but attempted to build a new statewide organization, holding its 1914 state convention in Waco and nominating a slate of statewide candidates. Consistent with his past positions, Lyon approved a resolution by the delegates declaring that "the Progressive party in Texas shall be officered, controlled, and governed by white voters exclusively and (we) denounce the insincerity of the Democrats in inviting negroes into their recent primaries."[27] Meanwhile, the regular Republicans, led by McDowell, chose a new state chairman and nominated its own slate of statewide candidates. The new state chairman was Phil Baer of Paris, a Taft loyalist who had been named US marshal in one of the last appointments of the Republican president. As expected, disaster was to come once again in November, when together the Progressive and Republican candidates for governor received only 6 percent of the total votes cast, far fewer than those obtained by the Socialist Party candidate.

In April 1916 Lyon passed away, but the Progressive forces carried on for one last-ditch effort to create a permanent party and return Roosevelt to the White House. Both the Progressives and the Republicans held spring state conventions and elected delegates to their respective national conventions in June. When the Progressives attempted to nominate Roosevelt again, however, he refused to be a candidate, and their efforts came to an end.

At the second Republican state convention in August, many of the Bull Moose dissidents were welcomed back, but it was clear that they were not in control. When a resolution was introduced calling for a literacy requirement, it was defeated by the Republican delegates. The literacy requirement was viewed as an effort to exclude blacks and poor whites, and its defeat indicated that at least temporarily "the 'Black and Tan' was back in control of the party; the Progressive attempt to limit the Negro in the Southern party had come to naught in Texas." [28] Once again united, the party nominated Rentfro B. Creager of Brownsville as the Republican candidate against Governor James "Pa" Ferguson. Although unsuccessful in his race for governor, Creager would play a vital role in the party for the next thirty-four years.

THE CREAGER YEARS

Creager was the often challenged but long-surviving leader of the Republican Party of Texas from 1920 until his death in October 1950. Born in Waco in 1877, he was the nephew and namesake of Robert B. Rentfro, who was one of the Republican leaders in South Texas during the latter part of the nineteenth century. Rentfro served as customs collector by appointment of President Benjamin Harrison and in 1888 he was elected to the Texas House of Representatives, where he served one term.

Creager graduated from Southwestern University in 1898 and from the University of Texas Law School in 1900. Following his uncle's lead, he obtained a presidential appointment as customs collector in Brownsville in 1908 and retained that position during the Taft administration. He was a follower of state chairman Lyon and served as part of the unsuccessful Roosevelt delegation to the 1912 Republican National Convention. The experience of being denied a seat at the convention made a lasting impression on Creager. "At the National Convention of 1912, the pro-Taft delegation was seated. Creager learned then an organizational lesson he never forgot: that any bolters or non-conformists to party control are more dangerous to the party than the opposing political party, and are to be dealt with summarily."[29]

As a measure of unity in 1916, both the Lily White forces and the Black and Tan faction backed Creager's gubernatorial candidacy. Once again, there were fleeting hopes that a Republican victory was possible, and Creager undertook an active campaign throughout the state. According to one historian, "The South Texas Republican endorsed woman suffrage, straddled the issue of prohibition, accused Governor Ferguson of misusing public funds, and condemned President Wilson's policies toward Mexico. These vigorous attacks against the Democratic party had almost no effect on the Texas electorate, however."[30] When the election results were in, the Republican candidate had won 49,198 votes, or merely 13.5 percent of the total votes cast. From the perspective of the time, however, the campaign was a success as Creager received four times as many votes as John W. Philp, the party's candidate for governor two years earlier. Moreover, this allowed the Republicans to become, once again, the second party in the state, a position they had lost to the Socialist Party in 1912 and 1914.

Creager remained active in party politics after his defeat, although he never again ran for public office. While national committeeman MacGregor and many other Texas Republican leaders backed Governor Frank Lowden of Illinois for the presidential nomination in 1920, Creager lined up behind the candidacy of Senator Harding of Ohio.[31] He had been introduced to Harding by Frank E. Scobey of San Antonio, an active Republican and personal friend of the senator who had moved to Texas from Ohio, where he had been elected sheriff of Miami County.[32] Creager's endorsement of the candidate who would ultimately win the nomination and presidency gave him even more influence in the party.

Once again the Texas Republicans were divided when the state convention met in May 1920. After the state executive committee refused to recognize challenges to white delegations from thirteen counties, the Black and Tan faction followed McDonald and E. H. R. Green to a rump convention.[33] The dissenters named a slate of national convention delegates favorable to General Leonard Wood for the presidential nomination. At the Chicago convention, the delegation led by Baer and MacGregor was seated.[34]

The officially recognized Texas delegation in Chicago was split, casting votes for eight different candidates on the first ballot. Creager had received national recognition, however, by making the only seconding speech on Harding's behalf. Creager and Scobey convinced 19.5 of the state's twenty-three votes to switch to Harding on the decisive ninth ballot, and all twenty-three were cast for the eventual nominee on the winning tenth ballot. Historian Roger Olien explained the early relationship between Creager and Scobey: "Though Creager's political maneuvers delivered the convention votes to Harding, Scobey was responsible for having brought Creager into the Harding camp long before the national convention. Scobey's connection with Warren Harding, moreover, was strong, personal, and of long duration."[35]

While the national party now had its candidate to reclaim the White House, all was not harmonious back in Texas. After the national convention, the split within Texas Republican ranks continued, resulting in the regulars nominating one slate of state candidates while the Black and Tan element selected its own slate. The result was an easy win for Democratic nominee Pat Neff, and presidential candidate James Cox kept the state in the Democratic column. The gubernatorial vote was Neff (D) 290,672; J. G. Culberson (regular R) 90,102; H. Capers (Black and Tan R) 26,128. Meanwhile, Cox bested Harding 288,933 to 114,384 in Texas, one of only eleven states carried by the losing Democratic presidential nominee. Although they did not carry the state, Republicans were once again in control of the White House, and federal patronage was available again to the party faithful.

THREE

CREAGER AND WURZBACH

The Patronage Wars

The decade of the 1920s saw Texas Republicans briefly resurface on the state political scene. After the eight years of the Wilson administration, the Republican Party had regained control of the White House and, with it, the ability to make thousands of patronage appointments. For Texas Republicans, this meant an opportunity to recapture postmasterships and many other offices throughout the state. While Warren Harding did not come close to carrying Texas in his 1920 victory, he did win twenty counties, the largest of which was Bexar. His vote total in Bexar County helped to produce Texas's first Republican member of Congress in the twentieth century, as Guadalupe County Judge Harry Wurzbach upset the incumbent Democratic member. Four years later Calvin Coolidge kept the presidency in Republican hands, Wurzbach was re-elected to a third term, the party picked up its lone seat in the Texas legislature, and the GOP candidate for governor won over 40 percent of the vote. Unfortunately, the party was unable to build upon these encouraging developments, and by the end of the decade it was back to a position of relative irrelevance. Control of patronage had taken precedence over any efforts to build a viable competitive political party.

By his early support of President Harding, Rentfro B. Creager had gained an important ally in the White House. Throughout the decade of the 1920s, while the Republican Party controlled the presidency, Creager would be faced with opposition within the party from a number of sources, not the least of which came from a Texas member of Congress. From 1900 to 1950 Wurzbach was the only Republican to win election to Congress from Texas.[1] Wurzbach represented a district centered on San Antonio and served first from 1921 to 1929. When supposedly being defeated for re-election in 1928 with 49.7 percent of the vote, he challenged the outcome before the US House of Representatives, and one year later he was seated. Wurzbach then won his last term in the 1930 election and died in office in 1931.

A REPUBLICAN MEMBER OF CONGRESS FROM TEXAS

Wurzbach was born in San Antonio in 1874 and graduated from the Washington and Lee University School of Law before serving in the US Army during the Spanish-American War. He was elected Guadalupe County attorney in 1900 and county judge in 1904, serving a total of sixteen years before being elected to Congress in 1920. When the results came in, not only had the Republicans recaptured the White House, but Wurzbach had defeated the incumbent member of Congress, Carlos Bee, by some 3,500 votes. Wurzbach would be the first Republican elected to Congress from Texas in more than twenty years, and he was successful at a time when not a single Republican served in the Texas legislature.[2] According to Paul Casdorph, "the party was generally pleased with Wurzbach's election, even if Creager and the regular organization were not. The latter feared that Wurzbach, by exercising congressional courtesy, would interfere with their control of the patronage."[3]

As early as January 1921 some of Wurzbach's supporters were already making evident the conflict with Creager over patronage matters. Writing to Senator Harry New of Indiana, Sherman C. Kile maintained that "we have in the party some men of influence who were disappointed when Texas elected a Republican to Congress, as it interfered with their plans to control patronage in the state."[4] Remembering the critical support Creager had provided at the national convention and taking the counsel of his former Ohio associate Frank Scobey, the new president indicated that Creager would be his patronage coordinator for Texas, rather than national committeeman Henry F. MacGregor or the party's only member of Congress from the state.

As the Republican Party reclaimed the presidency after eight years in the wilderness, federal patronage was once again a highly sought-after benefit. Wurzbach believed that as the only elected Republican in the state he should be consulted on appointments not merely in his district but throughout the state. Creager, however, had been an early and vocal supporter of Harding prior to and at the national convention. Following the election the president-elect and his wife traveled to Brownsville, where they visited with Creager and went fishing off Port Isabel.[5] By April 1921 Creager was named state chairman and, due to his early support of Harding, became the key Republican contact in Texas. "After the President chose Creager over Congressman Harry Wurzbach and National Committeeman H. F. MacGregor of Houston as his 'referee' on patronage matters in Texas, Creager, called the 'Red Fox' of the Rio Grande Valley, assumed a leadership of the state party that would last for three decades."[6] MacGregor, who had served as national committeeman since the Taft-Roosevelt campaign of 1912, passed away in 1923 and was replaced by

Creager on the national committee. Wurzbach, however, was to continue as a challenge to Creager's domination of the party until his own death in 1931.

It is evident from contemporary correspondence that patronage matters took up much time and effort for both Wurzbach and Creager. Moreover, patronage issues created serious conflict between them. Writing to one job seeker in October 1921, Wurzbach made clear his attitude toward Creager and his allies: "I would prefer to support you for political reasons, because the men who are supporting Judge Harris are my bitter political enemies and have been doing everything in their power to discredit me."[7] Creager attempted to destroy Wurzbach by denying him patronage considerations even within his congressional district, resulting in Wurzbach attempting to recruit a candidate for state chairman against Creager, an effort that never succeeded.[8]

Creager continued to have support at this time from President Harding's associate Scobey, as well as from Eugene Nolte, an active Republican living in Wurzbach's district who would later succeed Creager as state chairman. As 1922 began, Representative Wurzbach indicated to one of his key supporters that the political battle must be carried out against his intraparty rivals: "We must eliminate Nolte and Scobey in the coming primaries and perhaps also make a fight this year in Creager's senatorial district."[9] Claiming that he had done nothing against Creager and the state party, Wurzbach was forced to defend himself when writing to a key Republican who had obtained a federal appointment as district manager of the Veterans Bureau: "I have not, at any time, laid any obstacles in the way of the State Organization, or its leaders, but the latter have, on the other hand, ever since my election, and some of them during my campaign, shown a disposition to oppose and belittle me in every conceivable way."[10] Nevertheless, at a time when nominations were still being made at a party convention, Wurzbach was concerned that the Creager forces in his district might attempt to deny him renomination, a fear he expressed to another supporter as late as June 1922.[11] The battle between Creager and Wurzbach became so vocal and public that President Harding was forced to intervene, arranging a meeting in July 1922 that resulted in a temporary truce lasting through the November election.[12]

Encouraged by the GOP split, the Democrats of San Antonio rallied behind state senator Harry Hertzberg to recapture the lone Republican congressional district. The Hertzberg campaign used the race issue to attack Wurzbach in three ways. When the representative gave a speech to a Negro association in Washington, Hertzberg had a supporter take down the comments, and he released them to the *San Antonio Light*, claiming that Wurzbach favored the social mixing of the races, a controversial position at the time in much of the nation. Wurzbach was forced to return to San Antonio and give two speeches denying any such comments.[13]

Hertzberg's second charge against the Republican was that he was the only Texas member of Congress to support the Dyer anti-lynching bill when it passed the US House of Representatives in January 1922. In a debate before the election, Hertzberg called the bill an attempt to reestablish Reconstruction throughout the South. In response, "Wurzbach affirmed that he had indeed voted for the Dyer Bill and promised that he would vote for it again at the next session of Congress because, he told the restive audience, 'Whenever I think of a lynch mob, I think of that mad mob which cheered at the crucifixion of Jesus Christ.'"[14] Wurzbach had carried the day on this point, but Hertzberg was not through.

The final charge was that Wurzbach had responded to a black constituent's request for a job recommendation by suggesting she pay a social call on Wurzbach's wife when in Washington. To many southerners of the time, such an invitation was viewed as race mixing when racial segregation was the accepted social and legal policy. After much maneuvering, Hertzberg was unable to produce any such letter, and Wurzbach convinced the public that the letter was a forgery.[15] Following the election, Wurzbach brought a libel suit against Hertzberg and was successful, resulting in the Democrat being required to pay all court costs.[16]

The charges brought by the Democratic candidate against Representative Wurzbach for being too supportive of blacks was also reflective of the disputes going on within the Republican party. To some extent, the Wurzbach-Creager feud was a continuation of the Black and Tan and Lily White split that had existed in the party since Reconstruction. There is no question but that Wurzbach was more favorably disposed to protecting the rights of African-Americans than were most Texas politicians of his time. Writing to one constituent in 1922, he claimed: "I not only state but boast that I am the friend of the Negroes and am greatly interested in their welfare and betterment and have a very poor opinion of a white man who is not."[17]

Wurzbach was the rare southern member of Congress who had the courage to address the National Association for the Advancement of Colored People (NAACP) convention in 1924 and to vote for the anti-lynching bill. According to one writer, "Congressman Wurzbach voted anti-lynching and for that his enemies called him a black man. As his niece Emily Wurzbach Mickler said, 'Uncle Harry and Poppa were very tolerant people. You see, that's one thing they had against Uncle Harry, they said he was a 'nigger lover.'"[18] In the Black and Tan faction's final challenge for control of the state convention and to be seated at the 1928 Republican National Convention, Wurzbach stood with them and against the Lily White forces.[19] Throughout his six campaigns for Congress, he retained majority support from the relatively small number of blacks voting in his district.

It was only with the intervention of President Harding that the friction between the Creager and Wurzbach forces was lessened during the 1922 campaign. One month after the brokered meeting of the two principals Creager wrote a "personal and confidential" letter to the San Antonio postmaster, whom he had been responsible for having appointed, pledging his support to Wurzbach. A copy of the letter was sent to Wurzbach for maximum effect.[20] Yet the support was more rhetorical than actual. Less than a month before Election Day, Wurzbach's campaign chairman telegraphed Creager for help: "We are in urgent need of financial aid. Nothing received from State Committee and are two thousand dollars in debt. We urge you to come to our immediate relief. Please answer." No funds were forthcoming from the state organization, but national committeeman MacGregor did send one hundred dollars to the campaign later that month.[21] Despite the organized effort of the Democratic Party—and the quieter effort by some of his fellow Republicans—Wurzbach was re-elected to his second term by a vote of 19,083 to 15,760 over Senator Hertzberg.

In September 1923 national committeeman MacGregor died, and Wurzbach sought to elect another candidate to the position. The Wurzbach faction's candidate was Thomas P. Lee of Houston, who had been a close associate of MacGregor and allegedly his preferred replacement. According to Wurzbach, Lee was the natural successor to MacGregor. Wurzbach maintained, "I am making no fight on Creager or the organization. It is Creager and his following who are fighting us. Mr. Lee has served as national committeeman, in fact, since Mr. MacGregor was incapacitated by illness. It was Mr. MacGregor's wish that Mr. Lee succeed him, and we are simply seeking to have affairs continue as they have been for some time."[22] When the votes on the state Republican executive committee (SREC) were counted, however, it was clear who was in control of the Texas party. Creager became the national committeeman, and his ally Nolte of Seguin was named to succeed him as Republican state chairman.

Creager then became embroiled in charges of land swindles in the Rio Grande Valley, publicized by Senator James Heflin of Alabama. After much negative publicity, including testimony before a Senate committee by buyers alleging land fraud, no court action was ever taken.[23] Creager's aggressive control of federal patronage did, however, alienate Scobey, his ally from the

Harding campaign, who became a supporter of Wurzbach in internal party matters.[24]

A TRUCE AND A REAL CAMPAIGN FOR GOVERNOR

As the presidential election approached, the truce between Creager and Wurzbach continued to the extent that Wurzbach was made part of the Texas delegation to the 1924 Republican National Convention, and Creager remained publicly supportive of Wurzbach's re-election. Nevertheless, the Black and Tan faction held a separate state convention and selected its own slate of delegates, but they were not seated by the national committee. Wurzbach was easily re-elected to Congress, and Julius Real won another term in the Texas Senate from a district overlapping much of Wurzbach's congressional district.[25] While not carrying Texas, Coolidge easily retained the White House for the Republican Party and ensured continuing battles over federal patronage between Creager and Wurzbach.

For many Texas Republicans, however, the focus of much attention and interest in 1924 was the contest for governor. When Governor Pat Neff chose not to seek a third term, several candidates filed for the Democratic primary, resulting in a runoff between Felix D. Robertson and Miriam "Ma" Ferguson. It was a choice from hell for many Democrats. Robertson, from Dallas, was a prohibitionist and member of the Ku Klux Klan. Ferguson was the wife of a disgraced former governor, James "Pa" Ferguson, who had been barred from seeking office but who also had built a reputation as being opposed to the Klan.[26] After Ma Ferguson won the runoff, the SREC met to choose a new person for their party's gubernatorial nomination to replace Lee, who had withdrawn.[27] The choice was between US Attorney Henry Zweifel of Fort Worth and George C. Butte, dean of the University of Texas Law School. Although Butte won the nomination, Zweifel would subsequently play a central role in Texas Republican politics. The party's new nominee was a graduate of Austin College and the University of Texas who had also studied at the University of Heidelberg, Germany. He had previously made a name for himself opposing some of the educational policies of Governor Pa Ferguson.[28]

Butte maintained, "I am not now and have never been a member of the Ku Klux Klan. I have not now and never will have any alliance with it."[29] Though neither Butte nor the Republican state organization sought their public support, there was little doubt that the Klan organization would do anything to oppose the wife of its bitter enemy, former governor Pa Ferguson. All across the state the Klan strongly backed the Republican candidate. As one party activist reported to state chairman Nolte, "At the big Klan rally here, composed of both men and women on the occasion of their endorsing Dr. Butte, they advocated that even if he was not elected Governor ... in any event they would gain a valuable friend."[30]

For the first time since Reconstruction, the Republican candidate made a serious challenge to Democratic domination of state politics. In the end, Butte came up short, however, losing by a margin of 422,563 to 294,911. In what would be a precursor of the 1928 presidential contest, the Republican candidate failed to carry many of the traditionally GOP areas while winning a total of fifty-five counties across the state. Butte's backing from the Klan naturally lost him many African-American votes, while Ma Ferguson's reputation as being opposed to prohibition won her support among many other voters. According to Tom Love of Dallas, leader of the Good Government Democratic League, which backed Butte, "The Republican Germans and negroes (about 75,000 of them) voted solidly for Ferguson. If they had voted for Butte, he would have been elected."[31] Indicative of this trend were the results in Wurzbach's district, where the vote was 30,779 for Ferguson to 22,768 for Butte, while the Republican member of Congress won a third term by a margin of 31,784 to 19,165 for his Democratic opponent.

Throughout 1925, Creager endeavored to solidify his position with the Coolidge administration as its chief patronage referee for the state, as well as ensure that he had control of the state party organization. When an effort was being launched to form Republican women's clubs around the state, Creager made clear that no such activity should be undertaken without it first being approved by what he described as "an organization created under the laws of the state that is recognized by the state authorities and by the national authorities of the Republican Party."[32] Creager was particularly sensitive to the formation of women's clubs because the first one in the state had been formed in 1920 as the Republican Women's Club of Bexar County and was a key contributor of volunteers for the Wurzbach for Congress campaign. According to one report, "always a booster of the club, Wurzbach gave members much credit for his political success and spoke often at their meetings."[33] In a letter to national committeewoman Florence Griswold, Creager wrote that he would not countenance any effort to organize such clubs without approval from the state party organization, stressing that "it is absolutely necessary that this legally created and legally recognized official of the Party have cognizance of all party activities in the state."[34] As far as he could ensure it, nothing was going to be done to organize Republicans throughout Texas without the knowledge and consent of Rentfro B. Creager.

1926: PATRONAGE CHARGES AND
PRIMARY CHALLENGES

As another election year began in 1926, the battle between Creager and Wurz-bach intensified. The legislator determined that his battle with Creager was only one example of a more pervasive problem involving southern Republican parties and patronage for delegate votes at the national convention. Only by rooting out such practices could the party ever develop into a serious political force in the South.

In late January Wurzbach outlined his position in a letter to one of his constituents: "It seems the rotten system prevailing of exchanging Southern patronage for Southern Delegates to National Conventions is pretty firmly embedded as the policy of the Republican Party. I am trying to impress upon the Republican leaders that until that condition changes there is not the slightest hope of that party making any substantial gains, either in Texas or in the South generally. I think you can realize what a tremendous job for one lone Republican to try to bring about a change in the system so long established."[35] The following week Wurzbach met with President Coolidge, explained his perspective on the Texas political situation, and came away believing that in the future all appointments in his district would be made upon his recommendation. This was not sufficient, however, as he maintained in a letter to his law partner: "I am going to insist further, that any appointments made outside of my District that my recommendations be given equal consideration with the recommendations made by the Republican State Organization."[36]

The Creager forces had determined that something must be done to remove the continuing challenge from Wurzbach. Some one hundred supporters of Creager held a meeting and decided that they would recruit a candidate to challenge Wurzbach in the Republican primary that state law dictated must be held in 1926. Scobey, formerly a Creager ally but now supportive of Wurzbach, warned the legislator, "you had better get your friends busy all over the district, because this is going to be the fight of your young life."[37]

On March 3 Wurzbach decided it was time to elevate the challenge into a national campaign. He launched an all-out attack on southern Republican patronage operations. From the floor of the US House of Representatives Wurzbach maintained that Creager's motivation was personal benefit and his fundraising from federal appointees was nothing more than a raid on the federal treasury. According to Wurzbach, "under the guise of voluntary party contributions tribute is levied by the 'organization' upon the salaries of many, if not most, of the Federal appointees in Texas.... These demands are often in the form of quarterly installment notes." As the legislator explained to a national audience, "Patronage is the beginning and end, the alpha and omega, of political interest and activity of Republican State organizations in Texas and other Southern states. In exchange for the patronage they receive they deliver the delegate votes to Republican National Conventions.... It is a spoils system pure and simple, without one redeeming quality."[38] Wurzbach claimed that party officials do not want Republicans elected because that would "interfere with the division of the spoils." The focus of attention had now expanded from Texas to the entire South and was generating national coverage.[39]

A few days later five state party leaders, including Creager and Nolte, sent off a blistering response to Senator William M. Butler of Massachusetts, chairman of the Republican National Committee and a personal friend of President Coolidge. The letter attempted to answer the charges made by Wurzbach and denounced him as an unfit representative for the Republican Party.[40] This letter prompted a response from the National Republican Congressional Committee defending their fellow legislator and warning the state party leaders against any opposition to his re-election.[41] As Representative Henry E. Barbour of California maintained in a letter to Leonard Withington, secretary of the state organization and one of the signatories on the response to Senator Butler, "judging by results, it would appear to me that Representative Wurzbach has done more for the Republican Party in Texas than your organization has ever been able to accomplish."[42]

Buoyed by the defense offered by his fellow members of Congress, Wurzbach determined to launch a concerted effort to take over the state party. As reported by Norman Brown:

> both R. B. Creager and Congressman Harry M. Wurzbach sought control of the state party machinery and appealed to national party leaders for assistance. (Congressmen Will R. Wood of Indiana and John Q. Tilson of Connecticut) told the White House that federal patronage should not be used to destroy a Republican majority in the House of Representatives, as was being done in Texas, and that all the rest was a smoke screen to obscure the real issue. In turn, Creager charged that Wurzbach, under the encouragement of Tilson and Wood and in combination with ... "Gooseneck" Bill McDonald, the black political boss, was making an open and avowed fight for control of the state organization.[43]

Maintaining that the primary offered the first time that a choice could be made by the state's Republican voters, Wurzbach called on rank-and-file "real

Republicans" to file for county chairman across the state.[44] To help carry out his challenge to the existing leadership, he recruited Judge E. F. Scott of Corpus Christi to seek the party's gubernatorial nomination.

With the gauntlet thrown down, Creager and Nolte intensified their efforts to recruit a candidate to run against Wurzbach in the upcoming primary.[45] During the first week of May, Creager and Nolte held a two-day caucus of state party leaders in the 14th congressional district, and upon its completion they announced that they had a candidate to oppose Wurzbach. Fred E. Knetsch, a thirty-year-old county attorney from Seguin, hometown to both Wurzbach and Nolte, was the state organization candidate to defeat the only Republican congressman from Texas.[46] To coordinate its plans on a statewide basis, the state organization then held a meeting in Fort Worth on May 22, conveniently timed to precede the state postmasters convention in Dallas on May 24–26, 1926.[47]

The seriousness of the political moves to remove Wurzbach from the Texas congressional delegation was evident in an exchange involving the appointment of a volunteer county chairman for Aransas County. When a vacancy developed, J. M. Hoopes of Rockport wrote to state chairman Nolte asking to be considered. The response he received came not from Nolte but rather from Robert F. Coon, the campaign manager for Fred Knetsch. Coon's telegram to Hoopes made clear what would be expected of him if he were to be appointed county chairman: "I assume you know the Republican Party Organization of the Fourteenth District and of Texas is earnestly urging the nomination of Fred E. Knetsch to Congress from this District. Will you join us in the support of Mr. Knetsch? If so, can arrange to have you appointed county chairman of the county at once. Please wire my expense."[48] When Bexar County Republicans met in June, the intensity of feelings was such that a disturbance broke out, resulting in fourteen police officers being called to restore order. In the resultant shuffle, one party member displayed a gun, a move that the press sensationalized as a threat to Wurzbach. Whether a serious threat or not, the action did nothing to improve the public image of the Texas Republican Party.[49]

Meanwhile, the issue of race raised its head once again. In a speech in Seguin, Knetsch alleged that Wurzbach once applied to be a member of the Ku Klux Klan. When Wurzbach heard of the charge he immediately sent a letter to the newspapers in his district denying the claim and challenging Knetsch to provide proof of any such effort. He recited his support for the anti-lynching law in Congress and emphasized his constituent services to all who lived in his district. Appealing to East San Antonio blacks in particular, the legislator attacked the Lily White Republicans, such as Creager and

Nolte, who "would sell them back into slavery if the opportunity ever presented itself."[50]

As the congressional primary campaign approached its conclusion, the Republican state organization held a rally for Knetsch at Alamo Plaza, attended by Creager, Nolte, and other party officials.[51] Among the small number of Texans who would vote in the Republican primary, the charges against their representative simply would not stick. Wurzbach won every county in his district, building a margin of roughly five to one over Knetsch. Judge Scott carried the district in his campaign for the gubernatorial nomination, and a Wurzbach supporter won out over the Creager-backed Bexar County Republican chairman.

The results statewide were not as encouraging to the Wurzbach forces, however. In a minuscule turnout, the Creager organization candidate, Harvey Haines, won the gubernatorial nomination in a vote of 11,352 to 4,081 for Scott. According to Wurzbach supporters, the small turnout was intentional to discourage people from associating with the Republican Party. In a critique of the primary, the Guadalupe County Republican Party maintained that statewide, "only a few of the voters were given a chance of freely expressing their choice, outside of those dispensing federal patronage by the ring. Places of holding primary elections were not made public, but deliberately concealed from the voters."[52] Meanwhile, the Creager organization viewed the primary as a resounding success, claiming that it was held in 177 counties and was a defeat for Wurzbach, "who campaigned the state against the personnel and policies of the regular state organization."[53]

When the November election took place, Dan Moody, who had defeated Governor Ma Ferguson in the Democratic primary runoff, easily bested the Republican nominee with a vote of 231,933 to 32,444. Wurzbach soundly defeated his Democratic challenger, A. D. Rogers, and returned for his fourth term in Congress. His was the only meaningful Republican victory that year. Writing to an associate after the election, Scobey described the plight of many Texas Republicans who desired a competitive party organization: "Under the Creager machine the Republican Party in Texas has become almost extinct. . . . You cannot play against the Ku Klux Klan one time and be for them in the next campaign. All the organization Creager has is on paper. Creager is in bad with the leaders in the house but he is in good with Coolidge because Coolidge thinks he can deliver the vote in 1928."[54] Whether Creager could produce victory in November mattered less than his ability to control delegate votes at the national convention for any potential presidential candidate who needed to first be nominated. Even a paper organization such as the one

Creager controlled was allotted an important bloc of delegates at the Republican National Convention.

Having defeated Creager's efforts to remove him in the primary and the Democrats' campaign against him in November, Wurzbach was prepared to continue the fight to bring about change in the state party. Writing to former county chairman Tom J. Darling of Temple, the congressman declared, "We must arrange to meet and discuss the welfare of our Party, which all must admit, is in a desperate condition."[55] Little did the legislator know that the most serious challenges to his continued political involvement were yet to come.

THE HOOVER NOMINATION BATTLE

In the summer of 1927, President Coolidge and his wife went on an extended trip to South Dakota, where the president visited with Gutzon Borglum and reviewed his plans for placing the visages of four presidents on the rough rock of Mount Rushmore. While in Rapid City, he held a conference on August 2 with twenty members of the press corps. Each of the journalists was provided with a brief statement: "I do not choose to run for president in 1928." When asked if he would respond to questions, the president's predictable answer was no.

Although Coolidge had never made evident his plans for 1928, most Republicans had anticipated that he would be a candidate for a full second term. The news from South Dakota surprised most political observers, and many felt it was merely a ploy to garner increased support and attention.[56] The pressure for Coolidge to run again continued through the fall, especially from those Republican political leaders who viewed the re-election of an incumbent as more favorable than electing a new candidate. On December 6 a meeting of Republican leaders was held at the White House, and Coolidge knew that he had to bring finality to the discussion about the upcoming election. Once more, he issued a declination: "My statement stands. No one should be led to suppose that I have modified it. My decision will be respected. After I had been eliminated, the party began, and should continue the serious task of selection of another candidate from among the numbers of distinguished men available."[57] There was no question now that the decision was irrevocable. There would not be another Coolidge campaign for the presidency in 1928 or any other year.

With the Shermanesque statement from the president, Secretary of Commerce Herbert Hoover officially announced that he would be a candidate for the Republican presidential nomination. When Hoover announced, "Creager did not even bother to consult with the Texas state chairman, Eugene Nolte, before announcing that Hoover would receive all the votes of the Texas delegation to the national convention."[58] In a one-page news release from Washington on December 9, the national committeeman declared that his first choice of a Coolidge re-election was no longer a viable alternative. Creager explained, "So long as there was any chance that the president might accede to the overwhelming demand of the people, I favored a call to him but his statement Tuesday was a revelation of personal desire that I feel it would be presumptuous to disregard. He has renounced an unprecedented national tribute and has placed himself among the immortals." Then he made evident his support and that of the delegates he controlled by declaring, "I am for the nomination of Herbert Hoover as the Republican candidate for president in 1928. I believe he will have the support of Texas Republicans and that the Texas Delegation to Kansas City will be solidly for him." In typical Creager fashion the news release pointed out that he had seconded the Harding nomination in 1920 and was an early backer of Coolidge in 1924, before claiming that the party now had a permanent state headquarters and a "party organization in nearly every one of the 254 counties."[59]

The Creager declaration that the state was solidly behind Hoover did not sit well with a number of local GOP leaders. Wurzbach and Scobey viewed this as an opportunity to line up additional supporters around the state in their effort to remove Creager. In an editorial the *Houston Post-Dispatch* indicated that it saw the Creager action as heating up the ongoing dispute in the party: "With smouldering enmities ready to flare, Mr. Creager's recent espousal of the Hoover candidacy fanned the flames. The Wurzbach faction made common cause with a group of prominent 'regulars' led by C. C. Littleton of Fort Worth.... This group favors an uninstructed delegation to the Kansas City pow-wow—a delegation not openly hostile to the Hoover candidacy but free to support Vice-President Dawes, for instance, if the winds of fortune should favor him." The editors concluded, "if the tide runs against Mr. Hoover nationally, Mr. Creager may find himself at the tip end of a long and high limb, with the Littleton faction ready to saw it off."[60]

The national committeeman had to mend fences. In a letter to state chairman Nolte he took the offensive by claiming that Texas had to be a leader among Republican ranks. Although he had previously called for a conference of party leaders should Coolidge not run again, Creager maintained that the president's final statement in December required quick action on his part. "I am sure that you will agree with me that the Texas Republican party has 'reached its majority' and can be expected to do something finer and more courageous than 'waiting to see how the cat will jump.' Therefore I made public endorsement of Mr. Hoover, believing from conversations and letter in which you have expressed your views to me, that you would approve of my action." He went on to claim that "leaders in the party and other leading citizens have expressed their congratulations on the early stand of Texas." Among a number of reasons Creager gave for supporting Hoover, one was telling: "Mr. Hoover is essentially an organization man. He has been that all his life. He appreciates the need of political organizations and only asks that they be clean and patriotic."[61]

At a January meeting of the SREC in Dallas, the committee voted to endorse Herbert Hoover by a margin of 27 to 1. Creager's overwhelming control was evident in that many of the votes were cast by proxies held by the party leaders. The lone dissenting vote was cast by C. C. Littleton of Fort Worth, who "entered a vigorous protest against what he termed the 'domination' of Texas Republicanism by national committeeman Creager and state chairman Eugene Nolte."[62]

The campaign for an uncommitted slate of convention delegates became the latest weapon for the Wurzbach forces. In an early February letter to the legislator, Scobey concluded that "from information I have, believe Hoover's fight is slowing up but I believe we will have a fight to beat him."[63] Although he was allied with Wurzbach, Littleton, William "Gooseneck Bill" McDonald, and Captain Jack Elgin in promoting an uncommitted slate, Scobey clearly favored Vice President Charles Dawes for the presidency and endeavored to convince him to enter the race. That same month he wrote to Dawes and reported, "The situation in Texas is looking good. My late friend, Creager, said everyone had to be for Hoover and the people did not like that. We are going to try to have an uninstructed delegation. If it was so you could become a candidate we could muster your strength more effectively, especially with the American Legion."[64] Dawes was not interested in taking on such a challenge and indicated in response that he favored Illinois governor Frank Lowden for the nomination. Wurzbach then announced that he would spend several days in the Dallas–Fort Worth area building a statewide organization for an uncommitted slate. He claimed that a clear majority of Texas Republicans supported sending an uninstructed delegation to the national convention.[65]

Throughout the spring a number of states held Republican presidential primaries, but the results were mixed for the Hoover candidacy. Unpledged delegates won the nation's first primary in New Hampshire, followed by Lowden carrying North Dakota and his home state of Illinois while Senator George Norris was winning Wisconsin and his own state of Nebraska. In early contests Hoover won overwhelmingly in Michigan and Massachusetts, but his first competitive victory was not until Ohio on April 24, where he won 68.1 percent of the vote. The Ohio win was followed by competitive losses in both Indiana and West Virginia, but he garnered more delegate votes by running basically unopposed in Maryland, New Jersey, Oregon, and his home state of California. With the limited number of primaries concluded, Hoover was clearly in the lead, but the contest remained an open battle for the nomination.

On May 10 congressional district conventions were held across Texas prior to the May 22 state convention in Dallas. The Wurzbach forces contended that these district meetings were authorized to select delegates to both the state and national conventions. Creager maintained that state law required the state convention to choose all delegates, including both the four at-large positions and those representing the eighteen congressional districts. Along with the Creager allies declining to seat several delegations where national convention delegates had been chosen at the district meetings, this technical distinction became the basis of the Wurzbach challenge to the Creager delegation at the national convention.

Prior to the state convention Creager traveled to San Antonio and met with some of his local supporters, including state chairman Nolte. Creager announced in advance of the convention the names of those who would be national convention delegates, assuring the media that they would not include Scobey and Elgin, Wurzbach supporters chosen at the 14th congressional district convention. He told the *San Antonio Express* that there was no possibility of the Wurzbach faction prevailing. "It will be proven conclusively that there is not a vestige of authority either in party rule or Texas statute for the holding of a district convention to send delegates to a national convention of any political party. The state is the unit.... I don't mind saying in advance that Messrs. Elgin and Scobey will not be sent to Kansas City as delegates from Texas, but that Drs. Thomson and Terrell will be sent."[66] Creager declared that his faction of the party would control 90 percent of the delegates to the state convention and pointed out that a majority of the Republican National Committee, where any delegation challenge would first be heard, had endorsed Hoover's candidacy.

When the Republican convention convened in Dallas on May 22, it was clear that the Creager forces would use every tool available to maintain power and ensure a national convention delegation committed to Hoover. Contested delegations were sent from twenty-two counties, and all were decided in favor of the Creager forces, and many against Black and Tan delegations constituted mainly of blacks. As one historian noted, "All the techniques of convention control were in evidence. Police were used, and badges were denied many to stop them at the auditorium door.... A listing of devices used in this convention to keep control included the voting of pocket counties, the flagrant use of proxies, the prejudiced selection and decision of contested delegations, the denial of badges for admittance, police strong-arm methods, and control of the convention rostrum."[67]

It was a time when convention rules allowed much leeway, including the use of pocket county delegates. Since a contest of a county delegation could come only from someone residing in that county, voters from smaller and more distant counties could come and present themselves as state convention delegates without ever having held a county or precinct convention, knowing there would not be anyone else from their county who could contest their delegation. According to the minutes of the 1928 state convention, fifty-one counties, covering much of the Panhandle and West Texas, sent uncontested delegations to the convention without ever having held precinct conventions. An additional technique used by Creager supporters was the securing of proxies from smaller counties where no local voter was willing to attend the state convention. Thus a nearby county chairman might be able to cast proxy votes allocated to several different counties.[68]

When Littleton of Fort Worth, a leader of the Wurzbach forces, attempted to protest the treatment given to the black-majority delegations not seated, he was ejected from the convention hall. At this point, one of the convention doors was smashed, and the police were called into action. As the *New York Times* reported:

> Those demanding an uninstructed delegation forced the reading of a minority report upholding their position and it was then that trouble started. Mr. Littleton was seized by a policeman as he entered through the smashed auditorium door, and J. E. Elgin of San Antonio, a member of the State Executive Committee, likewise was led out.... Mr. Elgin was led out when he sought to have Littleton recognized as Temporary Chairman. Mr. Creager rushed to the platform and roared that the convention was not going to be "taken away from us."[69]

Littleton was arrested and briefly detained for allegedly destroying public property. Wurzbach then walked out of the convention. At this point one of the leaders of the Black and Tan faction called out, "All Republicans follow me!" and shortly thereafter a rump convention was convened in a nearby hall.[70] After being released on bond, Littleton became presiding officer of the rump convention, whose members elected four at-large delegates to the national convention and ratified the selections made at the district conventions.[71] The Wurzbach-Littleton forces would continue their battle by appealing to the Republican National Committee, asking to be seated as the legitimate delegation from Texas.

When the two delegations made their case before the national party committee, the question arose as to whether a party organization existed throughout the state. Creager made the claim that there were county chairs in 247 of the state's 254 counties, but it was quickly challenged by Elgin, representing the uninstructed-delegation forces. Elgin presented affidavits from 140 county clerks testifying that there was no Republican county chairman or organization in their counties. The charge was damning but irrelevant to the Hoover supporters on the committee.[72] Historian Richard Sherman writes, "In nearly every instance the committee's decision favored Hoover, often to the disadvantage of Negro politicians. For example, the pro-Hoover delegation from Texas, led by R. B. Creager, was seated in place of a racially mixed group, with the result that the Texas delegation to the national convention was for the first time entirely white. Although the lily-whites were not awarded every contested seat, the decisions tended to put the black-and-tan regulars on the defensive."[73] The overriding question for the Republican National Committee was neither whether a delegation represented a viable state organization, nor whether it was inclusive of both blacks and whites, but whether the delegation was totally committed to Hoover's nomination. Two weeks earlier Creager had maintained that there were at least fifty-seven Hoover supporters on the national committee, and in their actions on seating contested delegations he was proved correct.[74]

One week later the convention credentials committee sustained the action of the national committee in a vote of thirty-four to fifteen, refusing to seat the uninstructed delegation. As one historian summarized the situation, "Amidst the din of charges and countercharges of corruption, the lily-white, pro-Hoover faction, led by the suave R. B. Creager, squared off against the anti-Hoover black-and-tan regulars. . . . As expected, the committee seated Creager's lily-white delegation."[75] Representative Wurzbach, who lost his position as a delegate, immediately announced that he would appeal the decision to the convention floor. When that vote was taken, the Creager forces were victorious once again in a vote of 659.5 to 399.5, indicating that the Hoover forces were in control of the convention. At that point, all serious opposition to his nomination ended, and Hoover was nominated on the first and only ballot with 837 of the 1089 delegate votes cast.[76]

For the first time in its history the Republican Party of Texas had sent an all-white delegation to the national convention. Included along with Creager and Nolte were Houston banker Thomas P. Lee, engineer and former Hoover associate James F. Lucey of Dallas, and Fort Worth attorney Henry Zweifel. All twenty-six delegates were white males, while five females were included among the alternate delegates. There were no delegates, male or female, with Mexican-American names. Perhaps as a commentary on the prevailing prejudices of the time, to some unnamed Texas reporters it was "the finest body of men that has ever represented a southern state in a Republican convention."[77]

To some observers the battle at the 1928 national convention was between the pro-Hoover Lily Whites, who controlled the state party, and the anti-Hoover Black and Tans led by William M. "Gooseneck Bill" McDonald.[78] But the division was not so clear cut. While in Texas the pro-Hoover forces were clearly the Lily White faction in state politics led by Creager, those seeking an uninstructed delegation were organized more by Wurzbach, Scobey, and Littleton than by McDonald or other traditional Black and Tan faction leaders. The dispute was more accurately another in the long-standing conflict between Creager and Wurzbach over patronage and party control. Moreover, while the pro-Hoover forces were the Lily Whites in Texas, this was not the case in all southern states. Being for Hoover's nomination was accounted for by more than race, as was the situation with the pro-Hoover Black and Tan delegations from Mississippi and Tennessee that were seated over Lily White challengers.

Once the national convention was completed, Wurzbach turned his attention to the re-election campaign against his Democratic opponent, Bexar County Judge Augustus McCloskey. Attending the August state convention, Littleton received a positive welcome when he pledged his support for Hoover.[79] Not all was sweetness and light with others who had lost out in Kansas City, however. At a news conference in Fort Worth on July 16, McDonald and J. M. O'Hara officially announced their defection from the Republican Party and their support for Al Smith. O'Hara, who had been organizational director for the uninstructed-slate effort, claimed that "the traditions and principles of the Republican Party as practiced by Lincoln, Roosevelt, Lowden, and Dawes have been subjected to the policies of Boss Vare and the autocratic administration ring, dominated by Andrew Mellon." He went on to claim that they would deliver 250,000 voting Texans to the Smith campaign.[80]

THE 1928 GENERAL ELECTION

For the first time in history, a Republican presidential candidate carried Texas as Herbert Hoover bested Governor Al Smith. According to historian T. R. Fehrenbach, it was the three Ps of Protestantism, prohibition, and prosperity that won the state for Hoover. "The rural belts were Southern and fervently Democratic in loyalty; Republican to most Texans was still a dirty, capitalist word. But Smith's Catholicism and views on liquor hit the loyal Democrat farmer where it hurt most."[81] In a postelection analysis Creager maintained that prohibition was the main reason the party lost the German vote and picked up votes from other rural Texans. To him the defection of black voters to Smith was not a great loss: "The negro vote has been declining in Texas for some years.... Probably not to exceed 6 or 7 percent of the adult negro population ever votes.... The negro is a political liability to the Republican in the South. Fewer of them are voting, most of those who do want money in one way or another, and their affiliation ruins the standing of a party with the overwhelming majority of voters."[82] Creager failed to explain that the decline in African-American votes was due to the requirement to pay a poll tax by January 31 prior to the November election, combined with the actions of the Democratic Party in excluding blacks from voting in their primary. Such factors contributed greatly to the decline in political involvement among blacks.

While Creager took credit for the Hoover victory, many observers believe it came about due to the efforts of the anti-Smith Democrats, or Hoovercrats, who convinced Texas voters to split their tickets.[83] The Republican candidate for senator, T. M. Kennerly, polled a respectable 130,172 votes against Tom Connally, who had defeated Senator Earle B. Mayfield in the Democratic primary runoff. Nevertheless, Kennerly obtained only 18.7 percent of the vote, while Hoover carried the state. In the contest for governor, Republicans came up far short once more, but their candidate, W. H. Holmes of Amarillo, did poll 123,337 votes, thus requiring the holding of a Republican primary election again in 1930.

Creager's early support of Hoover was designed to ensure his continued role as patronage referee in Texas once Hoover kept the White House in Republican hands. For this to happen, however, more was needed than a Hoover win. Creager still had to contend with Wurzbach, who had established strong relationships with some close Hoover associates. The experience of 1926 had shown that it would be difficult, if not impossible, to deny renomination to Wurzbach even without a primary in 1928. In such a situation, "from Creager's point of view, it was imperative to retire Congressman Wurzbach in the

November elections in 1928, while carrying Texas for Hoover."[84] Recognizing that they could not openly endorse the Democratic candidate for Congress, Creager and Nolte provided McCloskey with assurances of their tacit support and attempted to dry up as many sources of campaign funds for Wurzbach as possible.

Wurzbach kept in close contact with the national party leaders to ensure their continued support and to seek additional funding. In early September he wrote to the secretary of the Republican National Committee to explain that he represented what he considered the "wettest" district in the state, one that would likely go to Smith in the presidential contest. Nevertheless, he believed his chances of re-election were good: "Bexar County polls about four thousand negro votes, and although the Democrats are making desperate efforts to line them up for Smith, I believe that we will hold a large majority of them in line by calling attention to the fact that the Texas Legislature about a year ago passed legislation preventing negro participation in Democratic primaries."[85] One week later Wurzbach wrote to the chairman of the Republican National Congressional Committee seeking a contribution and pointing out that "My opponent will have strong financial support and I have the best of reasons to believe that some of this financial support is coming from the Creager-Nolte following. Unquestionably, the Republican patronage crowd is fighting me under cover."[86] This claim was repeated in a telegram to another national party official in late October, in which Wurzbach reported, "I expect to win. Federal officeholders fighting me under cover."[87]

Wurzbach's optimism was unfounded, in terms of both support from his constituents and the determination of his political enemies. After early unofficial returns gave the edge to Wurzbach, the political machinations began. From election night to mid-January the vote totals changed almost continuously as recapitulations were reported from various counties. What had been a re-election by 427 votes became a defeat by some 600 votes in January, when McCloskey obtained a certificate of election from the Texas Secretary of State and was sworn in as a member of the US House of Representatives.[88]

Wurzbach immediately challenged the election on two fronts. A grand jury indicted McCloskey and some local Democratic officials for election fraud.[89] During the trial, the deputy county clerk of Bexar County admitted that he had entered false reports, saying that he "did it to protect my friends and was double-crossed."[90] Six precinct judges testified that the returns had been altered in Bexar County. The official returns of at least fourteen precincts were ignored by the canvassing board in favor of tally marks submitted by the deputy county clerk. In his defense, McCloskey did not deny that the returns were altered but maintained that he personally did not alter them. While McCloskey was found not guilty, the testimony brought forth in the trial weighed heavily against him.[91]

The second and more successful path for Wurzbach was to challenge the election before the House of Representatives. After having served four terms in Congress, Wurzbach had built up positive relationships with many of his fellow Republicans. Moreover, the evidence presented in the Bexar County courthouse made it difficult to defend the fairness of the McCloskey election. A special committee on elections was appointed, but its work dragged on until it finally reported in his favor in February 1930, whereupon Wurzbach replaced McCloskey for the remainder of the two-year term.[92] McCloskey's political career was over, and Wurzbach would be back in Washington to represent his district and continue as a nemesis for Creager.

THE FINAL CONFLICTS

During the year in which Harry Wurzbach was out of Congress, two more serious charges were levied back and forth between the two rival party leaders. In early 1929, Republican senator Smith Brookhart of Iowa, chairman of the Senate Post Office subcommittee, began hearings on the sale of federal patronage in southern states. Focusing on Texas, one witness claimed that Creager had provided protection against Prohibition raids on certain hotels in Dallas and Fort Worth. Another witness, Lloyd E. Hill, testified that he had signed a promissory note for $1,200, payable to Creager, when he sought the position of postmaster for Fort Worth. In response, Creager called the charges ridiculous and added, "I understand that Hill has been actively identified with my political opponents."[93]

The following month Wurzbach testified before the subcommittee and claimed that promissory notes payable to the Republican state organization from May 1921 to January 1929 amounted to more than $200,000. He maintained that the use of promissory notes indicated clearly that the contributions were not voluntary. Senator Brookhart reported that his subcommittee had identified 350 such notes, over two-thirds of which had been signed by postal employees.[94] Wurzbach then personally identified nine additional signers as holders of other federal patronage appointments, including a US attorney, a US marshal, and a customs collector.[95]

In a strongly pro-Creager column, Irvin S. Taubkin of the *New York Times* claimed that despite the testimony before the Brookhart subcommittee, the "organization, well captained by R. B. Creager, holds its head unbloodied and unbowed." Taubkin alleged that most of the political opinions expressed in the state favored Creager and that Wurzbach had not gained support apart from his own followers. What the hearings had accomplished, according to Taubkin, was "to have stirred to renewed effort all other foes of Creager and his machine."[96]

When called to testify before the subcommittee on March 1, Creager turned the tables and charged that Wurzbach had received illegal campaign contributions from federal appointees during his 1926 primary campaign. Creager produced checks from a postmaster in Houston and another from C. K. McDowell of Del Rio, a former county judge and Republican state chairman.[97] He challenged the Brookhart committee to present whatever evidence they had concerning himself and Wurzbach before a federal grand jury.[98] Two days later a grand jury in Waco indicted Wurzbach for alleged violation of the Corrupt Practices Act. Creager denied any involvement in the indictment process.[99]

Senator Brookhart did not accept Creager's denial of involvement and claimed that the grand jury action involving Wurzbach was designed as a diversion from the investigation into Creager's own patronage practices. As Brookhart maintained, "He showed by statements before the committee that he knew the indictment of Wurzbach had been obtained, even though it was not yet public, and had been obtained by a United States Attorney he had appointed, John D. Hartman. From the record I have reached the conclusion that he was responsible for the indictment of Wurzbach for the purpose of stopping the investigation."[100] Brookhart then entered into the record some thirty letters submitted by Creager that praised him, but the senator had his staff add notations of the promissory notes previously signed by each of the writers.

As part of the indictment of Wurzbach some twenty-four affidavits were submitted from individuals who were serving as federal employees when they contributed to the Wurzbach primary campaign in 1926. The legislator did not deny receiving the funds but maintained that since they were made for a party primary contest, federal prohibitions did not apply.[101] After US District Judge DuVal West dismissed the indictment, Creager refused to concede the matter. He sent a telegram to Lawrence Richey, secretary to the president, asking that the Justice Department appeal the dismissal to the Supreme Court: "Wurzbach and his friends have openly charged indictment was result political persecution and that district attorney and his friends knew the statute did not apply.... In the light of charges made by Wurzbach and Brookhart it is particularly important and common justice demands decision be had by supreme court."[102] The Hoover administration acceded to Creager's request, and the matter was appealed to the Supreme Court, which held, in a unanimous decision written by Associate Justice Oliver Wendell Holmes Jr., that prohibitions on contributions from federal employees apply to all elections, including primaries. Therefore, the indictment was reauthorized, and the case against Wurzbach would proceed.[103] Before a trial could begin, however, Wurzbach passed away.

In June and July the Brookhart subcommittee held hearings in San Antonio and Dallas where Creager presented a number of character witnesses and defended his actions as Republican national committeeman. At the San Antonio hearing Creager claimed that the committee was exceeding its authority and said he would not be bluffed by Senator Brookhart.[104] When the committee reconvened in Dallas, the decorum of the hearing was challenged on several occasions. Creager called out, "Beck is a nigger lover," when Harry Beck of Dallas, a leader of the Black and Tan faction, labeled the Creager machine as a "pie counter" interested only in controlling patronage.[105]

It was evident from the progress of the hearings that Brookhart was determined to limit Creager's influence in Republican politics. One of his objectives was to convince President Hoover and his key aides that Creager's access to patronage should be ended, an action that the president was unwilling to take.[106] This created some tension in the party when it appeared Hoover was willing to eliminate Black and Tan control of some southern state parties while continuing patronage machines controlled by Lily White factions such as in Texas.[107] The national committeeman's attacks on Beck during his testimony before the Brookhart committee did nothing to lessen the impression that blacks and those willing to work with them were no longer welcome in a Republican Party controlled by Creager. Six years later, addressing an August 1936 meeting of the SREC, Creager reinforced once again his views on inclusiveness in the party when he stated, "I believe it is wise, particularly in the South, that the leadership of the Republican Party still remain in the hands of the whites."[108]

Meanwhile, in the aftermath of the Senate subcommittee's hearings on corruption in southern Republican politics, two articles appeared in *Collier's* magazine implicating Creager. In the first article the author explained how job seekers were required to sign promissory notes payable to Creager that were then collected by a bank. According to the article, "several high books are required to contain the pledges of over a thousand Texas citizens who had promised to pay certain sums to Creager's political organization in Texas."[109]

One week later the magazine published an article by Texas writer Owen P. White that focused on Sheriff A. Y. Baker of Hidalgo County and his allegedly corrupt machine.[110] As Democratic leader in Hidalgo County, Baker was presented as being in alliance with Creager to ensure each other's political positions. When a group of taxpayers in the county attempted to nominate a reform ticket at the Republican county convention of 1926, Creager ensured that a rump convention held by five delegates loyal to him was recognized as the legitimate county convention. This eliminated the possibility of nominating the reform ticket to oppose Baker in the general election. Moreover, the rump convention would ensure a pro-Creager delegation at the Republican state convention.[111]

Some claimed that Creager acceded to the wishes of Sheriff Baker because he feared that otherwise the taxes on his sizeable landholdings in Hidalgo County would be raised substantially. Still others saw it as simply a means to ensure continued control of the party in the Rio Grande Valley and to prevent the rise of a reform group that might focus its next efforts against him. With his reputation besmirched in a nationally circulated popular magazine, Creager reacted by filing a $500,000 libel suit against the Crowell Publishing Company and its distributors. During the jury trial in Creager's hometown of Brownsville several witnesses said that it was generally known that Creager and Baker had an understanding. On May 15, 1930, the jury returned a verdict in favor of the defendants.[112]

When the Brookhart subcommittee issued its final report in March 1930, it charged Creager with extorting political contributions from federal officeholders and job seekers as well as undermining the growth of the Republican Party in Texas. The report further called on the Justice Department to review the evidence presented to the committee and determine whether proceedings should be started against those who violated the federal Corrupt Practices Act by bartering or selling public offices. Focusing specifically on Texas, the report concluded that "Creager's only interest in building up a two-party system in the State of Texas is to perpetuate himself in office as national committeeman of that State." It was for this reason, claimed the subcommittee's report, that "Creager did everything he possibly could to defeat Congressman Wurzbach" so he would have total control of federal patronage in Texas.[113]

Once the fraudulent results of the 1928 congressional election were overturned and Wurzbach reclaimed his congressional seat, he received over a thousand letters of congratulations, each of which he answered. Reviewing some of these documents reinforces the commitment Wurzbach had to his African-American constituents. In response to a congratulatory telegram from one San Antonio voter, he noted, "It is unnecessary for me to say how much I appreciate the loyalty of the colored voters of Bexar County. They have always stood by me and I have always tried to represent them fairly."[114] Thanking the general secretary of the Baptist Landmark Association of Luling, the legislator told them that "the colored voters of Guadalupe County have always been most loyal to me, and I shall in the future, as I have endeavored in the past, to merit their good will and support."[115]

By the time of the 1930 general election both Wurzbach and Creager had been badly bloodied but were still standing. With an indictment reactivated and a trial planned for the future, Wurzbach nevertheless easily won election to Congress by a margin of some 8,000 votes. He had been vindicated with his constituents, but he would not live to complete his term. Creager's reputation had been damaged by the Brookhart investigations, the sensationalized exposés of his political machine, and the loss of the libel suit. Yet he still had the support of the Hoover administration, and he continued as the patronage referee for appointments in Texas. Creager would continue to control Texas Republican politics for nearly two decades more.

On November 6, 1931, Wurzbach died in San Antonio at the age of fifty-seven from complications following an appendicitis operation. When his bier was placed in the San Antonio municipal auditorium, an estimated fifteen thousand persons paid their respects, and thousands more attended his funeral at St. Mark's Episcopal Church.[116] As one of his constituents described him, "Mr. Wurzbach possessed as much natural charm, affability, and accessibility, as any man I have ever met.... One was perfectly at home with Mr. Wurzbach within a few minutes."[117] During his six terms in Congress Wurzbach won the admiration and respect of his colleagues as well as the support of his constituents in Texas. Yet in his battles with Creager, he and his supporters continually came up short.

In retrospect, the battles between Creager and Wurzbach that consumed the attention of Texas Republicans for the decade of the 1920s can be viewed as a lost opportunity to build a viable Republican Party in the state. On a national level, Republicans controlled the White House and both chambers of Congress for the entire decade. Focusing almost exclusively on control of patronage, neither Wurzbach nor Creager was determined to build more than a paper statewide organization or to recruit candidates who might have a possibility of election. Only in 1924, when the Republican candidate for governor ran against Ma Ferguson with the tacit and even open support of the Ku Klux Klan, did the party's statewide candidate win a presentable though losing vote. By the time of the Hoover re-election campaign, any opportunity for assembling a viable political force in the state had been lost, and the party entered two long decades of neither political influence nor patronage.

FOUR

FROM ROOSEVELT TO TRUMAN

Three factors helped solidify Rentfro B. Creager's position in Republican politics until the late 1940s. With the rejection of the Black and Tan delegation at the 1928 national convention, the final challenge from its faction had concluded. While a few blacks would remain active in the party, the Lily White leaders had won out.[1] No longer would Creager face a concerted challenge to his leadership from William "Gooseneck Bill" McDonald and his supporters.

The deaths of four prominent Texas Republicans contributed to another void in competitors for control of the party machinery. Two Creager lieutenants and two of his strongest opponents would no longer be involved in intraparty battles. Leonard Withington, who had been the key staff person at the state organization headquarters in Dallas, passed away at the age of forty-five on February 3, 1930. Less than three years later, state chairman Eugene Nolte died at forty-six in January 1933. The most serious continuing challenger to Creager's domination of the party, Representative Harry Wurzbach, had died in November 1931, and earlier in the year another of those allied against Creager in intraparty combat, Frank E. Scobey of San Antonio, had also passed away.

Then in 1933 the Democratic Party regained the White House; they would hold it continuously for the remainder of Creager's time as national committeeman. The overriding reason to be associated with the Republican Party for many Texans, federal patronage, was now swept away. Only forlorn hopes for the party's return to power would sustain those dependent on government positions. Creager would now be the unchallenged leader of Texas Republicans but without the ability to dispense federal or state patronage.

For Creager to remain in control of the state party, it needed to remain a small and close-knit organization with few competitors for his rule. This would continue to be his method of ensuring influence in national party affairs throughout the remainder of his life. The classic example of discourag-

TABLE 4.1. TEXAS VOTES FOR PRESIDENT, 1932–1948

	Democrat	Republican	% GOP
1932	767,585	97,852	11.2
1936	730,843	104,728	12.5
1940	861,390	201,866	19.0
1944	820,048	191,372	16.7
1948	750,700	282,240	24.6

In 1944 the Texas Regulars slate of electors won 135,661 votes, for 11.8 percent of the total. In 1948 the States' Rights ticket received 106,909 ballots, for 9.3 percent. Other minor candidates received votes in each of the elections from 1932 to 1948.

ing involvement in the party by up-and-coming leaders was Creager's advice to Lloyd Bentsen Sr., whose father had been an active Republican in South Dakota. After Bentsen moved to South Texas, he sought out Creager, who was then serving as state chairman. Not wanting to encourage any competition for patronage from the Republican administration in Washington, Creager advised Bentsen to join the Democratic Party and help keep Texas a one-party state. Rationalizing that his recommendation was in the best interest of the state, Creager maintained that in this way the Texas congressional delegation could gain greater seniority and, therefore, more influence in the legislative process. A vibrant Republican Party might recruit candidates who could challenge these incumbent Democratic legislators and threaten their ability to build up seniority. The rest is history, as the Bentsen family went on to play an important role in twentieth-century Democratic politics.[2]

In many ways, without the appeal of patronage or the ability to elect public officials, the Republican Party of Texas from the start of the New Deal into the 1950s was basically a political club, with its few members committed by ideology, family, tradition, business contacts, or prominence. For performances on Election Day, the box score displayed no runs, very few hits, and lots of errors. Nothing explains the quick turn of fortunes for the Republican Party in Texas more than the 1932 presidential election. After having carried the state in his successful campaign four years earlier, President Herbert Hoover could retain the support of only 11.2 percent of Texas voters when he ran for re-election. Although he received the votes of 367,036 Texans in his 1928 campaign, only 97,852 were willing to give him a second term in the White House. For the remainder of the Roosevelt and Truman years, no Republican presidential candidate was able to obtain support from as much as one-fourth of the Texas vote.

An overview of the elections from the New Deal era through 1952 indicates how irrelevant the Texas party was to the election of public officials during that period. For the six general elections involving a contest for United States Senator, the Democratic party won every race by such an overwhelming margin that only once did the Republican candidate win over 25 percent of the total votes cast. H. J. "Jack" Porter of Houston, who would become a major force in the party by mid-century, received 32.9 percent of the vote against Representative Lyndon B. Johnson. Johnson had defeated former governor Coke Stevenson by eighty-seven questionable votes in the Democratic primary. Including the Porter showing, the average Republican percentage in the six races was 10.7 percent, slightly more than one in ten votes cast.

Of the 210 US House of Representatives elections from 1932 to 1950, the GOP had candidates filed in only forty-seven, or fewer than one-fourth of all possible contests. And even when a candidate did file for office the party's Election Day performance was abysmal. In only three of these forty-seven candidacies did Republicans win as much as 25 percent of the vote, including that of Ben Guill, who had won a special election in May 1950 only to be defeated in the November general election. Guill was the sole Republican over these twenty years to run a competitive race, with 47.5 percent of the vote in his unsuccessful effort to retain his seat in Congress.

While the Republican Party could retain its status without nominating any candidates for the US Senate or House of Representatives, its ability to remain a functioning legal entity required that it nominate a candidate for governor in each election. In the ten biennial contests for governor, Republicans ran candidates every time but achieved more than 25% of the vote only once, in 1932. In fact, eight of the ten candidates did not reach as high as ten percent of the vote. Only the election involving Miriam "Ma" Ferguson

TABLE 4.2. TEXAS VOTES FOR SENATOR, 1934–1948

	Democrat	Republican	% GOP
1934	439,375	12,895	2.8
1936	774,975	59,491	7.1
1940	978,095	59,340	5.7
1942	260,629	12,064	4.4
1946	336,931	43,750	11.5
1948	702,985	349,665	32.9

Minor candidates also received votes in each election except 1946.

TABLE 4.3. VOTES FOR TEXAS GOVERNOR, 1932–1950

	Democrat	Republican	% GOP
1932	522,395	317,590	37.7
1934	428,734	13,703	3.1
1936	782,083	58,842	7.0
1938	358,943	11,309	3.1
1940	1,019,338	59,885	5.5
1942	280,735	9,204	3.2
1944	1,007,826	100,287	9.1
1946	345,513	33,231	8.8
1948	1,024,160	177,399	14.7
1950	367,345	39,793	9.8

Minor candidates also received votes in 1932, 1934, and 1948.

in 1932 gave Texans a reason to consider the Republican candidate, Orville Bullington, who received 37.8 percent of the vote. As would be expected, no Republican candidate was elected to any of the myriad other statewide offices over this period of time.

The party's mediocre performance in gubernatorial elections meant that in 1934 only one primary was held in a handful of counties, involving the grand total of 1,554 voters statewide.[3] Under the Terrell Election Law (1905), a party was required to conduct a primary when its candidate for governor obtained at least 100,000 votes in the preceding election. After their candidate, B. J. Peasley of Tyler, obtained slightly over that number in 1944, the Republican Party leaders convinced the legislature to amend the law and require a primary only after a minimum of 200,000 votes was received in the general election, thus avoiding a primary in the next three gubernatorial election cycles.

Throughout the New Deal years no Republican served in either chamber of the Texas legislature. Likewise, Republicans were absent from virtually all of the state's 254 county courthouses. As historian Roger Olien summarized this period in Texas political history, it was "an extended period of hibernation" for the party in Texas.[4] What occupied the leadership of the state party was involvement in national Republican politics and especially control of the delegations to the various national conventions.

Creager was now the undisputed leader of the Texas Republican Party, but his defeat of internal competitors must have seemed at times a pyrrhic victory. No longer were there any state or federal elected officials in Texas. Nor were there any appointed officeholders from whom promissory notes of financial support could be collected. Faced with a shortage of funds, the state organization was forced to close its headquarters office in Dallas. Then in May 1935 Creager filed a voluntary petition for bankruptcy as mounting debts from failed investments overcame his existing assets.[5] He had hit bottom both politically and personally. Creager would recover, but his position and prestige suffered.

PRESIDENTIAL NOMINATING POLITICS

However, there was always presidential nominating politics to occupy Creager's attention. In 1935 Hoover made soundings about seeking the presidential nomination once again. Creager was among the party leaders the former president approached, but this time he remained uncommitted. Like many others who had supported Hoover in the previous two campaigns, he believed that running Hoover again would be a mistake. As various other candidates openly sought the nomination, "Hoover waited hopefully for deadlock," but none was to occur.[6] When the delegates convened in Cleveland, Governor Alf Landon of Kansas easily won on the first ballot.

Once again the Republican Party performed abysmally in the November election. Landon obtained the support of only 12.5 percent of those voting in Texas, while C. O. Harris received 7 percent in the election for governor, carrying only Kendall County, by a margin of two votes. Perhaps the only lasting positive accomplishment for the party in 1936 was the formation of the Texas Young Republicans under the initial leadership of Carter H. Stovall of Dallas.[7]

With another presidential defeat and few or no elected party members back home, Creager's position was similar to that of other southern Republican leaders of the 1930s and 1940s. These party faithful were described by V. O. Key Jr. in his 1949 classic, *Southern Politics in State and Nation*:

> The Republican chairman or national committeeman is apt now to be a businessman, of considerable wealth, who frankly regards his Republicanism as a hobby, an expensive hobby.... Most of them are overwhelmed by the futility of it all, but they keep the faith in a quiet spirit of dedication not unlike that of the Britisher who, although living in the jungle surrounded by heathen, dresses for dinner.[8]

Having fought off potential challengers to his position in Texas, Creager turned his attention to national Republican politics and the quadrennial battles for the presidential nomination.

After the overwhelming loss of 1936, Republicans witnessed the development of a conflict between the party's most recent president and its most recent presidential nominee. "The ex-President considered the election results a vindication of his strategy and an invitation to wrest control of the party from the Landon liberals who had flirted with the New Deal."[9] Hoover called for a midterm convention dedicated to drawing up a statement of principles around which the party could present a unified opposition to the New Deal. Landon opposed the idea on several grounds, including the belief that such a gathering might highlight disagreements within the party just as the 1938 campaign was under way.

While not endorsing another campaign for Hoover, Creager was supportive of the former president's idea of a national gathering. When the Republican National Committee met in November 1937, Creager told the media that the party's executive committee was strongly committed to holding a midyear conference.[10] By early 1938 a compromise was reached to distribute a survey to local leaders, followed by regional conferences and a final series of meetings in August 1938. The final report from all this effort was not issued, however, until Spring 1940, and it had little impact.[11]

After the Republican Party made a comeback nationally in the 1938 congressional elections, the drive for another Hoover nomination began again. In April 1939 media reports surfaced that "Colonel R. B. Creager, Republican National Committeeman from Texas and one of the original Hoover supporters, is reported to be leading the drive among Southern Republicans."[12] Despite these claims, little support was found for another Hoover effort, and Texas sent an uninstructed delegation to the 1940 convention in Philadelphia. In the end Creager served as a floor leader for Senator Robert A. Taft in his first losing presidential nomination campaign. The nomination eventually went to businessman Wendell Willkie, but "six ballots were required before Willkie received the nomination, and Texas under the firm control of Creager cast its twenty-six votes for Taft on every roll call."[13] It would not be the last time Creager and his allies would line up behind the candidacy of the senator from Ohio.

Once the convention ended, Texas Republicans gave their support to Willkie in the faint hope that he might defeat Franklin D. Roosevelt's unprecedented effort to obtain a third term in office. Opposition to Roosevelt and several of his New Deal policies had surfaced in Texas Democratic circles at least since his Supreme Court–packing efforts of 1937. After serving eight years as vice president, John Nance Garner believed that it was his time and turn to receive the Democratic nomination for president, but Roosevelt's decision to seek a third term ended that possibility, as well as Garner's role in the administration. In the face of an overwhelming renomination effort, all forty-six Texas delegates to the 1940 Democratic National Convention cast their presidential votes for John Nance Garner, an indication of both support for one of their own and disapproval of a precedent-setting third term for Roosevelt.

With the votes, if not the open support, of anti–New Deal Democrats throughout Texas, Republicans saw an opportunity to increase their vote in November. As historian George Norris Green notes, it was an odd situation when both the Democratic governor and the sitting vice president refused to endorse the candidacy of their party's incumbent president.[14] Although Willkie received roughly twice as many votes as the Republican Party's candidate in 1932 and 1936, his total constituted less than 20 percent of all votes cast in the November election.

A year after the re-election of President Roosevelt to his third term, Japanese forces attacked the American naval base in Hawaii. For the next several years the nation was focused on its efforts in both Europe and the Pacific. While many Republican leaders had been clearly noninterventionist, if not isolationist, prior to the bombing of Pearl Harbor, Willkie had supported many of Roosevelt's more interventionist policies. As the war began, Willkie continued to be a prominent Republican supporter for FDR's foreign and military policies and was joined by most other Republican leaders, who agreed that "politics ends at the water's edge."[15]

Although he gave his backing to the war effort, Willkie very much wanted to be the Republican Party's nominee for president again. In early 1943 his book *One World*, which advocated active US involvement in world affairs and the creation of a postwar international organization, received wide distribution.[16] For four months it sat atop the *New York Times* best-seller list. Meanwhile Willkie maintained an active correspondence with Republican leaders across the country and prepared for the 1944 primary elections. One Texan with whom he attempted to line up support was Eugene "Mike" Nolte Jr. of San Antonio, son of the late state chairman of 1923–1933. The younger Nolte had been the party's candidate for the Railroad Commission in 1942 and would later run for governor. Unlike his father's consistent loyalty to Creager, Nolte had an on-again, off-again relationship with the national committeeman. Willkie implied that he had Nolte's backing when he wrote in early 1944, "I certainly appreciate your fine support and am sure that with fellows like you on the team, we can win out this time."[17]

Creager was definitely not a supporter of Wendell Willkie or his interventionist policies. Just as he had been in 1940, the national committeeman was aligned with the Taft forces in the party and their candidate for the nomination, Governor John W. Bricker of Ohio. An agreement had been reached in 1940 that Senator Taft would seek the nomination that year in return for his support of a Bricker candidacy four years later, an agreement that Taft and his supporters kept. Bricker's strategy was to line up votes from convention and caucus states, building on what he anticipated to be a base of support from southern delegations and his own Ohio. To this end, Bricker was a featured speaker at the May 1944 Republican state convention in Houston, an appearance lined up by Creager.[18]

Wendell Willkie's campaign focused on the early Republican primaries to show that he had support beyond the party elite. His first major effort was in Wisconsin, a state that was known for having strong noninterventionist sentiment among its progressive Republicans. When the results of the April 5 primary came in, they were an unmitigated disaster for Willkie, and his campaign promptly ended. Willkie came in fourth, with only 4.6 percent of the vote. General Douglas MacArthur won overwhelmingly with 72.6 percent of the vote, as he did one week later in neighboring Illinois. But the MacArthur vote was from the heart and not the head. Totally involved in the Pacific war, the general was in no position to return and become an active candidate for the presidency. The Republican Party would need to find a candidate elsewhere, and its focus was turning to Ohio and New York.

Thomas E. Dewey had sought the nomination previously, in 1940, but had subsequently been elected governor of New York. Dewey had come to national attention first in 1935 as the crusading special prosecutor and later district attorney for New York City. In 1938 he lost a close race for governor, but he was successful on his second try. While Dewey had little support in a Texas party controlled by Creager, his national campaign manager, Herbert Brownell, allied Dewey's candidacy with an ongoing anti-Creager faction led by Hobart McDowell from San Angelo and W. C. "Colley" Briggs from Paducah. In a letter to Brownell, Briggs described the Creager faction as "reactionary and isolationist."[19]

Brownell could make headway only with those on the outside of state party leadership, but that did not seriously detract from his candidate's ability to gain the nomination. Dewey ended up receiving all of the state's convention delegates after Bricker, the favored conservative candidate, withdrew before any votes were cast.[20] Bricker then became the vice presidential candidate on a Dewey-Bricker ticket. When the delegation returned to Texas, however, they faced new opportunities and challenges.

Once again the conservative element in the Texas Democratic party was dissatisfied with the direction of the Roosevelt administration and unwilling to concede to his ambition for a fourth term in office. Rather than file a candidate against Roosevelt, the conservatives' strategy was to select a slate of electors pledged to not support FDR in the Electoral College. Led by former governor Dan Moody, with support from Senator W. Lee "Pappy" O'Daniel, the conservatives prevailed in the first state convention in May. On a key vote of 940 to 774, the conservatives were empowered to select a slate of delegates to the national convention, and they proposed electors committed to supporting a candidate other than Roosevelt. This resulted in most of the Roosevelt supporters leaving the convention for a rump convention that selected its own slate of national convention delegates.[21]

At the Democratic national convention in Chicago, the credentials committee voted to seat both Texas delegations with half a vote for each delegate. Both the conservatives and the rump Roosevelt forces threatened to walk out, but in the end the two delegations were seated. While the rump Loyalists cast all of their twenty-four votes for Roosevelt, the conservative Texas Regulars split twelve for Roosevelt and twelve for Senator Harry Byrd of Virginia.[22]

When the Texas Democrats returned home and held their second state convention, the conservatives were outvoted by those loyal to the president, and the delegates selected a new slate of Loyalist electors. This led the Texas Regulars to petition the courts to allow their slate to remain on the ballot as the official Democratic slate of electors. When this failed before the Texas Supreme Court, the Texas Regulars formed themselves as a separate party and filed their slate of presidential electors with the Texas Secretary of State.[23]

Thus began an abortive effort to bring together the two competing slates of anti-Roosevelt electors. Various meetings were held between Texas Regulars and officials of the Republican National Committee. The Dewey forces put pressure on the Texas party to propose a workable compromise to avoid having two competing anti-Roosevelt slates on Election Day. One reporter summed up the dilemma: "The aim of the Republicans is to elect Dewey. The insurgent Democrats want to defeat Roosevelt. It adds up to the same thing, but the anti-New Deal Democrats apparently do not want to wear the Republican collar, for they remember how long it took some Democrats of Texas to live down bolts to Hoover."[24] Meanwhile, the Texas Regulars tried to convince the Republicans to withdraw their slate of electors from the November ballot. When asked about it, Creager replied, "I can say they would like to have that done. It will not be done."[25] He did admit, however, that a method to combine Texas forces opposed to Roosevelt's re-election was being considered.

As the election drew ever closer, Creager made a proposal in mid-October to replace twelve of the party's twenty-three electors with Texas Regular electors who would agree to cast their votes for Dewey. This arrangement was never consummated, and on October 18, Creager declared that it was too late for a mixed ticket of electors to be agreed upon.[26] Great confusion resulted as defections occurred back and forth, with some Texas Regulars announcing their support for the Republican slate while others, such as GOP leader Henry Zweifel of Fort Worth, calling on Republicans to vote for the Texas Regular slate. Some commentators have held Creager responsible for failing to accomplish unification with the Texas Regulars, not only for the 1944 election but also as an opportunity to bring some existing state leaders and elected officials into the Republican fold.[27] The end result of the inability to join together had little impact on the outcome of the presidential race in Texas but may have delayed the Republican Party's ability to make inroads with conservative Democrats. The combined total of votes for both slates amounted to 326,664, 28.5 percent of the total, as Roosevelt easily carried Texas and the nation on his way to a fourth term.

CREAGER CHALLENGED ONCE MORE

Prior to another presidential nominating contest, Creager had to confront some new challenges to his domination of the Texas party. When John Philp abruptly resigned as state chairman due to illness in May 1946, Creager was caught without an obvious candidate. George Hopkins, a state Republican executive committee (SREC) member from Dallas, sought the appointment, and Creager acceded, in the belief that his own eventual candidate could gain the post at the state convention.[28] When the 1946 state convention took place in August, Creager experienced two momentary setbacks. First, Creager was resigned to accepting the continuation of Hopkins as state chairman. In the intervening months since his appointment, Hopkins had lined up support from various sources statewide and had not crossed Creager on any substantive issues. Zweifel had made moves to become chairman, but in the end Hopkins was re-elected. Creager would soon regret that outcome.

Additionally, Creager's candidate for the gubernatorial nomination, Alvin H. Lane, was upset by surprise candidate Eugene "Mike" Nolte Jr. in a vote of 178 to 150.[29] The media and most political observers had assumed that Lane had the nomination locked up, since he was Creager's choice. That was not to be as the delegates selected a rather nontraditional nominee. A beer distributor and nightclub owner, Nolte had been the party's candidate for state land commissioner in 1942 and had received the expected minimal level of voter support. However, Nolte brought with him a family history of involvement in the party, which helped him obtain the votes of many delegates around the state. His father, Eugene Nolte Sr., had been Creager's state chairman and chief ally in the battles against Wurzbach. Two years earlier, in 1944, Mike Nolte had joined Creager in defeating a pro-Dewey element in Bexar County. But in 1946 he believed it was his time to receive honorary designation as the party's candidate for governor.[30]

After the convention ended, Nolte told his employees, many of whom served as Bexar County precinct chairs as well as beer truck drivers, "It was a rough fight. There was lots of opposition but I finally won in the nominating room and then we took it to the floor and we won there, getting about 200 out of 254 counties."[31] Making the most of the situation in which he found himself, Creager quickly pledged his "active and energetic" support to Nolte's campaign while the candidate promised an active effort with headquarters in major cities across the state.[32]

While Nolte did undertake a statewide effort to rally support, reality quickly set in, and he remembered that he was the gubernatorial nominee of a political party that had last won such an office by a handful of votes in 1869. On the Monday before the November election, Nolte conceded, stating to one reporter, "I have no illusions. Beauford Jester will be our next governor. I made out like I was going to win. You know I traveled 5,000 miles, making speeches all over the state in big and little towns."[33] The final vote was overwhelming: Jester 345,513; Nolte 33,231. Once more the party was far from being competitive.

There were, however, the beginnings of a move to develop a two-party system in the state. In January 1947 Captain J. F. Lucey, an independent business owner from Dallas who was a personal friend of Hoover, announced the formation of the Republican Club of Texas, with plans to establish local units throughout the state. Naturally, Creager saw this movement as a direct challenge to his control of the party. He claimed that any such clubs should be formed only with the cooperation and involvement of the state organization.[34] Publicly Creager portrayed the dispute as caused by those opposed to the selection of Hopkins as state chairman and the nomination of Nolte for governor, overlooking what appeared to be the obvious target of the new organization. Nolte called the Republican Club "a group of Dallas millionaires dissatisfied with the beating Alvin Lane took."[35]

After Bexar County Republican Party chairman Joe Sheldon hosted an open meeting of the new Republican Club, Creager and Nolte convinced the county executive committee to remove Sheldon and replace him with a Nolte loyalist.[36] While the Republican Club of Texas continued organizing across the state, the Creager forces maintained their counterattack. A few months later state chairman Hopkins removed Ralph Currie, a club supporter, as Dallas county chairman. Then, when the SREC met in July, Creager's supporters removed general counsel Lane and finance chairman Marrs McLean from their positions in the state organization. Both had been involved in the initial formation of the Republican Club of Texas.[37]

In September leaders of the Republican Club vowed to "fight to the finish against the strong party control in the hands of Hopkins, national committeeman R. B. Creager of Brownsville, and Eugene Nolte Jr. of San Antonio."[38] Shortly thereafter Lane filed a lawsuit contesting the removal of Currie as Dallas County chairman. Lane alleged that Hopkins's "primary interest is to keep the Republican Party in Texas a small, streamlined organization. My primary desire is to promote the growth of the party."[39] The Texas courts, however, refused to intervene in what they regarded as a private matter to be settled within the political party.

In the organization's newsletter, the Republican Club alleged that "the 'Old Guard' has pledged the Texas delegation to Governor Thomas E. Dewey of New York." Although Nolte was flirting with Dewey but ended up supporting Taft, and Hopkins was indeed a Dewey backer, the claim certainly did not apply to Creager, who maintained, "The Texas delegation will support the candidate whom we think can win. That is the objective. To win."[40] Creager had chosen wisely in 1920 with his early endorsement of Harding, and had followed that up with loyalty to Coolidge in 1924 and another early endorsement of Hoover in 1928. In 1940, however, he held the Texas delegation for Taft through six roll-call votes until Willkie ended up with the nomination. Creager's loyalty to Taft and his conservative principles seemed to outweigh his comments about backing a winner as he lined up votes for Taft again in 1948 and laid the groundwork for another Taft campaign in 1952.

When Nolte invited Republican Club leaders and old-guard forces to a peacemaking barbecue at La Villita in San Antonio, some five hundred Republicans attended. While others made a plea for harmony, Creager told the crowd, "The regular Republican party organization is going to stay in control and to hell with the outsiders that are trying to break in."[41] That same month, Lucey passed away, and with him the financial and organizational base of the Republican Club movement was gone. Although others tried to keep it alive, the organization failed to exist as a political force by early 1948.[42] As one reporter described the situation, Creager was "back firmly in the saddle in Texas after something of a revolt earlier this year, but the end of the warfare appears to have been conditioned on his not insisting on a Taft delegation if it appears in the spring of 1948 that Mr. Taft will not make a strong nominee."[43] The reality was that another challenge to Creager's control had been overcome, but he would once again end up leading a strongly pro-Taft delegation to the 1948 national convention.

1948: DEWEY VERSUS TAFT

Presidential politics once again took center stage as the year 1948 began. Herbert Brownell, who had been campaign manager for Dewey in 1944 and then served until 1946 as chairman of the Republican National Committee, attempted to line up support in Texas for his candidate. State chairman Hopkins was a committed Dewey supporter, as were some party leaders in West Texas. Former Minnesota governor Harold Stassen, who would make his only serious challenge for the presidency in 1948, had some dedicated supporters in the Panhandle and scattered throughout other areas of the state. But as in 1940, Creager was firmly behind Taft, and therefore so too was the state organization he controlled.

The precinct conventions were held in May, and both the Dewey and Taft forces organized their supporters, resulting in several contested delegations at the county and state conventions. The hard-nosed politics in Bexar County was a precursor of what was to take place across the state four years later. By 1948 Nolte had switched his earlier support for Dewey and was now firmly aligned with Creager and the Taft campaign. Nolte refused to release the locations of the precinct meetings in Bexar County, forcing the Dewey supporters to obtain a court order requiring him to post the locations at the courthouse. Nolte finally complied, but not until the actual day of the precinct meetings. When the county convention was held, "Nolte contested the precinct results, and the Nolte-appointed county chairman threw out elected delegates and replaced them with Nolte-backed Taft supporters."[44]

When the SREC met prior to the state convention, the members voted to remove fourteen of the nineteen county chairmen appointed by Hopkins and replaced them with individuals loyal to Creager and the Taft campaign. Thirteen contested delegations, including those from Bexar and Dallas counties, were decided by the credentials committee, which seated the Taft delegates, with only two small contested counties being awarded to the Dewey forces.[45] When the full convention convened, "Creager firmly controlled the state convention, which declined to seat county delegations unfavorable to Creager."[46] To avoid the possibility of a bolt and a credentials challenge at the national convention, Creager consented to the selection of Hopkins and one other Dewey supporter as delegates, along with one Stassen advocate, Ruthelle Bacon of Amarillo. This ensured that Taft would receive thirty of the state's thirty-three delegate votes.[47]

While the Dewey forces had to admit defeat in their attempt to win a majority of the delegate votes from Texas, they would be successful once again at the national convention. Moreover, their efforts to recruit supporters throughout the state helped to create "a bloc of committed partisans with a vested interest in the GOP's future," a development that would eventually lead to the shift from patronage politics to an attempt to win elective office.[48]

After Dewey won the party's nomination, the second state convention was held in August in Waco. With Republicans optimistic about the chances for a Dewey victory in November, the issue of patronage and who would control it came to the fore once more. It was estimated that there could be about two thousand patronage appointments in Texas that would once again be in Republican hands. As reporter Allen Duckworth noted, "Original Dewey men like state GOP chairman George Hopkins, Dallas, don't think Creager should be the one because he backed the wrong horse in the nominating race—Senator Robert A. Taft."[49] The expectations of a Truman loss were widespread. His party had been split, with dissenters from the left backing the Progressive Party candidacy of former vice president Henry A. Wallace, while many Southern Democrats were bolting to the Dixiecrat movement led by South Carolina governor J. Strom Thurmond. Meanwhile Republicans were fairly unified behind the man who had already run one race for president and who was governor of the nation's most populous state.[50]

When the delegates assembled in Waco, Hopkins was no match for Creager. "The Republican faction led by state chairman George Hopkins of Dallas was ground to bits by a well-oiled Creager political machine."[51] Hopkins's candidate for state chairman, Hobart K. McDowell of San Angelo, was defeated by Creager's choice, Henry Zweifel of Fort Worth, in a vote of 214 to 50. As the convention proceeded, Hopkins was defeated on vote after vote but used every opportunity to publicly criticize the national committeeman. "Creager did not engage in debate with Hopkins. He sat quietly, a few feet away from the chairman, puffed a cigar, heard himself denounced again and again. But the voting went his way."[52]

For governor the convention selected Lane, who had sought the nomination two years earlier but had lost to Nolte. As political writer Duckworth noted, "The Lane nomination was a victory for another Hopkins foe. Hopkins had ordered him fired last year as Republican state counsel."[53] The shifting alliances among the various players was clearly evident at the 1948 convention. Lane had been Creager's candidate in 1946, then allied with the Republican

Club movement, which led to his removal from his state party position, only to come back into the national committeeman's good graces. Nolte, who had run against the Creager-backed Lane in 1946, then had favored Dewey early in the campaign season, was now solidly on the Taft and Creager team. Meanwhile Hopkins, who had allied with Creager against the Republican Club effort, was now without any political influence in the party.

The convention also nominated a Creager ally from Brownsville, Carlos Watson, for US Senator in a holding action until a stronger candidate could be recruited. Houston oil producer H. J. "Jack" Porter had been named chairman of a candidate recruitment effort and met with retiring senator W. Lee "Pappy" O'Daniel in an effort to convince him to seek another term, this time as a Republican. When that approach failed and no other suitable candidate could be found, Porter was convinced to make the race, and Watson stepped aside.

It was difficult to find prominent Texas business leaders willing to associate with the Republican Party, a problem Porter confronted in his search for a senatorial candidate. During the Roosevelt administration, with Democrats in control of the White House, Senate, House of Representatives, and virtually every elective office in Texas, there was little incentive to associate with the Texas Republican Party. While many wealthy oil industry leaders were opposed to various policies of FDR and his associates, their opposition was expressed within the confines of the Democratic Party. One of the first prominent leaders in the oil industry to clearly identify as a Texas Republican was Marrs McLean, originally of Beaumont and later of San Antonio. In 1938 McLean had accepted the position of finance chairman for the Republican Party of Texas; he continued in that role off and on until 1952.[54]

With Harry Truman in the White House and Republicans resuscitated nationally with the congressional victories of 1946, a few other wealthy oil industry leaders began to consider the GOP alternative in Texas. Behind the scenes Roy Cullen worked with Jack Porter to help convert the Texas party into an avenue for election to public office rather than simply a patronage machine. After Porter became the GOP candidate for the Senate in 1948, Cullen publicly endorsed him. Most wealthy oil industry leaders, however, gave their money and their votes to Lyndon Johnson.[55]

Republicans were more optimistic than usual about their chances in the senatorial contest due to the outcome of the Democratic primary. When O'Daniel decided not to seek a second term, several candidates filed for the nomination. This resulted in a runoff between Representative Johnson and former governor Coke Stevenson. After the late returns came in from Box 13 in Jim Wells County, where the votes were cast in alphabetical order, Johnson had won statewide by eighty-seven votes. As historian T. R. Fehrenbach concluded, "There was probably no injustice involved. As in most close races in Texas, Johnson men had not defrauded Stevenson, but successfully out-frauded him."[56] One result was that Stevenson endorsed Porter and made several speeches on his behalf.[57] Porter took his nomination seriously, hired a professional campaign staff, and campaigned full-time against Johnson, linking him to the Truman administration. His campaign ran ads in most daily newspapers across the state, and Porter rallied local Republicans who realized that he had a better chance of winning the seat than Dewey had of carrying the state.

As the results came in on Election Day, Republicans were shocked to learn that Truman had been returned to the White House, but less surprised that he had easily beaten Dewey in Texas.[58] Their candidate for the US Senate had also lost, although Porter had received more votes than Dewey and more than any previous Republican candidate except Hoover in his 1928 campaign. Porter received nearly twice as many votes as Lane, the party's gubernatorial candidate, and carried eleven counties while making a competitive showing in Dallas, Harris, and Bexar counties.

Porter came away from the 1948 campaign convinced, as were many others in the state, that with strong candidates and an effective campaign operation the Republican Party might become a competitive force in state politics. Porter's first move was to help reorganize the Young Republicans, which had first been organized by Carlos Watson and Thomas E. Ball in 1930 but had faded into inactivity during the New Deal era. The Young Republicans would serve as a base of support and activity for the younger voters who were becoming politically involved in the post–World War II period.[59]

THE END OF THE CREAGER ERA

Dewey's failure to capture the White House in a four-way contest was not the only loss for the Republican Party in 1948. Campaigning against what he labeled a do-nothing Congress, Truman had led his party to an across-the-board victory. Nationally the Republicans lost seventy-five seats in the House of Representatives and nine members of the Senate, ending the brief majority they had held in both chambers for two years. As is often the case, much of the blame was directed at the chairman of the Republican National Committee, in this case Representative Hugh Scott of Pennsylvania. With any opportunity for dispensing patronage gone, Creager turned his attention once again to national party politics, serving as the spokesperson for the Taft people on the national committee. In this capacity, he was one of the leaders in a move to seek Scott's resignation. When Scott finally announced in July that he was stepping aside, backers of all three elements in the party—the Dewey, Taft, and Stassen supporters—wanted nothing done that would rock the boat.[60] In the end, Guy Gabrielson, national committeeman from New Jersey, won the nod and became national chairman.

Texas Republicans did receive some encouraging news in May 1950, although it would turn out to be simply a momentary high point. When Representative Eugene Worley resigned from his district in the Panhandle, eleven candidates filed for the special election, including one Republican, Ben Guill, a real estate broker from Pampa. The contrasting reactions to the Guill candidacy from Creager and Porter were symptomatic of the divisions in the party. Porter, who had been an organizer of the Texas Independent Producers and Royalty Owners (TIPRO), rounded up about one-fourth of Guill's campaign funds, mainly from independent oil producers in the Houston area. Meanwhile no financial support was forthcoming from either the state or the national party because, as Olien notes, "Creager was not interested in helping Guill get to Washington."[61]

With the Democratic vote scattered among several candidates and no requirement for a runoff if no one received a majority, Guill came out on top, becoming the first Republican in nearly twenty years to win a seat in Congress from Texas. National party leaders soon made the most of the victory. According to chairman Gabrielson, "Voters of the Texas Panhandle have demonstrated that the South shares the disgust of the rest of the nation over the Truman Administration program of socialism."[62] Unfortunately for Guill, he was to lose re-election only six months later in the November general election.

While some minor skirmishes developed at the 1950 state convention in Galveston, Creager was once again in control. As in all previous nonpresidential election years, more Texans voted in the Democratic primary, where the real choice for public offices would be made, than voted in the November general election. Ralph Currie, who had been removed as Dallas County chairman two years earlier, was nominated for governor. Currie mustered fewer than forty thousand votes, constituting less than ten percent of the total votes cast. Meanwhile, Edward T. Dicker became a state representative from Dallas, the first Republican in the Texas legislature since 1930. Dicker's tenure was also short-lived: he was defeated for re-election in 1952, and the legislature went back to total Democratic control.

Prior to the general election, on October 28, 1950, Creager died in Brownsville at the age of seventy-three. Creager had been the dominant force in Texas Republican politics for more than thirty years. A master at national convention politics and the dispensing of patronage when the party controlled the White House, Creager had done little to build a viable party organization in the state. According to Michael Bowen, "His ruthless management style, not any sort of mandate from the grassroots of the party, allowed Creager to remain at the top of the Texas GOP."[63] Summing up his record as party leader, V. O. Key concluded, "Nothing in the operations of the Creager organization dispels the belief that it desires no electoral victories."[64] Creager's dominant objective was to control the state organization, not to expand the party's base in terms of either supporters or elected officials. From the experience of dealing with Harry Wurzbach, Creager learned that elected officials became competitors for the dispensing of patronage. More supporters of the party only increased competition for whatever patronage could be distributed.

Although one can question whether there was any viable path that would have made the Republican Party of Texas a competitive force, clearly Creager was not interested in exploring the possibility. In his battles with Representative Wurzbach, the focus was always on controlling patronage from a Republican administration in Washington. After Roosevelt and then Truman became president, Creager's dominant concern was national party politics, with control of the state organization an essential requirement for continued influence. Creager had left his mark on the Republican Party of Texas, but it was a mark of failure in terms of any efforts to present an alternative choice to the state's electorate. The Creager regime had ended, and the party was about to enter a new phase of internal conflict but one that would begin moving it toward building a competitive political force.

FIVE

THE EISENHOWER YEARS

As the 1950s began, presidential politics became the focus of attention once again for many of the individuals active in the Republican Party of Texas. This decade, however, would be quite different from nearly all the preceding ones in the history of the party. Twice during this decade, the state's electorate would choose a Republican candidate for the presidency, a result obtained only once previously in the Hoover election of 1928. But more important in the long run was the recruitment and activation of a new cadre of volunteer activists, individuals who would serve as candidates, managers, and campaign workers for an emerging political force over much of the remainder of the twentieth century. None of this would have come about without a change in the direction of the party from patronage to elections, a change brought about by the elevation of new party leaders in the aftermath of the 1952 presidential nominating contest.

THE TAFT-EISENHOWER BATTLE

Conflict within the Republican Party of Texas ended up being one of the key factors in the eventual nomination of Dwight Eisenhower as the Republican presidential candidate in 1952. In many ways it was a battle between Henry Zweifel and Jack Porter as much as it was between Eisenhower and Robert A. Taft.[1] With the death of R. B. Creager, the state Republican executive committee (SREC) met on November 21, 1950, to name a new national committeeman. State chairman Zweifel was the candidate of the old guard, with backing from Carlos Watson, Orville Bullington, and most of the Creager organization, which still maintained a clear majority on the SREC. Porter announced for the position with the support of Alvin Lane, Ralph Currie, and the party's two most recently elected public officials: former member of Congress Ben Guill and new state representative Edward Dicker. Ever the maverick, Mike Nolte also indicated his interest in the position. Before the votes were cast, both Nolte and Porter withdrew, and Zweifel assumed the position Creager had held for nearly thirty years.[2] Bullington, a former gubernatorial candidate, then took over as state chairman of the party.

Although Porter withdrew from the contest for national committeeman, it was clear that he had developed a deeper and continuing interest in revitalizing the state party, and he had the energy and the personal finances to devote himself to reshaping it. His campaign for the US Senate two years earlier had provided him with statewide contacts, but not the support of the old-guard Republicans on the SREC. What he did have was the support of those Republicans committed to winning elections. Over the next two years Texas Republicans engaged in what was "basically a contest between the old faction of the party which sought only control of the federal patronage, and the new faction which had a real desire to build a genuine two-party system party in Texas."[3] What Porter needed to gain traction within the party was a presidential candidate around whom he could rally support. That candidate would be a native of Texas who was known as a war hero for his leadership in World War II.

Some wealthy Texas oil industry leaders attempted to rally support for a presidential candidacy by General Douglas MacArthur without much success or direct interest from MacArthur. It was another retired general who became their standard-bearer, someone they could support as a Republican candidate while retaining their ties to the Texas Democratic Party.

Dwight David Eisenhower had served as president of Columbia University from 1948 to 1953, taking a two-year leave of absence to become the first supreme allied commander of the North Atlantic Treaty Organization (NATO). While at Columbia, Eisenhower established the American Assembly project to harness the views of leading businesspeople, political leaders, and intellectuals on problems and issues confronting the nation. In many ways the first think tank, it provided a vehicle for Eisenhower to develop contacts throughout the country and involved extensive fundraising to underwrite the program. This effort has been described as a shadow campaign that laid the groundwork for support in his eventual 1952 presidential drive.[4]

On one of Eisenhower's fundraising trips to Texas for the American Assembly project, Porter met with the former general and came away convinced that he was the candidate to support. From 1950 on Porter dedicated himself to lining up support for Eisenhower. "Eisenhower's candidacy was exactly what Porter needed for his own purposes. With the Texas Republican organization still firmly in the hands of the pro-Taft old guard, Porter, like Creager in 1920, needed a candidate who would carry him into power.... Porter would have to do more than support Eisenhower; control of the delegation to the national convention was every bit as important as backing the winning candidate."[5] Behind-the-scenes maneuvering took place during most of 1951, and by November the lines were more clearly drawn. Senator James Duff of Pennsylvania toured the state as part of a Draft Ike movement, and Porter began publicly organizing Eisenhower for President activity. He hired three full-time field workers to build grassroots support and to explain the process of participating in precinct, county, and state conventions where delegates would be selected for the national convention. Many of those who were re-cruited were presidential Republicans who had always voted in the Demo-cratic primary. This time they were being asked to attend a precinct meet-ing, many of which would be held in a longtime Republican's living room.[6] Although Texas oil industry leaders were attracted to Eisenhower's personal character and his widespread name recognition as a war hero, many were motivated more by his support of the Texas position on the tidelands dispute over whether the state or the federal government controlled oil deposits off the Texas coast in the Gulf of Mexico.[7]

Once it was evident that Porter would lead the Eisenhower effort in Texas, Zweifel announced his support for Senator Taft and was named his state campaign manager. Unlike Porter, who attempted to recruit new supporters, "Zweifel had no interest in expanding the Texas Republican Party if the new recruits did not agree with him."[8] Zweifel was quoted as saying he would "rather lose with Taft than win with Eisenhower."[9] Clearly for him it was a contest of Zweifel versus Porter for control of the party organization. Porter's overall objective was the same. In December 1951 he admitted that this was his goal in a letter to Eisenhower. "It is just this simple: if I control the state convention, I can name the delegation, and if Henry Zweifel of Fort Worth controls the state convention, he can and will name the delegation."[10] It was clear that either Porter or Zweifel would be leading both the national con-vention delegation and the state party organization for the next four years.

In an attempt to suppress Porter's efforts, the SREC, firmly in the hands of Zweifel and state chairman Bullington, voted at its February 1952 meeting to require a pledge from all who participated in the May 3 precinct meetings. The pledge stated: "I am a Republican and desire to participate in Republi-can Party activities in the year 1952." Although the pledge was not legally binding, its proponents felt that the mere fact of having to declare oneself a Republican in Texas would discourage some voters from crossing over and supporting Eisenhower. Porter objected to the pledge, but to no avail. He asked the longtime party leaders, "Is it more important to perpetuate a small party in Texas or expand it and win an election?" To many Taft supporters, the answer was evident.[11]

On May 3, 1952, some 2,200 Republican precinct conventions were to be held in Texas, each one electing delegates to one of 230 county conventions, which, in turn, were to elect 984 delegates to a state convention on May 27 in Mineral Wells. Building on broad support for Eisenhower among the electorate at large, Porter and his forces convinced many who had never been involved in politics to attend these Republican precinct conventions. As the date approached, the Taft forces feared that these "New Republican" Eisenhower supporters would overwhelm them at many precinct conventions. Zweifel urged his supporters to walk out when outnumbered and hold rump conventions elsewhere.[12]

When the precinct conventions were held across the state, thousands of Eisenhower supporters swamped the longtime Republicans who were supporting Taft. In some precincts where only a handful had attended four years earlier, more than five hundred showed up in 1952. In most counties it was the Eisenhower forces that prevailed, resulting in the Taft backers bolting, reconvening in another location, and selecting a Taft slate of delegates to the county convention.[13] "In Fort Worth, state (Taft) chairman Henry Zweifel bolted the convention held in his home, where he was defeated as precinct chairman by a vote of 63 to 50. Zweifel crossed the sidewalk and held a rump convention on the curb."[14]

Frank Crowley and his wife Martha showed up at the home of the pro-Taft precinct chairman in East Dallas where the precinct convention was being held. "He said we weren't really Republicans. The Taft delegation in our precinct consisted of the precinct chairman, his wife, and their son." When the Eisenhower supporters managed to get in the house, the precinct chairman and his family retreated to a back room and held their own precinct convention. Crowley later became a Republican county commissioner and county judge in Dallas County. "What we had done here in the precincts in Texas had the telling effect of gaining Eisenhower the nomination and, ultimately, the Presidency," according to Crowley, "so no one ever had to come preach to us afterward about the importance of grassroots organization."[15] One of the rare exceptions to the Eisenhower dominance was San Antonio, where Nolte and Marrs McLean carried out extensive outreach to motivate Taft supporters. The end result of the precinct meetings across the state was a series of credentials challenges at the county, state, and national conventions.

Days after the precinct meetings, county conventions were held across the state, and once again the outnumbered Taft forces held rump conventions in many places, while the Eisenhower backers bolted in a few isolated counties.[16] The result was contested delegations to the state convention from thirty-one counties, including Dallas, Harris, Bexar, Tarrant, Travis, Cameron, and Potter counties, representing some 512 of the convention's 984 delegates. When the SREC met on May 25, the Eisenhower forces maintained that "in most of the contested counties the Taft forces bolted after being outvoted in the main conventions." McLean, a leading Taft financial backer, countered by claiming that Democrats were encouraged to attend the Republican precinct meetings.[17]

In twenty-nine of the thirty-one contested county delegations, the SREC voted to seat the Taft supporters, deferring to the Eisenhower delegations only in Galveston and Lavaca counties. Even this slight victory for the Eisenhower forces was overturned, however, when the convention credentials committee, led by Nolte, replaced the Galveston and Lavaca delegations with Taft supporters. After the credentials committee vote, Nolte predicted that Porter would "probably import a lot of hoodlums Tuesday to take over the convention."[18] Meanwhile, Eisenhower leader Howard G. Swan of Galveston asked, "How many conventions must you be thrown out of before you qualify as a Republican in Texas?"[19]

There was no question as to who was in control of the party machinery. To Zweifel, "this is a fight for Americanism and the American way of life and will be so regarded by history." As one reporter analyzed the situation, "In a demonstration of pure machine control, the committee kicked Eisenhower delegations right and left and awarded control of Tuesday's state convention to Zweifel and his Taft backers. A bolt and rival convention is the only opening left to Jack Porter of Houston and his pro-Eisenhower followers."[20] The following day the delegates gathered for the state convention. Outside the hall, supporters of General Eisenhower held up signs saying "Taft Crooks Enter Here" and "Rob with Bob" as the newly seated Taft delegates entered. When the full convention was convened to order, with the challenged Taft delegations seated, the delegates turned down a request to override the actions of the credentials committee in a vote of 762 to 222.[21]

After the vote on the credentials committee report, Dallas Eisenhower leader Alvin Lane announced, "Hundreds of lawfully elected delegates to this convention have been thrown out by this committee and we will not stay here any longer." With that announcement more than two hundred Eisenhower supporters who had been seated walked out and reconvened in the Mineral Wells community hall, along with the five hundred supporters not seated at the official convention. This rump convention then selected thirty-three

Eisenhower and five Taft delegates to the national convention, a proportion reflecting what they claimed had been the distribution of support at the original county conventions.[22]

Back at the official convention, the remaining Taft delegates selected an uninstructed delegation dominated by Taft supporters. This list was heavy with the names of old-guard Republican leaders, including Zweifel, Nolte, McLean, Bullington, and Watson, along with former state chairman George Hopkins and Julius Neunhoffer of Kerrville. One new name appearing on the delegate list was of an individual who would later play a critical role in the party's development: John Tower of Wichita Falls.[23]

Leaving Mineral Wells, the Eisenhower forces made the most of the alleged theft of delegates by transforming the issue into a national crusade for honest elections. *Time*, *Life*, and *Newsweek* magazines all publicized what had occurred in Mineral Wells, as did the wire services covering the events for newspapers across the nation. Among the media supportive of Eisenhower, the *Dallas Morning News* editorialized that it was not surprised by what Zweifel and his supporters had undertaken. "He is merely preaching what the Republican State Executive Committee has practiced through many years. This little group of sixty members has done exactly as it pleased, regardless of the will of the majority of Texas Republicans."[24] The uproar over the "Texas steal" became a rallying cry that the Eisenhower forces would take to the national convention in Chicago.

Prior to the meeting of the Republican National Committee, whose members would initially determine convention credentials, the Taft forces proposed a compromise of twenty-two Taft and sixteen Eisenhower delegates from Texas, an arrangement that was approved by a vote of sixty to forty-one. Porter rejected the compromise and vowed to challenge it before the convention credentials committee and on the convention floor if necessary. According to Paul Casdorph, "the nationwide outcry against the Taft controlled national committee decision literally engulfed them."[25]

Both sides made formal legal presentations before the national committee and the convention credentials committee. In both cases, however, the Taft forces were in the majority and voted to seat the split delegation of twenty-two Taft and sixteen Eisenhower supporters.[26] This Taft victory was short-lived however. With challenges to the Georgia, Louisiana, and Texas delegations, Governor Arthur Langlie, an Eisenhower supporter from Washington state, convinced all twenty-five Republican governors to endorse a fair-play resolution preventing any challenged delegation from voting on credentials issues. When Langlie's resolution was brought to the convention floor as the first item of credentials matters, it passed by a vote of 658 to 548. This resulted in the loss of sixty-eight Taft delegates on future credentials votes.

Next up was the vote on Georgia's contested delegation. When the Eisenhower forces won in a vote of 607 to 531, the Taft campaign caved and moved to accept the Porter delegation from Texas.[27] Shortly thereafter, Eisenhower went over the top in pledged delegates and won the nomination on the first and only ballot. The Texas delegation then elected Porter as national committeeman for the next four years, and Zweifel left Chicago no longer a leader in the state party.[28]

Once back in Texas, Bullington called a unity meeting for July 19 in Dallas, where Porter and Zweifel pledged harmony and Tower called for a unified Republican campaign. Bullington then announced his resignation as state chairman, and the SREC filled his position by selecting Taft loyalist Watson over Eisenhower leader Lane. Eventually Porter succeeded in moving the party's headquarters to Houston, where it remained until 1961.

CROSS-ENDORSEMENTS:
DEMOCRATS AS REPUBLICANS

The political whirl continued with another round of precinct and county conventions to select delegates to another state convention in August. In many counties it was a repeat of the events of May, with factional fights and disputed delegations. This time the focus of the dispute centered on whether the Republicans would cross-endorse the Democratic statewide candidates in what appeared to be a quid pro quo for their support of Eisenhower. The political positions of the two-party factions were somewhat reversed. The old guard, led by state chairman Watson, maintained that "it is necessary that we nominate our own candidates for state offices if we are going to have a two-party state."[29] Meanwhile, it was Porter, the advocate of building a competitive party, who was now calling on the GOP to endorse a slate of Democratic officials rather than provide a choice to the Texas electorate.

There was substantial opposition to any such deal among longtime Republicans, with the Tarrant County chairman calling it "a sellout of the Republican Party" and Nolte threatening to create a separate conservative Republican party that would nominate its own slate of candidates.[30] As the party's delegates assembled in San Antonio for another state convention, the SREC settled the disputes over contested delegations by seating most regular convention groups, whether old guard or Eisenhower supporters. Meanwhile,

Nolte assembled the old guard forces to work out their plans for the convention.[31] Former state chairman Hopkins predicted "developments of an explosive nature" centered on opposition to Porter, who represented the force they had been fighting for four years.[32]

When the delegates finally assembled on August 26, however, all was sweetness and light. The motion to cross-endorse the Democratic statewide slate passed overwhelmingly with the proviso that if any candidate declined, the SREC would name a new Republican candidate. Watson agreed to step aside from the contest for state chairman, and Lane was elected unanimously. "Lane's election marked the first time in modern political history that a Texas Republican chairman was selected without the blessing of the Creager machine or its successor, the Zweifel machine."[33]

Texas Democrats were also divided as they approached the 1952 presidential election, but their main focus was on their differences with the Truman administration. When a dispute arose over the tidelands in the Gulf of Mexico, Texas attorney general Price Daniel, soon to be a candidate for the US Senate, pushed for Texas, rather than the federal government, to have control over them. Daniel and other state leaders claimed that Texas should have control up to three marine leagues beyond the shore, an area where substantial oil deposits were located. The state's claim was denied in federal court, up to and including the US Supreme Court. Allan Shivers, along with Senator Lyndon Johnson and Speaker Sam Rayburn, had attempted to develop a compromise, but with no success. As Shivers later recalled, "we successfully passed two bills through the Congress of the United States to quit claim these lands to Texas, and they were both vetoed by then President Truman."[34]

At the first Texas Democratic convention of 1952, the liberal faction, led by Maury Maverick, walked out, held a rump convention, and sent its own competing delegation to the national convention. Meanwhile, Governor Shivers led the conservative forces in the party, controlling an uninstructed delegation to the Democratic National Convention. At the convention, also held in Chicago, Senator Estes Kefauver of Tennessee, a candidate for the presidential nomination, met with Shivers in an effort to gain the support of the Texas delegation. When that failed, Kefauver announced that he supported ousting the Shivers delegation and seating the rump group led by Maverick, a position also taken by Averell Harriman of New York, another contestant for the Democratic presidential nomination. In the end, the Shivers delegation was seated and cast all fifty-six votes for Senator Richard Russell of Georgia as the nomination went to Governor Adlai Stevenson of Illinois.

Shortly after the national convention, Shivers traveled to Illinois and visited with Governor Stevenson concerning the Texas claim to the tidelands. The Democratic nominee was accompanied by Arthur Schlesinger Jr. and had previously discussed the issue with several federal officials, all of whom were against the Texas position. Since Shivers had no success at his meeting, "when I came back I announced that I could not support Stevenson for election as president of the United States and said why."[35] As the Democratic governor later noted, "I think it was one of the most difficult decisions that I ever had to make during the time that I was active in politics,... and I did a lot of soul-searching on it before making the decision."[36] When the Democratic state convention was held on September 9, it passed a resolution that urged "every Democrat in Texas vote and work for the election of Dwight D. Eisenhower for president and Richard Nixon for vice president."[37]

Led by Shivers and Senate candidate Daniel, the Democrats for Eisenhower organization took the lead in corralling support for the GOP presidential candidate. The conservative Democratic establishment, including elected officials, newspaper publishers, mayors of major and smaller cities, financial backers, and former governors all endorsed the Republican presidential nominee and gave his campaign a level of acceptability never before obtained by a Republican candidate. Eisenhower's support went beyond the presidential Republican element that first appeared in the 1920s. Serving as state Democrats for Eisenhower finance chair in both 1952 and 1956 was Harrell Edmund "Eddie" Chiles, who would be a major contributor in future Republican campaigns and whose wife, Fran, would serve as Republican national committeewoman during the Reagan administration.[38]

All statewide Democratic candidates save one ran on both the Democratic and Republican tickets in the November election. In effect, the Eisenhower campaign and the national Republican Party had made a pact with the devil. Focused entirely on reclaiming the White House after twenty years in the wilderness, they were willing to sell the Texas party down the river. Even Porter, the advocate of building a viable competitive party in place of the tightly controlled patronage operation long present in the state, was willing to go along to achieve the overriding objective of electing a presidential candidate. Porter viewed this as a tactical move on the path to creating a two-party system. Thus, it was Porter who called on Texas Republicans to endorse all the statewide Democratic candidates and refrain from challenging nearly all incumbent Democratic members of Congress, while the old-guard patronage Republicans were the ones advocating the naming of a separate slate of GOP candidates.

CONTINUING SUPPORT FOR TEXAS DEMOCRATS

It was clear that it was more than wealthy oil industry leaders who were abandoning their Democratic loyalties in supporting Eisenhower. With Governor Shivers and all but one statewide Democratic candidate endorsing Eisenhower, support for his candidacy can only tangentially be viewed as in any way supportive of a competitive Republican Party in Texas. No single person was more responsible for retaining a conservative presence in the Texas Democratic Party than Shivers, whose success in co-opting the Eisenhower candidacy helped prevent the spread of a viable Republican Party throughout the 1950s, limiting its successful growth to Dallas and a few other urban outposts around the state. Whether their income came from oil or other avenues, the very wealthy of Texas remained loyal to the Texas Democratic Party even with a Republican they had supported in the White House.

Among the wealthy Texans who remained active Democratic supporters in the 1950s and 1960s were retailer Stanley Marcus, Troy V. Post of Braniff International Airways, C. R. Smith of American Airlines, landowner and oil industry leader John D. Murchison, George R. Brown of the Brown & Root Construction Company, developer Raymond Nasher, attorneys Billy Goldberg and Robert Strauss, and insurance company owner and backer of liberal causes Bernard Rapoport. Still other wealthy Texans, including banker and rancher Dolph Briscoe, newspaper publisher Bill Hobby, radio executive Gordon McLendon, insurance executive and landowner Lloyd Bentsen Jr., and major Braniff stockholder William Blakley, became Democratic candidates and officeholders.

As late as the 1970s, most of the very wealthy of Texas still retained their loyalties to the state Democratic Party. In his work on *Fat Cats and Democrats*, G. William Domhoff concluded, "They may vote Republican nationally, or even give $1000 or $2000 to an Eisenhower or a Nixon, but they will continue to consider themselves Democrats and work to control the Democratic Party in their home localities."[39] Even as late as the 1980s, Houston developer Walter Mischer was the most prolific fundraiser in Texas for Ronald Reagan's presidential campaign while also being a leading source of funds for Democratic officeholders Barbara Jordan, Lloyd Bentsen Jr., and Mark White.[40]

BREAKING WITH THE ESTABLISHMENT

Few wealthy Texans were without some connection to the oil industry, whether as royalty holders, petroleum engineers, or providers of oil field services and equipment, or directly involved in production. A few successful oil industry leaders such as Porter were among the early financial backers of the Texas Republican Party in addition to contributing directly to GOP candidates and their campaign committees. Brothers Harry and Richard D. "Dick" Bass were key fundraisers for the Republican Party in Dallas. When Harry Bass became Dallas County GOP chairman in 1957, he promoted automatic monthly deductions of small amounts to provide a continuing base of support for the county party organization and ensure that it did not rely solely on a few wealthy donors.[41]

At the state level, the Republican Party of Texas subsisted not on the beneficence of a few wealthy backers but rather on support from middle- and upper-middle-class Texans, mainly in the more urban areas of the state. This support came from an active direct-mail solicitation program that produced average contributions of less than thirty dollars. Many of these funds came from homemakers who felt more comfortable identifying as Republicans than their husbands who depended on business interactions with the dominant Democratic establishment. Despite being portrayed as the party of the rich, as late as 1980 the state party organization had fewer than two hundred individuals who contributed as much as a thousand dollars a year, a handful of donors giving five thousand annually, and none contributing more than ten thousand. Some wealthy donors chose to provide substantial sums directly to candidates and their campaign committees.

Those who did provide major contributions at mid-twentieth century included individuals in the aerospace and electronics industries, independent investors, attorneys, and those in the ranching and banking industries. As Dallas began developing as a base of support for Republicans, the party involved Texas Instruments investors J. Erik Jonsson (later to become mayor of the City of Dallas) and Fred Agnich (later a state representative and Republican national committeeman), savings and loan executive L. E. Guillot, and prominent attorney William "Billy Mac" McKenzie.

It was only after the 1978 breakthrough election of William P. Clements Jr. as governor that major donors began identifying directly with the Republican Party, although much of the financial support went not to the party organization but to the autonomous "Governor Clements Committee," formed initially to eliminate the remaining debt from the governor's campaign. By the end of the twentieth century the two most prominent major donors to the party and to GOP candidates were not wealthy oil industry leaders but physician and inventor James Leininger of San Antonio and homebuilder Bob Perry of Houston.

THE EISENHOWER VICTORY

On Election Day Eisenhower received 53.2 percent of the vote in Texas, carrying the state's urban areas while losing the more rural counties by a small margin. His support was weak in the counties with a heavy black population and in the more strongly Dixiecrat counties of four years earlier. Donald Strong wrote, "Whatever else may be concluded of Eisenhower's victory it was, like Hoover's," ensured by "the Republicanism of white voters who had little preoccupation with race."[42] Nevertheless, a good number of Eisenhower's votes appeared to come from presidential Republicans who still identified with the state Democratic Party, and in reality "it had not been a Republican victory that carried the state for Eisenhower in 1952, but a strong conservative Democratic one."[43] Governor Shivers declared the election a protest vote that would not lessen Democratic dominance of state politics. According to Shivers, "it is a vote for the man. It is a vote against Trumanism, and is a vote for an honorable peace and better government."[44] This sentiment was evident in the bumper stickers displayed on pickup trucks and cars throughout the state that proclaimed "I'm a Democrat, but I like Ike."[45] As Shivers summed up the events of 1952, "Daniel went to the Senate, I was re-elected governor and Eisenhower was elected president of the United States. The Congress of the United States passed another quit claim bill, Eisenhower signed it, and we got the tidelands."[46]

The end result of the November 1952 election was to put a Republican back in the White House while continuing the near-total Democratic domination of Texas politics. As one Texas historian concluded, "Republicans owed their victory in the 1952 presidential election to conservative Democratic voters who otherwise remained loyal to their party. Shivers and his fellow leaders continued to support the traditional one-party system and to control government at the state and local level."[47] In reality, the Eisenhower win was a victory by and for the conservative Democratic establishment. Polly Sowell, an early Republican activist who would later serve as state party vice chairman, concluded that by running on both party slates "the Democrats effectively kept the Republican Party from growing during the 50s when Eisenhower was elected. It was all very cleverly done."[48] Most Texas Republicans, however, viewed it as a harbinger of future success. According to state chairman Alvin Lane, "the Republican Party is the friend of the South and will be recognized as such.... We are going to take a little breather. Then we are going to work for the next two years to make this a real two-party state with real candidates."[49]

EISENHOWER IN OFFICE

As Porter became national committeeman, he faced a number of concerns. Although he had been a vociferous supporter of Eisenhower in the battle against Taft and the old-guard Republicans, as well as in the November election, he soon discovered that he would not have the dominant role in patronage matters that had been played by Creager and previous national committeemen. The Eisenhower White House quickly determined that the key person to consult on patronage issues in Texas was not Porter or any other Republican official, but Shivers, the Democratic governor of the state.

The new president's chief of staff, Sherman Adams, believed that the ability to carry Texas was due to the efforts of Shivers and the Democrats for Eisenhower effort, a view that was shared by Herbert Brownell, a longtime party operative who became attorney general in the Eisenhower administration. Once ensconced in office, "Eisenhower largely ignored the state's embryonic Republican party, choosing instead to cooperate with Shivers and the conservative Democratic establishment."[50] According to historian Roger Olien, "As a result, the Democrats from the Citizens connection entered the front door of the White House while Texas Republicans queued up for scraps at the Republican National Committee."[51] Although only a few Texans received key appointments in the administration, all were Democrats, including Oveta Culp Hobby as Secretary of Health, Education, and Welfare, a prominent cabinet position.[52]

The preference of the White House political operatives for dealing with Shivers and his Democratic allies continued throughout the eight years of the Eisenhower administration. When Attorney General Brownell, a key strategist of the Dewey and Eisenhower campaigns and former Republican national chairman, came to Texas for a strategy meeting in preparation for the 1956 re-election campaign, he met not with Porter but with Governor Shivers. In fact, Brownell did not even notify Porter of his meeting with the Democratic governor.[53]

The policy of ignoring the Texas Republican Party and its leaders not only soured the party faithful toward their president but also hampered the ability of the party to grow and become a serious competitive force in the state. Olien views Porter's lack of influence over patronage appointments as an important factor preventing the party from gaining respectability in the state during the Eisenhower administration: "The political consequences of the inability of Porter and the Texas Republicans to control patronage went beyond the denial of places to party faithful and the attendant failure to groom strong candidates for state and congressional offices. Equally significant was the fact that Jack Porter and other party leaders could not demon-strate to influential state conservatives that the Republican party in Texas was to be taken seriously."[54] To many of the political, civic, and business leaders of Texas, Republicans were still viewed as somewhat outside the norm. De-spite the Eisenhower victory it was deemed socially unacceptable in various parts of the state to be identified as a Republican. Writing in 1963, Clifton McCleskey could claim, "Segments of the community crucial to Republican success, especially those engaged in some manner in serving the public, are often reluctant to become too closely identified with the GOP because of the fear it would lead to the erosion of their economic and even social position in the community."[55]

Thanks to Shivers's position that ideological convictions trumped parti-san loyalty, Eisenhower was able to carry Texas in both of his elections, and Nixon nearly won in 1960, losing by some 46,000 votes to a ticket featuring a Texan as the vice presidential nominee. Meanwhile, conservatives continued to dominate in the Democratic primary, thereby preventing the Republicans from developing a clear-cut alternative. This strategy proved unbeatable for many years and allowed the conservative faction to remain in control of the Democratic nominations and, with them, most statewide and local offices.[56]

William Murchison, who was an editorial writer for both the *Dallas Times Herald* and the *Dallas Morning News*, as well as a columnist and a keen ob-server of Texas politics, maintains that Shivers typified the strong southern Democratic and populist approach to politics that was dominant through-out much of Texas. This view was represented nationally by Senators Richard Russell of Georgia and Harry Byrd Sr. of Virginia, individuals who perceived themselves as "keepers of the faith" of southern traditions.[57]

The idea of conservatives staying in the Democratic Party and voting in the Democratic primary was pushed hard by the *Dallas Morning News* and especially Dick West, longtime director of the editorial page. In concert with Governor Shivers, West believed the conservative future remained within the Democratic Party to constrain liberal impulses. It was far more important to nominate conservative candidates in the Democratic primary because the Democrats were very likely to win in November.

Shivers had facilitated the growth of a special breed of Texas voters, the presidential Republicans, but in so doing had helped to ensure the continued conservative dominance of the Texas Democratic Party and had hindered the development of a viable state Republican challenge. In Murchison's view, "Shivers was concerned more with the ends than the means for the mainte-nance of conservative government in Texas. In his mind it was clear that con-servative Democrats could control Texas government and keep it conservative." Voting for a GOP presidential candidate was acceptable, but the state's politics needed to stay Democratic. In this context, both Shivers and White House political operatives played critical roles in continuing the conservative Democratic dominance of Texas politics throughout the 1950s and, in effect, until the end of the 1970s.[58]

Starting soon after the election, liberal and labor loyalists organized to gain control of the Texas Democratic Party, first with the Democratic Organizing Committee, founded in May 1953 with the aim "simply to return the Democratic Party to the Democrats."[59] Beginning in 1954, and especially in the 1960s, these liberal Democrats would occasionally throw their support to a Republican candidate who was running against someone they viewed as an unacceptable conservative Democrat. By 1958, the group Democrats of Texas was organized to gain control of the 1958 Democratic state convention. While the organizational names would change, similar groups of liberal Democrats would remain a factor in Texas politics for the next twenty years.[60]

In addition to the cold shoulder from the White House and the Shivers administration, Porter had to confront internal conflicts over the next few years. Although he had been supportive of the cross-endorsement strategy in 1952, when all but one statewide office saw the Democrats win on both tickets and the GOP oppose only one Democratic congressman, Porter now advocated running Republicans for all congressional seats in 1954. Meanwhile, some of the old-guard Republicans who had wanted to run GOP candidates in the previous election now were expressing opposition to Porter's more aggressive strategy. Former state chairman Bullington wrote President Eisenhower in November 1953 to complain about Porter's plans for opposing the incumbent Democratic members of Congress, most of whom were part of the "conservative coalition" that supported much of the administration's legislative agenda.[61]

Since Shivers had obtained nearly 470,000 votes on the Republican ticket, roughly one-fourth of his total, the GOP was forced to conduct a primary election in 1954 for the first time since 1936. Political commentators viewed the filing deadline as one opportunity to answer the question "Are Texans really turning Republican or did they just like General Eisenhower?"[62] Despite Porter's best efforts, the party could recruit candidates for only five of the state's twenty-two congressional seats and twelve of the 150 Texas state house districts. Among the candidates for state representative were two Republicans in Wichita County, one of whom was a twenty-nine-year-old professor from Midwestern University, John Tower. These sporadic efforts to field candidates led to criticism of both Porter, who was on a cruise for most of May 1954, and the administration in Washington.[63] Even more discouraging was the fact that the party could recruit volunteers to conduct a Republican primary in only 150 of the state's 254 counties and attracted a statewide total of 9,606 voters, roughly two percent of the number who had voted for Shivers on the Republican ballot in 1952.[64]

In the statewide races on the November 1954 ballot Tod R. Adams, the GOP candidate for governor, won only 10.4 percent of the vote, while Watson, running against Senator Lyndon Johnson, received support from 15 percent of voters. It appeared to one observer that "the Republican party, standing alone and without the benefit of cross-filing and Eisenhower, had dropped back to its normal insignificance in state politics."[65]

Texas Republicans did have one significant victory in 1954, however. In a contest for an open seat representing all of Dallas County, Bruce Alger became the lone Republican in the state's congressional delegation. The main thrust of Alger's campaign was that he was an Eisenhower Republican; his campaign stickers simply stated, "Back Ike—Vote for Alger for Congress." His opponent for the seat was Wallace Savage, who as chairman of the Texas Democratic Party two years earlier had been a leader in Democrats for Eisenhower. Savage, a former Dallas mayor, had defeated a liberal candidate in the party primary. According to one report, "Liberals here grew so irate that the plan to cross the party line in Tuesday's general election resulted."[66]

As one GOP leader noted a few years later, "If I had to trace the one thing that got the Republicans going on a statewide level, I would say it was the election of Alger. For the first time we saw that we could elect a man to Congress from the Republican party."[67] Alger attracted the support of a number of young middle- and upper-middle-class homemakers in Dallas, bringing into the party many new activists who would continue to play roles throughout the next several decades. In an obituary on Alger's death in 2015, political reporter John Gizzi maintained that "Alger, in fact, was the forerunner of the 'tea party' conservative of today."[68]

The Eisenhower election and Alger's subsequent campaign in 1954 saw the involvement of large numbers of women volunteers. As one observer noted, "at a time when women had fewer opportunities to pursue fulfilling careers, Republican activism was a socially acceptable and satisfying intellectual outlet." These moderate conservative women with talent and time available provided the institutional framework for local Republican organizations not only in Dallas but also in other urban areas of the state, the places where a middle-class-oriented conservatism had gained support.[69]

Having experienced breakthrough victories for their cause, many of these newly activated women formed the Texas Federation of Republican Women in October 1955. Beryl Milburn of Austin presided over the meeting at which the federation was formed and later became vice chairman of the Republican Party of Texas. Looking back on their efforts in the 1950s, Milburn noted, "I really think that the Republican Women's Clubs were the real levers that got people going because the women were freer economically to join and be Republicans than their husbands were" at a time when the business establishment in the state was overwhelmingly committed to the Democratic Party.[70]

Meanwhile, the national Democratic Party was committed to purifying the Texas congressional delegation. At a delegation meeting in March 1955, Democratic national chairman Paul M. Butler singled out the lone Republican, saying "We intend to see that you do not return, Mr. Alger. We're raising lots of money and will have plenty on hand." The new legislator's response was simply, "He dignified me with lots of attention. It surprised me. I didn't realize I was so important."[71] Alger would defy the Democrats' plans and go on to serve ten years in Congress until he was defeated in the Johnson landslide of 1964.

Just as Creager had faced a series of intraparty challenges to his leadership, so too did Porter. State chairman Lane, who had been a strong ally in the Eisenhower-Taft showdown, reached the conclusion that Porter was attempting to micromanage the party organization in much the same way as Creager had done. Lane was unwilling to be a figurehead state chairman and resigned after less than two years in office. At one of the rare meetings called for the SREC, Lane was replaced by John Q. Adams of Harlingen, the preferred Porter candidate, in June 1954.[72]

Porter also had a difficult relationship with the newly active Republican women's organizations. When the Fort Worth Republican women's club criticized the nomination of Watson as the party's token candidate against Lyndon Johnson in 1954, Porter called them backseat drivers. As author Meg Grier concluded, Porter "didn't take kindly to the idea that women should have more of a say about running the party."[73] One year later, when the state federation of women's clubs was formed, a longtime Republican leader in Amarillo noted Porter's desire for complete control of party affairs: "It looks like a big fight is shaping up for the women in the organization of the National Federation of Republican Women's Clubs for Texas. Porter has made it clear that no one can hold an office in the federation unless she supports him. Sarah Menezes and Mike McCarty are fighting his stand, but I fear they will not get very far."[74]

Disillusionment with Porter's leadership also developed among some party members opposed to maintaining a close relationship with the Shivers faction in the state Democratic Party. In the 1954 Democratic primary Governor Shivers was opposed by liberal candidate Ralph Yarborough, and many

Republicans felt their party leadership had encouraged GOP supporters to vote in the other party's primary. When fewer than ten thousand voted in the Republican primary it was apparent that many who traditionally voted Republican were helping Shivers fend off a challenge from the left. To Porter's critics, providing assistance to the continued conservative dominance of the Democratic Party lessened any possibility of the Republicans becoming an independent competitive force in state politics.[75]

One unnamed political activist described as "a long-time prominent figure in Texas Republican party affairs" predicted that conservatives, upset with the direction of the two national parties and the Eisenhower administration, would split from both major parties before the 1956 election. As one newspaper article summarized the situation, "Those Old Guard forces fought bitterly for the selection of Senator Taft in 1952. They will remain 'out in the cold' as long as the Eisenhower hegemony prevails. If Eisenhower is renominated, the opinion was that these Old Guard leaders would be ripe for the effort to join conservatives in setting up their own party and putting their own nominee before the voters."[76] It was clear that opposition to Porter and Eisenhower remained strong among some of the former Taft supporters. Likewise, in a July 1956 letter to the political editor of the *San Antonio Light*, Nolte claimed that there was little healing of the wounds from 1952. "Too many fine Republicans retain memories of the debauched Chicago convention; they remember how bona fide Taft delegates were ruthlessly unseated and were hooted and jeered as they left the hall by the motley crew of Fair Deal-liberals who had seized control of the convention."[77]

Most Texas Republicans, including those who had backed Eisenhower in the 1952 nominating battle, shared a political philosophy and outlook that was clearly more conservative and individualistic than the elements in the Eisenhower administration who were attempting to promote a "modern Republicanism" that accepted a more active federal government. Alger spoke of his support for the principles of individual liberty espoused by writer Ayn Rand and economists Ludwig von Mises and Friedrich Hayek.[78] Writing to Rita Crocker Bass, Peter O'Donnell Jr. maintained, "The problem of government today is to prevent the federal government from encroaching on states' rights and intervening in every aspect of the private lives of our citizens."[79]

This outlook was more than the traditional states' rights approach long advocated by southern Democrats and segregationists. In many ways it was libertarian in its emphasis on individual rights and limited government intervention in the economy. The major responsibility of the federal government was national defense, and to this end the new conservatism differed from the views espoused by the late Robert Taft, long the spokesperson for conservatism in the Republican Party. Those conservatives assuming leadership positions in the Texas party during the 1950s were firmly anti-Communist and advocated an active role for the United States in defending Western civilization. By the end of the decade, these views would be popularized by writer William F. Buckley Jr. and Arizona senator Barry Goldwater, the candidate around whom most Texas Republicans would rally in the next few years.

Despite the internal turmoil, Eisenhower once again carried Texas in 1956 and was re-elected with the support of Shivers and most conservative Democratic officeholders. This time there was no cross-endorsement of candidates for statewide office. The Republicans nominated William Bryant for governor to run against Democratic senator Price Daniel and write-in candidate W. Lee "Pappy" O'Daniel, the former governor. Bryant's roughly 260,000 votes meant the party would be required to hold a primary again in 1958, but his total accounted for only 14.8 percent of votes cast. Five GOP candidates ran for Congress, but only Alger was successful. Alger beat off a serious challenge from Dallas district attorney Henry Wade, to be re-elected with slightly over 55 percent of the vote. In the end, the 1956 results produced "a rather poor record for a party which professed to be in the process of becoming a serious rival to the Democratic Party in the politics of the state."[80]

THAD HUTCHESON: CANDIDATE AND CHAIRMAN

Alger continued to be the only candidate elected to an office of more than local substance during the decade of the 1950s, but in 1957 the Republicans thought they might have a chance to produce a major breakthrough in a special election for the US Senate seat of Price Daniel, who resigned upon being elected governor. The contest involved twenty-one Democratic candidates and one Republican, with victory going to whichever candidate came in first. The election boiled down to a competition among conservative legislator Martin Dies, Republican attorney Thad Hutcheson, and liberal stalwart Ralph Yarborough, loser in three previous gubernatorial campaigns. In such a divided field, some Republicans believed that their candidate could win. "In Hutcheson the Republicans found a candidate they could all support. He was, moreover, not only personable but enthusiastic as well, the sort of candidate who could elicit the best efforts of supporters and volunteer workers."[81] Unfortunately, Hutcheson ended up in third place with 219,591 votes. In a historic breakthrough Yarborough won the election and gave new hope to liberal dreams of taking over the Texas Democratic Party.

While disappointed with his 22.9 percent of the total vote, Republican activists saw the Hutcheson campaign as one more building block in the process of establishing a statewide competitive party. In the multicandidate field Hutcheson had carried eighteen counties, including Bexar, Midland, Victoria, and a handful of smaller and historically German counties. After the special election state chairman John Q. Adams announced his resignation, and the SREC chose Hutcheson to take his place. As the new state chairman, Hutcheson pledged that he would help bring about a "Texas brand of Republicanism that can help shape the course of the national party along conservative lines."[82] Among those congratulating Hutcheson was John Tower, the SREC member from Wichita Falls who four years later would be elected to the Senate from Texas as a Republican.[83]

Reality set in once again with the 1958 election season. In a memo to party leaders five days before the filing deadline, Hutcheson pleaded for more candidates: "Our effectiveness in Texas as a minority party, our position for the 1960 presidential year, depends in large part on our running a representative slate this year."[84] The end result of the recruitment effort saw the Republicans run twenty-nine candidates for state representative, three for the Texas Senate, and three for congressional districts.

Forced to conduct another primary, the party managed to recruit volunteers to conduct the election in only sixty-eight counties and attracted some 16,000 voters, two-thirds of whom lived in Alger's congressional district in Dallas. In an effort to keep conservatives out of the Democratic primary, labor leader Grover Cantrell filed as a Republican against Alger, contributing to the higher-than-normal GOP primary turnout in Dallas. Alger easily won renomination and then went on to defeat Harold Barefoot Sanders in November.[85] Meanwhile, some 1,300,000 Texas voters took part in the Democratic primary held in all 254 counties, where newly elected senator Yarborough fended off a challenge from conservative Democrat William Blakley with almost 60 percent of the vote.[86] By September the GOP had a county chair in only 140 of the state's 254 counties as they attempted to compete with the Texas Democratic Party on Election Day.

In the 1958 Republican primary the party had nominated Roy Whittenburg of Amarillo as their candidate for US Senate, but several party leaders were not happy with the choice. By early August the state's newspapers were reporting that party leaders were discussing the possibility of Hutcheson replacing Whittenburg as the GOP candidate. Such a move would require Whittenburg to voluntarily step aside, but the *Dallas Morning News* quoted him as saying: "I have no intention of withdrawing."[87] In response to requests that he become the candidate, Hutcheson said, "What these people do not seem to understand is that Roy Whittenburg was nominated our candidate in the Republican primary. . . . I intend to wage a vigorous campaign in his behalf."[88] Nevertheless, the pressure on both Whittenburg and Hutcheson continued. Tower expressed his views in a letter to Hutcheson a few days later: "I am very much in favor of your supplanting Mr. Whittenburg on the ticket. I feel that if we can get the funds, we can conduct an even better campaign than we did last year."[89]

Later that month Hutcheson sent a confidential memo to a special sub-committee of party leaders. Whittenburg had publicly advocated the election of federal judges and had called for a censure of President Eisenhower for sending troops to Little Rock during the school integration crisis, positions not supported by most party leaders.[90] In his memo Hutcheson reported, "With reference to the matter which we considered in executive session at the meeting in Austin on August 11, 1958, I have received a letter from the person involved advising that he has no intention of reversing his position on the problem we discussed and further advising that he has no intention of withdrawing. No further explanation was offered. Under the circumstances, I feel that we are free to release a resolution repudiating the position taken by this individual on the matter discussed."[91] No public statement was forthcoming from the state party leaders on the Whittenburg situation, and prior to the September state convention in Wichita Falls, Hutcheson made it evident again that he would not be a candidate. Meanwhile, the draft platform prepared by the convention resolutions committee declared that the party "views with alarm the activities of the recent 85th session of the U.S. Congress and heartedly approves the Eisenhower administration."[92]

The controversy over Whittenburg did not end with the state convention, however. While several party leaders, including Hutcheson, wanted to denounce their senate candidate, and especially his advocacy of electing federal judges, others felt that silence was golden. In a letter to the state chairman, Joe Sheldon of San Antonio made the case for saying nothing: "It is my humble opinion that if we should start a battle with Whittenburg we would give him undeserved publicity, and I am thoroughly convinced that *we* would get the worst of it from the standpoint of politics and votes. Nothing would please me more than to repudiate Whittenburg and give him a scathing denunciation, . . . all of which he so richly deserves. However, I think the best interests of the party is what we should consider." Sheldon went on to make evident his opposition to Whittenburg by adding, "Personally, I would like to burn him at the stake, but as I said, it is not a question to satisfy my personal desires, but to do what we believe is best for the Party and the candidates."[93]

Hutcheson decided to remain silent, and Whittenburg, in a basically self-funded campaign, won only 24.1 percent of the vote against the liberal Democratic senator. Nevertheless, he performed better than gubernatorial candidate Edwin S. Mayer of San Angelo, who received 11.9 percent of the vote and, with only some 94,000 votes, saved the GOP from having another primary in 1960. Alger was once again the only successful Republican legislative candidate. In Kerr County Julius Neunhoffer became the state's sole Republican county judge.

In his postelection report to state party leaders Hutcheson warned that "we must help keep party leadership from being tempted to 'turn left' in their search for votes."[94] This position was reinforced by Tower in a subsequent letter to the state chairman: "I am concerned about the view on the part of many that if the Party is to approach any degree of electoral success, it must swing further to the left. This observation defies reason.... Me-too-ism, while failing to contribute to Republican electoral fortunes, has demoralized many of the Party's constituents.... I believe that it is Eisenhower's failure to provide us with party leadership and his efforts to remain aloof from party politics that is largely responsible for the mess we find ourselves in."[95] Tower's view was widely shared by many in the party and would result in substantial support for Senator Barry Goldwater at the 1960 Republican National Convention, as well as for his presidential nomination battle four years later.

Thad Hutcheson continued as an active leader of the party throughout 1959 and most of 1960. Indicative of the political environment of the time, the state chairman's January 1959 memo reminded party leaders of the January 31 poll tax purchase deadline. "Every Republican official must join in the campaign to see that every Republican and conservative voter has purchased his poll tax or obtained his exemption certificate.... Our drive this year will be important as a 'dress rehearsal' for the all-important 1960 Poll Tax Sales Drive."[96] After leading efforts to prepare the party for the next presidential election and serving as a delegate to the 1960 Republican National Convention, Hutcheson announced he would not seek another term as state chairman at the September state convention.[97] But he was persuaded to remain in office through the November elections before being replaced by Tad Smith of El Paso.

As the 1950s closed and the end of the Eisenhower administration approached, Texas Republicans did not find themselves in a much better position than they had been in previously. Having a Republican in the White House had done little positive for the party. Shivers and the conservative Democrats had benefited the most from patronage, the prestige of association with the incumbent president, and the visibility of a federal appointment. The cross-endorsement of 1952 had eliminated any possibility of presidential coattails, and the desire to keep conservatives in control of the Texas Democratic

Party had discouraged participation in subsequent Republican primaries and conventions. Little help came from the national party or the White House. "The Eisenhower administration showed only scant and sporadic interest in promoting its party in Texas. Though Eisenhower's candidacy had swelled the ranks of the presidential Republicans, he was not inclined to use patronage or other prerogatives in the interest of the party in Texas."[98] As Tower viewed the situation, "It's not so much we muffed it. It's just that Eisenhower felt more beholden to the conservative Democrats who supported him than he did to the Republicans. And Eisenhower was not politically-oriented—he was not a party-builder because he didn't understand the party leadership responsibility the President has."[99]

At the same time, the party had elected and re-elected one member of Congress from Dallas and, in so doing, had attracted a small band of younger conservatives who would help begin the process of changing the state's politics over the next few decades. Moreover, as historian T. R. Fehrenbach noted, "Republicanism gained a respectability it had not enjoyed" since the party's early years after the Civil War.[100]

In February 1960 Porter announced his resignation as Republican national committeeman from Texas. Writing Thad Hutcheson, Porter concluded, "I do not feel I am physically able to fully discharge the duties of the National Committeeman during this all important election year."[101] Porter's campaign for the US Senate in 1948 against Lyndon Johnson was one of the few serious contests waged by the party over the first fifty years of the twentieth century. He had been the critical organizer for the Eisenhower forces that eventually overcame the old-guard establishment and moved the party from an emphasis on patronage to political campaigns. Ironically, when Eisenhower won, Porter was able to dispense little patronage, and the only successful political campaigns were the Alger victories.

Porter stepped aside from a leadership role in the party in 1960 and was replaced by his close associate and fellow Houstonian, Albert Fay. Born in Louisiana, Fay moved with his family to Houston in 1928, and he graduated from Yale University in 1936. After serving in the Navy during World War II, Fay and his brother were engaged in a number of business interests. Fay would serve as national committeeman until 1969 and was the party's candidate for land commissioner in both 1962 and 1966.[102]

Porter did continue his involvement in politics, however, serving as a delegate to the Republican National Conventions of 1960 and 1964, and as a key backer of the 1968 effort to corral Texas delegate votes for Reagan. Away from day-to-day political involvement, Porter lived to see Reagan elected and re-elected to the White House before passing away in late 1986. His legacy in-

cluded being an organizer and the first president of Texas Independent Producers and Royalty Owners (TIPRO), as well as changing the focus of the
Texas Republican Party. As his obituary in the *New York Times* indicated,
Porter "was instrumental in transforming the Texas Republican Party from a
small group into a potent statewide organization."[103]

Throughout the eight years of a Republican in the White House who had
twice carried the state by considerable margins, the Texas party had succeeded
in electing only one of the twenty-two members of Congress from Texas and
had nary a seat in the Texas legislature or any statewide elective office. The
number of county officeholders who were Republican was less than 1 percent
of the state's total. Credit for the continuing conservative control of the Texas
Democratic Party, and the concomitant failure of the Republican Party to
reach critical mass, can be given to both Shivers and the political operatives
of the Eisenhower administration. Working together, they helped to prevent
the birth of a viable Republican opposition.

What the decade of the 1950s did produce for the Republican Party of
Texas, however, was a new cadre of political activists comprising both campaign volunteers and future candidates. New Republican leadership emerged
in the state's urban areas, including both native Texans and transplants to the
state, individuals who would contribute to creating a competitive force in
Texas politics over the coming decades. It was in the 1950s that a relatively
new movement developed in American politics, with the arrival of the amateur as a political activist. As James Q. Wilson explains in his classic work
The Amateur Democrat, such individuals were motivated more by issues and
ideology than by patronage and position: "An amateur is one who finds politics intrinsically interesting because it expresses a conception of the public
interest. The amateur politician sees the political world more in terms of ideas
and principles than in terms of persons. . . . The professional, on the other
hand—even the 'professional' who practices politics as a hobby rather than
as a vocation—is preoccupied with the outcome of politics in terms of winning or losing."[104] The rise of the amateur in Texas politics during the 1950s
challenged the longtime dominance of the Post Office Republicans and their
efforts to limit the growth of the party organization. Although the movement
was present in various areas of the state, it was in Dallas that it first took hold
with Alger's election in 1954 and the subsequent growth of a potent political
organization. No one individual better epitomizes this development and its
impact on Texas politics than the individual who would manage Alger's 1958
re-election and then become the Dallas County Republican chairman.

ENTER PETER O'DONNELL JR.

Peter O'Donnell Jr. was born in 1924 as the son of a wealthy cotton broker originally from New Orleans. He graduated from Highland Park High School and then began his undergraduate studies at the University of the South in Sewanee, Tennessee, in the fall of 1941. His college days were interrupted by three years in the Navy during World War II, during which he was a communications officer in Puerto Rico, Guam, and North Africa, reaching appointment as a lieutenant junior grade. After completing his military service, he re-enrolled at Sewanee in September 1946, where he was inducted into Phi Beta Kappa and graduated in June 1947. O'Donnell later attended the Wharton School of the University of Pennsylvania and received his MBA in finance and banking. After a brief time with E. F. Hutton and with a small Dallas bank, he became a private investor.[105]

In 1952 Peter O'Donnell married Edith Jones of Abilene, daughter of Ruth Legett and Percy Jones. Her father had been an early investor in West Texas real estate and had accumulated his fortune through land and mineral interests, cotton, and ranching. Edith came from a Republican-leaning family and volunteered for Alger in his initial race for Congress in 1954.[106] Two years later Dallas County GOP chairman Paul O'Rourke asked Peter O'Donnell to become chair of Precinct 143, at the time described as "a wealthy and important enclave which included many of the most influential and politically powerful citizens in the state."[107] At first Peter declined, but when Edith agreed to help, he accepted the post one month before the 1956 general election.[108]

Peter O'Donnell immediately stepped up and took on additional tasks in the county party. He served as campaign manager for Alger in both of his successful re-elections, in 1958 and 1960. In what was a disastrous year for Republican candidates nationally, Alger defeated state representative Harold Barefoot Sanders in 1958 as O'Donnell organized "one of the most closely coordinated campaigns the area had seen."[109] The thirty-four-year-old O'Donnell's reputation as an up-and-coming Republican leader was growing.

In October 1959, Dallas County GOP chairman Maurice Carlson, president of Reliance Life and Accident Company, announced that he would not seek re-election the following May. Soon thereafter Carlson resigned abruptly, and the Dallas County executive committee selected Peter O'Donnell as the new county chairman. With the necessary resources of time and money, plus intelligence and a high degree of organization, O'Donnell was the perfect choice to move Dallas in a Republican direction. "From his first day in office Peter O'Donnell set his sights on actual Republican victories at the polls—and recognized the need for good candidates and a real organization to achieve those goals."[110]

Upon assuming office O'Donnell made it clear that any Republican appeal must be on the basis of more than merely advocating a two-party system. It was conservative philosophy, and not merely good government, that motivated him. O'Donnell explained, "I'm a Republican because I'm a conservative. And the fundamentals of the conservative creed are private property, free enterprise and limited government."[111]

Bobbie Biggart, who served as volunteer chair for the county party from 1958 to 1960, remembered that "Peter always got the most out of people. He would participate in every function of the party, from phoning and walking door-to-door to planning events and fundraising."[112] Although O'Donnell's elevation came only with Carlson's resignation, his predecessor had been well aware of the new county chairman's abilities. In a 1963 interview Carlson described O'Donnell as "probably the best organizer in the Republican Party. He has the financial resources to carry out his ideas and he isn't dependent upon these finances or upon any individual or groups.... With great organizational ability and unlimited financing a man can go far as a political leader. He has gone far and will go further."[113] Indeed, as the Republican Party entered the 1960s, O'Donnell's star did rise as he assumed increasingly important positions in state and national politics.

What O'Donnell was able to accomplish in Dallas County could not have occurred without the active participation of women. The 1950s was a time of fewer professional women and more homemakers—women whose substantial responsibilities in managing a household and raising children allowed a flexible daily schedule that left time for civic and community involvement. It was in such an environment that several women assumed essential roles in building a base of support for the expanding Republican Party of Texas.

As campaign manager for Alger, Peter O'Donnell came up with various projects for involving these volunteers. One typical example was Alger Tag Day, which involved eighty women who met at 7:00 a.m. at the Baker Hotel in downtown Dallas on a workday one week before the 1958 election. These women volunteers recruited by Peter O'Donnell and attracted to Alger's campaign ranged in age from eighteen to thirty-five. After remarks by Alger and O'Donnell, the women set up folding tables outside various office buildings and gave out Alger tags and literature as workers arrived. By 9:30 this first phase was completed, and at 10:00, the women moved to street corners to distribute literature and campaign materials. Once this task was completed, the women assembled for a closing gathering, where Alger's campaign manager told the volunteers that victory was at hand. The end result was the distribution of some thirty thousand tags, fifteen thousand brochures, and two hundred yard signs.[114]

WOMEN VOLUNTEERS AND
PARTY ORGANIZATION

Dallas was the center of this enhanced activity, much of it generated not only by the 1952 presidential campaign but also by Alger's various campaigns throughout the decade. Like many others, Edith Jones O'Donnell first volunteered in the 1954 Alger campaign, two years before her husband, Peter, accepted his first political office as precinct chair. Among the many other early activists were Martha Crowley, Mary Ann Collins, Bobbie Biggart, Sally McKenzie, Margot Perot, and Jo Kanowsky. As Gwen Pharo, a former assistant to Speaker Sam Rayburn, concluded: "I don't think there would be any Republican Party in Texas without the women who went against the habits of the times and became very active in Republican politics.... The women of Dallas truly made politics socially acceptable."[115]

When he became Dallas County chairman, Peter O'Donnell was well aware of the contributions made by women activists, and, as Anne Armstrong observed, "He really reached out to women who he thought could be effective and helpful."[116] Women volunteers provided a reliable force to help change the direction of Dallas County politics. For Peter O'Donnell, "The stand-up-and-be-counted people and the workers were women. They were able. They worked hard. They were dependable. We were looking to get a job done. We had a huge volunteer effort. We knew that they could perform."[117]

The growing influence of women in Republican politics was not limited to Dallas. As Meg McKain Grier explains when discussing the early efforts of Mary Lou Grier, "Women like my mother-in-law and her friends went against the norms of the 1950s and 1960s and pursued their political interests.... Through campaign and Party work, women developed areas of expertise and trained others. They organized precinct, county, and state party structure, ran campaigns, raised funds, worked with the press, ran for office themselves."[118] According to Bette Jo Buhler of Victoria, women were at the forefront of the effort to change the focus and direction of the party: "If the old guard in 1948 didn't want any new Republicans, there was this new group in 1952 that wanted to open it up. It made a big difference."[119]

Betty Andujar of Fort Worth, who would later become a state senator and Republican national committeewoman, began her political involvement by volunteering in the 1952 Eisenhower campaign. For many, it was the start of a lifetime of involvement in building a viable political force. Andujar maintained that "We didn't have a Republican Party until after Eisenhower had been president, and then there was a small effort."[120] Ruth Schiermeyer of Lubbock started her political career as a junior high student for Eisenhower; Katie Seewald of Amarillo was another who first became active as an Eisenhower precinct attendee and delegate to the state convention in Mineral Wells.[121]

Not all of the future female leaders of the party were for Eisenhower, however. Nancy Palm first became involved as manager of a successful slate of Houston school board candidates in 1951. This led to continued involvement, she explained in an interview: "By 1952 I was a precinct organizer for Taft. So that would tell you where I was in the spectrum of Republican politics."[122] Among those active in San Antonio were Flo Kampmann, Janelle McArthur, and Joci Straus, whose son Joe would later serve as Speaker of the Texas House of Representatives. Kampmann had been cochair of Hutcheson's 1957 campaign for the US Senate and was named vice chairman of the state party in 1958.[123] Still others whose activism began in the 1950s were Katie Heck of Midland, Barbara Howell of Fort Worth, Jane Anne Stinnett of Lubbock, and Marjorie Meyer Arsht of Houston.[124]

All across the state women were beginning to assume important roles in the development of the party. By October 1955 a sufficient number of Republican women's clubs had been organized across the state to allow a federation of clubs to be established and recognized by the national party. Thus came into being the Texas Federation of Republican Women, an important support organization for the party that has continued as a force to the present day. Convening the first gathering of the federation was Beryl Milburn of Austin, an up-and-coming leader who would later become president of the federation, vice chairman of the state party, and chair of the Ford campaign in the 1976 Texas primary.[125] Milburn later concluded, "I really think that the Republican Women's Clubs were the real levers that got people going because the women were freer economically to join and be Republicans than their husbands were. They were very devoted and dedicated. Republicans were ideologically committed."[126]

One prominent example of this development of dedicated new volunteer activists is Rita Crocker Bass, later to serve as first lady of Texas as the wife of William P. Clements Jr. Born Rita Crocker in Newton, Kansas, in 1931, she moved with her family to Texas at the age of ten. Her father, Mason Crocker, was in the cattle business and brought his Midwestern Republicanism with him, serving many years as McCulloch County GOP chairman. Rita Crocker attended the Hockaday School and completed one year at Wellesley College before transferring to the University of Texas at Austin. At UT she majored in Spanish and minored in government and history, graduating in 1953 as a member of Phi Beta Kappa.[127]

While in college, she rang doorbells for Eisenhower in 1952, then she continued her political involvement after marrying Dick Bass and moving to Dallas. By 1958 Rita Crocker Bass was a precinct chair and one of the area coordinators for the 1958 Alger Tag Day project.[128] She would go on to hold many important campaign positions throughout the 1960s and 1970s, including serving as Republican national committeewoman from 1973 to 1975. Rita and Dick Bass had four children, but by the 1970s they were pursuing separate paths. They divorced, and in 1975 Rita Bass married Clements, who was then serving in the Department of Defense as part of the Ford administration. As one writer commented, "she was a political veteran long before she married Governor Bill Clements in 1975, at home with campaign fundraising, bringing home the vote for long-shot Republican candidates in a Democratic state and meeting the demands of appointive office at the national level."[129]

THE LITTLE PROFESSOR

While volunteer campaign workers were essential to the development of a viable state party, even more critical was the identification of potential winning candidates. Alger was the only successful candidate throughout much of the decade but a number of others were developing for future campaigns. Frank Crowley, John Leedom, and O. H. "Ike" Harris were building credentials and obtaining political experience in Dallas, and others were doing the same across the state. Two individuals in particular were active during the 1950s and would go on to play important roles in state and national politics: John Tower and George H. W. Bush.

After assuming a position on the faculty at Midwestern University, Tower played an active part in the Texas Republican Party throughout the 1950s. He was on the slate of national convention delegates pledged to Senator Taft that was denied credentials at the Chicago convention in 1952. Two years later he was a candidate for state representative in Wichita Falls. Throughout most of the 1950s Tower was a member of the SREC, a position he would continue to hold until launching his 1960 senatorial campaign. His role in the Eisenhower re-election campaign was acknowledged by an invitation to sit on the platform when Vice President Nixon spoke at a campaign rally in Houston that September.[130] Jack Porter subsequently thanked him for his efforts in the campaign, noting, "Texas Republicans have a team of which we can be well proud. You have been and still are an important part of that team."[131]

When Hutcheson became state chairman after his 1957 Senate campaign, Tower congratulated him and pledged to continue his efforts to build the state party.[132] Two months later, however, he expressed his concern over the direction of the national party in a letter to national chairman Meade Alcorn. While stating his support for integration, Tower contended that civil rights should not become a partisan issue.

> I feel that the injection of the Civil Rights Issue into party politics would deal a damaging blow to the progress we have made toward breaking one-party control in the South.... I believe that the Republican Party in Texas has taken a moderate stand on the issue in recognizing that the decision of the Court in the Brown case is the supreme law of the land and must be complied with, while at the same time recognizing that the Southerners must have some time to readjust to the overthrow of a social tradition that, however evil, is not entirely of their own making.[133]

He would continue to advocate policies to implement the law of the land while still recognizing the difficulty of bringing about lasting change in southern society. His concern was that partisan attacks on southern Democrats would be counterproductive in the long run and reinforce a perception that the Republican Party was merely a party of the North and East.

In his commitment to building a viable political force, Tower took on the responsibility of newsletter editor for the state party and became chair of both the arrangements and platform committees for the 1958 state convention. The young professor had already developed a reputation as "the most expert phrase-maker and draftsman in the Republican Party," according to state chairman Hutcheson.[134] As a delegate to the 1960 Republican National Convention, Tower represented Texas on the platform committee and worked to lessen the influence of Nelson Rockefeller and his supporters on the final document.[135] Tower's performance in Chicago would be only a precursor to the role he would assume less than one year later.

THE SENATOR'S SON

Although Tower would be the first to break through the barrier to victory in the 1960s, still another important contributor to Republican success was settling in to West Texas. George and Barbara Bush moved to the Midland-Odessa area in the late 1940s, bringing with them a commitment to the Republican Party. Bush's father, Prescott Bush, would soon thereafter lose a close race for US Senate in Connecticut but then rebound with the party's nod for an uncompleted term in 1952, defeating Abraham Ribicoff by 37,000 votes and then earning re-election in 1956 over Thomas J. Dodd. Prescott Bush served in the Senate from 1953 to 1963 before deciding not to seek another term.[136]

While building his business in Midland, George developed an interest in advancing the Republican cause locally. In 1952, at his father's request, he organized an airport rally for Senator Nixon, then a candidate for the vice presidency, in what appears to be Bush's first public partisan effort in Midland. Bush assumed the role of Midland County finance chair for the Eisenhower campaign in both 1952 and 1956.[137] Barbara Bush recalled their efforts to become involved in local Republican politics at a time when the state was solidly Democratic: "There was no Republican politics in which to become active. In fact, there were hardly any other Republicans." When the party held one of its rare primary elections in 1954, the Bushes were among the few to participate. As Barbara Bush recalls the event, "I can still remember when George and I volunteered to work at the polls during a primary election. Exactly three people voted Republican that day. The two of us and a man who you could say was a little bit inebriated and wasn't sure what he was doing."[138]

With little in the way of local politics, George Bush became district finance chair for the state party in 1957. One year later the party was looking to him as a possible congressional nominee. After analyzing the results of the party's effort in 1956, Bush demurred from becoming a candidate.[139] By early 1959, George Bush had determined that the family would move to Houston. When notifying Porter that he would be resigning as district finance chair, Bush observed that "Midland has been mighty good to the Bush family and we are going to miss it here tremendously since we are lucky enough to have a great many friends."[140]

After the move to Houston in 1959, Bush continued his involvement in Republican politics and was appointed by county chairman Fred Weston to serve on the Harris County candidates committee along with Albert Fay, T. E. Kennerly, and Clive Runnells. The new Houston resident was one of a group invited to meet with Rockefeller, the new Republican governor of New York, at a private reception later that year.[141] As the 1960s began, Bush was actively involved in raising funds for Tower's general election Senate campaign. It would be only a few years later when he too would become a senatorial candidate.

The 1950s were a difficult decade for the Republican Party of Texas. While it had succeeded twice in carrying the state for the GOP presidential candidate, little progress had been made in electing officials to other positions. However, a base was developing in some of the state's most urban counties, especially in Dallas where Alger had broken the Democratic hold on the state's congressional delegation. Moreover, a new cadre of amateurs had been attracted to political involvement, individuals who would play more important roles over the next thirty years. As the 1960s began, the slow process of building a political party that could win elections would soon be underway. Thanks to Lyndon Johnson, a major breakthrough in acceptability for the Republican Party would soon take place.

SIX

THE 1960S BREAKTHROUGH

The decade of the 1960s was one of tremendous upheaval and transition, not merely in Texas and not exclusively in politics, but throughout all of American society. In many ways it was a divided decade, with the first few years a continuation of the conformity and traditions carried over from the 1950s, but ending up with a nearly unrecognizable society at the close of the decade.

Change was coming in society as a whole, including within the Texas Republican Party. After eight years of an Eisenhower administration that did little to help build a viable party in Texas, the dissatisfaction with the lack of party growth was spreading toward other party leaders. In January 1960 party activist Lee Griffin expressed the views of many when he described his grievances in a lengthy letter published in the *Beaumont Enterprise*. Rather than focusing on the national administration, he laid most of the blame for the party's failure to grow on the national committeeman:

> Mr. Jack Porter and his coterie have had almost eight years in which to build even a resemblance of a strong grass-roots Republican movement. As far as I can see, all that they have accomplished is the formation of another wing of the conservative Democrats. . . . A functioning Republican Party will never emerge from the leadership of men who are content to shuttle back and forth to Washington, bask in the warmth of the Eisenhower affability, accept the crumbs of patronage that fate or Lyndon Johnson may allow them to gather from the floor and at the same time play "footsie" with the conservative Democrats.[1]

One week later Jack Porter announced his resignation as national committeeman, saying "my health will not permit me doing all the work" needed to continue in office.[2] Porter had accomplished much with his challenge to the old-guard Post Office Republicans and with the key role he played in the nomination and election of Eisenhower. But the party to which he dedicated much of his time, talent, and treasure was still far from being a competitive force in state politics. Many years would pass before one could honestly describe Texas as a two-party state.

THE 1960 CAMPAIGN

The year 1960 was one of those rare occasions in which, under state election law, the party was required to hold three state conventions. Since there was no Republican primary in 1960, delegates to a May convention in McAllen named the party's candidates for the November general election. A second convention was held one month later in Galveston to elect delegates to the Republican National Convention. Finally, in September delegates were convened once again to choose party officers, adopt a platform, and certify candidates for the general election.[3]

At the May convention Texas Republicans were focused not only on the upcoming presidential contest but also on mounting a challenge to Senator Lyndon Johnson, whose re-election campaign was underway even while he also sought the Democratic presidential nomination. Many party activists wanted Thad Hutcheson to mount another senatorial campaign, but there was also one active candidate seeking the nomination, a young college professor from Wichita Falls who had been building a record of party involvement. As Beryl Milburn, a leader among the growing organization of Republican women, summarized the situation, "We thought, 'John Tower has no chance. … He's not a very attractive kind of person.' We wanted Thad Hutcheson to run again. He wouldn't do it. We begged him. Finally, we gave the nomination to John Tower."[4]

Given the record of Texas Republican candidates over the previous eighty years, few political activists expected him to win. According to Tower, "we were dismissed as naïve visionaries and worse. The idea that the entrenched Texas Democratic Party would ever be forced to share political power was considered by the experts about as foolish as 'a dog walking on his hind legs.'"[5] To many political observers Tower was simply "too young, too short, cool and aloof, dressed almost foreign to the Texas scene," a candidate who had "never held an elective office of any kind, and representing a small minority party."[6]

Although somewhat skeptical of his chances for actually defeating Johnson, party leaders saw value in mounting an aggressive campaign for the Senate at a time when they hoped to carry the state for the party's presidential nominee. Dallas County chairman Peter O'Donnell Jr. was not reticent about giving advice to the party's senatorial candidate. As the fall campaign began, O'Donnell wrote to Tower with "a few suggestions at this time" about the candidate's speeches, recommending that he "write out a basic ten-minute speech." For content, O'Donnell suggested he dwell on his personal background because "as a minister's son, I think you might be in a position to quote some scripture, particularly in the rural areas." Tower should remember, "The man in the street feels very strongly that Lyndon Johnson has betrayed him and sold him out. Keep hitting this."[7] The Tower campaign literature claimed that "running for two high offices further proves Lyndon is politically immoral," while the Republican candidate was "Tower: A Texan who puts Texas first."[8]

When the party convened in San Antonio for its June convention, the forces favoring Senator Barry Goldwater attempted to line up delegate votes on his behalf but then joined in backing Vice President Richard Nixon. In the end, the twelve hundred delegates pledged the state's fifty-four votes to Nixon for president and Goldwater for vice president.[9] Although some one-third of those selected as national convention delegates leaned strongly to Goldwater, by the time the Texas delegation arrived in Chicago there was little doubt that Nixon would be the party's presidential nominee.[10] Most of the controversy centered around the proposed platform on which Nixon would run, as Governor Nelson Rockefeller of New York made demands for a number of planks perceived as more liberal on civil rights and critical of the Eisenhower policies on national defense.

Tower represented Texas on the platform committee and its civil rights and immigration subcommittee. At a time when many African-Americans were Republicans, some controversy developed over the strong civil rights plank proposed by Nixon. While disagreeing with some of the wording, state chairman Hutcheson claimed most southern delegates "disciplined ourselves and our views to recognize that this is a national convention seeking a national platform." From Hutcheson's perspective, "we from a specific geographical area have no right to construct a platform on this or any other problem exactly in accordance with our views."[11] But this was not enough for Rockefeller, who was dissatisfied and viewed the draft platform as "still seriously lacking in strength and specifics" on both civil rights and national defense. On the Friday before the convention was to start, the Rockefeller forces threatened to take their challenge to the convention floor. To avoid such an open split, Nixon asked to meet with Rockefeller at the governor's personal residence in

New York City and basically agreed to all the platform changes demanded by Rockefeller. Thus came into being the infamous Compact of Fifth Avenue, which rejected the work of the platform committee in several key areas.[12]

Nixon was now in a bind. By agreeing to Rockefeller's platform demands he had raised the ire of many delegates, who saw the deal as one more example of backroom politics. By accepting language critical of current policy on national defense, he had created opposition from President Eisenhower, who viewed it as a direct challenge to his stewardship of the nation. Yet backing away from the compact could result in a challenge from Rockefeller, not merely on platform issues but possibly as a candidate for the presidential nomination. Over the next few days Nixon's strategists in Chicago negotiated with Eisenhower aides staying with the president in Newport, Rhode Island, and also with the Rockefeller forces in New York. After much rewording, an agreement was reached on the national defense language. As Theodore White reported, "The same afternoon of Tuesday that saw the passage of the Rockefeller civil rights platform saw the passage of the new defense platform as approved by both Rockefeller and Eisenhower. Thereafter, Mr. Rockefeller withdrew his threat of floor fight and announced to his restive and turbulent New York State delegation that he was definitely withdrawing from the race for President."[13] The result of this agreement between Nixon and Rockefeller was an uprising among many of the delegates, especially those in the southern delegations.

On Tuesday, the Texas delegation met and approved a resolution proposed by Hutcheson, Representative Bruce Alger, and national committeeman Albert Fay declaring that the delegation "now considers itself free of instructions on nominations for the presidency—and each delegate will be considered free to vote his or her own convictions."[14] Efforts were under way to draft Goldwater to seek the presidential nomination. In a planned compromise, Governor Paul Fannin of Arizona placed the senator's name in nomination, at which point Goldwater strode to the podium and asked that his name be withdrawn. Goldwater called on the delegates to support Nixon but urged them, "Let's grow up, conservatives. If we want to take this Party back, and I think we can someday, let's get to work."[15] His remarks were a clarion call for conservatives that would result in Goldwater's nomination four years later. When the roll call was taken, Texas cast all fifty-four votes for Nixon.

In the build up to the September state convention in Galveston, sentiment began to develop for O'Donnell to become a candidate for state chairman. O'Donnell's abilities had already been recognized by his appointment, while he was serving as Dallas County chairman, to the influential headquarters committee of the state party and as a delegate to the 1960 national convention.[16] Heading up this effort was Tad Smith, El Paso County GOP chairman. In response, O'Donnell did not dismiss the campaign on his behalf but praised Hutcheson for "the effective way in which he has brought before the public the principles and objectives of the Republican Party."[17] Shortly thereafter Hutcheson informed the state Republican executive committee (SREC) that he could not serve another full two-year term.

One week before the state convention, the Committee for O'Donnell for State Chairman was announced with a steering committee of Smith, Joe Pratt of Victoria, Blanche Martin of Denison, and Jo Kanowsky and Bobbie Biggart of Dallas.[18] However, the campaign of 1960 came to naught as Hutcheson agreed to seek re-election and then resign after the November general election.[19]

On December 31, 1960, Hutcheson resigned due to the pressures of family and business. He looked back on the 1960 campaign as "a thorough, hard-hitting, enthusiastic, effective team effort that showed our Party has, in the last ten years, grown to maturity as a political party and has a wealth of talented and dedicated people to lead it at the County, District, and State levels." On a more personal note, Hutcheson acknowledged Tower's support by saying, "When help was needed you were always there to help me as a loyal friend and supporter. I will not forget this and hope to see you as our next U.S. Senator."[20] Several possible candidates were mentioned to succeed Hutcheson, including county chairs Peter O'Donnell of Dallas, John Goode of Bexar, and Tad Smith of El Paso, as well as 1960 gubernatorial candidate William Steger of Tyler. When the state committee met in January, they selected Smith of El Paso to lead the party organization.[21]

WELCOMING LYNDON JOHNSON

On the Thursday before the November 8, 1960, election, the Democratic campaign ran an advertisement in the *Dallas Times Herald* welcoming Senator Johnson to Dallas for a campaign luncheon the following day at the Adolphus Hotel. The ad bore the names of some four thousand Dallas residents. Almost immediately an uproar developed when "many of the persons whose names appeared on the advertisement angrily protested the use of their names," while other names "were the same as persons who are dead."[22] It appeared that the Democrats had mailed or telephoned opt-out requests, so a failure to respond negatively resulted in an individual's name being listed. Among those listed were a number of Republican activists and supporters, including attorney Duncan Boeckman, business leader Trammell Crow, and Lawrence

Neely, whose wife worked at Republican headquarters. Several indicated that they had specifically turned down the request. Others commented, "I've never voted for Lyndon Johnson and never intend to," "we're Nixon-Lodge people," "I haven't voted Democratic in 40 years," "I did not authorize it. In fact, I have an Alger sign in my yard," and "I called them last week and told them not to run it."[23]

A survey by the *Dallas Morning News* reported that some 625 of the 4,000 names appearing in the ad were of individuals who did not grant approval for their use. Those who protested in writing or by telephone to the Dallas newspapers or were reported by relatives to be dead constituted more than 15 percent of the names in the advertisement.[24] Needless to say, the appearance of so many unauthorized names in a Democratic ad one week before the presidential election caused an uproar among Republican volunteers.

It so happened that the Johnson luncheon occurred on the same day as the Nixon-Lodge Tag Day, whose dates had been set months earlier. The project was modeled after the successful tag day first employed by O'Donnell during the 1958 Alger re-election campaign.

> The Friday lunch-time tagging shift was sidetracked for quite a while, as sign-carrying anti-Johnson crowds gathered on the Baker Hotel's Akard Street side. . . . The uproar moved to the Commerce Street side of Hotel Adolphus, then inside the Adolphus and almost to the door of the ballroom, where the Johnsons were to be honor guests at a luncheon. Women in Democratic campaign outfits hollered back at the anti-Johnson shouters. They also made up part of a convoy with linked arms which brought the Johnsons from the Baker, where they had a room, to the Adolphus.[25]

Among those taking part in the anti-Johnson rally was Representative Alger, who appeared in newspaper pictures holding a sign declaring "LBJ sold out to Yankee socialists."[26] Alger was downtown to give a pep talk to his tag day volunteers; noticing the demonstration, he had walked across the street to greet and join the assembled protestors.

Johnson saw the political possibilities in challenging the demonstrators head on by walking unescorted with Lady Bird from the Baker to the Adolphus, dismissing police guards, and taking "almost 30 minutes to inch their way through the Republican demonstrators."[27] At the luncheon Johnson chastised the Nixon supporters. "It makes me sad to know that we have people—attractive people, nice people—who can be so frustrated, and so discourteous and so desperate. I can understand it. He who has any knowledge of history has seen groups rise to power and demonstrate it as it was demonstrated today."[28] Later that night at a rally in Houston, Johnson said, "It was sad in Dallas—you wouldn't have believed you were in Texas."[29]

Johnson made no mention of the deceptive advertisement that poured fuel on the fire and precipitated much of the anger of the pro-Nixon demonstrators. Nor was Johnson willing to take an alternative route from the Baker Hotel to the Adolphus and thus avoid a direct confrontation between the two competing groups of demonstrators. The media focus on Johnson's response was so pervasive that over the weekend before the election Republican get-out-the-vote callers were provided with a fact sheet "to set the record straight," maintaining that "the so-called 'goon squad' was comprised of 300 young ladies of Dallas who had volunteered in early September for a Nixon tag day effort."[30] Callers were advised not to introduce the issue but to respond, if asked about it, by stressing that neither the senator nor his wife was jostled and that there was no heckling of Johnson's speech or interruption of his schedule. The Alger campaign was forced to run a full-page advertisement on the Monday before Election Day responding to the charges of harassment. The campaign stressed once again the deceptive Johnson advertisement that included the names of deceased individuals, bringing "insult to the memory of their loved ones."[31]

The end result of the situation was that for much of the nation Johnson came across as the victim of right-wing Republican hatred. The picture would be used by the left once again three years later in the aftermath of the assassination of President John F. Kennedy. Dallas was labeled a hotbed of rabid right-wing extremism even though the president's killer was a committed Marxist with only tenuous ties to Dallas. Unfortunately it continues to be used to associate the city with extremist politics to the present day.[32]

KENNEDY CLAIMS THE WHITE HOUSE

On Election Day the Kennedy-Johnson ticket was able to squeeze out a tight victory and return the state of Texas to the Democratic column. Many political observers shared the view of former governor Allan Shivers: "I think if it had not been for Johnson, Kennedy would not have been elected and I think to Lyndon Johnson can be given most of the credit for getting that ticket elected. I know they would not have carried Texas if Johnson had not been on the ticket."[33] The southern moderate, Johnson, had softened the perceived liberalism of the Catholic senator from Massachusetts, reassuring a sufficient number of traditional Democratic voters in predominantly conservative Texas.

The margin of victory for Kennedy over Nixon was roughly 46,000 votes in Texas, and questions arose concerning the counting of paper ballots in a number of counties. State chairman Hutcheson and national committee-man Fay petitioned for a "fair and legal recount" in all counties using paper ballots.[34] The party claimed that some 100,000 votes had been thrown out by local officials and not counted, resulting in an official challenge of the re-sults.[35] Neither the request for a recount nor the challenge to the allegedly uncounted votes met with success. The Nixon campaign withdrew its request for recounts in Texas, Illinois, and a few other states.

Meanwhile, the senate candidate dismissed by most political observers ended up receiving 926,653 votes, more than any other GOP state candidate had ever received. His total vote came within 200,000 of that received by Nixon, and he carried twenty-five counties, with his best showing in Dallas as he won the county by a margin of more than 31,000 votes. Tower had lost the senate race. but he had positioned himself as a strong candidate for a future campaign, including the one that would take place as Johnson vacated his senate seat for the vice presidency.

THE 1961 SENATE SPECIAL ELECTION

With Johnson's resignation from the senate, Governor Price Daniel appointed William Blakley to serve until a special election could be held. Blakley was a conservative Democrat and a personal friend of the governor who had previously been named the interim senator by Shivers in 1957 and had served until the special election won by Ralph Yarborough. Blakley had not entered that special election, but one year later, in 1958, he had unsuccessfully challenged Yarborough in the Democratic primary. Daniel had made the offer of a second appointment in 1961, expecting Blakley to decline. "There were no strings attached to the offer but I think it was pretty well understood that I thought whoever accepted it should make the race and that it ought to be considered with that in mind. I was surprised when Blakley accepted it, only because I considered his acceptance an indication he would run."[36] This time Blakley agreed to be a candidate in the special election, joining seventy others on the ballot, only one of whom was a Republican. After a liberal Democrat had won the 1957 special election with roughly one-third of the total vote, conserva-tives in the legislature changed the law to require a majority vote for election. Thus if none of the seventy-one candidates obtained a majority, a runoff be-tween the top two finishers would be required.

Building on the name identification obtained in his strong showing against

Johnson, Republican Tower was able to finish first in the special election but well short of a majority. His opponent in the runoff was interim senator Blakley. After having lost the White House only months earlier in a close election, national Republicans saw Tower's first-place showing as a potential opportunity to bounce back and break the Democratic monopoly of the South. Among those endorsing Tower in the runoff was former president Dwight D. Eisenhower, who met with the candidate in Gettysburg and made a five-minute campaign film for him.[37]

Tower's campaign stressed the need for a two-party system, especially in light of the liberalism of national Democrats, as well as pushing for an end to the power of the political bosses who were viewed as controlling the state Democratic Party.[38] He was aided in the runoff by Democratic supporters from both the left and the right. While the liberal *Texas Observer* openly endorsed Tower, other liberal activists said they would "go fishing" rather than vote for Blakley.[39] The conservative Democratic candidate was totally unacceptable to those who wished to see their party controlled by liberals supportive of the national Democratic Party. This approach was summed up by banker Walter G. Hall in his keynote address to the liberal organization Democrats of Texas: "Wouldn't it be nice to have all those who really believe in Republicanism opposing us honorably, and you may be sure vigorously, rather than having to continue this practice of having to watch more closely the traitors in our own party than we do the honest Republican opposition."[40] Meanwhile, former governor Coke Stevenson headed up United Conservatives for John Tower for U.S. Senator, a committee that included a number of prominent Democrats, such as Mildred Moody, wife of Dan Moody, another former Democratic governor.[41]

With fewer than 900,000 voters taking part in the runoff, Tower eked out victory by slightly more than 10,000 votes to become the first elected Republican US senator from Texas and the first Republican senator representing Texas since 1877. Tower did best in the urban areas, while Blakley carried most of suburban and small-town Texas. Nevertheless, Tower was able to eat into the conservative but traditionally Democratic areas of the state. Of the thirty-two counties carried by Blakley in his 1958 primary against Yarborough, twenty-two were carried by Tower in the 1961 runoff. Many of these, such as Ector, Midland, and Randall counties, would soon develop into GOP strongholds, while others, such as Comal, Gillespie, Kendall, and Kerr, were located in the traditionally Republican German Hill Country.

The Republican senate candidate was able to capture the support of many younger Texans and homemakers, two key elements in the party's Dallas success in the 1950s. According to Betty Andujar, a Fort Worth homemaker who would later serve as a state senator and Republican national committee-woman, Tower's grassroots campaign was "almost entirely women because, after all, the men were working."[42] Among the many younger Texans who would later play a key role in the party was Chase Untermeyer, then a high school freshman in Harris County. Untermeyer remembered: "Art Kelly, later the chief aide to State Senator Walter Mengden, was at the time president of the small Spring Branch Young Republican Club. . . . Art organized a group of us to ring doorbells in a precinct in deepest Spring Branch, identifying potential Tower voters, whom we called on Election Day to get to the polls." As Untermeyer recalled, "My role was tiny, but it enabled me to feel part of a truly historic moment in American politics. Such was the minuscule size of the Texas GOP in 1961 that teenagers and homemakers could be valued players, simply because we formed the political workforce."[43]

The growing Republican presence in Dallas County, which Nixon had carried with the help of a highly organized effort led by O'Donnell, was also a major contributor to Tower's victory in the runoff as he carried it with over 56 percent of the vote. Once elected, Tower called on O'Donnell, the recent Wharton School graduate and campaign strategist, to help set up his Washington office. O'Donnell stayed on as administrative assistant for the next two months, helping Tower to recruit and hire a staff, before returning to Dallas to prepare for the 1962 primary and general election.[44]

The significance of Tower's victory would be seen over the coming years even as Republicans were unable to elect any other top-of-the-ticket candidates until 1978. According to some analysts, "Tower's victory proved, to some at least, the world would not end if Texans were to elect Republicans, a debatable phenomenon for those who would 'sooner vote for a yeller dog than for a Republican.'"[45] To a reporter for the *New York Times*, "the result seemed to be the culmination of a trend going back for decades. In this trend, agrarian Democratic regularity has been steadily weakened by a population influx of Northerners and a shift in the balance of power from the country to cities, with a burgeoning of sentiments forgetful of the Civil War and inclining more toward Northern party lines."[46] Still others thought the Tower victory proved that the Republican Party "was not simply a protest party or a safety valve for the raging Democratic civil war, but a power that the state must recognize."[47] Over the next twenty-three years as US senator, John Tower would serve as a mentor to many younger Republicans who served on his legislative and campaign staffs and through his support of various conservative and party organizations.[48]

BUILDING ON A VICTORY

One result of the Tower victory was to encourage a number of conservatives to pledge loyalty to the emerging political party. In the early 1960s a mood change was going on in Texas. Conservative Democrats were getting old and becoming politically extinct. Few new people were joining the ranks, and the younger generation was not as attached to the ways of the old South. According to William Murchison, longtime editorial writer for the *Dallas Morning News*, there was a sense that the state was in a new situation and had to adjust to a new way. It was becoming clear that it was futile to rely on the Democratic Party for the representation of conservative viewpoints. Looking back on that period of time, Murchison explained, "Conservative Democrats were rudderless and without a program. The conservative Democratic influence was on the way out since Bill Blakley lost to Tower. They were a dying breed and did not know it. In a changing, dynamic Texas there was no longer a need for their services."[49] Throughout the state, "resignation rallies" were held where, with evangelical fervor, Texas voters publicly converted to the Republican ranks. A few were past candidates and officeholders, including Jack Cox, a former state legislator who had run for governor in the 1960 Democratic primary.[50]

In June the party leadership voted to move the state headquarters from Houston to Austin. The move was opposed by Houston party leaders, including Porter, Fay, and Hutcheson, but supported by most others, such as O'Donnell and Tower, as well as Milburn and Marion Findlay of Austin. The relocation was seen as providing a "tremendous psychological impact," with the minority party moving into the state capital and close to the Capitol press corps.[51] The party also hired its first full-time executive director, Jim Leonard, who had previously been a candidate for state senate and was the traveling aide to Tower during the special election campaign.[52] Texas Democrats were organizationally unprepared for competition while "Republicans moved to consolidate their unexpected success in 1961 by building, for the first time, a professional operation that would allow for sustained activity.... These efforts were designed explicitly to promote the party as a full-time operation, in both election years and off-years."[53]

By the end of 1961 the party had won two more special elections as Ken Kohler of Amarillo and George Korkmas of Alvin filled vacancies in the Texas House of Representatives, becoming the first two Republicans to serve since the single term of Edward Dicker ended in 1953. Combined with the Tower election, these victories and the success of the resignation rallies led the party to believe that 1962 could be a breakthrough year.[54]

The shifting alliances among the Texas electorate in the 1960s still left the Democratic Party as the dominant force, but it now confronted periodic challenges from the emerging Republicans. Sean Cunningham has described the prevailing political outlook in Texas as "cowboy conservatism." The Democrats' ability to project this outlook for much of the twentieth century had kept them the majority party. According to Cunningham, "The Democratic Party dominated Texas politics until the 1960s and 1970s in large part because it was seen as the party of populist cowboy conservatism. . . . This perception fomented loyalty and loyalty evolved into tradition; Texans trusted the Democratic Party. . . . The vast majority of white Texans supported the Democratic Party simply because they believed the Democratic Party supported them."[55] By the early 1960s, however, Texas was becoming more suburban and middle-class, witnessing an influx of residents from two-party states, and confronting a national Democratic Party viewed as liberal-dominated. In such a situation "a majority of Texans began to lose confidence in the Democratic Party and increasingly questioned their partisan loyalties."[56] The situation after the Tower breakthrough was summed up by Allen Duckworth, political editor of the *Dallas Morning News*, in a column on June 18, 1961: "The Republicans of Texas are a long, long way from conquering the state, but they have established a small beachhead."[57]

THE 1962 CONTEST FOR GOVERNOR

In the 1960 election, William Steger, the GOP candidate for governor, could attract only 27.2 percent of the vote, but his 612,913 votes meant that the party was required to hold a primary in 1962. In the optimism of the time, the party was able to recruit sufficient volunteers to conduct a primary election in 218 counties, a new record.[58] The Tower victory had led to an increased interest in the Republican nomination, and the party experienced a contest for the gubernatorial nod between Roy Whittenburg, an Amarillo rancher and publisher who had been the party's 1958 candidate for US senator, and Jack Cox of Breckenridge, a former Democratic state representative and gubernatorial candidate.[59]

Cox was among those who had participated in the 1961 resignation rallies and had switched his affiliation to the Republican Party after giving up on keeping the Democratic Party conservative. On September 10, 1961, Cox announced his change after concluding that "the present Democratic Party is dedicated to a course which can lead only to the destruction of the basic political and civil rights guaranteed by our Constitution." He went on to declare,

It should not be a question of party loyalty; rather it is a question of an individual citizen being loyal to the basic principles of government in which he believes and *then* determining the established political party in which and through which these basic principles of government—and a way of life—can be put into operation in an orderly and successful manner. After prayerful consideration, I have concluded that I can best serve Texans and the nation and the future of my children by supporting and working in the Republican Party.[60]

Explaining his decision to a reporter, Cox said, "I felt for a long time that I could be instrumental in changing the course of the national Democratic Party.... I no longer believed this possible. I believed the place for me was in the Republican Party."[61] Cox had been encouraged in his decision by a two-hour conversation with Senator Tower, who stressed the value of conservatives uniting within one party.[62] When the decision was announced, Tower publicly welcomed Cox into the party, declaring, "It is certainly a wholesome thing for such a prominent conservative Democrat to recognize that the Republican Party affords the only effective vehicle for those with conservative political persuasion and conviction."[63]

A graduate of the University of North Texas, Cox had served as a state representative from 1947 to 1953 and six years on the Texas Commission for Higher Education. He ran against Governor Daniel in the 1960 Democratic primary, receiving 40.5 percent of the vote. With the backing of Tower and O'Donnell, Cox decided to seek the Republican nomination for what he hoped would be a rematch with Daniel. Following the lead of Goldwater and Tower, Cox outlined his conservative views on government in a brief book titled *This I Believe ... and the Pursuit of Happiness*, which was widely distributed throughout the state.[64] Cox was able to bring with him the support, if not the party affiliation, of several conservative Democrats. In February former governor Stevenson, a Democrat who had previously supported Tower in his special election campaign, told a political associate, "I will vote in the Republican primary. I will support Kellis Dibrell and Jack Cox, both in the primary and in the general election."[65]

The conversion of Cox, who hailed from Breckenridge in Stephens County, and former governor Stevenson, from Junction in Kimble County, was significant in that it brought support from rural parts of Texas that had been overwhelmingly Democratic. Republican voters in many rural counties were so uncommon that Paul Burka related a story about a supposed election in South Texas where those counting ballots came to a Republican ballot and declared, "What's this?" Near the end of the count they found another Republican ballot, leading the election judge to declare, "That settles it. Let's throw it out. The guy voted twice."[66]

By March 1962 Dallas County GOP chairman O'Donnell began managing Cox's campaign for governor. While remaining in Dallas, O'Donnell took a hands-on approach to his task. He assumed responsibility for deciding which invitations should be accepted, noting in a letter to Cox's personal assistant that "I do not think you should accept any invitations after June 2 until we have time to plan where we are going."[67] A few weeks later he wrote to "remind you that there are to be *no* appearances scheduled for Jack unless he speaks (except Press Club Gridiron dinners)."[68] Following a report that Cox had arrived one hour late for an event in Amarillo, O'Donnell wanted to know what happened. "Also, I was informed that several things that had been on schedule in Fort Worth on April 11 were cancelled by Jack that day. I think this is very poor policy. I strongly recommend that everything scheduled be met as scheduled."[69] A review of the campaign correspondence makes it clear that O'Donnell would oversee every detail of the campaign, including matters as small as authorizing payment of $47 to the postmaster.[70]

On primary day Cox sailed past Whittenburg by a vote of 99,170 to 16,136 and began to prepare for the fall campaign. An even closer outcome was in the race for lieutenant governor between former FBI agent Kellis Dibrell of San Antonio and Temple business leader O. W. "Bill" Hayes. Despite an endorsement from Tower, Dibrell lost to Hayes by a vote of 56,012 to 55,209.[71] It was now settled that the statewide Republican ticket would be headed by Cox for governor and Hayes for lieutenant governor.

Cox would not get his rematch with Daniel, however. In the Democratic primary the governor's efforts at achieving a fourth term ran aground. A slew of candidates felt the time was right to challenge Daniel's effort to set a new record for longevity in the governor's office. Among them were the controversial major general Edwin Walker, Attorney General Will Wilson, and former highway commissioner Marshall Formby. The top two finishers making it into a runoff were Don Yarborough and John B. Connally, with the incumbent governor finishing third. Yarborough was a young liberal attorney who had previously sought the nomination for lieutenant governor in 1960 and had the backing of labor and of Senator Ralph Yarborough, with whom he had no family relation but who was a close ideological associate. Connally was a protégé of Vice President Johnson and had resigned as secretary of the Navy in the Kennedy administration to make the race. The runoff was perceived as a clear contest between the growing liberal element in the party, best exemplified by Senator Yarborough, and the moderate conservative forces loyal to Johnson and his allies. The final vote in the runoff was Connally 565,174 to Yarborough 538,924, a margin of less than 27,000 votes.

This time the November election would be between Cox, the former Democrat representing the newly resurgent Republicans, and Connally, the former Kennedy administration official derided by both liberal Democrats and conservative Republicans as "Lyndon's Boy, John." As related by historian Roger Olien, "Cox mounted the most strenuous GOP campaign for governor in Texas history. Under the industrious and methodical management of Peter O'Donnell, Texas Republicans carried on a lengthy, expensive, and effective drive for Cox. Unlike so many of his predecessors, Cox was no token candidate."[72] To Republican activist John Knaggs, "Cox was a tough challenger who knew how to punch and counterpunch."[73]

Before the fall campaign could be completed, however, the Republican Party had to conduct another state convention. With a sitting US senator and the special election victories of two state representatives, Texas Republicans were excited and enthusiastic about the upcoming election. According to one report, "the Republican State Convention was, by far, the largest ever held in the state. Observers noted that there was excitement and enthusiasm that had been missing in previous conventions."[74] Clearly, the party had moved from its almost total emphasis on patronage to dedication to electing candidates to public office.

In August state chairman Tad Smith announced that he would not seek another term at the September 18 convention. However, he did agree to remain in office through the fall campaign. To achieve this, the SREC amended the party rules to "provide that all statutory functions of the State Chairman shall rest in the newly elected State Chairman, but all remaining functions — i.e., authority and responsibility for the campaign, the Headquarters and the like — shall be vested in the retiring State Chairman until after the election."[75]

The leading candidate to succeed Smith was O'Donnell, who lined up the support of Tower, Alger, Cox, and Smith himself. As the convention approached, however, what appeared to be developing was a battle between the two major areas of Republican strength, Dallas and Houston. Ever since Jack Porter achieved control of the party in 1952, Houston had been the location of the party headquarters, and he had been succeeded by another Houstonian, Albert Fay, as national committeeman while Thad Hutcheson was the party's senatorial candidate and state chairman in the late 1950s. Now the SREC had moved the party's headquarters to Austin, and Dallas was being viewed as the center of Texas Republican activity. O'Donnell leadership would only solidify Dallas's importance in the party.[76]

Less than two weeks before the convention a challenger appeared in the person of Don Napier, a forty-one-year-old vice president of a steel company in Fort Bend County whose wife, Mary Ann Napier, was serving on the SREC. His opposition to O'Donnell was tactical, not ideological. While O'Donnell believed in concentrating party resources on winnable races, Napier maintained that support should be given to all Republican candidates. In his campaign letter to convention delegates he maintained that the party's purpose was to elect candidates at every level. "We have this year an excellent and qualified slate of Republican candidates at *every* level who deserve and must receive wholehearted support, financially and otherwise, from the State Headquarters to the Precinct organization."[77] While still Dallas County chairman, O'Donnell was serving as campaign manager for Cox's gubernatorial campaign. Napier saw this as a clear example of favoring one campaign over the efforts of other Republican candidates, a bias that would be magnified were O'Donnell to become state chairman.[78]

Napier played on a recent controversy over the state party's support for candidates. In June Harris County GOP chairman James Bertron criticized the planned distribution of state campaign funds, with 70 percent going to Cox and the remaining 30 percent split evenly between lieutenant governor candidate Hayes and congressional at-large candidate Desmond Berry. No state funds were allocated to other statewide, congressional, or legislative candidates. As Bertron explained, "I could never agree with Peter O'Donnell's stated feeling, i.e., 'Okay, so you elect another congressman from Texas. So what?'"[79]

The tactical differences were magnified by an August memo from Smith to all Republican candidates in which he advised: "Separate, individual campaigns are essential. Joint appearances or multiple candidate rallies should be avoided." He went on to claim, "If you are going to win, you must develop your own identity. Multiple candidate rallies submerge, rather than enhance, your individual identities. They emphasize the Republican slate, rather than the individual merits of the individual candidate."[80] But for many party activists, including a number on the SREC, pushing the party and its slate was exactly what should be done.

Additionally, Don Napier maintained there should be a more decentralized party decision-making process. As he explained to the media, "The main thing I'm pushing for is that the party should be operated through the state executive committee. I think the state chairman should act through the executive committee."[81] Geographically it appeared that Napier's likely support would be concentrated in Houston and parts of West Texas.

As the delegates assembled in Fort Worth they were met with placards and signs for both candidates. O'Donnell went about meeting delegates and seeking votes, stressing his record of building a solid organization in Dallas County, carrying the county for Nixon, Tower, and Alger in 1960 and then for Tower in the 1961 runoff.[82] His credentials as a conservative were solid: he was serving on the national advisory board of Young Americans for Freedom, as well as being a trustee for the Intercollegiate Society of Individualists, two leading young conservative organizations of the time.[83] At the last moment before votes were cast, Napier withdrew from the contest, and O'Donnell was unanimously elected state chairman.[84] In the battle between the state's two largest cities, Dallas had bested Houston within the Republican orbit. It would remain the dominant force in the party for at least the next fifteen years.[85]

Once the party leadership issue was settled, the delegates heard from their US senator and their gubernatorial candidate. Tower criticized the Kennedy administration's foreign policy by claiming, "Humiliating as it is, the most powerful nation in the world is acting like the most craven. The President's foreign and military policies are most confusing and perplexing to Americans everywhere."[86] Meanwhile, Cox charged that Texas was in "political bondage" and set the tone for his campaign as one that would "return the political power to the people. It is a winning idea and I think we are winning."[87] Cox's overriding themes were that Texas needed a governor who was "independent of Washington control," which would not occur if the state's voters chose "Lyndon's Boy, John" Connally.[88]

Just as Tower was able to do in 1961, Cox appealed to a number of liberal Democrats who viewed Connally as part of the conservative Democratic establishment. With such a close loss, and with enmity toward Connally running high, one of Don Yarborough's campaign aides formed Texans for a Two-Party Texas, and for the second time began the process of rallying liberal support for a statewide conservative Republican candidate. As one participant in the effort explained, "The issues were clear to all parties involved. The two-party leaders knew that liberal and conservative protest votes for Cox might bring about his election paving the way for the two-party system. The conservatives knew this also and worked to keep it from happening."[89]

In July, both Cox and Connally addressed the state AFL-CIO convention, and while "Cox drew some surprisingly favorable comments after his speech," the delegates gave what was described as a weak endorsement to Connally.[90] Liberal Democratic leader and small-town newspaper publisher Archer Fullingim saw not a dime's worth of difference between the two candidates. "We have two Republicans running for Governor! Real Democrats will scratch the Republican who is running on the Democratic ticket.... We've got to smoke all the Republicans out of the Democratic Party, and make them admit that they are Republicans and run under their true Republican colors, like Cox."[91] Little did Fullingim know that only eleven years later that is exactly what Connally would do when he declared himself a Republican.

Another prominent liberal who met with Cox and endorsed him after Don Yarborough lost the runoff was George I. Sanchez. Sanchez was a former president of the League of United Latin American Citizens (LULAC) and professor of Latin American studies at the University of Texas at Austin. In a letter of endorsement, Sanchez maintained that "Jack will do a tremendous lot of good for the Latin American and the Negro, something that his opponent, by the very nature of his associations and their record, will not do." He went on to explain that this time it was not enough to simply refrain from voting for the Democratic candidate: "I 'went fishing' when it was a choice between Blakeley [sic] and Tower. This time it is a different matter. We have a constructive option—Jack Cox. I am taking that option. I urge you, respectfully, to do the same."[92]

While a number of liberals were supporting Cox, a number of conservative Democratic Party leaders feared that a decline in support for Connally might weaken continued conservative control of the party. George W. Sandlin appealed to conservative party leaders by stressing the need for conservative precincts to turn out a heavy vote for Connally so conservatives would have more voting strength at the 1964 Democratic state convention. According to Sandlin, "the Republican-liberal coalition is very simple. The liberals will vote heavily in their precincts for Connally—and also help the Republicans get the conservative Democrats not to vote for Connally in their precincts. The liberals win both ways on this strategy—one, they control the county and state Democratic conventions in 1964 and at the same time claim credit for electing Connally; and two, if by chance Cox should win, then their liberal candidate will have a better chance to win the Governor's race in 1964."[93]

By late October the Texas Democrats knew that they had a real battle on their hands to retain the governor's mansion. After losing one senate seat to the Republicans they were committed to retaining their dominance of state politics. One tactic employed was to claim that anyone who voted in the Democratic primary was required to vote Democratic in the general election. As Tad Smith noted, "What a confession of weakness! Apparently the Connally forces fear they can't win if Texans really vote their convictions." In an analogy drawing on the world situation at the time, Smith went on to declare, "Khrushchev can force Russians to vote the one-party ticket. Castro can force Cubans to vote the one-party ticket. But nobody can force Texans to vote the one-party ticket."[94]

Desperate situations required desperate measures in the Democratic camp.

On the letterhead of "John Connally for Governor—San Antonio," a message went out to voters in minority neighborhoods: "We have a fight on our hands against a man with EVIL intentions toward the Negro People of Texas."[95] With such measures Connally was able to build his largest county-wide lead in Bexar County, besting Cox by nearly 20,000 votes.

When the votes were counted in November, Connally had defeated Cox by roughly 130,000 votes, with the Republican candidate receiving 45.6 percent of a record off-year voter turnout. Cox carried both Harris and Dallas counties and came in first in 55 of the state's 254 counties. His strong showing helped the party re-elect Alger, elect Ed Foreman to a West Texas congressional district, and come within two thousand votes of seeing William Steger, the party's 1960 gubernatorial candidate, capture a congressional seat in East Texas.[96]

Meanwhile the party broke through to elect six state representatives from at-large districts in Dallas County and one from Midland. One member of the Dallas delegation was O. H. "Ike" Harris, a thirty-year-old graduate of the University of North Texas who had served in the Air Force for three years before receiving his law degree from Southern Methodist University, where he was president of the student body. Harris was defeated for re-election in 1964, then lost a close race for the state senate in 1966 before winning a special election for the senate in November 1967. He continued to hold a senate seat until his retirement in 1995; he was the first Republican to become dean of the Texas Senate as its longest-serving current member.[97]

While winning seven new seats in the state legislature, the party was unable to retain the two districts it had captured in 1961 special elections, as Ken Kohler of Amarillo and George Korkmas of Alvin both lost their bids for re-election. Among county officials, the party was successful in electing six county commissioners and three county judges, including Barbara Culver of Midland, the only female county judge in the state at the time. Indicative of the regard in which Republicans were held in the early 1960s was Culver's answer when asked whether she faced a problem with voters accepting the idea of a woman being county judge: "The beautiful thing was that being a Republican was so much worse. They got off of being a female pretty quickly."[98]

O'DONNELL TAKES CHARGE

As 1963 began, O'Donnell was state chairman. His first task was to develop a permanent organization at the party headquarters now located in the state capital. Building on his business school training, O'Donnell emphasized "the long view" and prized "quality over quantity," the latter trait generating opposition from those who believed that all Republican candidates should receive party support.[99] O'Donnell convinced Marvin Collins, who had been his executive director at the Dallas County party, to relocate to Austin and head up the state party's operations. Collins was "well-schooled in the O'Donnell methodology of planning and executing organizational programs with precise goals, deadlines, and reports."[100] For several years through the 1960s, Collins would serve as the "chief executive" of the state party, carrying out the overall strategy outlined by the "chairman of the board," O'Donnell.

When O'Donnell assumed the chairmanship, an important transition in party influence and control was already under way. Traditionally in a state party focused on federal patronage, the most powerful party leader was the national committeeman. This had been the situation from the time of Norris Wright Cuney and on through Cecil Lyon, Rentfro B. Creager, and the tenure of Jack Porter. With the shift in emphasis towards winning elections in Texas, the role of the state party chairman gained increased significance. O'Donnell's background and his emphasis on planning, execution, and organizational development enhanced the importance of the state chairman as leader and spokesman for the party. While federal patronage remained important to the party, coordinating campaigns for public office and presenting the party's positions to the media and the state legislature became higher priorities. Since the 1960s the state chairman, rather than the national committeeman, has overseen party operations and has been held responsible for the party's performance.

At the January meeting of the SREC, O'Donnell was among those attempting to analyze the party's performance. He concluded that in future elections a uniform plan for the entire state was needed, one that emphasized a door-to-door rather than a telephone canvass, and that stressed the value of organizing more women's clubs, which, he concluded "do 95% of the work." Cox told the committee "We are disappointed but we are not discouraged," noting that "715,000 votes should be enough and I never dreamed the vote would be so high."[101]

DRAFTING GOLDWATER

The new emphasis on winning elections and developing a true opposition party did not mean, however, that presidential nominations and national convention politics would be overlooked. There was one national party leader who was clearly a unifying personality among Texas Republicans, and that person was Senator Goldwater of Arizona. Throughout the late 1950s, Goldwater's speeches, writings, and senatorial actions had created a following for him nationwide. The senator's advice to conservatives at the 1960 national convention, that they should grow up and organize for the future convention, was taken to heart by the Texans.

George W. Strake Jr., later to be Texas secretary of state and GOP state chairman, recalls two events he attended after returning to Houston in 1961. One morning he was invited to a meeting with Republican leaders Fay and Porter where the topic was how to best promote Goldwater for the vice presidential nomination. That evening he attended a Republican women's club meeting at the home of Joanne King Herring. When the topic of Goldwater came up, the women in attendance made it clear that their interest was in Goldwater for president, not vice president. It was evident to Strake that the Republican women were more aggressive and willing to reach higher than the longtime politicos, who were more cautious in what they thought could be achieved.[102] With such solid grassroots support, a serious effort began to nominate the Arizona senator for president.

From the time of the initial meeting of the nascent Draft Goldwater movement in October 1961 at the Avenue Motel in Chicago, Texas was represented among the small group of national conservative political activists plotting his nomination. Robert Morris, president of the University of Dallas, attended that first meeting and was joined by Republican national committeeman Fay and GOP state chairman Smith at the second gathering two months later.[103]

By the fall of 1962 most Texas party leaders, including Smith, Hutcheson, Fay, O'Donnell, and especially Tower, were firmly in Goldwater's camp and committed to seeing him become the nominee for president in 1964. Tower's victory in May 1961 was seen as a reflection of the appeal of Goldwater conservatism throughout the state. In Texas Goldwater was not perceived as an outsider but was in many ways the establishment candidate. Putting this movement in perspective, Olien concluded, "the Goldwater movement in Texas was led by seasoned party leaders, it was not the work of a conspiratorial clique of newly arrived political extremists."[104]

Just as past party leaders from Cuney to Porter had seen early advocacy of a presidential nominee as the path to increased influence, so too did O'Donnell. While they were focused on Goldwater, the long-term objectives of O'Donnell and Tower were to break the eastern domination of Republican national politics while advancing the conservatism prevalent in the South and Southwest. It was more than geography that motivated this drive; it was ideology and a commitment to conservative principles. The Goldwater campaign was a tactical move toward more long-term strategic goals. According to Knaggs, "It was easier for O'Donnell to build a stronger party around Goldwater's impending candidacy than to sell abstract conservative principles. Thus, the destinies of the Texas GOP and Goldwater became tightly intertwined."[105]

Once he became state chairman, O'Donnell replaced Smith in the group planning to recruit Goldwater as the party's presidential candidate, attending the so-called secret meeting in December 1962 that led to the eventual creation of the National Draft Goldwater Committee. O'Donnell later recalled, "We held more meetings—a great many more—in the next four months. But never once did we have a word of encouragement or even any contact with the senator. We knew he had the strength, but we didn't have an organization we could go with." Ever the advocate of detailed planning and strong management, he said, "Finally, I said that unless we got something started I was pulling out."[106]

It became apparent that the effort could not remain informal and secret for much longer. A decision was reached to go public and organize a national network of supporters. More than merely a member of the group, O'Donnell was named chair of the national committee and presided at a news conference announcing the group's formation on April 8, 1963, in Washington.[107] As F. Clifton White, one of the original planners and eventual executive director of the National Draft Goldwater Committee, explained, "Peter was the ideal man for the top Draft post. As Republican chairman of the fifth most populous state in the Union, a traditionally Democratic stronghold that was now very decidedly shifting toward the GOP, he commanded the admiration and respect of Republicans everywhere." O'Donnell was viewed as a campaign professional and not merely an ideological advocate, an important characteristic for displaying the seriousness of the draft effort. White added, "I couldn't see how Barry Goldwater—or any other leading Republican in his right mind—could possibly thumb his nose at Peter O'Donnell."[108] Having only been recently elected state chairman, O'Donnell had already developed a national reputation as "young, aggressive and impatient."[109]

Throughout 1963 O'Donnell played a critical role in the development of a Goldwater candidacy, a role that would extend his influence beyond the borders of Texas and result in the drafting of a somewhat reluctant candidate.[110] O'Donnell could devote his time to this cause since he knew that within the Republican Party, Texas was clearly Goldwater country. In a March 1963 survey by a Dallas newspaper, 91.2 percent of GOP county chairs were reported to have preferred Goldwater as the party's nominee in 1964.[111] At a meeting of the SREC later that spring, O'Donnell reported on the success of the Draft

Goldwater effort. "Our people are tingling with excitement. I have been receiving long distance calls from all over the nation. A year ago, it was said that Kennedy was unbeatable. But people are not thinking that way now." The committee passed a resolution commending O'Donnell for his work and reaffirmed a resolution first adopted at the 1962 state convention endorsing Goldwater for president. At the same meeting, Tower pledged his wholehearted support to the Arizona Senator: "I want my position made plain. I am supporting him for nomination for president."[112]

By the fall of 1963, one report indicated that in Texas, Kennedy "dropped in voter popularity polls from 65 to 46 percent in less than a year. Senator Barry Goldwater's score has jumped from 22 to 39 percent, and Texas is abuzz with Goldwater enthusiasm."[113] Veteran political writer Bo Byers concluded: "If Goldwater becomes President Kennedy's challenger—as Texas Republicans fervently hope—the Republicans could roll up Texas majorities in the presidential, gubernatorial, and U.S. senatorial contests."[114]

In late October, O'Donnell appointed state representative Dick Morgan of Dallas to be chair of the Goldwater campaign in Texas, with Mrs. J. C. (Barbara) Man of Wichita Falls as cochair. At this time, however, Goldwater had not declared himself to be a candidate, and there was no direct contact between the senator and the draft committee. Nevertheless, O'Donnell was not reluctant to give advice to Goldwater. In an interview published in the *Saturday Evening Post*, Goldwater volunteered that he thought the federal government should sell the Tennessee Valley Authority.[115] A few months later O'Donnell met with the senator and handed him a confidential memo taking Goldwater to task for shooting from the hip, advising him to steer clear of addressing sensitive issues head on. According to O'Donnell, "if you spell out your position on all issues at this time, you will have fewer new things to say come October. Also, you will be presenting a nice, fat target to some group or other every time you take a stand."[116]

Goldwater ignored the advice and, as White, director of the Draft Goldwater Committee, noted, "The only purpose it served in 1963 was to further estrange Peter from the Senator and his inner circle. Goldwater did not take kindly to advice. Moreover, Kitchel and the others regarded it as a sign of impetuosity and disloyalty for anyone outside their circle—and even some of those within it—to presume to offer advice this forthrightly."[117] Later that fall O'Donnell and Tower met with Goldwater again and presented him another confidential memo. With various liberal candidates being proposed in an effort to prevent a Goldwater nomination, the two Texans proposed a strategy to head this effort off. They recommended that Goldwater offer the vice presidential slot to Pennsylvania governor William Scranton: "instead of fighting your way through all those primaries you can wrap up the nomination right now by getting Scranton to announce as your vice presidential running mate. He will have nothing to lose and everything to gain."[118] The senator dismissed the possibility.

A similar fate befell O'Donnell's recommendation in December that the campaign not enter the New Hampshire primary. After spending several days in the state meeting with political operatives and local volunteers, O'Donnell had found a disorganized campaign that, on primary day, came in second to a write-in effort for former senator and United Nations ambassador Henry Cabot Lodge Jr. By the time of Goldwater's formal announcement in early January 1964, the Draft Goldwater Committee ceased its operations, and O'Donnell's involvement became focused almost entirely on gaining delegates from the South, as well as his responsibilities as state chairman.

Writing to Tower and other Draft Goldwater committee members in January 1964, O'Donnell reported on what he saw as disorganization in the campaign: "What is at stake? An unsuccessful drive for the nomination will provide the vehicle and excuse for the Republican liberals and moderates to purge the Republican Party of conservative officials and not a few conservative officeholders."[119] One more memo from O'Donnell to Goldwater emphasized, "the survival of the conservative element in our party depends on your success." By now, however, O'Donnell was among those responsible for the draft movement who were outside the inner circle, "mowed down by the Arizona Mafia" of longtime friends and associates of Goldwater who came to dominate the campaign.[120] According to one report, "Kitchel coldly informed Peter O'Donnell there would be no place for the Texas Republican leader on the Goldwater for President Committee staff."[121]

Beyond the inner workings of the presidential campaign, support for Goldwater remained strong and fervent. When the SREC met in January, a survey by the *Houston Chronicle* showed all thirty-two responding favored Goldwater. O'Donnell predicted that Goldwater would beat Johnson in Texas and in the nation. "As reason replaces emotion, analysis will show that Johnson will be easier to beat than Kennedy. The popular part about Kennedy was his style and his family. His program was unpopular."[122]

BUILDING A STATE TICKET

Unlike the past, however, more was happening among Texas Republicans than presidential nomination politics. By 1963 the GOP had a presence, albeit small, in the Texas House of Representatives, with seven members as the regular session began. The party's numbers had increased with the special election victory of Chuck Scoggins of Nueces County in May, followed by those of Hughes Brown and Jack Sampsell of Dallas County in November. Morgan, one of the Dallas legislators, maintained that the Republicans functioned more as a party united by common principles, while Democratic legislators were beholden more to various special interests: "All the Democratic Party does is preside over a primary, then each nominee goes elsewhere for his funds, and as a result he does get obligated. The Republican Party gave me $3,000; my largest contribution apart from that was $100. I suppose I am obligated to the party, but principle-wise. As a result, I consider the Republican Party the party of the people, and the Democratic Party now the party of special interests."[123] Although their numbers were small, by sticking together and allying themselves with those interested in promoting realistic and viable solutions, the Republican delegation was able to influence the direction of state government.

Having elected a US senator, two members of the US House, and the first state legislators in a decade, as well as making a respectable showing for governor, Texas Republicans were optimistic throughout 1963, looking forward to a Goldwater versus Kennedy ideological battle for the presidency in the coming year. As Knaggs recalled, "Those were heady days for Texas Republicans. . . . They were fighting for the conservative cause, a basic change in direction for their nation and a more independent brand of conservatism for their state. Their momentum was strong and growing stronger every day."[124] While Dallas, with its lone member of Congress and eight freshmen Republican legislators, remained the center of Republican strength, the party's reach was expanding into other areas of the state, with a new member of Congress from West Texas and state legislators from Midland and Corpus Christi.

A new political force was also developing in the state's largest county, Harris, in 1963. Dallas had developed a vibrant Republican force by the mid-1950s, but Houston's politics had remained dominated by conservative Democrats. By 1960, however, Harris County was changing, with some 30 percent of its residents born outside Texas and 25 percent of its population minorities. As one writer concluded, "demographic factors gave the liberal Democrats a fairly stable base of support. These developments also aided the Republican party locally. As a result of Republican party activity, conservative Democrats began to move into the Republican party."[125] While Porter, Hutcheson, and Fay placed most of their attention on state and national politics, a few others were attempting to build a viable local political force.

Among those prominent in the early-1960s growth of the Harris County GOP was Marjorie Meyer Arsht. A lifelong Republican, Arsht first became active in the Tower campaign and then was recruited to run countywide as a state legislative candidate in 1962. Although unsuccessful as a candidate, she "sought to increase involvement in the precinct conventions and executive committee meetings. She created a program that became known as the neighbor-to-neighbor fund drive.... Due in large part to Arsht's efforts, participation in Republican primaries and other party functions continued to grow."[126] By 1962 the Harris County Council of Republican Women's Clubs had been formed, and the following year the clubs set up booths in stores and shopping centers to sell poll taxes and attempt to register additional Republican voters at a time when payment was required months in advance of the election.[127] The small cadre of dedicated Republicans had become substantial enough to help elect Bill Elliott to the Houston City Council. He is considered to be the first Republican elected to a city government position in Houston.

After moving his family and his new business from Midland, George H. W. Bush was now settled in Houston. Zapata Offshore Company, a spinoff of the original Zapata Oil, which Bush had helped form in Midland in 1953, was now established, and he could devote more time to political activities. While still in Midland, Bush had been involved in fundraising for the state party at a time when his father was a US senator from Connecticut. Party leaders had attempted to recruit him as a candidate for a West Texas congressional seat in 1958. Now he was being asked to assume a more prominent role in party politics with the Harris County Republican Party.

The new Houston resident agreed to serve on the Harris County candidates committee prior to the 1960 elections, joining Fay, T. E. Kennerly, Clive Runnels, and county chairman Fred Weston. He became actively involved in raising funds for Tower's 1960 campaign and for a November 1961 dinner featuring Representative Walter H. Judd of Minnesota, the keynote speaker at the 1960 Republican National Convention.[128]

James Bertron followed Weston as county chairman. Like many in Harris County at the time, Bertron favored providing support for all Republican candidates, rather than emphasizing a few high-profile positions. This tactical approach put him in opposition to O'Donnell and those who had concentrated the state party's resources on the Cox gubernatorial campaign. Back home Bertron found himself fighting off the influence of those active in the John Birch Society, an extreme right-wing organization headed nationally by Robert Welch.[129] As viewed by two biographers of the Bush family, "Bertron was trying to broaden the base of the party by promoting conservative economic issues and appealing to the business community. But the Birchers were making it difficult, with talk of blowing up the United Nations, violently resisting the income tax, and claims of a global conspiracy."[130] By early 1963 Bertron announced that he was moving to Florida, creating an opening in the position of county chairman.

Soon thereafter, George H. W. Bush decided to become a candidate for the vacant office. In a letter to his college classmate, Representative Thomas "Lud" Ashley of Ohio, Bush noted, "I am running, yes, for chairman of the Republican Party of Harris County.... I think I'll win—though I now have misgivings. Actually, it is a challenging job and one which, if done right, could show results."[131] Bush drew an opponent in Russell Pryor, a commercial real estate broker and party activist. The two aspirants presented themselves to a meeting of area GOP activists on February 13 in advance of the county executive committee meeting to select a new chairman.[132] Before the vote took place, however, Pryor withdrew from the contest, and Bush was elected unanimously. Pryor would remain an active leader in the county for many years, serving on the SREC while his wife, Molly, was district director for Senator Tower before becoming Harris County Clerk.

Bush began his term by reaching out to the various factions in the party and attempting to attract more minority support for Republicans. These efforts brought congratulations from George W. Strake Jr., who noted, "your action in appointing the various committee heads from the several different factions within the party will have untold good results."[133] Also among those sending letters of congratulations to the new county chairman were O'Donnell, Cox, and James A. Baker III. Foreshadowing his own future efforts, Baker said, "You are the type of conservative individual who, in my judgment, should go actively into politics. If more of us followed your example, this would, indeed, be a better political world."[134]

When local business executive Lloyd H. Smith sent Bush a copy of a pro-Goldwater article by William A. Rusher appearing in *National Review*, Bush responded by asking for additional copies to distribute to his advisory committee, and said, "I am convinced that we need a conservative presidential candidate in 1964, although if you asked me to be completely honest I would not say that I think we are going to get that." Bush recognized that the party in Texas was conservative, but that much of the Eastern Republican establishment was not. "I think there is no question that our party here in Texas is conservative. The only thing I am determined to do is see that we are responsibly so."[135]

On March 30 Senator Goldwater was the featured speaker at a county party fundraising dinner. Upon his arrival he was greeted by a delegation of Young Republicans urging him to seek the presidency and was met by a number of reporters.[136] Recognizing the success of the event, Bush wrote that "this has certainly given us a wonderful boost in several ways. Goldwater's visit charged up our people with a great deal of enthusiasm."[137]

While some on the far right claimed that Bush was a Rockefeller Republican, his letter to Republican National Chairman William E. Miller made it evident that he would never support the New York governor as the party's candidate for president. A few days after Nelson Rockefeller married Margaretta "Happy" Murphy, Bush maintained that "The Republican Party must not hand its highest position of leadership, responsibility and trust to a man who does not value the sanctity of the home.... It is his business now but as President it would be the business of every school child in this country. Our first lady should not be one who has left her four children; our President should not be one who has left his wife of 31 years."[138] Bush's view was shared by many others, including his father, former senator Prescott Bush. Whether Rockefeller ever had a serious possibility of gaining the party's nomination or not, the situation concerning divorce and remarriage was a major personal liability for any presidential candidate.

After the Draft Goldwater Committee was announced, Bush circulated a petition calling on the senator to seek the nomination and soliciting a dollar contribution from each of the Harris County executive committee members, noting that it was "a request from our State Chairman, Peter O'Donnell." The leadership of the state party and most of its grassroots supporters were for Goldwater, but not everyone was in agreement. After the Harris County party's finance chair, Craig Peper, referred to leaders of the Goldwater movement as "right-wing extremists," Bush called for his resignation and restated his personal support for the draft movement.[139]

Throughout the remainder of the year, Bush concentrated on strengthening the Harris County party organization and bringing together disparate factions as much as possible. One area where he was committed to expanding the party's reach was to the county's African-American population. After meeting with a small group of black Republicans, Bush received a proposal for establishing a party headquarters in Houston's third ward, a predominantly black area where the party had little infrastructure.[140] Bush convinced the party to fund the start-up costs of such an effort, and later that year the Greater Houston Republican Alliance was formed, with Thomas E. Dixon as temporary chair and a headquarters at 1918 Wheeler. Bush stressed that the new effort was not a segregated arm of the county party, emphasizing that "the Alliance will organize precincts and Negro leaders will sit on county Republican committees."[141]

Meanwhile, with the new emphasis on contesting elections in Texas, O'Donnell took on the task of putting together a statewide ticket. He wanted to ensure that the party had a strong, viable, and well-financed candidate to run against Senator Ralph Yarborough, whose liberal voting record was viewed as inconsistent with the conservatism of Texas voters. One associate of O'Donnell's suggested he speak to "a fellow named Bill Clements. He's made a lot of money out of a drilling contract in Argentina, and I think he's interested in public service."[142] O'Donnell met with Clements and asked him to consider running for the senate. Over the next few months the two discussed the matter several times, on some occasions involving Senator Tower. Clements finally said no, proposing that they speak with one of his business associates in Houston and promising that "if you can get him to run, I'll be his state finance chairman." That business associate was Bush. As O'Donnell recalled later, "I went down to Houston to see George, and of course he was dying to run. I thought it was fabulous. I'd gotten a great candidate and a great finance chairman on the same day."[143]

Bush, however, was not the only possible candidate for the senate in 1964. Cox, who had run a strong campaign for governor two years earlier, could not decide whether or not he would mount another effort for public office. Party leaders wanted Cox to make another race against Connally for governor but could not get a firm commitment from him.[144] Cox's focus was not on a rematch for the governor's mansion. As he told the *Houston Chronicle* in August 1963, "At this moment I'm not a candidate for anything. If I should be a candidate in 1964, it will be for the U.S. Senate."[145] A few weeks later Bush let it be known in a letter to friends and supporters that he would be a candidate: "After talking with John Tower and other state leaders this week, I have decided to go ahead and make my announcement around the middle of next week for the United States Senate."[146]

Cox's indecision had led O'Donnell, his campaign manager in 1962, to Bush. It was frustrating the desires of other supporters, including attorney C. Douglas Forde Jr. of Dallas. Forde urged Cox to run and to announce his candidacy, saying that the needed funds could be raised but that the longer he waited the more support Bush would gain. According to Forde, "You have a record of fighting the fair deal–new frontier philosophy whereas Bush is totally unknown, [this] would guarantee your winning the primary. You would then be a lot more help to the Goldwater effort in Texas than Bush would be were he the victor in the primary."[147]

It would not be until February 6, 1964, that Jack Cox finally announced as a senate candidate. A few weeks later he named state representative Henry Stollenwerck of Dallas as his campaign chair, along with a steering committee that included a number of individuals who would be active in party leadership over the next several years, including Russell Pryor, Fred Gray, and Nancy

Palm of Houston, as well as Raymond Tapp, Taffy Goldsmith, Tom Medders, Roy Whittenburg, Bette Jo Buhler, Anne Armstrong, Polly Sowell, Walter Wilkerson, Jamie Evans, and Julian Zimmerman.[148]

Two other candidates came forth to seek the Republican nomination to oppose Yarborough, both from the Dallas area. Milton Davis, a leader in the campaign against Kennedy's health care proposals who would later become president of the Texas Medical Association, announced his candidacy in late 1963. Davis was a supporter of Bruce Alger, who wished him well and advised him: "Stress your conservatism and the necessity of returning the leadership of this nation to those who believe in conservative principles and constitutionally limited government."[149] Also seeking the nomination was Robert Morris, a fervent anticommunist and newspaper columnist who had served two years as president of the University of Dallas. Morris had been part of the original group that resulted in the formation of the Draft Goldwater Committee.[150]

One catastrophic and historic event would intervene before the 1964 campaign could begin: the assassination of President Kennedy in Dallas on November 22, 1963, which would change so much in American society. The shock of the killing of the president was overwhelming for many Americans, who rallied to the new president in an effort to unify the country at a time of national mourning. The political implications of these events could not be overlooked. With Johnson assuming the presidency, even those liberal Democrats who had long opposed him in Texas were now supporters. One leader of the liberal forces remarked, "In my humble opinion, the Democratic Coalition must absorb President Johnson, or be absorbed by him. Whatever our dislikes for LBJ, as a ruthless state hatchet man, and I yield to none in the intensity of mine, he is now President of the United States.... The President must swing liberal, at least through the 1964 general election, and I think we should swing with him before he swings away from us."[151]

With both liberal and conservative Democrats rallying behind the successor to the slain president, the challenge for Republicans was overwhelming. As O'Donnell concluded in a later interview, "The Kennedy assassination affected us the most because it happened here and you had a Texan become president of the United States. Lyndon Johnson had been very unpopular. All of a sudden, one day—bingo—he's popular. Our situation changed overnight."[152] In early 1964, optimism—however naïve it may have been—still reigned supreme among many Texas Republicans.

Once Bush announced for the Senate he began traveling the state extensively, meeting with potential donors and supporters. One such trip was to Dallas for a meeting with H. L. Hunt. Bush hoped for his support and a sizeable campaign contribution but came away with a large brown envelope containing only several issues of *Lifeline*, a publication funded by Hunt and "produced to advance the Bircher cause."[153] Hunt ended up supporting Cox for the nomination. Meanwhile, Clements remained true to his word and donated $7,200 to Bush's primary campaign.[154]

In an early 1964 appearance before the North Brazoria County Republican Club, Davis used homespun sayings and slogans, Robert Morris was described as forthrightly conservative, and Bush sought "moderation, prudence, and a return to issues concerning Texas." According to one reporter, the audience members "laughed with Dr. Davis, applauded heavily for Morris, and were indulgently polite with Bush."[155] Once Bush's Senate candidacy was under way, a contest developed to replace him as Harris County chairman. Indicative of the overall mood in Republican circles, both candidates seeking the office supported Barry Goldwater for the presidential nomination.[156]

Spring 1964 was an interesting time for the growing band of Republican supporters in Texas. Not only were they experiencing a heated four-way contest for the Senate nomination, but the nation was in the midst of a lively presidential nominating battle. Determined to hold their first presidential primary, albeit a beauty contest in which no delegates would be won or committed to any candidates, the SREC placed the names of all four announced candidates—Goldwater, Rockefeller, Senator Margaret Chase Smith of Maine, and former Minnesota governor Harold Stassen—on the ballot. Smelling a rat in a state whose leadership was firmly committed to Goldwater, Rockefeller requested that his name not be included, but his request fell on deaf ears.[157]

When the votes were counted, to no one's surprise the Arizona senator posted an overwhelming victory with 104,137 votes (74.7 percent of the total) while Rockefeller could garner the support of only 6,207 (4.5 percent) primary voters, with Stassen winning 5,273 votes and Smith 4,816. The surprise of the primary, however, was the 12,324 write-in votes cast for Lodge, who had pulled off an upset in the New Hampshire primary. Focusing attention back on the Goldwater victory, O'Donnell concluded that the vote showed him to be "far and away the favorite of grass-roots Republicans in Texas as well as the party leaders."[158]

Meanwhile, the race for the Senate nomination was less conclusive. Bush ended up with 62,985 votes (44.1 percent), to 45,561 (31.9 percent) for Cox, 28,279 (19.8 percent) for Morris, and 6,067 (4.2 percent) for Davis. With no candidate obtaining a majority, a runoff was required between Bush and Cox. Morris threw his support to Cox and formed the Coalition of Conservatives to Beat the Bushes, claiming that Bush was too liberal for Texas.[159] Nevertheless, a number of Davis and Morris supporters sent a letter to primary voters endorsing Bush. Among the names of former Morris backers were Dallas business executive Fred Agnich and homebuilder David Fox.[160] In the June runoff Bush won 49,751 votes to 30,333 for Cox.

When the Republican state convention was held in Dallas one week later, it was clear that all the state's national convention delegates would be pledged to the Arizona senator. As Goldwater arrived to address a crowd of more than eleven thousand in the Dallas Memorial Auditorium, he received a standing ovation lasting more than five minutes.[161] Now it was on to San Francisco to secure the nomination for the favored candidate. Already new assignments were being made, as Rita Bass was appointed cochair of the Texas Goldwater for President Committee and would later be named national canvass chair for the Goldwater ticket.[162] Sally McKenzie of Dallas was selected by O'Donnell to serve as state canvass chair and was instructed to make a weekly report of her efforts to Bass. True to his emphasis on detail and organization, O'Donnell added, "enclosed is a list describing the information wanted under each column. Please mail your list each Friday to Rita, beginning Friday June 3.... Each Monday I will be able to determine what progress or lack of progress has been made organizationally."[163]

At the Republican National Convention in San Francisco, Senator Tower served as chair of the Texas delegation, made up of fifty-six delegates firmly committed to Goldwater. Tower was provided the honor of seconding the nomination for the Arizona senator and represented the state on the platform committee, fighting off amendments offered by liberal party members.[164] The party's gubernatorial candidate, Jack Crichton, received some national recognition when he was selected to chair the committee on permanent organization at the convention. During the convention, former senator Prescott Bush met with a number of delegates and talked up his son's candidacy.[165]

Throughout the fall the party undertook an intensive organizational effort and opened campaign headquarters in a number of cities across the state. O'Donnell was committed to a major effort to identify every possible supporter of Goldwater and established coordinated canvass and ballot security efforts modeled after the successful programs he had initiated in Dallas County. Meanwhile, a network of Youth for Goldwater clubs was organized on several campuses. Party county chairs were invited to use these volunteers because they were "well suited for the legwork involved in many campaign jobs, and they may be employed usefully in areas such as Car-Branding and headquarters work."[166] Among the many young Texans who would be active in the Goldwater campaign were Ronald B. Dear, later general counsel for the state party and a leader in the various Reagan presidential campaigns, and

Ed Emmett, who subsequently became Harris County judge.[167] Despite the fact that Goldwater was running against a president from Texas who had assumed office only months earlier after the tragic events in Dallas, enthusiasm among Republican supporters remained high.

While the Goldwater effort had been a major focus for O'Donnell ever since he became state chairman, he was also committed to turning out the vote for Bush in the senatorial contest. The Bush campaign was able to garner the support of some conservative Democrats who had been active in the campaigns of Eisenhower and Nixon but were unwilling to go against their fellow Texan Johnson. Among the most prominent of these was former governor Shivers. Meanwhile, the Democrats were flooding the state with posters proclaiming simply "Vote Texan, Vote Democratic, Vote Ralph Yarborough."[168] In his effort to rally supporters, the liberal senator attacked Bush as a "carpetbagger from Connecticut who is drilling oil for the sheikh of Kuwait to help keep that harem going" and called him "a Republican candidate who is the contractual driller for the international oil cartel."[169]

Bush's eldest son, George W., recalled the efforts put forth to help elect his father to the Senate in 1964, including the outreach to traditionally Democratic rural areas of the state. "He chartered a bus nicknamed the 'Bandwagon for Bush.' I traveled with him on a bus trip to West Texas, where we stopped in Democratic strongholds such as Abilene and Quanah.... We would pull into a town square, and a country band called the Black Mountain Boys would start playing in hopes of drawing some kind of a crowd. The Bush Belles, an enthusiastic and brightly clad group of housewives would pass out campaign pamphlets." For many rural Texans it was a new experience to witness someone other than a Democratic candidate for public office. As George W. Bush recalled, "Dad would mount the podium and give a speech. Some in the audience applauded and cheered. Others just looked startled at the sight of a real-life Republican."[170]

When the votes were counted, it was a landslide for Johnson in Texas and in most other states. Goldwater was able to carry only fourteen of the state's 254 counties, losing even Dallas. In a letter to Nixon shortly after the election, Bush expressed the opinion of many Texas Republicans when he concluded, the "Goldwater philosophy was not rejected. It was the false image that people had about Goldwater and the Johnson presence on the ticket."[171] Despite the loss of the national ticket, Texas Republicans remained firmly in the conservative camp.

The senatorial campaign was closer as Bush won 1,134,337 votes to Yarborough's 1,463,958. In losing, Bush had obtained nearly two hundred thousand more votes than the Goldwater-Miller ticket and had set a new high-water mark for votes for a Republican candidate in Texas. Bush was convinced that Johnson was responsible for his defeat, telling one reporter, "When President Johnson came to Texas and put his arm around Ralph Yarborough that was the end for me. The President was and is enormously popular in Texas."[172] Nothing could indicate the difference in the character of the two senatorial candidates more than their remarks after the election. Ralph Yarborough declared, "I think my opponent ought to pack up his suitcase and go back where he came from. He carried on the vilest and most defaming campaign I have ever seen."[173] Meanwhile, Bush accepted responsibility for his defeat, telling the *Houston Post*, "I have been trying to think whom we could blame for this and regretfully conclude that the only one I can blame is myself. I extend to Senator Ralph Yarborough, who I believe beat me fair and square, my best wishes."[174]

Once again, Texas Republicans had mounted a major effort geared toward statewide victories and came up short. As the year 1964 came to a close, some in the party were convinced that a reassessment of strategy and goals was needed.

SEVEN

AFTER GOLDWATER

The Goldwater debacle hit the Republican Party of Texas hard. As Roger Olien concluded, "the wild-eyed extremist label which was successfully pinned on Goldwater stuck to Republican candidates in Texas."[1] Not only had Johnson carried the state in a landslide, but his margin helped ensure the re-election of Senator Ralph Yarborough over an up-and-coming business owner and political leader from Houston who would occupy the White House a quarter of a century later. Both Texas Republican members of Congress were defeated for re-election, and the party held on to only one of the 181 state legislative seats.[2]

The Texas GOP learned the futility of relying on presidential Republicans, as the Shivercrats and other conservative Democrats retreated to support their traditional party. Robert Anderson and Oveta Culp Hobby, cabinet members during the Eisenhower administration, endorsed Johnson, as did former governors Allan Shivers and Price Daniel, who had led the support for Ike in 1952. Even worse than the actions of the Shivercrats, the defections included a number of known Republicans. Heading up Republicans for Johnson was former state representative Edward T. Dicker, who maintained that Goldwater's nomination "disturbed me no end." Dicker had been the sole Republican in the Texas legislature from 1951 to 1953 and was cochairman of the Eisenhower campaign in Texas in 1952.[3]

In the aftermath of the national loss, calls were being made to replace Dean Burch, who had been named national chairman after Goldwater's nomination.[4] Initially, many of the ideological conservatives among the Goldwater backers sought to retain Burch as chairman. If the votes were not present for this, they wanted another Goldwaterite to replace him. Peter O'Donnell was proposed by some to be that candidate. In the end, the votes to retain Burch could not be found, and Goldwater agreed to accept Ray C. Bliss, Ohio GOP state chairman, as the new national chairman.[5] Bliss was a technocrat who had helped build the Ohio party, a professional politician who placed winning elections ahead of philosophical consistency. Over the next four years Bliss would emphasize organization building that allowed the party to be in a position to win back the White House only four years after the landslide defeat of 1964.

While O'Donnell's name was being floated by some as a possible successor to Burch, back home in Texas he was facing the criticism that follows an overwhelming defeat. Some of the complaints came from those who had opposed Goldwater's candidacy, including Carlson, O'Donnell's predecessor as Dallas County GOP chairman. According to Carlson, "the Goldwaterites lost the presidential election before the gavel fell for adjournment at the Republican convention in San Francisco. When Barry Goldwater delivered his acceptance speech he also delivered his political valedictory." Carlson maintained that to rebuild the party, "all participants who went along with them the past few months should step aside."[6] Bill Elliott, then serving as a Republican on the Houston City Council, told the media that he advocated new leadership for the state party.[7] In response to these challenges Senator John Tower, both a strong advocate for the Goldwater nomination and a close associate of O'Donnell, questioned the wisdom of listening to those with little party loyalty. "It seems to me unlikely that those who failed to support the party ticket could be effective rallying points for party unity."[8]

Perhaps more serious were the attacks from those who had backed the presidential ticket but criticized O'Donnell and the state party leaders for their heavy involvement in the Goldwater campaign at the expense of Texas candidates such as George H. W. Bush and the various congressional candidates, including incumbents Bruce Alger and Ed Foreman.[9] On November 20, seven prominent Texas Republicans called for the resignation of all party leaders who refused to reject what they labelled "Goldwater ultra-conservative Republicanism." Most prominent among the group was Thad Hutcheson, former state chairman and Senate candidate.[10] Some of the criticism was a continuation of the Dallas versus Houston rivalry for party control. Just as they had two years earlier, when they backed Don Napier against O'Donnell at the state convention, some of the strong conservatives from Houston believed the party had placed too much time, energy, and resources on the presidential campaign to the detriment of other contests.

O'Donnell weathered the storm and remained as state chairman. After all, he had the support of the party's only statewide officeholder and had built up relationships with the state Republican executive committee (SREC). When Keith Shelton, political writer for the *Dallas Times Herald*, sent a survey to SREC members and county chairs in late November, he asked their opinion on O'Donnell's leadership and whether he should continue in office. A typical response was that of Mason Crocker, McCulloch County chairman, who expressed a high opinion of the state chairman's leadership and said he felt O'Donnell should continue in office.[11]

The Goldwater campaign brought many new volunteers and donors to the party, and for those people O'Donnell was viewed as their leader, thus strengthening his position. Steve Bartlett, later member of Congress and mayor of Dallas, was one of the high school students activated by the Goldwater effort. As he recalled years later, "1964 was the year the Republican Party achieved the spirit—the sense of determination and sense of purpose—to make us a real political force in Dallas County." Looking back on the many campaigns in which she was involved, Rita Clements concluded, "Goldwater was the easiest candidate I ever recruited for."[12] O'Donnell and the other party leaders were committed to keeping these new enthusiasts involved in the party, an approach that in some instances created internal problems for the party.

THE TOWER RE-ELECTION

A few days after the election, top party leaders assembled in Austin to discuss the road ahead. Having been one of the most fervent supporters of the Goldwater candidacy, Tower offered to stand aside for another candidate if the group felt that would be best for the party. O'Donnell spoke for the group in rejecting the idea outright. His advice was for the party to circle the wagons around Tower. As recalled by John Knaggs, at the time a key state party staffer,

> Every effort would be made to retain all the volunteers and contributors who had come aboard for Goldwater and Bush, melding them into Tower supporters or participants in the party organization, which would function almost solely for the benefit of Tower. If that base could be secured, it would provide a strong building block for Tower's reelection, a goal O'Donnell obviously believed to be vital. Emphasis would be on Tower's campaign to the exclusion of a governor's race or any other for statewide office.[13]

In reality, given the outcome of the recent election, clearing the field of any other serious statewide candidate would not be a difficult task.

In February 1965 O'Donnell met with the state party staff in Austin and reported to Tower, "We are all in agreement that our Number One objective is your re-election, and all our programs have been tailored to this end."[14] Once again O'Donnell stressed that the party must have quotas, deadlines, and reports to ensure that all essential tasks were being completed in a timely fashion. The Tower re-election would be the overriding objective for the state party for the next two years. One month later O'Donnell wrote the senator again, outlining what he saw as the essentials for the campaign and telling Tower what he must do to be re-elected.[15] Shortly thereafter, Rita Bass agreed to develop a timetable for an undecided voter program. According to O'Donnell, in the previous election "easily a third of the voters showed themselves to be undecided as a result of our canvass, yet we had no detailed program on how to win them over."[16] Carrying out these plans would be Nola Smith, statewide undecided chair for the 1966 campaign.

That summer O'Donnell wrote Tower expressing his concern that insufficient attention was being devoted to resolving organizational issues, including the decision-making process for the campaign. Among the subjects yet to be settled were the management of the campaign, the finance chair and plan, and the hiring of an advertising agency, as well as determining responsibilities for research, scheduling, and advance work. In typical O'Donnell fashion, he stressed "the necessity of job descriptions for all persons to serve in the campaign covering responsibilities, goals, timetables, relationship of the Washington office, Austin office, Republican State Headquarters, and your state campaign office to each other."[17]

Key personnel of the state party and the Tower campaign began meeting every Sunday afternoon at the Forty Acres Club in Austin, managed at the time by Jack Cox. Among the regular attendees were O'Donnell, Knaggs, and Marvin Collins for the state party, with Jim Leonard, Ken Towery, and Tower representing the campaign. The group would review events of the previous week and outline plans for the future. Knaggs recalls that the efforts of the state party and the Tower campaign were totally integrated.[18]

In the aftermath of the Goldwater campaign, a number of new recruits with little past involvement in politics became active in the party. Members of the John Birch Society were particularly involved in the Harris County party, and the county chairman came under criticism for allowing them to gain influence in the organization. In June Robert Gilbert resigned as chairman, and a contest developed between James B. Bowers, backed by the Birchers, and James M. Mayor, supported by longtime Republicans. Among political observers nationally it was perceived as an attempt by Birch Society members to take over the party in the state's most populous county. When a special meeting of the county executive committee was called to select the new chairman, O'Donnell and Tower flew to Houston to endorse Mayor before the vote.

They were joined in their efforts by former county chairman George H. W. Bush and national committeeman Albert Fay. The meeting extended into the early morning hours before the party leaders' favored candidate was elected in a vote of ninety-five to eighty.[19] The Harris County election would be the most visible, but not the only, effort by Birch Society members to gain control of the party apparatus.[20]

In January 1966 state leaders received some sobering news as to how their party was viewed by Texans. When asked whether the Republican Party's support would influence people in how they voted, 11 percent said it would make them more likely to vote for the candidate, and 25 percent said it would make them less likely. Conversely, Democratic Party support would make 32 percent more likely to support a candidate and only 8 percent less likely. As the authors of this survey concluded, "The Democratic Party support helps define the character of the state, and in this sense: to a Texan the Democratic Party is something which is locked into tradition. It hasn't really very much to do with whether one is a moderate or a conservative or a liberal. By the same token, the fact that the Republican Party produces an over-all negative reaction is little more than confirmation of the same point, or the same analysis."[21] A second survey that spring showed 64 percent of Texans identifying themselves as Democrats, with only 25 percent thinking of themselves as Republicans. In no voter subgroup—by geography, age, race, ethnicity, or income—were there more Republicans than Democrats.[22]

Reacting to these findings and the 1964 loss, party leaders decided to prioritize Tower appearances and organizational efforts. Party staff prepared an analysis developing eight categories of counties depending on size and voting history for either Cox 1962 or Bush 1964. As the report noted, "if we proceed to form an organization in all 254 counties, we will be faced with the problem of restraining workers in counties where a lot of noise will only hurt the Senator." Too much Tower activity in certain counties was viewed as potentially increasing turnout among people who would likely vote against the Republican candidate. The two categories where less organizational emphasis and very few candidate appearances would be placed included several suburban counties that would subsequently become rock solid for the party, including Collin, Ellis, Hunt, Kaufman, and Williamson.[23]

While Tower's re-election was clearly the main priority, party leaders recruited qualified candidates for most statewide elective offices, partly to ensure that no loose cannons would distract attention from the overriding themes of the Tower campaign. Seven congressional districts would be contested also in 1966. George Bush attempted to rebound from his Senate loss by seeking office in Houston's 7th congressional district, while Bob Price made his second try for the Panhandle-dominated 18th district, where he had received 45 percent of the vote in 1964. O'Donnell convinced Jim Collins, who had recently stepped down as president of Fidelity Union Life Company, to seek the 3rd congressional district seat in Dallas County.[24] According to one political observer, "He could see what was coming down the line and wanted to be on the winning side." Collins was described as "a crossover between the older conservative Democratic approach and the new suburban Republicans" since he was so folksy and friendly that you didn't care that he was not a great orator.[25]

Rebounding from the disastrous defeat of 1964, the party was able to recruit a presentable number of candidates for lower-visibility positions. At the state legislative level, nine senate districts would be contested in 1966, and forty-two Texas House of Representatives districts would have a Republican candidate. A scattering of counties ran candidates for county commissioner, while nine counties fielded GOP county judge candidates, including the party's incumbents in Harrison, Kerr, and Midland counties.[26]

The Democratic contest for the nomination to oppose Tower quickly fizzled out. In September 1965, Attorney General Waggoner Carr, a key figure in the conservative Democratic establishment, announced his candidacy. Meanwhile, Representative Jim Wright of Fort Worth made soundings around the state but backed off by December and filed for re-election. This left liberals in the party with no strong alternative to Carr, a candidate many deemed unacceptable. In the Democratic primary, Carr defeated the little-known John R. Willoughby by a margin of 902,223 to 226,568, while turnout in the Republican primary was less than 50,000 votes.[27]

O'Donnell's emphasis on organization was evident throughout 1966. He relied heavily on a core of dedicated and experienced female volunteers. Once again, Rita Bass played a leading role as state organization chairman, with Ginny Pearson, wife of George Pearson, as turn-out-the-vote chairman, Nola Smith heading up the undecided voter program, and Sally McKenzie again serving as state canvass chairman. Shortly after accepting her assignment, Pearson was told by O'Donnell to submit weekly reports to Bass because they needed to "establish a system of periodic checks" to make sure all was being accomplished on time.[28]

For those dedicated to re-electing Senator Tower, summer was not a time merely for vacations. O'Donnell instituted Operation Early Bird as an under-the-radar effort to canvass potentially favorable neighborhoods. As he explained to the canvass volunteers, "Please *do not* publicize our summer canvass in your local press. It does not help us to tell our opposition what we are doing—and that is certainly the effect of giving the newspapers all (or even part of) the details of our organizational programs."[29] O'Donnell's commitment to the canvass was total, and he dedicated a good deal of his own time to taking part and motivating the volunteers, much as he had done when serving as Dallas County GOP chairman. According to the Tower campaign newsletter for August 1966, the state chairman canvassed with fifty-six volunteers in Austin on July 28. "Peter O'Donnell is showing his enthusiastic support for this program by having canvassed in Dallas and in Austin and by scheduling himself for an evening of Early Bird campaigning in Houston on August 3." A later newsletter indicated that O'Donnell had traveled to Longview and Sherman to help with the door-to-door canvass and had also visited Corpus Christi, El Paso, Amarillo, Fort Worth, and San Antonio.[30]

These intensive organizational efforts were welcomed and recognized by Senator Tower, who made a number of appearances with his volunteers during the campaign. As he noted to one reporter, "One thing I think a politically-savvy Republican has over a Democrat in Texas, in a hotly-contested election, is that Democrats are so accustomed to running in Democratic primaries that they're not oriented to running in general elections—while we're totally oriented to general elections. The Democrats are used to getting a few of the old party bosses who run various areas, lining them up and saying that's an organization. They haven't developed the technique of working precincts the way we Republicans do."[31] Throughout the fall, the GOP concentrated on Tower's campaign and did little to promote its candidate for governor and other statewide offices.[32] Symbolic of this emphasis was the cover for the September state convention program, which featured a picture of the senator and the campaign slogan, "He's doing a good job for Texas."[33]

Meanwhile, it was evident that many liberal Democrats were not anxious to elect Carr. When asked about his support for the Democratic senate candidate, Senator Yarborough told his supporters, "I'm going to make as many speeches for Waggoner Carr in his campaign as he's made for me in my seven statewide campaigns," adding that "I have no personal (bad) feeling about Tower. As a matter of fact, I sort of like him."[34] With Johnson in the White House and a Republican as the other senator from Texas, Yarborough had a key role in any patronage and appointment decisions involving the state. Were Carr, a conservative Democrat, to be elected, Yarborough's influence would be lessened.

Adding to Carr's troubles was the relationship between Governor John Connally and many liberals in the Democratic Party. After much bickering over party matters, a sizeable number of liberals walked out of the state convention in Austin to chants of "To hell with John Connally," reassembling on the capital grounds to adopt a resolution approving the idea of voting for Tower as a protest against conservative control of the Texas Democratic Party.[35] According to a report in the *New York Times*, "About 850 liberal Democrats bolted the state Democratic convention in Austin yesterday. They said they might endorse Republican Senator John G. Tower, an extreme conservative, for re-election, rather than back the Democratic nominee, Attorney General Waggoner Carr."[36]

A group of liberals calling themselves the Democratic Rebuilding Committee refused to back Carr and endorsed Tower's re-election. Their motto was simple: "Sometimes party loyalty asks too much."[37] Distaste for Carr and a desire to drive conservatives out of the Democratic Party led David Richards, at the time husband of Ann Richards, to do the unthinkable. "We'd rather go down in flames than be trapped supporting reactionary Democratic candidates. Thus it was that I cast my one and only vote for a Republican candidate for public office. I am sure that many Texas liberals joined me."[38]

Tower also was supported by the Committee for a Two-Party Texas, organized by a group of Mexican-American Democrats in San Antonio.[39] Meanwhile, the leader of the Amigocrats for Tower defended his endorsement of a Republican by saying if Democratic governor Shivers could rally support for Eisenhower in 1952, then he could lead a group of Democrats for Tower in 1966.[40] As one observer noted, "More than any other GOP politician of his era, John Tower attempted to attract Mexican-Americans into the party. He succeeded beyond anyone's expectation."[41]

As part of a pincer movement on Carr, a number of conservative Democrats, led by former Texas attorney general Will Wilson, also defected to the incumbent Republican senator. Wilson had finished fourth in the 1961 Senate special election and also in the 1962 Democratic gubernatorial primary. An effort under the rubric of Democrats for Tower was organized to recruit the support of Shivercrats who had previously backed Eisenhower and Nixon, although the former governor remained committed to Carr. Wilson would subsequently become a Republican and serve as an assistant attorney general in the Nixon administration.

With defections from the left and the right, Connally was motivated to rally his supporters behind the Democratic Senate nominee. By October Connally's key political lieutenants had been placed in control of the Carr campaign, and the president had made it known that he strongly supported Carr's election. With their control of the state and the state Democratic party under challenge, Connally and Johnson combined an appeal to party loyalty with political arm-twisting to rally support for Carr.[42] Mark White was a volunteer for Waggoner Carr and recalled attending a rally for the candidate where "every single prominent elected official in Texas" was present and endorsed his candidacy.[43]

Despite their best efforts, the Democrats came up short as Tower was re-elected by a comfortable margin of 841,501 to 643,855, with 56.7 percent of the statewide vote. Tower carried Dallas County with nearly two-thirds of the vote and won all of the six largest counties in the state. Reflecting back on the election later, O'Donnell described the 1966 Tower re-election as his biggest success as state chairman.[44] Carr was unable to retain the support he had received in the Democratic primary; he garnered 258,368 fewer votes in November than he had won in May. As one reporter described the results, "Carr went down to defeat through the passive coalition of Republican conservatives and Democratic liberals."[45]

Meanwhile Connally easily won a third term with over a million votes as all the other Republican statewide candidates were defeated. The party did score some significant legislative breakthroughs, however. Both Bush and Price won their congressional races while Jim Collins ran a close race against an incumbent conservative Democrat, ending up with 47 percent of the vote. Former Democratic state representative Hank Grover was elected as a Republican state senator from Harris County, the first party member to serve in that body since 1929. In the Texas House, Frank Cahoon of Midland, who had been left as the only Republican after the 1964 debacle, was joined by Malouf "Oofie" Abraham of Canadian and Chuck Scoggins of Corpus Christi.

LOOKING AHEAD TO 1968: NIXON OR REAGAN?

As the year 1967 began, there was a change in the administration of state party operations. Marvin Collins, who had worked with O'Donnell in the Dallas party and since 1963 as executive director of the state party, announced he was stepping aside. O'Donnell accepted the change with deep regret, concluding "I'm sure that everyone who knows him will agree that he deserves a generous share of the credit for the progress we've achieved." Replacing Collins was Al Allison, a Harvard graduate who had previously served on Tower's staff and in 1966 was executive director of the Harris County GOP.[46]

Intensive targeting for the 1968 elections began with an effort to analyze past elections and recruit qualified candidates. Jerry Stephens, a young staffer at the party office, accumulated election data and prepared opportunity sheets based on the performance of Cox in 1962, Bush in 1964, and Tower in 1966, in all congressional and state legislative districts.[47] O'Donnell attempted to balance the equation of multiple candidates and winnable elections in a memo to party officials: "The supply of good candidates is limited, just as is our supply of money, volunteers to support them, and good districts in which to run. Therefore, since we are dealing with scarce items, we must carefully plan and allocate their use in order not to waste valuable resources, on the one hand, and on the other to maximize our opportunity for success in 1968 and beyond."[48]

Meanwhile O'Donnell appointed eight task forces led by prominent Republicans to hammer out policy recommendations that could be incorporated into the party's 1968 platform. Among those involved in the process were Will Wilson, former state attorney general, and Vernon McGee, former director of the influential Legislative Budget Board.[49] With targeting of districts under way and the development of specific policy recommendations being formulated, what the party needed now were candidates. The effort to recruit a statewide slate, and especially a candidate for governor, would consume much time and effort over the remainder of 1967.

Presidential nominating politics—the perennial pastime of Texas Republicans for nearly a century—was the focus of increasing attention by some party leaders. As early as February 1966, O'Donnell concluded, along with two Goldwater financial backers, Jeremiah Milbank and J. William Middendorf, that "siding with Nixon was a reasonable choice." In April O'Donnell held a meeting at his office in Dallas with Middendorf, former Alabama GOP chairman John Grenier, Mississippi national committeeman Fred LaRue, and Fred Agnich, at the time Dallas County chairman. According to Middendorf, "Our purpose was to launch 'Project X.' The label was more in fun than an effort at secrecy, but our goal was serious: to determine whether Dick Nixon was the best hope to win back the presidency and, if not, to decide who was."[50] As one political observer of the time noted, "Peter O'Donnell was smart and committed, highly focused in advancing his principles. O'Donnell was a realist, he wanted to win, and he had been burned by the Goldwater loss."[51]

At the winter meeting of the Republican National Committee in December 1966, O'Donnell worked with LaRue to encourage favorite-son candidacies from the various delegations. This was seen as a strategy to keep the party's options open until there could be a consensus on a presidential candidate. Behind the scenes, however, the real purpose in encouraging these efforts was something different. According to Rick Perlstein, "In New York, Richard Nixon smiled. LaRue and O'Donnell were his secret agents. Sowing a dozen or more presidential 'contenders' starved the five or six who actually *were* contenders of attention, leaving Nixon to plot behind the scenes in peace."[52]

O'Donnell and LaRue convinced Gaylord Parkinson, chairman of the California party and proponent of the "Eleventh Commandment" (Thou shalt not speak ill of any fellow Republican), to meet with Nixon in New York. After they met, Parkinson agreed to head the Nixon for President Committee whenever it was made public. At a gathering of delegate-recruiting leaders with Nixon in January, O'Donnell reportedly made the observation: "Collecting delegates is just like washing dishes, you gotta take 'em one by one." With their activities in deep cover, Nixon referred to O'Donnell as "the non-chairman of a nonexistent group."[53]

Back home in Texas, O'Donnell maintained, "While I like Mr. Nixon and think he is well qualified to serve as President, at this time I am not committed to his candidacy. Further I think the interests of Texas Republicans can best be served by going to the 1968 Republican National Convention pledged to support Senator John Tower as a favorite son."[54] With Tower playing the role of favorite son, some of his supporters in other states began to view him as a serious presidential possibility. From Los Angeles came word that Peter J. Malatesta, a nephew of entertainer Bob Hope, was forming a Tower for President committee. Learning about this effort, O'Donnell wrote to Malatesta and informed him that this was not the proper time to start any such effort, noting that "I have discussed this with Senator Tower, and he agrees with me."[55]

By the fall of 1967, O'Donnell was becoming disillusioned with what he viewed as the disorganization of the Nixon campaign and was willing to consider alternative candidates. In September O'Donnell called Tom Reed, who had been given the task of exploring the possibilities of a Ronald Reagan presidential campaign. At the same time Tower called Reagan directly and asked for a meeting. One week later Tower, O'Donnell, and Anne and Tobin Armstrong met with the Reagans and their key operatives at the governor's residence in Sacramento. When the Texans asked Reagan if he was going to run, Reagan gave an evasive answer, proffering the view that the office often seeks the man. This was not the answer they sought; they didn't want to commit themselves to someone who would not become an active candidate. As Reed concluded, "It was a disastrous non-conversation. The Texans left perplexed and unconvinced."[56]

After this inconclusive meeting with Reagan, at the September meeting of the SREC O'Donnell warned that if Reagan and Nixon, whom he saw as appealing to the same audience, ended up fighting each other, the nomination could go to Nelson Rockefeller. For this and other reasons the state chairman reiterated his support of the favorite-son strategy to create internal harmony within the Texas party. In remarks later in the meeting, Tower agreed that the favorite-son strategy was the appropriate path for the party to take, but handicapped the race a little differently. Tower thought Michigan governor George Romney was "suffering some self-inflicted wounds," Rockefeller's failure to support the party's ticket in the last two elections limited his standing among party leaders, and the principal contenders for the nomination were Nixon and Reagan.[57]

The following month, Tower met with Reed and informed him that he had been offered a leadership position in the Nixon campaign, a position he would accept unless he had some assurance that Reagan would become a declared candidate. None was forthcoming, and Tower accepted the position with Nixon. As Reed analyzed the situation, "Reagan left the impression with every party factotum he met during that last week of September that his campaign was a vague and headless monster, and that he was going to improvise as the convention approached. That is not what these old pros needed to hear. They did not want to get caught on the losing side of a struggle for the nomination. By early October, all were reluctantly joining what they felt to be Richard Nixon's inexorable ride to nomination, the only realistic alternative to a Rockefeller recapture of the party."[58]

Despite his indecision, a continuing effort was under way to convince Reagan to become an active candidate, a step he remained reluctant to take. Among those Texans advocating a Reagan candidacy were former national committeeman Jack Porter, former state chairman Thad Hutcheson, and Houston oil industry executive Larry Reed.[59] Porter had been attracted to Reagan for several years, having sent to Tower in February 1962 a copy of Reagan's October 1961 speech to the American Bankers Association titled "Losing Freedom by Installments."[60] O'Donnell decided that if a movement for Reagan could not be stopped, then it should be controlled. In December party leaders met in Houston, and O'Donnell told them that if there was going to be a Reagan effort in the state, "it ought to be steered away from extremes and, most important, be under their control. By the end of the Houston Club session one of those present, J. R. (Butch) Butler, had been drafted."[61] An independent oil operator from Houston, Butler was named chairman of Texans for Reagan, and his effort attracted support from a number of party leaders, especially in Houston and West Texas.[62]

Among those supporting a Reagan candidacy was Bob Price, one of two Republicans in the state's congressional delegation. At the same time Reagan was gaining support among the state's conservative Democrats. Longtime Democratic state senator Grady Hazlewood endorsed Reagan for president in April 1968. While the Potter County Democratic Committee demanded his resignation for endorsing "an extremist candidate," the local electorate continued to support Hazlewood, and many began the shift to the GOP.[63]

In January 1968 Richard Nixon undertook a tour of Texas, stopping in Dallas, Houston, and San Antonio, where he was well received by audiences. Senator Tower accompanied Nixon on his trip, praising him extensively but maintaining that he was not endorsing Nixon over other possible presidential nominees. After an evening event in San Antonio, Nixon headed on to meet with Republicans in Dallas and Houston. As one reporter summarized the visit, "Before his campaign day ended here late this afternoon, the former Vice President had received a rousing ovation from 3,000 Dallas Republicans, repeated bursts of applause from a slightly smaller but no less exuberant group of Houston Republicans and a warm embrace in both places from the state's most powerful Republican, Senator John G. Tower."[64] Nevertheless, Tower maintained that he would still retain his favorite-son candidacy to keep open the delegation's options on an eventual presidential nominee.

While Tower and O'Donnell were giving covert support to the Nixon effort, those promoting Reagan were also rallying his backers throughout the state. In March Butler solicited financial and political support for the effort, claiming that "Governor Reagan will make a most effective candidate and an outstanding president."[65] The Reagan effort picked up the open support of former national committeeman Porter and state senator Grover, as well as the latent backing of national committeeman Albert Fay. Fay's support for Reagan produced an internal dispute for the position on the national committee as O'Donnell announced that he wished to replace Fay and have former Texas Instruments president Fred Agnich succeed him as state chairman. As one reporter summarized the split, "At the base of the dispute is a disagreement over whether Texas Republicans should support Richard Nixon or California Governor Ronald Reagan for the GOP presidential nomination, rather than any actual fight between O'Donnell and Fay."[66] While acknowledging their differences, O'Donnell maintained that "any division suggested along Nixon-Reagan lines is incorrect. Both Fay and I support Tower as the state's favorite son candidate."[67]

In April a private meeting was held in Houston to try to smooth over relations within the party. In addition to Fay and O'Donnell, those attending were Tower, Bush, retired general John Bennett of San Antonio, and Harris County GOP chairman Dudley Sharp. While no resolution of the national committeeman position came out of the meeting, party leaders worked to convince O'Donnell to defer any challenge to Fay until after the November elections.

The bugaboo of a liberal Rockefeller candidacy and a return to party control by the hated eastern establishment soon surfaced as a rallying point for the Reagan forces and as an attack on O'Donnell. John Trice, a candidate for the party's gubernatorial nomination, claimed that O'Donnell sought control of the national convention delegation so he could make a deal with Rockefeller. Trice believed there would be a floor fight at the state convention in June. "I don't see how we can avoid it. It is a question of whether we will remain a conservative delegation in Texas or be relegated to being a 'yes man' to O'Donnell for whatever deals he makes." Trice claimed that Nixon's chances were weakened by Johnson's decision not to seek another term and that LBJ's action "leaves Republicans a choice between Governor Rockefeller and Governor Reagan. Governor Reagan can win the Republican nomination for president if he has the solid support of the Texas delegation. Without Texas, he cannot win, and Governor Rockefeller would be the Republican nominee." Tying it all together and bringing the discussion back to his own efforts, Trice claimed that if another candidate were to win the nomination for governor, "it will leave a delegation of hand-picked, pre-selected delegates under the control of Peter O'Donnell who might make a deal with Rockefeller."[68]

Shortly thereafter, Cox confirmed that he had been encouraged to run against O'Donnell for state chairman at the September state convention but denied any interest in such a contest. He did note, however, that "the word is that the state chairmanship will be contested," and noted that in addition to the differences over the presidential nomination, part of the controversy centered on O'Donnell and other party leaders recruiting and endorsing Paul Eggers as a gubernatorial nominee.[69] Finally on May 15 Fay wrote to Tower and pledged that if the senator requested his resignation after the November election, he would so submit it to the SREC.[70] With Fay's letter, the dispute over the national committee slot was set aside, only to arise again after the 1968 election. The Fay-O'Donnell split became enmeshed with not only the presidential nominating contest and the choice of a gubernatorial candidate, but also the long-standing struggle for control of the party between Dallas and Houston.[71]

The Reagan efforts in Texas, as in many other states, were hampered by the position of their preferred candidate. Throughout the spring, Reagan continued to remain a noncandidate, even writing to O'Donnell in April saying that he had not and would not authorize any action on his behalf in Texas.[72]

Despite his denial of an active candidacy, Reagan did allow his name to remain on the ballot in states where removing it would be difficult. His supporters hoped that an increasingly strong showing in the few so-called mandatory primaries would produce momentum for a last-minute candidacy. After winning only 10.4 percent of the vote in Wisconsin, Reagan rebounded to 21.3 percent in Nebraska, his high-water mark in those states where his name and those of others appeared on the ballot. Texans for Reagan declared the Nebraska showing a symbolic victory and an indication that he was a formidable candidate for the nomination.[73] When he did no better in Oregon, Butler "reckoned Reagan had done as well as he could considering the nature of the Oregon political terrain which, from his vantage point, looked like a 'socialist state ... where they spend Federal money like it was going out of style.'"[74]

Since there was no presidential primary in Texas in 1968, the state's fifty-six delegates to the national convention were selected at the party's June conclave in Corpus Christi. The delegates passed a resolution confirming Tower as the state's favorite son in an effort to keep the delegation unified, but the final disposition of the state's votes in Miami Beach remained to be seen. It was clear that while many, if not most, would follow the lead of O'Donnell and Tower, there were a number of Reagan supporters in the delegation. Butler claimed that the state convention "was a tremendous victory" and reported that "Governor Reagan is gratified with the support he received in Corpus Christi which resulted in the selection of more delegates committed to him than in any other state, with the exception of California."[75]

As the national vote counts were assembled by the three major campaigns, the Nixon strategists concluded that they needed first-ballot votes in Miami Beach too badly to allow any Texas votes go to Tower.[76] Thus on July 1 Senator Tower released his favorite-son hold on the delegation and publicly endorsed Nixon.[77] Meanwhile O'Donnell recruited Bill Clements to head up the Nixon fundraising effort in Dallas, and by the time of the convention he had met his goal. As O'Donnell noted, "If he tells you, 'I can do it,' you can bank on it. I can see his face right now when he looked at me and said 'I can do it.'"[78]

With Tower's release of the delegation the battle was on to win their support for either Nixon or Reagan. Not all elected officials followed Tower's lead into the Nixon camp. Representative Price announced that he would support Reagan if he were a candidate at the time of the convention. Subsequently, in Miami Beach Price gave one of the seconding speeches for the California governor. Butler maintained that "Senator Tower's announcement presents the members of the Texas delegation with a new responsibility and a great opportunity." He urged the delegates to support Reagan as a new face who would appeal especially to southern voters at a time when Alabama governor George Wallace was attempting a third-party candidacy.[79] The Reagan forces engaged Ron Dear, a young law student already deeply involved in conservative Republican politics, to travel the state, meet with various delegates, and try to convince them to support Reagan. At the same time Tower and O'Donnell were working to firm up support in the delegation for Nixon. According to one delegate the pressure from Tower was intense: "He really ground it in to them—telling them that a vote against Nixon was a vote against him."[80]

While the battle in the Texas delegation centered on the former vice president and the California governor, there were isolated supporters of other candidates. Entrepreneur Sam Wyly of Dallas indicated that he might vote for Senator Charles Percy of Illinois, a personal friend, while national committeewoman Flo Kampmann of San Antonio ended up seconding the nomination of Rockefeller.[81] With the Nixon forces attempting to ensure a first-ballot victory and the Reagan and Rockefeller backers seeking to push the nomination to a second or third ballot, the drive was on in Miami Beach for every possible delegate vote. Tower and O'Donnell claimed they had forty solid votes for Nixon, while Butler maintained that he could count at least nineteen of the fifty-six for Reagan.[82]

It was retail politics in Miami Beach as Reagan met with ten of the pro-Nixon delegates from Texas, attempting to win them over to his side. When O'Donnell cancelled the delegation caucus scheduled for Wednesday of convention week, Cox called the action "high-handed, ridiculous and definitely designed to help Nixon.... They kept saying there would be a free and open discussion of the presidential aspirants but this was never held."[83] In the end, when the roll-call was taken, Texas cast forty-one votes for Nixon and fifteen for Reagan, allowing the former vice president to win on the first ballot by a slim margin of twenty-five votes.

The conflict and controversy in the Texas delegation was not over with the nomination of Nixon, however. Tower and O'Donnell were two of the close advisors of Nixon who met the following morning to discuss vice presidential possibilities. As state chairman, O'Donnell was in a difficult position, with two of his elected officials, Senator Tower and Representative Bush, supposedly under consideration for the second slot. O'Donnell endorsed both, "perhaps fatally for their chances" when focusing on one or the other would have increased their possibility of being selected. Some observers viewed this as a problematic situation, especially for a state party that did not have a single candidate considered likely to win a statewide office in 1968.[84]

It was a major surprise to O'Donnell, and to much of the nation, when

Nixon named Maryland governor Spiro Agnew as his running mate. Agnew had a reputation as a more liberal Republican from a border state and had originally backed Rockefeller for the presidency. While he would become controversial as vice president, at the time of the convention he was not well known, even to those who follow politics closely. The choice also left scars among the Texas leadership. According to one reporter, Tower "feels strongly that he might well have been the vice presidential nominee had it not been for Cox's endorsement of Reagan, after heading a 'Tower for favorite son' drive, and O'Donnell endorsing Rep. George Bush of Houston as well as Tower for vice president. O'Donnell's giving the freshman congressman equal billing with the nationally known senator led many to believe that the Texas party was split in its allegiance to the two men."[85] The end result was that the incident "caused a bitter rift, which both men later tried to minimize, between Tower and Bush."[86]

Leaving Miami Beach, three Texas Republican leaders—Tower, Bush, and Cox—all felt that they had been shortchanged by O'Donnell in one fashion or another. Yet all had to pull together if they were to mount a serious statewide campaign for the presidency and for their gubernatorial candidate. Despite the personal and political differences, all agreed that the party could carry the state for Nixon and possibly elect other candidates to state and local offices in 1968. Neither Johnson nor Connally would be on the ballot, and the independent candidacy of George Wallace would be pulling some yellow-dog Democrats away from their party's nominee. It was time to move on from presidential-nominating politics and concentrate on a state ticket.

BEYOND THE PRESIDENCY

On November 11, 1967, a number of special elections were held to fill vacancies in the Texas legislature. In Dallas former state representative Ike Harris easily won a state senate seat without a runoff while six other Republican candidates made it into a runoff for Texas House seats. In Travis County Maurice Angly was elected to the Texas House to become that county's first Republican official, while in Harris County Sonny Jones and Glenn Purcell won open seats, and state representative Bill Archer announced that he would be seeking re-election as a Republican. Tower had received some criticism from O'Donnell for what O'Donnell viewed as the "half-hearted support you gave Ike Harris" at a press conference in Dallas. The chairman concluded, "If the Republicans had supported your campaign in '66 the way you are supporting Ike Harris, I doubt very much you would have been successful."[87] With Harris's victory to become the second GOP state senator, any breach in the Tower-O'Donnell relationship was quickly healed.

At the beginning of 1968, Texas Republicans were once again optimistic as to their chances for a future breakthrough. Not only had they re-elected Tower and succeeded in winning two congressional seats in 1966, but they also had increased their state legislative representation through the 1967 special elections. They would add to their state representation with the victory of John Lowrance from a Dallas state representative district in June. With a strong presidential candidate and the likely absence of Connally from the governor's race, a gubernatorial victory was possible.

There was, however, one overriding problem, and that was the difficulty in recruiting a winnable candidate. GOP leaders had searched far to find such an individual, but with little success. Neither Tower nor Bush was willing to leave Washington. Party converts such as Cox and former attorney general Will Wilson were interested but not convinced they could win. Veteran Austin political observer Jimmy Banks claimed that, among longtime Republicans, "many of them had never quite forgiven Jack Cox and Will Wilson for having once been Democrats. That was one factor which prevented either Cox or Wilson from being anointed as the GOP nominee for governor in 1968."[88] O'Donnell made another stab at convincing Bill Clements to make the race. In an ironic comment that would be reversed ten years later, it was reported that "He was practically in, then unexpectedly pulled out, declaring that he didn't really have the political background, instincts and drive necessary."[89]

Some Republican leaders even approached former Democratic member of Congress Joe M. Kilgore, a long-standing close supporter of Lyndon Johnson. O'Donnell and a key Tower aide, Ken Towery, met with Kilgore, who expressed interest in such a race. However, when Kilgore said he would expect to be party leader as governor but could never support candidates against some of his old congressional friends, "this brought to an abrupt end a rather brilliant idea for the Republicans to 'draft' for governor a man whose philosophy was closely akin to their own and who offered their best chance for success." Hearing of the failure to recruit Kilgore and the lack of support for either Wilson or Cox, one disgruntled SREC member complained, "Some of the party leaders had rather lose with an old-guard, lifelong Republican than to win with a well-known 'convert' from the Democratic Party."[90]

As the filing deadline came ever nearer, only two individuals had declared for governor on the Republican side: John Trice, a thirty-five-year-old Dallas attorney who had been the party's 1964 candidate for attorney general and was a thorn in O'Donnell's side, and Wallace Sisk, a little-known attorney from

Houston. Neither one excited the party leaders. Finally, a few days before the deadline, Paul Eggers, a forty-eight-year-old tax attorney from Wichita Falls, announced his candidacy. Eggers's only political experience was as a GOP county chair, but he was a close associate of Tower and was widely viewed as having the backing of O'Donnell.

On May 4 the party held a primary in 192 counties, with the gubernatorial race the only statewide contest, although the party did field unopposed candidates for all statewide nonjudicial positions and for sixty-nine of the 150 state representative districts. In another low-turnout Republican primary the final vote was Eggers 65,501, Trice 28,849, and Sisk 10,415. Indicative of the party regulars' support of Eggers, he was able to carry all but ten of the 192 counties where primary votes were cast.[91]

With Eggers heading up a statewide ticket and Nixon at the top of the ballot, Republican leaders believed they had an opportunity to make the long-awaited breakthrough in state politics. O'Donnell reportedly sought to raise a million dollars for the Eggers campaign, an amount that would allow major media penetration in the geographically expansive state.[92] His efforts in raising the funds came up short, as most campaign contributions were directed to the effort to carry Texas for Nixon, and the gubernatorial candidate was left with a campaign budget of only half a million dollars.

While Eggers had won his primary handily, it was a different picture on the Democratic side. Seeking to succeed Connally were six prominent candidates: Lieutenant Governor Preston Smith, frequent liberal spear carrier Don Yarborough, defeated senate candidate Waggoner Carr, wealthy rancher and banker Dolph Briscoe, Secretary of State John Hill, and Eugene Locke, considered to be the Connally candidate. Yarborough ended up first, but in a runoff with Smith. As John Knaggs, one of Eggers's campaign consultants, noted, "The Eggers' camp hoped Yarborough would win the runoff, providing a clear philosophical difference, but Smith won, posing a race between Smith, the 'caretaker of the stagnant one-party system,' and Eggers, 'the forward-looking conservative offering vigorous new leadership for Texas.'"[93]

Under the direction of campaign manager Marvin Collins, long a close O'Donnell associate, Eggers put together a campaign team that included a number of up-and-coming political activists, including Pete Roussel, Roger Wallace, Jim Oberwetter, Jim Francis, Gary Griffith, Jerry Stephens, and Eleanor Arnold, all of whom would continue to play important roles in the Texas party throughout the remainder of the twentieth century. Eggers made more than two hundred campaign appearances across the state and reached out to young voters, African-American community leaders, influential Hispanic organizations, and Democrats who wished to move conservatives out of the Democratic Party. As in the Tower and Cox elections earlier in the decade, Eggers developed an alliance with the two-party Democrats, such as those active in the Democratic Rebuilding Committee. According to these liberals, "the election of a Republican governor in 1968 will attract hundreds of thousands of conservatives into the 1970 Republican primary, taking them out of our primary. Otherwise Texans will be faced with two years of Preston Smith and lobby-dictated rule. Real Democrats will never have a strong voice in their own party until a two-party Texas is a working reality."[94]

While the *Texas Observer* endorsed the Republican gubernatorial candidate in an October 18th editorial, in a presidential election year it was much more difficult to encourage split-ticket voting.[95] Texas liberals disliked not only conservative Democrat Preston Smith but even more so conservative Republican Nixon. In such an environment "cross-pressures were soon evident among liberal-labor ranks in which pro-Eggers sentiment was growing but anti-Nixon sentiment was strong. Thus the ticket-splitting had to be promoted and that was not easy for so many leaders who had so often preached straight Democratic voting in presidential years."[96] One liberal activist noted this conflict when he explained, "We have more leadership-types solidly on this program than ever before. . . . Our problems are of an entirely different kind than in '66 and in '62. This time we've got to really take the message to the grass roots, re-write the message into a ticket-splitting proposition instead of a 'go-fishin' deal."[97]

As the fall campaign season began, Republicans were heartened by the special election victory of Jim Collins in a Dallas congressional contest. Yet the closeness of the presidential contest led O'Donnell to write Tower, asking him to concentrate his time and efforts in Texas. "In my judgment, we are in a tight race here. . . . It is in Texas that you have your maximum political influence. You are our only officeholder elected statewide. I think you need to utilize your prestige and popularity in Texas to guarantee that Texas goes for Nixon."[98]

On Election Day, Nixon came up nearly forty thousand votes short in a three-way battle with Hubert Humphrey and George Wallace but was able to claim the White House without the electoral votes of Texas. Eggers received more votes than Nixon but lost to Smith by some four hundred thousand votes, ending up with 43 percent of the total, a respectable but losing performance. Much of the media and most political observers were impressed with Eggers and viewed him and Bush as future leaders in the party.[99] All three GOP members of Congress and two state senators were re-elected, while the party's candidates won eight seats in the Texas House of Representatives, including a freshman from Midland, Tom Craddick, who would go on to become the first Republican speaker of the Texas House in 2003.

By the end of the decade, it was evident that Dallas and Harris counties remained the source of the most votes, and the most elected officials, for the party. In the 1968 elections each area had elected one member of Congress (Collins of Dallas and Bush of Houston) and one state senator (Ike Harris and Hank Grover, respectively), while Harris County was home to four GOP state representatives (Bill Archer, Sonny Jones, Jim Earthman, and Will Lee), and the Dallas state house delegation remained totally Democratic. In the presidential race, Nixon bested Humphrey by more than sixty thousand votes in Dallas and by nearly twenty thousand in Harris County. The party's gubernatorial candidate, Eggers, carried both counties also, with a larger margin from the Houston area. Republican candidates were doing well in areas of middle-class, white-collar workers, many of whom had migrated from other parts of the nation. The suburban growth of the 1960s was still occurring within the major metropolitan counties and was only beginning to slowly spread out to what are now the suburban counties surrounding Dallas, Tarrant, Harris, Bexar, and Travis counties.

In the aftermath of the disappointment resulting from the 1968 election, the knives were out once again. Those opposed to O'Donnell's leadership claimed that party funds were withheld from the Eggers gubernatorial campaign and diverted to the Nixon presidential effort. Eggers had been outspent by Smith in their relatively close contest, with Eggers spending about $550,000. Some Eggers supporters believed O'Donnell was responsible for diversion of campaign funds away from the Eggers campaign and toward the presidential effort. Even former Democratic governor Allan Shivers praised the showing made by Eggers, but claimed, "one thing he didn't have was the support of the entire Republican organization. They wanted to carry Texas for Nixon more than they wanted to elect Eggers."[100]

While those who followed Texas politics widely believed that O'Donnell had withheld funds from Eggers, the claim was denied by the gubernatorial campaign managers. Marvin Collins and John Knaggs maintained that "over 80 percent of our financial support came directly or indirectly from Mr. O'Donnell and other state party leaders and from funds raised by the finance office of the Republican state headquarters."[101] However, money was only one element in the criticism directed toward the state chairman. Some party activists, while praising O'Donnell's talent and dedication, maintained that he consistently placed an overriding emphasis on presidential politics, just as had his predecessors among party leaders. Such a policy, they believed, only lessened the possibility of potential gains at the state level. Among those concerned about the direction of the state party were a number of younger Republicans, strong supporters of Eggers, and the leadership of the Harris County party.

When O'Donnell called a postelection meeting of the SREC, a group of dissidents held a secret meeting in advance of the official sessions. Their hope was that a political leader, as opposed to someone with a business background, could be recruited to serve as state chairman. For some, that person was Cox, who might be enticed to assume the volunteer position with a pledge to underwrite his travel expenses. Still others thought Eggers would make the best choice for chairman. In the end, no movement to oust O'Donnell took hold, and he presided over a relatively peaceful two-day meeting of party leaders in early December.[102]

During the meeting, differences in approach and emphasis were apparent, however. A letter from Paul DesRochers, state finance chairman, served as fuel for the fire of internal dissent. DesRochers advocated placing the state party's major financial effort on winning the US Senate race in 1970 to the exclusion of other priorities, claiming that "to undertake the full effort for more than one candidate may not be practical."[103] Addressing the Republican leaders, Tower maintained that the GOP could win both the Senate and gubernatorial race in 1970 "if we put our minds to it." He urged all Republicans to unite and recruit a strong slate for the next election, warning them, "I hope we won't indulge in personality conflicts and petty nitpicking within the party, because our goals are too important to be lost in this sort of strife."[104]

While national committeeman Albert Fay expressed the belief that Connally's strong backing of Humphrey was responsible for delivering the state to the Democrats, Tower placed more blame on the vote for George Wallace, the American Independent Party candidate in the race. Calling Wallace a demagogue, Tower received applause from the audience when he said the Alabama governor "is not a sincere man.... He seeks to build his own power base.... He doesn't deserve the confidence and support of anyone who calls himself a conservative."[105] Also apparent at the meeting was a continued interest among the party workers in promoting another candidacy by Eggers. Having received the most votes of any statewide Republican candidate, the onetime unknown tax attorney from Wichita Falls had become a Republican celebrity. Several executive committee members wore "Eggers '70" campaign buttons and urged him to run again for governor.[106]

In early January 1969, political writers Rowland Evans and Robert Novak devoted their nationally syndicated "Inside Report" column to what they described as "serious factionalism" in the Texas GOP. According to their sources, the criticism was directed at both Tower and O'Donnell and was emanating from diverse elements within the party. Most vocal were a group of activists who had backed Reagan for president and were dismayed by the two party leaders' endorsement of Nixon prior to the national convention. The Reaganites included former gubernatorial candidate Cox, former national committeeman Jack Porter, and billionaire Bunker Hunt.

The intraparty sniping extended to others as well, and included more moderate Republicans such as entrepreneur Sam Wyly, a major fundraiser for the party, who advocated moving the party leftward on civil rights to increase its appeal to minority voters. Still others associated with Representative Bush thought that the party needed to reach out beyond its base of suburban, middle-class voters. Evans and Novak described the result of the O'Donnell strategy: "the Republicans now seem limited to a country club party with built-in minority status." Their reports indicated that there was a growing rivalry for political leadership between Bush and Senator Tower.[107]

With O'Donnell still in control of the state party organization and Fay refusing to step down as national committeeman, any changes in party leadership would not occur for several months. What did take place, however, was a consolidation of state patronage matters, which were shifted away from the national committeeman, where they had been centered for a century, and to the state chairman. To advise and consult with the Nixon administration on a myriad of appointive positions, a five-member committee was named, comprising O'Donnell, Tower, state vice chairman Anne Armstrong, Texas Federation of Republican Women leader Beryl Milburn, and former gubernatorial candidate Bill Steger.[108] Conspicuously missing from the committee was national committeeman Fay or anyone else from Houston. Those opposed to O'Donnell's leadership quickly turned their focus from the past campaigns to his control of the Texas patronage process in the new Nixon administration.

Leading the attack on O'Donnell's leadership of the party this time was the fiery chairman of the Harris County Republican Party. Nancy Palm was a graduate of Vanderbilt University who had moved to Houston with her physician husband in 1951 and had become active in school board politics. With the Goldwater effort in 1964, Palm "established herself solidly in the Republican camp," starting as a precinct chair and working her way up to county chairman in 1967.[109] One party activist of the time described her as a "resolute" woman who "became to Harris County what O'Donnell had been in Dallas, the consummate organizer."[110] When asked a few years later what was different about the party in Harris County, Palm responded, "If I had to put the finger on one thing, I would say it was on organization, on the strong Republican women's clubs, and on the strong precinct organizations."[111]

According to Chase Untermeyer, an activist at the time who would later be elected to the Texas House from a Houston district, Palm believed strongly that electing local officials was how you built a political party, and she had accomplished much in establishing a Republican presence in Harris County.[112] While the party was experiencing losses at the statewide level in 1968, Harris County Republicans were electing a member of Congress, a state senator, four state representatives, and a county commissioner, as well as carrying the county for the presidential and gubernatorial candidates. Palm's approach was to reach beyond the country club Republicans and integrate former conservative Democrats into the party organization. As one party leader of the time recalled, "She could count on the total loyalty of the former Democrats, to the dismay of the old-line Republicans, who kept leading their lives as they had in the old days, going to the ballet and the opera and leaving the nitty-gritty of politics to subordinates."[113]

While defending President Nixon for his handling of patronage matters, Palm laid the blame on O'Donnell for the state's failure to receive any cabinet-level appointments. She claimed that after "seven years of inept leadership in the Republican hierarchy, it is slight wonder that President Nixon went to a former conservative Democrat turned Republican, Will Wilson, for his sole major Texas appointment." The lack of significant GOP victories in Texas was viewed by Palm as the reason for the state party's limited success in obtaining appointments in the Nixon administration: "Despite the expenditure of millions of dollars and purported strengthening of the party structure, O'Donnell has failed to elect a single statewide candidate in his seven year tenure."[114]

The Harris County party chairman blasted O'Donnell's patronage committees as "mere window dressing" and said that the big three of Texas influence were Senator Tower, Representative Bush, and national committeeman Fay. "I do not believe in government or party politics by 'cronyism' which is what Mr. O'Donnell is attempting to foist on the public of Texas."[115] A few days later, in a memo to party officials, Palm claimed that the county party had been denied state-produced materials during the campaign and that the state party's regional field representative was told not to assist the Harris County party effort. Describing the county party's relationship with O'Donnell, she wrote, "In every way, he has deliberately circumvented the legally elected structure of the Harris County Republican Party." While praising the efforts made locally, Palm was convinced that "a change in the attitudes and priorities of the state leadership is essential to increase the effectiveness of the GOP throughout the state."[116]

O'Donnell's response was swift and decisive, as he announced he would bypass the elected party leadership in Harris County and work through a special committee that he would appoint. Palm was not surprised by his approach, writing, "He is simply continuing a policy he has followed for the last nine months."[117] The open warfare between the two party leaders caused former national committeeman Porter to write Tower and advise him that "you cannot afford the luxury of Peter O'Donnell as State Chairman," given his penchant to ignore the local party leadership.[118]

Cooler heads soon prevailed, and a truce was in effect as the focus of attention turned to a special election for the Texas House of Representatives in the Hill Country west of San Antonio and Austin. This area of considerable German settlement had traditionally provided a higher level of support for Republican candidates. In the election John Poerner, referred to as a Republican and running with the party's volunteer support, was successful on February 27, 1969.[119] The state party's magazine featured his victory and a picture of him being "welcomed to Republican ranks" by some of the GOP representatives.[120] The excitement did not last long, however, and the results ended up as another defeat for O'Donnell. After being sworn in on March 4, Poerner quickly changed his party designation to Independent and subsequently filed for re-election as a Democrat.[121]

At the SREC meeting on May 3, Fay resigned as national committeeman after Nixon and Tower urged him to step aside so O'Donnell could assume his position on the national committee. In what was described as a "three hour bloodletting," Fay failed in an effort to have his successor chosen from the Texas congressional delegation, and thus ended a dispute with O'Donnell that had gone on for more than a year.[122] The SREC then unanimously chose O'Donnell as the new national committeeman and began planning to choose a successor as state chairman at the June meeting.[123]

Meanwhile the small GOP delegation in the Texas legislature expressed "a uniform concern with the party's neglect of local and legislative officeholders," causing O'Donnell to arrange a breakfast meeting with them, "the first time they have received such recognition from party leadership." According to one reporter, "they complain privately that O'Donnell never consulted them during the session until the chairmanship issue arose. They also contend that he has failed to staff the state headquarters with personnel qualified to provide aggressive backup efforts for the lawmakers." Representative Malouf Abraham was quoted as saying, "O'Donnell has done a good job, but he has concentrated on Tower, Bush, and the presidential races."[124]

In the contest to replace O'Donnell as state chairman, former gubernatorial candidate Bill Steger announced his interest, backed by a committee of supporters headed by Polly Sowell of McAllen and Bill Rector of Wichita Falls. Soon thereafter Millard Neptune, who had been a candidate for the railroad commission in the 1968 elections, also expressed his desire to serve. When the SREC met, it was apparent that the party was closely divided. Steger bested Neptune in a vote of thirty-three to thirty, while Beryl Milburn of Austin became vice chairman by defeating Betty Andujar of Fort Worth by a margin of thirty-four to twenty-nine. Both Steger and Milburn were allies of O'Donnell and served on the statewide patronage committee named by the state chairman. Milburn had been a trailblazer for the party, helping to establish the Texas Federation of Republican Women, and was one of the few party members to run for state representative in 1958.

With the selection of Steger as state chairman, Norman Newton Jr. became executive director of the party. Newton would play an essential role in Texas Republican politics for more than thirty years, becoming director of a newly organized support group in 1974, the Associated Republicans of Texas, whose emphasis on legislative and county elections saw the party gain a majority of elected positions by the end of the twentieth century. According to some observers, the party had acquired a measure of stability, with "a state headquarters prepared to take advantage of the growing electoral competitiveness in the state."[125] Throughout the remainder of 1969, party attention centered on putting together a slate of candidates for the 1970 election.

Some Republican activists attempted to convince Cox to take on another gubernatorial campaign. Having lost three previous statewide races, two in primaries and one in the 1962 general election, Cox was reluctant to run unless he had the support of the party's leadership.[126] Many of those party leaders, however, were more interested in convincing Eggers to engage in a rematch with Governor Smith. Only when he was convinced that sufficient financial support for a serious statewide effort was available did Eggers agree to run again. By year's end Eggers was in the race and Cox declined to be a candidate. In the 1970 primary, Eggers trounced the little-known Roger Martin, a retired Navy commander from Gainesville, with 93 percent of the vote.

Similar positioning was going on in the quest to find a strong candidate against liberal Democratic senator Ralph Yarborough. This time, Yarborough would not be running with a landside-winning Johnson at the top of the ticket. While it was clear that Representative Bush wanted to run against the liberal senator, as late as October 1969 he was still telling supporters that a decision had not yet been made.[127] Some months earlier Bush had met at the White House with the president. Facing a hostile majority in both congressional chambers, Nixon was committed to creating a GOP Senate majority. The president encouraged Bush to seek the Senate seat and pledged his support.[128] Yet any such campaign would involve giving up a much-desired spot on the House Ways and Means Committee and a sure re-election in what had become a Republican congressional district. Finally in January 1970 Bush announced his rematch against Yarborough.[129]

Bush was opposed in the primary once again by Robert Morris, the former president of the University of Dallas who had been a candidate for the nomination in 1964. As he had six years earlier, Morris attacked Bush for allegedly being insufficiently conservative. The primary contest was not even close, with Bush winning 87.6 percent of the vote. The rematch with Yarborough would not take place, however, as former Representative Lloyd Bentsen Jr., with the overt backing of Connally and the covert support of Johnson, defeated the incumbent senator in the Democratic primary.[130]

At the beginning of 1970, Texas was the largest state and the only one of the ten most populous without a Republican governor. State chairman Steger was committed to changing that situation, as well as to electing other candidates in the upcoming election.[131] In addition to Bush and Eggers at the top of the statewide slate, the party nominated Byron Fullerton for lieutenant governor and Edward Yturri for attorney general. Yturri was a young Mexican-American from Corpus Christi who had been active in party affairs since the initial Tower campaign. His opponent would be incumbent attorney general Crawford Martin, who was seeking a third term in office. Fullerton was on leave from his position as assistant dean of the University of Texas law school and was running against lieutenant governor Ben Barnes, a thirty-one-year-old protégé of Connally and Johnson. Fullerton claimed the Democratic leaders' plan was "aimed at putting Barnes in the White House" and Texans needed to escape "the grip of the Johnson-Connally-Barnes political power axis."[132]

Texas Republicans fielded candidates in eleven of the state's twenty-three congressional districts and fifty-nine of the 150 Texas house districts, as well as for a number of county level positions, mainly in the larger urban areas of the state. While Eggers once again was unable to raise sufficient funds to undertake an aggressive advertising campaign, his supporters were optimistic that they could defeat Governor Smith. Under the direction of campaign manager Eddie Mahe, the Eggers effort had attracted the involvement of several up-and-coming Republicans, including Richard Parker and Doug Harlan. According to one reporter, "the Eggers campaign has jelled to the point that Republican party insiders are confidently reporting Eggers has 'turned the corner' as a candidate." Mahe reported that a May voter survey had Smith at 45 percent support and Eggers with 40 percent, while other responses "showed Eggers much more closely resembles what the voters want in a governor than does Smith."[133]

Meanwhile Bush refocused his campaign effort after learning his November opponent would be the more establishment-backed Bentsen rather than the liberal hero senator Ralph Yarborough. Bush knew he had to energize his base of conservative Republicans and avoid losing those conservative Democratic voters who had been leaning in the party's direction. Once again, women volunteers would be a key to mobilizing support and turning out voters for his campaign. Among the many volunteers lined up for his effort was Rita Bass, state chairman of the 1970 Bush Belles program. In her directions to local leaders, Bass told them, "we plan to recruit thousands of Bush Belles across Texas to make a real public relations impact on George Bush's campaign. The more women we have wearing the Belle scarf and button and talking up George's campaign, the greater the chances of success in November."[134]

Nixon kept his promise of support by campaigning for both Bush and Eggers in Dallas and Longview, while Vice President Agnew held campaign rallies for the GOP ticket in Dallas, Amarillo, and Lubbock. Bentsen tried to play on Texas chauvinism by describing the vice president as "a Maryland politician trying to get a fellow from Connecticut elected senator and one from Indiana elected governor."[135] If Bentsen and Smith were to win, it would be critical to keep as many conservatives as possible in the Democratic column, and attacking the Republicans as carpetbaggers had always worked in the past.

At the same time, Tower had been able to win in 1961 and 1966 with the support of both conservatives and disaffected liberals. Once again Texas liberals found themselves with an unacceptable Democratic nominee; indeed he was one who had the audacity to defeat their sitting senator and liberal icon. From out of state came the recommendations of nationally known liberals to their counterparts in Texas. Harvard professor John Kenneth Galbraith wrote to "urge Texas liberals to vote for George Bush—and to defeat Lloyd Bentsen." The very liberal senator from Alaska, Ernest Gruening, declared, "Were I voting in Texas I would find it impossible not to rebuke and repudiate such poisonous tactics as those practiced by Bentsen by voting for George Bush."

Within the state Kaye Northcott, editor of the *Texas Observer*, made evident the strategy of those liberals who wanted to drive conservatives from the Democratic Party and thus gain dominance for their ideological position. Northcott claimed, "I'll be casting a predominantly Republican ballot in the Fall. The Rebuilding Committee argument that liberals should vote Republican because a stronger GOP might lure conservatives into the Republican ranks, leaving the Democratic Party to the Democrats, is the only alternative Texas liberals have this Fall to cast a possibly constructive vote. . . . Bush is definitely the lessor of two evils."[136] Unhappy with both Smith and Bentsen and opposed to seeing conservatives win under the Democratic Party label, the "two-party Democrats" would once again urge their small band of supporters to vote for the conservative Republican candidates. Unfortunately for both these liberals and the conservatives in the Republican Party, the tactical move would fall short of electing either Bush or Eggers, and once again, the more conservative Democratic candidates were dominant on Election Day.

Two factors contributed to the loss of both the Senate seat and the governorship. The strong involvement of the White House tended to limit the ability of either Texas candidate to gain the votes of disaffected liberals, whose dislike of both Nixon and Agnew caused them to back away from Bush and Eggers. Even more important was the presence on the ballot of a constitutional amendment allowing localities to decide whether to allow liquor by the drink. This issue brought out the more infrequent, and Democratic-leaning, voters who normally would not participate in a nonpresidential election. As Jim Francis, one of the Bush campaign workers, noted, "If there was one factor that defeated Bush, it was the question of allowing liquor by the drink and the East Texas Democrats opposed to it came out in droves."[137] So, too, did those in the more urban areas who favored allowing liquor sales, especially increasing the Democratic vote in some minority precincts.

Bush and Eggers ran close to each other in terms of the total vote (slightly over one million votes each), share of the total vote (46.6 percent), and the counties they carried. As a senatorial candidate again, Bush held on to nineteen of the thirty-four he had carried against Yarborough in 1964, while picking up eight additional counties, including Harris, Travis, and Montgomery. Of the twenty-seven counties carried by Bush in 1970, Eggers had a majority of the votes in nineteen, while he also carried Denton and Tarrant counties. Republican support in statewide elections had developed in the various urban areas of the state as the party's candidates were winning majorities in both Dallas and Harris counties, along with a swath of smaller urban areas in West and East Texas. Midland, Ector, Lubbock, Randall, and Potter counties in the west could normally be counted in the GOP column, as could Smith and Gregg counties in the east. To these urban strongholds, Republican candidates could add their traditional support in various Hill Country and Panhandle counties.

Asked to comment on his loss, Bush took total responsibility, telling one reporter, "I have a horrible problem in figuring this thing out. I can't think of anyone to blame except myself. Like Custer who said there were just too many Indians, I guess there were too many Democrats."[138] It was the heavily Democratic vote in rural areas that made the major difference between the two candidates, a vote differential that was also reflected in the gubernatorial contest. According to Bush, "We thought we had more inroads there, but we obviously hadn't."[139]

One of the young conservatives involved in the second Bush senatorial campaign was Robert Estrada of Brownsville, an individual who would play an important role in Republican politics for the remainder of the twentieth century. Estrada became involved in the Young Republicans while attending the University of Texas at Austin, and after graduation he became a reporter with a television station in Harlingen. When a communications position with the Republican Party of Texas was offered in early 1970, he accepted. The immediate impact for Estrada was that "during that 1970 senatorial campaign, I really got to know Bush and developed a relationship with him as he traveled throughout the state.... Next to my father, George H. W. Bush was most important in shaping my values. The values I observed beginning in that 1970 campaign and the mentoring throughout the years made lasting impressions on me." Nineteen years later, after Bush won the White House, Estrada became a special assistant to the president working in presidential personnel.[140]

While running competitive but losing races statewide, the party's performance in congressional districts produced no gains in representation. Bob Price and Jim Collins were re-elected, and Bill Archer retained the seat previously held by Bush. Five of the eight other GOP candidates obtained over 35 percent of the vote, well short of victory or competitiveness, but at the time better than many observers anticipated. The GOP Texas House delegation grew slightly to a total of ten representatives as Harris County elected three new members (Walter Mengden, Bill Blythe, and Sid Bowers) to join the re-elected Jim Earthman, Sonny Jones, and Will Lee. Dallas contributed its first legislative victory since 1962 with the successful campaign of business executive Fred Agnich.[141] Three other state legislators from around the state (Maurice Angly of Travis County, Tom Christian of Armstrong County, and Tom Craddick of Midland County) were re-elected to match the party's highest total elected since 1962.

As the year ended, a number of announcements from the White House made dramatic changes to the future of the Republican Party of Texas. On December 1, Nixon appointed Steger as a US district judge for the Eastern District of Texas. Steger resigned as state chairman of the party and awaited senate confirmation of his selection.[142] Steger's appointment was approved by the Senate, and he served for the next thirty-five years as a federal judge.[143]

Next was the announcement that Bush would become the nation's ambassador to the United Nations, giving the defeated senatorial candidate a high-profile position in the Nixon administration.[144] Nevertheless, some Bush supporters viewed the appointment "as sort of a throwaway item" with Henry

Kissinger at the State Department determining foreign policy.[145] However, as with the selection of Steger, this appointment would remove another party leader from direct involvement in Texas politics.

The final appointment made in December 1970 was the most dramatic and consequential of all. On December 14 Nixon announced that he would nominate Connally to become secretary of the Treasury Department. With this appointment, Nixon had removed from state politics the leader of the conservative Democratic faction and the one individual most responsible for the election of Bentsen to the Senate. Serving as a cabinet member in the Nixon administration would make it difficult, if not impossible, for Connally to continue his involvement in Texas Democratic politics. As O'Donnell viewed the situation, "This assures that President Nixon is going to carry Texas in 1972 and it means Senator Tower will be re-elected."[146] It also meant that a high-profile Texas Democrat would be part of the Nixon administration at a time when Tower would be seeking re-election. Not all longtime Republicans were pleased by the appointment. Upon hearing that Connally would join the Nixon cabinet, Edwin S. Mayer of San Angelo abruptly resigned from the SREC. He would be replaced by Ernest Angelo Jr. of Midland, who would later become mayor of Midland and cochair of the Texas Reagan presidential campaign, and then serve for twenty years as Republican national committeeman.[147]

What these three appointments also meant was that O'Donnell remained on the scene as the most prominent Republican leader and was once again the focus of attack for those disappointed in the party's failure to elect any statewide candidates other than Tower. As Ron Calhoun of the *Dallas Times Herald* summarized O'Donnell's situation, "He still has a big say in patronage and strategy. He controls the purse strings, and has put up a big slug of his own over the years, . . . but there are those who would like to hang his scalp from the highest political wigwam."[148]

There were renewed complaints of what some viewed as O'Donnell's high-handedness and concentration of power. According to one reporter the party was organizationally in disarray and financially challenged, and had a constituency of disenchanted activists: "Dissention in party ranks has given impetus to a move to oust national committeeman Peter O'Donnell of Dallas, the party's chief money raiser and one of President Nixon's longtime friends and advisors. . . . Many party regulars blame O'Donnell for the licking the state party took in 1970, the year that was supposed to mark transition of the Texas GOP into a full-fledged political party and Texas a two-party state."[149]

As the 1960s ended, it appeared that the Republican Party of Texas had made slow and limited progress to becoming a competitive force in state politics. No longer was patronage the overriding motivation for involvement in party politics. Taking its place, however, were internal divisions over strategy and tactics, between the power centers of Dallas and Houston, and over differing concepts of conservatism, all of which seemed to engage a considerable amount of the time and resources of party activists. The party had elected and re-elected a US senator, increased its delegation in the US House of Representatives from one to three, and established a small beachhead in the Texas legislature. More areas of the state were now organized for the party, and Republican candidates could count on a base of support statewide. Yet competitive races lost were still losses. It would be another decade, with a continuation of the highs and lows of victory and defeat, before the party would break the Democratic stranglehold on state government.

EIGHT

THE HIGHS AND LOWS
OF THE 1970S

The year 1971 saw scandal, redistricting, and a more significant GOP legislative presence in Austin dominate the political discussion. As the newly elected Democratic officials were being sworn into office at the Texas Capitol, lawyers from the US Department of Justice were filing suit in Dallas for what became known as the Sharpstown stock fraud scandal. Beginning as a Securities and Exchange Commission investigation of loans to state officials by the Sharpstown State Bank, the scandal soon engulfed a number of Democratic officials, including then-Speaker of the Texas House, Gus Mutscher.[1]

In reaction a group of legislators opposed Mutscher's leadership of the House and pushed for various pieces of reform legislation. Known as the Dirty Thirty, this group of conservative Republicans and liberal Democrats attempted to create roadblocks against Mutscher and his allies.[2] The Speaker of the House struck back by having his supporters create a redistricting plan designed to eliminate many of his opponents. In their plan, however, Mutscher's allies had split twenty-three county lines, in conflict with provisions in the state constitution concerning the composition of House districts. That led a group of Midland Republicans, including state Republican executive committee (SREC) member Robert Monaghan, Mayor Ernest Angelo Jr., and Representative Tom Craddick, to file a challenge in state court. When the court upheld their position, the responsibility for developing an acceptable plan was thrown to the Legislative Redistricting Board (LRB) comprising the speaker, lieutenant governor, attorney general, comptroller, and land commissioner, all Democratic officials.

The LRB's plan for the first time divided Harris County into single-member districts but left other urban counties with county-wide, multimember districts. Such multimember districts were designed to allow conservative Democrats to remain dominant and, by requiring county-wide election, increase the cost of mounting a campaign for the state legislature. Another lawsuit was then filed against the LRB plan by both Republicans and liberal Democrats.

Lead attorney for the GOP was Tom Crouch of Dallas, while state senator Oscar Mauzy and David Richards, at the time married to future governor Ann Richards, represented the liberal Democratic cause. The conservative Democratic defense was coordinated by Frank Erwin, an Austin lobbyist, and Leon Jaworski of Houston, at the time president of the American Bar Association. A panel of three federal judges heard the case and overturned the LRB plan, ordering the drawing of new districts. Subsequently, another court order mandated the creation of single-member districts for Bexar and Dallas counties.[3] Republicans were now ready to make a major push to elect candidates from a number of Texas House districts.

Meanwhile, John Tower was gearing up for another re-election campaign. In May 1971 Tower's team organized a major fundraising dinner in Dallas with William P. Clements Jr. as dinner chair. With some 1,500 in attendance, the event raised over $250,000 for the Tower 1972 campaign. Throughout the year, the senator traveled the state with an emphasis on small to medium-sized counties, where in past elections the Democratic officials had turned out the vote for their party's candidates. Tower did not want to be nickeled-and-dimed to death as past GOP statewide candidates had been throughout rural Texas. With Dick Agnich as his administrative assistant in Washington and Nola Smith as state director in Austin, Tower made the most of incumbency with nonpartisan civic appearances throughout the state, making his presence known to as many Texans as possible.

O'DONNELL MOVES BACKSTAGE

In early 1972 Texas Republicans received a major surprise when Peter O'Donnell Jr. announced his resignation as national committeeman, ending fifteen years of high-level party involvement. O'Donnell's move came less than three years after his bitter battle for the position with Albert Fay, which had forced Fay's reluctant resignation in May 1969. In announcing his resignation, O'Donnell said it was for personal reasons and because he believed it was time for new leadership. While Tower was quoted as simply saying "I regret his resigning," national committeewoman Anne Armstrong was effusive in her praise for her colleague. The Kenedy County rancher commended O'Donnell by noting, "His record is unequaled for generously giving of his talent and resources to build a Republican party within our state. At the national level, he has been among the most effective voices in promoting interests of Texas."

Similar statements of praise and regret came from state chairman George Willeford and vice chairman Beryl Milburn.[4]

Behind the scenes, theories on the reason for O'Donnell's withdrawal from the national party position were numerous. Some speculated that he was about to be named to a position in the Nixon administration. As one Dallas Republican activist claimed, "I believe he's got something in the Nixon administration, maybe a high position in the Defense department."[5] From an opposite perspective, others thought that O'Donnell had stepped aside because he disagreed with the Nixon administration's policies on defense and busing, resulting in a possible rift between the White House and the state party.[6] Still others maintained that they saw the footprints of Tower and Nixon supporters in the drive to convince O'Donnell to resign. One line of reasoning was that O'Donnell had failed to deliver Texas for Nixon in 1968, and the president wanted someone with more muscle to make sure the state would go Republican in 1972. According to one reporter, "The fact that Nixon did not carry Texas against Humphrey in 1968 was a distinct embarrassment to the Texas GOP, which O'Donnell headed."[7]

Another view was that O'Donnell was simply weary of the criticism directed at him during his years leading the state party. According to this view, O'Donnell was "tired of being the scapegoat for everything that goes wrong in the Texas Republican Party." One report claimed that the leader's "roughshod method of handling Texas party affairs ... gave O'Donnell an empire-builder reputation among foes. Legislative officeholders in the GOP, along with 1968 and 1970 gubernatorial nominee Paul Eggers, blamed the party's failure to adequately finance statehouse campaigns on O'Donnell's predominant interest in national affairs."[8] Over the years, many party activists complained that he ignored the party base and attempted to build from the top down, resulting in a lack of candidates for many county and statewide races.[9]

To some it was simply time for a changing of the guard, as O'Donnell had noted in his resignation. From this perspective, "a split has been developing in the party for some time, with the O'Donnell faction on one side and a younger more aggressive group pounding on the door from the other."[10] Whatever the reasons for his resignation, O'Donnell left a legacy of accomplishment as well as frustration, as he stepped from the center stage to a role as advisor, strategist, confidant, and financier for other Republicans. The *Dallas Morning News* editorialized upon his departure from the Republican National Committee (RNC) that he had served "as one of the foremost leaders of the GOP in this state. And the party is going to miss that leadership. For 15 years, Peter O'Donnell was a major force in developing and holding together the party in Texas, and during that time he also was the one leader chiefly instrumental in setting the stage for a two-party system in this state."[11] Despite all the differences over strategy and tactics, one party activist put O'Donnell's record in perspective by concluding, "There wouldn't be any Texas Republican Party without Peter O'Donnell. . . . Peter has been responsible for the growth of this party so far."[12]

O'Donnell's influence within the party and in remaking Texas politics was far from over with his stepping aside from the RNC position. The leading individual to replace him was state representative Fred Agnich of Dallas, the person who had been O'Donnell's original choice to succeed him as state chairman. Agnich quickly expressed his interest in becoming national committeeman and was regarded as the logical choice by some party leaders. Still others who had differed with O'Donnell on campaign strategy thought the nod should go to Eggers.[13] When the SREC met one month after O'Donnell's resignation, Agnich was unanimously elected as the state's new national committeeman.[14]

ENTER HANK GROVER

In many respects 1972 may be seen as the beginning of a serious open conflict within the party that had previously surfaced in the 1964 senatorial primary and, more specifically, in the 1968 battle between the forces aligned with Richard Nixon and those backing Ronald Reagan. Throughout the 1970s the rivalry between Houston and Dallas became transposed into differences over tactics redefined as ideological crusades. To some it was a conflict between conservatives and moderates. To others it was a difference between country club Republicans and Lions Club Republicans. Chase Untermeyer, then a reporter but later to be a major player in Republican politics and government, summed up these distinctions as basically the ins versus the outs: "The so-called Dallas-Houston split of the Texas Republican Party is alternatively explained as one of ideology (Houston more conservative, Dallas more moderate), of political tactics (Houston more doctrinaire, Dallas more pragmatic), of tone (Houston more strident, Dallas more sophisticated), and of orientation (Houston more interested in state contests, Dallas more in national). But the antagonism reduces itself to the oldest political motivation of all: Us vs. Them."[15]

In retrospect, as the internal disputes involved Republicans from all parts of the state, it appears to have been centered more on campaign tactics and approaches than on substantive differences in political philosophies. Sure, there remained a tiny minority in the party who would accept the labels of liberal or moderate, but the vast majority of Texas Republicans considered themselves conservatives. By the beginning of the twenty-first century, pinning the label *liberal* on any Texas Republican candidate was merely a feeble attempt to prove oneself somehow more ideologically pure. Nevertheless, differences existed on how best to present the conservative philosophy and how best to build a political party and elect candidates to office. It is a conflict that continues to the present day, without the specific geographical differences, in the Texas Republican Party.

As primary season began, the Nixon re-election team was headed up by cochair J. Erik Jonsson, cofounder of Texas Instruments and recently retired mayor of Dallas, and business leader Bill Clements, with O'Donnell on board as an advisor.[16] Julian Zimmerman was chair and Flo Atherton cochair of Friends of John Tower, and the senator's re-election campaign manager was Nola Smith, with Brad O'Leary handling finances and John Knaggs as the public relations consultant. Starting in the spring of 1972 and continuing through the fall the Nixon and Tower campaigns would be closely coordinated. Rita Bass was recruited to serve as state organization chair with the responsibility of heading up a major unregistered voter drive in targeted precincts, followed by a get-out-the-vote effort in the fall for the Nixon and Tower campaigns.[17]

Despite the losses of 1970 optimism was running high in Republican circles, resulting in the party's ability to recruit candidates for thirteen senatorial and seventy-four house districts, as well as thirteen of the state's twenty-four congressional districts.

HANK GROVER AND THE PARTY ORGANIZATION

While Tower was unopposed for renomination, six individuals filed to run in the Republican primary for governor. In a spirited race state senator Henry "Hank" Grover came in first with 32.6 percent of the vote, followed by former national committeeman Fay (21.3 percent), Austin College administrator David Reagan (17.6 percent), and Tom McElroy of Dallas (17.2 percent), with two other candidates receiving the remaining support. Although he finished third and was out of the runoff, Reagan, who was not related to the California governor, had substantial support from party insiders, with Gary Bruner as campaign manager, Jack Warren as finance chair, and Lubbock mayor Jim Granberry as overall campaign chair.[18]

In the subsequent runoff Grover was able to increase his total vote while Fay's support declined to produce a two-to-one margin for Grover. Although both Grover and Fay were from Houston, had backed Ronald Reagan for president in 1968, and were not supporters of O'Donnell, they did represent different elements of the Republican party base. Fay was described by some as coming from the country club wing of the party, while Grover represented the more numerous Lions Club constituency.[19] Perhaps even more of a factor in his runoff performance, Grover had won the backing of Nancy Palm, Harris County chairman and O'Donnell's nemesis. Committed to growing a party from the grassroots, Palm had built a solid organization in Harris County that in 1970 elected a member of Congress, a state senator, six state representatives, and a county commissioner.[20]

Once he secured the party's nomination for governor, Grover launched into an aggressive effort to take over the party organization. He was convinced that both chairman Willeford and vice chairman Milburn had supported Fay in the runoff, and he wanted them replaced. According to state law, in presidential election years the June state convention focused on national issues and finalizing delegates to the national party convention, while the second convention in September provided for the election of state party officials. Nevertheless, Grover determined that he wanted an immediate change in the party's leadership, claiming Willeford and Milburn belonged to a "little clique" of party leaders headed by O'Donnell who "have run this party for years like a closed society and want to keep running it that way."[21] According to Grover, "It is obvious that Willeford and Milburn are not committed to my victory."[22] Both Willeford and Milburn made it evident that they had no intention of resigning and turning the party organization over to Grover.

As the delegates began assembling in Galveston, efforts were underway to create a truce between the party leaders and the party's nominee for governor. One reporter wrote that the scene on the day before the conclave began as "all unity and harmony."[23] To this end, Midland mayor Angelo had arranged a meeting between Tower and Grover, but no progress was made.[24] Nevertheless, Tower remained optimistic that a divisive convention could be avoided. A key aide to the senator later recalled, "Tower met with Grover privately the night before the convention and believed that no serious split would occur, that he and Grover could cooperate as each pursued his own campaign. But for whatever substantive or subtle reasons, Grover went through with his threat the following day during a dramatic speech to the convention."[25]

With no advance notice, Grover stunned the delegates in his speech to the convention by demanding that Willeford and Milburn be replaced. He called on the delegates to "pass a resolution instructing the State Republican Executive Committee to convene as soon as possible to appoint a chairman and vice-chairman to unify the party for the great victory that awaits us in

November."[26] When the Grover-backed proposal was submitted to the resolutions committee, chaired by Representative Bill Archer, it was defeated in an eighteen to six vote. Grover's supporters on the committee then prepared a minority report to take the battle to the convention floor.[27]

Grover's strongest support at the convention came from Harris and Bexar counties, as well as from a scattering of delegates in other areas of the state. Bexar County GOP chairman Van Henry Archer (no relation to Bill Archer) claimed that O'Donnell was attempting to "control this party with an iron fist" and accused Willeford and national committeeman Fred Agnich of "exhibiting their brand of power politics." Harris County GOP chairman Palm made evident her dissatisfaction with the party leadership by declaring, "John Tower has the right to choose the leadership he wants at this convention, even if Agnich and Willeford are grossly inept."[28] Palm warned, however, that she viewed Tower's continuing involvement in party politics as possibly harming his re-election. Referring to the party leaders, she told one delegate, "We still got John Tower's poor fool up there.... Let John stay in bed with Beryl and George."[29]

At a time when policy positions and differences over campaign tactics had superseded patronage concerns for most Republicans, especially in light of the removal of postmasterships from politics and other civil service reforms, some in the party still saw the ability to select federal appointees as an overriding concern. Palm insisted that Tower's concern over control of patronage meant that he did not want to have a Republican governor in Texas who would gain influence on White House appointment matters.[30]

When the Grover forces brought their minority report to the floor, Bill Rector of Wichita Falls moved to table the resolution. After a voice vote, permanent convention chair Rudy Juedeman of Odessa ruled that the ayes prevailed. That led James E. Lyon of Houston to seek recognition, but he was initially ruled out of order before being allowed to address the delegates. Lyon maintained that the fight was in no way a struggle between Tower and Grover. It was difficult for many observers, however, to see it as anything else. As Willeford noted, it had "started as a Grover-Willeford thing but this afternoon Grover decided to take on Senator Tower and I felt it was my duty to defend Senator Tower's position as the party's leader."[31]

Although Juedeman gaveled the convention to an end, the dispute between Grover and the party leadership continued. Meeting with Republican women in Austin on the day following the convention, national committeewoman Armstrong criticized Grover for attempting to take control of the state party. "Henry Grover does not have the right to take over the party leadership. I will work for Grover's election as governor, but oppose his efforts to take over the party."[32] Meanwhile, vice chairman Milburn made it clear that she had no intention of voluntarily resigning and urged Grover supporters to keep their focus on the governor's race. Addressing the same gathering of women, Milburn claimed, "if he and his Houston supporters are more interested in gaining party control than they are in winning elections, I seriously urge them to consider how much harm this will bring both to the party and to its candidates this fall."[33]

Despite the various calls for unity, attacks on party leaders continued. In Houston a group named New Republicans for Progress called for the resignation of county chairman Palm, claiming such a move was needed to bring about harmony within the party.[34] Grover continued his attacks, saying country club Republicans only wanted a token candidate for governor and were opposed to him because "they don't control me." He claimed, "the party organization is so weak Tower doesn't even work through it. The quality of opposition from Willeford doesn't amount to much. You know, I'd rather have him in there than somebody who's smart."[35]

Not content with limiting his criticism to party leaders, Grover attacked his predecessor as a gubernatorial nominee, an individual who had twice received over one million votes to achieve the highest total recorded for a GOP state office candidate up to that time. According to Grover, "If we'd had a more competent, qualified candidate running for governor in 1968 than Paul Eggers, I think Nixon would have carried the state." Willeford responded in a July 21 letter to Grover by expressing his irritation over the attacks on Eggers. He urged Grover to explain his charges to "all of the hard-working, dedicated Republicans in the state of Texas who will feel offended at the cracks you have taken at our party organization."[36] As onetime ally Angelo recalled years later, "Hank was his own worst enemy. He couldn't get along, let personal things interfere in the political realm."[37]

In August Zack Fisher of Memphis, Texas, became the new executive director of the state party, replacing Jim Kane. Fisher had run a courageous but losing campaign in 1970 against powerful Democratic state representative Bill Heatly, nicknamed "the Duke of Paducah."[38] Fisher's first task was to finalize plans for the second state convention, to be held in Dallas the following month. By the time of that convention all indications were that Nixon was far ahead of his Democratic challenger, Senator George McGovern of South Dakota. McGovern was experiencing major defections from conservative and moderate Democrats across the country, and his campaign proved to be especially weak in Texas, despite the efforts of a band of young liberal supporters with political futures ahead of them, including Bill Clinton, Hillary Rodham, and Garry Mauro.

A temporary truce was in place within the party as Republicans oozed enthusiasm for their ticket and hoped to make some critical breakthroughs. Despite their previous differences state chairman Willeford told the delegates, "Hank Grover is an attractive, intelligent, articulate candidate. I admonish you to get behind Hank Grover." From Willeford's perspective, 1972 could be the time when Republicans finally were a major force in state politics. According to the chairman, "We're never going to be a viable party until we get a foot in the door of that state house in Austin. A Republican governor could clean out some closets in that Capitol, some closets that haven't been cleaned out since Reconstruction."[39]

No gathering of Republicans at the time would be without controversy, however. In this case it erupted from a wire service report that quoted Armstrong claiming that Grover could not win the governorship. Although Grover called the report "ridiculous" and pointed out the support Armstrong had provided to his campaign, this was insufficient for Palm, who demanded, "If she was misquoted, then she should say so. She either should retract it or be removed from office." That required Armstrong to return to the convention podium and reiterate her support for Grover: "I said it earlier and I'm glad to say it again. Hank Grover is on the upswing and he's going to come out on top November 7." Armstrong concluded her remarks by noting, "We must, we can, we will win for Hank Grover; and when we triumph on November 7, that's the great day when this state will become a two-party state."[40]

While Grover put aside his push for replacing Willeford and Milburn, both of whom were re-elected without any opposing candidates, it was clear that dissension remained in the ranks. Four of the thirty-one senatorial district caucuses refused to nominate Willeford, and five declined to support Milburn. According to one report, "more than a third of the delegates loudly shouted 'No' when the names of Willeford and Mrs. Milburn were called." With the Nixon campaign reaching out to voters dissatisfied with McGovern's liberalism and opposition to the war in Vietnam, Milburn urged the delegates to be receptive to newcomers: "If we don't welcome them, I'm afraid we will miss a very real opportunity to expand our ranks on a permanent basis.... They should not be expected to serve an apprenticeship nor a term in purgatory for their past allegiances."[41]

In response to the Sharpstown scandal, the party's platform advocated a "meaningful code of ethics for all public officials and an effective financial disclosure law for all state officials with adequate enforcement provisions." The ethics plank also called for the regulation of lobbyists who interact with state government officials. The party went on record supporting a federal constitutional amendment to ban forced busing and a state constitutional amendment guaranteeing equal rights for women. While the national campaign was seeking to gain support from labor union members, the state party reinforced its support of the Texas right-to-work laws. The one significant controversy during the platform deliberations concerned a draft plank proposing to reduce first-time marijuana possession from a felony to a misdemeanor. Midland mayor Angelo moved that this provision be eliminated in the belief that the delegates were too widely divided in their opinions. After much debate the reference to marijuana was deleted and the platform approved.[42]

NIXON AND TOWER, ONCE MORE

As the fall campaign began, optimism ran high in the Nixon camp, and most political observers believed that Tower was in a good position for re-election. In the Democratic primary John Connally's candidate, Barefoot Sanders, had defeated former senator Ralph Yarborough, who was attempting to make a comeback from his defeat in 1970. Connally had made it clear that as a Democrat he was endorsing only one Republican—Richard Nixon, in whose cabinet he was then serving.

Within the Tower campaign, however, there was worry and uncertainty. A late summer poll taken by Decision Making Information (DMI) showed Sanders with a 48 to 36 percent lead over the incumbent senator. Campaign aide Knaggs noted that "Only a trusted handful would know the favored Tower was well behind."[43] In the traditionally Democratic state if it came down to a choice between two acceptable candidates, Sanders had the advantage. Thus the task of the Tower campaign was to show Sanders to be a liberal, an effort that was aided by his longtime association with former US attorney general Ramsey Clark, a fervent opponent of American policy in Vietnam and leading supporter of McGovern's campaign. When Nixon made three appearances in the state, Tower was close by his side. Meanwhile at every opportunity Republicans linked Sanders with the unpopular McGovern and the antiwar Clark. By late September the DMI survey showed that the campaign had turned the situation around as Tower now led Sanders by a margin of 44 to 30 percent, with a sizeable number undecided and a small percentage supporting the candidate of La Raza Unida.[44]

Most of the political media were unaware that Tower had been substantially behind in August but had taken the lead by late September. Just when the internal Tower campaign surveys showed the senator with a substantial lead, the *New York Times* claimed that Sanders had "a strong chance to defeat Republican Senator John G. Tower in the November election" and that the Democratic candidate "appears to have made such dramatic gains in the last month that many Texas political experts believed that Senator Tower's re-election is in doubt." Noting that in his previous victories Tower had obtained critical support from liberal Democrats who would not give their votes to a conservative Democrat, the paper claimed that the liberal focus was now almost exclusively on the presidential race. "The liberal leaders who set up organizations to support Mr. Tower in his first two elections are too busy this year trying to carry Texas for Senator McGovern."[45] In the end, liberal endorsements would not be needed for a Tower victory.

When the votes were counted, Nixon had won in a landslide not only in Texas but in every area of the nation. In the Lone Star State Nixon gained two-thirds of all ballots cast, for a margin of more than one million votes over McGovern. Tower ended up with a comfortable margin of 310,000 votes to win a third term in the Senate. Perhaps the biggest surprise, however, was the close outcome of the race for governor, where Hank Grover, running a poorly financed and organized campaign, came within a hundred thousand votes of becoming the first Republican governor in the twentieth century. Not surprisingly Grover failed to take personal responsibility for his loss. He and many of his followers blamed Tower, claiming that the senator and the presidential campaign had drained needed funding from the gubernatorial race. Given Grover's attempts to oust party leaders, his challenging of Tower's influence in the party, and his attacks on the party's two-time gubernatorial nominee, it should have been of little surprise that many longtime Republicans gave their time and money to other candidates in 1972. Grover would continue to be a thorn in the side of many other Texas Republicans over the next quarter century.

In addition to carrying the state for their presidential nominee and re-electing their US senator, Texas Republicans picked up an additional congressional seat when Alan Steelman defeated Representative Earle Cabell of Dallas. The thirty-year-old Steelman conducted a vigorous door-to-door campaign and was aided by the strong Republican showing throughout Dallas County.[46] The Dallas GOP state legislative delegation grew from one to seven as Bob Davis, Frank Gaston, Ray Hutchison, Al Korioth, Bob Maloney, and Richard Reynolds joined Fred Agnich. In neighboring Tarrant County, Betty Andujar became the third Republican member of the Texas Senate and the only female member at that time. Andujar, who had previously run for state representative, credited her victory to voter reaction to the Sharpstown scandal.[47]

In Harris County the party held onto the state senate seat vacated by Grover when it elected Walter Mengden while adding five new state representatives: Kay Bailey, Ray Barnhart, Milton Fox, Don Henderson, and Larry Vick. According to Bailey, who would later marry fellow freshman legislator Ray Hutchison, "Sharpstown made people aware of what has been happening in Texas in general for a long time."[48] Meanwhile, Bexar County sent its first Republicans to the state legislature when it elected James Nowlin and Joe Sage as new state representatives. All in all, the Republican legislative delegation in Austin grew to three in the Texas Senate and seventeen in the Texas House of Representatives, a high-water mark for the party, but still far from serving as a viable opposition to Democratic dominance.

It appeared the party was finally beginning to build a county presence. After the election Republicans held a county office in twenty-seven counties, including Bexar, Dallas, Harris, Midland, Ector, Potter, and Randall counties. Republicans had reached a new high-water mark with five county judges and seventeen county commissioners in addition to the twenty state legislators, four members of Congress, and one US senator. With Nixon being re-elected in a landslide and the party in control of the White House for the next four years, the future looked bright for the Texas Republican Party, but dark clouds were building, and the result would be a disaster in the next election.

As 1972 came to a close and the new year began, a number of events affected the Texas political scene. In December, Armstrong stepped down as national committeewoman to accept a position as counselor to the president and Milburn resigned as vice chairman of the state party. When the SREC met in February, the members elected Rita Bass of Dallas to replace Armstrong and Polly Sowell of McAllen as the new party vice chairman.[49]

Two days after the second inauguration of Richard Nixon, former president Lyndon B. Johnson died, and an era of Democratic Party control in the state came to an end. Johnson and his key lieutenant, John Connally, had been the dominant force in the Texas party for the past twenty-five years, holding off challenges from both the left and the right. Meanwhile, as the second term began for Nixon, Dallas business owner Bill Clements accepted an appointment as deputy secretary of Defense. Clements had been Texas cochair of the Nixon re-election campaign and was a friend and business associate of O'Donnell. No longer national committeeman, O'Donnell remained active behind the scenes in the political world and spent four months in Washington, living in the same apartment building as Clements. The two men frequently went to work together and often dined together, while O'Donnell helped recruit staff members for Clements.[50]

CONNALLY SWITCHES SIDES

In May 1973 former governor John Connally announced that he was be-coming a Republican. Connally had served for one year as secretary of the Treasury in the Nixon administration, a position he resigned to head up Democrats for Nixon in the 1972 campaign. He claimed that the Democratic Party was now "so far to the left that it had left the majority of the American people."[51] Now the major figure among conservative Democrats in Texas had defected to the other political party.

Republican leaders welcomed Connally and viewed his move as a positive step in expanding the party's reach to Texas voters. State chairman Willeford saw Connally's switch as a tremendous asset to the party's efforts at candi-date recruitment, while Fred Agnich predicted that a number of others would follow Connally's lead.[52] Soon after the announcement, the SREC held a re-ception for John and Nellie Connally in Austin, at which Tower welcomed Connally into the party. As Knaggs saw it, Tower "was the veteran Texas GOP general, speaking to his field grade officers about the proud defector standing nearby who had held general's rank in the opposing army." Former national committeeman Albert Fay summed up the senator's advice: "Tower's saying Connally is welcome to join the church, but don't start out trying to lead the choir."[53] Later that year the state party held a major fundraising event called the Welcome John Connally Reception and Dinner in Dallas. It was cochaired by RNC members Rita Bass and Fred Agnich, Tower served as the master of ceremonies, and Senator Barry Goldwater gave the keynote speech.[54]

Political observers noted the importance of the Connally switch. One writer summed up the situation: "The John Connally switch is significant in that it was the first attempt by an extremely successful Democrat to de-nounce the Democratic Party completely and seek a new home in the oppo-sition party."[55] Historian Sean Cunningham placed the former governor's decision in perspective by noting, "John Connally's Texas was the Texas of the space age—of skyscrapers, technology, and beginning in May of 1973, Republicanism. Connally's decision to switch parties reflected what was be-coming a much more common impulse among conservative Texans."[56] How-ever, there was no mass movement of Democrats to the GOP after Connally's announcement. According to one report, "the only semi-quasi-notable con-servative Democrats to follow him were ex-House Speaker Rayford Price and State Representative Skip Scoggins of El Paso."[57] To some observers, many of Connally's supporters had already made the move to the Republican Party as conservatives defected from the Democratic fold over the previous twenty years beginning with the Eisenhower campaign.[58] Still others noted that Connally's move came at a time of turmoil and scandal associated with the Republican administration. As Admiral Bobby Inman remarked, "Many conservatives more than likely would have switched party allegiance because of John Connally if it hadn't been for Watergate."[59] More biting was the comment of former senator Yarborough, who said "It's the first time in recorded history that a rat swam towards a sinking ship."[60]

A CANDIDATE FOR GOVERNOR

A sinking ship might well have been an apt description of the situation as Republicans moved from one crisis to another throughout the remainder of 1973 and 1974. Soon after the 1972 election, Grover announced that he would be running for governor again in 1974. After coming close to victory, Grover was well-known across the state, had the support of key party leaders in Harris and Bexar counties, and had the ability to generate media attention with his sometimes outlandish criticisms of fellow Republicans. Grover's relationship with many party leaders had not improved since his defeat. As one reporter summed up the situation, "Regarded as a thorn in the side of the GOP establishment, Grover has little use for the Tower-dominated leadership coalition and it, in turn, has little use for him."[61] Only one other candidate surfaced to challenge Grover, Jim Granberry, SREC member, orthodontist, and former mayor of Lubbock. Granberry formally announced his campaign in June and characterized Grover as a fringe candidate, describing him as "divisive" and unwilling to appeal to the Mexican-American and African-American electorate.[62]

With neither Grover nor Granberry attracting the support of many party leaders, by summer the focus of attention centered on George H. W. Bush, then serving as chairman of the RNC. In March he had been quoted as saying, "I absolutely am not going to do that," but by August his position had become, "I am inclined at this moment not to do that."[63] One advisor to Tower counseled that Bush should not run for governor since he concluded that Granberry would not withdraw and Grover had announced that he would run. He believed that "Grover would wage a bitter, divisive campaign against him." Bush would be attacked as the handpicked candidate of a party establishment that was only interested in controlling the party, not electing a governor. Moreover, Grover would attempt to link Bush with Nixon and Watergate at a time when scandal and controversy was erupting in Washington.[64]

Meanwhile other party leaders were attempting to convince Bush to run.

State chairman Willeford and national committeewoman Bass began to line up prominent conservative Democrats to call or write Bush and urge him to run.[65] Bush responded with a handwritten note to Bass, saying, "The fact is I really am torn up on this, but I am very clear on one thing; namely how lucky I am to have you helping me sort it out."[66] Bush's indecision was reflected in other correspondence at the time. To Young Republicans leader Neil Calnan, Bush wrote "I am trying to make a determination as to whether all that governor's thing makes sense. It's not an easy decision."[67] In mid-October, he informed Thornton Hardie Jr. of Midland, "I am giving serious thought to this matter, but I'm just not sure whether the governor's race is winnable."[68] Meanwhile, both Tower and Connally met with Bush in Washington and encouraged him to run. According to one reporter, "Tower and other leaders reportedly feel Bush is the only 'credible' candidate who could possibly pull off a victory in a year of scandal."[69]

In October political consultant Bob Mallas prepared a report on a potential governor's race, pointing out a number of weaknesses in Governor Dolph Briscoe's administration and record. He concluded, "At this point in time with modest campaign effort, despite the 'Watergate attitude,' Bush could defeat Briscoe."[70] Immediately upon receiving the report, Bass forwarded it to Bush for his consideration. Bush read the report and thanked Mallas for his efforts but wrote that he was leaning against running for governor.[71] Nevertheless, by early November media reports indicated that Bush was tired of serving as chairman of the national party during the scandals of Watergate and was taking a private poll to help him decide whether to seek the governorship.[72]

As word spread of a possible Bush candidacy, Grover claimed that he would "beat the hell out of him" if Bush were to oppose him in the Republican primary.[73] Two weeks later Bush had decided finally to remain as chairman of the RNC.[74] It was not the Grover threat that kept Bush out of the race, but the long-standing prioritization by many Texas Republican leaders of national rather than state politics. Once elected, Tower had become a national spokesperson for the conservative cause and a power broker at conventions. Shortly after becoming state chairman, O'Donnell became national cochair of the Draft Goldwater committee and began his time as a kingpin in the national party. According to some, a similar case could be made for Bush: "George Bush, son of a senator, was a Washingtonian by nature and ambition. Once he was elected to Congress from Houston in 1966, he never 'returned' to Texas in a spiritual sense." When the opportunity came to run for governor, Bush "turned it down chiefly from desire to operate out of Washington and New York rather than Austin."[75]

Bush's decision caused the party establishment to turn elsewhere for someone who could defeat Grover. At a November meeting between party leaders and a group of GOP state legislators, the idea of a Tower candidacy received a generally unenthusiastic reception, with most believing he was more valuable to the state and the party in the US Senate. Soon thereafter, Tower made it clear that he was not running for governor, and the focus shifted elsewhere once again.[76]

With Bush and Tower eliminated as possibilities, national committeeman Fred Agnich and others began encouraging state representative Ray Hutchison of Dallas to enter the race. On December 1 Agnich convened a meeting of party leaders in Austin and tried to convince them to promote a Hutchison candidacy.[77] That action set off Granberry supporters, who charged the party leadership with intervening in a primary contest. Former gubernatorial aspirant David Reagan said party vice chairman Polly Sowell had asked him to serve on a steering committee for Hutchison. He claimed that Sowell had told him that Agnich was supporting Hutchison. According to Reagan, "she said she and other party leaders, including Agnich, had decided that Hutchison would make the best candidate." As to Agnich, Reagan noted, "I don't know how he can keep a straight face and say he is not involved. It's absurd."[78] Business executive Julian Zimmerman, a former Tower finance chair and early backer of Granberry, claimed that a Hutchison candidacy would only benefit Grover. He believed that "the real reason they have rejected Jim Granberry is that he didn't go hat in hand and ask their permission to run."[79]

On December 11 Hutchison held a series of news conferences in Austin, Dallas, and Houston, where he formally became a candidate for governor. It would be a short-lived campaign, however. On January 4, 1974, he withdrew, admitting that his campaign "created a divisiveness within the Republican Party totally contrary to that objective of unity which I envisioned in my original announcement."[80] Meanwhile a third candidate had surfaced in Odell McBrayer of Fort Worth. McBrayer had been an assistant district attorney and an unsuccessful candidate for district judge but was little known to Republican activists and had little party support.

One more twist to the search for a gubernatorial nominee came in March when Grover withdrew with an attack on Tower, Anne Armstrong, and other leaders of the party. He accused them of torpedoing his chances and giving him no assistance in paying off his campaign debts from the 1972 effort. Grover claimed that the party leaders "have no intention of making any effort to win the governor's race in 1974."[81] The end result was a 1974 Republican primary attracting less than seventy thousand voters. Granberry became, by

default, the accepted candidate of most active Republicans and trounced Mc-
Brayer with 77.6 percent of the vote.

THE IMPACT OF WATERGATE

While all the machinations over a gubernatorial nominee took place, changes
were occurring in the party organization. In January 1973 Brad O'Leary had
become executive director of the state party. O'Leary was a professional
fundraiser who had worked in the 1972 Tower campaign and would assume
that role again in various campaigns for many years.[82] Criticism of the party
leadership continued, and in August state representative Bill Blythe of Houston laid the blame for Grover's loss in 1972 squarely at the feet of state chairman Willeford. Blythe called for Willeford to resign, and Nancy Palm recommended the position go to James A. Baker III, a Houston attorney and close
friend of George H. W. Bush.[83] But the state chairman was not ready to step
aside under pressure from the Grover forces, and after a leadership meeting
in Dallas it was decided he would remain in office.[84]

One month later Willeford changed his mind. He informed Bass, "After
soul searching for days, I have decided to resign as Chairman of the Executive Committee of the State Republican Party effective November 19."[85] Some
observers claimed that Tower had pressured him to resign, but "Throughout
his stormy two-year reign, Willeford was often the whipping boy in abrasive
party squabbles that pitted Houston and Bexar County factions against the
established leadership, composed of Tower, the SREC and other key Republican office-holders."[86] When the SREC met on November 19, Jack Warren of
Tyler was the unanimous choice for state chairman. It would be his responsibility to lead the party through the tumultuous year that was to come.

The drip, drip, drip of scandal in Washington began to build throughout
1973. The first target was not Nixon but his vice president, Spiro Agnew. In
February a federal grand jury in Baltimore began considering charges that he
had received kickbacks on government contracts and engaged in income tax
evasion. Eventually Agnew was charged with having accepted bribes while
he was serving as Baltimore County executive, Maryland governor, and even
vice president. On October 10, 1973, Agnew pleaded no contest to a single
charge of failing to report income, a plea that was accepted by the court on
the condition that he resign as vice president.[87] Nixon quickly announced
that House minority leader Gerald R. Ford was his choice for vice president.
After congressional hearings Ford was confirmed by overwhelming votes in

both the Senate and the House of Representatives, and on December 6 he assumed office. While most Americans were supportive of the selection, Grover criticized Nixon's choice by declaring, "I never believed he could be so politically stupid."[88]

In the aftermath of the Agnew resignation, Texas Republicans were despondent. Looking ahead to the state elections in 1974, Beryl Milburn maintained, "Our people are disheartened, and whether they can rise above that we're going to have to wait and see. Republicans are weak, we don't have a lot of depth. If a frontrunner can't make the race, we don't have a lot to fall back on." Meanwhile, Palm saw the November election as "far more difficult than in the past because of Watergate. I think any realistic politician — if he makes a serious appraisal — is going to be quite hesitant to get into the race."[89] It appeared that the party had quietly and unofficially adopted what could be called an enclave strategy to save whatever current officeholders it could while not expecting any major breakthroughs into new territory.[90]

It seemed as if every week during 1973 and into the summer of 1974, more and more revelations came forth about the Watergate break-in and the subsequent cover-up. Despite his denials, the evidence pointed to the president's involvement in efforts to hide the facts. After extensive televised hearings on Watergate in both the Senate and the House, on July 27, 1974, the House Judiciary Committee approved the first of three articles of impeachment.[91] One week later, audio tapes from the White House were finally released and revealed the extent to which Nixon had been directly involved in the cover-up. Nixon's support in Congress quickly evaporated, and on August 9 he resigned the presidency, turning over the White House to Vice President Ford.[92]

One of the new president's first responsibilities was to choose an individual to serve as vice president. The number of names floated by political observers was endless. As other possibilities were filtered out, one that remained in contention was George H. W. Bush, who had substantial support among House members led by Bill Archer, Jack Kemp, and several other younger legislators. A survey of congressional preferences tallied Bush 101 and Nelson Rockefeller 68.[93] The rumored support for Bush within the White House was so strong that one reporter bluntly declared, "President Ford will select Republican National Committee chairman George Bush of Houston as his vice president, probably by Friday, informed sources here are predicting. Bush has the inside track over former New York Governor Nelson Rockefeller and Arizona Senator Barry Goldwater, and is gaining strength hourly, the sources say."[94]

In the end, the predictions of a Bush vice presidency proved untrue as Ford selected the nemesis of conservative Republicans, Nelson Rockefeller. Once again, Bush had come up short. As he explained to his close friend Baker, "Yesterday was an enormous personal disappointment. . . . I take personal pleasure from the great official support, but I take even more from the way our friends rallied around. None did more than you to help me with a problem that burned my soul and conscience. The sun is about to come out and life looks pretty darn good."[95] Among the many Texas Republicans who had attempted to rally support for his selection was national committeewoman Bass. In a note to her, Bush added a handwritten observation, "Tough to lose out *again* but there was some great warm support. Best, GB."[96]

Ford's choice of Rockefeller was "the final blow of 1974 to the old guard, solid Goldwater and solid anti-Rockefeller to the core since 1964."[97] The air was out of the balloon, and, save for those totally dedicated to the party, the search for volunteers and campaign helpers was nearly impossible. When the small cadre of party faithful gathered for the state convention in September, it was clear that Palm's warning would soon come true as opposition to Ford was fast developing. In an effort to divert direct attacks on the Ford administration, Tower stepped forward to serve as the chair of the convention, and state senator Ike Harris was named to head the platform committee. In a nonpresidential election year, Tower wanted the focus of the platform and the convention to be on state issues and the gubernatorial race. His task was made all the more difficult, however, when on the eve of the convention Ford announced that he was granting amnesty to draft dodgers and deserters from the Vietnam war. The senator met with the platform committee twice to urge that no statements on national issues be included.[98]

Although Harris got the committee to report a platform dealing solely with state issues, two minority reports were taken to the convention floor. When Van Henry Archer of San Antonio presented a resolution supporting Ford's pardon of Nixon, Tower ruled that it failed on a disputed voice vote.[99] Then came a second minority report from state representative Ray Barnhart of Harris County. Barnhart's proposed resolution criticized the president's stand on amnesty and the selection of Rockefeller, noting "very deep concern over the direction of the new Administration and apparent compromises of basic conservative principles." Passed on a close voice vote, it was viewed as a defeat for Tower and a precursor of the divisions to come in the 1976 presidential nominating contest.[100]

In the end the best efforts of Tower, Harris, and gubernatorial candidate Granberry to have the delegates focus on the upcoming state campaign were to no avail. They found themselves in an environment where the White House was making appointments and taking positions inimical to the conservative beliefs of many, if not most, Texas Republicans. These grassroots party activists simply could not put aside their differences with the direction of the national Republican administration and concentrate solely on a state election their party had been unable to win in more than one hundred years. As reporter Ron Calhoun of the *Dallas Times Herald* noted, "The idea was to put on a show of unity and gig the Democrats but Texas Republicans wound up dividing their house and rebuking their President."[101]

Less than six weeks after the state convention, Election Day brought generally bad news for the Texas Republican Party. After its strong showing in 1972, the impact of scandal and controversy in Washington contributed to a major setback in 1974. In the race for governor, incumbent Democrat Briscoe won the state's first four-year term as Granberry ended up with 31.1 percent of the votes cast. Granberry's 514,725 total votes was roughly one-third the amount received by Grover in his losing campaign two years earlier. The party lost one of its four members of Congress when Bob Price failed to gain re-election from the Panhandle district and had a net loss of one in the Texas House. The longer-term good news, however, was that the party picked up the office of county judge in the state's two largest counties, Dallas and Harris. In Dallas County Commissioner John Whittington knocked off twenty-five-year veteran county judge Lew Sterrett, while in Harris County, Jon Lindsay began what would be a twenty-year tenure as chief administrative officer of the state's most populous county.

RECOVERING AND RENEWING

In the aftermath of the 1974 election losses, Julian Zimmerman decided that something needed to be done to provide more support for local and state legislative candidates. Zimmerman had been chairman of the Granberry campaign for governor and was well aware of the difficulty of raising funds in the aftermath of Watergate. From his perspective, if the Republican Party was going to become a competitive force in Texas it needed to recruit and support candidates who could help build a local presence. That meant finding and funding individuals with community ties and influence who would make winnable legislative and county office candidates. To convince such community leaders to run on the Republican ticket would require an entity that could provide both financial and campaign management assistance.

In late December Zimmerman shared his thoughts with Tower, and although the senator was noncommittal, he did not throw cold water on the idea. Tower then discussed the idea with a number of his allies in the party and found them receptive. Meanwhile Zimmerman recruited Norman Newton Jr., a former executive director of the state party and manager for the Granberry campaign, and they in turn invited a number of Republican activists and financial supporters to a planning meeting in March. When the initial meeting was held in Irving, some one hundred Republicans were there, and formally created the Associated Republicans of Texas (ART). Zimmerman, a former federal housing administrator who was then president of Lumbermen's Investment Corporation, was named chairman, and Newton was charged with developing an office and small staff to carry out the organization's objectives.

ART's status was secured when Tower formally endorsed the organization later in the spring of 1975.[102] Tower's position on how best to build the party had gone through a transformation, and in a February interview he suggested that legislative and county races should have priority, with the party concentrating "the bulk of its resources" on such contests. Moving away from the previous top-heavy or trickle-down theory of party growth, Tower concluded that the time was right for a change in strategy, declaring "I think we should build from the grass roots and broaden our local base."[103]

The new group's board of directors mixed together political activists with individuals who had gained prominence and success in business or community service. Former ambassador John Hurd agreed to head up the ART finance committee, and past gubernatorial candidate Paul Eggers agreed to serve as a director. Committed to increasing the party's presence in the Texas legislature, ART focused on targeting winnable districts, recruiting qualified candidates, assisting with survey research and campaign management, and providing direct financial assistance. To avoid divisiveness in the party, ART agreed not to endorse or otherwise aid candidates in a contested primary, a pledge that would not prevent them, however, from recruiting candidates when a district was deemed winnable.

PASSING THE TORCH

In May 1975 state chairman Jack Warren passed the word to a few party leaders that he would be resigning. State vice chairman Polly Sowell instructed Zack Fisher, then serving as executive director, to inform the staff of the pending change and to set the date for a SREC meeting in June to choose a successor.[104] Shortly thereafter Warren made it official in a letter to Rita Clements (formerly Rita Bass) and other party officials, saying, "It has been a labor of love, some headaches, many friends, a few soreheads, and, very rewarding."[105] Clements, who had married William P. Clements Jr. on March 8, 1975, would also step aside from her role as national committeewoman a few months later.

As soon as Warren made it official, Ernest Angelo Jr., mayor of Midland and a member of the SREC, announced his candidacy. Angelo claimed that the party needed to exercise "real leadership and direction.... We need to take a definite approach to solving state problems. We need to stand for something,... to have some credibility." A few days later state representative Ray Hutchison of Dallas entered the race. Hutchison, who had announced for governor in 1974 and then had quickly withdrawn, refused to say whether he would seek statewide office in 1978. He maintained that in the absence of any state officeholders other than Tower, the party must "step into the breach and become more visible."[106]

While both aspirants said it was too early to discuss presidential preferences, Angelo made it clear that he would want to dump Vice President Rockefeller from the 1976 ticket. Reports began surfacing that Tower was supporting Hutchison for state chairman, but Tower denied the claim. The discussion led Angelo to write his fellow SREC members: "Senator Tower's leadership is not an issue! The Senator and I have always had an excellent, open relationship. He has assured me as late as June 12 that he has no intention of personal involvement in the selection of a new State Chairman."[107]

When the SREC met in Austin on June 29, Walter Wilkerson of Conroe nominated Hutchison with a second by Fort Worth state senator Betty Andujar, while Angelo was nominated by county judge Barbara Culver of Midland and seconded by Don Jansen of Houston. In a secret ballot Hutchison received backing from thirty-eight committee members, while Angelo had the support of twenty-five, mainly the more conservative members of the SREC.[108]

Warren was not the only party leader to step aside in the early part of 1975. Longtime Harris County GOP chairman Palm announced her resignation effective July 1 and was replaced by former state representative Barnhart of Pasadena. Palm had been the chairman for seven critical years and had built the county party into a major political force. As Chase Untermeyer, later a state representative from Harris County and much later ambassador to Qatar, noted decades afterward, "When Nancy Palm was Harris County chairman she believed strongly that electing local officials was how you built a political party. Recruiting Jon Lindsay to run for county judge in 1974 was a key in building the GOP in Harris County. His election opened the door to other opportunities for party success locally."[109]

Tower wrote to Palm, "No Republican County Chairman in Texas or in the nation has worked harder, or more successfully for Republican candidates from the court house to the White House than you have. The work you have done in Harris County is known not only throughout the state, but also among political professionals throughout the country. Friends and political foes alike acclaim you for your skill at grassroots organization, the meat and potatoes of party politics."[110] Mary Jane Smith, now a political consultant for judicial races and wife of federal circuit judge Jerry Smith, was one of many who earned their political spurs working for Palm. As she recalled, "Nancy was just a tremendous person, one of a kind, whose dedication to grass roots politics turned around Harris County."[111]

Known to friends and political opponents alike as NaPalm for her combative nature, Palm had a work style that corresponded with that of another female activist in Harris County and state Democratic politics, Billie Carr. A leader in the liberal wing of her party, Carr was a skilled organizer who served on the Democratic National Committee and was often cited in tandem with her Republican rival. Carr's dedication to party politics was evident in a precinct worker manual she compiled and published in 1975: *Don't Default to the Bastards: Organize! A Common Sense Handbook for Left-Wing Democrats*. With Palm and Carr leading their respective forces in political combat, the late 1960s and early 1970s were a lively time in the transition of Harris County politics as it moved away from a history of conservative Democratic domination.[112]

By the fall of 1975 a third prominent Republican leader announced her resignation. After more than twenty years of intense involvement in positions of leadership, Rita Clements stepped down from her position on the RNC. Newly married to the deputy secretary of Defense, Bill Clements, she would be spending most of her time in Washington, but a few years later would serve an important role as an advisor in her husband's gubernatorial campaign. At the November meeting of the SREC, Pat Archer, wife of Houston member of Congress Bill Archer, was chosen as the new national committeewoman by a margin of thirty-three to thirty, with one abstention, over state senator Andujar.

THE BENTSEN PRIMARY

Meanwhile political developments were taking place in the Texas Democratic Party. Senator Lloyd Bentsen Jr., still in his first term, decided that he would seek the presidency in 1976. Bentsen would be up for re-election that year, but like Lyndon Johnson some sixteen years earlier, he knew that whether or not his presidential nomination efforts were successful, he could still seek re-election to the Senate. To enhance his possibilities of gaining the presidential nomination, Bentsen's allies in the Texas legislature enacted a presidential primary law applicable to both parties. By winning his home state's primary, Bentsen could display popular appeal and improve his possibilities in other states. Texas Republicans chose to elect their delegates from the state's twenty-four congressional districts, with only four at-large delegates picked at the state convention. This meant that on the Republican side the contest for the presidential nomination would be taken to the voters rather than determined by the smaller number of party activists motivated enough to attend precinct, county, and state conventions.

Bentsen's campaign never took off, and he withdrew from the presidential race eight days after the filing deadline but remained on the ballot, attempting to win delegates and gain leverage at the national convention. Another southern Democrat would win the Democratic nomination and go on to capture the White House in 1976. With Bentsen out of the competition, the Democratic presidential primary had less appeal to Texas voters, many of whom would shift to the heightened battle on the Republican side. Bentsen now could focus his attention on re-election to the Senate.[113]

While Bentsen was weighing the possibility of a presidential race, Representative Alan Steelman of Dallas determined that he would seek Bentsen's senatorial seat. Steelman had knocked off an incumbent member of Congress in 1972, and then, in the face of Watergate and a Democratic redistricting map, had won re-election in 1974 against a strongly backed challenger. During his short tenure in Washington, he had "won the respect and admiration of his colleagues in both parties" and had run "an exceptionally efficient office filled with talented people; Marvin Collins, his administrative assistant (and a former campaign manager for George Bush), is considered one of the ablest staffers on the Hill in either party."[114] Despite his reputation as a hard worker in Washington, when Steelman decided to shift his focus to a statewide campaign, he was "bucking some big odds in going after Lloyd Bentsen's U.S. Senate seat."[115]

In the Republican primary Steelman trounced two little-known opponents with 70.5 percent of the votes cast. It would be the high-water mark for his campaign; he came up a half million votes short of Bentsen in November, polling 42.2 percent of the vote in what turned out to be another disappointing year for Texas Republicans. The party had fielded candidates in nineteen of the state's twenty-four congressional districts, but only two incumbents, Jim Collins and the unopposed Bill Archer, were successful. Bob Price lost his attempt to regain his Panhandle seat, and Ron Paul, who had won a special election earlier in 1976, was ousted after only a few months in Congress. Among the other losing candidates only Jim Reese, former mayor of Odessa, and Nancy Judy, a Dallas County commissioner seeking to hold Steelman's seat for the GOP, reached 45 percent of the vote. The Texas legislative races saw slight progress, as the party picked up two new House of Representatives seats, including their first ever from El Paso, Tarrant, and Lubbock counties, to boost their total to nineteen while keeping three seats in the Senate (Andujar of Tarrant, Harris of Dallas, and Mengden of Harris county). The results of 1976 showed the party to be a political force in the state's largest counties, with little success elsewhere.

FORD VERSUS REAGAN

While the party was attempting to recruit candidates for a number of state and local races, the major thrust of political attention throughout most of 1975 centered on the presidency. Would the appointed president be nominated and elected to a term on his own? What about the former California governor and his reported interest in seeking the presidency? In the face of internal party opposition, would vice president Rockefeller seek another term? As the year progressed, it became clear that President Ford was seeking a full term of office and that he would be opposed by Reagan.

By the fall of 1975 the President Ford Committee was in place to secure his nomination and election under the leadership of Howard "Bo" Callaway, a former member of Congress and gubernatorial candidate from Georgia. In a weekly report to the president, Callaway indicated that former Tower campaign aide Roger Wallace had been hired as executive director of the Texas committee, and a headquarters opening had been scheduled for November 1.[116] A few days later, the president wrote to Rita Clements to thank her "for your willingness to help spearhead my campaign in Texas and I want you to know that I am grateful for your support."[117] Soon thereafter the Texas campaign was underway, with Tower as state chairman and Anne Armstrong as cochairman, while former party vice chairman Beryl Milburn took on the role of campaign director. Although she had resigned as national committeewoman, Clements retained an active role in Republican politics. After she offered her assistance to the Ford campaign, Bo Callaway wrote to tell her, "We are excited about several things in the campaign where we see the opportunity for you to make a great contribution. We need your enthusiasm and I'll be in touch with you shortly."[118]

Meanwhile, as early as 1974 Reagan was meeting with prospective supporters and potential staff, keeping his options open. By the summer of 1975 it was becoming evident that Reagan was giving serious thought to challenging Ford. In July Senator Paul Laxalt of Nevada announced the formation of Citizens for Reagan. According to Craig Shirley, "By this point, Reagan was on a course he probably could not reverse, even if he had wanted to. The personal insults from the Ford White House were more than he could stomach, and he certainly had the ideological reasons to make the race."[119] Throughout the fall Ford partisans continued to doubt that Reagan would run. As Ron Nessen, press secretary to the president, recalled the situation, "At first, the Ford White House refused to believe that Reagan would challenge an incumbent conservative Republican President. When the reality of the threat sunk in, various strategies were tried to discourage Reagan from entering the race and to win his constituency over to Ford."[120]

By early November Rockefeller had announced that he would not seek another term as vice president, thereby removing a major roadblock to conservative support for Ford. In so doing, however, Rockefeller cagily did not make any reference to Ford's presidency; nor did he rule out the possibility that he might seek the presidency himself.[121] A few days later Reagan made it official by formally announcing his challenge to Ford. The mainstream media was not impressed. As James Reston wrote in the *New York Times*, "The astonishing thing is that this amusing but frivolous Reagan fantasy is taken so seriously by the news media and particularly by the President. It makes a lot of news, but it makes no sense."[122]

Reagan's national campaign manager, John Sears, traveled to Houston to line up leadership for the Texas campaign. He held a meeting with a number of Harris County GOP precinct chairs and then met privately with Barnhart, at the time Harris County chairman. Sears told Barnhart that Reagan wanted him to head up the campaign in Texas. Barnhart agreed to do it but realized he needed cohorts from other areas of the state.[123] He quickly signed up Midland mayor Angelo as a cochair and then, on the advice of Congressman Jim Collins, recruited Barbara Staff, at the time president of the Dallas County Council of Republican Women. The three cochairs were from Houston, Dallas, and West Texas, but they certainly were not household names to most Texans, even those who closely followed politics. As Angelo explained, "We were trying to get people who had higher positions in the state than we had, but we couldn't find anybody to get involved. So we finally decided that we might as well do it ourselves."[124] Staff viewed the pending contest as one involving the establishment backing Ford and a band of grassroots insurgents supporting Reagan. Her task was to recruit the women volunteers who could make the difference and produce a victory for Reagan.[125]

On November 21 the Texas Citizens for Reagan Committee was announced, with the three cochairs and regional chairs who included six members of the SREC.[126] Substantiating Barbara Staff's observations, when the

President Ford Committee Texas steering committee was released, it contained the names of twenty-nine SREC members. Also included on the Ford committee was a long list of former state party officials and county chairs, along with several of the small number of Republicans in elective office.[127] While Tower was in El Paso to address the annual convention of the Texas Federation of Republican Women, he responded to the Reagan committee's announcement, appearing to dismiss the challenge to the president. His hope was that it would be a contest on issues rather than personalities, in which case he was convinced that Ford would be the winner.[128]

As the presidential election year began, both sides were attempting to put a positive spin on their candidate's chances. Ford's director, Milburn, was optimistic because the president had lined up most of the longtime party leaders, who could turn out the votes in a primary that normally attracted few voters. "I don't think the people in Reagan's campaign are capable of or know how to organize this state and win a Republican primary," she claimed. Reagan's director, Ron Dear, who had been an executive with two national conservative organizations and legislative assistant to member of Congress Bill Archer, saw the situation quite differently. According to Dear, "This primary is not going to be won on the old line Republican vote.... People who are motivated enough to break old voting habits and come into the Republican primary for the first time this year are going to be people who are emotionally committed to Ronald Reagan."[129]

Texas was allotted one hundred delegates to the 1976 Republican National Convention. The Texas presidential primary was conducted in such a way that votes were cast not for the actual presidential candidate but for four individual delegate candidates in each of the state's twenty-four congressional districts, with the remaining four delegates selected at the state convention. This process gave both of the candidates an advantage. Ford had lined up the more recognizable names among regular Republican voters as delegate candidates pledged to his nomination. It was hoped that such individuals would attract voter support on the appeal of their own names. Among the Ford delegate names were a number of SREC members and county chairs, as well as business and community leaders such as Trammell Crow, Robert Mosbacher, former El Paso mayor Fred Hervey Jr., Robert West, and publisher Jimmy Allison, along with former statewide candidates Paul Eggers, Byron Fullerton, and Zack Fisher, and county judges John Whittington of Dallas and Julius Neunhoffer of Kerr County.[130] Meanwhile the only widely recognizable names on the Reagan delegate list were state senators Andujar and Mengden, along with banker James E. Lyon, former Texas Supreme Court justice W. St. John Garwood, and Midland County judge Barbara Culver.

Reagan's advantage in this delegate election process stemmed from the nature of the two campaigns and the intricacies of the recently enacted federal election law. As Shirley compared the campaigns, "Ford had a top-down operation, with party loyalists taking their marching orders from state GOP leaders. Reagan had a bottom-up coalition with grassroots activists banging on the door and trying to force the party leadership to let them in."[131] The Ford camp had the financial resources to set up phone banks in the top twenty-six counties, where it was expected that up to 90 percent of the vote would be cast.[132] In contrast, the Reagan statewide effort was strapped for cash and needed to be innovative to compete with the resources and public stature of a sitting president. Houston attorney Jerry Smith realized that each delegate candidate could raise and spend funds for their own campaign, acting as if they were independent candidates. This freed up the responsibility of the statewide Reagan campaign and depended on the delegate candidates to fund their own local efforts.[133]

Reagan could not match Ford in money or endorsements but had the enthusiasm of his grassroots troops. In Texas and elsewhere, "it was the same story. A small group of dedicated conservatives were backing Reagan while the state GOP and local party apparatchiks were supporting Ford. These grassroots conservatives did not know that 'it could not be done,' so they simply did it."[134] One regular volunteer at the Houston Reagan headquarters was an eighteen-year-old high school student named Steve Munisteri, who later recalled, "I just got very fired up about Reagan. Ford was a nice man, but dull. I felt like we needed a dramatic shift in direction for the country and he didn't seem to be the type that would lead the charge for that."[135] Some thirty-four years later, Munisteri would be elected chairman of the Republican Party of Texas. He was one of many young conservatives who spent hours working for Reagan during the 1976 primary, retained their political involvement, and went on to other positions in party and elective office. Just as the Goldwater campaign had done some twelve years earlier, the Reagan effort provided an infusion of new supporters and workers into the party.

After defeats in the New Hampshire, Florida, and Illinois primaries, the continued viability of the Reagan challenge was much in doubt. To rally their troops, the Reagan cochairs wrote to their campaign leadership in mid-March, claiming that their candidate had run "astonishingly strong in those earlier primaries" and informing them that "the Texas quota is only 66 of our 100 delegates." They charged that the contest had become one for control of the party. "The same folks who have controlled the official Republican Party structure, both nationally and state-wide, for the past dozen years, are fighting for their political lives—and fortunes—to continue that control. The objective is pure power."[136] One day after the memo was sent, Reagan won his first primary in North Carolina, and the battle for Texas was on.

By mid-April, it appeared that Reagan had a clear advantage in Texas, with more than three hundred thousand voters anticipated to take part in the Republican primary. However, media reports claimed that "Mr. Reagan will find it hard to match the forecast of his local managers, who predict that he will win two-thirds of the state's 100 delegates." According to Peter O'Donnell, unofficial advisor to the Ford campaign at that time, "I think it's a good deal closer than many people think."[137] The Ford forces were not willing to concede Texas, and the president made a tour of key cities in the state, hoping to rally his supporters. As one report indicated, "Political observers here believe that heavy last-minute campaigning by President Ford has cut substantially into Ronald Reagan's early lead in Texas, turning tomorrow's Presidential primary into a cliff hanger that they said was too close to call."[138]

When the results came in on May 1, it was a landslide for Reagan. In a massive turnout for Republicans, some 465,000 ballots were cast for convention delegate candidates, with Reagan's backers receiving two-thirds of the total. Only in the low-turnout congressional districts of inner-city Houston and San Antonio were the Ford delegate candidates competitive, but even in the closest district Reagan's slate won 56.5 percent of the vote.[139] Reagan lost only three small-turnout counties in South Texas (Jim Hogg, Kenedy, and Webb) out of the 210 counties participating in the GOP primary. He had captured all ninety-six delegates allocated by congressional districts and would subsequently garner the four remaining at-large delegates at the state convention.

In response Tower released a concession speech on behalf of the Texas Ford campaign, congratulating Reagan on his decisive victory but reaffirming his belief that Ford would win the nomination and election. Tower expressed doubt about the impact of the Texas win, saying, "The unanswered question is whether this victory gives Governor Reagan viable momentum or whether national perception of him as a result of this campaign makes his victory a Pyrrhic one."[140] President Ford simply said, "We lost. We expected to get a fair share of the delegates. We didn't."[141] Others in his campaign organization were less charitable. In an unsigned memo to Jerry Jones, special assistant to the president, one Ford backer claimed that Reagan's success in Texas was due to "skillful organization by extreme right wing political groups in the Reagan camp operating almost invisibly through direct mail and voter turnout efforts conducted by the organizations themselves." According to this analysis, "We are in real danger of being out-organized by a small number of highly motivated *right wing nuts*."[142] The battle for the presidential nomination would now continue onward to the national convention in Kansas City.

1976 STATE AND NATIONAL CONVENTIONS

Before heading to the Midwest, Texas Republicans had to hold a state convention to elect four at-large delegates and propose resolutions to be considered as part of the national platform. In consideration of the primary results, state chairman Ray Hutchison deferred to Barnhart as presiding chair of the convention. While a number of prominent Texas Republicans—Tower, John Connally, and national committeeman Fred Agnich, among others—sought to be national convention delegates, Hutchison indicated that he would step aside from any such role. It was clear to all observers that "In this new Texas GOP, Ray Barnhart and Ernest Angelo called the shots, and loyalty to Reagan was prized above prominence and experience."[143] In this context, both Angelo and Barnhart told Tower that he would need to pledge his support to Reagan if he wished to be an at-large delegate. Having been designated as a Ford floor leader for the convention, this was something Tower was unwilling to do. Barnhart relayed the same conditions to Connally, who declined the offer.[144] Agnich expressed a willingness to endorse Reagan and had his name nominated by Dallas city council member John Leedom, who had been elected as a Reagan district delegate, but then Agnich withdrew when it appeared a loss was inevitable.[145]

The end result of the maneuvering for the four at-large delegate positions was the selection of Ron Paul, victor in a special election to Congress months earlier; Michel Halbouty, a respected oil industry leader from Houston; Fran Chiles, wife of Fort Worth industrialist H. E. "Eddie" Chiles; and J. Evetts Haley, West Texas author of the controversial 1964 paperback *A Texan Looks at Lyndon*. Apart from Paul, of the one hundred delegates sent to the national convention, only Andujar, Mengden, and Culver were currently holding public office after being elected as Republicans. As far as the national convention delegation was concerned, this was a new breed of Republican leaders.

Although they were not chosen as national convention delegates, both Tower and Connally addressed the delegates. Tower's message centered on the need to work together behind whichever presidential nominee was selected. Connally used his time to attack the Democratic domination of Congress and predict that the coming election would produce Republican victories.[146] The changing of the guard was apparent not only in the selection of the four at-large delegates but also in the election of Texas members of the RNC. Angelo was a unanimous choice to succeed Agnich, and Senator Betty Andujar won overwhelmingly against Barbara Howell of Fort Worth to replace Pat Archer as the national committeewoman.

Three weeks before the national convention, with most delegate vote counters estimating that Ford was within a handful of clinching the nomination, the Reagan camp made a radical announcement. On July 26 Reagan introduced Senator Richard Schweiker of Pennsylvania as his choice for a vice presidential running mate. At the time Schweiker, whom most political observers viewed as a liberal Republican, had been a Ford delegate from Pennsylvania. The announcement was meant to shake up the political equation, and it certainly did. While the Schweiker choice never did free up delegates in the Northeast for Reagan, it did upset numerous conservatives. In the Texas delegation Angelo and Barnhart had to put out several fires as the dyed-in-the-wool conservatives found it difficult to accept a liberal Republican as the vice presidential candidate, even with a conservative like Reagan at the top of the ticket.[147]

One day after the announcement of Schweiker as Reagan's vice presidential choice, Connally traveled to the White House and visited with the president in the Oval Office, and then Connally and Ford met with the press in the Rose Garden, where Connally announced his endorsement of the president. With any possibility of a vice presidential selection by Reagan now out of the picture, Connally decided it was time to endorse Ford in the hopes that he might become his choice for the second slot on the ticket.[148] In fact, Connally was one of approximately twelve Republicans from various delegations being wooed and considered by Ford in his effort to reach a majority of convention delegates. To stop Ford's dangling of the vice presidential selection as an appeal to undecided delegates, the Reagan strategists proposed an amendment to the party rules, requiring a presidential candidate to announce the vice presidential choice before nominating ballots were cast. This became known as Rule 16c. After the Ford forces defeated it in the convention rules committee, a minority report was brought to the convention floor. In a vote that closely mirrored the final vote for the presidential nomination, the proposed rule change failed, 1,068 to 1,180, and Ford had secured the nomination.[149]

With Ford's nomination settled, the focus of attention turned to the choice of a vice presidential running mate. Connally had asked O'Donnell to organize an effort to recruit support for his selection by Ford. O'Donnell agreed and set up a coordinated effort in Kansas City, attempting to contact delegates who would express their support for Connally to the Ford campaign operation.[150] With his recent experience as state chairman and national committeeman, O'Donnell had a number of contacts in other delegations throughout the South. His influence within a Texas delegation populated by newcomers, as well as those who had opposed him in previous internal party battles, was less apparent. Yet he was able to call on a core of Texas Republican activists to assist him.

A number of Texas Republican activists who had supported Ford and thus were not delegates at the convention came to Kansas City to help O'Donnell in this effort. As Polly Sowell, vice chairman of the state party, recalled the experience, "There were several of us who went to the Kansas City convention with the purpose of getting Connally on the ticket. That was our mission and, of course, we failed. We went around and talked about Connally with people from other states but, of course, the only person to make that decision was President Ford himself."[151] Rita Clements was another party activist who answered the call from O'Donnell. As he wrote to her shortly after the convention, "I am indebted to you for coming to Kansas City to help with the Connally operation. You did a great job getting important events scheduled and dealing with JBC III. We couldn't have done it without you."[152] While Tower was not a delegate and was ineligible to serve as floor manager for Ford, he was included in the vice presidential selection process and pushed for Connally, but to no avail. In the end Ford chose Senator Robert Dole of Kansas to join his ticket.

Texas Republicans returned from Kansas City ready to battle the Democrats in November. Before that could happen, another state convention would be held in September. While Dole and Connally, now chair of the Texas President Ford Committee, attempted to rally the delegates for the November election, a lively contest for state chairman was taking place. Current state chairman Hutchison was opposed by Harris County chairman Barnhart in what appeared to be another Ford versus Reagan battle. Dole refused to get involved, declaring at a press conference, "I think the Texans can resolve that. They're big boys and they're going to resolve that."[153] Connally, on the other hand, publicly endorsed the sitting state chairman and telephoned several delegates on Hutchison's behalf.[154]

While Hutchison had been neutral in the presidential primary, he was clearly perceived as the establishment candidate against Barnhart, cochair of the Reagan forces. Once again it was a battle of geography, with Hutchison from Dallas and his opponent from Harris County. While Reagan won the hearts and votes of those who participated in the primary, Barnhart was unable to translate that into support from a majority of the party activists elected as delegates to the state convention. When the votes were counted, Hutchison bested Barnhart by carrying eighteen of the state's thirty-one senatorial districts and narrowly topped him in total votes by a margin of 843 to 792. Among the many banners at the convention, one in particular summed up the mood of many Texas Republicans: "My Heart Goes to Reagan, My Vote Goes to Ford."

Once the state convention was over, nearly all Republican activists rallied behind the president's election effort. The Ford campaign in Texas was headed by Connally, with O'Donnell as state vice chairman and Doug Lewis, the recent party executive director, heading up the campaign staff.[155] Although less than two months remained for the presidential campaign, it appeared to one astute observer that "the warfare between supporters of President Ford and supporters of former Gov. Ronald Reagan of California, which led to a bitterly divisive primary appears to have ended."[156] Nevertheless, the Ford campaign was unable to overcome the state's Democratic tradition, and Jimmy Carter carried the state with 51.6 percent and a margin of nearly 130,000 votes.

The year that had begun with such high hopes for Republicans ended in disappointment as they lost another US Senate election, saw their House delegation in Washington reduced to two members, and failed to carry the state for the GOP presidential nominee. The immediate picture looked dim, but the Republican cause had made lasting progress. Though Reagan's primary challenge was unsuccessful, it changed the dynamics of Texas politics. According to historian Sean Cunningham, "more than any other figure, Ronald Reagan deserves credit for the success of the modern Texas Republican Party. His regular presence at party fundraisers and civic organizations in Texas, beginning in 1967 and continuing almost unabated through 1980, coupled with the skilled, crafted charm of a former Hollywood actor, transformed the public's image of conservatism and the Republican Party."[157]

As Gilbert Garcia noted, "With one dramatic presidential campaign, Reagan lured tens of thousands of Texas Democrats and political fence sitters into the GOP fold for a single day, and before long many of them began to identify themselves as Republicans."[158] In the words of another Texas reporter, "he set in motion a political revolution in the Lone Star State that broadened the Texas Republican Party from a country club-dominated organization into a populist movement led by social conservatives."[159] The image of the party had been changed, the base of the Texas party had been broadened, and although they were unable to pull off many victories in 1976, with a little luck and better timing, Texas Republicans were on their way to a landmark victory only two years later.

NINE

BREAKING THE GLASS CEILING

As 1977 began, John Tower and his advisors were gearing up for another re-election effort, and this time there would not be an incumbent Republican president on the ballot with him. Moreover, his involvement in the Ford campaign still left hard feelings among some of the party activists who had supported Reagan in 1976. Among the diehard backers of Hank Grover there remained a belief that Tower did not support Grover sufficiently in the 1972 gubernatorial campaign. This situation led Tower to engage in a process of fence mending within the party during much of 1977, hoping that the result would be a unified effort in the upcoming state elections. One of his first outreach efforts to party activists took place in January when he traveled to Houston and met with the Harris County GOP leaders, many of whom grilled Tower and challenged him on his support for Ford and perceived lack of support for the Grover campaign.[1] Similar meetings, usually in more friendly territory, were held across the state.

When the state Republican executive committee (SREC) met in February, the party adopted a detailed and lengthy plan for 1977 geared toward preparing for the 1978 elections. While not overlooking the importance of re-electing Tower, the party was now beginning to devote substantial resources to county and legislative races, candidate recruitment, and campaign management training. Supplementing the state party's efforts to build a base of local candidates and officeholders was the work of the Associated Republicans of Texas (ART).[2] While some in the party had been critical of the group's formation three years earlier, by 1977 state chairman Ray Hutchison clearly recognized the important role ART could play in recruiting, training, and financing local and legislative candidates. Hutchison also brought about the creation of the Texas Republican County Chairmen's Association (TRCCA) as a vehicle to encourage the building of a more professional party organization throughout the state.[3]

By the fall of 1977 the internal divisions that had developed over the Ford-

Reagan primary contest appeared to have subsided, with Jack Orr, executive director of the state party, describing factionalism as "almost zero. We're about 90 percent unified."[4] Two special elections in December gave additional encouragement to party activists as S. L. Abbott won election for the 71st House district, covering parts of El Paso and Far West Texas, while former member of Congress Bob Price picked up a vacant state Senate seat from the Panhandle. This enthusiasm carried over to the filing deadline as Republican candidates appeared in twenty-one of the state's twenty-four congressional districts and in sixty-eight Texas House districts.[5]

When neither George H. W. Bush nor Anne Armstrong expressed an interest in seeking the governorship, Hutchison designated a treasurer for a prospective campaign and resigned as state chairman. At that point, the field temporarily looked clear for Hutchison, who had announced for governor in 1974 but then backed out one month later. In a contest that had some of the Ford-Reagan and Dallas-Houston divisions, the SREC selected Harris County chairman Ray Barnhart over Collin County judge Nathan White to replace Hutchison as state chairman.[6]

Behind the appearance of unity in the party, Grover was once again making noises, this time about a possible statewide race in 1978. His supporters undertook a drive to pay off the remaining debts from his 1972 campaign, and some observers thought he was gearing up for another try at the governor's office.[7] When Grover spoke at a conservative conference in Dallas, he claimed to be considering another race for governor or even possibly a challenge to Tower for the Senate nomination. According to Grover, "More people are urging me to run against Tower. I'm not convinced he will run for re-election. Tower has real problems in the party."[8] Grover's possible candidacy did not sit well with all his previous backers, however. Nancy Palm was now clearly on the Tower team, raising money for the Harris County party by stressing the need to re-elect the senator.[9] When word reached Palm that Grover was seriously planning to run against Tower in the GOP primary, "Nancy Palm came to Austin and said, 'I'll keep him out.' And he stayed out."[10] While Palm did keep Grover out of the Republican primary, he still harbored a desire to get even with Tower, and in February 1978 he announced that he would run against the senator as an independent, bypassing the party primary. In the end, Grover failed to obtain the necessary 16,549 signatures from registered voters statewide and thus never did appear on the 1978 ballot.[11]

It was clear that Tower was in the fight of his life for what would turn out to be his final six-year term in the US Senate. Taking nothing for granted, Tower's state director Robert Estrada would pick up the senator on Friday afternoons at Dallas/Fort Worth International Airport and travel with him around the state to various civic and campaign events, then drive him back to the airport for the return trip to Washington. As Estrada recalled, "During the early months of 1978, we spent nearly every weekend in the rural areas of the state. I'm sure we went to all 254 counties in that campaign."[12]

Under the direction of new state chairman Barnhart, the state party held a successful fundraising banquet in October with attorney and Bush confidant James A. Baker III and banker and Reagan campaign financier James E. Lyon as dinner cochairs. While the special guest was Tower, the featured speaker was Reagan, the candidate whose 1976 campaign had been cochaired by Barnhart.

Barnhart brought a number of Reagan supporters to the state party staff but also retained several who had worked there under the leadership of Hutchison. Coby Pieper, son of a SREC member and a staff member in the 1976 Reagan effort, became political director, while Gary Hoitsma, another former Reagan campaign worker, was hired as communications director. Hoitsma would resurrect a monthly party newspaper, relabeled the *Texas Advocate*, which was sent to all party activists and donors over the next five years, playing an important role in building a sense of camaraderie among GOP supporters. Finally, Barnhart hired a young assistant professor of political science from Arkansas State University to serve as the new executive director of the party. Wayne Thorburn had been a Reagan delegate to the 1976 Republican National Convention from Arkansas. He would continue as director of the Texas party for the next five and a half years.[13] With Barnhart's ascension to the chairmanship, the insurgent Reagan supporters were now part of the establishment and would continue to play important roles in the party leadership from this point forward.

NOMINATING A GOVERNOR

Meanwhile Hutchison was developing a campaign structure for his effort to win the governorship. He brought to the campaign a number of strong attributes. Within the small circle of regular GOP supporters, he was well known from his time as state chairman, a position that allowed him to travel and build relationships with party activists throughout the state. Among the Texas media, he had built a reputation as a conscientious legislator; he had been named to *Texas Monthly* magazine's Ten Best list for both sessions he served in the Texas House. After Hutchison's second session in 1975 the magazine declared him "the consensus choice as the House's most outstanding member."[14] With other recognizable names in the party avoiding a race for governor, Hutchison had every right to expect that he would become the Republican nominee against Governor Dolph Briscoe in 1978.

It was not to be for Hutchison, however. Along came another well-connected and well-financed aspirant for the governor's office: William P. Clements Jr. of Dallas. Clements was a business associate and friend of Peter O'Donnell Jr. Clements's wife, Rita, had served on the board of the O'Donnell Foundation since its founding in 1957 and had been a key worker in the party while O'Donnell was county and state chairman.[15] As early as 1964 O'Donnell had attempted to recruit Clements as a candidate for statewide office, but to no avail. Clements had been a finance chair and fundraiser for various candidates, however, and was deputy secretary of Defense in the Nixon and Ford administrations. While he was not widely known among Texas Republicans, his wife, Rita, had developed many contacts in the party through her years of active involvement and leadership, including serving as Republican national committeewoman from 1973 to 1975.

Clements had founded and was chief executive of SEDCO, a multimillion-dollar oil services and equipment company. When he accepted appointment to his position in the Pentagon he had turned over leadership of SEDCO to his son, Gill. Now back in Texas, he had the time and resources to devote himself to further public service. In November 1977, Clements took part in an energy forum at Southern Methodist University that also included Senator Harrison "Jack" Schmitt, the former astronaut who had been elected from New Mexico the previous year. Schmitt spent the night as a guest at the Clements home, and after the university event the discussion turned to politics. The senator noted that while previous GOP candidates for governor had come close, no one was able to close the deal on Election Day. He suggested that Clements might be the one to break this losing tradition. Clements dismissed the idea out of hand, and they called it a night.[16]

Retiring to their bedroom, Bill and Rita Clements continued to discuss the possibility of a campaign for the next hour. According to one report, "If Clements had any doubts about his abilities as a candidate or whether he had a chance to win, Mrs. Clements put them to rest."[17] As political reporter Carolyn Barta observed, "Rita was not only enthusiastic about the governor's race, she was well grounded in the Republican Party and possessed rare practical knowledge of Texas politics. In her, he had the perfect political partner."[18] By the next morning, Clements had determined to seek the gubernatorial nomination. Bill and Rita then headed to meet with O'Donnell to inform him of the decision and inquire as to whether the longtime Republican leader believed Clements had a chance of succeeding. O'Donnell was both optimistic and enthusiastic about a Clements gubernatorial campaign.

Once Bill Clements had committed to the race, O'Donnell started putting together a campaign plan and a team to implement it. Among those Clements asked to join his team was Jim Francis, who had been executive director of the Dallas GOP, headed by William "Billy Mac" McKenzie. Francis agreed to become finance director for the Clements campaign. As he later recalled his decision, "I knew Bill Clements would put in whatever money we needed and with a staff put together by Peter O'Donnell and a candidate who was smart, we could win. The whole issue in the primary was who can win and Hutchison couldn't take that issue away from us."[19]

O'Donnell became chair of what the campaign called the God Squad, comprising Bill Clements, Rita Clements, pollster Lance Tarrance, Tom Reed, and George Steffes. Reed was a Californian who had been involved in Reagan's two gubernatorial campaigns and had served as secretary of the Air Force while Bill Clements was at the Pentagon. Steffes had been Reagan's legislative aide in Sacramento. Also playing a key role in the campaign was Omar Harvey, a former IBM executive who would serve as campaign manager in the primary and then head up the general election effort in rural counties.[20] After the primary the inner circle was expanded somewhat. In the end, however, the two individuals whose opinion counted the most were veteran party leaders Rita Clements and Peter O'Donnell. As Francis recalled, "Peter O'Donnell worked day and night on that campaign."[21]

Two weeks after the discussion with Jack Schmitt, Bill Clements announced his candidacy on November 16, 1977. The initial response was skepticism from much of the media and many party activists. Few Texas Republicans knew Clements, and among those who did there were questions as to whether he had the personality to be a successful candidate. According to George H. W. Bush, "When I first heard he was going to run, I was not sure he would adjust to it."[22] Longtime Republican Millard Neptune, then serving as Travis County GOP chairman, was even more direct in a letter to Clements: "My advice would be that you withdraw as quickly and gracefully as possible. ... I visit with lots of Republicans and find that most of them, like me, are completely puzzled as to why you surreptitiously announced your candidacy without at least making an inquiry as to your chances and as to what your candidacy would do to Republican chances generally."[23]

Clements's first challenge was to become better known among the party activists who would constitute much of the low-turnout primary electorate. Reed analyzed the likely distribution of primary votes and proposed that the campaign be organized through ten geographical regions. Major emphasis would be placed on the regions centered around Houston (26 percent of the 1976 primary total) and Dallas–Fort Worth (32 percent). No other identifiable area of the state contributed more than eight percent of the 1976 Republican primary turnout.[24] While the candidate, Bill Clements, concentrated on the areas where most primary votes would be cast, Rita Clements campaigned in many of the smaller counties, where her past party work had already resulted in personal relationships. As she noted, "It was very helpful to have the political experience I had. A lot of the people in the Republican Party—the workers, the Republican club members—said 'Who is Bill Clements?' They really didn't know. A lot of them knew me better than they knew him."[25]

Reed assumed the role of campaign manager, responsible for overseeing the administrative details of the campaign while Stuart Spencer was the outside campaign consultant and strategist. Spencer and his business partner, Bill Roberts, were also from California and had been involved in numerous Republican campaigns.[26] With many party activists loyal to Hutchison, the Clements campaign relied more extensively on paid staff coordinating elaborate campaign events. As Ann Quirk (later Ann Quirk Erben) recalled, the campaign had to offer a free meal or entertainment to draw a crowd: "No one turned down a free lunch. Clements spent a lot of money to get people to come to events."[27] Spending money drew people to hear the candidate and brought credibility to the Clements effort.

Money was one key ingredient that separated Clements from Hutchison and from previous Republican gubernatorial candidates. At a February news conference in Austin, Clements promised to create a campaign organization in all 254 counties, a claim dismissed as puffery by many in the media. Referring to his predecessors, he said, "Every one of them ran out of gas in the fourth quarter. . . . I'm not going to fold."[28] This became the battle cry throughout the primary as Clements stressed that he, not Hutchison, would have the resources to execute a winning campaign in the fall. According to Francis, the campaign built its entire strategy in the primary on winning in November. There were two good men; the issue that separated them with the primary voters was who could win.[29]

Also in February, Clements commenced a series of meetings with George Strake Jr., a well-known business leader and philanthropist in Houston who described himself as a Goldwater conservative and had been part of the Reagan delegation to Kansas City. After overcoming Strake's initial skepticism, Clements asked him to be his state campaign chairman. Strake said that when he agreed, "That started a life-changing journey for me and my family." Strake would go on to serve as secretary of state in the first Clements administration, followed by five years as the state party chairman.[30]

Clements's support was weak among the small band of Republican elected officials. As a former legislator and state chairman, Hutchison had built up a reservoir of support over several years. State representative Bill Blythe of Houston was the only state legislator to endorse Clements in the primary, while a majority openly backed Hutchison. Many elected officials perceived Clements as part of the big rich, someone who was contemptuous of the political class. Clements viewed himself as a business executive who had run the Pentagon and thus was qualified to run state government. To him Hutchison was merely a state representative. Chase Untermeyer recalled that "When Clements spoke to the Young Adult Republican club in Harris County, he said that state legislators were 'just a dime a dozen,' as a reference to Hutchison's qualifications."[31]

While the primary contest for the gubernatorial nomination was taking place, Republicans had a number of other campaigns to consider. One objective for party leaders was to lessen the divisions from the 1976 presidential contest, not an easy task in a state where, as George H. W. Bush put it, "we have Republicans who still are not speaking to each other because they were on different sides of the Taft-Eisenhower fight in 1952."[32] For Tower to be reelected and other candidates to succeed, a sense of common purpose would need to be established.

Houston attorney James A. Baker III, who had served as campaign manager for Ford after a time as undersecretary of Commerce, was gearing up for a serious effort to become Texas attorney general. As political writer Adam Clymer noted, "the candidacy of James Baker for Attorney General is the clearest example of a party trying to get together. He is close to Mr. Ford and to Mr. Bush as well, but he cultivated and impressed Mr. Barnhart and other Reagan backers and traveled to California to consult with Mr. Reagan himself before announcing his candidacy."[33] As a further indication of the effort to bring disparate forces together, Baker hired as his campaign manager Frank Donatelli, until that time national executive director of the conservative group Young Americans for Freedom.

After an extensive effort at candidate recruitment, the party fielded individuals for twenty-one of the state's twenty-four congressional districts and sixty-eight of the 150 Texas House districts.[34] A number of these districts saw GOP primary contests, the most combative of which was in the 19th congressional district of West Texas, where George W. Bush of Midland was making his first campaign effort against former Odessa mayor Jim Reese and retired lieutenant colonel Joe Hickox of Lubbock. In the May primary Bush came in first but short of a majority, then bested Reese in the subsequent runoff. While Reagan had endorsed Reese, the former California governor quickly attempted to heal any breach. One day after the runoff, Reagan called Bush, saying "George, this is Ron Reagan. Congratulations on proving me wrong.

I just want to let you know that I'll do anything I can to help you win the seat."[35]

What became evident as Republicans campaigned across the state was the unpopularity of President Jimmy Carter, who quickly became "the man Texas Republicans want to run against."[36] Writing in the party's monthly newspaper, Gary Hoitsma claimed, "After one full year in office, President Carter finds himself in serious political trouble. The consensus of journalists and pollsters seems to be that Carter is losing popularity as certain problems continue to plague the administration. . . . At the heart of President Carter's political problems lies a growing feeling on the part of many that he simply 'doesn't have a grasp' on the job."[37] In a memo to the party's candidates, executive director Thorburn urged them to run against Carter. "There is now a broadly perceived lack of confidence in Mr. Carter's ability as our nation's Chief Executive, his Administration in general and its policy initiatives—or lack thereof. The breadth of such perception indicates that the American people, along with many world leaders, now sense a degree of paralysis permeating the Administration."[38]

While most political activists and observers were focused on the 1978 election, behind the scenes two prominent Texas Republicans were preparing for the 1980 presidential contest. George H. W. Bush created his own political action committee, the Fund for Limited Government, and hired a former College Republicans leader, Karl Rove, to staff it. Operating out of Houston, the Fund provided support to other candidates and paid for Bush's political travels.[39] John Connally's efforts were more high-profile as he made campaign appearances and speeches to business associations around the country. With two potential presidential candidates from Texas, home-state support would be divided, while the candidate who had overwhelmingly carried the state in the most recent primary was Reagan.[40]

Meanwhile Texas Democrats were involved with two lively primary contests for governor and US senator. Member of Congress Robert Krueger Jr. of New Braunfels bested former state senator Joe Christie of El Paso for the opportunity to oppose Senator Tower. Governor Briscoe, who had developed a reputation as a moderate conservative, was upended by Attorney General John Hill, who had support from the growing liberal faction in the Texas Democratic Party. Hill made it clear that there would be a changing of the guard in the party: state chairman Calvin Guest "would have to go, and Hill people would take over party leadership posts."[41] The message could not be clearer: conservatives were out and liberals now dominated the state Democratic Party.

There was no upset or surprise in the Republican primary, however. Tower was unopposed for renomination, and Clements breezed to an easy victory over Hutchison by a margin of 115,345 to 38,268.[42] Hutchison had managed to carry twenty-one counties, the largest of which was Bowie County, where a total of 204 votes were cast in the Republican primary. Clements carried 162 counties, and the two tied in an additional three. Indicative of the challenge for any Republican candidate, however, was the fact that no one could be found to conduct a primary in sixty-eight of the state's 254 counties. This lack of GOP infrastructure in roughly one-fourth of all Texas counties would be a major concern for Clements as he approached the November election.

Hutchison quickly endorsed Clements, and the party activists who had supported him came on board with little reluctance. At a May 9 press conference at the Capitol, Clements promised an all-out campaign, saying "my opponent is in for a real fracas. If he thinks this is going to be some kind of cakewalk, I can assure him he's gotten hold of a hot enchilada."[43] An unsigned report on the Hill campaign noted that the Democratic gubernatorial candidate had spent $1.3 million to defeat Briscoe and, like all Democratic candidates for the past hundred years, anticipated an easy win in November. According to the report, "Hill's camp thinks neither Clements nor Tower have a prayer of winning in November.... They should concentrate on Baker's attorney general race for they have a chance to win that one. This probably stems from the fact that Hill despises Mark White."[44]

THE GLASS CEILING CRACKS

With the primary contest behind him, Clements reorganized his campaign operation and brought in Nola Smith Haerle as campaign manager, a position she had held in the 1972 Tower re-election effort. The campaign's policy committee would now comprise Haerle, O'Donnell, Reed, and Spencer, as well as Rita and Bill Clements. For three weeks in June, Clements and his key staff lived at the Sheraton Crest Hotel in Austin. A number of political leaders, including state senator Ike Harris and former gubernatorial candidate Paul Eggers, were involved in the effort to ensure that Clements was prepared for the fall campaign against the Democratic nominee. As Harris recalled, "We talked issues; we talked about problems, strategy. People came in to visit him, too. We set up a lot of meetings with ... well, the first time we went to Austin, we had a meeting of all the so-called establishment lobby. We put on a cocktail party. I introduced him there, because I knew most of them and he didn't."[45]

In early June the five Republican statewide candidates met with state party leaders and discussed a joint effort for victory in November. Each candidate would run his own campaign, and the state party would have the responsibility for a coordinated drive to register new voters and conduct a ballot security program, while the September state convention would highlight the effort to elect the Republican "team for Texas" in November.[46] It was clear that the unpopularity of the Carter administration would be used against the Texas Democratic candidates. At the June SREC meeting in Amarillo, Clements told the party leaders that he would "hang Jimmy Carter around Mr. Hill's neck like a dead chicken."[47]

The Clements campaign determined that their candidate needed to introduce himself to voters and line up support in the state's 230 smaller counties. Francis, who had been an advance worker in the 1968 Eggers campaign for governor, explained how that campaign spent most of the summer months in rural Texas. Out of this discussion, Project 230 became the name given to this targeted approach, and Clements called on Omar Harvey to carry it out.[48] Given the defeat of a conservative Democratic incumbent whose best showing had been in these smaller counties, this approach took on an added importance. Upset with their governor, many conservative Democrats were receptive to appeals from Clements. One key early recruit was David Dean, Briscoe's general counsel, who agreed to serve as deputy campaign manager and helped line up former Briscoe county leaders for the Clements effort. As Francis noted, "David Dean and the Democrats & Independents for Clements effort played a major psychological role in showing the seriousness of the campaign and its chances for victory."[49]

George Bayoud, a recent college graduate, was hired for the general election effort and told to pick up a motor home in Garland and drive it to Austin. The motor home would serve as a movable campaign office for Clements. Bayoud spent the next six weeks driving the motor home to rural areas of the state, where he would make local arrangements and meet Clements, who would fly in for events in the various small towns of Texas. Over the next few weeks, when few were focused on politics, the Clements campaign toured the rural counties, meeting with local officials at county courthouses, visiting the radio stations and weekly newspapers, and holding events to introduce the candidate to voters.[50] As Clements's pollster Lance Tarrance noted, "Bill did something no other Republican candidate had the discipline or the patience to do—to go into the rural counties. It was a brilliant move, to do it in the summer, when the Democratic guard was down and people weren't watching."[51]

One of Clements's first stops in the Project 230 tour was a dinner meeting with some twenty West Texas conservative Democrats at the Uvalde home of

Governor Briscoe's daughter and son-in-law, followed by a reception at the First State Bank of Uvalde, which Briscoe owned. As Carolyn Barta noted, "Even though Briscoe did not endorse Clements, that event sent a powerful message to Briscoe friends and supporters."[52]

When the summer months began, a poll by Tarrance showed Hill with firm support from 40 percent of likely voters and Clements with strong support at 25 percent. Nearly one in four who identified as Republican was drifting to Hill, who was also getting support from 50 percent of those who described themselves as ticket splitters. By the time of a mid-August survey, Clements had improved his showing among Republicans but was still losing half the ticket splitters to Hill. In the mid-September poll, one-third of likely voters remained undecided, but among all voters Clements had closed to within two points of Hill.[53] Clements's summer strategy of concentrating on the smaller towns of Texas seemed to be making inroads into the base of traditional Democratic support. This was not evident, however, to the Hill forces, who were described by some observers as "naively overconfident" and more concerned with transitioning from the office of attorney general to the governor's mansion than with winning an election in November.[54]

By the fall months the Clements campaign claimed that in more than 170 counties former Briscoe county or regional coordinators were now working on Clements's behalf. In addition, Briscoe's daughter and son-in-law openly endorsed Clements, assuring many conservative Democrats that it was okay to vote for the Republican candidate. Meanwhile, Janey Briscoe told a *Dallas Times Herald* reporter that Clements would make a better governor than Hill but that party loyalty alone would cause her to vote for the man who had defeated her husband.[55]

Clements brought on a number of campaign professionals, including Spencer of California and state senator Nancy Brataas of Minnesota, to assist in the general election effort. Brataas had developed a systematic approach to voter identification and turnout using phone banks with both paid and volunteer callers working out of thirty-five locations statewide. After early surveys to identify voter intentions, nearly a million phone calls were made from mid-October to early November geared toward turning out all possible Clements supporters. This effort had a side benefit in that those voting for Clements also had a high likelihood of supporting Tower in his re-election effort. As John Knaggs observed, "The two campaigns appeared to have complemented one another. The phone banks of the Clements campaign energized the urban conservatives and Tower's old ties to the Mexican-American community prevented that door from being closed to Clements as solidly Democratic."[56]

At the 1978 state convention in Dallas, Barnhart was opposed for re-election as state chairman by John R. Butler Jr. of Houston. Butler, an oil industry executive, was the son of J. R. "Butch" Butler, whom O'Donnell had chosen to head up Texans for Reagan in the 1968 campaign. Although both candidates had ties to Reagan, Barnhart was clearly the candidate of the Reagan forces leading up to the 1980 presidential contest, while backers of both Bush and Connally tended to line up behind Butler. The final vote was not close, as Barnhart carried twenty-two senatorial districts, receiving 1023.8 votes, to Butler's nine districts and 600.2 votes. In winning the 1978 race Barnhart picked up majorities from nine senatorial districts that had supported Hutchison at the previous convention, adding to the thirteen he carried in both races. Butler was strongest in the Dallas area, while Barnhart's support was more evenly dispersed. The convention vote would not be a predictor of the 1980 presidential primary, however, as Bush would subsequently carry many of the areas that had supported Barnhart at the state convention.[57] Also elected in a somewhat closer contest for vice chairman was Dorothy Doehne of San Antonio. Doehne defeated SREC member Amalie Cobb of Beaumont, a Bush supporter whose husband, Howell Cobb, was later named a federal district court judge. Doehne would continue to serve as vice chairman under both Barnhart and Chester Upham until May 1983.

Member of Congress Jack Kemp was the featured speaker at the convention, but the delegates also heard from all the statewide candidates, as well as Representatives Archer and Collins. Tower exhorted the dedicated Republican activists by calling on them to go "once more, my friends, into the breach." The program included workshops on various aspects of campaign organization, and Nancy Palm came out of retirement to head up the statewide voter registration effort labeled Volunteers Organized for Trustworthy Elections.[58] The delegates approved a rule establishing a presidential primary and apportioning delegates by congressional district, calling on the party to conduct a primary election "regardless of whether or not the legislature approves a separate primary law."[59]

With the summer outreach to small towns completed, Bayoud was assigned to do advance work for the campaign in the larger cities. He recalled one event in particular, a major campaign rally in September on the University of Texas campus in Austin with Ford and Clements that drew some four thousand people. Ensuring a friendly crowd for two Republican politicians on a campus in liberal-dominated Austin was a major accomplishment for the campaign. Bayoud had been president of the Texas Cowboys while at the university and was able to draw on their members for assistance with the campus event. After the rally Ford and Clements flew to Dallas for a fundraising dinner where they joined other Republican dignitaries.[60]

Three days after the convention the Clements campaign carried out the largest and most financially successful dinner in Texas political history when some 1,300 individuals took part in a $1,000 a plate dinner at the new Hyatt Regency hotel in downtown Dallas. Among the head table participants were Ford, Connally, Reagan, George H. W. Bush, and Anne Armstrong. In his remarks Ford called Clements "the best general manager of the Defense Department I have seen in my 18 years in Washington. If Bill can do that job so effectively, he is qualified to be chief executive of the great Lone Star State of Texas."[61]

As the election approached, *Texas Monthly* released its final poll. Hill was ahead of Clements by a margin of forty-five to thirty-four, with roughly one-fifth of likely voters still undecided. Hill felt he had an insurmountable lead and claimed, "There is no way I will lose. It's all over. We think we have enough votes to win regardless of the turnout. The polls show I'm going straight up." Hill's own internal poll, released on October 31, had him ahead by a margin of 51 to 35 percent.[62]

Meanwhile, Tarrance was using what was at that time a new technique in polling called tracking. A small number of respondents were called each night and then the results from five nights were rolled into a statewide survey, so any possible changes over time could be seen. "When the tracking polls showed Clements faltering in the last week in the Dallas–Fort Worth area, he added a visit to the area and stepped up advertising there."[63] All across the state, the phone banks were calling identified supporters and urging them to vote. The state party had organized groups of attorneys in key areas across the state to ensure a fair count was made. As Election Day ended, O'Donnell and Francis were up almost all night calling lawyers to keep the vote count going. In one county in Southeast Texas the sheriff had closed down the count and taken the uncounted ballots home. The campaign got a court order to restart the count. With Democrats in control of nearly all county courthouses, such an effort was mandatory.[64]

On the morning after the election, the final results showed that both Tower and Clements had squeezed out victories. Both candidates carried the Big 6 counties by slightly more than fifty thousand votes while breaking even in the twenty-nine suburban counties surrounding those urban enclaves. Small town Texas counties remained Democratic, but not as strongly as had been the case in all previous elections save the Nixon landslide. While Tower lost those rural areas to Krueger by 56,774 votes, Clements cut his loss to 48,777. The outcome was basically settled in the other smaller metropolitan counties around the state, where Tower built a lead of 11,911 votes and Clements beat Hill by 10,622. The end result was a statewide Tower margin of 12,227 and a Clements win by 16,909 out of nearly 2.3 million votes cast. Without the strong gubernatorial campaign of Clements and its extensive get-out-the-vote efforts, it is possible that Tower would not have been re-elected.

Tower did much better than many political observers and the media expected in the Rio Grande Valley. According to Bob Estrada, Tower had delivered for years to those areas of the state and not merely given lip service to them. In the three most populous counties (Cameron, Hidalgo, and Nueces), Tower won 47.2 percent of the vote, compared to the 40.5 percent he had received in his 1972 campaign, resulting in a net deficit of only 5,541 votes from these traditionally Democratic and heavily Hispanic counties.[65]

Leading the Hispanic effort for Tower was a campaign section called Nosotros con Tower. The senator received an award from the GI Forum and a warm reception when he spoke at a LULAC convention. Tower's media guru, Lionel Sosa, had put together an effective Hispanic media campaign that helped increase support for Tower. The firm even produced a corrido called "El Corrido de John Tower" that sang his praises in Spanish.[66]

A postelection analysis for the Clements campaign indicated he was able to attract support from 83 percent of self-identified Republicans, 44 percent of conservative Democrats, and 58 percent of those who viewed themselves as ticket splitters. It appeared to many observers that Hill gave away the ball game by acting as if he were governor after winning the primary, appearing arrogant and overconfident while the Democratic organization became complacent. According to Hill's campaign manager John Rogers and consultant Jack Martin, there was a postprimary complacency that resulted in the Hill campaign never taking the offensive. With their internal polls showing an 11 percent Hill lead, the campaign saw no need to take Clements seriously. In the end, the Clements operation was able to ensure a high GOP turnout while Democrats were not motivated to vote for a candidate expected to win easily.[67]

By breaking the glass ceiling that had prevented Republicans from winning the governor's mansion for over one hundred years, Clements had introduced a new level of party competition in Texas. As Sean Cunningham concluded, "The victory was a watershed for Republican acceptability in Texas. Fueled largely by the momentum of Reagan's 1976 bid and Texans' dissatisfaction with Carter, Clements hastened the reconciliation of divisions that had left the Texas GOP temporarily fractured after 1976." While Clements experienced the victory, "Reagan, more than any other political figure in the state, tore down the barriers of loyalty and tradition that had kept many Texans voting Democrat for so long."[68]

On the day after the election, Clements held a news conference at the

Capitol. The governor-elect had a hard time even getting in the door because of the mob of reporters who had showed up to hear the first Republican governor in 104 years.[69] Clements summarized the situation by declaring, "My election marks a new day for Texas. We literally have turned a page in history and the political scene in Texas will never be the same."[70] As Rita Clements noted after the election, "For a number of years you have seen these conservative Democrats and independents voting for a Republican president or for Senator Tower, but they hadn't made that big break and voted Republican on the state level. This year they did make that break for the first time and it will have a tremendous impact."[71]

While the other statewide candidates were not successful, Baker ran a competitive race against Mark White for attorney general. As White recounted a few years later, "Jim was an honorable fellow.... He did a good job. He ran a strong campaign. It was one in which I was running scared every day because he was the best candidate I think the Republicans had ever put out down there."[72] Less than three years after the campaign, Baker would become chief of staff to a Republican president.

Meanwhile, the party doubled its number of members of Congress by electing Tom Loeffler to the seat vacated by Krueger and returning Ron Paul to a district he had previously won in 1976. Four other congressional candidates came ever so close but fell short of victory, as Tom Pauken lost by 852 votes to Representative Jim Mattox, while Jack Burgess, George W. Bush, and Leo Berman all received over 46 percent of the vote in open districts. Texas would send nine freshmen members to the House of Representatives after the 1978 elections, including five conservative Democrats (Phil Gramm, Kent Hance, Joe Wyatt, Charles Stenholm, and Marvin Leath), three of whom would become Republicans in the next decade. In local races, four GOP county judges were re-elected, in Harris, Collin, Kerr, and Lipscomb counties, while five new Republicans took over in Midland, Randall, Smith, Gray, and Mason counties.

Republicans also made a net gain of three state representatives when Ed Emmett won a Harris County district, Bob Leonard and Bob Ware were victorious in Tarrant County, and Tom DeLay picked up a district in suburban Fort Bend County, while Buzz Robnett kept the seat vacated by Joe Robbins of Lubbock in Republican hands. S. L. Abbott was the only incumbent to lose, having been ousted in a close vote from his El Paso area district. Soon thereafter Gerald Geistweidt won a special election to a seat representing thirteen West Central Texas counties, and Representatives Anita Hill of Garland and Clay Smothers of Dallas switched parties, bringing the GOP total to twenty-five House members. The party's state senate representation increased to five after Bill Braecklein of Dallas became a Republican.

The Emmett election is a clear example of how the party was able to attract young, aggressive candidates who wanted to influence the direction of state policy. Emmett had considered the possibility of a campaign before, and as 1978 approached, he decided to run against state representative Joe Allen, a Democrat who had never been opposed by a Republican. Emmett determined that only a grassroots campaign could take advantage of Allen's lack of campaign exposure in past elections. He knocked on 19,404 doors, taking each precinct and neighborhood seriously in an area of northeastern Harris County not known for its GOP support. When he met with the state party staff, he was told that his district was not winnable and was therefore not targeted for support. Emmett then met with the Associated Republicans of Texas (ART) and convinced them to support him if he could raise ten thousand dollars. He borrowed that sum from his father-in-law, ART made the promised contribution, and Emmett paid back his campaign loan. All told he spent some $26,000 on the campaign to defeat a twelve-year incumbent Democrat. Emmett is proud of the fact that "Barbara Bush agreed to personally support three candidates, one of whom was me, for whom she sponsored coffees. The other two candidates she supported lost, George W. Bush and Jim Baker." Two years later Emmett returned the favor and was one of two state representatives to endorse George H. W. Bush for president at a time when most Texas Republican state legislators were backing Connally. Emmett later served three terms as Harris County judge.[73]

State chairman Barnhart viewed the 1978 elections as a turning point in the history of Texas politics. "The gains made by Republican candidates at every level point to the undeniable fact that our party has come of age in Texas—traditionally one of the most powerful Democratic bastions in the nation. 1978 will be seen as the dawn of a viable two-party system in our state, and Texas stands to benefit immeasurably from it."[74] The year 1978 began a period best described as a two-party interlude during which neither party could take victory for granted and Republicans came to be competitive for more and more elective positions.[75]

When Clements took office, one reporter spoke about the challenge facing the new governor: "He knows the Republican party's fate may very well be resting upon his shoulders. It's taken more than one hundred years for a Republican to win the governorship in Texas and if Clements bungles the job, it might be another hundred years before they get another shot at it."[76] Looking back several years later, Carolyn Barta concluded that Clements showed "that not only could a Republican be elected governor but he could function in the traditionally Democratic environment that was state government.... His ability to deal successfully with conservative Democrats created the environment that made conservatives comfortable in switching parties. As a result, he hastened the emergence of Republicans down to the courthouse level."[77]

One of Clements's first critical decisions was whom to name as secretary of state, perhaps the most visible of the appointed state positions. After serving as campaign chairman, George Strake was prepared to return to his business and community commitments in Houston. While on a much-needed family vacation, however, Strake received a call from the new governor asking him to be secretary of state. When they met again in Austin, Strake tried to beg off, but realizing the historical significance of a position once held by Sam Houston, Strake agreed to take on the assignment.[78]

A NEW GOVERNOR TAKES OFFICE

With Clements in the governor's mansion, a change in the dynamics of Republican politics was evident. Traditionally a governor controlled the state Democratic Party machinery and named the state chairman. While the new governor was busy organizing his administration, some in the GOP who were opposed to the conservatives now in charge of the party felt that Clements should control the state party organization. These individuals were concerned that the party under the leadership of Barnhart would work to ensure that Reagan's backers controlled the state's delegation to the 1980 Republican National Convention. The drive to hamper Barnhart's influence united the supporters of both potential presidential candidates from Texas, George H. W. Bush and John Connally.

As had been the case in previous years, much of this opposition to Barnhart, the former Harris County GOP chairman, took on a Dallas-versus-Houston tone. Indeed, his major opponents on the SREC were from Dallas, including one who told Rita Clements, "It is my plan to continue to weaken his credibility." When Barnhart sought approval from the SREC for obtaining a $75,000 loan to consolidate debts remaining from the 1978 campaign, the anti-Barnhart faction could garner only nineteen votes (out of sixty-four members) against the proposal.[79] The efforts against Barnhart would continue without the governor's direct involvement for, as one SREC member advised, "We believe that it would be judicious for Clements not to take any role or participate in any political controversies within the SREC at this time."[80]

Although it was not directly involved in party politics, the Governor

Clements Committee was established after the election as an independent group whose main responsibility was to raise funds to pay off the campaign's $7.2 million debt. Interest alone on the campaign debt was mounting at approximately $500,000 a year, making the need to raise more funds urgent. The task could be more easily accomplished with Clements as governor rather than a candidate. Shortly after the election Clements met with Jim Francis, who had been finance director in the campaign, telling him, "I want you to be in charge of politics for me and you're in charge of everything in Texas and Tom Reed is in charge of everything outside the state."[81] In one of his first decisions as head of the Governor Clements Committee, Francis retained Karl Rove's company to be in charge of direct mail for the committee, while raising major dollars became the responsibility of a staff that included Herb Butrum, Pat Oles, Milo Burdette, and George Bayoud. One year later, when Francis left to return to Dallas, Bayoud, at the age of twenty-five, was named to succeed him. Having paid off the 1978 campaign debt, the committee was able to move on to other challenges.[82]

The second challenge for the committee was to use the influence of the governor's office to develop the political muscle needed for changing the state's politics. Tobin Armstrong, husband of Anne Armstrong, was recruited to head up appointments and was given a mandate to require a political clearance on all appointees to ensure that they supported the governor and to build credentials for future candidates. As Francis recalled, "With appointments, we started getting Republican judges, with a particular emphasis on Dallas and Houston and the other metropolitan areas." The strategy was to crack the local courthouse as part of a systematic approach to changing the state's politics and creating a two-party state.[83]

Once again, behind much of the conflict within the state party organization was presidential politics. After Reagan's resounding primary victory in 1976, his supporters had consolidated a majority on the SREC and in state party operations when Barnhart became chairman. Both George H. W. Bush and Connally had strong advocates on the SREC and among the party activists who did not want to see the state's delegates awarded to Reagan in 1980. One possibility to stop Reagan was for Clements to launch a favorite-son candidacy, the approach that had been taken by Tower in 1968. To this end, he had sent a request to party leaders asking them not to "ally themselves with other political operations." But as one SREC member advised the governor, a decision on a possible favorite-son candidacy would need to be made in early 1979. "The problem seems to be that the Reagan people are putting their campaign machinery in place and are applying a great deal of pressure on the former Reagan leaders to continue to support Reagan." According to this analysis, "It is obvious that the Reagan campaign has a full head of steam. If a favorite son activity is to succeed, it must be started immediately. However, such an activity bears many serious risks."[84]

Throughout the next few months Clements was more concerned with state government matters and his relations with the Texas legislature than with any possible 1980 presidential politics. Not only was he confronted with an overwhelmingly Democratic state House and Senate, but his business background and lack of appreciation for legislative norms sometimes caused further difficulties in his first year in office. His difficult relationship with the legislature was compounded by his veto of an innocuous bill changing the dates for deer season in Comal County, a bill filed by well-liked Democratic state representative Bennie Bock. Not only did Clements veto the bill, he did so when the legislature was still in session, thus allowing the House and Senate to override his veto. The small contingent of Republicans thought that they should support the governor of their party on the veto, even though in the internal culture of the Texas House this placed them against the popular and powerful conservative Democrat who introduced the bill. Clements's veto was indeed overridden, and those in control of the Texas legislature had sent the new governor an important message.[85]

By April an opportunity arose for Clements to replace a strong Reagan partisan with someone more aligned with himself as chairman of the state party. When a vacancy occurred in the Texas Highways and Public Transportation Commission, the governor nominated Barnhart. This was a natural appointment for Barnhart, who had been in the construction business and had long expressed an interest in transportation issues. Barnhart informed Republican leaders of his nomination and urged the SREC to elect Chester R. Upham Jr. of Mineral Wells, the governor's choice, to replace him.[86] Two weeks later the Texas Senate confirmed Barnhart's appointment, and he resigned as state chairman. Having re-elected the state's senior senator for a fourth term and elected a governor, Barnhart could point with pride to his accomplishments as state chairman: "Our Texas Party is organizationally sound, economically stable, blessed with one of the finest headquarters staffs in the nation, and—so importantly—structured and governed according to By-Laws which are workable, fair, and neutral."[87]

On May 19, in a voice vote with no other candidates, the executive committee elected Chet Upham as the new state chairman. Upham was a fifty-four-year-old former county chairman, SREC member, and state finance chair, positions reflecting a lifetime of Republican party involvement. Co-owner of Upham Oil & Gas Company, he was at the time serving as president of Texas Independent Producers and Royalty Owners (TIPRO), a major force in the state for independent oil operators and lease owners. Furthermore, his wife, Virginia, was currently serving on the SREC. The transition from Barnhart to Upham could not have been smoother. While the party was now led by an individual of the governor's choosing, Upham retained all the state party's staff and the budget under which it was operating. In terms of presidential politics, the former Reagan cochair of 1976 had been replaced by someone who had a long-standing friendship with George H. W. Bush but who pledged to remain neutral in the upcoming presidential contest.

THE PRESIDENTIAL CONTEST GEARS UP

Presidential politics played an important part in the deliberations of the Texas legislature during its 1979 regular session. After his close convention defeat in 1976, most political observers expected Reagan to seek the presidency again and, in all likelihood, to be the frontrunner for the Republican nomination. Among those challenging him, however, would be two Texans. George H. W. Bush was actively organizing for his anticipated campaign, while John Connally had made it known that he would seek the nomination and was raising considerable campaign funds from inside Texas and elsewhere. Also joining the field were senators Howard Baker, Bob Dole, and Larry Pressler; representatives John Anderson and Phil Crane; and business executive Ben Fernandez. Meanwhile, on the Democratic side, Governor Jerry Brown of California and Senator Edward Kennedy were planning challenges to President Carter for the 1980 nomination.

In late April Bush formally announced, claiming, "I believe the record of the Carter administration is so impotent that any Republican candidate will have a good shot. I believe I have the best shot."[88] Soon thereafter Bush announced a national steering committee that included Texas party leaders Flo Atherton, Albert Fay, Ambassador John Hurd, and former member of Congress Alan Steelman; sports figures Bob Lilly and Nolan Ryan; business leaders Norman Brinker, Will Farish, Ray Hunt, and Ben Love; and University of Texas law professor Charles Alan Wright.[89] Other key supporters were Mary Teeple of Austin, who had known the Bush family since growing up in Midland, and Houston attorney Hal DeMoss, later to be named to the 5th circuit, U.S. Court of Appeals. Although Bush was personally known to most active Texas Republicans, only two state legislators, Ed Emmett of Kingwood and Chase Untermeyer of Houston, were willing to endorse him at a time when most of the GOP delegation backed Connally or Reagan.[90]

The pending lively battle on the Republican side—with two Texans and

Reagan especially—posed a serious challenge to continued conservative dominance of the Texas Democratic Party. With so many conservatives attracted to the Republican candidates, conservative legislators feared defeat at the hands of liberal challengers in the Democratic primary. Those elected to the Texas legislature in 1980 would have the responsibility of redistricting the state, potentially further affecting conservative Democratic influence. Finally, those conservatives who voted in a GOP primary could not participate in Democratic precinct and county conventions; the result would be an advantage for liberals in their efforts to control the party machinery.

To deal with this problem of possibly losing conservative influence, Lieutenant Governor Bill Hobby and House Speaker Billy Clayton advocated a split-primary bill establishing a presidential primary in early March open to all voters, with the regular state primary moved back to July. This arrangement would allow Texans to vote in one party's primary in March and another party's primary in July. Benefiting from this divided primary would be not only the conservative Democratic legislators and party officials but also Connally, whose conservative Democratic supporters could vote for him in the GOP presidential primary and return to support other conservatives in the later Democratic state primary.

Opposition to such a plan came from all the other Republican presidential candidates and many liberal Democrats. The Texas AFL-CIO and the SREC's committee on legislative action both issued statements in support of a same-day primary, as did the Republican Party of Texas. As the official GOP newspaper editorialized: "Separating the presidential from the state primary, allowing crossover voting, moving the primary date closer to the general election—these are nice sounding but misguided proposals now before the legislature which threaten the Republican Party's presidential primary plan as adopted by a unanimous vote at last year's state convention."[91] Nevertheless, in Hobby and Clayton the split-primary proposal had the support of the two most powerful forces in the Texas legislature. Moreover, according to some sources, Clements could never accept why a separate primary was bad for the Republican Party. According to then–state representative Untermeyer, "all that it would have taken was for him to say he would veto the bill," and it would have died a quick death.[92]

As the legislative session approached its end, it became apparent that those opposed to a split primary could muster enough votes to prevent it from receiving the two-thirds vote required to bring it to the Senate floor. Hobby then attempted to call up another bill that did not include the split primary but had a broadly defined caption. Once it passed through the Senate, Clayton would have it amended on the House floor to create a split primary and send it back to the Senate for concurrence, where only a majority vote would be needed.[93] At this point twelve liberal Democratic senators went into hiding, thereby breaking the quorum needed to conduct Senate business. They soon acquired the name Killer Bees, a designation originally given by Hobby to a group who filibustered against a strip-mining bill. As he later recalled, "I started calling them the 'Killer Bees' because no one knew when they would strike next."[94]

While the twelve senators remained in hiding for four days, Hobby called on the Texas Rangers to locate the recalcitrant legislators while threatening to take away their committee assignments or even declare their seats vacant. Finally a deal was reached, and the missing senators returned while the concept of a split primary lacked the needed two-thirds to bring it to a vote. At a news conference upon their return to the Senate, Killer Bee Carl Parker of Port Arthur noted, "They talk of how embarrassing this is, how the Senate looks. Well, how does the whole state look when the rules are changed specifically for one presidential candidate (Connally)."[95] Meanwhile Senator Betty Andujar, then also serving as Republican National Committeewoman, saw the Killer Bee episode as precipitating the "final transition of power in the Texas Democratic Party from the conservatives to the total liberal wing."[96]

Through the remainder of the year the Texas Republican Party placed a major emphasis on volunteer training and preparations for the 1980 presidential election. While three-day campaign management seminars were held in Austin in June and September, fourteen precinct organization workshops were conducted around the state, and the Texas Federation of Republican Women held their own campaign volunteer workshops in El Paso, San Antonio, and Houston. To provide additional financial support to legislative and local candidates, the state party's campaign committee created the Texas Club for donors who gave three hundred dollars a year. Members received an insider newsletter called the Lone Star Political Report to keep them informed of developments in key state legislative campaigns. All proceeds were used for direct contributions to targeted candidates.

The party also witnessed three state legislators join their ranks as state senator Bill Braecklein and representatives Anita Hill and Clay Smothers, all of Dallas County, became Republicans. In November Clements named Will Garwood to become the first Republican to serve on the Texas Supreme Court. Garwood, whose father previously served on the court and in retirement became treasurer of the state GOP, filled the unexpired term of Sam D. Johnson, whom President Carter had appointed to the 5th US Circuit Court of Appeals. Garwood was required to seek election in 1980 and came within a few thousand votes of retaining his position on the court. Subsequently he too would receive an appointment to the 5th Circuit Court of Appeals.

In preparing for the next election, the state party developed a detailed strategy report showing Republican progress to date and outlining why the state was at a turning point in its political history. The party's plan of action centered on four priorities: building a strong grassroots organization, attracting new support, recruiting and training candidates, and promoting winning campaigns. To achieve these objectives, executive director Wayne Thorburn urged party leaders to adopt an aggressive and comprehensive program for 1980. He saw the task as deciding "whether the political party organization will play a role in the election process or become irrelevant to the election of Republican candidates."[97]

According to Thorburn's analysis:

> More and more people call themselves Independent voters and say that the parties are unimportant organizations. They vote for "the man" and not for the Party. They give their money to candidates they like rather than to us. At the same time, successful candidates believe that they were elected on their own merits, without any important assistance from the Party. They set up their own organizations, raise their own funds, and run their own campaigns. And, the simple truth is too often that this is the only way they could win.
>
> If we believe that the party should be an important force in politics, that there should be responsibility in government, that a party label means something more than merely a label, then we must provide the services needed by our candidates and become an essential element in their campaigns. Simply stated, do we want to help elect our candidates or do we want them to run solely on their own, depend on other interest groups for support, and feel little allegiance to the Republican Party as an organization? Moreover, if we fail to adequately assist our candidates and they lose, it is the Republican Party which will take the blame and the role of the party organization will be discredited."[98]

When the SREC met in December, it adopted a comprehensive plan of action and the budget required to carry it out. Party leaders realized that 1980 could well be an opportunity for significant gains for Texas Republicans.

As the year began, the state party continued its training and outreach efforts. In February several state legislative candidates participated in a candidate workshop in Austin where the speakers included Karl Rove, then serving on the governor's staff, and Rick Rodgers, political director for the party. In March and July campaign management seminars were held for those interested in working on congressional and state legislative campaigns. Meanwhile the Mexican American Republicans of Texas held their February conference in Austin, with remarks by Bob Estrada, state director for Senator Tower, and G. G. Garcia, special assistant to Governor Clements. Garcia advised the members, "Mexican Americans must look beyond Clements and Tower and build a permanent organization so that politicians will actually seek their backing."[99]

To reach African-American voters, the party distributed issues of the *Texas Republican Alternative*, which included a list of thirty appointments made by Clements in his first six months in office. Another article discussed the dedication of a historical marker commemorating Norris Wright Cuney at Prairie View A&M University. At the ceremony then–state chairman Ray Barnhart and Jim Bowie, chair of the Black Republican Council, described the role of Cuney as the only African-American to serve as state chairman of a Texas political party. As Barnhart stated, the marker was "dedicated to the belief that the voters of no group of Texans should be considered automatically in any one party's column and to providing all voters with a strong alternative to the Democratic Party here in Texas."[100]

NOMINATING A PRESIDENT

By the filing deadline for the 1980 primary, four presidential candidates met the requirements to be placed on the ballot: George H. W. Bush, Connally, Reagan, and Howard Baker. Much of the discussion, however, centered on the possibility of another candidate entering the race and one or more of the four possibly dropping out. Tom Reed, a Californian who had been a key advisor in Clements's election, was now serving as head of the Draft Ford Committee. Reed spoke with Clements, who reported, "I've been talking with some of the other governors. None of us think Reagan can win in the fall. Let's get Jerry Ford back in."[101] In early March the Texas governor made a secret trip to California to meet with the former president and three Ford advisors to discuss the possibility of Ford entering the race. Once back in Texas, Clements contacted Connally, who was considering withdrawing from the contest, to see if he would serve as a stand-in for Ford on the Texas ballot. Connally advised him "there wasn't any way that President Ford can have a surrogate and get any delegate vote in Texas."[102] While some Republicans were urging Ford to enter the race, the simple arithmetic of delegate votes made its possibility of success highly unlikely. Any roadmap to gaining the nomination depended on gaining delegates from Texas and Ohio as well as winning the winner-take-all primary in California against former governor Reagan. In addition to meeting with Clements, Connally was reported to have discouraged Ohio governor Jim Rhodes from any effort to back a Ford candidacy.[103]

On March 5 Baker removed himself from the nominating contest, and three days later Connally officially dropped out of the race also. One week later Ford made public his decision not to seek the nomination. While many now believed Reagan would win the nomination, he still faced challenges nationally from John Anderson and Bush, but only from Bush in Texas.[104]

National Committeeman Angelo was devoting almost full time to the Reagan campaign and organized a news conference at DFW Airport, where Connally endorsed Reagan. The two former governors then attended an airport reception and traveled to Longview for a thousand-dollar campaign fundraiser. Angelo viewed the Connally endorsement as "a nice thing overall, both for the primary and the general. It makes Reagan's candidacy that much stronger."[105]

Prior to the May 3 primary, both Reagan and Bush made campaign appearances in several visits to Texas, on one of which they each met with Governor Clements in Austin. It was rumored that Reagan was considering Clements for vice president, but it was quickly denied by all concerned.[106] Meanwhile, Bush made a major push to win his home state as a last-ditch effort to be competitive with Reagan. The Bush campaign spent some seven hundred thousand dollars in the state on a television blitz, while Reagan, approaching the cap on his spending limit, devoted only two hundred thousand dollars to the Texas effort.[107] The spending disparity and the general consensus that Reagan had locked up the nomination caused consternation and concern for Ernest Angelo, then serving as both Republican National Committeeman and head of the Texas Reagan effort.

The May 3 primary set a record for turnout among Republicans, with more than 525,000 participating. Reagan's support throughout rural and smaller urban areas of the state allowed him to carry most of the state's congressional districts handily and to capture the three delegates allocated to each district. Bush's support was more concentrated in the Dallas, Austin, and Houston areas. The statewide vote total was Reagan 268,169 and Bush 250,219, a margin of only 17,950 votes. In terms of what counted, however, Reagan was awarded sixty-one delegates to Bush's nineteen.

Once the presidential primary was over, Texas Republicans fell in line behind Reagan. As state chairman Chet Upham noted, "I personally feel Ronald

Reagan will be our nominee. I do not see any way that he will not be. Reagan has it wound up."[108] On Monday Clements enthusiastically endorsed Reagan and predicted he would carry Texas and win the White House.[109] In addition to the presidential contest, the same-day primary included a record number of candidates for congressional and state legislative positions. Republicans contested eighteen of the twenty-four congressional districts, eighty-eight of the 150 Texas House seats, and thirteen of the sixteen state Senate positions on the ballot that year.

When some six thousand Republicans met in Houston for the June state convention, the prevailing attitude was unity, a point stressed not only by the speakers—such as Tower, Clements, and members of Congress Jack Kemp, Barry Goldwater Jr., Bill Archer, Jim Collins, and Ron Paul—but also by the state party leadership. As Jane Ely reported, "State party chief Chet Upham led the unity front, with Republican National Committee members Ernest Angelo and State Senator Betty Andujar and SREC vice chairman Dorothy Doehne closing the ranks with him. Upham, Doehne, and Angelo—also the leader of the Ronald Reagan forces in Texas—presented their united front at an afternoon press conference where each stoutly maintained the choice of a running mate should be left entirely to Reagan, the certain party nominee for president."[110] In the spirit of unity, national committeeman Angelo was re-elected to another four-year term, while Fran Chiles replaced Senator Andujar as committeewoman.

A fun convention event that foreshadowed the coming election was the Peanut Stomp, including a Democratic Party Platform Toss, in which a number of Republican state representatives competed for the golden cow chip prize. The honor was won by Lubbock's Buzz Robnett. Donkey dartboards were also available for use by attendees, and entertainment was provided by the Houston Oilers' Derrick Dolls and the Clogg Hoppers dance troupe.[111] On a more serious note, delegates participated in a series of workshops with topics ranging from national issues to nuts-and-bolts political organizing. The delegates formally elected the eighty delegates and eighty alternates who would represent the state at the national convention that summer in Detroit.

When the Texas delegation reached the national convention, they found mostly a celebration. Unlike the situation four years earlier, Reagan had sewn up the nomination, and the only suspense was over the vice presidential selection. After much maneuvering around the possibility of Ford as vice president or an even more unrealistic copresidency, Reagan broke precedent and announced his choice of George H. W. Bush ahead of the customary point in the convention schedule. With Clements as chief executive, Angelo as delegation chair, Tower as platform committee chair, and Bush as the vice presidential nominee, Texas's key place in national Republican politics was evident to all.[112]

RECLAIMING THE WHITE HOUSE

Next up on the schedule was a second state convention, held in San Antonio in early September. Heading the lineup of speakers was vice presidential nominee Bush, as well as Connally, Tower, Clements, Anne Armstrong, and Senator Orrin Hatch of Utah. Both state chairman Upham and vice chairman Doehne were re-elected unanimously. Perhaps the more important aspect of the gathering, however, was noted by James McCrory of the *San Antonio Express-News*: "A strong Hispanic presence emerged as the most significant development at the Republican State Convention in San Antonio."[113]

Ten days after the September convention, Reagan kicked off his effort to carry Texas with an appearance in San Antonio on September 16, Mexican Independence Day. He was joined at the event by Senator Tower and former presidential candidate Benjamin Fernandez. The campaign's Hispanic outreach effort included a number of appearances around the state by Columba Bush and television personalities Desi Arnaz and Joe Santos, as well as Fernandez and El Paso native Fernando Oaxaca, a leader of the Republican National Hispanic Assembly.[114]

The Lone Star Tribute was held in Houston to raise funds for the fall campaign, ending up with more than $2.8 million for the Texas Victory Committee, the coordinated statewide campaign effort. Some 2,500 supporters heard from Reagan, Bush, Ford, Clements, Tower, Connally, and Armstrong. As the party's fundraising director, Jan Naylor, noted, the event "made political history in the U.S. in that it was the biggest political fundraiser ever held."[115] Just prior to the dinner, some four thousand attended a noontime rally on the University of Texas at Austin campus to hear from Ford and Bush.

Between proceeds from the dinner and other fundraising, over $3 million were raised for the first statewide Victory Committee, an organizational fixture of all elections since then. This allowed the campaign to establish volunteer phone banks throughout the state, mount a coordinated ballot security program, send millions of direct mail pieces, and undertake Victory Roundup tours across Texas.[116] Former US attorney John Clark of San Antonio headed up the ballot security effort, while a GOP voter registration drive in targeted counties produced 271,000 new voters. Reagan undertook a two-day swing through San Antonio, Harlingen, Corpus Christi, and Houston, following up on a previous trip to El Paso. Meanwhile Tower and Clements led late October visits to most major metropolitan areas while television personalities Desi Arnaz and Joe Santos were the featured participants in a Hispanic-oriented tour of South and West Texas.

Angelo, Texas campaign manager for the Reagan-Bush ticket, concluded "This is the best organization ever put together for a statewide campaign. We're not falling all over ourselves."[117] Peter O'Donnell Jr. came out of political retirement to serve as comptroller for the Victory Committee. As Rove recalled, "Every expenditure had to be approved in advance with a paper trail, so there were no surprises. Everything in the campaign had to be measured against goals, from the number of volunteers recruited for each phone in each phone center to the number of county steering committee members to the number of yard signs displayed in each target precinct.... We set goals for everything, then set things right where we were falling short."[118]

To reach out to all possible supporters, Democrats and Independents for Reagan-Bush was formed, headed by former governors Allan Shivers and Preston Smith. Most of its prominent members were conservatives who no longer had influence within the Texas Democratic Party and were making the initial move toward affiliating with the GOP. As the state party's executive director noted, "Frankly, we cannot continue to grow and win elections without attracting literally thousands of involved Texans who previously called themselves Democrats. I truly believe that we have become the conservative party in Texas, the party of the future."[119]

The Texas Reagan campaign contracted for a voter survey in late September and early October. When the results came back, they showed Reagan ahead of Carter by some fifteen to seventeen points. Angelo and Clements decided not to release the results out of a concern that overconfidence might lessen the commitment of volunteers. The following week, CBS news released the results of their poll and declared the Texas race too close to call, with Carter slightly ahead.[120]

In a heavy turnout, the Reagan-Bush ticket carried 56 percent of the vote in the general election, winning by a margin of more than 700,000 votes. The 1980 victory for the presidential ticket was a turnabout in Texas politics. From the Eisenhower victories in the 1950s up until the late 1970s, the Republican percentage in Texas had always been below the national GOP percentage. From Reagan's win to the present, the Republican presidential ticket has done better in Texas than the national average and has carried the state in each of those elections.

Down ballot, Jack Fields added to the GOP congressional delegation by defeating Democratic member of Congress Bob Eckhardt in Houston, while four new Republicans were elected to the Texas Senate: Mike Richards in Houston and Buster Brown from Lake Jackson, along with Dee Travis and John Leedom from Dallas County. Thirteen new state representatives produced a 50 percent increase in the party's Texas House delegation, while the number of Republican county officials nearly doubled, to 166 statewide. Unfortunately, Will Garwood, whom Clements had appointed to the Texas Supreme Court, lost an exceedingly close race, and Bob Price was unable to gain re-election to the Panhandle state Senate seat.

All in all, as state chairman Upham observed, "1980 was the year the Republican Party of Texas solidified the two-party status of Texas. Great gains were made in our congressional delegation, our state senate and legislature. ... The reluctance to 'Vote Republican for a Change' is fading fast."[121] Over the next few years, Reagan's presidency would produce even more Republican support. With control of both the governor's mansion and the White House, things were looking up for Texas Republicans as a new decade began.

TEN

THE REAGAN-BUSH YEARS

It was a cold and windy day as many Texas Republicans gathered with their compatriots at the Capitol grounds in Washington on January 20, 1981. They were there to witness the inauguration of Ronald Reagan as the 40th president of the United States, as well as to see fellow Texan George H. W. Bush assume the office of vice president. It was the start of a twelve-year period that would see many Texas Republicans assume important roles in our national government, a period when Texas politics would move inexorably in a more Republican direction.[1]

With Reagan's victory at the top of the ticket, Republicans gained a majority in the US Senate for the first time in twenty-six years but still faced a House of Representatives populated by more Democrats and led by Speaker Thomas P. "Tip" O'Neill. Nevertheless, as had been the situation throughout the twentieth century, neither party was ideologically consistent; each had both liberal and conservative members in its midst. The Democratic delegation in the House from Texas included a core of conservatives, called Boll Weevils, who were to provide key votes to the Reagan administration as it passed the historic tax cut of August 1981, a fiscally conservative budget, and other key proposals. Among these Texas Democrats were Marvin Leath, Charles Stenholm, Phil Gramm, and Kent Hance. The latter two would become Republicans a few years later.[2]

Meanwhile Republicans were increasing their numbers in the Texas legislature through the party switches of state representatives Ray Keller of Dallas and George Pierce of San Antonio in May, and Senator Bill Meier of Euless, who crossed over and became the eighth GOP state senator in June of 1981. Meier previously had headed Democrats and Independents for Reagan-Bush in 1980 and subsequently would win the GOP nomination for attorney general in 1982.

The decade of the 1980s was a period of substantial growth for the Republican Party of Texas. With the breakthrough election of Bill Clements two years earlier, the state began a period of two-party politics, an objective long sought by Republican partisans but one that would fade away as the century came to an end. From 1978 to the elections of 1996, the state's politics remained competitive but was moving in a Republican direction. Each party held one of the two US Senate seats for much of the time, while the office of governor shifted back and forth from Clements (R) to Mark White (D) to Clements again (R) to Ann Richards (D) to George W. Bush (R). Among these governors Bush would be the only one to win re-election. It was not to be a continuous shift—Republicans experienced some serious setbacks, especially in 1982—but the state was clearly becoming more favorable to GOP candidates at all levels.

With the decennial census having been completed, 1981 was a redistricting year for congressional and state legislative districts. Population growth throughout the 1970s meant that Texas representation in the US House of Representatives increased from twenty-four to twenty-seven. After much intense maneuvering in the legislature, a conservative congressional districting plan sponsored by Democratic senator John Wilson and House Speaker Billy Clayton was enacted with the support of Governor Clements.[3] Redrawing state legislative lines was more complicated, however. While Clayton passed a House redistricting plan favorable to conservatives, the Senate's outcome was much more Democratic leaning, wiping out some of the GOP gains achieved one year earlier. Clements vetoed the Senate's plan, throwing it to the Legislative Redistricting Board (LRB) comprising the governor, lieutenant governor, comptroller, land commissioner, and speaker of the House. The end result was that the LRB enacted a similarly Democratic-friendly plan.

As is the case with most redistricting decisions, appeals were made to the federal courts. US district judge William Wayne Justice and circuit court judge Sam Johnson overturned the congressional redistricting, with district court judge Robert Parker dissenting. Justice and Johnson had been appointed by a Democratic president, and Parker was a Republican appointment. The federal court then drew a new plan that was in effect for congressional elections until 1992. In response to the state legislative redistricting, both the state GOP and the Associated Republicans of Texas (ART) challenged the redrawing of state Senate lines but were unsuccessful.

THE 1982 ELECTIONS

Once redistricting was completed, Texas Republicans turned their attention to fielding candidates for the 1982 election. At lunch with the governor, Secretary of State George Strake made known his interest in running for lieutenant governor, telling Clements, "I've been thinking about it and I'm willing to run as a long shot. But I don't want to do it if you think it will jeopardize your re-election." The governor enthusiastically supported the idea, and Strake made preparations to run. In October Strake stepped down as secretary of state and was replaced by David Dean, the conservative Democratic attorney who had played an important role in Clements's 1978 victory.[4] Having been successful statewide in 1978 and 1980, the party put forth a strong statewide ticket, with Senator Meier for attorney general, Senator Mike Richards for comptroller, and member of Congress Jim Collins for US Senate.

Meanwhile the Democrats nominated a slate described by political commentator Kyle Thompson of the *Fort Worth Star-Telegram* as "much more liberal than any state ticket offered in modern times."[5] Indicative of its growing importance in the party, four candidates from the party's liberal wing were slated for down-ballot positions and would continue to play important roles in Texas politics over the next decade and a half. Member of Congress Jim Mattox was nominated for attorney general, along with Travis County Commissioner Ann Richards for treasurer, party executive director Garry Mauro for land commissioner, and writer and political commentator Jim Hightower for agriculture commissioner. Rounding out the slate were Senator Lloyd Bentsen Jr., who was seeking a third term, Lieutenant Governor Bill Hobby, Comptroller Bob Bullock, and Attorney General Mark White as the candidate for governor.

On November 13, 1981, the Republican Party of Texas sponsored a Salute to a Stronger America dinner in Houston honoring ten presidential appointees from Texas and James A. Baker III, White House chief of staff. Cochaired by oilfield equipment executive H. E. Chiles and homebuilder Bob Perry, it raised more than one million dollars to help the party prepare for the upcoming state elections. The featured speaker was President Reagan, with John Tower, Bill Clements, John Connally, and the five GOP members of Congress from Texas also in attendance. Evangelist Billy Graham capped off the evening with a benediction. The following morning table sponsors were guests at a private brunch with Vice President Bush and his wife, Barbara, at the Houstonian.

One week later Governor Clements launched his re-election campaign with business financier T. Boone Pickens as state chairman. George Bayoud moved over from the Governor Clements Committee to head up finance operations, while Dary Stone, who was later replaced by Jim Francis, served as campaign manager, and Peter O'Donnell Jr. once again was in charge of keeping the campaign on budget and working toward implementation of the campaign plan.

With the recent victories of 1978 and 1980 in mind, the state party launched a concerted effort to elect more Republicans in 1982. In addition to aggressive candidate recruitment in conjunction with ART, five campaign management seminars were held to provide trained coordinators for state legislative and county contests. By the end of the fall the state party's campaign committee had provided almost a million dollars to various Republican campaigns, and the party's staff was providing ongoing technical assistance to a number of candidates.[6] Attorney Thad Hutcheson Jr., whose father had been the party's candidate for the Senate in 1957 and later served as state GOP chairman, headed the state party's coordinated Election Accuracy Program, focusing on voter registration and ballot security. Providing staff support for the project was Margaret LaMontagne (later Spellings), who would become a key aide to George W. Bush and serve as US secretary of Education from 2005 to 2009, before becoming president of the University of North Carolina.

The Republican Party of Texas undertook an active outreach to Hispanic voters headed by Catalina Vásquez Villalpando on the state party staff, with key assistance from Eddie Aurispo, special assistant to Governor Clements; Bob Estrada, state director for Senator Tower; and Hollis Rutledge, a long-time Republican activist. Some years later Villalpando would be appointed treasurer of the United States by President George H. W. Bush. Several issues of a tabloid newspaper, *Hispanic Times of Texas*, were published by the state party and featured the various Hispanic appointments by both Governor Clements and President Reagan. In addition to the state party efforts, each of the statewide candidates had a Hispanic outreach coordinator on staff. Clements, Strake, and Meier each addressed the May state convention of the League of United Latin American Citizens (LULAC), where the state party sponsored an appreciation breakfast and it was announced that Reagan was appointing Guadalupe Quintanilla, an associate professor at the University of Houston, to the US Civil Rights Commission. In his second term, Reagan would appoint the first Hispanic to a cabinet position when he selected Lauro Cavazos, president of Texas Tech University, to serve as secretary of Education.[7]

In June the Republican Party of Texas produced and purchased television spots in ten media markets telling voters to "Keep the Texas Way Working—Vote Republican." The theme of the ads was that a sharp change had occurred in the Democratic Party, that it was far more liberal than it had been in the past, and that the current crop of liberal Democrats did not understand the Texas way. The spots were announced with a series of press conferences across the state in the markets where the spots would be shown. This was the first time that either state political party in Texas had undertaken a generic ad campaign to boost support for the party and its entire slate of candidates. Another effort to promote the statewide slate took place in the fall as the state party produced and mailed some 950,000 tabloids titled *The Texas Way* to voters in 192 targeted counties. The publication was designed to keep voters in the Republican column as they went down the ballot. Postelection analysis showed that Strake and Mike Richards had retained more than 85 percent of the vote for Clements, a much higher percentage than lower-ticket candidates had kept in past elections.[8]

In July longtime Clements associate Tom Reed presented a revised campaign plan for the governor based on his belief that Democratic gubernatorial nominee Mark White would run his campaign more against President Reagan and his policies than against Clements, given the perceived unpopularity of some of Reagan's programs and the impact of the recession being felt across the nation. When survey respondents were asked for the most important issue, they mentioned the economy most often. While Reagan and his policies were associated with the recession, he retained his personal popularity among the public. Unfortunately, this was not true of Governor Clements. As Reed summarized, "A large number of Texans do not like the Governor personally, although they do agree that he has a record of achievement." With White being perceived as a centrist, some slippage in support among white conservative Democrats was to be expected in 1982.

Despite his belief that White would emphasize national issues, to Reed the campaign was developing as a "Clements versus Clements" race based on how people viewed the governor. A successful re-election effort had to focus on competency, contrasting Clements with a less-than-competent attorney, White. Clements needed to be governor and talk about his accomplishments and how he was "fighting for Texas" while others in the campaign would attack White.[9]

THE DEMOCRATS ATTACK

While Clements was seeking re-election, Representative Collins of Dallas defeated state senator Walter Mengden of Houston for the senatorial nomination to oppose Bentsen. Unfortunately, Collins's broad, sweeping effort to brand Bentsen a liberal was a hard sell and ignited the flames in the Bentsen camp to wage an all-out effort for the entire Democratic ticket. As popular incumbents with ties to the state's business establishment, Bentsen and Lieutenant Governor Hobby were able to attract substantial financial support from major donors, funds that were then used for a coordinated Democratic campaign that helped to both re-elect Bentsen and Hobby and bring down the state's Republican governor.[10]

Bentsen and his supporters realized that for the Democratic candidates to win they needed to increase turnout above what it had been four years earlier, especially in the African-American and Hispanic communities. While both parties operated paid and volunteer phone banks throughout the fall, the Democrats' efforts were focused specifically on elderly, black, and Hispanic voters. According to one Democratic phone bank worker who later wrote to Governor Clements, the canned spiel used by the callers stressed the fear of unemployment and the potential loss of Social Security benefits. She was surprised by the number of respondents who planned on voting a straight Democratic ticket because they perceived Democrats to be delivering the most direct benefits to them.[11]

In addition to the phone warnings of impending doom, the Texas Democrats distributed flyers in black neighborhoods with mock gravestones for Martin Luther King Jr., James Chaney, and Medgar Evers under the heading "They died for your right to vote," while "Ronald Reagan and Bill Clements have been a disaster for Black Texans." Calling on history, the flyer claimed: "In 1932 as the soup and bread lines grew larger, more jobs were lost, more farms and businesses were lost. Mr. Hoover told the people to 'stay the course,' to hang in there. Now in 1982 Mr. Reagan and Mr. Clements are preaching the same doctrine of hopelessness and singing the same song of despair. The people didn't buy it in 1932, and they won't in 1982. Those who are lucky enough to have a job help those who don't by voting Democratic next Tuesday." Another flyer carried the headline: "Breadlines! The Sign of Republicans."[12]

Across the state, mailings referred to as "Telegrams" were sent to Democratic voters from White, Senator Bentsen, and Lieutenant Governor Hobby, claiming, "Ronald Reagan and his rich friends are betting that you won't vote on Tuesday. . . . Your vote for all Democrats will let Mr. Reagan know that enough is enough. . . . That the people of Texas want to get this country moving forward again." It concluded with a plea to support all statewide and local Democratic candidates.

The Democratic attacks were effective, and November 1982 turned into a serious setback—if not a disaster—for Texas Republicans. This came as a surprise to most Republicans, who were conditioned by the recent victories to expect success again in 1982. As Clements campaign manager Francis noted, "Our polls showed us ahead and they were off dramatically. Nightly tracking polls showed us up six points on the day before the election."[13] Although Clements won 282,109 more votes than he had in his 1978 victory, his total was short of what was needed for re-election. The Democratic turnout effort helped to attract more than three million voters to the polls, an increase of 34.7 percent over the number who had voted four years earlier. The governor was 231,931 votes short of the total cast for White.

Among political observers there was general agreement that federal issues played a dominant role in getting people to the polls as the Democrats stressed unemployment, Social Security, and the state of the economy. In the view of columnist Carolyn Barta, "In some ways the 1982 election was turning into a mirror image of 1978. Where Clements had blamed the country's problems on Jimmy Carter in 1978, Texas Democrats were blaming Reaganomics for the economic suffering of 1982."[14] This resulted in the higher than normal number of straight-ticket voters, with one analyst estimating that Democrats received two-thirds of such votes. The number one reason cited by voters supporting White was that he was a Democrat.[15]

Turnout was especially heavy in a number of minority precincts. As Francis recalled, "On election day, the campaign got reports that it was raining heavily in Houston but people were standing in line outside the polling places in minority precincts."[16] Although Clements had carried Harris County by 23,000 votes in 1978, he lost in 1982 by more than 9,000. A 7,000 lead in Tarrant County became a 4,000 deficit in the re-election effort. The state's small-town and rural areas reverted to their strong Democratic heritage and provided a sizeable margin for White along with substantial leads for Senator Bentsen and the other statewide candidates.

One of the factors contributing to the loss was that utility bills had increased substantially, and Clements was blamed for this. As columnist Kyle Thompson noted, "White vigorously attacked Clements on the utility fuel adjustment charges, convincing a lot of voters that he would snap his fingers after becoming governor and that part of their bills would simply disappear."[17] For Karl Rove, it was the state of the national economy, as well as the Texas-specific utility issue, that were the keys to Clements's defeat. "In the end, . . . the national economy was in the tank and there was a Republican in the White House. Texan families were paying record-high utility bills. White blamed the economy on the GOP and wrapped those utility bills around Clements's neck just as Clements had wrapped Carter around his opponent in 1978."[18]

The governor hurt himself even more when he said he couldn't find a qualified housewife to appoint to the Public Utility Commission. The gender gap that would plague Republican candidates nationally was exacerbated as the Democrats publicized the comments. Clements lost heavily among working women and homemakers who only had a high school education, while splitting the vote among college-educated women.[19] Pollster Jan Van Lohui-zen noted, "We had a severe problem with women (voters). Clements is not exactly a charmer."[20]

Indicative of the Texas Democratic Party's continuing ability to be all things to all people, Clements won the votes of only 65 percent of self-described conservatives and polled only 30 percent among those who labeled themselves as moderates, while losing the small body of liberals 87 percent to 9 percent.[21] Although Clements had earned the endorsement of most daily newspapers, as well as former governors Allan Shivers, Preston Smith, and John Connally, this support was not converted into votes on Election Day.

Some observers believed the campaign lacked focus and had no overriding message. According to Tony Garrett, deputy press director, "The campaign was all over the map on issues. There wasn't an issue we wouldn't address. We may have gone down too many rabbit trails."[22] Still others felt that Clements's personality and his confidence in re-election hurt the campaign effort.

There was little doubt that Bentsen and Hobby felt threatened by the slate of Republican candidates and devoted their resources to a united Democratic campaign. White acknowledged the effectiveness of the Bentsen-coordinated effort a few years later: "Lloyd Bentsen was a big help because he kept push-ing through his campaign to the very end. It was one of those truly team efforts."[23] As John Knaggs noted, "the unified Democrats made it a party against party contest with political winds blowing their way."[24] Bentsen beat Collins by more than a half million vote margin, while Hobby held off the drive by Strake.

All five GOP members of Congress were re-elected, but after redistricting the party lost three of its state senators and gained no new state representa-tives. The number of Republican district and county elected officials increased significantly, however, from 103 after the 1978 election to 260 following the 1982 election. Dallas County was one bright spot for the party, providing a 32,000-vote margin for Clements, securing victory in four of five county-wide races, and holding fifty out of fifty-nine judgeships and three of five positions on the commissioners court after the election.[25] As the state party's executive director noted, "Our party is much stronger now than it was when we entered the 1978 election campaign. We have more officeholders, stronger county organizations, more dedicated and trained volunteers, and a larger base of support among the Texas electorate. Our momentum has stalled and we have been temporarily set back. But we are in a position to come roaring back in future elections."[26]

One indication of the party's growth could be seen in the relative impor-tance of the primary and general elections. In past years many voters felt that the contest for public office was between candidates in the Democratic primary. More and more Texas voters believed that the real election was now the us-versus-them contest in November. The Republican Party was clearly in the ballpark as the main opposition force in Texas politics. Although its statewide candidates lost, the 1982 election was a milestone in the development of a two-party system in Texas. It was hard for the party's dedicated volunteers to accept this reality at the time, but significant GOP victories were on the horizon and would be achieved two years later. The election of 1982 proved to be the last year in which Democrats would sweep all the statewide races, a situation that had previously existed for over a century.

THE AFTERMATH OF 1982: INTERNAL DIVISIONS

The overwhelming loss of November provided an opportunity for those on the far right to call for a change in party leadership. No longer having the backing of a Republican governor, state chairman Chet Upham became their target. Some on the right saw this as an ideological rather than a factional dispute, maintaining that Upham and the state party were insufficiently conservative.[27] Still others saw it as a continuation of the battle between Bush and Reagan supporters.[28] Whatever the ultimate motivation, the election loss and the resulting campaign debt carried forth by the state party was a chance for the outsiders to demand a new chairman.

Over the next five months the battle raged between the Upham supporters, led by national committeeman Ernest Angelo, and the forces seeking his ouster, led by State Republican Executive Committee (SREC) member James Brandon of Amarillo. At the December 1982 meeting of the SREC in Austin, some members asked Upham to resign, which he refused to do, pointing out that he had been elected by delegates to the party's state convention. According to one report, "Upham's critics blame him for Clements' unimaginative campaign, and hold him responsible for having 'allowed' the governor to disassociate his campaign from those of the other Republican candidates."[29]

When a group of SREC members met in January, one claimed that the state party was "gearing for a Bush for President campaign in 1984." Another admitted, "the main issue is control of state party." For one of these hard-right conservatives, "Reagan is under control of the Eastern power bloc" while another "does not think Reagan is doing a good job."[30] These views were consistent with those expressed by some national New Right leaders, including Howard Phillips of the Conservative Caucus and direct-mail guru Richard Viguerie, who claimed that the president was engaging in "almost a stampede to the left." A meeting of hard-right leaders, including Phillips and Viguerie, was organized by Houston attorney Clymer Wright but was canceled.[31]

One Upham backer traced the dispute back to 1979, when, he claimed, "a small but vocal group attempted to gain control of the Reagan campaign," opposed Clements's recommendation of Upham originally, attempted to oust member of Congress Jack Fields as temporary convention chair in 1982, and tried to change the rules on selection of national convention delegates, taking the choice away from the presidential candidate and placing it with the state party.[32] Another party official remarked, "It's an attempt to control the party for the 1984 convention. If Reagan chooses to run, it could be to block George Bush's re-nomination as vice president and in the event Reagan doesn't run, it could block Bush" from getting the presidential nomination.[33]

It would be incorrect to describe the conflict as being between Reagan supporters and party moderates because the lineup of supporters for Upham belied this division. Stalwart Reagan backers Angelo, Nancy Palm, and national committeewoman Fran Chiles lined up with the chairman, whom Chiles called a "scapegoat" for Clements's loss. As Palm concluded, "They might as well face the fact that George Bush was Reagan's choice and has been a very loyal, very excellent vice president whether they like it or him or not."[34]

When the SREC met next in Corpus Christi on February 5, the dissidents claimed that thirty-four of the sixty-four members wanted Upham's resignation, but the chairman refused to step aside. In a measure of dissatisfaction, the SREC voted thirty-eight to twenty-four to reject Upham's recommended appointments to the state party's campaign committee and deferred action on approving a state party budget. Palm, former Harris County GOP chair and a longtime leader of Texas conservatives, spoke against the delaying action, asking "Will we be crucified in the media by voting down our state officer? To do this to our chairman is a very serious action." Palm's advice was not heeded, and the party was forced to operate without an approved budget for the year.[35] Upham saw the vote as part of a move to force him out but said he had no intention of resigning. "At our last meeting in December, I received the major credit for the loss of Bill Clements. But they forgot to give me credit for Ronald Reagan's victory in 1980, even though I don't think my role was that important in either of them."[36]

With Dallas the site of the 1984 Republican National Convention and both Reagan and Tower slated to be on the ballot, Texas had particular importance to the national party. As pollster Lance Tarrance noted, "the SREC intraparty squabbling is immature politically and causing the party to waste valuable time from the '84 elections."[37] Upham received an important boost when a letter came from President Reagan saying, "You have consistently displayed the kind of leadership which is essential in making the Republican Party a forceful and commanding presence in the Lone Star State.... I look forward to our continued partnership in achieving those goals we have set."[38]

By March efforts were underway to develop a compromise. At a meeting of his supporters in Dallas, Upham announced he would step aside in the interest of party unity if an overwhelming majority of the SREC would support Strake as the new chairman. His position was that resigning without an agreed-on successor who had a strong majority on the SREC would be counterproductive. Those at the meeting urged Upham not to resign but agreed to poll the SREC to see if Strake could garner sufficient support.[39] Strake had said he would consider the position "only if it comes to the point that nobody else can be agreed upon and a large majority want me to do it."[40] By the time the telephone poll was completed, a substantial majority could not be found willing to support Strake. Upham then announced, "I have concluded, therefore, that I will continue to serve as State Chairman and am absolutely committed to completing the term to which I was elected by the September 1982 State Convention."[41]

Prior to the April 9 SREC meeting a statement reaffirming support for Upham was signed by 155 county chairs, two-thirds of all current officeholders, whose counties had provided two-thirds of the delegates to the previous state convention. Meanwhile a poll by the *Dallas Times Herald* revealed the split among SREC members was twenty-five wanting Upham to remain in office, twenty-seven desiring his resignation, four remaining neutral, and six refusing to answer.[42] In response, Upham offered once again to step aside if at least forty-eight SREC members agreed to support Strake as the new chairman and state vice chairman Dorothy Doehne also resigned.[43]

The following day, when fifty-one SREC members pledged their support to Strake, and Doehne reluctantly agreed to resign, Upham announced he would resign effective April 30 when Strake could be formally elected. After the compromise, the committee unanimously endorsed both the party budget and Upham's appointments to the budget oversight and campaign committees.[44] In leaving his position, Upham called on "all Republicans to forget their differences and give George Strake, Jr., our incoming state chairman, the unity and support he deserves and must have to lead our party to the election victories that are now only opportunities."[45] The bitter four-month internal dispute ended on April 30 in Houston as the SREC officially elected Strake as the new chairman and named Diana Denman of San Antonio as vice chairman. The party's executive director also resigned and accepted an appointment in the Reagan administration as regional director for the US Department of Education.

Once in office, Strake met with financial backers H. E. Chiles, T. Boone Pickens, and James Lyon to discuss the party's financial situation. Chiles asked how much money Strake needed to do the job right, and he said one million dollars. Strake left the meeting with a pledge that those present would provide it, and they did.[46] He was on his way to paying off the party's remaining debts from the 1982 campaign. Once again, at least temporarily, there was peace in the valley.

As the new state chairman, Strake made it a priority of his role to encourage conservatives to switch parties. He spent a considerable amount of time traveling around the state meeting with conservative elected officials and urging them to become Republicans. This movement to the GOP continued over the next thirty years and resulted in the GOP holding a majority of elected positions by the early part of the twenty-first century.

ENTER PHIL GRAMM

While the party was wrestling with internal leadership issues, some encouraging political developments were taking place that would have a significant impact on the party's ability to expand its base of support in the state. Phil Gramm, a professor of economics at Texas A&M University, had first challenged Senator Bentsen in the 1976 Democratic primary and then had become one of a group of conservative Democrats first elected to the US House in 1978. Two years later, along with Kent Hance, he became a sponsor of key legislation backed by Reagan. Angelo visited with and worked on both Gramm and Hance to change parties, but they continued to believe there was a place for conservatives in the Democratic Party.[47] Gramm's support for Reagan's budget and tax proposals resulted in the Democratic leadership stripping him of his seat on the influential House Budget Committee in late 1982. Feeling ostracized by his own party, Gramm was ready to consider becoming a Republican.

Jim Francis, who had been Clements's campaign manager, and national GOP operative Charlie Black met with Gramm about changing parties and how it could best be accomplished. Black recommended that Gramm resign from Congress, then immediately run as a Republican in the special election caused by his resignation.[48] On January 5, 1983, Phil Gramm switched parties, resigned his seat in Congress, and announced for the special election. He claimed, "I cannot in good conscience work with a party that seeks to limit my effectiveness on behalf of those I represent in its effort to perpetuate the spending spree which has crippled our nation, threatened our position of world leadership and robbed our workers and retirees."[49]

Perhaps it was appropriate that on Lincoln's birthday, February 12, 1983, Phil Gramm won the special election in the 6th congressional district with 55 percent of the vote against a field of ten candidates, thereby negating the need for a runoff. Gramm's victory in that special election set the foundation for his ability to win the nomination and election for senator when John Tower declined to seek another term in 1984. His move also paved the way for other conservative Democrats, including Hance, to switch to the Republican Party, and it helped convince many voters that there was only one home for Texas conservatives. According to one writer, Gramm's action "may be the most significant of all party switches in the state of Texas" as "picking a political party affiliation became an important decision for Texas politicians for the first time. Gramm made party affiliation a litmus test for political ideology." By making a clear distinction between the philosophies of the two parties, "Gramm's party switch stripped all conservatism out of the Democratic Party. The politicians in Texas today did not suddenly become conservative. Rather, they just became Republican because Phil Gramm had established there was no room in the Democratic Party for conservatives."[50]

Throughout the remainder of 1983, the state party continued to conduct workshops to train volunteers and campaign workers, undertook efforts to recruit candidates, and helped prepare for hosting the 1984 Republican National Convention. Angelo was named by the national committee to serve as arrangements chair for the convention and involved a number of longtime Texas Republicans in the effort to ensure a successful event. His appointment was an honor for the state, as the role of arrangements chair was normally filled by the Republican national chairman.[51]

One of the lasting contributions to party success during Strake's time as chairman was the development of the Optimal Republican Voting Strength (ORVS) formula by Royal Masset, a longtime consultant for and staff member of the party. As Strake commented upon Masset's passing in 2016, "Without a doubt, Royal did as much or more than any other person that I know, whether that be elected official or ordinary citizen, to transform Texas into a solid Republican state. He did this in many ways but the one that stands out in my mind is his discovery and application of ORVS. His development of ORVS was incredibly helpful in showing us winnable political seats from dog catcher to governor."[52]

The ORVS formula provided a statistical measure of the likely Republican support in any election district from county to state legislative to congressional. As Strake explained, "ORVS allowed us to recruit the all-American type of candidates rather than simply the community dissident when we could show by numbers that a Republican had a solid opportunity to win. It also helped us tremendously when raising money for our candidates, being able to show that a district could be won."[53]

Strake was also responsible for initiating an organized paid phone bank operation to raise funds for the state party. The process began with the list of primary voters, from which known high-dollar donors were eliminated. Phone callers were hired after a phone interview because telephone manners were the key qualification needed. According to the chairman, "After three years of our phone bank operation, the party went from a base of 15,000 donors to around 120,000 donors."[54]

Both the state and national parties continued their efforts to reach out to the Hispanic community and encourage more involvement in Republican activities. These efforts were assisted when President Reagan named Esther Gonzalez-Arroyo Buckley to the US Civil Rights Commission. Buckley, a high school math and science teacher, was also the Webb County Republican chairman and a strong supporter of Senator Tower. Vidal Cantu, a Laredo city council member and former GOP county chairman, described her as a "workaholic." He said, "She does her homework. She stands for human rights as far as our people are concerned. You don't talk about Mexican-Americans down here. We are the system." Buckley continued to serve on the Civil Rights Commission for nine years.[55]

THE JOHN TOWER ERA ENDS

As the year proceeded, all expectations were that Senator Tower would seek a fifth term the following year when the Reagan-Bush team would be on the ballot for re-election. In April President Reagan spoke at a Tower fundraiser in Houston that brought in one million dollars for the senator's campaign account. By June, however, rumors began to circulate that Tower might not run again.[56] Then on August 23, at a news conference in the Texas House of Representatives, the state's senior senator announced that he would retire after nearly twenty-four years in the United States Senate while still at the relatively young age of fifty-eight.[57]

Almost immediately member of Congress Ron Paul announced his candidacy to replace Tower, and one month later Representative Gramm made it official that he would be a candidate also. As John Knaggs noted, "Gramm's campaign hit upon one of those powerful theme lines that enhance substantially the effectiveness of mass media advertising, 'Common Sense ... Uncommon Courage.' That catchy language capsuled Gramm's recent political history in a memorable manner."[58] Also entering the fray were wealthy business owner Rob Mosbacher Jr. and former gubernatorial candidate Hank Grover. When the primary was held, Gramm overwhelmed his opponents with 73.2 percent of the vote, while Paul obtained 16.5 percent, Mosbacher received 7.8 percent, and Grover was left with the support of less than 3 percent of GOP primary voters.

Meanwhile six Democrats saw Tower's retirement as a rare opportunity to compete for an open seat in the US Senate. The three serious candidates were Lubbock member of Congress Kent Hance, former member of Congress and 1978 Senate candidate Bob Krueger, and state senator Lloyd Doggett. These three candidates were viewed as representative of the conservative, moderate, and liberal factions in the Democratic Party, respectively. When the 1984 primary was held, Hance came in first and Doggett second, but all three candidates were separated by fewer than two thousand votes.

In the subsequent runoff Krueger endorsed Hance, and both Hance and Doggett increased their vote totals from what they had in the first primary. Hance carried some two hundred of the state's 254 counties but was overwhelmed in the major cities. By 1984, with Reagan in the White House, Republicans had made significant inroads into local elections in Dallas, Harris, and Tarrant counties, resulting in many conservatives voting in the Republican primary, making them unable to vote in the Democratic runoff. On runoff night, fewer than four hundred votes separated Doggett and Hance, with Doggett ahead. The Hance campaign paid for a statewide recount, but the margin for Doggett increased to 1,345 votes. After being endorsed by Krueger and successfully carrying nearly 80 percent of the state's counties, Hance was shocked when he did not win the nomination.

During the Democratic primary campaign Hance was constantly hassled about positions he took as a member of Congress. It became clear to him that in some areas of the state liberals were in control of the Democratic Party and unwilling to accept anyone who did not toe the line ideologically. One person whose actions helped convince Hance to eventually change parties was Democratic state chairman Bob Slagle. According to Hance, "Slagle called me nothing but a Dixiecrat and trashed me constantly in the primary and runoff." It was clear to Hance that Slagle wanted a purely liberal Texas Democratic Party.[59]

Having declined to run for another Senate term, Tower agreed to serve as chair of the Texas Reagan re-election campaign, with party activist Martha Weisend of Dallas as cochair. Tower had not backed Reagan prior to 1980, but Weisend came to the effort with a long history of involvement that began with the Goldwater campaign after she moved to Texas in 1964. She first volunteered for Reagan in his abortive 1968 nomination run and then again in both 1976 and 1980. Member of Congress Steve Bartlett maintained, "Martha combines being a brilliant strategist with being an effective organizer, and that combination is rare."[60] With the pairing of Tower and Weisend the major elements in the party were satisfied and focused on re-electing the president.

In June the party held its first of two uneventful state conventions in Fort Worth. Senator Paul Laxalt of Nevada was the keynote speaker, and his speech was supplemented by remarks from Vice President Bush, Senator Tower, and members of Congress Phil Gramm and Tom Loeffler. Dallas Congressman Steve Bartlett served as convention chair. That summer a successful Republican National Convention was held in Dallas, focusing national attention on the growth and success of the Dallas GOP, led by county chairman Fred Meyer. At the second state convention, held in Corpus Christi in September, member of Congress Jack Kemp provided the keynote speech, and Representative Bill Archer of Houston served as convention chair. While Strake was unanimously elected state chairman, vice chairman Diana Denman held off a serious challenge from Texas Federation of Republican Women leader Lou Brown of Midland.

After the downturn of 1982 it was apparent that Reagan was once again standing tall in public support as many Democrats and Independents rallied to his re-election effort. In July Texans for Reagan was announced, with the support of former Democratic governors Shivers and Smith, along with former Democratic members of Congress Frank Ikard, Omar Burleson, and O. C. Fisher. Tower claimed that the Democratic platform "drives the national Democratic Party even further away from the views of many Texans who have been accustomed to thinking of themselves as Democrats."[61] As the campaign progressed, even more elected Democrats came out for the president's re-election, including the leader of the Texas House of Representatives. "The migration of noted Democrats to the Republican camp culminated when Texas House Speaker Bill Clayton announced his support for the Reagan-Bush ticket in the Fall of 1984, although he did not officially switch parties until a year later."[62]

The state party was feeling optimistic as the fall campaign began, but they were taking nothing for granted. Once again they mounted a major get-out-the-vote drive with paid and volunteer phone banks across the state. The co-ordinated Victory Committee operation raised 2 million dollars to carry out its programs on behalf of the Reagan-Bush ticket, the Gramm Senate campaign, and the various other party candidacies across the state. State GOP political director Kevin Moomaw coordinated efforts to elect more Republicans to the state legislature. In a measure of the seriousness of their concern, the party convinced former justice of the Texas Supreme Court Will Garwood to head up the ballot security program, designed to ensure that all legal ballots were counted correctly.[63]

Although early polls showed Reagan significantly ahead in Texas, Democrats refused to write off the state, realizing that any coordinated effort patterned after their success in 1982 would benefit their senatorial, congressional, state legislative and county candidates as well. One new component of the Democrats' drive became possible when they were able to acquire a list of all persons who received unemployment benefits over the previous eighteen months. These individuals became a target for voter registration efforts, and they were mailed a form and then contacted with a follow-up call. The same callers were then used for the get-out-the-vote effort directed at those with a tendency of voting Democratic. According to state chairman Slagle, "there are 330 phones. We call from 5 to 9 Monday through Thursday, 9 to 5 on Saturday and noon to 8 on Sundays."[64]

Election Day 1984 produced a much more favorable outcome for Republicans than the one two years earlier. President Reagan was re-elected in a landslide, winning forty-nine states and obtaining 64 percent of the vote in Texas. Gramm defeated Doggett by over 900,000 votes, with 59 percent of the total cast. Barely losing were Railroad Commission candidate John Thomas Henderson, with 49.7 percent, and Court of Criminal Appeals candidate Virgil Mulanax with 49.0 percent, while Supreme Court candidate John Bates obtained 45.9 percent against former attorney general and gubernatorial candidate John Hill.

Six freshman Republicans were elected to Congress, giving the party a net gain of four new districts. Joe Barton took the seat vacated by Gramm, while Tom DeLay captured the district formerly held by Ron Paul. Larry Combest replaced Hance in West Texas, while Beau Boulter won the Panhandle district, Mac Sweeney captured a Central Texas seat, and Dick Armey ousted a Democrat in an area centering on Arlington. Republicans picked up their first state senator from Bexar County with the election of Cyndi Taylor Krier. The GOP reached a new high-water mark in the Texas House of Representatives, with nineteen freshmen among a delegation of fifty-two Republicans in the 1985 session.[65]

Not only did Dallas and Houston produce top-of-the-ticket margins for Republican candidates, but the party's sweep went down ballot. Every Democratic judge in Dallas lost, while every contested judicial race in Harris County went to the GOP. As Paul Burka, political editor of the *Texas*

Monthly, noted, "For the first time ever, Republican candidates were viable in every portion of the state and at every level of the ballot." All across the state, "from the top of the ticket to the bottom, it was a wipeout." There was only one clear conclusion from the election for Burka: "The ultimate meaning of the 1984 election is that the cycle of two-party politics has established itself in Texas.... Texas has become a true two-party state, and its politics will be swept along in national currents."[66]

Even at a time of great electoral success there were still some disgruntled Republicans. One writer claimed that the party concentrated almost entirely on federal issues and offices, failing to respond to issues of state importance. It was claimed that when the Democrats in the state legislature undertook a total overhaul of the state education system and enacted the largest tax bill in any state in history, the state GOP remained silent. According to commentator Scott Bennett, "It is truly amazing that these fiercest of Reagan supporters have failed so completely to hear their hero's call for a 'new federalism' in which *state* governments will play an increasing role."[67]

Still others on the SREC complained that Strake was using his position as state chairman to promote his possible candidacy for governor, while others associated with the Reagan-Bush campaign felt that the party did not do enough in gathering voter data for the election. According to one report, "Much of the animosity toward Strake is directed just as much at John Maxwell, executive director, and Byron Nelson III, press coordinator, both brought in by Strake last year." As national committeeman Ernest Angelo noted, "It is a little ironic that we'd be having a significant amount of dissatisfaction when the party's just gone through one of its most significant victories."[68] In the end, when the SREC met in December, all was sweetness and light as harmony prevailed.

As 1985 began, Mosbacher, who had been a candidate for the senatorial nomination the previous year, agreed to serve as finance chair for the state party, while Henry Santamaria continued as the party's treasurer. Republicans found themselves once again in debt after an election, with nearly $500,000 left unpaid by the Victory '84 effort. Through the efforts of Senator Tower, Dallas GOP chairman Meyer, and Martha Weisend this balance had been whittled down to less than $165,000 by early 1985. Chairman Strake hired attorney Jane Matheson to replace John Maxwell as executive director, and Wayne Massey became the new organization director on the state party staff.

During the sixty-ninth regular session of the Texas House of Representatives, with their delegation's size increased to fifty-two, Republicans played a more critical role than in past sessions. While the legislature continued to operate in a nonpartisan fashion, with some GOP members appointed to chair committees in both the House and Senate, the ideological lines between the two parties were slowly becoming more clearly defined. The Young Conservatives of Texas (YCT) rating of House members on selected issues showed only seven of the ninety-one Democrats with scores of 75 percent conservative or higher, while five of the fifty-eight Republicans scored below 75 percent.[69] Yet the Democratic delegation remained nearly as divided as in the past. After reviewing the ratings compiled by the *Texas Observer*—a liberal counter to the YCT measure—Chandler Davidson noted, "Democrats in both houses varied widely in their support of the measures. Around one-third tended to vote liberal, and one-quarter voted conservative. The remaining 40 percent or so were in the moderate category. The Republicans' overall difference from the Democrats was striking. In neither house was a single one of the fifty-eight Republicans in the liberal category."[70]

At the SREC's first meeting of 1985, held in Brownsville, Strake emphasized that it would be a year of recruitment and research. In an effort to increase GOP numbers in both the state legislature and county government, Royal Masset, political director for the state party, put together a series of campaign management reports on topics such as targeting winnable districts, reviewing the opponent's public disclosures, developing name identification and a campaign plan, the importance of integrated planning, and various other topics. These were made available to party leaders and potential campaign workers, as well as those being recruited to become candidates. Masset, who had developed the ORVS method of targeting winnable districts, used this formula as an important tool in the party's recruitment efforts.

KENT HANCE AND THE 1986
GUBERNATORIAL CONTEST

In the aftermath of the Reagan landslide, several officeholders changed parties and became Republican, a trend that would continue for the remainder of the century. One person was of particular interest, the conservative member of Congress who had come within a whisker of being the Democratic Party's nominee for the US Senate in 1984, Kent Hance. Despite the various rumors of a Hance move, as late as April he was saying he would not switch: "I've been asked, 'would you never, ever switch?' In politics, you learn never to say never—but I don't see that in the cards."[71] As he reflected on the situation, however, Hance realized that a change in party was required if he were to have any further influence on the direction of the state and nation. Thus on May 3, 1985, at a news conference in Washington attended by Senator Gramm, Hance announced that he was becoming a Republican.

Prior to the decision and announcement, Hance had met with Gramm, Bill Clements, and Jim Francis. Hance's view was that "Jim Francis was a key person in getting me over the finish line" of the switch. Hance believed that his party change was "the beginning of the end for the Democratic Party in Texas."[72] One clear example of the impact of his switch can be seen in his home area of Lubbock County, where in 1984 the primary turnout was overwhelmingly Democratic, but only four years later a majority of votes were being cast in the Republican primary, increasing from 6,609 to 22,736 GOP primary voters. Democratic political consultant George Christian, who had worked closely with President Lyndon Johnson, admitted that Hance's move was "a blow to the Democratic Party, no question about it. It's symptomatic of the problem the Democrats are having holding onto their conservative wing in Texas and elsewhere. It's serious business."[73]

In April Gramm convinced President Reagan to nominate Democratic member of Congress Sam B. Hall Jr. to fill a vacancy on the District Court for the Eastern District of Texas, hoping that his nomination would encourage more conservatives to change parties and that Hall's seat could be filled by a Republican. The party nominated former Texas A&M quarterback Edd Hargett to run in the special election against attorney Jim Chapman. Hargett had the greater name identification, but "Chapman proved to be a better campaigner than expected, carefully positioning himself on the conservative side of the social issues that seemed to have the most salience in East Texas."[74] Chapman ended up with 51 percent of the total in a heavy-turnout special election, winning by fewer than two thousand votes. The move to gain more GOP representation in Congress would have to wait a little bit longer.

Hance's switch was one move in the chessboard of gubernatorial nominating politics prefacing the state election of 1986, a year in which neither US senator would be on the ballot but all state elected officials would be, with the governor's office as clearly the most visible. Throughout most of 1985 Clements had dismissed the idea of running again, so some Republicans explored other possible candidates. With some of his past supporters encouraging an effort to reclaim the governor's mansion, Clements asked Weisend to survey Texans' attitudes toward his running again. Weisend went about surveying Republican activists and met with Bill and Rita Clements and Peter O'Donnell to report that of the likely GOP primary voters surveyed, 53 percent supported Clements. "After looking at the geographical analysis,

O'Donnell concluded that the primary belonged to Clements—but he challenged him to be sure he wanted the job again."[75]

In May a delegation of Dallas GOP activists, including Bill Elliott, Gary Griffith, Ken Nelson, Jay Patterson, and James Huffines visited Clements and told him they were forming a Draft Clements committee. One year earlier, former state GOP chairman Chet Upham had printed and distributed fifteen thousand bumper stickers proclaiming "Gee, I Miss Gov. Clements," and they were showing up on cars and pickup trucks around the state. Clements neither encouraged nor discouraged the draft effort but did agree to consider a candidacy.[76] Shortly thereafter George Bayoud, David Dean, and Dary Stone visited with the former governor and encouraged him to run again. Their advice was: "If you're going to do this, you need to tell Hance and Loeffler before they start up their campaign efforts."[77] By then it was too late to close that door, however, as both Hance and Loeffler were already organizing for a campaign.

After his party switch Hance was being encouraged to seek the governor's office, and he met with several active Republicans, including Rove and Francis, as he considered another campaign. Hance signed up business owner H. R. "Bum" Bright, who had been a close business associate of Clements, to serve as finance chair, with Francis as a key campaign consultant. Lance Tarrance, who had helped convince Hance to switch parties, would be the polling consultant in his gubernatorial campaign. Houston business owner Mosbacher and Austin SREC member Kay Danks were volunteer cochairs of the pending campaign. A majority of SREC members signed up to support Hance, and by late July, when he was not yet an official candidate, he announced a 450-member Dallas County steering committee.[78]

Meanwhile, Loeffler had made the decision to leave Congress and seek the governorship. Richard McBride, who had managed Gramm's Senate campaign, became campaign manager, while Brad O'Leary headed the finance operation and Bob Teeter served as pollster. Loeffler also snagged Tobin Armstrong, husband of Ambassador Anne Armstrong and appointments director when Clements was governor, as his overall campaign chair. By mid-July the Loeffler campaign sent out a fundraising letter signed by members of Congress Bill Archer, Tom DeLay, and Jack Fields, who admitted, "This is an unusual and, for some of us, an unprecedented request to make so far in advance of the election.... We believe Tom will make an outstanding Governor." Enclosed with their letter was a list of twenty-four GOP state legislators who had agreed to endorse Loeffler's campaign for governor.[79]

On July 26, 1985, Clements held a news conference in Dallas to become the first official candidate for governor. Weisend of Dallas and business executive Jack Rains of Houston were announced as cochairs of the campaign, with Ed Cassidy as campaign manager and Bayoud as finance director, with Dallas banker Robert Stewart serving as finance chair.[80] Soon thereafter, the campaign released the names of sixty prominent Republicans serving on the campaign steering committee. Those listed included former state party chairmen, as well as business leaders T. Boone Pickens, H. E. Chiles, Ray Hunt, Bob Perry, and Wales Madden, along with football heroes Roger Staubach and Bob Lilly.

There were differing opinions as to what motivated Clements to agree to a third campaign for governor. Francis, who had worked closely with him since his first campaign, believed that the key influence was Clements's wife Rita, whose history of political involvement and contacts throughout the state led her to believe that he could reclaim the governor's mansion. According to Francis, "Peter O'Donnell would not have urged Clements to run. Clements may have asked him whether he had a chance and O'Donnell said yes. It was Rita who urged him to run again."[81] Hance believed that Rita and Weisend convinced Clements that Hance and Loeffler could not win and that his candidacy was the best opportunity to defeat Mark White. As Hance recalled, "At that time, none of us realized how politically wounded Mark White was."[82]

Shortly after announcing his candidacy, Clements sent a letter to those who had been appointed to state government positions during his term as governor, admitting to difficulties in his previous campaign: "My campaign came across as mean-spirited and arrogant. We failed to explain our record and to run a positive race. So Texans came to believe I was out of touch with them and their concerns." He wrote further, "In the months ahead, I must reassure Texans that I am not content to talk simply about what I did as Governor. I will also talk about the new challenges Texas faces and the vision I have for our state's future."[83] This analysis of the 1982 campaign was shared by 1986 campaign cochair Rains in a memo to Clements stressing problems in approaching volunteers from past campaigns. According to Rains, "Many feel their past efforts were not appreciated. . . . Let me urge you to begin a program to mend some fences with your '78 and '82 supporters." He added that "Rita can be a great asset to the campaign in overcoming this problem."[84]

One month after Clements announced, Loeffler became an official candidate for governor. As pollster Dick Wirthlin noted in a Clements campaign document, "Loeffler's argument is that he is a young leader who has never lost an election and will bring the Reagan revolution home to Texas."[85]

On October 8 Hance became the last candidate to officially announce. According to the Wirthlin analysis, "The entire Hance strategy is to try to prod

Clements to lose his temper, shoot from the lip, or allow himself to be put in a situation where he appears arrogant and mean. Kent Hance will wrap himself in Gramm's coat as tightly as he can. His speeches are full of references to Gramm and Reagan."[86]

After Clements claimed Hance and Loeffler might drop out before the primary, Rove outlined what he saw as the strategy of his opponents: "The opposition wants you to blow up, lose your temper, and lash out at another Republican.... The slip-up they hope for must be capable of being sold to voters as an attack by you.... Loeffler and Hance know they cannot appear to be the aggressors.... So Loeffler and Hance want something they can sell as evidence of your short fuse and arrogance."[87]

All the major pieces were now in place for a lively contest involving the former governor who had come into office pledging to speak for the Texas ticket splitters, the young member of Congress with a lifetime commitment to the Republican Party, and the newcomer to the GOP who represented the growing number of conservatives moving away from their historic political home. GOP state chairman Strake could see both the assets and potential liabilities of this intensive primary battle among three prominent political figures. "For the first time in history our nomination is worth having. It's given us headlines we've never had before. It's a pleasant change if only we can keep from shooting ourselves in the foot."[88]

It was Strake's responsibility to see that this primary battle did not leave the party so divided that it could not unite to defeat the incumbent Democratic governor in November 1986. By October Strake and GOP national committeeman Angelo held a confidential meeting in Dallas with Clements and Hance, where they asked them to sign an agreement to campaign on issues and not on personal attacks, having previously obtained concurrence from Loeffler, who remained in Washington on congressional business. All three candidates took the pledge and mostly it held up throughout the winter and on to the May 3 primary.[89] But a concern over uniting the party after the primary was foremost in the mind of O'Donnell, a key Clements supporter. O'Donnell asked Tower to join Gramm and Clements on a tour to promote party unity by visiting some larger senatorial district conventions in May, two weeks after the primary. Tower agreed, and the unity tour helped to heal wounds.[90]

Meanwhile the Democratic primary for governor was becoming a measure of the popularity—or unpopularity—of Governor White. Among the five candidates opposing White for the nomination were two former defeated Republican candidates and two more serious contestants. Don Crowder was a Dallas area attorney and law partner of Attorney General Jim Mattox, who described him as "a progressive, populist individual" who "saw politics as a means of attacking some of the hypocrisy that exists in our society. His run for governor was a Don Quixote challenge—he ran with very little money."[91] A more serious challenge came from Andrew C. Briscoe III, a second cousin to former governor Dolph Briscoe. Andrew Briscoe believed that there were enough protest votes, especially from teachers upset with White's educational reforms, to keep the incumbent governor from obtaining a majority, and thus force a runoff.[92] On primary day, however, White squeaked through with 53.8 percent of the vote, followed by Briscoe with 22.7 percent and Crowder at a disappointing 11 percent. White's lackluster performance among his own party's voters was a precursor of trouble in November. Shortly before the November election Andrew Briscoe endorsed Clements.[93]

While Governor White was barely breaking a majority against a field of rather weak opponents, Bill Clements was rolling up a larger margin with 58.4 percent of the vote, carrying 177 of the 231 counties holding a Republican primary. Loeffler obtained 21.7 percent of the vote, with Hance coming in at 19.9 percent, each carrying twenty-seven counties. No candidate was able to obtain a majority in three other GOP contests, for lieutenant governor, attorney general, and railroad commissioner, forcing lively runoffs. In the end, the little known David Davidson captured the nomination for lieutenant governor, state representative Milton Fox won nomination for a seat on the Railroad Commission, and state district judge Roy Barrera Jr. secured the nomination for attorney general. Barrera, the first Republican elected judge in Bexar County, was seeking to become the first Hispanic elected to statewide office in Texas.[94]

Beyond the statewide offices, the Republican presence was growing. Up from a total of 454 candidates in 1984, the 1986 Republican primary saw 1,026 individuals seek nomination. According to state chairman Strake, this helped produce the record GOP primary turnout as these candidates "brought their friends and neighbors to the polls with them."[95] Strake saw the most lasting impact on party fortunes among the state legislative contests. "I think we have an outstanding chance of getting at or near a majority, and once we do that and we get some control over redistricting, then this will be a Republican state in my opinion."[96]

According to the Texas Poll, Republicans were approaching parity with the Democrats in terms of voter identification. Both generational and migration factors were contributing to this Republican growth. Among Texans under the age of forty-four, there were more Republicans than Democrats. Lifetime Texans remained strongly Democratic (41 percent Democratic versus 27 percent Republican), while those who had lived in the state ten years or less were much more Republican (24 percent Democratic versus 39 percent Republican).[97] The party's base remained heavily urban as more than 50 percent of the primary vote came from the six most populous counties (Bexar, Dallas, El Paso, Harris, Tarrant, and Travis), while the rural and small town areas of the state were still strongly Democratic. Yet changes in these voting patterns were soon to come. As Paul Burka observed, "Conservative Democrats who have been abandoning their party in fall elections in ever-increasing numbers, abandoned it in the spring primaries for the first time. This is the death knell for the old order of the Democratic party that has been the source of every governor of Texas since 1938 except Bill Clements."[98] Over the next twenty years this movement would turn rural Texas from a Democratic stronghold to a solidly Republican area.

With the primary behind them, Republican leaders gathered in Dallas for the biennial state convention. Rallying the troops at the late June confab were Vice President Bush, Representative Jack Kemp, Senate Majority Leader Bob Dole, and most of the Texas GOP congressional delegation. Leadership elections were lively as at one point, party chairman Strake was undecided on whether to seek a second full term and before he announced his decision, vice chairman Diana Denman launched her campaign for the office. Because party rules dictate that the chairman and vice chairman must be of differing sexes, she recruited Houston SREC member Steve Munisteri to run for vice chairman. Strake decided to run again, and Denman backed out of the contest and filed for another term as vice chairman just before the votes were counted.[99] With Denman out of the race for chairman, Austin minister Sam Hoerster opposed Strake, who won easily in a vote of 3,882 to 744. Meanwhile Denman won re-election by defeating Strake's vice chairman candidate, Kay Danks of Austin, in an exceedingly close vote of 2,367 to 2,300.[100]

With the convention over, it was back to organizing for the November election, setting up phone banks, arranging campaign events, raising funds, and planning media appearances. One of the most heated moments of the summer came in August when Democratic state chairman Bob Slagle charged that by holding stock in a company that did business with Libya, Clements was giving "aid and comfort" to terrorists who "harm and kill innocent children." Clements campaign manager George Bayoud called the charge "shocking, disgusting, irresponsible and gutter politics."[101] The following day, a *Dallas Morning News* editorial said Slagle's charge was a cheap shot and called on Governor White to disavow the chairman's statement.[102] Former president Ford was shocked at "this desperate political attack" and said Clements "served me and his country as deputy secretary of defense. He is, indeed, a true patriot."[103] Despite these charges, public opinion surveys conducted for the Clements campaign by Decision Making Information (DMI) showed the Republican's lead remained steady, from a margin of fifty-six to thirty-seven in June to fifty-five to thirty-one in August and fifty-two to thirty-six in September as the closing weeks of the campaign began.[104]

In October Clements and White held their only debate of the campaign. Hance was recruited to serve as a stand-in for White during the debate preparations. While state taxes and the no pass, no play educational reforms were major issues, White's purchase of a Japanese company's jet plane became a topic of discussion. When Clements was asked how he would balance the budget by cutting waste, he quickly responded "To cut waste, I'll sell the jet," then pulled out a list of fifteen items he would cut.[105]

Carolyn Barta described the Clements effort in 1986 as a textbook campaign. "The incumbent was down in the polls. The challenger was sticking to his script ('jobs, jobs, jobs'). Most of the race was being waged on TV. The strategy was not to make a mistake, because Clements was ahead and would win if he didn't make a mistake in the final days." As Election Day approached, the polls began to tighten, leading to heightened tension among the campaign workers. Yet on election night, all three networks at the time declared Clements the winner shortly after the polls closed.[106] Clements had recaptured the governor's mansion with 52.7 percent of the total vote and a margin of nearly 230,000 votes more than White. Clements's vote was up 460,000 over his totals in 1982, while White's vote total decreased by nearly 120,000. Of the state's 254 counties, Clements carried 194. Most significant for the future of Texas politics, although Clements had fallen off slightly from his 1978 performance in the big six counties, he had increased his percentage in suburban, small-town, and other metropolitan counties. Republicans were beginning to lose their advantage in the most urban counties but gaining strength in each of the other three categories of counties, most notably in small-town Texas.

Clements was able to win most of the traditional Republican areas except White's home territory of Harris County. The Republican candidate carried many of the traditionally Democratic rural counties and reduced the Democratic margin in rural Central and South Texas. Rove noted, "The Republican share of the rural vote grew tremendously in the 1980 Presidential election, receded somewhat in 1982 and came back with a vengeance in Phil Gramm's 203-county sweep in 1984." Success at the top of the ticket was making lower-ballot contests more competitive throughout the state. As Rove observed, "The willingness of rural and metro counties to cast Republican gubernatorial, Senatorial and Presidential votes is now being echoed by the election of Republicans to local offices."[107]

TABLE 10.1. BILL CLEMENTS'S GUBERNATORIAL VOTE PERCENTAGE BY
TYPE OF COUNTY IN HIS THREE GUBERNATORIAL CAMPAIGNS

Type of county	1978	1982	1986
Big six (N=6)	52.4%	49.6%	50.2%
Suburban (N=29)	50.9	46.9	56.9
Other metro (N=21)	51.2	46.8	54.1
Small-town (N=198)	45.6	39.5	56.8

While Clements reclaimed the office of governor, all other GOP state-wide candidates were defeated. However, attorney general candidate Roy Barrera Jr. came the closest of any candidate to pulling off a down-ballot victory. Running against incumbent Jim Mattox, he obtained 47.2 percent of the total vote to Mattox's 51.6 percent, losing by a margin of 146,000 votes. Meanwhile the party held on to its ten members of Congress and six state senators, while increasing their state House delegation to fifty-six.[108]

On January 20, 1987, Clements was inaugurated for his second term. Ironically, none other than John Hill administered the oath of office. After being defeated by Clements in 1978, Hill had been elected as chief justice of the Texas Supreme Court in 1984. Clements had a testy relationship with Lieutenant Governor Bill Hobby and the legislature during 1987, centering partly on the governor's efforts to balance the state budget.[109]

As vacancies occurred in various state positions, Clements was once again able to make key appointments that would have an impact on the party's future. In September Clements appointed former member of Congress Hance to the Railroad Commission. Hance would then become a candidate for election in November 1988, adding a well-known name to the party's statewide ticket in a critical presidential election year. A few months later, in January 1988, the governor named attorney Thomas Phillips to be chief justice of the Texas Supreme Court upon Hill's resignation. One month later Barbara Culver of Midland was also appointed to the Supreme Court, and for the first time two Republicans sat on the state's highest civil court.

A TEXAN BECOMES PRESIDENT AGAIN

As another presidential election approached, Texas moved its primary date to early March, along with a number of other southern states. The move was a concerted effort by southern Democratic state legislators to have more influence in the nominating process of both major political parties. The Democratic field seeking to recapture the White House included senators Gary Hart, Paul Simon, and Al Gore, along with governors Bruce Babbitt and Michael Dukakis, House Majority Leader Dick Gephardt, and the Reverend Jesse Jackson. Among the more serious GOP candidates were Vice President Bush, Senator Bob Dole, Representative Jack Kemp, and televangelist Pat Robertson. With no incumbent seeking re-election and a wide swath of candidates in both parties, a heavy primary turnout was expected.

For the first time Republicans would have three incumbent statewide officeholders—Railroad Commissioner Hance and Supreme Court justices Phillips and Culver—seeking re-election. Four candidates surfaced to oppose Democrat Lloyd Bentsen, who was seeking a fourth term in the US Senate. Business leaders Wes Gilbreath of Houston and Ned Snead of Georgetown were novice candidates self-financing much of their campaigns, while former state representative Milton Fox was building on contacts made in his losing campaign for a seat on the Railroad Commission two years earlier. Surprisingly to party activists, Panhandle member of Congress Beau Boulter also jumped into the nominating contest. His decision to give up what was viewed as a safe congressional seat irked a number of his past supporters, and in the end the Democrats recaptured his district.

Along with Hance's position, another slot on the three-member Railroad Commission was up for election in 1988. Four candidates, including former state representative Ed Emmett, who had sought the nomination two years previously, filed for the party's nod. Lively primary contests were also under way for two other positions on the Texas Supreme Court.

When the primary was held on March 8, Vice President Bush came out on top with 648,178 votes, followed by Robertson at 155,449 and Dole with 140,795 votes, Kemp having withdrawn from the race before primary day. Most significant of all was the GOP turnout of 1,014,956 voters, nearly twice the previous high reached two years earlier. After eight years of a Reagan presidency, more conservative Texans were now affiliating with the Republican Party by voting in its primary.[110] Both the overall turnout and Bush's sweep of all delegates was a surprise to most campaign strategists. Less than nine months before primary day the Bush campaign plan was predicated on the belief that "a turnout of between 500,000 to 600,000 voters can be anticipated." Emphasizing that GOP support was strongest among young voters and those who had lived in Texas less than ten years, Bush campaign planners concluded that "the number who have ever met George Bush personally" had declined, and that "to most voters, Bush is a distant figure they have seen on television … and not a neighbor from another part of their state."[111]

Runoffs would be needed to determine the party's nominees for US Senate, Railroad Commission, and one of the Supreme Court positions. In the runoff, Boulter received the nomination to oppose Senator Bentsen, Emmett was victorious for the Railroad Commission nod, and Nathan Hecht got the party's endorsement for the Supreme Court seat. In addition to the statewide slate, GOP candidates were nominated for more state and county offices than ever before in the state's history.

Before the June state convention it appeared that a battle for state chairman was brewing among Bush and Robertson supporters. Strake had determined that he would not be a candidate for another two-year term. Bush supporters and many other Republican activists were promoting Dallas GOP chairman Fred Meyer, and he officially announced for the state position in late March. Meyer said his goal was to "establish the Republican Party as the majority party in the state."

Meanwhile Robertson held a private meeting with sixteen prominent supporters, where he encouraged them to try for the chairmanship if they thought they could be competitive. Dallas oil and gas producer Roy Farrell, who had been Robertson's state campaign chair for the presidential primary, was considering a bid to replace Strake. According to one participant in the meeting, "One proposed slate would have Farrell run for state chairman, current vice chairwoman Diana Denman run for national committeewoman and Dallas lawyer Tom Pauken run for national committeeman. All three attended the meeting." Pauken later denied he was running for any party post but said he would not support Meyer. He claimed, "I'd be happy to support a conservative candidate for state chairman, and I don't care who he or she supported for president. Fred is not a conservative Republican."[112]

During the week of the state convention in Houston, an Americans for Robertson rally was planned for the same evening as several conservative groups were holding a traditional values rally. This created consternation among several Religious Right activists. As Bill Price of Texans United for Life noted, "The battle is over. There should no longer be Robertson supporters. It's time to be Bush supporters."[113] For some Robertson supporters his massive loss in the primary was not the final determinant. They were committed to securing as many delegates as possible to the national convention regardless of the primary vote.

In the buildup to the state convention, Bush and Robertson forces had locked horns attempting to control county and senatorial district conventions, where decisions on delegates to the state convention would be made. Several of these gatherings saw those on the losing side walk out and hold rump conventions resulting in challenges before the state convention credentials committee. Depending on the situation, both Bush and Robertson contingents were among the rump delegations challenging those named at the official gathering. While most of these disputes were settled in committee, one Robertson backer in Travis County who had helped organize a rump convention continued his challenge of the elected county chairman's seating all the way to a floor fight, where the Robertson backer lost in a voice vote. "By the time the state convention was held in June, party officials estimated 40 percent of the 6,000 delegates were Robertson enthusiasts."[114]

Despite the earlier projections of a challenge from the Robertson backers, Meyer was elected state chairman on a voice vote, as was his choice for vice chairman, Holly Decherd of Austin. Two supporters of Bush were opposed for the national committee positions, however. Incumbent national committeeman Ernest Angelo, long associated with Reagan, was unsuccessfully challenged by Farrell of Dallas, Robertson's statewide primary chair, while longtime party activist Penny Butler of Houston defeated state GOP vice chairman Denman of San Antonio.[115] Angelo's delegate vote was 2,968 to 1,793 for Farrell, while Butler prevailed with 2,567 votes to 1,885 for Denman.[116]

The convention's keynote speech was given, appropriately, by the vice president, who said the choice for president in 1988 came down to two different visions of America, with Michael Dukakis's "views and values ... too often, in my judgment, out of the mainstream." The crowd responded with enthusiasm.[117] Also addressing the delegates were Robertson, who called for a united effort to defeat the Democratic ticket, and three Cabinet secretaries: Bill Bennett (Education), Don Hodel (Interior), and Elizabeth Dole (Transportation). Also making brief appearances at the podium were all the statewide Republican candidates.

The state convention elected a delegation of all Bush supporters to the Republican National Convention in New Orleans. Leading the delegation was Governor Clements, who headed up an at-large slate that included Senator Gramm and most of the state's GOP members of Congress, along with state party officials Strake, Angelo, Butler, and Meyer. While Tower and O'Donnell reflected names from past Republican campaigns, future efforts were also represented in the delegation by Kay Bailey Hutchison, George W. Bush, and Karl Rove. Many of the delegates were longtime Bush supporters but also in the delegates were a number of Reagan backers from 1976 and 1980, including Steve Lilly of Nacogdoches, Dorothy Doehne of San Antonio, John Leedom of Dallas, and Wayne Thorburn of Austin. Perhaps the only major surprise at the New Orleans convention was the selection and nomination of Indiana senator Dan Quayle to join the ticket as candidate for vice president.

As the fall campaign began, Republicans knew that with popular senator

Lloyd Bentsen on the ballot as the vice presidential candidate nothing could be taken for granted. Texas Democrats came out of their national convention enthusiastic and proud to be represented on the national ticket. They still viewed themselves as the majority and dominant party in the state and were convinced that they could return Texas to the Democratic column in the upcoming presidential election, as well as remain in control of most state and local elective offices. To do so, however, they would need to be aggressive in their attacks. At a Democratic rally in Houston after the second Bush-Dukakis debate, Attorney General Jim Mattox claimed, "George Bush is phony. He's engaging in name-calling. He's being very deceptive. He represents everything that is bad and evil about politics."[118] The knives were out and would be thrown for the remaining weeks of the campaign.

However, the Democratic attacks appeared to be missing their targets. An October survey of 624 registered student voters at the University of Texas at Austin showed Bush with a 56 percent to 37 percent lead over Dukakis.[119] Surprisingly, Bush's performance among these young voters on the traditionally more liberal UT campus in Austin was in line with his overall statewide standing. In a separate October poll by SRI Research for the *Fort Worth Star-Telegram* and Dallas broadcaster WFAA, Bush was leading his Democratic opponent by 58 percent to 37.2 percent. The vice president led in all areas of the state except El Paso, Beaumont, and the Rio Grande Valley. His best big-city showing was in the Houston area, with a 63 percent to 33 percent advantage, and was topped by even larger margins in Lubbock, Amarillo, and Tyler. Meanwhile, in the contest for US senator, Bentsen had a 60 percent to 32 percent lead over Boulter.[120]

On Election Day the pollsters were proved right as a majority of Texas voters chose Bush and Bentsen, and the state continued to reflect its newfound level of two-party competition. While Bush beat Dukakis by a vote of 3,026,829 to 2,352,748, incumbent Democratic senator Bentsen (running for both vice president and re-election to the Senate, as Lyndon Johnson had done twenty-eight years earlier) easily topped Boulter by a margin of 3,149,806 to 2,129,228. The statewide contests for Railroad Commission and Supreme Court were evenly split between the two parties. Hance was elected to the Railroad Commission, but Emmett lost the other contest for a seat on the commission to incumbent Democrat Jim Nugent. Likewise, Republican candidates won three seats on the Supreme Court with the victories of Chief Justice Phillips and challengers Hecht and Eugene Cook. However, Justice Culver lost her office to former member of Congress Jack Hightower; Paul Murphy was defeated by Lloyd Doggett; and Raul Gonzalez, the first Hispanic elected to statewide office, retained his position on the Court.[121]

After being narrowly defeated in the 1984 Democratic primary for Senate and losing a Republican primary campaign for governor in 1986, former member of Congress Hance was once again successful. He had been opposed by state representative Clint Hackney of Houston, a popular legislator, but still won by slightly more than five hundred thousand votes. His victory and the margin by which it was achieved gave him encouragement to seek the gubernatorial nomination again in 1990.[122] The GOP also increased its numbers in the Texas legislature, picking up two more state Senate districts for a new total of eight while adding three more state representatives to give them fifty-seven members in the seventy-first regular session. Unfortunately, the party was set back in its congressional delegation, as member of Congress Mac Sweeney lost the 14th district in Central Southeast Texas to Greg Laughlin, who would later become a Republican, and the Panhandle's 13th district, which had been represented by Boulter, switched back once again to the Democrats.

Nationally Republicans had accomplished the difficult task of holding on to the White House after a two-term presidency. With a Republican governor and US senator and the breakthrough into other statewide elective positions, Texas Republicans were optimistic as they prepared for the 1990 election. It became evident early on that Clements would not be a candidate for another term as governor, a situation that might well open up some of the statewide offices currently held by Democrats seeking to advance to the governor's mansion. Additionally, the state legislature elected in 1990 would be responsible for drawing new district lines to reflect the results of the 1990 census. By gaining more legislative representation, Republicans could have more of an impact on redistricting.

By the start of the seventy-first regular session, Republicans were becoming a serious force in the Texas legislature not only because of the increase in GOP numbers but also due to changes in the composition of the Democratic delegation. As one reporter noted, "signs of a fundamental change in Texas politics could be seen: the power of the traditional conservative Democrat was receding, leaving a political void between an increasingly liberal Democratic Party and an increasingly strong Republican Party."[123] During what would be Clements's final legislative session, George Bayoud served as chief of staff, with former state representative Mike Toomey leading the governor's legislative liaison team. For years the legislature had basically overlooked and set aside the governor's proposed budget and worked off of the document submitted by the Legislative Budget Board, which comprised key House and Senate members. For the first time in 1989, Bayoud convinced the governor to simply adopt the legislative board's proposed budget rather than submitting one of his own. After the session ended, Clements chose Bayoud to be secretary of state, replacing Jack Rains, and Toomey moved over to serve as the governor's chief of staff.[124]

THE 1990 RACE FOR GOVERNOR

With no incumbent running for re-election, the governor's race attracted a strong field of candidates in both parties. One of the first to begin organizing was Railroad Commissioner Hance, who lined up Rove as overall campaign strategist with Jim Francis, Reggie Bashur, and Carol Treadway as key operatives and Dallas business leader Trammell Crow serving as finance chair.[125] Hance officially announced in mid-August 1989, claiming "I am the one candidate who does not need on-the-job training." One month later Hance began his campaign with a lead of thirty-three to twelve over his nearest challenger, with most likely Republican primary voters still undecided.[126]

Among the three serious rookie candidates, rancher and oil industry investor Clayton Williams was definitely the most colorful and had the most heavily financed campaign, much of it self-funded. As the campaign developed, he "soaked the airwaves with a good-old-boy image that appealed to the conservative Republican electorate. 'Texan from central casting' one supporter said of the stereotypical Texas image Williams projected."[127] Williams was proud of his image as a nonpolitician who was similar to the average Texan despite his vast personal wealth. "People claim I'm going after the Bubba vote. Hell, I am Bubba," he proclaimed at one news conference.[128]

Consistent with his self-description, Williams emphasized what he viewed as the practical over the philosophical in his stance on issues. He promised that in his war on illegal drug use he would teach young violators "the joy of busting rocks." The candidate claimed that as a successful business owner he knew firsthand "how to fight the politicians and the bureaucrats" and would make sure that he obtained "more bang for the buck" when spending state government funds. In explaining why he would succeed as governor, Williams reminded voters that "I am a salesman. I've even sold life insurance. You can sell anything if you can talk a guy into putting his beer money into premiums so that after he's dead his wife can live happily ever after with another man."[129]

As the campaign got under way and the extent of Clayton Williams's personal financial commitment to winning became evident, Hance backer Francis concluded that Williams was going to do to Hance what Clements had done in his initial nominating contest of 1978 against Ray Hutchison: outspend him enough to ensure the nomination.[130] Hance had raised 3.5 million dollars for the primary but estimated that Williams had spent a total of 17 million in the primary and general election, much of it personally contributed.[131]

Also in the race for the GOP nomination was Dallas attorney Tom Luce, best known for assisting H. Ross Perot to coordinate Governor Clements's war on drugs initiative, as well as Governor White's Select Committee on Public Education, which pushed for the no pass, no play policy for high school athletes. Luce's political consultant was Kevin Moomaw, former political director for the Republican Party of Texas, and he had key support from O'Donnell and Perot. Nevertheless, Moomaw emphasized that "Luce is his own man, and he's done a lot of things. People know him and know that he's been associated with Perot, . . . and if Luce is connected with him, Luce has got to be one of the best."[132] Promoted as "the thinking man's candidate," Luce was without question the one candidate who most resembled a policy wonk, with his detailed position papers on major issues. As primary day approached, he was able to obtain endorsements from ten major newspapers throughout the state.[133]

Soon Luce recognized that his major opponent would be Williams, with his populist appeal and his personal millions. From Luce's perspective, "I think we will become the majority party of Texas in the 1990's, and this election will say a lot to the voters about the direction we are taking and how we propose to govern. Clayton Williams is talking about the past, not the future. He is playing off a yearning rather than addressing the issues."[134] As the decade progressed, Luce proved correct in his prediction for the growth of the GOP. It soon became the clearly dominant political party despite its upcoming loss of the governor's mansion, a loss that, as of 2020, has not occurred again.

The final major candidate seeking the GOP nomination was Houston business leader Rains, who was also seeking election for the first time. Rains had served as 1986 campaign cochair for Clements, who later appointed him secretary of state. Rains was hoping to draw support from his home base of Harris County and from the various contacts he had made during his close association with Governor Clements. Despite being the only candidate from an area that provided a major share of the GOP primary vote, Rains had difficulty funding his campaign. His effort was fraught with other problems as well. For example, when he announced a ten-point program to improve education, reporters noted that it included only nine points. Rains said it had been prepared by aides educated in a faulty school system.[135]

On the other side three major candidates filed for the Democratic nomination. Current attorney general Mattox and state treasurer Ann Richards had first been elected in 1982. That was the year in which four liberals captured election to statewide office, an indication of the growing left-wing domination of the Texas Democratic party. Also entering the race was former governor White, who was seeking a comeback much like Clements had done four years previously.

Mattox brought to the campaign a reputation as a street fighter, with his slogan Texas Tough and his record of personally watching twenty-nine executions. He pestered the media to inquire about Ann Richards's alleged drug use, and in a televised candidate debate she twice refused to answer the question. In advance of the campaign Richards released her autobiography, *Straight from the Heart*, which gained her much talk-show coverage.[136] Prior to the book's release, which described her recovery from alcoholism, Richards gained national exposure at the 1988 Democratic National Convention with her attack on Vice President Bush: "Poor George, he was born with a silver foot in his mouth."[137] As Dennis Sheehan, Tarrant County Democratic chairman, described Richards's situation, "When she gives a speech, it is like having Johnny Carson come to town. She draws a crowd and has them rolling in the aisles, but there is no way to know whether the folks turn out because she's a good show or because they're going to vote for her."[138]

Throughout the fall and winter White struggled to gain traction and overcome Democrats' memories of his previous administration and subsequent loss in the rematch with Clements. At times polls of likely Democratic primary voters showed him running close to the top, but his support fell off significantly as the date of the primary approached.

With seven major candidates for governor, the state's primary contests were expected to draw roughly 2.5 million voters to what had become the preliminaries in Texas politics during the two-party era. As political scientist Richard Murray noted, "You have at least two or three candidates running in each primary strong enough to win but every one of them has the kind of weaknesses that could cause a lot of voters to shift away from them. The campaign is being played out in the fog and I think it will be down to the wire."[139]

Meanwhile Republicans were running a full slate of qualified candidates for other statewide offices, led by Gramm, who was seeking a second term in the US Senate. Every statewide elected office, save for three seats on the Court of Criminal Appeals, drew multiple applicants; it was the longest ballot and most heavily contested GOP primary in state history.

On March 13, 1990, the two major parties held their primary elections. When the votes were counted, the final outcome was unclear in several races. That was not the situation, however, for the GOP gubernatorial nomination, as Williams corralled 520,104 votes, for 60.8 percent of the total, with Hance a distant runner-up with 132,142 votes (15.5 percent), Luce at 115,835 (13.5 percent), and Rains with 82,461 (9.6 percent). Three other minor candidates combined garnered support from 4,779 Republicans, resulting in a total primary vote approaching 900,000. In the race for the attorney general nomination, state senator Buster Brown squeaked by with 359,721 votes, just barely reaching a majority of 50.1 percent. Dallas district judge Patricia Hill gathered 200,255 votes, Tex Lezar had 109,549 votes, and Bobby Steelhammer garnered support from 48,643 primary voters. Former state representative Kay Bailey Hutchison gained the nomination for state treasurer, while Beau Boulter bounced back from his loss to Bentsen and was nominated for the Railroad Commission. A candidate with the same name as a former president and a former state treasurer, Warren G. Harding Jr., defeated two other candidates for comptroller with 60.6 percent of the vote. All three positions on the Texas Supreme Court had GOP primary contests, with incumbent chief justice Tom Phillips, district judge John Cornyn, and attorney Charles Ben Howell securing the party's nomination.

A few races remained undetermined at the end of the primary, resulting in runoffs for land commissioner and agriculture commissioner, where two candidates in three-way contests gained roughly 47 percent of the vote. Business leader Wes Gilbreath fell short of a majority in his contest for land commissioner with Grady Yarbrough and William James John, but won his runoff by a two-to-one margin. Likewise, former Democratic state representative Rick Perry, seeking the nod for agriculture commissioner against Richard McIver and Gene L. Duke, won his nomination in the runoff by a sizeable margin. Perry's success in the primary was a signal to other conservatives that they were welcome in the Republican Party. As Rove recalled, "Democrat Rick Perry had planned to retire from the legislature until his best friend, David Weeks, and I talked him into switching parties and running for the GOP nomination for agriculture commissioner."[140] After the runoffs, the Texas Republican Party was ready to field its most complete statewide ticket yet, leaving only one position on the Court of Criminal Appeals without a GOP contestant.

On the Democratic side, a runoff would be needed to determine the nominee for governor. Treasurer Richards came in first with 580,191 votes, gaining support from 39 percent of primary voters but far short of the needed majority. Close behind was Attorney General Mattox with 546,103 votes (36.7 percent), while former governor White ended up in third place and out of the runoff with 286,161 votes (19.2 percent). Richards was able to expand her support in the runoff to 640,995 (57.1 percent), while Mattox's vote totals fell off to 481,739 (42.9 percent). Surveys showed that the fierce battle between Richards and Mattox had turned off many voters. Over the next several months polls showed Williams with a substantial lead over Richards.[141]

1990: SETBACKS AND SIGNIFICANT VICTORIES

As the general election campaign got underway, Williams had millions of his own money that he was willing to spend and with which he hired a team of first-rate political professionals.[142] Despite his money and his skilled advisors, however, Williams continued to have foot-in-mouth disease. Shortly after the primary, Williams invited reporters to his ranch near Alpine. When heavy rain and high winds caused the postponement of a roundup, the GOP candidate declared, "Bad weather, it's like rape. If it's inevitable, just relax and enjoy it."[143] The negative feedback from the media and especially women voters was considerable. The response to his comments substantiated the earlier prediction of journalist Dave McNeely, who claimed "I think that will be Ann Richards' big secret in 1990. When they get in that voting booth, there are many women who are going to vote for a woman if one is on the ballot, no matter what their husbands may do."[144] His prediction came true in November as many normally Republican women switched over to vote for the Democratic candidate for governor.

Williams's gaffes began to build up. When asked about his position on a constitutional amendment on the November ballot designed to expand the governor's powers, Williams admitted he was unaware of it. In response to another question, he proclaimed that he had paid no income tax in 1986. Referring to Richards, he claimed he would "head her and hoof her and drag her through the dirt" as if she were a cow on his ranch. He later refused to shake her hand at a joint appearance and called her a liar. By the end it was clear that Richards was not winning the race; rather, Williams was losing it.

As late as early October, Williams was still ahead among men by the sizeable margin of 60.5 percent to 27.3 percent while breaking nearly even among women (42.9 percent to 44.5 percent for Richards). On Election Day his lead with men was still substantial at 56.0 percent to 44.0 percent, but he had declined among women to fall behind Richards 41.0 percent to 59.0 percent. As Sue Tolleson-Rinehart and Jeanie R. Stanley noted in their book on the Richards campaign, "In the end, Clayton Williams made her job easier by finally breaking the 'cowboy code' so many times that he became unacceptable to many who would otherwise have been his natural—and loyal—Republican constituency."[145]

While Richards was making inroads with female voters, Williams had an appeal to other segments of the electorate. For one, he was running at a time when the Republican Party was gaining in its appeal to Texans and was running on a ticket headed by popular US senator Gramm. With a strong statewide slate and more serious contenders for state legislative and county positions, the friends-and-neighbors appeal of these other candidates was expected to bring out more GOP-leaning voters. A second advantage Williams had was his relationship with Mexican-Americans. As one reporter noted, "Williams has the strongest ties to Hispanics of any modern Texas Republican.... Williams, who delivered six or seven minutes of his Fort Worth (Republican state convention) speech in a slow, drawling Spanish, may cut into the Hispanic vote."[146] Finally, Williams had an especially strong appeal in Aggieland because he would be the first governor to have graduated from Texas A&M University.

Indicative of the two-party era, Ann Richards won by a close margin of 99,239 votes out of the 3,892,746 votes cast, recapturing the governor's mansion once more for the Democratic Party. What was different about this contest was the composition of the vote for each candidate in terms of geography. While Houston and Dallas had been voting Republican in many elections since 1961, Richards carried not only them but also the other four most populous counties, providing her with a net vote advantage of 143,133, more than her overall margin of victory against Williams. Outside the Big 6 counties, Williams succeeded in carrying twenty-one of the twenty-nine counties surrounding Dallas–Fort Worth, Houston, San Antonio, and Austin. These suburban counties provided him with a net advantage of 38,563 votes, while he split the twenty-one other metropolitan counties spread around the state, carrying twelve of the twenty-one but falling behind Richards in this category by 4,670 votes.

That left the remaining 198 small-town and rural counties. Paul Burka made special note of a development that was appearing in state politics and ran counter to the historical distribution of party support: "The major change in Texas politics is the change in the old conventional wisdom that the Democrats would always lose the urban areas and win the rural areas.... Probably the single most startling fact of politics in the modern era has been the Republican gains in rural Texas."[147] This phenomenon first occurred in the 1986 gubernatorial election when Clements carried rural Texas in his rematch with White. It showed up again in 1990 when Williams ended with a 10,001 vote advantage over Richards from the state's 198 small-town and rural counties. Williams carried 152 counties to Richards's 102, but the final statewide tally showed Richards to be the victor by a margin of less than one hundred thousand votes.

Although the governor's race was the focus of most attention, several other statewide contests were settled in the November election. As expected, Senator Gramm won easily by a margin of 872,370 votes more than his opponent, state senator Hugh Parmer of Fort Worth. Gramm's overwhelming support was reflected in his ability to carry 223 of the state's 254 counties. The GOP candidates for lieutenant governor and attorney general ran competitive races, but they garnered only 45.0 percent and 45.1 percent respectively. However, four other statewide candidates did bring home GOP victories. Supreme Court chief justice Phillips easily defeated fellow Court member Oscar Mauzy, while Cornyn joined the Supreme Court by defeating perennial candidate Gene Kelly. Even more significant breakthroughs came in the elections of state treasurer and agriculture commissioner, as Hutchison and Perry achieved down-ballot victories for Republicans.

The victories of Hutchison, Perry, and Cornyn brought to statewide prominence three individuals who would play important roles in the growth and success of the Republican Party of Texas well into the twenty-first century. Despite the party's ability to re-elect Gramm, win four down-ballot statewide contests, and see a flawed gubernatorial candidate lose by fewer than a hundred thousand votes, Republicans came away from the election with three fewer seats in the Texas House of Representatives and no gains in their congressional and state senate delegations. Progress had been made, but it was balanced by the loss of the governor's mansion and a setback in the effort to become a more substantial presence in the Texas legislature. These losses meant that once again Democrats would be in control of redistricting in 1991, and thus able to limit any potential GOP legislative growth for the next ten years.

With Ann Richards in the governor's mansion, Republicans in the legislature were once again confronting a solid Democratic leadership as they attempted to influence public policy. There would be more setbacks nationally in the next election, as the party would lose the White House after twelve years in office. At the same time, back home in Texas, Republicans were beginning their move to become the dominant force in state politics. While Richards remained personally popular, her administration of state government was challenged by a number of controversies and mini-scandals. As Hance noted, "She is well liked but like the aunt that no one in the family wants to run the business."[148] This perception would weigh on her ability to be re-elected in 1994.

While the 1990 election proceeded, two major events were occurring in other parts of the world. First was the demise of the USSR and the separation from Russia of a number of components of the Soviet Union, combined with the reassertion of independence by countries that had been behind the Iron Curtain. Throughout this period of uncertainty and confusion, President Bush led with a forceful and diplomatic hand, ensuring that those seeking freedom would be supported. Defeating communism had been a hallmark of the policies of President Reagan, and now, shortly after the conclusion of his term of office, Reagan's chosen successor was seeing it occur.

The second critical development on the world stage was the invasion of Kuwait by the forces of Iraq's dictator, Saddam Hussein. The Bush administration brought together a coalition of nations to attempt diplomatic efforts to remove Iraqi troops from Kuwait, followed by a military response that drove them back across the Kuwait-Iraq border. These efforts began in late summer 1990 and continued through the end of February 1991. With the success of Desert Storm, the president's popularity reached new heights. Throughout the first five months of 1991, Bush's favorability ratings never dipped below 70 percent; they reached their zenith of 89 percent in early March.

The news was not as positive on the domestic front. Although he had famously pledged "Read my lips, no new taxes" when he ran for office, President Bush was forced by the Democratic Congress to approve the raising of new tax revenues to deal with the growing deficit. Shortly thereafter, the nation entered the recession of 1990–1991, and Bush was blamed for what was viewed as a weak economic recovery. Knowing they could not challenge him on his foreign policy record, Democrats followed the advice of James Carville, who declared, "It's the economy, stupid."

1992: MORE SETBACKS AND SIGNIFICANT VICTORIES

As the 1992 presidential campaign began, Bush was challenged from the right within his party by Patrick Buchanan and from somewhere else by independent candidate and billionaire business leader H. Ross Perot. Buchanan reminded Republicans of the broken pledge to oppose any new taxes, but also campaigned on a range of what became known as social issues—demands for a reduction in immigration and opposition to multiculturalism, gay rights, and abortion. While Buchanan lost every Republican primary in which his name appeared on the ballot, he was given a prime-time speaking slot at the Republican National Convention in Houston, allowing him to gain more national exposure for his rightist views. Meanwhile, as the fall campaign developed, Perot focused on his opposition to free trade, budget deficits, and the national debt, and was motivated also by what many viewed as a personal animosity toward the Bush family and George H. W. Bush in particular.

Among Texas Republicans, George H. W. Bush remained a hometown boy, personally known to many of the longtime party faithful. In the March Republican primary, the president overwhelmed Buchanan and three other candidates by winning 69.8 percent of the eight hundred thousand votes cast. State chairman Fred Meyer's prediction that the president would win big came true as he also received all 121 delegates from the state. The only other statewide positions on the ballot were for one member of the Railroad Commission and three members each on the Supreme Court and the Court of Criminal Appeals. In the close contest for Railroad Commission, Barry Williamson of Midland bested former Austin mayor Carole Keeton Rylander by twenty thousand votes for a 51.5 percent to 48.5 percent victory and the Republican nomination.

At the June state convention, President Bush was the keynote speaker, rallying the troops for the fall campaign and preparing for the Republican National Convention, which would, once again, be held in Texas. Social conservatives dominated the platform discussions and strengthened the party's anti-abortion and anti-homosexuality planks. Additionally some observers claim that social conservatives and evangelicals gained a majority on the SREC at the convention.[149] State chairman Meyer was elected to a third term, and the new vice chairman was Gayle West of Pasadena, while both Ernest Angelo and Penny Butler were re-elected to represent Texas on the Republican National Committee.

The 1992 Republican National Convention was held in August at the Astrodome in Houston. Defeated presidential contender Buchanan gave the opening-night speech. In his controversial address he proclaimed that there was "a religious war going on in our country for the soul of America" and then spelled out his socially conservative views on a number of issues. This was also the last year in which Reagan would address the delegates, telling them, "Whatever else history may say about me when I'm gone, I hope it will record that I appealed to your best hopes, not your worst fears, to your confidence rather than your doubts." In their acceptance speeches President Bush and Vice President Quayle attempted to set the tone for the re-election campaign and saw a subsequent bounce in their poll standings against Democrat Bill Clinton and independent candidate Perot.

Although Bush carried Texas once again, he came up short in the national election, losing to Clinton by a vote of 370 to 168 in the Electoral College. Perot obtained over 18 percent of the popular vote, coming in third, but he was unable to carry any states and received no Electoral College votes. With 40.6 percent of the total vote in Texas, Bush carried his home state by a 215,000 vote margin over Clinton (37.1 percent) and Perot (22.0 percent).

In down-ballot races, the Texas GOP upset a number of Democratic incumbents. In a congressional district running west from San Antonio, Republican Henry Bonilla ousted Representative Albert G. Bustamante to become the party's ninth member of Congress among the thirty representing the state. Several other Republican congressional candidates ran viable campaigns, including Chip Taberski, a former local television sports anchor, who came within five thousand votes of winning the El Paso–based district. For one of three slots on the Railroad Commission, Williamson trounced Lena Guerrero, a former state representative who had been appointed to the commission by Governor Richards. Williamson's margin of victory was more than eight hundred thousand votes.

In the Supreme Court contests two of the three incumbents were defeated, as Republican Craig Enoch bested Justice Oscar Mauzy, while Republican incumbent Eugene Cook lost to Rose Spector. Only Democratic justice and former member of Congress Jack Hightower was re-elected. The other statewide contests saw Republican candidate Lawrence Meyers win one of the three Court of Criminal Appeals positions by defeating incumbent judge Pete Benavides. While the GOP picked up an additional four state Senate seats to bring their total to thirteen of thirty-one, the House delegation only increased from fifty-eight to fifty-nine when state representative Pedro Nieto of Uvalde switched parties to join the GOP in 1993.

As the Reagan and Bush administrations came to an end, Texas Republicans were beginning to see long-term signs of growth even in the midst of losing the governor's mansion and the White House. By the late 1970s Texas had become a two-party state, switching party control of the governor's office every four years, sending members of both parties to the US Senate, and increasing Republican representation in the congressional and state legislative delegations. Even more important to the party's future were the inroads being made among county elected officials, stretching out from urban areas to suburban and even some rural areas of the state. Change was on the way, and 1993 would bring an important victory for Texas Republicans in their drive to become the dominant force in Texas politics.

ELEVEN

GEORGE W. BUSH AND THE
REPUBLICAN MAJORITY

As 1993 began, Texas Republicans were in a funk. Having lost the governor's mansion two years earlier, they now found themselves shut out of the White House, which was doubly disappointing since the presidential loser was their friend and fellow Texan George H. W. Bush. In reality, however, the Texas GOP was on the verge of two critical election victories that would lead to the party's almost total domination of state politics by the end of the century.

The mood of disappointment and despair changed quickly as incoming president Bill Clinton selected Senator Lloyd Bentsen Jr. as secretary of the Treasury. After twenty-two years holding one of the two US Senate seats from Texas, Bentsen would be vacating it, creating the need for a special election on May 1, 1993. As governor, Ann Richards had the responsibility to appoint an individual to serve until a new senator was elected, and she chose Robert Krueger to fill the position on an interim basis.

ELECTING A SECOND GOP SENATOR

Given the traditional longevity of Texas senators, it was no surprise that twenty-four candidates filed to compete in an all-party election with no primary to sort out the political parties' nominees. Among the Republicans seeking the office were members of Congress Joe Barton and Jack Fields and state treasurer Kay Bailey Hutchison. Barton had first been elected to Congress in 1984 to fill the seat vacated by Phil Gramm. Fields had defeated longtime Democratic member of Congress Bob Eckhardt in 1980 and had been easily re-elected every two years since then. Hutchison had a long history of involvement in Texas politics, beginning with her time as a political reporter for KPRC-TV in Houston, then as press secretary to Republican National

Committee cochair Anne Armstrong, followed by election as the first female Republican state representative in 1972, a losing primary campaign for Congress in 1982, and finally election as state treasurer in 1990.[1]

During the special election campaign Barton stressed his ties to Senator Gramm, Fields claimed to best relate to blue-collar workers, and Hutchison noted that she had already won a statewide contest and was the only woman in the race.[2] Campaign strategist Karl Rove believed that Hutchison "was very well positioned for the 1993 special election. She had name recognition through winning a tough race in 1990 for state treasurer that she was not expected to win." With her record in office as treasurer, Hutchison could say, "Look, I've taken these conservative principles, such as fiscal responsibility, and actually followed through on them, cutting government spending and actually doing a better job."[3]

Hutchison could draw on her previous years as a state representative from Houston as well as her more recent involvement as a member of the state Republican executive committee (SREC) from Dallas, where she lived with her husband, former GOP state chairman Ray Hutchison. Heading up her campaign for the senate was Jim Francis, a Republican campaign activist who had held similar leadership roles in the Bill Clements and Kent Hance gubernatorial campaigns, as well as Gramm's victorious Senate race in 1984.[4]

Barton's campaign and his supporters were maneuvering to have the SREC give its blessing to a candidate prior to the May special election. However, when the SREC met, the members voted thirty-six to twenty-eight by secret ballot not to endorse any candidate. Hutchison had urged her supporters to vote for no endorsement to avoid splitting the party.[5]

The multicandidate field also included two competitive Democratic candidates in Krueger and Richard Fisher. Krueger had been elected to Congress in 1974 and re-elected two years later before challenging Senator John Tower in 1978 and losing an extremely close race to the incumbent Republican. Six years later Krueger lost the Democratic nomination for senator but bounced back to win a seat on the Railroad Commission in 1990. Governor Richards's appointment of Krueger to fill Bentsen's Senate seat gave Krueger a slight advantage of incumbency but also the responsibility of being in Washington and casting votes during some of the time leading up to the May 1 special election.

Fisher was an investment banker in Dallas who had previously worked on Wall Street and had been a special assistant in the Treasury Department during the Carter administration. He had been an advisor to the 1992 Reform Party presidential campaign of fellow Dallasite H. Ross Perot, and according to the *New York Times*, "He ran on an agenda of government reform torn largely from the pages of Perot's platform."[6] Fisher was also the son-in-law of former member of Congress Jim Collins of Dallas, who had been the GOP nominee against Bentsen in the 1982 senatorial election.

Although twenty-four individuals had filed for the election, only one other candidate won a substantial number of votes: José Angel Gutiérrez, founding member of La Raza Unita political party and former Zavala County judge. With a total vote of slightly more than 2 million, Gutierrez received 52,103 votes, and only two other candidates' totals reached five figures.

In the May 1 election, Hutchison barely edged out Krueger, 593,338 to 593,239, a margin of ninety-nine votes. Barton, Fields, Fisher, and Gutiérrez finished in that order but all far behind. That meant there would be a June 5 runoff between a Republican and a Democrat, each of whom had drawn roughly the same number of votes in the initial contest.

For the runoff campaign, both candidates drew on celebrity support to motivate their supporters to turn out. Hutchison was joined by actor Charlton Heston for appearances in Dallas and College Station, while Krueger held an early voting rally with feminist Gloria Steinem and aired television commercials by Cybill Shepherd, known by Texans for her role in *The Last Picture Show* and the subsequent film *Texasville*.[7]

Despite the closeness of the first round, the runoff election was no contest, as Hutchison received 1,188,716 votes to Krueger's 576,538, for a margin of 67.3 percent to 32.7 percent. Krueger's runoff total was 16,701 votes fewer than he had obtained in the first election, while Hutchison more than doubled her total. As the *New York Times* report on the election noted, "Her victory is the largest margin ever for a Republican in a statewide race in Texas. It is all but certain to turn her into a Republican star, the kind of living proof that party leaders are searching for to show that they can match the Democrats with talented female politicians."[8]

After having won a special election for the Senate in 1961, and then retaining the seat in each subsequent election, the Texas GOP had now won another special election to hold both US Senate seats from the state. Additionally Hutchison would be at the top of the statewide ballot in 1994 when Republicans would seek to remove Ann Richards from the governor's mansion.

A GOVERNOR'S CONTEST DEVELOPS

Among those exploring the gubernatorial race was George W. Bush. He had considered seeking the nomination in 1990 but backed away while his father was president. Now with Clinton in the White House, family considerations had lessened and his brother Jeb was gearing up for a race for governor in his home state of Florida.

Throughout 1993 George W. Bush met privately with close associates and advisors to assess the political climate and decide whether to launch a campaign. Among those with whom he consulted were Francis and Rove. Francis concluded that people liked Richards but disliked her policies, warning Bush that any successful candidate had to treat Richards courteously and avoid the aggressive approach taken by Clayton Williams in 1990. Rove, who had consulted on Hutchison's special election victory, believed the state was moving in a more Republican direction and that Bush had a path to victory if he was disciplined and concentrated on a few key issues. Still others, even within Bush's close family, had doubts as to whether he could defeat Richards. "Nearly all those closest to George W told him to wait four years until she was out of office to challenge someone less popular."[9]

Meanwhile Rob Mosbacher Jr., son of the Commerce secretary during the George H. W. Bush administration, started making noises about running for governor. Mosbacher had developed a number of statewide contacts in his losing campaign for lieutenant governor in 1990 and as the head of the 1992 Victory Committee. With his family, business, and political connections, Mosbacher had the financial resources to mount a serious effort. After analyzing the situation, however, he backed away and left the field to Bush. In 1997 Mosbacher would lose a close race for mayor of Houston to Lee Brown.

Going into the 1994 gubernatorial campaign, Ann Richards had a job approval rating of 67 percent and over $4 million in her campaign account. Her backers were confident that she would be elected to a second term.[10] Even so, Bush believed that "While Texans were inclined to give her a second term, their support was driven by her personal appeal, not confidence that she could address the state's pressing problems."[11] A campaign that was forward-looking and concentrated on a few key issues of importance to most voters could be successful.

Richards did have weak spots, including, for some, her image as a prochoice feminist, a posture that hurt her in the Democratic primary, where her unknown opponent, Gary Espinosa, carried three counties and received 230,310 votes for 22.2 percent of the total. This was a clear signal to Rove that the governor was having difficulty uniting her own party behind her reelection. "You got a sense of Democrats being unhappy with her and telegraphing that by voting for another name on the ballot."[12] Meanwhile Bush was winning his primary over another little-known candidate, Ray Hollis, with 93.3 percent of the total GOP primary vote.

It was evident also that changes in the political environment were occurring, most recently in Senator Hutchison's special election margin of victory, but also in the closeness of Richards's own election in 1990, which she won by a margin of less than 100,000 votes against a flawed candidate. Changes in party identification were also apparent in a comparison of survey results from 1984 and 1994. As one group of political scientists reported, "We find that more Texans identify themselves as Republicans today than in 1984, nearly eliminating the historical predominance of Democrats in the state, and that party identification continues to influence Texans' voting choices. At the same time, the ideology of the Texas electorate in 1994 is almost exactly the same as it was in 1984. As many Texans report being conservative today as they did a decade ago."[13]

Ever since the mid-1980s, the youngest cohort of voters, age eighteen to twenty-nine, had remained strongly Republican in their party identification, although most considered themselves independent. It was the oldest voters, age sixty-two or older, who remained the most Democratic, but over time they were being replaced by more Republican segments of the population. Indeed, it had been a cadre of young and middle-aged voters in the 1960s and 1970s who had led the way in building a competitive Republican Party, and as they aged they continued to provide a growing base of support for the GOP.[14]

Looking back at the results of the 1994 election, commentator Paul Burka identified an additional factor expanding the Republican base: the movement of GOP-oriented voters to Texas as the state's economy expanded. "Population growth, not anger, explains the Republican advantage. . . . Much of the growth in Texas has occurred in Republican areas of big cities and their suburbs."[15] Even into the mid-1990s, the two largest cities in the state, Dallas and Houston, were still the center of a growing Republican voter block, while the rural areas and smaller urban centers remained in their historic Democratic tradition. Only slowly were Republicans gaining strength in many suburban and exurban counties, and it would not be until the early twenty-first century that many small-town and rural counties would swing to the GOP.

In planning the campaign for governor, Rove was well aware of these demographic and political changes taking place in Texas. "The state was in the midst of a pretty phenomenal partisan shift. Starting in 1978, the dominant political dynamic has been the growth of the Republican suburbs—the overnight transition in places like Williamson County, Collin County, Denton County from being semirural Democratic strongholds to burgeoning sources of Republican strength."[16]

THE 1994 REPUBLICAN STATE CONVENTION

Once the primary was over and the party's nominees for the November election were determined, attention shifted to the Republican state convention, to be held in Fort Worth in early June. State chairman Meyer had announced that he would not be a candidate for another term, and this decision brought forth three candidates to succeed him. Meyer had a long record of successful leadership in the party, including as chairman of the Dallas GOP when it became the dominant force in local politics, followed by six years as state party chairman. But, it was claimed, "To the Christian right, Meyer represented all the secular, economic conservatives who were insufficiently committed to the constitutional rights of the unborn.... The Christian right accused Meyer of never having been to a pro-life rally, their litmus test for party officers."[17]

Of the three candidates to succeed Meyer, member of Congress Joe Barton could be described as the establishment candidate, with endorsements from Meyer and senators Gramm and Hutchison. However, Barton's chances were hurt among some delegates by his commitment to continue representing his district in Washington while serving as state chairman of the Texas party. Barton had been elected to Congress in 1984 to succeed Gramm and had acquired a solid economic and social conservative voting record.

Tom Pauken had a long history of involvement in Republican politics, beginning with his time as chairman of the College Republican National Committee in the mid-1960s, followed by close, but losing races for Congress and an appointment as director of ACTION, a federal domestic volunteer agency, during the Reagan administration. Pauken was endorsed by former governor Clements and three recent former state party chairmen (Ray Barnhart, Chet Upham, and George Strake), yet "he and his backers viewed themselves as insurgents waging a grass-roots campaign against the hand-picked choice of the state's top Republican Party leaders." As political scientist Paul Lenchner viewed the situation, "What was familiar was that the two strongest candidates, Pauken and Barton, shared a staunch conservative philosophy. Their backers agreed on the issues, but were split on insider-outsider lines."[18]

While both Pauken and Barton could be described as social conservatives, a clear distinction was evident in Pauken's relationship to the Bush family. To Pauken there was a continuing ideological battle in the Republican Party that boiled down to whether one was a Reagan Republican or a Bush Republican. Pauken claimed, "The groundwork for the death of the conservative movement was laid by the selection of George Herbert Walker Bush to be Ronald Reagan's vice presidential running mate in 1980."[19] He maintained that Reagan was a true conservative but Bush was merely a pragmatist who had strayed from the path set out by the fortieth president.

Pauken had been appointed director of ACTION in 1981 but was unsuccessful in his attempts to acquire another position in the Reagan administration. He contended that James A. Baker III, at the time chief of staff to the president, was "in a position to block me from going any higher in a second Reagan term."[20] Syndicated columnist Robert Novak claimed, "Baker undercut him in dealing with left-wing activists, then killed an attempt by Ed Meese to put Pauken in charge of implementing the Grace Commission report to streamline government. Finally, Baker blocked his appointment as ambassador to the Caribbean Basin Initiative, effectively keeping Pauken out of the Reagan second-term administration."[21] It is no surprise that Pauken believed his campaign for chairman of the party was taking place "in spite of strong, private opposition from Bush and Rove."[22]

The third candidate stood apart as representative of what had historically been the base of the Texas GOP. She was solidly conservative on economic issues but adhered to a moderate stance on what were now called social issues. Dolly Madison McKenna had run a respectable race against Democratic member of Congress Mike Andrews from a Houston-area district in 1992. McKenna turned out to be the last pro-choice candidate for high party office as the newly mobilized grass roots moved the GOP inexorably into a more rightward position on abortion, religious issues, family values, and homosexuality. While many big-city and suburban Republicans of the 1950s to 1970s had been supportive of family planning efforts such as those of Planned Parenthood and ignored the issue of sexual preference, Republican orthodoxy now stressed a prolife position and a multitude of other social issues, including opposition to homosexuality.

In her speech to the convention delegates before the vote for chairman, McKenna pulled no punches in expressing her concern over the direction of the party: "There are those people in this audience that want the Republican Party to be a church. You are very welcome in the Republican Party but the Republican Party is not a church." McKenna's support was limited at the convention. Longtime party activist Roy Getting observed, "I call them the righteous right. It's a little frightening to find people that say if you don't agree with them you don't belong."[23] The base of the Texas party was changing, and social conservatives would soon become a dominant majority in internal party matters.

After the senatorial district caucuses voted 54 percent for Pauken, 39 percent for Barton, and only 8 percent for McKenna, the latter two candidates withdrew, and Pauken was elected by acclimation.[24] In a further departure from the past, incumbent vice chairman Gayle West of Houston was ousted by Susan Weddington, a social conservative activist from San Antonio. Consistent with the rightward movement of the party on these then divisive issues, the platform called for a total ban on abortion except to save the mother's life.

THE 1994 GENERAL ELECTION

As the race for governor geared up after the state party conventions, it was clear that Bush was running a disciplined campaign. In addition to his long-time advisor Rove, the triumvirate overseeing the campaign included manager Joe Allbaugh and communications chief Karen Parfitt Hughes. Allbaugh came from Oklahoma, where he had worked for US senator and later governor Henry Bellmon, while Hughes had most recently served as Texas GOP executive director under state chairman Meyer.

The Bush campaign focused on the four key issues of education reform, juvenile justice, poverty remediation, and tort reform. Rove noted, "What struck me about each of these issues, especially the original three, was Bush's way of framing them. His approach was conservative yet broad and inclusive. He didn't sound like a run-of-the-mill Republican."[25] Reggie Bashur, media consultant to the campaign, who had handled press relations in the campaign and administration of the last Republican governor, Clements, stressed this presence of an overall theme to the campaign. The four main issues "were all interconnected with Bush's basic philosophy and approach, which was more individual responsibility. He went out and got his sea legs by going into smaller towns and rural areas, getting more comfortable, more relaxed, and sharpening his presentation. That was all part of Karl's plan."[26]

While the issue focus remained consistent, Rove was also analyzing demographic and political trends to maximize the campaign's presence and influence in those areas of the state where the candidate could make inroads in his contest with Richards. Seeing the governor's weakness in a number of rural counties in the Democratic primary, Rove had an opening and urged the candidate to make a number of appearances in smaller cities and towns across the state before shifting his attention to the major media centers. This gave Bush exposure in areas where his presence was major news and allowed him to further develop his skills as a candidate.

The Richards campaign monitored every Bush appearance, hoping to catch him in contradictory statements or erroneous claims, or simply being stumped by a policy question. Chuck McDonald, Richards's campaign press secretary, recalled, "For six months [Bush] just went to Sweetwater and every little town in the state, itty-bitty places, making a stump speech. I assigned John Hannah III to go to all his events and tape-record them so we would get him saying something we could exploit as far as contradicting himself or not being able to answer questions. It was a gigantic wasted effort. He had his note cards, and he would show up and make his speech. There was no deviation. There wasn't a new sentence. He would greet John, and they'd say hi to each other and joke around. Then he would get up and make his speech, and it would never change. It was a good strategy."[27]

Throughout the campaign the Bush team worked tirelessly to keep the emphasis on the issue and philosophical differences between the two candidates. State senator Florence Shapiro of Plano told a gathering of the Texas Federation of Republican Women, "the Governor's race in 1994 is not a race about gender. It is a race about philosophies. . . . Philosophy is why we have chosen the GOP and that is why it is up to us to remind our friends to focus on the real issues and the leadership abilities of all our candidates in 1994."[28]

Bush was careful to give due deference to the governor. It was Richards who let slip a derogatory comment about her opponent that was spread statewide by the media. In August, at a campaign rally in Texarkana, Richards referred to Bush as "some jerk who thinks he can be governor." As campaign manager Mary Beth Rogers recalled the incident, "The story was all over the newspapers the next day, and it hurt us decisively. From that moment on, we knew—and so did Karl Rove—that we had probably ceded the high ground in the campaign to George W. Bush."[29]

Longtime Richards friend Jan Reid wrote that both Rogers and the candidate were affected by the fallout from the remark. Rogers told Reid, "That shook Ann's confidence in herself. It was a turning point for me too. It was when I thought this was really going to be hard to win. Because, in effect, Ann had done what Clayton Williams did. Which was to let that resentment build and run away about someone having the audacity to challenge her."[30]

Unfortunately for Richards it was not a one-off comment. She also referred to her Republican opponent as "Shrub" and "that young Bush boy," and claimed he was "missing his Herbert"—in reference to his father's two middle names. Fortunately for Bush, as one reporter noted, "All the barbs and his prior reputation notwithstanding, Bush turned in a truly remarkable performance. He did not lose his cool at all, and at times he laughed right along with Richards, basically telling voters that she sure was a funny lady, whom everybody enjoyed, but that he came from a party and held to a conservative philosophy that were more in line with what Texans wanted in government."[31]

The Richards campaign had the advantage of incumbency and the access that came with it, an ample budget based on four years of successful fund-raising, and the advice and counsel of several seasoned Democratic campaign professionals. Despite all this and a sizeable campaign staff, outsiders perceived the campaign as disorganized. While Richards spoke of her accomplishments in office, she was confronted with the proverbial question, "What have you done for me lately?" The Richards campaign had no concise answer and no vision for what could be accomplished in another four-year term as governor. The conclusion for Paul Burka, political editor of *Texas Monthly* and a keen observer of the state's politics, was that "Richards did nothing, and so it was Bush who defined the race. Her campaign had no battle plan, no theme, no message. She said little about her record … and even less about what she wanted to do in the next term."[32]

In mid-October, the only debate of the campaign took place in Houston. Richards repeatedly claimed that Bush's inexperience in government made him unqualified to be governor: "This is really serious. This is not a joke. We're talking about who is going to run the State of Texas. You have got to have had some experience in the public sector before you get the chief executive's job." Her opponent saw this as a personal attack that needed a strong response. Bush said "This business of trying to diminish my personality based upon my business career is, frankly, astounding to me. We ought to be discussing welfare reform, juvenile justice, ways to make Texas a better place for our children."[33]

Most political observers believed that Bush had done more than hold his own; he had shown that he had the personality, ability, and issue stances to be an effective governor. In his closing comments Bush reminded the audience that he was the conservative candidate, Richards was the liberal candidate, and he would work hard to prevent the re-election of President Clinton, whom Richards would continue to support.

Even strong supporters of Richards saw the debate as solidifying Bush's standing. From Reid's perspective, "the Dallas debate was a tipping point in the race. Starting that night, Bush developed a habit of holding his own, contrary to expectations, against an experienced and highly rated debater. Truthfully enough, he laid out his premise, 'I'm the conservative candidate and she's the liberal.'"[34] In a state where more than twice as many people viewed themselves as conservative as those who took the label liberal, and at a time when opposition to the Clinton administration would allow Republicans to gain a majority in the US House of Representatives, the drawing of the ideological distinction was critical.

As a final effort to rally support for her re-election, the Richards campaign rolled out an endorsement by billionaire Ross Perot only days before the November election. Perot referred to Richards as "the steel magnolia of Texas" and called her "one of the greatest governors in the history of Texas." Perot's appeal was clearly to the 22 percent of Texas voters who had supported him in his 1992 campaign for the presidency. Richard Murray, political science professor at the University of Houston, noted, "If the race weren't so close, you'd say it's a nothing. But this might be just enough to give her some momentum into the last five, six days—and she needs some."[35]

Many in the Bush orbit saw this as a further extension of Perot's personal animosity toward George H. W. Bush, which had been seen two years earlier in a campaign they credited with helping keep President Bush from re-election. Now the "sins of the father" were being cast upon the son in his gubernatorial campaign. For Bush communications director Hughes, "The interesting question is why a supposedly popular incumbent governor feels she needs last-minute help from a presidential candidate she did not endorse in 1992 yet refused to campaign with the President she did support, Bill Clinton."[36] Bush's retort was more to the quality of endorsements: "She's got Ross Perot. I'll take Nolan Ryan and Barbara Bush."[37]

Meanwhile the Democrats were attempting to keep Hutchison from winning a six-year term in the Senate after her special election victory only allowed her to complete the remainder of Bentsen's term. In the Democratic primary former attorney general Jim Mattox had led the field over Richard Fisher, who had been a candidate in the recent special election, and member of Congress Mike Andrews of Houston. Indicative of some Democratic voters' dissatisfaction with the candidates, unknown Evelyn K. Lantz had obtained 63,517 votes, for 6.2 percent of the total. In the runoff primary Mattox's vote declined by nearly seventy thousand while Fisher increased his total by nearly thirteen thousand votes and won the Democratic nomination. He provided little competition to Hutchison, who won by a margin of nearly a million votes as a top-of-the-ballot candidate, giving the down-ballot Republican candidates a substantial boost.

The governor's race ended with a sizeable victory for George W. Bush as he bested the incumbent governor by a margin of more than 334,000 votes. This was the largest difference between the two parties' candidates for governor since the disastrous Watergate election of 1974. As Richards campaign manager Rogers reflected on the race, "few Democrats saw the magnitude or long-term implications of Ann Richards's defeat."[38] Author Lou Dubose, writing some years later, concluded, "With the election of Bush as governor, the Democrats were finished in Texas, though they could not yet admit it to themselves."[39] For Richards's longtime associate Reid, "The outcome was not preordained. Ann blew that election all on her own, and a man who was a decent sort and a very good politician was propelled toward occupying the White House."[40]

While Hutchison won a full term in the Senate and Bush reclaimed the governor's mansion for the GOP, other results were mixed but basically favorable. Rick Perry was re-elected as commissioner of agriculture, and the Republicans gained total control of the Railroad Commission when Charles Matthews and Carole Keeton Rylander defeated two Democratic incumbents, Jim Nugent and Mary Scott Nabers, to join Barry Williamson. Meanwhile attorney Priscilla Owen picked up a Supreme Court seat, while Steve Mansfield and Sharon Keller were elected to the Court of Criminal Appeals. Banker David Hartman lost a close race for treasurer by 24,567 votes to Martha Whitehead, who had been appointed by Richards when Kay Bailey Hutchison vacated the position. In sum, Republicans had more statewide victories—eight—than they ever had previously. It was a precursor of what would be accomplished two years later.

GOVERNOR BUSH AND CHAIRMAN PAUKEN

When assuming the office of governor, George W. Bush confronted a legislature controlled by the opposition party, with a margin of eighty-eight Democrats to sixty-two Republicans in the House and a seventeen to fourteen Democratic advantage in the Senate. While partisanship was never as controlling a factor in the Texas legislature as it is in Congress, it was still an important consideration for any newly elected Republican governor. The two chambers were led by Speaker Pete Laney, a conservative Democrat from West Texas, and Lieutenant Governor Bob Bullock, an irascible longtime Democratic politician.

Bush had campaigned on the issues of tort reform, revising the juvenile justice system, and changing state funding for public education. If he were to achieve his legislative goals he would need more than simply the votes of Republican legislators. Finding himself in this environment, Bush determined that he would work on building a positive relationship with the speaker and the lieutenant governor, the two individuals who controlled the fate of any legislation. Every Wednesday morning when the legislature was in session, Bush, Laney, and Bullock would meet for breakfast and discuss the status of bills making their way through the legislative process. As Bush explained to one reporter, "Lieutenant Governor Bullock and Speaker Laney could have made my life miserable, but in so doing, it would have been a disservice to Texas. They could have sabotaged me, and I'm grateful they didn't."[41] Working diligently to win votes from conservative Democratic legislators while retaining the support of his fellow Republicans, Bush was able to see his major programs enacted during his first term as governor.

One place where support was tepid was the state party, where Pauken was now state chairman. As political observer Burka remarked, "The Republican state chairman has made the Republican governor's job far more difficult. But it is unlikely that Tom Pauken cares. A battle that requires having Democrats on your side is not worth winning."[42] Pauken's relationship with Governor Bush was formed in the context of what he saw as a continuing split between Reagan conservatives and Bush Republicans, going back to the internal party battles of the 1970s and 1980s. According to Burka, "The split between Bush and Pauken ... is emblematic of the main problem facing Texas Republicans as they verge on taking over the state. They still haven't decided who the real enemy is: the opposition party or the opposition faction within their own party."[43]

Whether the governor was a Democrat or a Republican, the tradition in Texas, just as with the president and the national party, was that the state chairman and the party apparatus was expected to be supportive of the party's chief executive. Pauken saw it differently and viewed himself as the leader of the true conservatives fighting those who would compromise and work with Democrats to pass legislation. This contributed to the ongoing relationship Pauken had with the Bush family and its supporters. From Pauken's perspective as expressed years later, "When Bush was governor, you either supported the Bush-Rove agenda as a Texas Republican or you were viewed as disloyal."[44]

The conflict between the governor and the state party chairman would continue for the next two years. As Burka viewed the situation, "politics is like a war in one sense: it requires good soldiers. Every officer can't be a general; every low-level staffer can't be Secretary of State. Pauken is too much a public critic and not enough of a loyalist ever to succeed at politics."[45] That, however, was not the way Pauken saw the situation.

Future conflicts between the party chairman and the governor would result in Bush being pushed aside and Pauken being named chair of the 1996 national convention delegation. The Bush-Pauken relationship also resulted in a division of the party's 1996 election efforts, with Pauken's staff administering the victory committee while Bush supported a slate effort led by Railroad Commissioner Barry Williamson called Leadership Texas '96.

During the 1997 legislative session, Pauken ran newspaper ads attacking "Governor Bush's Tax Increase" and warning GOP legislators "not to vote for the George Bush tax increase" in his efforts to defeat the Governor's 1997 tax reform proposals. He told one reporter, "I see no enthusiasm from Republicans in the legislature. The only reason any of them are supporting it is because the governor is behind it." Pauken called the proposal "a terrible idea."[46] Several other political observers noted, "At times it was impossible to tell whether the hit shots attacking the Republican governor's tax plan were faxed from the offices of Democratic Party Chair Bill White or Republican Party Chairman Tom Pauken."[47] The final legislation out of a Senate and House conference committee focused mainly on raising the homestead exemption for school district property taxes and did not resemble Bush's original proposal.

At the end of 1996 Pauken decided to offer himself as a candidate for Republican national chairman to replace the retiring Haley Barbour of Mississippi. Shortly thereafter he withdrew from the race and claimed that George H. W. Bush had encouraged former governor Clements to call GOP leaders around the country, urging them not to support Pauken's candidacy. An editorial in the *Dallas Morning News* questioned Pauken's suitability for the position: "Mr. Pauken's tenure as Texas GOP chairman does not provide much evidence to suggest he would be a base-broadener. In fact, he has irked some Texas Republicans for contradicting Republican Governor George W. Bush's course."[48]

At times it appeared that Pauken was opposed to anyone and anything associated with the Bush family, believing that he was carrying on the battle between the Reagan forces and the Bush supporters that had occupied the state party nearly twenty years earlier. Throughout his three years as party chairman Pauken claimed that Rove discouraged major donors from giving to the state GOP, thereby hampering his ability to expand the party's operations. In return, the state chairman ended the party's direct-mail fundraising contract with Karl Rove + Company.[49]

As chairman of the state Republican Party, Pauken was determined that George W. Bush would not advance beyond his current office of governor. He maintained, "It was evident from the very beginning of George W. Bush's first term as governor that his sights were set higher and that his actions as governor were designed to further his presidential ambitions."[50] When that presidential campaign came about, Pauken refused to back his governor and declared, "I'm supporting a true conservative."[51] Pauken dismissed Bush's ability to be chief executive, declaring, "It's critical we have someone with the intellect to handle the job. It's one thing to be a governor in a state when Lieutenant Governor Bob Bullock had most of the power, as during most of Governor Bush's tenure in office, but it's a totally different thing to be president."[52]

Once Bush became the forty-third president of the United States, Pauken's opinions of Bush did not change. In his 2010 book, *Bringing America Home*, Pauken concluded that Bush "was a lousy President of the United States. He made a mess of things in his eight years in the White House" because it was "a job for which he was ill suited."[53] Pauken told one reporter, "The Bush years were a huge failure, both economically and internationally." According to reporter Lloyd Grove, "Pauken says the Bushes, father and son, have done so much damage to modern Republicanism that not even Dubya's younger brother Jeb, the highly regarded former governor of Florida, is a leader he can follow."[54] Clearly Pauken's dislike for all things associated with the Bush family continued. In 2016 he expressed his concern over Land Commissioner George P. Bush, Jeb Bush's son, being named chair of the state party's victory committee.[55]

In the fall of 1997 Pauken stepped down as GOP state chairman and launched his campaign for attorney general. The following year's GOP primary saw him finish third in that race. Four years later Pauken tried to convince Phil Gramm to seek a fourth term in the US Senate in an effort to keep John Cornyn, the man who had won the 1998 campaign for attorney general, from becoming senator.[56] When reports surfaced that Senator Hutchison might resign to run for governor, Pauken expressed his interest in running for the US Senate.

In March 2013 Pauken began a campaign for governor, criticizing what he called Governor Rick Perry's crony capitalism at a time when Perry had not announced whether he planned to seek another term. Although it was Perry who had appointed him chair of the Texas Workforce Commission, Pauken explained, "I like Rick personally, but I am probably the only statewide appointed or elected official not to endorse him in the presidential race."[57] After Perry announced he would not seek re-election and Attorney General Greg Abbott declared his interest in seeking the position, Pauken withdrew from the race and closed his campaign effort by the end of the year.[58]

CANDIDATE PHIL GRAMM

While Pauken saw presidential ambitions in the moves George W. Bush made as governor, it was another Texan who would declare for president in 1995. As the 1996 elections approached, Phil Gramm was not concentrating on his campaign for re-election to the Senate. Rather, he and his aides had developed a step-by-step plan to gain the presidential nomination and then defeat President Bill Clinton in the general election.

When Gramm became the first to officially announce his candidacy in February 1995, reporter Richard L. Berke was impressed with Gramm's efforts to lock up support in his home state and gain backers in the early primary and caucus states. Berke viewed his efforts as "an impressive, unapologetically raw display of political might that he takes around the country. And it leaves no doubt how a two-term Senator from Texas who is known as more bully than charmer, who looks more like a round-faced, stoop-shouldered Muppet than a stately public servant, has propelled himself into the top tier of Republican contenders, at least at this early stage."[59]

As Texas's senior senator, ranking member of the Senate Committee on Banking, Housing, and Urban Affairs, and member of the Senate Budget Committee, Gramm had the ability to line up significant business and political support in his home state. While much of the state party's leadership backed Gramm, former governor Clements did not. In Clements's view, "Gramm is not well suited to be president. He is not broad-gauged enough; his views are too parochial. I like Gramm right where he is, in the Senate. He votes right."[60]

Gramm was able to amass a campaign treasury of more than $21 million, including a near-record take of $4.1 million at one fundraising dinner in Dallas. He won some early straw polls, including in Iowa, but many political observers believed "he invested millions early on and in securing the victories in what were technically meaningless contests.... Rather than casting himself as an underdog and rising up, he declared himself the big dog early on and went downhill from there."[61]

Almost exactly one year after officially announcing his candidacy, Gramm went head-to-head in the Louisiana caucuses with Patrick Buchanan and lost. Charlie Black, Gramm's chief strategist, described the situation as "kind of a game, where being a lot of people's second choice isn't enough. In the end, they opted for the more fiery, passionate presentation of their views that Buchanan gives."[62] The defeat in Louisiana, followed by his fifth-place showing in the Iowa caucuses proved to be the death knell for his candidacy, and one week before the New Hampshire primary Gramm withdrew from the presidential contest. Gramm's campaign for the presidency and his early exit from the race brought back memories of a similar effort by another Democrat-turned-Republican from Texas, the 1980 presidential nominating campaign of John B. Connally, also amply funded but without a broad and deep level of support.

Because his six-year term in the US Senate was up in 1996, Gramm remained a candidate for re-election. While running for president he had drawn two primary opponents for the Senate. Best known of those seeking to defeat Gramm was Henry "Hank" Grover, the party's candidate for governor in 1972 and persistent gadfly since then. Grover attacked Gramm as being insufficiently conservative, declaring he himself had a plan to "put America first" that included an oil import tax, outlawing abortion under all circumstances including rape, and bringing all American troops home from Europe to be stationed on the Mexican border to prevent illegal immigration and the importation of illegal drugs.[63] Gramm's other challenger was the little-known and lightly financed David Young, who attempted to take a more moderate stance on a wide range of issues, attacking Gramm as too close to what he viewed as the radical right.

In the Republican primary of 1996, neither Grover nor Young was able to make a dent in Gramm's Republican support, and he ended up with 85 percent of the votes cast. In fact, the better-known but highly controversial Grover came in last with only 72,400 votes compared to Young's 75,463. Both ran far behind Gramm's 838,339 votes. Unsuccessful in his presidential effort, Gramm was well on his way to his third and final term in the US Senate.

Meanwhile, on the Democratic side, the possibility of a Gramm presidential campaign opening up a Senate seat led two members of Congress to seek the Senate nomination. Jim Chapman had entered Congress in 1985 through a special election to replace Representative Sam B. Hall Jr. Representing Northeast Texas, he had a relatively moderate voting record while being part of the House Democratic leadership. John Bryant was first elected in 1982 to replace Jim Mattox in a Dallas-based district and was more associated with the liberal wing of the Texas party. Also entering the primary contest was Houston attorney John Odam and little-known teacher Victor Morales from small-town Crandall, outside Dallas. Surprisingly coming in first was Morales, who campaigned across the state in his Nissan pickup on a budget topping out in the thousands. With 36.2 percent of the vote in a four-candidate race, Morales gained a spot in a runoff primary against Bryant, whose 267,545 votes represented 30 percent of the total. With most of the Democratic Party leadership in Bryant's corner, Morales pulled another upset by winning the runoff by an 11,000-vote margin and 51.2 percent of the vote. Morales would be the Democratic nominee to take on Gramm in November.[64]

THE PRIMARY AND CONVENTIONS OF 1996

When Texas voters went to the polls for the two major parties' primaries on March 12, 1996, a funny thing happened. For the first time in the state's 151-year history, all 254 counties provided an opportunity for voters to cast a ballot in the Republican primary. Even more surprising, more Texans chose the Republican over the Democratic primary in which to cast their vote. The Republicans set a record as some 1,019,803 votes were cast in the GOP presidential contest, while only 921,256 voted in the Democratic presidential primary, the lowest total since the 1944 primary, held during World War II. Besting the Democrats in primary participation was a precursor of what was to come in November.

Senator Bob Dole of Kansas easily won the GOP presidential primary with 55.6 percent of the vote, besting Buchanan (21.4 percent), Steve Forbes (12.9 percent), and Alan Keyes (4.1 percent). Data from exit polling on primary day indicated that some 63 percent of GOP primary voters claimed to be moderate to somewhat conservative, and another 31 percent described themselves as very conservative. As Harvey Kronberg, editor of the *Quorum Report* political newsletter, observed, "Although it may chagrin many a Republican ideologue, the exit polls clearly demonstrate that most GOP voters were only slightly right of center and focused on traditional Republican issues. . . . Social and religious conservatives are a serious part of the Republican coalition. However, that does not appear to pigeonhole these voters into any kind of voting patterns."[65]

The difference between primary voters and party activists was apparent, however, when the state convention was held at the Alamodome in San Antonio. It was a distinction that would lead one social conservative to advocate selecting party nominees for public office by caucus and convention, eliminating the primary and its voter participation in the nominating process. While no accurate survey of the convention delegates was conducted, most estimates were that "religious conservatives occupied most of the delegate seats, with estimates of their presence running to 80% or more."[66]

Reflective of chairman Pauken's alignment with the social conservatives, the state party refused to rent space in the convention exhibit hall to the Log Cabin Republicans, an organization of gay party members. Among the most prominent events during the convention was a fundraiser for the Christian Coalition, listed in the official program activities on the convention's first night. It was listed as the Faith and Freedom Banquet, and "literally thousands turned out to raise money for the Christian Coalition and to hear and cheer and applaud and cheer Ralph Reed, the coalition's executive director."[67]

Dole, the eventual presidential nominee, did not appear at the convention. The featured addresses were given by defeated candidates Keyes, Forbes, and Buchanan. In a reminder of his controversial speech at the 1992 national convention in Houston, Buchanan appealed to the social conservatives with an anti-abortion message coupled with attacks on President Clinton for his support of increased immigration and for deploying American troops as part of United Nations peacekeeping missions.

Throughout the convention proceedings social issues dominated, especially abortion, with much of the uproar led by Bill Price, president of Texans United for Life, along with holdout supporters of failed presidential candidates Keyes and Buchanan. As one reporter noted, "there were more stickers here for Alan Keyes, who ran for President on a strict anti-abortion agenda, than for Mr. Dole. And Mr. Keyes and Patrick J. Buchanan drew far more cheers than Gov. George W. Bush and Senator Phil Gramm, two leading Republicans who oppose abortion but who have warned the party against being preoccupied over the issue."[68] Longtime political observer Jane Ely claimed, "Overwhelmingly, the delegates here cared far more about their religious beliefs, about promoting a philosophy, an encompassing way of life, than they did about raw politics."[69]

With term limits applied to the national committee positions, former Midland mayor Ernest Angelo retired after twenty years as Republican National Committeeman. In a battle between two social conservatives to succeed Angelo, SREC member Tom Cottar of Houston was defeated by Tim Lambert of Lubbock, president of the Texas Homeschool Coalition. Penny Butler of Houston completed the eight years she was allowed to serve and was replaced by Susan Feldtman, also from Houston.

State chairman Pauken was opposed by a candidate who claimed Pauken was insufficiently right-wing. Robert X. Johnson of San Antonio maintained that all Republican candidates should support the party platform and their campaign promises should be reflective of the stances taken by the state convention. If elected, Johnson pledged "to change the party rules to make Texas a caucus state, similar to Virginia, where the party platform is respected. That means our Party's candidates would be nominated by the delegates at the State Convention, not by the general body of voters in a primary election."[70] While Pauken was easily re-elected, the Johnson challenge was reflective of the increasingly right-wing mood of the delegates.

Richard Berke covered the convention for the *New York Times* and noted,

As a measure of the new conflicts roiling the Republican Party, consider how the battle lines have changed since this state's party convention two years ago. In 1994, the issue was over how Tom Pauken, who was backed by the Christian Coalition, wrested control of the party from mainstream Republicans. But this past weekend, Mr. Pauken emerged as a figure of relative moderation as he sought to keep Mr. Price and his allies from overshadowing the proceedings. And Fred Meyer, the longtime party chairman whom Mr. Pauken had replaced, has become such a political relic that he lost his bid to go to the San Diego convention as a Dole delegate.[71]

In the midst of the clear swing to the right on various social issues, a few delegates could be found wearing stickers that said "the MOD squad" to indicate that they were not enthralled with the platform stances on abortion, homosexuality, and religious liberty issues. They were satirized by the Young Conservatives of Texas, who claimed that the acronym stood for either "Made Over Democrats" or "Marxists on Drugs." However, as reporter Dave Mc-Neely concluded, "At last weekend's state convention in San Antonio, the delegates ... time after time thumbed their nose at the types of folks who have been the voice of the Texas GOP for years."[72]

The most intense battle at the convention was over who would be included in the state's delegation to the Republican National Convention in San Diego. In a strange way it was a reversion to the conflicts within the party over its first one hundred years. This time, however, the dispute was not over patronage or even over who would be the party's nominee for president. Rather, it all boiled down to how strenuous and inclusive the potential convention delegate was on the issue of abortion and whether the delegate would demand that Senator Dole choose a vice presidential candidate who was deemed sufficiently pro-life. In the midst of this conflict, "Thousands of Republicans at the state convention thrust their fists in the air and shouted each other down over the contentious question of whether some candidates—including Senator Hutchison, who has supported abortion rights—were too moderate on abortion to become part of the state's 123-member national delegation."[73]

Pro-life forces led by Price were able to gain sufficient support to mount a challenge on the convention floor to the inclusion of Kay Bailey Hutchison on the at-large slate of delegates. They circulated flyers declaring "No way, Kay—vote against any slate of at-large delegates that includes Kay Bailey Hutchison." In response to this challenge Hutchison's fellow senator, Gramm, threatened not to accept a delegate slot if Hutchison was not chosen. After a voice vote was inconclusive, Pauken called for a standing vote for the entire at-large slate. When the results appeared close, Pauken declared that the slate had prevailed, and Hutchison became a delegate to San Diego.

The opposition to Hutchison was not the only challenge to the desires of the Dole campaign organization. Other prominent Republicans who were rejected as national convention delegates included members of Congress Henry Bonilla and Mac Thornberry, 1994 state treasurer candidate David Hartman, former state chairman Fred Meyer, Dole campaign cochair Richard Collins, and campaign officer Brian Berry. Some delegates were not satisfied with these exclusions, however. One delegate from San Antonio objected to Senator Gramm and Governor Bush being named delegates: "These candidates don't have strong enough positions to stand up for a vice president who is pro-life." Once more, it all boiled down to one single issue, and some pro-life leaders threatened to withhold their support of the party's presidential candidate if they found his vice presidential candidate to be insufficiently pro-life.[74]

The headaches for Dole campaign operatives were not over once the delegates were chosen. Despite the overwhelming number of delegates pledged to Dole and the tradition of past recent delegations to the national conventions, "contrary to the wishes of the Dole campaign, Governor Bush was not selected to chair the Texas delegation to the national convention. Tom Pauken won that honor, and Dick Weinhold, executive director of the Texas Christian Coalition, was named vice-chair."[75]

Clearly there was a rift between the party activists who participated in the state convention and the party's top elected officials. The breach continued through the fall election campaign, but it did not limit the party's ability to win votes from the general electorate. As Governor Bush concluded regarding the events in San Antonio, "I know that activists showed up at the convention, and they're clearly a part of the Republican Party. The Republican Party is a lot broader than could be characterized just out of a convention."[76]

With the state convention over, Texas Republicans were now focused on the national convention in San Diego and, after that, the November election contests. The differences between Bush and Pauken would continue and result in a bifurcated election effort, but one that did not hamper the party's ability to make significant gains that would have a lasting impact on Texas politics. Indeed, 1996 would be a historic year for the political complexion of Texas.

TWELVE

THE YEAR THAT CHANGED
TEXAS POLITICS

As the 1996 general election campaign began, Texas Republicans found themselves in an unfamiliar situation: fellow party members were in control of the governor's office and both US Senate seats. Below the presidential contest, their statewide ticket would be headed by a popular two-term Senator. It would turn out to be a year of three important and historic firsts in terms of party competition. Setting the stage for this transformation of Texas politics was the Republican advantage among primary voters that spring.

This had been a gradual, almost inevitable change in Texas politics. While most Texans continued to identify themselves as conservatives, the Democratic Party was no longer a welcome home for conservatives. Beginning as early as 1976, it was evident that the more liberal faction in the Democratic Party had become the dominant force. Twenty years later, as political observer R. W. Apple Jr. noted, "the Democratic Party is increasingly dominated by blacks, Hispanics, trade-union members and the enclave of liberals around Austin.... It is now more likely than in the past that the Democrats will nominate left-of-center candidates, giving the Republicans further opportunities."[1]

The Democratic Party's movement leftward started a slow transition of conservative and moderate Texas political leaders to the Republican Party, a change that began in the 1960s, gained momentum with John B. Connally's shift in the 1970s, and was accelerated by the party switches of Phil Gramm, Kent Hance, Rick Perry, and others in the 1980s. To aspiring candidates and officeholders it became apparent that unless they held to orthodox liberal positions they had no future in the Democratic Party. As more and more political leaders shifted parties, they were joined by their supporters in the electorate, voters who first began casting ballots for some GOP candidates, then were supporting even more Republicans, and eventually were participating in the Republican primary. By 1996, for the first time, Republican primary voters outnumbered Democratic primary voters.

A second factor contributing to the increase in Republican support came from the movement of individuals into Texas. Migration patterns brought to the state many who had previously voted Republican and who retained that partisan loyalty as they moved to the big cities and suburbs, often relocated by their employers, who were now establishing bases of operations in Texas. It was this migration that contributed to the initial Republican successes in the big cities such as Dallas and Houston, which then spread to the suburbs outside the state's five largest cities.[2]

Somewhat contradictory to the present situation, it was younger voters who fed the growing Republican base leading up to the election of 1996. Some of this could be credited to the appeal and popularity of President Ronald Reagan to younger voters, an age cohort that he carried in his re-election campaign of 1984. Four Texas surveys taken from 1986 to 1994 all showed that voters age eighteen to twenty-nine were the most likely to identify as Republicans and least likely to call themselves Democrats. The most heavily Democratic group was Texans age sixty-two or older. Over time older "yellow-dog" Democrats were passing from the scene and being replaced with younger groupings of voters who held more positive views of the Republican Party.[3]

The personality and performance of George W. Bush as governor cannot be overlooked. Bush appealed to a broad swath of Texas residents and expanded the party's appeal. Through his ability to appoint individuals to various state boards and commissions, he introduced several future Republican leaders to state government, many of whom would go on to become GOP candidates and officeholders in future elections. In a legislature led by a Democratic speaker and a Democratic lieutenant governor, Bush reached out to work with them to achieve many of his legislative goals. This approach would enable him to lessen partisan opposition and promote an image of working for the best interests of all Texans.

The appeal of George W. Bush, evident in his defeat of a popular incumbent Democratic governor, his overwhelming re-election victory four years later, and his appearance on Texas ballots over ten years, helped to solidify the party's image and base of support. For the period of time when Texas Republicans became the dominant force in state politics, the party was clearly identified with George W. Bush, both as governor and as the forty-third president of the United States.

SEPARATELY WORKING TOGETHER

Despite his positive relationship with most legislators and his popularity among the state electorate, Governor Bush continued to experience conflict within the Republican Party. With George W. Bush in the governor's office and Tom Pauken continuing as state party chairman, it was apparent that the two would not be able to work together amicably. Governor Bush expected to head up the party's statewide campaign, as had Bill Clements when he was governor. If Bush and his father would be called on to raise funds for the statewide campaign effort, then the governor expected to provide direction as to how those funds would be spent. Pauken, on the other hand, was unwilling to turn over direction of the statewide campaign to anyone else.

A compromise was reached with Pauken and the state party organization responsible for the Victory Committee effort focused mainly on an identification and turnout effort relying on volunteer phone banks and home phoning programs. By Labor Day, the state party's program would set up forty-two phone banks covering forty urban and suburban counties, coupled with a home phoning program in rural areas. This program was supported through the normal fundraising operations of the Republican Party of Texas and coordinated by the party's staff under Pauken's direction.

A separate effort, called Leadership Texas '96, was headed by Railroad Commissioner Barry Williamson with the support of Governor Bush. Much of the funding for Leadership Texas '96 came from high-dollar fundraising events with former president George H. W. Bush, Senator Kay Bailey Hutchison, and Governor Bush. This entity was responsible for all coordinated campaign literature and paraphernalia for the Dole presidential campaign, direct mailings to voters, coordinated mailings for state legislative candidates, and the advance work and expenses involved in campaign appearances around the state by the governor and other surrogates for the presidential ticket. In each county, an individual was named to coordinate the local efforts of Leadership Texas '96 on behalf of the state slate of candidates.[4]

By Election Day Leadership Texas '96 had raised and spent more than 2 million dollars in support of the Republican ticket. Over 2 million letters and brochures were distributed to Texas voters, and two hundred Dole-Kemp county organizations were supported with literature, signs, and campaign paraphernalia. Leadership Texas '96 funded a radio blitz in key markets and staged campaign events with Governor Bush and other surrogates in seventy counties.

Two other coordinated efforts were underway during the election year to help elect more Republicans to state legislative and county offices. Associated

Republicans of Texas (ART), first organized in 1974, continued its effort to provide strategic and financial assistance to targeted GOP legislative challengers and key county-level contests. Originally formed with the assistance of Senator John Tower, it had become a fixture in the Texas political arena under the leadership of Norman Newton Jr. and Pat Robbins. ART was an important source of early start-up money for promising legislative campaigns, as well as providing critical late funding for campaigns deemed winnable. With effective targeting and data analysis, "the Party's smart, pragmatic funders found it fairly easy to direct spending only toward races where Republican candidates were viable and in need of help."[5]

Additionally, a separate political action committee with the support of GOP chairman Pauken, 76 in '96, was formed to raise funds and support Republican candidates for the state legislature. The 76 in '96 committee raised and spent nearly a half million dollars in an unsuccessful effort to produce a GOP majority in the Texas House of Representatives and thereby oust Speaker Pete Laney. These two committees supplemented the overall statewide efforts of the state party's Victory Committee and Leadership Texas '96.

THE CAMPAIGN BEGINS

While Republican presidential candidates had carried the state in the most recent four elections, all of which included George H. W. Bush on the presidential ticket, the 1996 presidential campaign began as a serious challenge for the party and its candidate, Senator Robert Dole of Kansas. Immediately after the traditional Labor Day campaign kickoff, the *Dallas Morning News* and *Houston Chronicle* released a voter survey showing Dole and President Bill Clinton running virtually even in the state. When asked who they would support for president, 44 percent of registered voters chose Dole, 41 percent indicated Clinton would receive their vote, and only 4 percent backed H. Ross Perot, the Reform Party candidate. Digging deeper, the poll found that Dole supporters were more likely to vote and were more strongly supportive of their candidate. Nevertheless, it appeared to be shaping up as a close contest in Texas.

Railroad Commissioner Williamson, heading up the Leadership Texas '96 effort, saw the results as being influenced by the recently concluded Democratic National Convention. "This is as close as Clinton will get in Texas. The poll comes right after the Democratic convention and after he bombed Iraq. Bob Dole will continue to increase his lead to 10 or 12 points here by the first of October," claimed Williamson.[6] In addition to the closeness of the Dole-

Clinton numbers, the poll was significant in showing what appeared to be the irrelevance of the Perot campaign in the Reform Party candidate's home state. Pollster Julie Weprin noted, "That great big sucking sound we hear is Ross Perot leaving the political arena in Texas. He's just not a player."[7]

Seeing possibilities of carrying the state where he and his future wife had worked during the 1972 president campaign of George McGovern, President Clinton scheduled an eighteen-hour campaign swing from Longview to Fort Worth to an evening rally and fundraiser in Houston. At the downtown Fort Worth rally Clinton declared, "If the people are willing to give me a fair shot and look to the future, yes, I think we can carry Texas because it's right for the American people."[8] In an interview with Texas media, Clinton maintained that Texas could be a source of votes as well as campaign cash for Democrats. "For too long the Democrats just sort of gave up on Texas. So they'd come to Texas and raise money and leave. I thought that was wrong. Texas is better off than it was four years ago. The state of Texas has done well under our policies."[9]

Whether it was due to his campaigning in the state or a more general reflection of the national political scene, Clinton was able to keep the race in Texas close. In late October, the Texas Poll indicated that the previous margin had not changed, with Dole at 42 percent, Clinton at 39 percent, and Perot moving up to 8 percent but still far out of contention for the state's thirty-two electoral votes. Those who identified themselves as Independents broke almost equally for Dole and Clinton. With these Independents and undecideds appearing to be the keys for carrying the state, Leadership Texas '96 moved into high gear. Allison Griffin of the Texas Dole campaign reported, "We're sending out over one million pieces of mail targeted to swing voters and phone bank calls going out to swing voters. Our message to swing voters is that Bob Dole's values are Texas values, a strong military, less government, and he believes in letting Texans run Texas."[10]

While the Dole campaign denied it was in trouble in Texas, a campaign swing was scheduled for Dallas and Houston, the first visit by either Dole or vice presidential candidate Jack Kemp since the GOP national convention. Leadership Texas '96 chairman Williamson claimed the visit was to thank supporters and rally the troops, though it was clear that winning over the remaining undecideds was of paramount importance. At Moody Coliseum on the Southern Methodist University campus, some seven thousand turned out to greet the GOP presidential candidate, who listed a number of questionable activities involving the Clinton administration and campaign before asking, "Where's the outrage in the media? There is no outrage. It starts today in Dallas, Texas. That's where the outrage starts."

Earlier in the day Dole attacked what he called the liberal media at a rally in Houston, accusing the media of promoting the Clinton campaign. "If they weren't propped up by the media every day, this election would've been over with two weeks ago. When will the American people rise up and say, 'Forget the media in America, we're going to make up our minds. We are not going to let the media steal this election.'"[11]

Trust became a major theme at the Dole campaign rallies. In Dallas the GOP presidential candidate was introduced by Governor Bush, who described Dole as someone who "understands Texas. He thinks like a Texan. And he's going to act like a Texan—meaning he's going to keep his word." Senator Hutchison introduced Dole at the Houston rally, telling the audience, "If you want a president you can trust, there is still time."[12]

When the late October Texas Poll showed a statistical dead heat, President Clinton made his final appearances in the state with major rallies in El Paso and outside the Alamo in San Antonio on the Friday before Election Day. Not to be outdone, and taking nothing for granted, the Dole campaign scheduled one last rally in Houston on the Monday before the election, featuring the presidential candidate, former president George H. W. Bush, Senator John McCain of Arizona, and Governor Bush. It was a final effort to rally his supporters and motivate them to turn out the vote the following day.[13]

STATEWIDE CANDIDATES AND CAMPAIGNS

Meanwhile, having secured the Democratic Senate nomination by beating two incumbent Democratic members of Congress, high school teacher Victor Morales continued to drive his white pickup truck to campaign events across the state, hoping he was on the road to victory in November. However, when KERA-TV and the *Dallas Morning News* invited the major-party candidates to a September 29 televised debate, Gramm quickly accepted but Morales did not. The Morales campaign objected to the date and format, wanting the debate to be held closer to Election Day and without questions from the media. The program would have been part of the Public Broadcasting System's "Debate Night," a series of programs airing nationwide that evening. With no agreement by the candidates, the organizers cancelled the event.

Gramm's campaign manager, Kevin Brannon, noted, "In previous elections, every major campaign for statewide office in Texas has been eager to participate in the KERA debates. We find it difficult to imagine snubbing KERA, the *Dallas Morning News*, and the people of Texas in order to accommodate Mr. Morales's personal agenda."[14] As two campaign observers noted later, "Morales made a major tactical error when he declined to debate Senator Gramm on September 29, 1996. The challenger understandably wanted a debate closer to the general election, but by turning down the opportunity Morales lost his one chance to appear side-by-side with his adversary."[15]

The following week, after the KERA debate controversy, the *Dallas Morning News* and *Houston Chronicle* poll showed Gramm with the support of 50 percent of registered voters, with Morales trailing at 39 percent. Moreover, Gramm had a higher favorability rating (58 percent to 44 percent for Morales), and most voters approved of his performance in office. Pollster Weprin noted, "Gramm is a known entity and he is well-liked. Morales has got a tough battle here. . . . Morales has not been able to break out in any other group other than the traditional hardcore Democrats, and not enough of them."[16]

Realizing that he had not closed the gap in support with Gramm, Morales began to shed his average nice guy image and attacked Gramm as a pawn of special interests, a liar, and an opponent of government programs. At one event he went even further, labeling member of Congress Henry Bonilla, a Republican and Gramm supporter, as a "coconut," implying that he was not a true Mexican-American. The slur generated a negative response in the media, and Morales was forced to admit, "I used terms I should not have used," but he refused to apologize to Bonilla.[17]

By mid-October, Gramm was in full campaign mode and undertook a seven-city bus tour through South Texas with Representative Bonilla at his side. Differentiating himself from Morales, Gramm claimed, "My opponent likes to come to the Valley and speak Spanish. I don't speak it very well, but let me tell you what I do speak. I speak opportunity. I speak equality. I speak the American dream. And I don't only speak it, I work for it."[18]

While Morales continued to gain national publicity as a Mexican-American teacher who had knocked off two members of Congress in the primary, he was failing to make inroads with Texas voters. From Gramm's perspective, "The image of a school teacher in a white pickup is no less appealing. It's just that people listen to this guy and say, 'My goodness, this guy's views are nowhere near my views.' . . . I do believe when he started talking about issues, people started to listen to what he was saying, and that's when he started to falter."[19] Morales's difficulty of squaring his image with his values was highlighted when he was endorsed by Perot's Reform Party and refused to say whether he would vote for Perot or Clinton when he cast his presidential ballot. After the media publicized his apparent indecision, he was forced to clarify his position by saying he supported his fellow Democratic candidate, President Clinton.[20]

Beyond the presidential and senatorial contests, Texas Republicans had nominated a strong slate of candidates for the Railroad Commission, Supreme Court, and Court of Criminal Appeals. This time the GOP had the advantage of having several incumbents on the statewide ballot, including Railroad Commissioner Carole Keeton Rylander and four incumbent Supreme Court justices. Both parties had launched aggressive campaigns to increase their party's numbers in the congressional delegation, efforts that were compounded by the court-ordered redrawing of thirteen district lines and a requirement that a candidate must receive a majority of the votes cast to avoid a runoff election. Pauken described the congressional races as "a trench warfare battle. We could win two or lose two. In a year in which it is not going our way nationally, that doesn't give us the kind of boost we had two years ago."[21]

The statewide and national races gained much of the media attention and publicity, but a multitude of state legislative and county races were taking place also. Republicans had recruited and nominated more candidates than they had in most previous years. They were committed to obtaining a majority in both the Texas Senate and House of Representatives and wanted to make inroads in county government. While ART had provided financial and strategic support to county and legislative candidates, Leadership Texas '96 was coordinating and paying for direct-mail campaigns in targeted state legislative districts. Texas Republicans were attempting to achieve something few thought possible only a short time before; they were striving to make the Republican Party the majority party in the state.

ELECTION DAY: THE STATE SHIFTS

For the first time in the state's history, every statewide elective position on the ballot was carried by the Republican candidate. At the top of the ballot, Senator Dole won the state's thirty-two electoral votes over Clinton and Perot, carrying the state by a margin of 276,484 votes. Williamson, chairman of Leadership Texas '96, credited Dole's success in Texas to the voters' emphasis on trust. "Character counts in Texas. We wanted a President we could be proud of. Character, integrity, and trust are important to Texans." His interpretation was supported by exit polls showing that voters trusted Dole more than Clinton and liked the GOP candidate's honesty. Among Dole voters, most mentioned honesty and trustworthiness as the quality that mattered most to them.[22]

Of all ten statewide contests on the ballot, the presidential race turned out to be the closest win for the Republicans. Senator Gramm was re-elected by a margin of nearly six hundred thousand votes while Rylander kept her position on the Railroad Commission with a lead of more than a million votes over former state senator Hector Uribe. Meanwhile four GOP Supreme Court justices were elected, including John Cornyn and Greg Abbott, two individuals who would later assume higher elective positions. Three Republican attorneys won their first terms on the state's Court of Criminal Appeals by comfortable margins, including District Judge Tom Price, who defeated Democratic incumbent Frank Maloney.

Republicans picked up two new congressional seats with the victories of former mayor Kay Granger in Fort Worth and Pete Sessions in Dallas. Although falling short of a majority in the Texas House, the GOP did add six new state representatives to cut the Democratic lead to eighty to seventy. With one special election to be held in a Lubbock-based state Senate district, the GOP had reached a tie in the thirty-one member Texas Senate. That special election in December would go to state representative Robert Duncan, who became the sixteenth GOP senator, producing a Republican majority in the Texas Senate, the first in over one hundred years. Meanwhile, Republican candidates won most countywide contests in Harris, Dallas, and Tarrant counties.[23]

In an election night speech to party supporters, Governor Bush declared, "the message to Texans is our state is Republican and proudly so. It does look like an overwhelming night for Republicans statewide." Despite the loss of the presidential contest nationwide, "the Republican Party racked up an impressive string of victories at nearly every level in this former Democratic stronghold," according to a report in the *New York Times*.[24] This conclusion was amplified by Bruce Buchanan, a political science professor at the University of Texas at Austin, who maintained that the Republican victories were "more of the trend toward a two-party system and we are beginning to edge toward one-party status on the other side of the spectrum. It's an impressive showing in the midst of a presidential year that went the other way by an impressive margin."[25]

THE IMPACT OF 1996

Few political observers, noting the Republican Party's ability to win all ten statewide contests in 1996, would have predicted that this would be the new norm in Texas politics. Surely, the Texas Democratic Party, long dominant in the state, would bounce back in 1998 or, at least, by 2000. After all, it still held most statewide executive offices, positions such as lieutenant governor, attorney general, and comptroller that would be on the ballot again in 1998. Moreover, across the state the vast majority of county and district offices were still occupied by Democrats, and the party retained its majority in the Texas House of Representatives and the state's congressional delegation in Washington.

Nevertheless, no resurgence of the Texas Democratic Party was forthcoming. One month after the successful 1996 general election, the GOP picked up its sixteenth state senator, for a majority in that chamber, when state representative Duncan won the 28th senatorial district with 56.8 percent of the vote on December 10, 1996. The following month, in a special election for the 5th senatorial district, state representative Steve Ogden won with 55.5 percent of the vote to give the GOP its seventeenth state senator.

In retrospect, clearly 1996 had been the turning point in the emergence of a Republican majority in Texas. Regardless of how one measures party competition, whether it be in the number of elections won, the percentage of the electorate choosing to vote in a party's primary, or the extent of straight-ticket voting for each party, the evidence shows that since 1996 Texas has been a one-party–dominant state. This new Republican surge at the turn of the twenty-first century has been greatest in suburban counties around Dallas–Fort Worth, Houston, San Antonio, and Austin—the areas of the state that continue to experience the most rapid growth in population.

At the same time, the GOP has seen increased success in the small-town and rural counties of the state where hundreds of elected officials have abandoned the Democratic Party. Often these close-knit communities where almost everyone is known by other county residents tend toward one-party politics. As the Republican Party became the dominant statewide force and more local residents were voting for the GOP presidential and gubernatorial candidates, these local officials switched party affiliation, often with several doing so at one time.

Beginning in 1996 Republican gains have occurred also in the medium-sized counties of the state, urban areas beyond the major metropolitan areas. Traditionally Democratic counties such as Jefferson (Beaumont), Nueces (Corpus Christi), and McLennan (Waco) have become strong sources of Republican support, not only in statewide contests but also in electing county and district officials. Only among the six largest counties of the state has the Democratic Party staged a comeback to dominance or even competitiveness. The movement in state politics that became evident in 1996 has been toward a Republican-dominant state but with pockets of strong Democratic support.

THE IMMEDIATE AFTERMATH

Throughout 1997 a small but consistent tide was moving across the state. State and county officeholders were leaving the Democratic Party and declaring themselves Republicans. In October eighteen elected officials switched at one time, including Judge Michael McCormick, presiding judge of the Texas Court of Criminal Appeals. McCormick explained, "I didn't do it for a politically expedient reason. I did it because I think it was the right thing to do." Noting that the GOP now held seven of the nine positions on the Court of Criminal Appeals, Governor Bush said, "This is a big deal for Republicans." As the *Dallas Morning News* reported, "a dozen Democratic officeholders met at a hotel to become members of the GOP, . . . and Republican officials say that political party conversion is a trend that will continue."[26]

The 1997 legislative session was relatively successful for Governor Bush as he worked closely with Speaker Laney and Lieutenant Governor Bob Bullock. In a *Washington Post* article reporter Sue Anne Pressley described Governor Bush as focused on state issues and building support for his legislative agenda. "By presenting himself as an eager and respectful pupil, he has managed to work well with the state's leading Democrats, notably House Speaker Pete Laney and the legendarily terse and strong-willed Lieutenant Governor Bob Bullock. And by zeroing in on issues that few Democrats or Republicans can quarrel with—tort reform, juvenile crime, illiteracy—he has emerged with an image as a doer."[27]

Anne Marie Kilday, former reporter and at the time communications director for the Texas Democratic Party, had to concede that Bush was performing well as governor. "George Bush has two things going for him—he has an excellent staff and he gets good advice, in terms of the media and not getting overexposed. And he takes that advice. He is well-handled." But such praise was not forthcoming from Bush's own party chairman. When asked to comment on Bush's tax restructuring proposal, Pauken declared, "It's a bad bill—it's a tax hike, not a tax cut. It seems what you would expect from a liberal Democrat."[28]

In the end, Bush was not able to achieve the tax reform he had advocated, thanks partly to Pauken's vigorous and vocal opposition. In an effort to defeat the Republican governor's tax plans, Pauken ran full-page advertisements in Texas newspapers and called on GOP legislators to vote against it. Pauken derisively called his party's governor a "Me-too Republican" and continued his feud with the Bush family.[29]

Pauken's continual critiques of the Republican governor, including having the state party run a newspaper ad condemning a key Democratic state legislator who supported Bush's tax proposals, led Bush confidant Karl Rove to send a memo to key party leaders. Rove wrote that he was upset that "Tom Pauken attacked the Governor not once, but *twice* last Friday," referring to quotes from Pauken appearing in the *Washington Post* and the *Baltimore Sun*.[30] Rove told a reporter that he sent the memo on his own without consulting the governor, claiming, "I wanted you to see our chairman's latest salvo at the governor."[31] The Austin-based political newsletter *Texas Weekly* described Pauken as "something of a lightning rod for Bush. Never close personally, they have become combative on some matters.... Pauken, in the process, has become a sort of political icon for social-conservative Christians who think Bush is either not far enough to the right on their concerns or too legislatively collegial to draw sharp GOP lines."[32]

Despite these attacks from Pauken, Bush retained his popularity with the Texas electorate, holding a three-to-one advantage over his likely 1998 opponent. Bush was viewed as being able to work with both parties in the legislature and was not blamed by the vast majority of voters for the defeat of his tax reform proposals. In more general terms, 60 percent of those in a statewide survey believed the state was headed in the right direction, while only 23 percent thought that things were on the wrong track.[33] Most voters viewed Texas government as in good hands.

In the summer of 1997 Pauken resigned as GOP state chairman to launch his campaign for the party's nomination for attorney general. Replacing him was his vice chairman, Susan Weddington, described as a 46-year-old Christian conservative activist. Dick Weinhold, chairman of the Texas Christian Coalition, said "She'll work very hard to get Republicans elected up and down the ballot. I certainly count her as one of our friends." Meanwhile former state chairman Fred Meyer vouched for her when he said, "She's conservative but I don't think she will fit the description of any of the terms they like to use. She's reasonable and she understands what the party's purpose is." With Weddington becoming chairman, the new vice chairman was David Barton of Aledo, an evangelical Christian activist and author.[34]

Weddington was chosen unanimously by the state Republican executive committee (SREC) in a fleeting moment of congeniality, becoming the first woman to head a major Texas political party. After three years of conflict with Pauken, Governor Bush welcomed the change in party leadership, saying, "I look forward to working with Susan.... I think she will be an effective party chairman."[35] Relations between the Bush administration and the party organization improved immensely as the calendar moved closer to the governor's re-election campaign in 1998.

Will Lutz, former editor of the conservative newsletter *Lone Star Report*, maintained that by the 1990s the Texas party had a split personality that led to differences in how individuals viewed politics. A newer and increasingly influential element viewed the GOP's role as promoting and enacting ideas with the party organization as a means to get things done, ideas that were reflected in the party platform, a document that should be binding on elected officials. The more traditional element that had been dominant for years saw the party as an organized entity to help get people elected to office, an organizational tool for the candidates to help them run against and defeat Democrats. According to Lutz, Pauken was closer to the first perspective, while Weddington and her successor, Tina Benkiser, were closer to the second view, but could not admit to it because many—if not most—GOP activists who attended district and state conventions were committed to the first perspective.[36]

When Pauken announced for attorney general, media reports claimed that Bush supporters were attempting to line up Supreme Court Justice John Cornyn to challenge him in the GOP primary. There were rumors of a Bush slate comprising Agriculture Commissioner Rick Perry for lieutenant governor, Railroad Commissioner Barry Williamson for comptroller, Secretary of State Tony Garza for land commissioner, and former state representative Susan Combs for agriculture commissioner. By the filing deadline two of these individuals had announced for other offices: Williamson had switched to the race for attorney general and Garza had become a candidate for the Railroad Commission.[37] Williamson's switch cleared the way for fellow Railroad Commissioner Carole Keeton Rylander to win the nomination for comptroller but created a three-way race for attorney general involving Pauken, Cornyn, and Williamson.

THE 1998 PRIMARY AND STATE CONVENTION

As the 1998 campaign season began, some Democrats believed that the party should not run a serious candidate against Bush in the belief that it would decrease Republican turnout and improve the chances of down-ballot Democratic candidates. Bush's general popularity and the positive relations he had developed with Democratic legislative leaders might well lead him to obtain a bevy of endorsements for re-election, making any campaign against him even more difficult. One leading Democrat who did endorse him early was Lieutenant Governor Bullock, who in November 1997 declared, "I respect and admire Governor George Bush and feel he deserves re-election to a second term. During my public career, I've served under seven governors, and Governor Bush is the best I've served under."[38]

Comptroller John Sharp, gearing up for a campaign for lieutenant governor after Bullock announced he would not run again, believed the Democrats should forego a serious campaign for governor in 1998. Taking the opposite perspective was Land Commissioner Garry Mauro. Mauro had won four statewide elections and had served over fifteen years in the General Land Office. Ever since working with Bill Clinton and Hillary Rodham in the 1972 Texas McGovern campaign, Mauro had looked forward to a race for governor. In the end, Mauro declared for the office and became the party's nominee for governor, but, as some Democratic observers noted, "The argument was a measure of just how dispirited and marginalized the Democrats had become in Texas."[39]

The Democrats' predicament went well beyond the debate over whether to run a strong campaign effort against Bush. The only statewide Democrats seeking re-election in 1998 were one Supreme Court justice and one Court of Criminal Appeals judge — not a single executive branch official. Earl Black, a political scientist at Rice University, maintained, "The elections this fall put the Democrats in their weakest position in state politics, perhaps ever. I can't recall a situation where the Democrats are more or less conceding the governorship ... and where they might end up losing all of the major statewide offices if Bush has the big victory it looks like he will." Added reporter Dan Balz, "Rarely have Democrats faced an election so divided and disorganized."[40]

For the thirteen statewide offices with Democratic candidates, only three had to win a primary, as the other ten were unopposed for nomination, including Mauro, Sharp, comptroller candidate Paul Hobby, state representative Richard Raymond for land commissioner, and six judicial candidates. Former attorney general Jim Mattox easily won the nomination over two minor opponents in his effort to regain his old office. State representative L. P. "Pete" Patterson defeated Ernesto L. De Leon for agriculture commissioner, and Joe B. Henderson easily won the Democratic nomination for one of the three positions on the Railroad Commission.

After the GOP won all ten statewide contests in 1996, interest in the Republican nominations was much more intense. Even Governor Bush drew a token opponent, who ended up garnering only 3.4 percent of the vote. There were several highly contested statewide races however, resulting in three of them going to a runoff. Perhaps the most competitive race was the contest for attorney general. Railroad Commissioner Williamson came in first, with 38.1 percent of the vote, and was forced into a runoff with Supreme Court Justice Cornyn, who obtained 32.2 percent. Pauken trailed with 29.7 percent of the primary vote.

Although Williamson came in first in the primary, he was unable to reach a majority in the subsequent runoff election. The third-place finisher, Pauken, sent a letter to his supporters telling them that while he would not endorse Cornyn, they should not vote for Williamson. Pauken claimed that Cornyn had run an honorable campaign, but Williamson had launched a personal attack on him by calling Pauken the arch-nemesis of Governor Bush.[41] In the runoff on April 14 Cornyn defeated Williamson by a margin of 57.9 percent to 42.1 percent.

The other hotly contested primary involved Secretary of State Garza and former member of Congress Steve Stockman, both of whom were seeking the GOP nomination for Railroad Commission. Garza, who had twice been elected county judge of Cameron County on the Mexican border, was the subject of a last-minute attack by Stockman emphasizing Garza's Hispanic heritage and claiming that if he were elected "we could see illegals in the oil and gas fields taking away Texas jobs." The mail piece criticized Garza's appointment as secretary of state by Governor Bush and attempted to link him to illegal immigration, drug trafficking, welfare cheating, voter fraud, and rape. As Garza noted in a response to the media, "This isn't even thinly veiled. It's clearly a racist attack meant to appeal to people's worst instincts. I think Republicans are smart enough to see through something that is so clearly 11th hour and desperate and has no relation to the issues at hand."[42] On primary day Garza was nominated with 53.1 percent of the vote to Stockman's 46.9 percent.

The two candidates most closely associated with the religious right—Pauken and Stockman—came up short in the 1998 GOP primary. Mark Sanders, a consultant for Pauken, concluded, "On a statewide level, the Moral Majority turned out to be a vocal minority. They just didn't show up.... I've always thought that the importance of the far right has been overestimated in primaries and this is proof positive that they have overestimated their strength."[43]

With the primary and runoff over, the focus turned to the Republican state convention to be held in Fort Worth on June 12 and 13. This time, while there were the usual battles over various platform planks and whether GOP candidates should pledge their support for all the platform commitments, overall harmony prevailed. Party chairman Weddington was described by one observer as someone who would make hard-right statements on any social issue as long as the statements did not affect any bill in the legislature. Lutz claimed, "She backed a party platform that was hard right as long as the party rules did not tie the elected officials to endorsing the entire platform." At the state convention a compromise was reached whereby candidates would be mailed the state party platform and asked to note any issues with which they disagreed, although compliance was voluntary and many candidates refused to submit any statement.[44]

Weddington and vice chairman Barton were re-elected without opposition. Governor Bush gave the keynote address, and the delegates heard from Senators Hutchison and Gramm, along with brief remarks from the various statewide candidates. With Bush sitting at the top of the ticket, Republicans were optimistic that they could repeat their statewide success of 1996 and increase their numbers in the Texas legislature and the congressional delegation.

THE FALL CAMPAIGN AND ELECTION

Early on, it was clear that Governor Bush was in a strong position for re-election. In June the Texas Poll showed Bush leading Mauro by 70 percent to 17 percent. Mauro challenged the results and reported that his own polls showed him behind by "only" thirty points. Meanwhile, having difficulty raising campaign funds, Mauro and Democratic loyalists continued to go door-to-door attempting to rally support, with Mauro claiming to have personally knocked on seven thousand doors by the middle of the summer.[45]

Governor Bush continued to run television commercials and line up endorsements from Democratic officeholders while solidifying his base of Republican support. He campaigned personally in traditional Democratic strongholds such as the Rio Grande Valley and El Paso, where his proficiency in Spanish allowed him to communicate on a different level with many voters. By fall, more than one hundred Democratic officeholders had endorsed his re-election, including Lieutenant Governor Bullock and El Paso mayor Carlos Ramirez.[46] On Election Day his campaigning in Hispanic communities would pay off handsomely.

In mid-October, Bush and Mauro met in their only debate at a time when polls showed the incumbent governor ahead by nearly fifty points. Mauro challenged Bush on his rumored interest in running for president rather than completing his term as governor, saying "I would like to see him let us know if he's going to be a full-time governor." Bush demurred, claiming, "I don't know if I'll seek the presidency or not. I understand the consequences of not making up my mind. I don't think there would be all this speculation going on if the people didn't think I was doing a good job as governor."[47]

While Bush kept his substantial lead over his opponent and most other statewide races appeared to have the GOP candidate ahead, there were at least two exceedingly close contests developing—the open races for lieutenant governor and comptroller. The most critical election in turning the state to one-party Republican dominance was the race to succeed Bullock. Were Bush to run for president and be elected, he would be turning over the governor's mansion to the lieutenant governor. Whoever would be elected in 1998 could possibly become governor by January 2001. In fact, that is what happened.[48]

It was a contest between two statewide officeholders, both of whom had held their positions for the past eight years: Comptroller Sharp and Agriculture Commissioner Perry. Sharp was viewed as a well-respected moderate acceptable to nearly all elements in the Texas Democratic Party, and in an early poll he had a six-point lead over Perry, with a sizeable number of undecideds. For Governor Bush, the contest was viewed as a test of his ability to help elect other candidates and build his party. As Rove later related, "Electing Perry was a goal to which we devoted a lot of money, energy, and attention, including the only two Texas fundraisers former President George H. W. Bush did in Texas that election."[49] In the closing days of the campaign, the former president did even more, cutting a television commercial in which he told Texans, "Everyone in our family strongly supports him. You have a good man. My heart is where Barbara's is, where George's is, in the Perry corner."[50]

As late as mid-October, the Texas Poll showed Perry and Sharp even at 37 percent each, with more than 20 percent undecided. With Bush far ahead, the governor's campaign turned to helping Perry cross the finish line with a victory. Rove recalled, "We stepped up phone bank efforts to identify households that supported Bush but were undecided in the lieutenant governor's race so the Perry campaign could focus on those persuadable voters. Households backing Bush and Perry got an all-out push to turn out via absentee and early voting or on Election Day, while voters backing Bush and Sharp got dropped from the turnout efforts."[51] Perry won by slightly more than sixty-eight thousand votes, a squeaker of a win, but one that set Rick Perry on the path to becoming the longest-serving governor in Texas history.

The Sharp-Perry contest in some ways was a portent of the future and in other ways the last hurrah for the Democratic Party in statewide contests. No individual other than Sharp better epitomizes the difficulties for the Texas Democratic Party in winning statewide contests. Not even a well-respected and experienced political leader such as Sharp could overcome the growing tide of Republican votes in 1998 or in the subsequent election four years later.[52]

The other exceedingly close contest was for comptroller, for which the Democrats had recruited Paul Hobby, a thirty-eight-year-old business leader from Houston. Although he had not been a candidate for public office previously, to say that Hobby came from a distinguished political family would be an understatement. Hobby's grandfather had been Texas governor from 1917 to 1921. His grandmother, Oveta Culp Hobby, served in Dwight Eisenhower's cabinet as the first secretary of the Department of Health, Education, and Welfare. Paul Hobby's father, Bill Hobby, had been lieutenant governor for eighteen years, from 1973 to 1991. In addition, for many years the Hobby family had owned the daily *Houston Post*, a newspaper that had ceased publication three years earlier, in 1995.

Hobby's Republican opponent also came from a well-known family. Carole Rylander was the daughter of Page Keeton, the longtime and revered dean of the University of Texas Law School. Having served six years as mayor of Austin, Rylander was elected to the Texas Railroad Commission in 1994, winning an unexpired term over the Democratic incumbent by a margin of 292,403 votes. Two years later, in 1996, she won a full six-year term by a margin of more than one million votes, only to turn her attention rather quickly to the 1998 race for comptroller.

Throughout the campaign, Hobby attempted to steer clear of the Democratic candidate for governor, while Rylander clung tightly to the coattails of Governor Bush. In the end Hobby was able to garner 635,000 more votes than Mauro, but that was insufficient to overcome the Republican candidate. Rylander was elected by a margin of 20,223 votes, the closest margin in an election in which most down-ballot statewide Republican candidates were winning by margins ranging from 249,005 to 707,904 over their Democratic opponents.

The 1998 election is also important in that since then, the Republican Party has gradually built a substantial lead over the Democratic Party in the number of straight-ticket votes cast by Texas voters. The limited data available from the thirty largest counties shows that 53.1 percent of the two-party straight-ticket votes in 1998 were Republican, with an even larger margin among the state's other counties. Clearly Perry and Rylander won only because of the advantage they received from straight-ticket ballots; they lost to their Democratic opponents among "pick-and-choose" voters.[53]

From the perspective of down-ballot Republican candidates it is unfortunate that the 2017 Texas legislature, in a partisan vote, eliminated the straight-ticket option beginning with the 2020 presidential election. The move was pushed by big-city Republican legislators and signed into law by Governor Greg Abbott, despite the fact that the Republican Party had built a massive statewide lead over Democrats among straight-ticket voters. From 2010 to 2016, the Republican statewide lead among straight-ticket voters ranged from 405,664 to 587,069, giving lower-visibility candidates for state executive and judicial offices a tremendous built-in advantage over their Democratic opponents. It is certainly possible that the elimination of this GOP advantage may result in a down-ballot statewide Democratic victory, something that did not occur from 1994 to 2016, when the Republican Party stressed straight-ticket voting. Its elimination will certainly increase the cost of down-ballot contests, as candidates will need to stress name identification and encourage voters to continue down the ballot to their lower-level positions.[54]

While the contests for lieutenant governor and comptroller were close, the remainder of the statewide races went heavily Republican. Governor Bush received 68.2 percent of the total vote, for a margin of 1,385,229 votes over Mauro, carrying all but fourteen of the state's 254 counties. Reaching beyond the traditional GOP base, Bush obtained 27 percent of the African-American vote and bested his Democratic opponent among Hispanic voters with 49 percent of the total votes cast for governor. Bush's overwhelming margin and his coattails in bringing home a GOP lieutenant governor, as well as all the other statewide officials, put him in good standing for a possible presidential run in 2000. By re-electing Governor Bush Texas voters were saying that they appreciated what he had done for the state and were not overly concerned that he might leave them for a greater assignment in the Nation's Capital.

Cornyn became the first Republican attorney general by a margin of 371,749 votes over Mattox, while David Dewhurst easily bested Raymond for land commissioner, Combs replaced Perry as agriculture commissioner, and Garza became a member of the Railroad Commission. GOP incumbents Greg Abbott, Craig Enoch, and Deborah Hankinson retained their positions on the Supreme Court, while Harriet O'Neill ousted the one remaining Democrat, Justice Rose Spector. Democratic Court of Criminal Appeals judge Charlie Baird lost to Republican Mike Keasler, while the GOP's Lawrence Meyers retained his position on the court and Republican Cheryl Johnson gained the final statewide slot by a margin of 542,759 votes.

As the 1998 election ended, Republicans were in control of all twenty-nine statewide elected positions, a situation that would not change in the next twenty years. The party added two more state representatives to bring the partisan margin down to seventy-eight Democrats and seventy-two Republicans, while the state Senate remained barely in GOP control at sixteen Republicans to fifteen Democrats. The party continued to make gains in county government, especially in the growing suburbs around the five largest counties. It was a new period for Texas politics as the state was at the start of the era of Republican dominance.

THIRTEEN

BUSH 43 AND GOVERNOR PERRY

It was clear to most political observers that by the late 1990s, Texas had moved from being a two-party, competitive state, in which control of the governor's mansion changed partisan complexion every four years, to a Republican-dominated state. The Texas Democratic Party retained a tenuous majority in the Texas congressional delegation and the state House of Representatives but these majorities would soon disappear. For a while the Democratic Party would continue to have more county and district officeholders, especially in the smaller, rural counties, but the political winds were now moving in a different direction.[1]

As the state's politics became more oriented toward the Republican Party, several county and state officeholders began announcing a change in party affiliation. Although these party switches had occurred periodically since the early 1960s, in almost every case from Democratic to Republican, the period from 1999 to 2015 would see an increasing number of reaffiliations as groups of elected officials in a county made the move in unison to the Republican Party. In September 1999, Lieutenant Governor Rick Perry and GOP state chairman Susan Weddington welcomed fifteen Democratic officeholders to the party at an Austin news conference. Perry, a recent party switcher himself, spoke from experience when he declared, "It takes tremendous courage and a strong commitment to conservative principles and ideals to make this change." Explaining the party's objective, Weddington added, "We are aggressively recruiting conservative, qualified candidates to the Republican Party. And it is not a hard sell for most because the Democrats' liberal leadership and policies have left them completely alienated."[2]

With a Republican lieutenant governor presiding over a sixteen to fifteen GOP majority in the Texas Senate and a closely divided House of Representatives (seventy-eight Democrats to seventy-two Republicans) led by Democratic speaker Pete Laney, Governor George W. Bush was able to achieve a successful and largely uneventful legislative session in 1999. This was accomplished by focusing on a few key issues and working closely with Perry, Laney, and other key members of the legislature.

Among the new provisions signed into law was a parental notification act sponsored by Senator Florence Shapiro of Plano, requiring that parents be informed before an abortion could be performed on any woman under the age of eighteen. The governor also signed the Religious Freedom Restoration Act, requiring that any governmental entity must show a compelling public interest before interfering with a citizen's right to religious practice. The provision of electricity to Texas citizens was opened to competition with the deregulation of the market, while the Children's Health Insurance Program (CHIP) was expanded, increasing eligibility to 200 percent of the state poverty level, or an income of $32,900 for a family of four. Taxes were reduced, and the state enacted a law prohibiting the long-standing policy of social promotion for failing students.

The session also provided an opportunity for Perry to establish his political identity in a broader arena. Following the irascible Bob Bullock as lieutenant governor, Perry took a different approach to leadership. As political strategist Bill Miller described his performance, Perry cast himself as a conciliator. "He's watched, he's observed, and he's moved slowly and carefully."[3] Confronting a slim one-vote majority, Perry required a high level of diplomacy as presiding officer to help shepherd Bush's legislative priorities through the Texas Senate.

With the end of the 1999 legislative session, the focus of Texas politics shifted to Bush's presidential candidacy. Three months earlier, in March, Bush had formed an exploratory committee that allowed him to begin raising funds and making appearances around the nation while still holding back from a formal announcement of candidacy. Then on June 12, at an appearance in the initial caucus state of Iowa, Bush declared, "I am running for President of the United States. There's no turning back. And I intend to be the next President of the United States." Bush also telegraphed a theme of his campaign when he described himself: "I am proud to be a compassionate conservative. I welcome the label. And on this ground, I will make my stand."[4]

Throughout his years as governor, Bush concentrated on a few key issues, cultivating an image of working across party lines to achieve his legislative goals. State representative Arlene Wohlgemuth, a leading social conservative in the Texas legislature, contended, "He would have lost his effectiveness had he been a religious right champion. I think he has been very wise politically." Chuck Anderson, director of the Texas Christian Coalition, said the governor had delivered on three issues of concern to his group: parental notification, the Religious Freedom Restoration Act, and tax cuts. "On most every issue we've had pretty much the same goals," declared Anderson.

Tom Pauken had been a consistent thorn in the governor's side, and Pauken was not the only one who felt Bush was insufficiently right-wing. Cathie Adams of the Eagle Forum felt ignored and taken for granted, claiming Bush kept her followers at arm's length. According to Adams, "The real reaching out, and the real, 'I want to work with you,' has been for Democrats." Donna Ballard of Houston, a former member of the state board of education, bluntly declared, "The facts are that he has not been a friend to conservatives in the state of Texas." However, Professor Bruce Buchanan of the University of Texas at Austin claimed that the social conservatives "have no leverage over him because the rest of the state is more moderate than them, in part, and because they have not gotten elected."[5] Bush continued to have broad support among most Texans, support reflected in his two victories for governor, followed by his twice carrying the state in his presidential campaigns.

In early 2000 Weddington stirred up some dissension in the party by abandoning the state chairman's traditional neutrality in intraparty contests. Weddington publicly endorsed Railroad Commissioner Michael Williams and Supreme Court Justice Alberto Gonzales, both of whom had been appointed by Governor Bush, as well as veteran Supreme Court Justice Nathan Hecht. All three had drawn opponents in the March 2000 GOP primary. Andy Draughn, running against Williams, said in response to Weddington's action, "I'm incredulous," while Gonzales's opponent Rod Gorman maintained, "I consider it unethical."[6] Defending Weddington's breach of normal practice, National Committeeman Tim Lambert claimed, "She has taken this unusual step because there are candidates for nomination who clearly have a background as Democratic activists and supporters." In Lambert's view the party would welcome former Democratic officeholders and activists into the party but not as candidates against longtime Republicans in the GOP primary. In defense of her actions Weddington claimed that Valerie Davenport and Rod Gorman, running for Supreme Court positions, were "stealth Democrats," while Railroad Commissioner Williams was a personal friend who had served as general counsel for the state party organization.[7]

The rationale of endorsing against stealth Democrats could not be used two years later when Weddington once again endorsed a candidate in an expensive and divisive primary for the state Senate. Weddington backed state representative John Shields in his challenge to longtime GOP activist state senator Jeff Wentworth of San Antonio. Wentworth won the intraparty battle and continued to serve until he was defeated ten years later by Donna Campbell of San Marcos in another divisive GOP primary.[8]

By the time of the March 2000 primary elections, both Bush and Vice President Al Gore had insurmountable leads for their presidential nominations. In the Democratic primary Gore defeated former senator Bill Bradley of New Jersey with 80.2 percent of the vote, while Governor Bush racked up 87.5 percent of the GOP primary vote, well ahead of John McCain and Alan Keyes. Once again more Texans chose to participate in the Republican primary rather than the Democratic primary.

It was a rather uneventful Republican primary in much of the state, with the only statewide competitive races being for three seats on the Court of Criminal Appeals. Two state Senate districts in East Texas saw lively nominating contests, won by Bob Deuell and state representative Todd Staples, races that in November could decide whether the GOP would hold its razor-thin sixteen to fifteen majority in the Texas Senate.

Senator Kay Bailey Hutchison was unopposed in her primary, and the Democratic Party establishment was having great difficulty in nominating a viable candidate to oppose her. Former state representative Charles Gandy, the party leadership's choice, barely squeaked into a runoff and then lost the runoff primary to perennial candidate Gene Kelly, whose only notable attribute appeared to be sharing his name with a well-known deceased actor and dancer. In November, having conducted virtually no campaign and lacking any significant Democratic Party support, Kelly lost to Hutchison by a margin of more than 2 million votes.

When the primary was over, Texas Democrats had nominated candidates in only four of the ten statewide contests, conceding to the GOP the Railroad Commission and three seats on the Supreme Court, along with one of the three Court of Criminal Appeals positions on the ballot. Meanwhile several Democratic state legislators were traveling to primary states to back Bush in his campaign for the presidency. As George Christian, press secretary to President Lyndon B. Johnson, explained, "For most Texans, it's a no-brainer. It's an acceptable, bi-partisan Texan running for President." Added Dan McClung, a Democratic political consultant, "Right now, our fight is not statewide. George W. Bush is popular. He's extremely well financed. And most Texans would prefer to have a President from Texas than fight about party politics."[9]

At the Republican state convention in Houston, Weddington was reelected as state chairman along with her vice chairman, David Barton. The more competitive elections were for Texas representatives on the Republican National Committee. With National Committeewoman Cathy McConn having stepped down to seek a congressional nomination, three candidates were vying for her position. Denise McNamara was backed by a number of social conservatives, including National Committeeman Tim Lambert, former Harris County GOP chairman Gary Polland, and Chuck Anderson of the Texas Christian Coalition. Also gaining support from social conservatives was LaNeil Wright Spivy, founder of the Texas chapter of Eagle Forum.

The third candidate for national committeewoman was Jill Mellinger of Dallas, backed by former state chairmen Fred Meyer, Ray Barnhart, and Chet Upham, as well as former national committee members Ernest Angelo, Fran Chiles, and Penny Butler. Despite this support from former state party leaders and others, Mellinger lost, and McNamara was successful. In the contest for national committeeman, Lambert was re-elected by defeating Mike McDougal, president of McDougal Realtors and brother of the mayor of Lubbock.

By the start of the twenty-first century it was evident that social conservatives were the dominant force among activists who attended Republican conventions. National Committeeman Lambert was also president of the Texas Homeschool Coalition, while the new national committeewoman, McNamara, came from an involvement in prolife activities. State chairman Weddington was employed by Kinetic Concepts, a firm whose founder was James Leininger, financial backer of many conservative religious and political causes and candidates. Vice chairman Barton was founder of WallBuilders, an organization promoting the religious aspects of the founding of the US and an active role for religion in public life.

As abortion became a litmus test issue for party leadership, the small band of Republicans for Choice disappeared from state conventions, along with the Log Cabin Republicans, an organization comprising mainly gay and lesbian party supporters, who had been denied, once again, the opportunity to rent a booth in the convention's exhibit hall.

Delegates to the 2000 state convention adopted a platform declaring that "homosexual behavior is contrary to the fundamental unchanging truths that have been ordained by God" and calling for the overturning of the Supreme Court's decision in *Roe v. Wade*. In an isolationist mood, delegates called for an end to participation in the United Nations, repeal of the North American Free Trade Agreement (NAFTA), and withdrawal from the World Trade Organization. Domestically they wanted an end to the Internal Revenue Service, a phasing out of Social Security, and a return to the gold standard.[10] It was evident at the 2000 Republican state convention that changes had taken place among the party's activist base.

Although Governor Bush was not at the state convention, his presidential candidacy was the one effort on which nearly all Texas Republicans could agree. Addressing the delegates were Laura Bush and senators Phil Gramm and Kay Bailey Hutchison.[11]

With Bush at the top of the ballot as the party's presidential candidate, November 7, 2000 could be viewed as another strong victory for Texas Republicans—but was it? In the presidential contest Bush carried the state easily by a margin of 1,365,893 votes over Vice President Gore. Even more impressive was the margin of 2,051,776 achieved by Hutchison, although her Democratic opponent was little more than a token candidate with a famous name.

The other two statewide candidates with Democratic opponents—Sharon Keller and Barbara Parker Hervey, running for two seats on the Court of Criminal Appeals—won by margins of over seven hundred thousand votes. Railroad commissioners Charles Matthews and Michael Williams and Supreme Court justices Nathan Hecht, Priscilla Owen, and Al Gonzales all retained their positions over Libertarian and Green Party opponents, and Charles Holcomb became a judge on the Court of Criminal Appeals. Williams became the first African-American to be elected to a nonjudicial statewide position in Texas history.

In the last election for legislative districts apportioned and drawn on the basis of the 1990 census, the state's US House of Representatives delegation remained seventeen Democrats and thirteen Republicans. While the party retained its majority in the Texas Senate, the Democrats kept a slim majority in the Texas House, despite more votes being cast statewide for GOP legislative candidates.

The uncertainty of election night was focused not on what occurred in Texas but on what was transpiring in Florida, where the vote counting and the call for recounts went on for more than a month before the US Supreme Court, in *Bush v. Gore*, ended the recount, allowing Florida to cast its Electoral College votes for Bush, thus making him president of the United States.[12]

TEXAS REPUBLICANS ENTER THE TWENTY-FIRST CENTURY

From his performance as governor and his ability to reach out and engage a wide range of supporters, George W. Bush had helped to convert a growing Republican Party into the dominant force in Texas politics. Now he would be in Washington, and power shifts would occur in the Texas GOP. Both in Texas and across the nation, the rhetoric of politics seemed to be moving more to simplistic and emotional appeals. While politicians have long tended towards generalizations, the forward-looking calls to confront a new frontier, build a great society, or view America as a beacon to all, a city on a hill, were replaced by pledges to turn back the clock to a perceived better time in the past. Whether from the left or the right, many voters believed the answers were easy to find but the politicians were simply unwilling to enact them. If college student debt was hampering young people, then make attending college free for all. If we need to keep drug smugglers out of our country, then build a wall. If there were Americans without health coverage, then mandate insurance as a requirement for all.

It was in such an environment that the Texas GOP continued to grow in terms of officeholders and influence over state government. The change was evident not only in statewide offices held by the party or control of the state legislature, but also in many of the state's counties. Republicans were building overwhelming majorities of county judges, sheriffs, and county commissioners in suburban, other metropolitan, and small-town counties, leaving the Democrats with a solid base of support in five of the six most populous counties and those along the Rio Grande border. Rural and small-town Texas, long the home of conservative and populist Democrats, was rapidly changing partisan allegiance.[13]

At the same time the geographical base of the Republican Party was changing, and with it the overall composition of the primary electorate. In 1978, when the GOP won the governor's office after a 104-year absence, 66.8 percent of all GOP primary votes came from the six largest counties; by 2012 these counties contributed only 30.6 percent of the total Republican primary vote. Meanwhile the percentage of votes from suburban counties grew from 7.5 percent to 27.5 percent while the contribution from small-town counties increased from 8.0 percent to 24.9 percent. Urban voters were no longer the dominant force in the process of selecting Republican candidates.

After a century during which most important decisions on selecting officeholders occurred in the Democratic primary, the arena of final choice had moved to the Republican side. Now it was those who voted in the Republican primary who were screening out candidates who wished to hold public office. By 2012, in more and more suburban, other metropolitan, and small-town counties, less than 10 percent of the primary vote was being cast on the Democratic side.

These changes in the party electorate would affect the kind of candidates who obtained the GOP nomination and subsequent election. More and more candidates with the support of social conservatives and fewer and fewer business-oriented, moderate conservatives would represent the party. As the GOP primary became the most important election, contests took place between individuals reflecting these two elements in the party. By 2012 it was clear that the social conservative wing was now dominant over those who had previously represented the party as a middle-class, business-oriented force.

All these changes were occurring during a time of great partisan continuity. The last Democrat had been elected to statewide office in 1994, and beginning in 2002 the state legislature was in total Republican control. Moreover, one Republican officeholder was situated in the governor's mansion for the first fourteen years of the new century.

THE PERRY ERA

On December 21, 2000, James Richard Perry was sworn in as governor of Texas after it was confirmed that George W. Bush would become the forty-third president of the United States. This began the longest continuous service of any governor of the state as Rick Perry commenced his fourteen years in the office. While Governor Bush had led the Republican Party to become a strong force in state politics, it would be during Perry's tenure that Republicans became dominant in federal, state, and county government across the state. Much of this would come about with total GOP control of all statewide offices and the eventual ability to redraw the state legislative and congressional district lines.

With Perry's elevation the Texas Senate chose a new lieutenant governor, naming Senator Bill Ratliff of Mount Pleasant over Senator David Sibley of Waco. Ratliff would serve as lieutenant governor and presiding officer until the 2002 election produced a new officeholder. Ratliff remained in the Senate for his legislative term but did not seek re-election in 2004.

REAPPORTIONMENT AND REDISTRICTING

While the Democrats held majorities in the Texas legislature they were able to control the decennial process of redrawing congressional district lines. The process was designed to magnify the number of districts that could be won by Democratic candidates, and perhaps the most effective plan was enacted in 1991. As political scientists Earl and Merle Black explained, "Holding the governorship and both chambers of the legislature, Texas Democrats completely controlled the redistricting process in 1991. As they had done in the past, Democrats protected their incumbents and consigned the Republicans to a few utterly safe seats."[14] According to *The Almanac of American Politics, 1994*, it was "the shrewdest gerrymander of the 1990s."[15] Throughout the 1990s, GOP congressional candidates regularly received a majority of the votes but ended up with fewer members of Congress. Texas Republicans were determined that they would not be shortchanged again when the next reapportionment of congressional seats and redrawing of district lines occurred.

After the calculations from the 2000 Census were reported, redistricting became a major political and governmental concern for both parties. From the time of the 1990 Census to 2000, Texas had grown from an estimated 16,986,500 residents to 20,903,000. Texas' population growth rate was greater than that of the nation as a whole, and thus the state gained two additional congressional seats, increasing the state's US House of Representatives delegation from thirty to thirty-two members.

When the Texas legislature met in January 2001, there was a slim Republican majority in the Senate and a Democratic majority in the House. No agreement could be reached on drawing the thirty-two new congressional districts. The task was referred to the federal courts, where a panel of judges created a map with minor changes to the existing districts to be used in the 2002 election. These court-drawn districts resulted in the election of seventeen Democrats and fifteen Republicans in the 2002 elections.

Republicans were convinced that they had been shortchanged by the actions of the federal court and were determined to redraw the congressional lines once they obtained a majority in both chambers of the Texas legislature. To help achieve this objective a new political action committee, Texans for a Republican Majority, was created under the leadership of US House majority whip Tom DeLay.

Meanwhile internal population movement and growth necessitated the redrawing of state legislative districts. While it is the responsibility of the Texas legislature to draw new districts of roughly equal population, the regular sessions of the Texas House and Senate adjourned without agreeing to any redistricting plans. This left the task of developing state legislative districts to the Legislative Redistricting Board (LRB), comprising the lieutenant governor, attorney general, speaker of the House of Representatives, comptroller, and land commissioner—all of whom were Republicans except Speaker Laney. The LRB plan for the Texas Senate was precleared by the US Department of Justice and upheld by the federal district court. However, the LRB's plan for the Texas House was denied preclearance, and the federal district court developed and imposed a new plan to be in effect for the 2002 elections. These new districts produced three additional GOP state senators, to increase the party's majority to nineteen to twelve, while for the first time since Reconstruction there would be a Republican majority—of eighty-eight to sixty-two—in the Texas House. Longtime state representative Tom Craddock from Midland, who had served continuously since 1968, became speaker.[16]

The 2002 elections produced a GOP majority in both the Texas Senate and House, and the legislature proceeded to redraw the court-drawn congressional districts in a manner more favorable to Republican candidates. Outnumbered in the House, fifty-two Democratic state representatives went into hiding outside Texas to prevent a quorum from being present. This kept a vote approving the GOP redistricting plan from taking place during the allotted time for the legislature's regular session.

Unable to complete the redistricting process in a regular session, Governor Perry called a special session. Democrats were able to prevent a Senate vote in the first special session, and the governor called a second thirty-day session. This time eleven of the twelve Democratic senators fled to New Mexico, and no plan could be passed. When the governor called a third special session, two Democratic senators attended and ensured a quorum would be present, allowing a congressional district plan to be enacted. The new plan would be in effect for the 2004 election, resulting in the election of six additional Republican members of Congress and a partisan split of twenty-one Republicans and eleven Democrats.[17]

THE DEMOCRATIC DREAM TICKET OF 2002

After having lost two consecutive gubernatorial elections and all statewide elective offices since 1994, Texas Democrats made a conscious effort to recruit the best possible candidates representing various demographic and geographic groups for the 2002 election. With Bush no longer in Texas and now situated in the White House, this would be his first presidential off-year election—a time often fraught with peril for the incumbent party. Just eight years earlier the Democrats had lost their longtime majority in the US House of Representatives with Bush's predecessor, Bill Clinton, occupying the White House.

Democratic hopes were enhanced not only by the fact that the party of the president frequently performs poorly in the midterm elections, but also because a number of statewide contests—for US senator, lieutenant governor, attorney general, and land commissioner—were open seats with no incumbent seeking re-election. Even Governor Perry had not been elected but rather, as lieutenant governor, had succeeded Bush upon the latter's elevation to the presidency.

State Democratic Party leaders were convinced that a multiethnic and multiracial statewide ticket would bring together sufficient diverse constituencies to ensure victory. For the US Senate contest, popular Dallas mayor Ron Kirk, an African-American, was encouraged to seek the party's nomination.

Multimillionaire banker and rancher Tony Sanchez of Laredo announced his candidacy for governor, while former comptroller John Sharp decided to make a second run for the office of lieutenant governor after having lost an extremely close election to Perry in 1998. Additionally, party leaders convinced Austin mayor Kirk Watson to run for attorney general while state senator David Bernsen of Beaumont gave up his seat to become a candidate for land commissioner.

This balanced and diverse ticket first had to overcome some major obstacles in the Democratic primary. In the Senate race, Kirk's path to the nomination was challenged by two serious opponents: Victor Morales, the high school teacher who had come from obscurity to run a competitive race against Senator Gramm in 1996, and member of Congress Ken Bentsen of Houston, nephew of former senator, vice presidential candidate, and Treasury Secretary Lloyd Bentsen Jr. No candidate obtained a majority in the primary as Morales came in first with 33.2 percent of the vote, barely besting Kirk's 33.1 percent and Bentsen's 26.8 percent. In the runoff, with greater financial resources and the support of party leaders, Kirk succeeded in garnering 59.8 percent of the vote to Morales's 40.2 percent and thereby secured the nomination.

In seeking the gubernatorial nomination, Sanchez was opposed by former attorney general Dan Morales, resulting in a contest between two Mexican-Americans from differing backgrounds and the nation's first gubernatorial debate in Spanish. Sanchez, a banker with oil and gas investments and an estimated worth of $600 million, outspent Morales at a ratio of forty to one, with much of his $20 million primary campaign self-funded. Morales, a Harvard Law School graduate from San Antonio who had served eight years as attorney general after terms in the Texas House, entered the race on the last day of filing and was unable to overcome Sanchez's massive financial advantage. When the primary was held, Morales corralled 330,873 votes, or 33 percent, compared to Sanchez's total of 609,383, or 60.7 percent of the Democratic primary vote.[18] The nominating battle did not end the conflict between Morales and Sanchez. By October Morales had endorsed GOP governor Perry as "the candidate in this campaign whose election would clearly be in the best interest of Texas."[19]

Sharp and Watson were more fortunate, as they faced no primary opposition to their nominations. Senator Bernsen easily defeated Reynaldo "Ray" Madrigal of Corpus Christi, a candidate who would surface again twelve years later to oppose state senator Wendy Davis for the Democratic gubernatorial nomination.[20]

Once the primary was over, Texas Democrats had their dream ticket balancing the state's various ethnic, geographic, and racial components, a ticket calculated on a belief that Texas voters could be appealed to on personal characteristics more than on policy perspectives and ideological differences. From the latter years of the twentieth century to the present, Texas Democrats have been counting on a surge in the state's Hispanic population to produce a majority for their candidates. The 2002 slate, with an African-American mayor, a Hispanic banker, and an Anglo veteran of state government, was designed to produce this Democratic majority. The stage was set to determine whether Republicans could continue their hold on state government or the Democrats would come back from the devastating losses they had suffered since 1996.

THE 2002 ELECTION

On September 11, 2001, America confronted the most significant attack on the nation since December 1941 as Islamic terrorists used three passenger flights to attack the World Trade Center and the Pentagon. A likely attack on the White House was diverted by brave passengers who succeeded in bringing a fourth plane down in a field in Pennsylvania. This began a battle against terrorism that continues to the present day, not only in the US but throughout most of the world.

In the immediate aftermath of 9/11, President Bush rallied the American people and gave comfort to those who had lost loved ones in the attack, and hope and commitment to the nation. In turn, most of the US population stood behind the president in this time of crisis, and his popularity reached new highs for the next few months. There is no way of measuring 9/11's impact on the November 2002 election, but it certainly made it something other than a standard presidential midterm election.

The contest for governor of Texas was described by one reporter as "one of the nastiest and most expensive governor's races in the nation." Democrat Tony Sanchez spent more than $54 million of his own money on the campaign, pouring roughly one million dollars a week into television advertisements across the state. As GOP state chairman Susan Weddington observed, "It's like nothing we've ever experienced. Just money, everywhere, trying to buy everything."[21]

Meanwhile, in the Senate contest between John Cornyn and Ron Kirk, Republicans were attempting to hold a seat that the GOP had controlled continuously since John Tower's special election victory in 1961. An early poll in May showed Cornyn and Kirk in a close race. A second survey in June had Kirk ahead by 8 percent, but with more than a third of all voters undecided in the race.[22] It was a contest that took on special significance for President Bush. A personal friend of the Bush family, Cornyn noted, "His father has done a couple of events for me. His mother is going to come in and do one. The first lady did an event for me in Austin. What it boils down to is he wants to make sure his legacy in Texas is protected."[23] The race had national implications also, as Republicans were attempting to regain a majority in the US Senate.[24]

On Election Day the dream ticket had become a nightmare for Texas Democrats. All the party's statewide candidates went down to defeat by wide margins, with only one, Sharp, losing by less than a half million votes. Sharp was the sole Democrat to corral more than two million votes from the 4,550,000 Texans who participated in the election, 46.0 percent of the total in his second attempt at becoming lieutenant governor. In the top-of-the-ballot Senate race, Kirk lost by more than 540,000 votes, while gubernatorial candidate Sanchez ended up 813,000 votes short of the total for Perry. The incumbent governor carried 220 of the state's 254 counties, including the Big 6 counties of Bexar, Dallas, Harris, and Tarrant, while losing Travis County by 213 votes out of 220,000 cast.[25]

To add to the Democrats' misery, the GOP picked up three additional state Senate seats to increase its majority to nineteen to twelve, while for the first time Republicans became the majority party in the Texas House of Representatives, after gaining sixteen new districts, for a margin of eighty-eight Republicans to sixty-two Democrats. Indicative of the Democrats' weakness and the packing of Democratic voters into a limited number of districts, of the sixty-two Democratic state representatives, forty-three had no Republican opponent on the general election ballot. Thus only nineteen of the sixty-two Democratic state representatives had defeated a Republican candidate on the path to election.[26]

When the Texas House of Representatives convened in January 2003 with its new Republican majority, one candidate for speaker had already lined up enough pledges of support to be easily chosen as presiding officer. Tom Craddick was the longest-serving GOP state representative, having represented his Midland district since first being elected in 1968. Craddick would continue as speaker until January 2009, and he continues as a member of the House in 2020.[27] Perry's relationships with the legislature were facilitated by his choice of Mike Toomey as chief of staff. Toomey had served in the Texas House with Perry and then became chief of staff to Bill Clements during his second term as governor.

TRANSITION AMID CONTINUITY

In 2003 Weddington stepped down as party chairman when she was appointed by Governor Perry to head up the newly formed OneStar Foundation, a nonprofit charged with furthering volunteerism and community service. When the state Republican executive committee met to choose a new leader, attorney Tina Benkiser of Houston won in a close contest with attorney Gina Parker of Waco.[28]

At the 2004 Republican state convention in San Antonio, Parker once again ran against Benkiser. Parker had the support of both National Committee members, Tim Lambert and Denise McNamara, as well as endorsements from Texas Right to Life and the Texas Homeschool Coalition, but was unable to defeat Benkiser.[29]

During the state convention, the Parker campaign sponsored an appearance by Alabama judge Roy Moore, whose battle to install a five-thousand-pound granite statue of the Ten Commandments in the rotunda of his state's Supreme Court building was a current political controversy. When a federal court determined its placement violated the First Amendment, Moore refused to remove the monument and was subsequently ejected from office for judicial misconduct.[30]

In the contest for the state's representatives on the Republican National Committee, McNamara was re-elected over Cathie Adams, Texas leader of the Eagle Forum, while Lambert did not seek another term. Attorney Bill Crocker of Austin was elected national committeeman by defeating Mark Cole of Houston, the candidate endorsed by Texas Right to Life and the Texas Homeschool Coalition.

While the official convention agenda focused on unity and inclusion, "beneath the show of harmony, the early political jostling for the 2006 governor's race was beginning." Both Senator Hutchison and Comptroller Carole Keeton Strayhorn made known their opposition to some of Perry's proposals and actions.[31] Perry ran into opposition among the delegates for proposing the legalization of video lottery terminals as a means to fund public education, but his support for cutting $9 billion in state spending rather than increasing taxes was applauded. As Ted Royer, spokesman for the Texas party, noted, "The governor continues to be very popular among Texas Republicans. He's a conservative leader who does what he believes to be the right thing regardless of what the others say. I think grass roots Republicans respect him for that."[32]

Despite the apparent support for Governor Perry at the state convention, it was not all smooth sailing for him politically over the next two years. Comptroller Strayhorn continued to criticize the governor, calling his budget cuts "mean spirited" and attacking new eligibility standards for CHIP.[33] When the state auditor's office extended its investigation of the comptroller's office, Strayhorn called it a "political witch hunt," claiming "I know where this started. It's right out of the governor's office that the intimidation and bullying continues." The governor's spokesperson denied that Perry was involved in the decision to audit the comptroller's office. In 2003, Strayhorn had briefly withheld certification of the state budget, maintaining that it did not balance. In response, the legislature moved two of the comptroller's functions to other agencies.[34]

At the same time Senator Hutchison was exploring the possibility of a race for governor. With two small children, Hutchison would prefer to be back home in Texas, and moving to the governor's mansion would be an appealing transition from life as a legislator in Washington, DC. Shortly after the 2004 election, Hutchison admitted, "I am thinking about doing it, but I haven't made a decision. I cannot tell you how much encouragement I am getting from people of all different areas of influence and interest."[35]

Some social conservatives in the Texas GOP had been critical of her record, especially when she cast her vote, along with four other Republicans, against the appointment of an Arkansas anti-abortion activist to the US District Court.[36] Yet Hutchison was the most popular politician among Texas voters, according to a Texas Poll released in September 2004. Statewide 62 percent viewed Hutchison as doing a good job, while Governor Perry had a favorable rating of 43 percent and Comptroller Strayhorn achieved a 45 percent approval rating. Among self-identified Republicans Hutchison's approval score was 77 percent, Perry was at 65 percent, and Strayhorn trailed at 48 percent favorability.[37]

Amid all the discussion of possible gubernatorial challenges two years later, President Bush was attempting to avoid his father's fate as he geared up for his re-election campaign. There was little doubt that he would once again carry his home state. The Texas Poll released in October 2004 showed Bush at 58 percent and Democrat John Kerry with 32 percent support, close to the eventual outcome of 61.1 percent for Bush to 38.2 percent for Kerry.[38]

Republicans were so confident of the outcome of the presidential race in Texas that they launched the Mighty Texas Strike Force to send volunteers to battleground states where they would campaign for Bush and other Republican candidates. Coordinated by former party vice chairman Polly Sowell, the effort sent party stalwarts to Nevada, Ohio, and other states that were eventually carried by Bush.

The only other statewide contests in 2004 involved three seats each on the Supreme Court and the Court of Criminal Appeals, and the re-election campaign of Railroad Commissioner Victor Carrillo, a Hispanic Republican who had previously been elected as Taylor County judge and who easily defeated his Democratic opponent for the Railroad Commission by more than one million votes. Democrats fielded only one candidate for the three Supreme Court positions and one candidate for the Court of Criminal Appeals, both of whom also lost by more than a million votes.

Major changes occurred in the state's newly redrawn thirty-two congressional districts, which swung from a seventeen to fifteen Democratic majority to a delegation of twenty-one Republicans and eleven Democrats. In two redrawn districts incumbent members of Congress were paired, resulting in the loss of two senior Democrats. In West Texas, Republican member of Congress Randy Neugebauer defeated longtime member Charles Stenholm, while Democrat Martin Frost lost his attempt at re-election to fellow member of Congress Pete Sessions in a new Dallas–Fort Worth area district. In East Texas, newcomers Louie Gohmert and Ted Poe ousted Democratic members of Congress Max Sandlin and Nick Lampson, while GOP candidates Michael McCaul, Mike Conaway, and Kenny Marchant picked up open seats. Adding to the Democratic losses was the party switch of longtime representative Ralph Hall, who won re-election as a Republican for the first time. The end result was six more Republicans in the state's congressional delegation.[39]

In summarizing the results, GOP chairman Benkiser said, "It was a great night from the White House to the courthouse. The sea of red was a great victory." Of the Democrats, Benkiser maintained, "They are out of touch with Texas values. We gave the message of hope and optimism."[40]

Texas Republicans were quite pleased by the support from Hispanic voters for the president's re-election. According to exit polling data, Bush received 59 percent of the Hispanic vote in Texas, an improvement over his 49 percent performance in 2000.[41] Railroad Commissioner Carrillo won the only other nonjudicial statewide contest in his re-election.

On the negative side, 2004 saw a turning point in the partisan leanings of Dallas County, long a Republican bastion, where the party had experienced its early successes in the 1960s and 1970s. Indicative of the change was the vote for president. Since 1952 the Republican presidential candidate had carried Dallas County in every contest except 1964, when home-state president Johnson bested Senator Barry Goldwater. In 2000 Bush beat Gore by more than 47,000 votes in Dallas county, but four years later he could eke out only a margin of 9,605 votes over Kerry. Bush's slim victory in 2004 would be the last time a Republican presidential candidate carried Dallas County. In

2016 Donald Trump lost the county to Hillary Clinton by a margin of nearly two hundred thousand votes.

From 1968 to 2006 only two Democratic gubernatorial candidates (Dolph Briscoe in 1974 and Ann Richards in 1990) had carried Dallas County. Since 2006 Democratic candidates have carried it consistently, with Governor Greg Abbott losing the county by more than 140,000 votes in 2018. Likewise, from 1974 to 2006, only one Democrat (Garry A. Weber) was elected as county judge; since then only Democrats have served as the county's chief executive. Lower down the ballot, Dallas County Democrats were making further inroads in county government as Democratic candidate Lupe Valdez became the county's first woman, lesbian, and Hispanic sheriff. Four other Democratic candidates were successful in judicial races. As Southern Methodist University political science professor Cal Jillson noted, "Democrats are on their way back. It's not that their party is well-organized or doing things that improve their chances of winning. It's the demographic changes in the county that are helping them to win."[42] The shift from a predominantly Republican county government to one dominated once again by Democrats was under way and would continue in full force over the next several years.

JANUARY 2005: THE TEXAS
LEGISLATURE IN SESSION

With Bush re-elected and beginning another four years in the White House, the focus of attention turned to Texas politics once again. In 2005 there would be a state legislative session and the buildup to what turned out to be one of the most unusual gubernatorial elections in the state's history.

When the Texas House convened in January, the GOP held the eighty-eight to sixty-two majority it had first achieved in the 2002 election, and Craddick remained as speaker. The party had lost two seats from the Big 6 counties, but it still retained a slight majority in these major urban counties and had picked up one additional district each from the suburban and other metro counties, giving the party a majority from each of the four categories of counties.[43]

Texas legislators and Governor Perry faced the possibility of a one to two billion dollar shortfall in anticipated income without an increase in some form of state taxation or even more drastic budgetary cuts than had already been made in 2003. Meanwhile, Comptroller Strayhorn was pushing for a teacher pay raise, while Senator Hutchison advocated restoring some of the funds that had been cut from the Children's Health Insurance Program (CHIP) two years earlier. The potential political challenges from these two statewide officeholders and the fiscal demands on the state placed Governor Perry in a difficult position. As Byron Schlomach of the Texas Public Policy Foundation viewed the situation, "Rick Perry is the most conservative governor since the first term of Bill Clements, but he has been beaten up pretty hard on the spending issues, and it is being reflected in the popularity polls."[44]

A proposal for legalizing gambling was raised once again, even though the House had earlier overwhelmingly rejected video lottery terminals and the Texas GOP platform said the party leadership "strongly opposed gambling, in any form, as a means to fund education." When the House passed a bill to revise the method of funding public education, Comptroller Strayhorn claimed it was the largest tax bill in history and still would not balance the state's budget. The proposal would increase a number of state taxes and create a new business tax while reducing property taxes for school maintenance and operations.[45]

Amid the discussions on improving public school funding, Governor Perry, Lieutenant-Governor David Dewhurst and Speaker Craddick attempted to rally support for education vouchers. Three differing bills to establish a voucher program were discussed before the House Public Affairs Committee, but none reached the floor. Not all Republicans supported vouchers, and the issue became a major campaign consideration in the 2006 Republican primary.

Disputes arose among Republican members over how best to reduce the tax burden on homeowners and businesses while still adequately funding public education. Efforts to put caps on local property appraisals and limit tax revenue increases by local governments ran into vigorous opposition from cities, counties, and school districts. In the end efforts at school finance reform failed, as did school vouchers and merit pay for public school teachers.

After expressing concern over school finance and tax proposals, Comptroller Strayhorn did certify the nearly $140 billion budget approved by the legislature. As she told reporters, "I am very comfortable that this budget balances. While I'm certifying the budget, it does not mean I agree with all the budget decisions."[46]

KINKY AND THE TOUGH GRANDMA

While the legislature was discussing and debating changes to state law, political developments were taking place in the lead-up to the 2006 state elections.

In early January, in an effort to freeze out any serious primary opposition, Governor Perry announced that every statewide elected official supported his re-election except Comptroller Strayhorn and the state's two US senators.[47] The various early endorsements of Perry did not scare off either Hutchison or Strayhorn, however. All three began 2005 with solid financial standing. Perry's campaign reports showed he had $7.9 million in his campaign treasury, while Hutchison had $6.7 million on hand, and Strayhorn sat on a balance of $5.7 million. Clearly none of the three was being outgunned financially fifteen months before the primary.[48]

Not fazed by the endorsements or the campaign treasuries, another well-known personality announced that he was launching a campaign to become governor. Richard S. Friedman, better known as "Kinky," said he was running for governor because of his concern over education and other issues. He sought a place on the November ballot as an Independent. Friedman, whose unofficial slogan was "How hard can it be?," was attempting to follow the pattern of California governor Arnold Schwarzenegger and former Minnesota governor Jesse Ventura in making the leap from celebrity to state chief executive. Friedman announced his candidacy in front of the Alamo, stressing its symbolism for Texas independence. To obtain ballot position as an Independent candidate in November, Friedman would need slightly more than forty-five thousand valid signatures from registered voters who did not participate in either the Democratic or Republican primary in 2006.[49]

Meanwhile former Houston area member of Congress Chris Bell announced that he would be seeking the Democratic nomination for governor, as would former member of Congress and Texas Supreme Court justice Bob Gammage and Fort Worth educator Felix Alvarado. With both Hutchison and Strayhorn considering a primary challenge to Perry, as well as a potential Independent candidacy by Friedman, it was clear that in 2006 it would be a major challenge for Rick Perry to retain his position as governor of Texas.

During the spring Hutchison's campaign committee hired the firm of Tarrance and Associates to survey likely Republican primary voters. Released in April 2005, the poll showed 59 percent leaning to Hutchison and 35 percent favoring the incumbent governor. Despite the favorable poll results, Hutchison announced in mid-June that she would not be a candidate for governor. At a late June rally of her supporters at Love Field in Dallas, Hutchison explained that she would seek re-election to the US Senate. She declared, "Gosh, I'd love to be governor of Texas. But I wanted to do what was right for Texas right now.... It may not be the right decision for me personally, but it is the right decision for Texas, and I do want to continue serving."[50] The reaction from Perry was a giant sigh of relief coupled with praise for Hutchison: "Senator Hutchison has been a true champion for Texas in Washington, fighting for the interests of our state. Her decision to seek re-election is great for Texas, and will help grow our Republican majority with her strong presence at the top of our ticket."[51]

Strayhorn did officially announce her candidacy, declaring "Now is the time to replace this do-nothin' drug store cowboy with one tough grandma." Strayhorn's declaration came shortly after Perry vetoed the public education provisions in the state budget and called for a special session devoted to school funding.[52]

Over the next several months Strayhorn attempted to expand her potential support by urging Democrats and Independents to cross over and vote for her in the Republican primary. She maintained at the time that the March 2006 GOP primary would be the only meaningful path to choosing the state's governor since no Democrat had won statewide office since 1994. But Strayhorn's pitch ran up against opposition from some party leaders. Jeff Fisher, executive director of the state party, accused Strayhorn of "courting liberals ... to vote in the primary like a one-night stand."[53]

As 2005 ended and the deadline for candidates to file approached, speculation centered on whether Strayhorn would continue to seek the Republican nomination. All that Mark Sanders, the comptroller's spokesperson, would say is, "Carole Keeton Strayhorn is a candidate for governor. She is a Republican. She will file for that office on Monday." In response, Perry's spokesperson, Robert Black, claimed, "If Carole Strayhorn leaves the GOP, it will represent the latest desperate act of a politician who has no core convictions or guiding principles. Political opportunism will have motivated Carole Strayhorn to abandon two parties and two sets of principles all in the name of furthering her own political ambition.[54]

Strayhorn gave her answer at the filing deadline by declaring "I am a Republican. But I know we must set partisan politics aside to do what's right for Texas. That is why I am running for governor as an independent." State GOP chairman Benkiser claimed "Grass-roots Republicans should be outraged that Carole Strayhorn has lied, deceived and now abandoned the very people who put her in office, all for her own selfish ambition."[55] After declaring her Independent candidacy, the comptroller was faced with the requirement of obtaining over 45,000 signatures from those who did not vote in either party primary, a task that could not begin until after the primaries and any resulting runoffs. She would be competing for signatures with Friedman, who had to overcome the same obstacle to have his name on the November ballot.

With the campaign year beginning, Strayhorn did receive an important endorsement from the Texas State Teachers Association (TSTA), the National

Education Association affiliate among the four educators' groups in Texas. TSTA had previously supported only Democratic candidates for statewide office. To gain their endorsement, Strayhorn had dropped her previous support for school vouchers.[56] A few months later Strayhorn would gain the nod of the Texas Federation of Teachers and the Texas State Employees Union. But when the AFL-CIO Committee on Political Education (COPE) met in May to make an endorsement, the battle was on as Bell blasted Strayhorn, who criticized Perry, while Friedman told the delegates he would reform state government to benefit working people. As one observer noted, "Most of the large crowd wore Bell stickers, and he received a standing ovation after his remarks. Mrs. Strayhorn got a smattering of applause, while Mr. Friedman received a standing ovation, and delegates laughed uncontrollably at his jokes." In the end, the union leaders stuck with the Democratic nominee and endorsed Bell.[57]

As Strayhorn's independent candidacy took shape, she gained support from other unlikely sources however, including former lieutenant governor Ben Barnes and 2002 gubernatorial candidate Tony Sanchez, both Democrats. Joining the campaign staff was Mark Sanders, coming over from the comptroller's office, and George Shipley, a longtime Democratic political consultant involved in both of Ann Richards's gubernatorial campaigns. Over the next few weeks Strayhorn's task was to convince donors and voters that she was a serious candidate who could defeat Rick Perry and to prepare to obtain voter signatures on her nominating petitions, a process that could not be implemented until after the primary runoff elections on April 11.

Meanwhile Friedman, widely known throughout Texas as a musician, comedian, and author of detective novels, was fundraising and organizing his own effort to obtain the signatures he needed to be on the ballot. In the months leading up to the election, Friedman combined political campaigning with entertainment. During the spring of 2006 he appeared in a short-lived television series called *Go Kinky* on the Country Music Television (CMT) cable network. Guests on the show included musicians Dwight Yoakam and Willie Nelson.

Once on the campaign trail Friedman stressed that he was serious about becoming governor. To achieve this goal he recruited the services of Dean Barkley, a political consultant who had been instrumental in wrestler Ventura's election as governor of Minnesota. Barkley would head up the campaign staff as overall director, with Bill Hillsman, another Ventura veteran, as advertising consultant, and longtime Friedman friend Jeff Shelby as deputy director.

The unorthodox campaign would gain the backing of several well-known names in Texas. In addition to Willie Nelson, other prominent supporters included defense attorney Dick DeGuerin, columnist Molly Ivins, and hair care multimillionaire Farouk Shami of Houston, who would himself seek the Democratic nomination for governor four years later. An early high-dollar fundraiser was held at socialite Carolyn Farb's River Oaks home, and the one-night event raised $150,000 for the Friedman campaign.[58]

Nothing could stop Friedman from sallying forth with one-liners, however. At age sixty-one, he declared that he was "too young for Medicare and too old for women to care." According to Friedman, "there's a fine line between fiction and nonfiction, and I believe I snorted it in 1976." When asked why he was running, his response was a simple and direct, "Why the hell not?" Across the state more and more pickups and old Volkswagen buses were displaying stickers proclaiming, "He ain't Kinky, He's my Governor."[59]

Promoting their names, raising money, and gaining pledges of support were the immediate tasks for both Strayhorn and Friedman since they could not circulate nominating petitions until mid-April. Fortunately for both candidates, turnout in the two major parties' primaries and runoffs was slight, at less than 1.2 million votes out of a total 12,722,671 registered voters, thus leaving a pool of some 11.5 million potential petition signers.[60] Those who did not vote in either the primary or runoff could sign only one nominating petition for a candidate for governor.

THE BATTLE FOR THE TEXAS HOUSE

The 2006 primary elections were held on March 7, with the subsequent runoff on April 11. There were few statewide contests in the GOP primary. Governor Perry (84.2 percent), Lieutenant Governor Dewhurst (78.3 percent), and Railroad Commissioner Elizabeth Ames Jones (65.6 percent) easily defeating token opponents, while the holders of other statewide executive offices and Senator Hutchison were unopposed. Likewise, only three of the state's eighteen GOP members of Congress faced primary opposition.

Surprisingly the statewide judicial offices generated the most competition. Supreme Court justice Don Willett barely defeated the controversial former justice Steve Smith, by a six-thousand-vote margin, while Sharon Keller, presiding judge of the Court of Criminal Appeals, bested fellow Appeals Court judge Tom Price with 52.8 percent of the primary vote. The contest for a place on the Court of Criminal Appeals was pushed to a runoff between incumbent Charles Holcomb and Austin state representative Terry Keel, while Dallas district court judge Robert Francis came in third. In the subsequent runoff, Holcomb retained his position, with 53.6 percent to Keel's 46.4 percent.

A major battle was taking place, however, in a number of state legislative districts focused especially on school vouchers and public school finances. Two prominent and wealthy financial backers provided support for a number of primary challenges to GOP incumbents deemed insufficiently supportive of vouchers. Houston homebuilder Bob Perry and billionaire physician James R. Leininger of San Antonio poured millions into the campaigns. Bob Perry's spokesperson, Anthony Holm, maintained that the state business climate, and not school vouchers, was the main factor in his becoming involved in the primary contests. According to Holm, he preferred candidates who were "individuals who will be good for the business climate in Texas and in particular those who support reasonable tort reform."[61] It was clear, however, that vouchers were the motivating factor for Leininger, who had personally underwritten scholarships for needy students to attend private schools in San Antonio.

Among those targeted by the committees backed by Bob Perry and Leininger were veteran legislators Delwin Jones of Lubbock and Charlie Geren of Fort Worth, along with Roy Blake Jr. of Nacogdoches, former Comal County judge Carter Casteel of New Braunfels, and Tommy Merritt of Longview. All five were known to be opposed to the use of state funds for education vouchers.

To influence a number of races, Leininger provided funds to a newly formed political action committee, which hired the consulting firms of veteran campaign consultant Milton Rister and former Midland County judge Jeff Norwood. Norwood's firm, Anthem Media, then worked for the primary opponents of state representatives Casteel, Geren, and Delwin Jones, among others. According to campaign finance reports, Leininger gave or pledged over eight hundred thousand dollars to the primary opponents of the five targeted GOP incumbents who had opposed legislation to create a pilot voucher program in Texas.

As the date of the primary approached, Leininger increased his donations, giving over three hundred thousand dollars to Nathan Macias, the opponent of Representative Casteel, as part of a total of $2.4 million to opponents of the five targeted incumbents.[62] For Representative Geren of Fort Worth the battle became personal when five of his colleagues endorsed one of his primary challengers, Chris Hatley, who received nearly $175,000 from one of the PACs that had received money from Leininger.[63]

While these efforts were underway to remove legislators deemed insufficiently conservative, still another political action committee, the Texas Opportunity PAC, was attempting to help keep in office six incumbents close to Speaker Craddick. The PAC, whose nominal chair was former GOP state chairman George Strake, undertook supportive efforts coordinated by political consultant John Colyandro, an associate of member of Congress Tom DeLay, and Mike Toomey, former chief of staff for Governor Perry. The six Craddick allies had been targeted by the Texas Parent PAC, which sought to replace legislators they viewed as not supportive enough of public schools.[64]

When the primary votes were counted, three of the incumbents targeted by voucher supporters (Geren, Jones, and Merritt) were renominated, while former representative Wayne Christian ousted Blake, and Representative Casteel lost by forty-six votes to challenger Macias.[65] Among those incumbents backed by the Texas Opportunity PAC, three (David Swinford, Betty Brown, and Leo Berman) were renominated, then re-elected in November. Three others were less successful. Representative Elvira Reyna lost to her challenger, Representative Scott Campbell was forced into a runoff and subsequently lost, and Representative Kent Grusendorf, who had received over $125,000 from the Texas Opportunity PAC, lost to educator and state board of education member Diane Patrick.

Grusendorf had been a House member since 1987 and was chair of the House Education Committee where he had been an advocate for school vouchers and charter schools. According to political science professor Allan Saxe of the University of Texas at Arlington, failure to pass school finance legislation over the previous several years came back to hurt Grusendorf in his battle against a local educator. Grusendorf's loss was seen as a serious setback for Speaker Craddick, as he lost one of his close allies and leadership team members.[66]

The end result of the primary battles between the supporters of vouchers and the backers of public schools, or the contest between those on Speaker Craddick's team and those labeled as more moderate Republicans, was a draw. Some of Craddick's key lieutenants, such as Grusendorf, would no longer be there, but others, such as Swinford, Brown, and Berman, won narrow nominating victories. There remained, however, a contingent of returning members, as well as some incoming freshmen, who were concerned over the direction of the House and Craddick's leadership as its presiding officer.

In addition to the various contested House primaries, an important race for an open state Senate seat occurred in Harris County when longtime Republican leader and former county judge Jon Lindsay decided not to seek re-election. This produced a four-way race involving what Richard Murray, political science professor at the University of Houston, described as "an insurgent, anti-tax outsider; two established members of the Texas house; and a (Houston) city councilman," providing "a nice slice of the modern Republican Party."[67] The runaway winner, with 68.8 percent of the primary vote, was the insurgent, veteran radio talk show host Dan Patrick. With this 2006 win in his first campaign Patrick was on his way to becoming lieutenant governor eight years later.

THE DEMOCRATIC COMPETITION

By 2006 it was clear that Texas had become, at least for the time being, a Republican state. The last statewide Democratic victory was twelve years in the past, and since then both chambers of the Texas legislature and the congressional delegation had had GOP majorities. In such an environment the most significant primary battles of 2006 were among the candidates for the Texas House of Representatives.

Although the Democrats had contests for top-of-the-ballot nominations, their primary attracted little more than a half million voters, the smallest total in nearly one hundred years. In the contest for the gubernatorial nomination, former member of Congress Chris Bell defeated Bob Gammage by a margin of 63.9 percent to 28.5 percent, but the races for US senator and lieutenant governor required runoffs. In the end, Houston attorney Barbara Ann Radnofsky defeated perennial candidate Gene Kelly for the Senate nomination, and Maria Luisa Alvarado, an Air Force veteran from San Antonio, became the Democratic candidate for lieutenant governor by beating former state representative and judge Ben Z. Grant of Marshall. Indicative of its decline as a competitive force, the Texas Democratic Party was contesting only ten of the sixteen statewide places on the ballot.

GAINING A PLACE ON THE NOVEMBER BALLOT

With both major parties having determined their nominees, it was time for the Strayhorn and Friedman campaigns to circulate nominating petitions and obtain a place on the November ballot. The campaigns went door-to-door, sought signatures on downtown street corners, and set up tables on college campuses and in concert halls around the state. The petition circulators needed to ensure that the signatures and addresses given matched the format shown on registration records if they were to count as legitimate. Moreover, valid signatures could not come from anyone who had voted in either the primary or runoff elections that year.

The campaigns were using similar methods to locate those who might sign the nominating petitions, although Friedman, the musician and comedian, relied more on bars, dance halls, and places that attracted younger voters, while Strayhorn's campaign sought out Independent voters and women who had not voted in either primary. As Mark Sanders, of the Strayhorn campaign, explained: "We'll be doing everything from county fairs to door-to-door. Malls, shopping centers, festivals—we'll be doing everything imaginable to collect the petitions." Friedman's campaign manager, Dean Barkley, was providing volunteers with "walking lists and maps and pre-printed petitions with all the information there except signature and the date."[68]

In addition to relying on a cadre of volunteers across the state, both campaigns hired professional firms to oversee paid circulators. According to Barkley, "We call it a supplement to the volunteer effort, just to make sure that if the volunteer effort doesn't pan out the way we think it's going to, we have a backup."[69] The Friedman campaign reported spending only twenty thousand dollars on paid solicitors, but did run radio ads seeking signatures, with Willie Nelson urging listeners to sign Friedman's petitions. On the other hand, Strayhorn spent over five hundred thousand dollars with two firms specializing in petition drives, which hired petition circulators.[70]

Prior to the May 11 deadline, Strayhorn turned in 223,000 signatures and Friedman submitted 169,574 names on nominating petitions. Friedman told his supporters as they unloaded the boxes full of petitions, "All I can say is, thank God for bars and dance halls." The office of Secretary of State Roger Williams would need to verify the signatures over the next few weeks before ballot position would be guaranteed.[71]

It was the latter part of June when the secretary of state's office certified that both independent candidates had submitted a sufficient number of valid signatures, although surprisingly, Friedman, who had relied more on volunteers, outpaced Strayhorn in valid signatures, 137,154 to 108,512. Both totals were well above the minimum of roughly 45,000 needed to qualify for ballot status. The final count led Jason Stanford, campaign manager for Democratic nominee Bell, to call Strayhorn "an Austin mirage. She can't win this race, and getting fewer valid signatures than a novelty country singer is just the most recent example of why."[72]

With Strayhorn and Friedman obtaining ballot access and the Libertarian Party nominating James Werner as its candidate, the November election for governor would be a five-way race with the winner needing only a plurality of the votes cast. Incumbent Republican Perry and Democrat Bell were the lead candidates due to the existing party infrastructure and attachment to a long-standing label, but neither one could ignore the two Independent candidates. A June survey of likely voters showed Perry with 35 percent support and his three major opponents bunched together, with Friedman at 21 percent, Bell with 20 percent, and Strayhorn polling 19 percent.[73]

SCHOOL FINANCE AND THE SPECIAL SESSION

While his two independent challengers were busy circulating petitions, Governor Perry was involved with his third special session dealing with education funding, a process made necessary by a Texas Supreme Court decision that upheld a lower court's order declaring the state's school finance system unconstitutional. The state was mandated to fix the funding system by a June 1 deadline or it would not be in compliance with the court's order.

Friedman weighed in on this issue by advocating the legalization of casino gambling and a 1 percent wellhead surcharge on oil and gas produced in the state. He also made known his opposition to continued use of the statewide student performance test called TAKS. None of his suggestions were introduced as bills during the special session then under way in Austin.[74]

The basis for most of the funding measures debated in the special session was an ad hoc Texas Tax Reform Commission comprising twenty-four members, appointed by Governor Perry in November 2005 to make recommendations on lowering property taxes while ensuring sufficient funds for public schools. Heading the commission was former comptroller John Sharp, a Texas A&M classmate of the governor and previous Democratic election opponent of both Perry and Lieutenant Governor Dewhurst. The commission's final report and recommendations were submitted in late March 2006, just prior to the governor calling the third special session.

When the legislature came back to Austin, there was much debate and discussion of various means to provide tax relief while also increasing the state's portion of funding for public schools. To raise additional funds a new business tax was enacted, the cigarette tax was increased, and the basis for calculating the sales tax on used cars and trucks was modified. The new revenue generated by these changes would be used to provide a two thousand dollar pay raise for teachers while also reducing property taxes. The final legislation provided an additional $1.46 billion a year in state funding for public education. It was signed into law by Governor Perry just prior to the Republican state convention and the beginning of his campaign for re-election.[75]

SAN ANTONIO IN JUNE

As delegates began to gather in the Alamo city for the biennial Republican state convention, an editorial in the *Austin American-Statesman* advised them to "bring a book" and plan on visiting the River Walk.[76] The writer erroneously assumed that because the dominant party controlled all statewide offices and a majority in the legislature the meeting of these dyed-in-the-wool activists would be a ho-hum affair, but it was far from that.

While nearly all delegates called themselves conservatives, they differed on several issues, including tax policy, immigration and border security, and the perennial issue of abortion. Some held themselves out as the final arbiter of conservatism. When state Senate candidate Dan Patrick was denied a speaking slot at the convention, he claimed, "It's disappointing that the conservative point of view will not be heard."[77]

Governor Perry's backing of a revised business tax to help fund public schools was bitterly opposed by many Republican activists. Two weeks before the convention the Harris County GOP executive committee adopted a resolution condemning the tax and voted to push for a plank in the state party's platform calling for repeal of the business tax. Leading the push were activists Steven Hotze and Norman Adams, along with Harris County tax assessor–collector Paul Bettencourt and state Senate candidate Patrick.[78]

As the convention was about to begin, former state chairman Tom Pauken, a longtime critic of George W. Bush, maintained that there were a lot of unhappy Republicans in the state: "There's no question in my mind there's a split on the tax bill. Nationally, people are unhappy with the spending, with the budget, with the trade deficits and immigration policy. So you have a lot of conservatives fighting among themselves." However, platform committee chair Kirk Overbey of Austin saw the challenge to Perry as less significant than the concern over specific issues: "There is a small group, a disgruntled group that is upset with the governor. I can say confidently that probably 90% of the members of this committee are very loyal to the governor."[79] As vocal tax opponent Adams explained, "I don't want anybody but Perry being re-elected. But I want to scare the pants off of him."[80]

Longtime party strategist Royal Masset expressed concern that the party was placing more emphasis on purity and less on outreach to the broader Texas electorate: "My fear is that we have forgotten some of the very lessons we learned when we were still trying to break through. It used to be that our candidates for office ran to serve the people of Texas. Now it seems that they run to serve the Republican Party. . . . We are the majority party now. We should be working now to increase that majority."[81]

In defense of his record in office and preparing for a heated contest against three opponents, Perry attempted to convince the delegates of the need for unity. He reminded them of the progress that had been made during his administration and explained why another four years in the governor's mansion was warranted. According to Perry, "With jobs at an all-time high, a top-ranked business climate, college enrollment and student test scores climbing, frivolous law suits dropping, teacher pay on the way up, property taxes on the way down and school finance solved by this Republican majority—the answer is clear."[82]

Those opposed to Perry's tax reform succeeded in bringing their position to debate on the convention floor, but the governor's allies were able to defeat them in a roll-call vote. While Perry saw the vote by the delegates as an affirmation of his position, tax critic Patrick viewed it differently: "If you're the governor in a contested, four-way race coming out of the convention with only a 55–45 victory over the centerpiece of your campaign, that's a very shallow victory."[83]

Taxes were not the only concern of the party activists. On the issue of immigration and border security Governor Perry expressed support for a guest worker program and opposition to a border wall. The delegates, however, wanted more direct action to secure the border, action they did not see coming from the national government. Perry maintained that the state needed to take on the responsibility itself and proposed installing video surveillance cameras at heavily frequented crossing spots. State chairman Benkiser said that the immigration issue would "just far overshadow everything" but that policymakers should "secure our border first and enforce our laws, and then we can talk about everything else."[84]

Some longtime Republicans cautioned against inflammatory language on the immigration issue. Reggie Gonzales of Houston, state chair of the Republican National Hispanic Assembly, admitted, "I don't like the rhetoric. Being a proud American of Mexican descent, I don't like the overtones."[85] A similar view was expressed by consultant Masset, who explained, "I am for very strong controls along the border, and I am not for amnesty. But I am definitely not for all this hateful rhetoric that we are hearing on this issue— that we are going to felonize them, that we should deport them. It's talk like this that is going to lose us the Hispanic vote, just like we lost the black vote in the last generation."[86]

Masset's warning of potentially losing the Hispanic vote was echoed by Tamar Jacoby, senior fellow at the conservative-oriented Manhattan Institute, who maintained, "There's a generation of young Latinos being politicized right now. They're not going to vote on immigration all their lives. If they think one party is hostile to people who look like them, even if that party has better answers to some of the things they care about, its going to be hard for them to pull the lever for that party." Jacoby noted that under Bush's leadership, both as governor and president, the party had been reaching out to welcome Americans of all ethnic and racial backgrounds. According to Jacoby, "Rove and the president built the reputation and they would like to save it. They are trying to save the party from people who are destroying the reputation of the party. It's like the old saying: It takes a lifetime to build a reputation but you can destroy it in a day."[87]

On the last day of the convention, the delegates adopted a platform that gave witness to the domination of social conservatives among the party activists. It called for a constitutional amendment to outlaw abortion and urged the repeal of the *Roe v. Wade* decision of the US Supreme Court. The platform opposed gay marriage and called for the denial of benefits to domestic partners while also barring homosexuals from adopting children or serving in the military. The GOP activists supported making American English the official language and requiring voter reregistration every four years, along with requiring voters to display a government-issued photo ID when attempting to vote. The platform called for withdrawal from the United Nations and opposed government-sponsored gambling, such as the state lottery, and was against any expansion of gambling in Texas.

THE FOUR CANDIDATES CAMPAIGN

As the fall campaign began, a number of Texans remained undecided in the race for governor. A late September poll showed Perry with 38 percent (up slightly from a June survey figure of 35 percent), while Strayhorn remained flat at 18 percent (down one from June), Friedman had slipped from 21 percent to 14 percent, and the Democratic Party's nominee Bell was now polling at only 15 percent (down from 20 percent in the June survey). It was clear that only slightly more than one-third of all voters favored re-election of the incumbent Republican governor. What was saving Perry was that those opposed to his re-election were dividing their votes among three major opponents, and state election law allowed a candidate to win without a majority. Unlike primary contests, there would be no runoff if no one received a majority of the votes cast.[88]

By Labor Day, all four campaigns had begun running television and radio campaigns, although Bell was hampered by a shortage of funds until the ar-

TABLE 13.1. 2006 VOTE FOR GOVERNOR

Candidate	Number of votes	Percentage of votes
Rick Perry (R)	1,716,792	39.0
Chris Bell (D)	1,310,337	29.8
Carole Keeton Strayhorn (I)	796,851	18.1
Richard "Kinky" Friedman (I)	547,674	12.4

Libertarian Party candidate James Werner obtained 26,749 votes, making up less than one percent of the total votes cast.

rival of a late influx of support from a few wealthy trial lawyer supporters. In an effort to reclaim his earlier momentum and attract new voters to the polls, Friedman undertook a statewide tour of college campuses, accompanied on some stops by former Minnesota governor and professional wrestler Jesse Ventura, who had won election as an Independent. As Friedman's campaign manager, Barkley, observed, "In order to win, Kinky has to expand the electorate."[89]

On Friday night October 7, the four major candidates (as the Libertarian Party nominee was excluded) appeared in the only debate of the campaign. It had competition from high school football games and many sports fans' focus on the next day's Texas-Oklahoma football match at the Cotton Bowl during the State Fair of Texas. Most political observers viewed the debate as a draw, concluding that Governor Perry had held his own and that none of the three other debaters had made appreciable gains among those who viewed the program.

What did appear to be happening, however, was that Friedman and Strayhorn were hurting Democrat Bell as much as, if not more than, Perry. Bell's campaign was desperate to convince Democratic voters to return to the party's candidate, believing that a unified Democratic vote, though still short of a majority, could topple Perry from the governor's mansion. In a dramatic move, Bell appealed to Friedman to step aside and quit the race, believing his supporters were more likely to shift to the Democratic candidate. Friedman dismissed the request out of hand, convinced he still had a chance of becoming governor.[90]

With both Friedman and Strayhorn drawing anti-Perry votes, Bell's campaign decided to draw on national Democratic figures as a way of convincing Texas Democrats that only by uniting behind Bell could they defeat Perry.

Former president Clinton was featured in radio ads running in major urban areas, while in late October Senator John Kerry campaigned with Bell in Austin and was featured at a high-dollar fundraiser for the campaign.[91]

Then came Election Day and the results from the Texas electorate. Against a divided opposition, Rick Perry was able to carry 215 of the state's 254 counties, including three of the state's six largest metropolitan counties. His success left Democratic candidate Bell with the most votes in only thirty-three counties, while Strayhorn had the lead in the remaining six counties.[92] Democrats were disheartened by the fact that Strayhorn had outpolled Bell in a number of counties, although she trailed him significantly in total votes. The comptroller finished second in 107 counties, while Bell was second in ninety-eight and Friedman came closest in ten counties.

Geographically Perry was challenged most by the Democratic candidate in the major metropolitan areas, while Strayhorn cost him support especially in small-town Texas. Perry had carried the Big 6 counties in his 2002 race against Tony Sanchez by a margin of 154,751 votes, but four years later, in the four-way contest, he trailed Bell in these same counties by 17,174 votes. The tide was beginning to turn against Republicans in these most urbanized parts of the state, especially in Dallas County.

In the twenty-nine suburban counties outside the state's major urban counties, Perry's margin over the Democratic candidate was cut from 349,073 in 2002 to a margin of 184,070. But in the state's twenty-one smaller metropolitan counties, Perry's vote lead over Bell was slightly greater than it had been against Sanchez. It was in the 198 small-town counties of the state where Strayhorn hurt Perry the most, cutting his advantage over the Democratic candidate from 202,871 in the previous gubernatorial election to only 126,692 votes ahead of Bell.

Perry had received an endorsement for another four-year term as governor, but from less than 40 percent of Texas voters. He could be grateful for the divided opposition he faced and for the support of a significant Republican base in key areas of the state. It would not be the last critical challenge Perry would face; nor would it be his last victory in a race for governor. More serious opposition would come in both the primary and the general election four years later.

At the top of the ballot was the contest for US senator, and Hutchison won another term by over 1.1 million votes (61.7 percent) against Houston attorney Barbara Ann Radnofsky. All other Republican statewide candidates were also victorious. The only statewide Democratic candidate within a half million votes of the opponent was William E. Moody, who lost to incumbent Supreme Court justice Don Willett by 257,703 votes. Moody was one of only two Democratic candidates nominated for the eight statewide judicial races on the ballot.

Republicans were less successful in some other races, as they lost five seats in the Texas House of Representatives while still retaining their majority and adding one to their Senate majority. The breakdown as of January 2007 was eighty Republicans and sixty-nine Democrats in the House, and twenty Republicans and eleven Democrats in the Texas Senate. In Dallas the county's last Republican county judge, Margaret Keliher, lost her re-election bid by slightly over five thousand votes.

Nationally Democrats regained a majority in the US House of Representatives for the last two years of Bush's presidency. Texas Republicans lost two congressional seats in quirky situations. With Tom DeLay stepping down from his House seat in June, Republicans were unable to nominate another candidate for his district. That required Republican Shelley Sekula-Gibbs, who won the special election to fill the remainder of DeLay's term, to run as a write-in candidate for the full two-year term. Sekula-Gibbs was able to convince 41.8 percent of voters to write in her name but lost to Democratic candidate Nick Lampson, whose name was printed on the ballot.

When the courts declared that the 23rd congressional district, long represented by Republican Henry Bonilla, was unfairly drawn to dilute Hispanic voting strength, they created new lines, opened the contest to new candidates, and required a runoff if no single candidate received a majority of the votes. Bonilla was far ahead of his opponents in the November contest but fell short of a majority, with 48.6 percent of the vote. For the December runoff national Democrats poured in the resources, and Bonilla was unable to convince a sufficient number of his supporters to return, with the result that Democratic candidate Ciro Rodriguez became the district's representative. The end result of these two elections was that the GOP retained a majority, holding nineteen of the state's thirty-two congressional districts.

Republicans entered the last two years of the Bush presidency at a time of reduced political clout and a transition away from having a fellow Texan in the White House. After a decade of growth and expansion they were now confronting setbacks in the Texas legislature and their congressional delegation, as well as in what had been their urban base of Dallas County. Meanwhile, the state party was experiencing financial difficulties as it prepared for another presidential year election.

FOURTEEN

THE BUSH ERA TRANSITIONS

It was 1964 when George H. W. Bush first became a candidate for public office, running as a Republican for the US Senate in his adopted state. Now, forty-four years later, after George H. W. Bush had served as vice president and president, his eldest son was about to complete his second term as president of the United States. This would not be the last connection between Texas public life and George Bush. In a few years another George Bush, "P" as he was called in reference to his middle name of Prescott, would enter the ranks as a candidate and officeholder, becoming commissioner of the General Land Office in the election of 2014. Re-elected four years later, he continues the family tradition.

From his election as governor in 1994 through his eight years in the White House, George W. Bush had done much to build the Republican Party of Texas into an open, inclusive, and clearly conservative political force. His efforts helped to make the party dominant at the state level, in terms of both statewide officials and the Texas legislature, and a growing force in counties of all sizes across the state. As he left the presidency, whatever direction the state party might take, it would begin from a position of broad and deep support among Texas voters.

A number of candidates were in the running to succeed Bush as president. When the Texas primary took place in early March 2008, however, it was already evident that Senator John McCain of Arizona was the leading candidate. By the time of the March primary his only serious challenger was Mike Huckabee, former governor of the neighboring state of Arkansas. Also on the ballot but out of serious contention were Texas member of Congress Ron Paul, former Massachusetts governor Mitt Romney, former Tennessee senator and actor Fred Thompson, Alan Keyes, and former New York mayor Rudy Giuliani, none of whom obtained as much as five percent of the primary vote. McCain ended up with a slight majority of 51.2 percent in the Texas primary, besting Huckabee's 38.0 percent of the 1,362,322 votes cast.

No other significant statewide contests were on the ballot, but once again a battle raged for state representative nominations. Seventeen Republican members faced challengers in the primary, and Nathan Macias, Pat Haggerty, Buddy West, Tom Latham, and Corbin Van Arsdale failed to win renomination. These primary defeats of incumbent GOP legislators were an early indicator of what would happen in the November election.

When the 2008 Republican state convention was held in Houston, it comprised a smaller contingent of delegates due to the relatively low number of votes cast for the GOP gubernatorial candidate in the previous election. While Paul had received less than five percent of the vote in the March presidential primary, his supporters were activated, and many were elected as state convention delegates. At the convention state chairman Tina Benkiser was opposed for re-election by Paul Perry, now a county commissioner in Ellis County. Paul Perry had the support of the more libertarian elements of the party, especially the backers of Paul's presidential campaign. Benkiser fought off the challenge and was successful in retaining her position.

According to Will Lutz, former editor of the *Lone Star Report*, Governor Perry's proposal for a statewide coordinated transportation pathway, the Trans-Texas Corridor, became a major controversy at the convention. The Trans-Texas Corridor was proposed to include auto and truck tollways, railways, and utility lines on a four-thousand-mile long supercorridor that would be up to 1,200 feet wide. Both libertarians and many rural Texans were opposed to it and feared the state's use of eminent domain would threaten property rights. Farmers and ranchers saw it as a threat to their operations, while environmentalists expressed concern over its impact on the countryside.[1]

The Trans-Texas Corridor proposal put Benkiser on the spot as she faced opposition from party activists while it remained a major objective of the governor. Despite the rumblings, Governor Perry's forces were able to tamp down opposition, and the party did not take a stance against the proposal. However, the support for this major infrastructure project was never sufficient to move it beyond the idea stage, and in 2011 the legislature formally canceled the project.

ELECTION DAY 2008

In the November 2008 election, McCain easily carried the state by a margin of 950,695 votes over Barack Obama, 55.5 percent to 43.7 percent. There were few other statewide contests, but Republican candidates were successful in all of them. John Cornyn won his second term in the US Senate by defeating Democratic state representative Rick Noriega and Libertarian candidate Yvonne Schick. Cornyn's margin of 948,104 over Noriega mirrored McCain's margin over Obama in the presidential race.

All three African-American GOP statewide incumbents—Railroad Commissioner Michael Williams and Supreme Court justices Wallace B. Jefferson and Dale Wainwright—were re-elected, along with four other statewide judicial incumbents. Republicans also gained back one of the congressional seats lost in 2006 as Pete Olson defeated Nick Lampson, recovering the 22nd congressional district, formerly held by Tom DeLay. Olson's victory gave the GOP representatives from twenty of the state's thirty-two congressional districts.

The results were not as favorable, however, in contests for the state legislature. In Tarrant County's 10th senatorial district incumbent Kim Brimer was defeated by Fort Worth City Council member Wendy Davis by a seven-thousand-vote margin. All nineteen other incumbent state senators who were up in 2008 were re-elected.

The Texas House situation was even less positive as the GOP lost five seats previously held by Republicans, cutting the partisan composition of the chamber to seventy-six Republicans and seventy-four Democrats. This advantage was razor thin as Representative Linda Harper-Brown from Irving had to survive a recount to ensure re-election by nineteen votes. The only pickups for the GOP came when Todd Hunter, a former Democratic legislator who changed parties, defeated incumbent Juan Garcia in a Corpus Christi district and the party reclaimed an open seat in Central Texas.

The closeness of the outcome in the Texas House elections became a major concern for the party and its legislators. As reporter Dave Montgomery observed, "The election seemingly left Democrats emboldened and unified and stirred further dissent among Republicans who have watched their House majority steadily erode since Craddick became speaker in 2003."[2]

Some saw the need for a reevaluation of the party's approach to public policy. Representative Dan Branch, re-elected from his Park Cities district in Dallas County, believed the party needed to place more emphasis on solving the everyday problems confronting Texas and less on statements about personal behavior. Branch believed that "Texas is a center-right, limited-government state. The larger message for us is, people don't want conservatism that's limited to rhetoric. If government's going to be in the space, it had better be effective."[3]

Still others felt it was time for direct action that would bring about a change in leadership. Speaker Tom Craddick had faced previous challenges to his position, and a critical one would be forthcoming. After the 2006 elections two Republicans and one Democrat announced they were running for speaker against Craddick. When efforts to allow a secret ballot failed, the opposition faded away and Craddick was re-elected in January 2007 by a vote of 121 to 27.[4] Four months later, near the end of the regular legislative session, GOP Representative Fred Hill attempted to make a motion to remove the speaker, but he was not recognized, a decision taken over the objections of the parliamentarian, who then resigned in protest. Hill's motion was not allowed, and Craddick remained speaker.[5]

A NEW SPEAKER

Conditions were different after the 2008 elections reduced the GOP to a bare two-seat majority in the Texas House. In January a group of Republican legislators met to agree on a challenger to Craddick's continued speakership. On the fourth secret ballot, Representative Joe Straus of San Antonio emerged as the consensus candidate. A few days later, with the support of the Democratic caucus and a smattering of anti-Craddick Republicans, Straus announced that he had enough votes to win. The coup had succeeded and Straus became speaker, a position he would retain for the next ten years until he retired from the House.

Straus was a relative newcomer to elective office and the Texas House, having first been elected in 2005 to fill the seat vacated by Elizabeth Ames Jones, who was appointed to fill a vacancy on the Railroad Commission. But he was a lifetime Republican from a family well-known in party circles. His mother, Joci Straus, first became involved in Republican campaigns in 1960 when she coordinated the Nixon Girls effort in San Antonio, and she continued to be active in party affairs from that time forward.[6] As a young man Joe Straus was an intern in the office of Senator John Tower, for whom his mother had raised funds and consulted on five campaigns. Later Joe Straus held positions in the administrations of Ronald Reagan and George H. W. Bush.

Although he came from a strong Republican lineage, Straus was not a stereotypical Texas Republican. He became the first Jewish Texan to hold the office of speaker and represented a more business-oriented and consensus-seeking element in the party. Longtime acquaintance Representative Branch of Dallas described Straus as "thoughtful, a listener. Plays his cards close. A lot of people have underestimated him or counted his vote too quickly." As one reporter described the situation, "The rise of Mr. Straus, a fiscal conservative who has not toed the conservative line on issues like abortion and gay rights, was widely seen as a defeat for the socially conservative wing of the party."[7]

Once in office Speaker Straus set a tone for cooperation and compromise when it was needed to advance legislation that was in what he viewed as the best interest of the state. Following a long-standing tradition of bipartisan working arrangements, a number of Democratic legislators were appointed committee chairs, but the key committees were still headed by Republicans. Throughout his ten years Straus faced criticism from social conservatives and Tea Party supporters. In 2013 two Republican legislators announced challenges to his continued service as speaker but withdrew before Straus was unanimously re-elected. Two years later Representative Scott Turner of Frisco launched a campaign against Straus but lost in a vote of 128 to 19.

Meanwhile Republican activists upped their opposition to Straus, running candidates who unsuccessfully opposed him in the Republican primary in 2012, 2014, and 2016. In each case, Straus obtained over 60 percent of the votes cast in his district. Unable to defeat him in either the House chamber or at the ballot box, the right-wing party activists passed resolutions of no confidence in the speaker at more than fifty party organizations across the state. Closer to home they convinced the Bexar County executive committee to censure him at a meeting in December 2017 after Straus announced he would not be seeking re-election. Precinct chair Vivian Brown called the censure "disgusting" and said, "You had 77 people out of the county of nearly 2 million that voted to censure the speaker, it's hardly a repudiation of him. They are so proud of themselves and all they did was tear down a fellow Republican."[8]

Those opposed to Straus would not stop there, however. The following month they brought a censure motion to the state Republican executive committee (SREC), where it obtained a two-thirds vote only with state chairman James Dickey and vice chairman Amy Clark casting the deciding votes. Dickey claimed he voted to censure Straus as a means to unify the party. Jason Embry, spokesperson for Straus, said that the speaker "expected these antics from some people when he opposed their bathroom bill and helped prevent the harm it would have brought our state. . . . Speaker Straus will continue working to support traditional Republican principles and re-elect Republicans who put their constituents first."

Not all Republican activists were pleased with the treatment given to a longtime Republican. SREC member Mike McCloskey lamented the situation. "I always thought our party was the one of dignity and class and to so disrespectfully kick someone of that prominence on his way out was disgraceful. The Republican Party of Texas has changed into something most mainstream Republicans would not recognize."[9]

A CHANGE IN PARTY LEADERSHIP

On September 26, 2009, Benkiser resigned as state chairman to join the Rick Perry re-election campaign as a senior advisor. Benkiser had been the subject of much criticism over transparency concerning the party's finances. According to some reports, the party was deeply in debt and was failing to pay its direct-mail firm and other vendors. She was criticized also for promoting Perry's re-election when party rules required impartiality among candidates.[10]

At the October meeting of the SREC, then–National Committeewoman Cathie Adams of Dallas was elected chairman to succeed Benkiser, defeating Melinda Fredericks of Conroe by a vote of thirty-six to twenty-five. Adams had been director of a crisis pregnancy center in Plano and in 1993 was named state president of the Eagle Forum, a right-wing profamily organization founded by Phyllis Schlafly, which developed out of her STOP-ERA efforts in the 1970s.

Adams's time as chairman would be contentious and brief. At the 2010 state convention she was defeated in her efforts to obtain a full term. Adams campaigned on her longtime battle against abortion, same-sex marriage, and the United Nations. But her appeal was insufficient, and she lost to Steve Munisteri, an attorney from Houston who had begun his involvement as a fifteen-year-old volunteer for state senator Hank Grover in his 1972 gubernatorial campaign. Munisteri later became active in Young Americans for Freedom, rising to serve on the organization's national board of directors. In 1980 he founded the Young Conservatives of Texas, a campus organization active on more than twenty campuses across the state.[11]

Munisteri's victory was facilitated by the last-minute withdrawal of a third candidate, Tom Mechler of Amarillo, who endorsed Munisteri. Although Adams had lost the ballot in most senatorial districts, she took the vote to the floor of the convention. While Adams retained the support of 2,950 delegates, Munisteri was able to obtain the votes of 4,170, or nearly 60 percent. Elected as vice chairman was Fredericks, whom Adams had defeated for the chairmanship some months earlier.[12]

Munisteri's first objective on taking office was to eliminate the party's debt, which had soared to roughly seven hundred thousand dollars, and to unify the party for the coming statewide elections. He appointed Beth Cubriel, a former key aide to Senator Cornyn, as the party's executive director. According to Lutz, "Munisteri was the right person at the right time. He reached out to various factions of the party. He reminded activists that the party has rules which must be followed and the chairman serves as an honest broker in the process."[13] By the end of 2010 Munisteri reported that the party was debt-free and could begin preparing for the next presidential election campaign.

CHALLENGING PERRY FROM BOTH SIDES

Before the 2010 state convention could be held, however, there was a contentious battle for governor. This time Perry was being challenged from two sides in his own party's primary. His main opponent was Kay Bailey Hutchison, the longtime senator and top vote-getter in the party. Hutchison represented the traditional Republican base of suburban, middle-class voters who had been the heart of the party in the late twentieth century. She had been elected first as a Republican member of the Texas House in 1972, one of seventeen GOP members in the body of 150. In 1990 she and Perry were the first two Republicans elected to a statewide executive office other than governor. Then in 1993, with Lloyd Bentsen's resignation to become secretary of Treasury, she won the special election to the Senate seat she currently held.

Hutchison had deep roots among the traditional Republicans who had worked to build the party in its early years of competitiveness. Many of these voters identified with the Republican Party of Tower, George H. W. Bush, and Bill Clements, candidates who had broken through the Democratic dominance of state politics. Her husband, Ray, had been the GOP state chairman during the mid-1970s, and together they personally knew the key Republican activists in counties throughout the state. These were the people now viewed by some as the establishment, a term of derision in the environment of twenty-first-century politics.

As one writer analyzed the situation, "Hutchison represented the blue-blood, country club Republican set that had dominated the internal GOP machinery before the rise of religious conservatives."[14] Indicative of this support, among those endorsing her campaign were former president George H. W. Bush, former secretary of state James A. Baker III, and former vice president Dick Cheney. A major fundraiser for the Hutchison campaign was held at the Georgetown home of baseball legend Nolan Ryan and his wife, Ruth.

These early trailblazers could not have made the Republican Party into the dominant force in Texas politics without the involvement of those who had come over from past involvement in the Democratic Party, which had been dominant for decades in the small towns and smaller urban areas of Texas. As they were rapidly changing party loyalties by the end of the twentieth century, the public figures they identified with included John Connally, Phil

Gramm, and Kent Hance, all of whom had successful careers first as Democratic elected officials. Perry himself had made the transition to the GOP only some twenty years earlier.

There was another component to this three-legged stool that was the twenty-first-century Republican Party of Texas. This third element comprised those with more libertarian leanings, a group that had been present in the party at least since the Goldwater campaign of 1964 but was more recently identified with the various campaigns and causes of member of Congress Ron Paul. Added to the mix were many of those activated by the Tea Party movement, which surfaced in 2009 and helped the GOP regain control of the US House of Representatives the following year.

With Hutchison representative of the longtime GOP viewpoint and Rick Perry reflecting the perspective of the former Democrats and social conservatives in the party, it was left to a newcomer to present the more libertarian outlook in the gubernatorial contest. Debra Medina, a small-business owner from Wharton, was a longtime supporter of Paul and would attempt to rally the support of those primarily, but not exclusively, concerned about tax and spending priorities. Medina proposed abolishing property taxes and raising the sales tax then sitting at 8.25 percent in most areas across the state.

As one reporter described her campaign, "Ms. Medina has been riding a wave of anger among conservatives who feel the federal government is spending too much to bail out banks and jump-start the economy. Like Ross Perot in the 1992 presidential race, Ms. Medina has touched a nerve in an anxious electorate looking for an alternative to the status quo. She has become the right-wing, anti-establishment candidate, calling for term limits and portraying herself in her advertisements as an ordinary Texas resident."[15]

While Medina posed a challenge from the right, Perry rightly saw his main opponent as Senator Hutchison and effectively portrayed her as Washington and not Texas. His supporters began referring to her as Kay Bailout Hutchison even though she voted against the second bank-bailout bill and the economic stimulus project. Political consultant Mark Sanders commended the governor for how he had positioned his campaign: "You have got to give Rick Perry and his team a great deal of credit for being the longest-serving governor in Texas history and still running a campaign as an outsider. Outsiders are what people want right now."[16]

As journalist Jay Root noted, "Despite spending a quarter-century in state elective office, Perry had begun to position himself as an outsider, a states' rights conservative who would keep the evil influences of Washington out of Texas. His opponent was turning out to be the perfect foil: a sixteen-year

Senate veteran who had seemingly carried enough pork through Congress to risk trichinosis. While it may have helped in past elections to be known for bringing home the bacon, it was radioactive in 2010."[17]

Perry ran what one observer called a near perfect campaign. According to political science professor James Henson, "Perry has just done everything right. He exploited the environment perfectly well, stayed on message, framed her early, and she never escaped it."[18] Posing the choice as among "an establishment conservative, an untested doyenne of the Tea Party movement and Perry, a social and economic conservative riding an anti-Washington wave,"[19] the campaign achieved an overwhelming primary victory for Governor Perry.

More votes were cast in the Republican primary than ever before, as nearly one and a half million voters came to the GOP polls. Despite having two serious opponents, Rick Perry was able to avoid a runoff by obtaining 51.2 percent of the vote, besting Hutchison's 30.3 percent and Medina's 18.5 percent. Most other statewide officeholders were unopposed in the primary, but Railroad Commissioner Victor Carrillo lost his renomination bid to accountant David Porter of Midland.

In other contests incumbent justice Eva Guzman defeated her opponent, Rose Vela, for another term on the Texas Supreme Court. With five candidates bunched together for an open seat on the court, former state representative Rick Green and attorney Debra Lehrmann were forced to a runoff, which Lehrmann won. There were fewer heated primary contests for state representative in 2010, but representatives Betty Brown and Tommy Merritt failed to obtain renomination, and Delwin Jones was defeated in a runoff with Charles Perry.

With the primary loss behind her, Senator Hutchison decided she would serve out the remainder of her six-year term, although she had previously indicated that she would resign. This caused some concern among those who were hoping to succeed her in the Senate. On the right there were vows to oppose her should she decide to run again in 2012, and ultimately she retired when her term ended in January 2013.[20]

NOVEMBER 2010

Perry had survived the major challenge to remaining as governor of Texas. The Democratic primary had attracted fewer than seven hundred thousand voters and had seen former Houston mayor Bill White defeat six opponents, the closest of whom, Farouk Shami, obtained only 12.8 percent of the vote. Despite his time as chief executive of the largest city in the state, White remained relatively unknown. As political scientist Cal Jillson observed, "White is not out of it but he has to run a good campaign in which he gets the kind of support that no Democrat has gotten in 15 or 20 years."[21] It was not to be.

In what was an impressive year for Republicans across the country, all the GOP statewide candidates were once again successful, all winning with at least a million-vote advantage over their Democratic opponents. The race for governor, however, was somewhat closer, as Perry bested White by 630,000, with 55 percent of the vote.

It was in the legislative contests that the Texas GOP made its most impressive gains. The party picked up three additional congressional seats to give the GOP a twenty-three to nine advantage in the delegation as three Democratic members of Congress were retired. Business owner Bill Flores ousted Chet Edwards in a district running from Waco to College Station, while Blake Farenthold defeated Solomon Ortiz in the Corpus Christi area. Along the border in a district that had long been represented by Republican Henry Bonilla, banker Francisco "Quico" Canseco retired Democratic representative Ciro Rodriguez.

The largest gains for the GOP came in the Texas House, where the partisan division went from seventy-six Republicans and seventy-four Democrats to 101 Republicans and forty-nine Democrats. Twenty-one Democrats seeking re-election lost to their Republican opponents. The GOP rookies included five Hispanic and one new African-American state representative.

Republican representation in the Texas House up through the end of the 1970s was concentrated in the upper and middle-income areas of the state's largest cities, especially Dallas and Houston, along with the midsized West Texas cities of Midland and Amarillo. Of the twenty-four GOP state representatives serving in 1979, nineteen were from the Big 6 counties. It was not until 1978 that Tom DeLay became the first suburban GOP representative, when he was elected from Fort Bend county.

With the 2010 election results the party had diversified its legislative delegation in several ways. Geographically only 36.5 percent of its legislators were from the Big 6 counties, while suburban counties now provided twenty-three Republicans and only two Democrats. Small-town counties had been overwhelmingly represented by Democrats in the late 1970s, but by 2011 the partisan division from rural Texas was eighteen Republicans and two Democrats. Likewise, those representing the state's other smaller urban counties had gone from twenty-nine Democrats and two Republicans thirty years earlier to a GOP majority of twenty-four to eight.

The 2011 legislative session also reflected a higher level of ethnic and racial diversity in the party, with one Asian-American, two African-American, and six Hispanic representatives. One more African-American, Scott Turner, would be elected to the legislature in the next session, to be joined later by Hispanic Republicans J. M. Lozano, Gilbert Peña, Jason Villalba, Rick Galindo, and John Lujan. Unfortunately, by 2019 the Texas GOP was down to one Hispanic, one African-American, and one Asian-American in the Texas House delegation, while it added its first Hispanic state senator in a 2018 special election. Although the Texas GOP congressional delegation included one Hispanic and one African-American, both of them announced they would not be candidates for re-election in 2020.[22]

PERRY FOR PRESIDENT

In an August 13, 2011, speech to the Red State Gathering in Charleston, South Carolina, Governor Perry announced his campaign for the presidency with an attack on President Obama. Perry told the crowd of conservative bloggers, "We don't need a president who apologizes for America. We need a president who protects and projects those values." Speaking to the same audience, senatorial candidate Ted Cruz told the group, "In his DNA, Rick Perry is a fighter. My prediction is Rick Perry will win the nomination and in November 2012 he will defeat Barack Obama."[23]

With ample resources and a professional staff on board, the campaign was on its way. But the strategy did not work out as planned. After some campaign appearances in Iowa and early primary states, Perry joined the field of candidates for a presidential debate in November. When he proposed cutting funding for three federal agencies, the governor could not recall the third agency and ended up declaring "Oops!"[24] The reaction of viewers and especially the media covering the campaigns was not favorable, and his performance led to the campaign's downfall. Ironically, the agency Perry could not recall was the Department of Energy, where he subsequently served as secretary during the Trump administration.

From the time of the November debate forward, Perry's campaign never took off. He placed fifth in the Iowa caucuses and, after little campaigning in the state, finished last in New Hampshire. By January 19, days before the South Carolina primary, Perry suspended his campaign, saying he saw no viable path forward. After exiting the race he endorsed Newt Gingrich, and then, after Gingrich also dropped out of the race, he endorsed Mitt Romney.[25]

ENTER TED CRUZ

By the time of the May primary in Texas, Romney had virtually locked up the presidential nomination, and while eight names remained on the ballot, only two received support in the double digits. Romney received slightly over one million votes for 69.1 percent of the total, with Ron Paul a distant second with 12 percent. The Texas delegation would go to the national convention in Tampa committed to Romney.

With Perry no longer a presidential candidate, the major focus of attention in Texas Republican politics concerned the May 29 primary battle for the US Senate seat being vacated by Hutchison. The senatorial race was much more contested than what remained of the presidential nominating contest. Several individuals filed to run, and the two leading candidates were Lieutenant Governor David Dewhurst and Ted Cruz, former solicitor general of Texas. Also in the mix with some financial resources and name identification were former Dallas mayor Tom Leppert and Craig James, a retired football player and ESPN television sports commentator. All four campaigned extensively across the state during the months leading up to the primary.

A number of Republican officeholders endorsed Dewhurst. His most prominent backer was Governor Perry, who claimed the state's success was "the result of good conservative leadership and a good conservative record. David Dewhurst has stood by my side as the lieutenant governor of this state for the last nine years. David's record is my record." Cruz drew on the support of Tea Party backers, such as Sarah Palin and Senator Rand Paul of Kentucky, along with senators Mike Lee of Utah and Jim DeMint of South Carolina and former Pennsylvania senator Rick Santorum.[26]

In the March primary Dewhurst came in first, but he had only 44.6 percent of the vote and thus was forced into a runoff with Cruz, who had received support from 34.5 percent of primary voters. Far behind were Leppert at 13.4 percent, James with 3.6 percent, and five other candidates trailing them. Dewhurst had more votes than Cruz in each of the four categories of counties, with small margins in the Big 6, suburban, and other metro counties, and his best showing in the 198 small-town counties, where he led Cruz by a margin of 183,171 to 93,115.

When the runoff was held, Cruz upped his vote total from 480,558 to 631,812, while Dewhurst's support slipped off precipitously, from 627,731 in the first primary to only 480,126 in the runoff. Only in the small-town counties did Dewhurst retain his advantage, and in only a few counties did he increase his vote totals over what he received in the first primary. With Dewhurst unable to remotivate his supporters to return for the runoff while

Cruz was able to corral additional votes, the young Hispanic attorney had upset the longtime Republican officeholder and was on his way to the general election.

In retrospect, the Cruz victory was a continuation of what had been experienced in the 2010 gubernatorial primary. Some supported Cruz in an effort to provide more diversity in the party on the rationale that what the US Senate didn't need was another aging white male legislator. The relatively small band of Hispanic Republicans rallied to his cause in an effort to expand their number of elected officials. Yet the overriding message from the Cruz victory was the same one heard in Hutchison's loss to Perry two years earlier. The Texas Republican primary electorate was no longer dominated by suburban middle-class and middle-aged business-oriented voters. It was now characterized by a more populist, socially conservative, and somewhat older electorate to whom establishment candidates were suspect.

The Cruz win over Dewhurst was noticed around the nation. Back home it sent "shockwaves through the state political establishment and sent the same message to Texas politicos as Tea Party wins have in other states: ambitious conservatives aren't going to wait their turns any longer." According to GOP consultant David Weeks, "You are going to see more contested races in the primaries. The Cruz race changed things."[27]

Once again there were a number of highly contested battles for state representative, this time resulting in the defeat of ten Republican incumbents. Although many were between moderate conservatives aligned with Speaker Straus and those further on the right who were opposed to him, the results were a mixed bag. Some House committee chairs loyal to Straus went down to defeat, but so too did some of his more outspoken critics. Indicative of the Republican electoral dominance and the importance of the Republican primary was the fact that sixty-five of the 150 newly drawn house districts had no Democratic candidate, while Republicans left thirty-four districts uncontested. The end result was that only voters in one-third of the state's districts had a choice between a Democratic and a Republican candidate for state representative.

Unlike the House districts, only two state senatorial districts were seriously contested. Former state senator Mike Galloway failed in his effort to defeat Senator Tommy Williams but did force him into a runoff. Twenty-year veteran senator Jeff Wentworth garnered opposition from both former Railroad Commissioner Elizabeth Ames Jones and physician Donna Campbell. Wentworth was a moderate conservative who had previously served as a state representative and a Bexar County commissioner. He had a long history of involvement in the Republican Party, and his father had been a candidate at a time when few Republicans sought office, let alone were elected. However, he was also pro-choice on the hot-button issue of abortion, a position that was becoming increasingly untenable in a party concerned with social issues.

Perhaps even more critical to his chances for renomination, Wentworth had failed to support a bill backed by Texans for Lawsuit Reform (TLR), and the organization poured money and resources into the effort to defeat him. In the primary Wentworth led with 35.8 percent of the vote but was forced into a runoff with Campbell. With financial help from TLR and significant Tea Party support, Campbell was able to defeat Wentworth and then go on to retain the seat in the Republican column in November.

NOVEMBER 2012

The fall campaign saw both Romney and Cruz win easily by almost identical margins. Romney outpaced President Obama by 1,261,719 votes while Cruz obtained 1,245,210 votes more than his Democratic opponent, former state representative Paul Sadler. In a contested race for an open place on the Railroad Commission, Christi Craddick, daughter of former speaker Tom Craddick, defeated Democratic candidate Dale Henry by a margin exceeding one million votes. For the six available places on the Supreme Court and Court of Criminal Appeals, the Democratic Party had slated candidates in only two races, and their candidates in both races lost resoundingly.

The results of the 2010 Census had caused a reapportionment of congressional seats that resulted in Texas gaining four additional members of the US House of Representatives, bringing the state's total to thirty-six. When the state was redistricted, both the Republicans and Democrats gained two more members. However, in the 23rd congressional district along the border with Mexico from El Paso to San Antonio, member of Congress Quico Canseco was ousted by Democrat Pete Gallego by a margin of nine thousand votes. This was the most highly contested and expensive congressional race in the state, with estimated total campaign expenditures as high as $7 million.[28]

The decennial redistricting of the Texas legislature brought about a number of changes in the Senate and House district lines. These changes contributed to some of the losses by incumbents in the primary. In November, under the new district lines, Democrats had a net gain of seven House seats, leaving the GOP with a ninety-five to fifty-five margin. In the only highly contested state Senate race, incumbent Democrat Wendy Davis defeated Representative Mark Shelton by a margin of six thousand votes to retain her Fort Worth–area seat.

BUILDING TOWARD 2014

As 2013 began, Republicans were reevaluating their situation nationally with a task force appointed by Republican national chairman Reince Priebus, called the Growth and Opportunity Project, in response to their recent losses of the popular vote in presidential elections, while continuing to be successful in state and gubernatorial elections. After extensive interviews across the country the task force issued a one-hundred-page document of their recommendations for improving the party's position. It was released to mixed reviews, referred to by some as an "autopsy report," and ignored by the time of the 2016 presidential election.[29]

Back in Texas, the party continued its progress in attracting officeholders to switch as the GOP added thirty-four county officials in early 2013, including two county judges and five county commissioners. However, the party was concerned about its ability to attract new supporters, especially given the changing demographics of the state. As Speaker Joe Straus noted, "We better watch our agenda very closely and try to appeal to more people. Politics is a game of addition. Just because we've had success in recent years doesn't mean we're guaranteed of success tomorrow."[30]

The message of inclusion and outreach was not lost on the leaders of the Republican Party of Texas, who, while witnessing growth in the number of elected officials, were concerned over the ability to preserve the party's majority in future elections. State chairman Munisteri was committed to involving more individuals from diverse communities in the activities of the Republican Party. Together Munisteri and national chairman Priebus hosted an all-day outreach summit in Houston to discuss ways in which the party could better market its message. Included were a number of Republican Hispanic and African-American elected officials. Of particular concern to Munisteri was the party's outreach to Hispanic voters, who were becoming an increasing share of the electorate.[31]

Reaching out to more Hispanic voters and recruiting candidates was a concern that went beyond the official party structure and extended specifically to the Associated Republicans of Texas (ART). Formed with the help of Senator John Tower in the 1970s, ART had been rejuvenated in 2010 with the help of Senator Cornyn, who recruited Dallas business leader George Seay and Austin attorney Hector de Leon to serve as cochairs. It had long been an organization of business and community leaders committed to electing Republican county officials and state legislators, and its full-time president was Jamie McWright, a former staffer for Cornyn. To reach more Hispanics, ART created the Hispanic Voter Network as a statewide group of probusiness and profamily conservatives.[32]

One individual especially concerned with Hispanic involvement in the Republican Party was George P. Bush, who was the grandson and nephew of two presidents and whose mother was born in Mexico. While meeting with various groups around the state in anticipation of a possible campaign for state office, Bush told the Institute for Policy Innovation in Addison, "We don't have to sell our principles to win the Hispanic vote." Bush was convinced that on a broad range of issues a significant number of Hispanic voters were in agreement with Republican Party positions.[33]

Among the elected Hispanic Republicans attempting to reach out to involve new voters in the party was state representative Jason Villalba of Dallas, who credited Ronald Reagan's steady but firm leadership in helping him shape his ideals. Though he believes that government has certain functions that it must perform well, Villalba is a firm believer in limited government: "I don't believe that the government knows how to spend my money better than I do." Like Bush, he maintains that there is a common concern on key issues that relates to voters of all backgrounds. Tone and language, however, are critical, as "It's important that Republicans recognize that we have to reach out to Hispanics in a new and fundamentally different way than we have in the past."[34]

It was Munisteri's belief that while recruiting candidates who reflected the composition of the state was important, the party also needed "boots on the ground" to engage in outreach to various communities around the state. In the summer of 2013, the state party hired nine full-time outreach representatives operating from locations around the state and planned to add nine more as the 2014 campaign year began.[35]

While Texas Republicans were reevaluating their situation and committing themselves to reaching out and involving various communities in party activities, Texas Democrats were making plans of their own, plans that they believed would allow them to reclaim Texas. In January 2013 a small group of Texas and out-of-state Democratic operatives announced the formation of Battleground Texas, a well-funded effort organized by Jeremy Bird, national field director for the Obama re-election campaign.

One who backed the new effort to build a more viable Democratic Party was Fort Worth state senator Wendy Davis, who explained, "I'm excited to see that at national levels, people are now looking at Texas and saying, 'That's where we need to make our next investment. That's where the next opportunity lies.'" Others encouraging the group included former Dallas mayor Ron

Kirk and Houston mayor Annise Parker.[36] An existing group, the DC-based Texas Democratic Trust, led by consultant Matt Angle, had raised millions of dollars since its formation in 2005, with most of its money going to support the financially struggling state party or in payments to political consultants. Now there would be competition for both Texas and out-of-state Democratic donors.[37]

One month after its formation Battleground Texas hired its first two operatives when it brought to Texas Jenn Brown, Obama campaign field director for Ohio, and Christina Gomez, a former digital strategist for the Democratic National Committee.[38] The group began its operations with an annual budget of $10 million, some of it from outside liberal backers but much of it from Steve and Amber Mostyn, wealthy Houston residents and longtime Democratic donors. Steve Mostyn is a former chair of the Texas Trial Lawyers Association, the bête noire of conservative Republicans.[39]

An unintended consequence of the media attention to Battleground Texas was that otherwise complacent Republican supporters became activated. According to GOP state chairman Munisteri, "There has been a great deal in the press on the Democrats' efforts to target Texas for the 2014 and 2016 elections, but what has been missed by the press in recent months is that Democrats have stirred up a hornet's nest within Republican Party ranks. As word of the Democrats' efforts and activities have spread within Republican circles, GOP activists have started to get off their sofas and are turning out for training seminars and organizational meetings in numbers that I have never seen before."[40]

TOM PAUKEN FOR GOVERNOR

While both Republicans and Democrats in Texas were analyzing and planning and preparing, in March 2013 former state chairman Tom Pauken announced he would be a candidate for governor in 2014, not waiting to see if Governor Perry would file for another term. According to Pauken the state needed someone who would reform the public education funding formula, end what he called "crony capitalism," and solve problems rather than divide people.[41]

Pauken insisted, "I like Rick Perry. I like Greg Abbott. I don't know what they're going to do. One or both may run. I'm going to run on issues."[42] Pauken first ran for public office in 1976 when he campaigned for a state Senate seat. He followed that race with close losses in 1978 and 1980 for Congress against Jim Mattox. He was also unsuccessful in a 1998 primary campaign for the attorney general nomination, finishing last in a three-way contest that John Cornyn won in a runoff.

In July, Rick Perry announced that he would not be a candidate for re-election in 2014. As the longest-serving governor in the state's history, he could be proud of his record. He called Texas "the envy of the nation." According to the governor, "Texas works because we have less government, less spending, fair regulations and lower taxes. We have built a pathway to prosperity through innovation and ingenuity."[43] Ray Sullivan, longtime Perry aide and spokesperson, noted, "He has held the line on government. He has created an economic engine that is the envy of the nation and has really stuck to his conservative principles and been successful doing so."[44]

Later that same month, Attorney General Greg Abbott announced his candidacy for governor at a rally in the La Villita area of San Antonio, the first stop in a ten-city tour. He declared, "When it comes to our freedom and our future, I will never, I will never stop fighting. That's why I am asking you—the people of Texas—to elect me as your next governor."[45] The choice of La Villita had significance for Abbott because his wife, Cecilia, is from San Antonio and would become the state's first Hispanic first lady. Speaking from personal experience, Abbott would return to this theme in his primary night victory speech when he noted that "the blending of cultures in the Lone Star State works. We are all one people. We are all Texans."[46] As one Hispanic Republican noted, "there's no greater definition of a bicultural family than his and that's kind of what Texas is. Nearly every Hispanic family I know has Anglo family members, and vice versa."[47]

Pauken was still in the race and challenged Abbott to a "series of Lincoln-Douglas style debates and community forums across the state so that voters can come to understand our differing views of how the Republican Party should govern."[48] But Pauken's campaign ended rather quickly. In December he wrote to supporters and informed them, "I can no longer in good conscience ask friends and fellow conservatives to continue to help me when there appears to be no realistic path to victory. Clearly, my message has not resonated with enough contributors, party leaders, and grassroots conservatives to show a pathway to victory."[49]

THE REPUBLICAN PRIMARY 2014

March 4, 2014, was an early date for the major parties' primaries. With Attorney General Abbott running for governor and Lieutenant Governor Dewhurst wounded by his Senate loss to Cruz, there were several open contests for statewide office as various individuals saw an opportunity to advance. Because numerous serious candidates were filing for these offices, there would likely be many runoff contests.

Turnout in both parties' primary elections was down compared to 2010, but the drop-off was more pronounced on the Democratic side, which fell 18 percent, from 680,000 to 555,000. In both years the Democrats' leading candidate for governor had no significant opposition. For Republicans the 2010 primary saw the three-way battle involving Perry, Hutchison, and Debra Medina, but in 2014 Abbott faced minimal competition, and GOP participation went from 1,490,000 in 2010 down to 1,340,000 in 2014, a 10 percent decline.

It is a truism in sports that you can't win if you don't play. The same is true in politics, and in 2014, the year after the much-ballyhooed Battleground Texas was formed to turn Texas blue, the Texas Democratic Party was ceding wide swaths of public offices to the GOP without a contest. It nominated candidates for only twelve of the fifteen statewide positions on the ballot, and more striking, voters in 40 percent of the state House and Senate districts up for election were without a Democratic candidate, almost guaranteeing a continued GOP majority in the Texas House before a single vote was cast.

Perhaps the most significant failure of Texas Democrats to compete was evident in the state's 254 counties, historically the center of Democratic politics. In 2014, the Democratic Party failed to file a single county office candidate in eighty-six counties, over one-third of the total. In another thirty-six counties, only a single Democrat was seeking election to any county office. Without a vote being cast, Republicans knew they controlled at least 165 county judge positions, with less than 20 percent of the state's 254 counties witnessing a contest between a Democrat and a Republican for county judge. This lack of Democratic candidates contrasted with the few areas where Republicans did not compete. Of the twenty-two counties without a GOP candidate, only Webb and Hidalgo counties had populations over a hundred thousand while Democrats lacked any county-level candidates in places as populated as Denton, Montgomery, Bell, Johnson, Randall, Grayson, Parker, and Comal counties.

What was also troubling to those who analyzed election data was the fact that Wendy Davis, opposed in the primary only by little-known candidate Ray Madrigal, lost twenty-five counties, including seven in West Texas, and sixteen in South Texas. The counties where Madrigal outperformed Davis included the heavily populated Democratic base counties of Hidalgo and Webb. It was not a fortuitous start to her campaign for governor.

In the Republican primary Greg Abbott received 91.5 percent of all votes cast, leaving his three opponents far behind. In addition to the race for governor and most statewide judicial elections, two others avoided a runoff. Senator Cornyn saw seven candidates file against him, but he was renominated with 59.4 percent of the vote, far outpolling member of Congress Steve Stockman, who received 19.1 percent, and the other six candidates who trailed even farther behind. Also avoiding a runoff was George P. Bush, who won the nomination for land commissioner by a margin of 937,987 votes to 346,949 for business consultant David Watts.

In seeking to retain his position as lieutenant governor, Dewhurst drew opposition from Land Commissioner Jerry Patterson, Agriculture Commissioner Todd Staples, and state senator Dan Patrick. Patrick's 41.3 percent and Dewhurst's 28.3 percent required a runoff, which Patrick won by nearly a two-to-one margin. As in some of the other primary races, the old-line moderate conservative candidate fell short of the Tea Party social conservative advocate.

The race for attorney general attracted state senator Ken Paxton, state representative Dan Branch, and Railroad Commissioner Barry Smitherman. Paxton finished first with 44.5 percent with Branch second at 33.5 percent. In the runoff, Paxton was nominated by a vote of 466,407 to 269,098. In a last-minute twist, the nomination for comptroller was won outright by state senator Glenn Hegar, who was fifty votes short of a majority in the first round but was nominated when the second-place candidate, state representative Harvey Hilderbran, withdrew from the runoff.

Among the five candidates for agriculture commissioner, former state representatives Tommy Merritt and Sid Miller made it to a runoff, while J. Allen Carnes, Joe Cotten, and Eric Opiela were eliminated. Miller won the runoff by a margin of 364,756 to Merritt's 320,835. For the one open seat on the Railroad Commission, former state representative Wayne Christian and Ryan Sitton, owner of a small engineering and technology company, were forced to a runoff after SREC member Becky Berger and Malachi Boyuls were eliminated in the primary. Sitton won the runoff with 400,259 to 298,659 for Christian.

Only three congressional districts had contested primaries. In Northeast Texas, longtime member of Congress Ralph Hall, who had first been elected in 1980 as a Democrat, drew six opponents and was forced into a runoff with former US attorney John Ratcliffe, who won the runoff primary. Many had expected that Hall would retire, resulting in the large number of candidates running for this district. At the time of the election Hall was ninety-one years old and one of two remaining World War II veterans to serve in Congress.

In the border district running from El Paso to San Antonio, former member of Congress Quico Canseco attempted a comeback and was opposed once again by former CIA operative Will Hurd. In the primary the two candidates were separated by 164 votes, far ahead of the third candidate, Robert Lowry. This time Hurd would come out on top in the runoff, outpacing Canseco 8,699 to 5,930. With Congressman Stockman having made an abortive effort to defeat Senator Cornyn, his congressional district was once again open, and it attracted twelve candidates to what was assumed to be a safe Republican seat. The top two candidates were Tea Party favorite Ben Streusand and dentist Brian Babin, a longtime GOP activist. Babin was successful in the runoff primary.

Two state Senate seats went to runoffs. Both were won by Tea Party candidates as Bob Hall ousted Senator Bob Deuell in East Texas, while the Fort Worth district vacated by Democratic gubernatorial candidate Wendy Davis was won by Tea Party activist Konni Burton over former state representative Mark Shelton, who had lost the Senate contest in the previous general election to Davis.

THE WENDY DAVIS PHENOMENON

After losing a close race for the Fort Worth City Council in 1996, Wendy Davis was elected in 1999 and developed a reputation as a diligent representative of her constituents' interests. Davis voted in several Republican primaries, gave money to and supported GOP member of Congress Kay Granger, and donated funds to George W. Bush's 2000 presidential campaign. Like many professional women, however, Davis was concerned over the Texas GOP's strong antiabortion position and its stands on other social conservative issues. Davis decided to challenge incumbent GOP state senator Kim Brimer in 2008 and defeated him by seven thousand votes. She was re-elected by virtually the same margin in 2012, when she defeated state representative Shelton.[50]

It was while serving her fifth year in the Texas Senate that Davis became a known figure to Texans and to liberal Democrats across the country. During the first called session of the 2013 Texas legislature, the Republican leadership was attempting to pass a proposal to require that abortion clinics meet the same accessibility and health standards as hospitals and surgical centers, to mandate that physicians performing abortions have admitting privileges at a nearby hospital, and to prohibit the performing of abortions after twenty weeks of pregnancy. The provisions of Senate Bill 5 had failed passage in the regular session, and Governor Perry had placed the issue on the special session call.

Special sessions are limited not only to the topics indicated in the call but to thirty calendar days. On June 25, 2013, near the end of the calendar time allowed, Davis undertook an eleven-hour filibuster to stop the bill restricting abortion services from passing. Although she was unable to continue her filibuster until midnight, the bill did not pass before the end of the session, and Governor Perry called a second special session the next day.[51] In July the bill was passed by both chambers and signed into law by the governor.[52]

The filibuster did not stop the restrictive law from being enacted, but it had made Davis a star among liberal and pro-choice activists and organizations nationwide. Battleground Texas was among the groups urging Davis to continue her efforts by becoming a candidate for governor. Jenn Brown, executive director of the Democratic group, declared, "You can't win big elections without great candidates. And Wendy Davis would be a great candidate for governor." Joining in the effort to draft Davis was Annie's List, a political action committee (PAC) dedicated to electing liberal Democratic female candidates.[53]

Davis was becoming a household name across Texas and in liberal households throughout the country. She appeared on the cover of *Ms.* magazine and was featured in *Vogue*. As James Henson and Joshua Blank of the Texas Politics Project at the University of Texas at Austin observed, "There may have been a moment when it made sense for Davis to bide her time for four years while Democrats gathered their forces. That option seems much less viable now as a result of her ever-increasing, newfound fame."[54]

On October 3, 2013, in Haltom City, Wendy Davis officially jumped into the race for governor, declaring, "Texas is a place where we aim high and we take big risks. We're builders, and doers, leaders, and dreamers. We love Texas, not only for how good it is, but for how great we know it can be." At that stage in the developing campaign, Attorney General Greg Abbott had already raised nearly $25 million that could be used in his campaign for governor. But Davis's celebrity and pro-choice stance guaranteed that she would be able to raise sizeable amounts from both Texas residents and out-of-state PACs.[55]

With Perry stepping aside, Abbott the only well-known candidate for the Republican nomination, and with no other prominent Democratic candidates likely to file, the two main contenders for the governor's office were evident as early as the fall of 2013. Shortly after the Davis announcement, a University of Texas/*Texas Tribune* poll was released showing Abbott with 40 percent, Davis with 35 percent, and Libertarian Party candidate Kathie Glass at 5 percent, with 20 percent of those individuals surveyed undecided. Davis was already well-known and had a favorability ratio of thirty-seven to twenty-four, almost exactly the same as Abbott's, which was thirty-six to twenty-four. Though neither was an incumbent, the two candidates were starting relatively well-known; less than 20 percent of respondents had no opinion of them.[56]

NOVEMBER 2014

As the fall campaign began, one of the major battles between Abbott and Davis was for the support of Hispanic voters. In fact, their first televised debate took place in Hidalgo County, the most populous county in the Rio Grande Valley, where the population was over 80 percent Hispanic. Abbott committed over one million dollars to Spanish-language radio and television advertising, while Davis spent less than $300,000. Lionel Sosa, Abbott's media consultant, explained that Hispanic voters look for "a candidate who knows and understands the community. Latinos put family first, they work hard, they have a strong work ethic.... What Latinos will ask is: Do I know you, do I understand you, can I feel what you feel?"[57] The objective of the Abbott campaign was to relate to the Hispanic community and be accepted. Once trust was established, a vote could be sought.

In addition to Spanish broadcast media buys, the Abbott campaign purchased a number of highway billboards featuring his Hispanic mother-in-law Mary Lucy Phalen, his madrina ("godmother"), who in both print and broadcast media spoke of Abbott's family values and declared, "He is someone you can trust."[58] Abbott received the endorsement of seven mayors from South Texas, including the mayors of Harlingen and McAllen. Former GOP state representative Aaron Pena and Hispanic Republican leader Hollis Vasquez Rutledge hosted a *pachanga* for Abbott in Mission. Rutledge was Hidalgo County GOP chairman and president of the Texas Republican County Chairmen's Association.[59]

One factor in Abbott's favor was that national surveys had shown Texas Hispanics to be more favorably disposed to Republicans than was the situation in many other states. In a 2013 survey by Gallup, 27 percent of Texas Hispanics identified as Republican, another 20 percent viewed themselves as Independent, and 46 percent called themselves or leaned Democratic.[60] In other recent gubernatorial elections Republican candidates, including Bush and Perry, had obtained over 40 percent of the Hispanic vote and it was not unreasonable for Abbott to seek that same level of support.

As the election approached, two opinion polls described different political environments. A late September survey sponsored by the nonpartisan Texas Lyceum showed Davis nine points behind Abbott. This gave hope to those who maintained that growth in the Hispanic voter pool, migration from other states, a more ethnically and racially diverse population, and urbanization would produce a Democratic victory.[61] Then came the results from the respected *Texas Tribune*/University of Texas poll conducted in early October. It showed Republican statewide candidates with an average level of support of 51 percent compared to 34 percent for their Democratic opponents, and Abbott leading Davis by a margin of fifty-four to thirty-eight percent.[62]

One week out from Election Day, some commentators were developing new measures of Democratic success short of outright victory. Would Wendy Davis surpass Bill White's 42.3 percent of the vote? Can Davis cut Abbott's advantage below the 631,086 votes that separated Perry from White four years earlier? In a state whose population is constantly growing, can Davis corral more votes than White did in 2010? These were the standards to judge the efforts of Battleground Texas and the other political committees who were convinced they could make Texas a Democratic state. Donors and volunteers would need to be reassured that any transformation of the state's politics in a leftward direction would take time and several election cycles.

On November 4, 2014, 4,727,208 Texans' votes were counted, over 2 million of whom had cast their ballots before Election Day. Despite all the media focus on the Davis challenge to continued Republican dominance and the increasing population of the state, the number of voters was down one quarter of a million (252,662) from the number participating in the 2010 gubernatorial election. Approximately one-third of those eligible to vote in 2014 had done so.

The results produced a landslide for Greg Abbott as he obtained the support of 2,796,274 Texas voters, contrasted with 1,865,896 who chose to support Wendy Davis. Statewide Abbott received 60.4 percent of the total, for a margin close to a million votes. Texas voters had turned back the efforts of Wendy Davis and her out-of-state backers to turn Texas blue. With strong candidates and a resuscitated party organization, the GOP continued its twenty-year record of winning all statewide contests in a system with twenty-nine statewide elected positions. As one commentator noted, "No Democrat has finished so far behind since 1998, a blowout in which popular incumbent George W. Bush swamped Garry Mauro."[63]

Abbott received 48.8 percent support in the Big 6 counties, carrying Bexar, Harris, and Tarrant counties while losing Dallas, El Paso, and Travis. Those who lived outside these major cities were more favorable to the GOP candidate. Abbott's suburban support was strong, 787,133 to 368,389 for Davis, far overcoming the lead Davis had in the Big 6 counties. He had 68.1 percent of the suburban vote, carrying all twenty-nine suburban counties.

In the state's twenty-one smaller metropolitan counties, Abbott carried all but Cameron, Hidalgo, and Webb on the Mexican border. The counties Abbott carried in this category contained the cities of Beaumont, Corpus Christi, Lubbock, Amarillo, Midland, and several others of substantial size. The GOP candidate obtained 64.6 percent of all votes cast in these twenty-one counties.

It was small-town Texas that most heavily voted for Abbott. In these 198 counties that had long been the base of the Texas Democratic Party, Abbott received 72.1 percent of the vote, besting Davis by a margin of 552,285 to 164,062. Clearly over the past thirty-five years there had been a dramatic shift in voter loyalties throughout most of rural and small-town areas of the state.

Abbott had improved substantially in all four categories of counties compared with the Perry-White contest of 2010. While Perry had beat White by 631,086 statewide, Abbott's advantage over Davis was 954,782 votes. Davis was able to carry only eighteen of the state's 254 counties, ten fewer than Mayor White carried four years earlier.

Despite the efforts of the well-funded Battleground Texas and the national media attention on Davis, the Republican victory was broad, wide, and deep. According to the NBC News exit poll, 54 percent of all female voters supported Abbott, along with two-thirds of male voters. A significant dividing factor, however, was marriage. Abbott had 62 percent of the votes of married women while polling only 42 percent of nonmarried women. The split among men was 68 percent for Abbott among those who were married, dropping to 54 percent of unmarried men.[64]

Abbott's strong push to continue making inroads among Hispanic voters resulted in the Davis margin decreasing to a lead of 55 percent to 44 percent among a segment of the electorate thought to constitute the future of the Texas Democratic Party. Abbott broke even among Hispanic men, with 49 percent of the vote, while losing women 61 percent to 39 percent. Despite the vaunted efforts of Battleground Texas to increase the rate of Hispanic voter participation, turnout among this growing pool of potential voters was down compared to four years earlier. In both elections Hispanics made up 17 percent of all voters casting ballots. Abbott's campaign strategist David Carney credited some of the success to the television advertisement featuring Abbott's Hispanic mother-in-law. By the time of the election, the Abbott campaign had increased its Spanish-language media buy to $3 million.[65]

The GOP candidate's support among that broad swath of voters labeled white or Anglo, making up two-thirds of the electorate, was overwhelming: he surpassed Davis by a margin of 72 percent to 25 percent. African-American voters, however, remained strongly Democratic, with the GOP candidate's support in single digits. At the same time, among that growing segment of the Texas population classified as Asian-American, a national exit poll showed Abbott beating Davis by a margin of 51 percent to 47 percent.[66]

Two other facts from the NBC exit polls spoke to the challenge facing Democrats and the opportunity for continued Republican dominance. Respondents indicated that on most political matters 44 percent considered themselves conservative, while 38 percent chose "moderate" and only 18 percent selected "liberal" as a description of their outlook. Texans also had differing views of the two political parties. Not surprisingly, there were considerable negative attitudes on both, but the Democratic Party was viewed unfavorably by 59 percent (with 38 percent favorable), while attitudes toward the Republican Party were split with 47 percent favorable and 49 percent unfavorable.

There was more to be decided than who would become the next governor of Texas. At the top of the ballot was the senatorial contest. Twelve-year incumbent John Cornyn racked up a margin of 1,258,000 votes more than his little-known Democratic opponent, receiving 61.6 percent of the total vote. The statewide candidate with the next highest advantage over his opponent was one with a familiar name: George P. Bush. In his first political race, Bush was elected land commissioner by easily defeating former El Paso mayor John Cook. Once again Republican candidates won all the statewide contests on the ballot.

Republican success in Texas extended also into legislative races as the party increased its advantage in the congressional delegation (to twenty-five Republicans and eleven Democrats), the state Senate (twenty to eleven), and the state House of Representatives (ninety-eight to fifty-two). The one state Senate seat picked up from the Democrats was the district vacated by Davis when she filed for governor.

A young, attractive candidate and former Texas A&M student body president, Will Hurd, recaptured the 23rd congressional district that had flipped back and forth ever since Henry Bonilla had held it for fourteen years. Hurd became the first African-American Republican in the Texas delegation. Two of the three state House districts captured from the Democrats were won by two more Hispanic Republicans, Rick Galindo of San Antonio and Gilbert Peña of Pasadena.

While the Texas GOP was successfully broadening its support, the Democrats were losing ground among the largest segment of the electorate both in terms of raw votes and number of elected officials. When the state legislature met in January 2015, there remained only seven white or Anglo Democrats in a delegation of fifty-two and only two of the eleven Democrats serving in the Texas Senate.[67]

At the level of county government, Republicans continued to make progress as the number of county judges increased to 199. All twenty-nine suburban counties were led by a Republican county judge, as were eighteen of the twenty-one smaller metropolitan counties. Among the Big 6, Harris and Tarrant each had a GOP county judge, while 150 of the 198 small-town counties were overseen by a Republican in the county judge's office. After decades of being in the minority, Republicans now had a clear majority of the elected officials in the state at all levels.

For this continued success commentators credited the efforts of the state party organization and its Victory Committee under the leadership of state chairman Munisteri. Competing with the well-funded Battleground Texas and Davis's national fundraising power, the GOP not only held its own but added to its list of elected officials. While primary contests for public office remained heated, during the six years of Munisteri's leadership the party had been financially successful, additional outreach efforts had been undertaken, and internal disputes had been kept to a minimum.

Abbott entered the governor's office with experience as both a Texas Supreme Court justice and attorney general. He added to that by hiring, as his legislative director, another broadly experienced hand. Randy Erben had been director of the Texas office of state-federal relations during the Clements administration, assistant secretary of state, acting assistant director of the US Department of Housing and Urban Development, and general counsel for Texans for Rick Perry. With Republican majorities in both the Texas House and Senate and an experienced legislative director, Abbott was off to a positive start.

Another Republican was now in the governor's mansion, and the Republican Party of Texas was preparing for the 2016 presidential election, when Obama would not be on the ballot. No one knew what the next presidential nominating contest and general election would hold for Texas Republicans.

FIFTEEN

DONALD TRUMP AND THE REPUBLICAN FUTURE

In March 2015 Steve Munisteri resigned as GOP state chairman to become a senior advisor to the presidential campaign of his longtime friend Senator Rand Paul of Kentucky. Over five years Munisteri had served nearly full-time as a volunteer, working closely with Executive Director Beth Cubriel to reestablish the party's financial stability, involve various communities and voter groups in party activities, and promote unity and commitment to the common goal of electing Republicans to public office. It was time to move on and heed the call of a friend for assistance and advice.

When the state Republican executive committee (SREC) met to choose a successor, they selected Amarillo business owner Tom Mechler, the party's treasurer and Munisteri's recommended candidate, to complete the unexpired term. Mechler was elected to the position at the 2016 state convention, defeating Jared Woodfill, a former Harris County GOP chairman who had been defeated for re-election in the 2016 primary. Mechler's time as chairman was challenging as he was vociferously and incessantly opposed by a small faction on the state committee. After two years as chairman Mechler determined that life was meant to be lived and not merely endured. Consequently he resigned his volunteer position to spend more time with his family and pursue his business commitments.[1]

Once more the SREC had to select a state chairman, and the choice came down to Rick Figueroa of Brenham, whom Mechler recommended, and James Dickey of Austin. Dickey prevailed in a vote of thirty-two to thirty-one. At the following state convention in 2018, Dickey easily defeated his challenger, Cindy Asche, by a margin of 65.4 percent to 34.6 percent.[2] A few months after the state convention Dickey convinced the SREC to change the state chairman's role from a volunteer unpaid position, which it had always been, to a full-time paid employment arrangement at an annual salary of $150,000.[3]

AFTER OBAMA: THE 2016 PRIMARY

While there were many candidates in the 2016 battle for the GOP presidential nomination, only one survived. The survivor was a billionaire business owner with no government experience, no political background, and no longstanding ties to the Republican Party. Donald J. Trump had made and lost a fortune in real estate and in marketing his brand—the name Trump—which appeared on hotels, men's clothing, wine, and even a network of "wealth creation" seminars called Trump University. Trump was able to motivate and activate a number of personal supporters, many of whom had never participated in Republican Party primaries.

By the time of the Texas primary, Trump had only two serious challengers for the nomination: Senator Marco Rubio of Florida and Senator Ted Cruz of Texas. The primary was held on March 1 and generated a large turnout of 2.8 million voters, with Cruz easily beating off the other twelve candidates whose names appeared on the ballot. Only Cruz, with 43.8 percent of the votes, Trump (26.8 percent), and Rubio (17.8 percent) were in double figures and would be allocated delegates to the national convention. When Rubio failed to carry his home state of Florida, losing it to Trump, his campaign was over.

The Texas primary was part of what was referred to as Super Tuesday, when ten states held a presidential primary and two other states had caucuses where delegates were chosen. In addition to winning Texas, Cruz won Alaska and Oklahoma. As other candidates began to drop out, Cruz increasingly became what was viewed as the most viable alternative to Donald Trump, the candidate who was winning the largest number of delegates. The Indiana primary, where then-governor Mike Pence indicated he would be voting for Cruz, was seen as the last effort to stop a Trump nomination. On May 3 Donald Trump won the state with 53 percent of the vote, with Cruz trailing far behind at 36 percent. The next day Cruz suspended his campaign, and Trump had a clear path to the Republican nomination.

The Texas primary on March 1 involved more than the presidential nomination contest as all candidates for the November ballot were nominated at the same time. Although a number of GOP members of Congress found themselves with primary opponents, all were renominated. The only statewide contests were for one seat on the Railroad Commission, where neither Gary Gates nor former state representative Wayne Christian obtained a majority, forcing a runoff subsequently won by Christian. Three incumbent justices on the Texas Supreme Court were seriously challenged, but all three were successful. The contests for two open seats on the Court of Criminal Appeals required runoffs, which were won by Mary Lou Keel and Scott Walker, while incumbent judge Michael E. Keasler easily defeated his opponent for renomination.

All the incumbent state senators up for election in 2016 were renominated, but there were lively contests for the open seats, eventually won by state representative Bryan Hughes in Northeast Texas and by Dawn Buckingham in the Hill Country. Once again there was a series of primary contests for the Texas House of Representatives, with outside groups and PACs providing financial support and technical assistance to candidates who were regarded as either supportive of or opposed to Speaker Joe Straus. Most of these contests were won by candidates endorsed by allies of the speaker.

NOVEMBER 2016

To little surprise of most Republicans, Donald Trump won Texas and received the state's thirty-eight electoral votes by 4,685,047 votes to 3,877,868 for Hillary Clinton and 283,492 for former two-term governor of New Mexico Gary Johnson, the Libertarian Party candidate. As a protest vote against Trump, a number of conservatives took the extra step of writing in the name of Evan McMullin, who was campaigning as a conservative alternative to Trump and ended up with 42,366 write-in votes.

Trump's vote total was less than that of six GOP candidates who were running for down-ballot statewide judicial positions, and his margin of 807,179 votes ahead of Clinton was smaller than that of all other statewide candidates, who were winning by more than one million votes over their Democratic opponents. In the Big 6 counties Trump was trounced, losing to Clinton by 655,164 votes. Trump made up for this deficit in the other areas of the state as he carried the twenty-nine suburban counties by a margin of 598,730, the smaller metro counties by 217,539, and the 198 small-town counties by a whopping 646,074. As in most other parts of the country, the votes of rural and small-town Texans went overwhelmingly for Trump.

What was evident in the election was that the Republican brand was more popular than the Trump brand. This can be seen most clearly in the votes for Trump at the top of the ticket and two candidates with virtually no name recognition further down the ballot. Appearing on the ballot after the presidential and congressional candidates and the other statewide elected positions was a contest for an open seat on the Court of Criminal Appeals. Other than attorneys, only a minuscule percentage of the electorate could name the two candidates or the function of this office. Both candidates had generic Anglo names, were defense attorneys, and were described as rookies who had not previously been candidates or served as jurists. Neither had much organized financial support or campaign organization, and they ran few if any media advertisements. Their election or defeat depended mainly on party identification and straight-ticket voting. The candidates were Scott Walker and Betsy Johnson.

In the November election Walker, the Republican candidate, obtained 4,790,800 votes, 105,000 more than the presidential candidate at the top of the ballot. While Trump won by 807,179 votes, Walker beat his opponent by a margin of 1,270,194 votes. Given how little-known Walker and Johnson were to the electorate, it is safe to conclude that a major factor differentiating them in the voter's mind was party affiliation. The conclusion is that while both were popular in Texas, the Republican brand, which contributed to Walker's success, was more popular in 2016 than the Trump brand. Over time, however, with Trump in the White House, the image and brand of the Republican Party nationally, as well as in Texas, became closely associated with the Trump brand.

Beyond the presidential contest there were no changes in the state's congressional delegation, with the closest race being Will Hurd's re-election by a margin of three thousand votes in the 23rd district. Both parties held their own in the state Senate contests, while four Texas House Republicans were defeated.[4]

O'ROURKE AND TRUMP

As Trump was inaugurated in January 2017, many Republicans were thankful that their party had reclaimed the White House and held majorities in both the Senate and House of Representatives. No longer facing divided government, they were hopeful that Republicans would achieve a reform and replacement of Obamacare, confront the problem of illegal immigration and border security, strengthen the nation's defense, and improve relations with US allies around the world. In many ways the next two years were frustrating as the president and his administration were often stymied in their efforts. Throughout it all, however, the personality, prejudices, and opinions of Donald J. Trump were front and center.

Many people believe that it was the candidacy of one Democratic member of Congress, Robert Francis "Beto" O'Rourke of El Paso, who attempted to become a US senator, that attracted a record number of voters to the November 2018 election. Whereas only 33 percent of eligible voters turned out for the gubernatorial election in 2014, over half of all possible voters took part in the 2018 election. Participation rose from 4,727,208 voters four years earlier to a total of 8,371,655, 53.1 of eligible voters, and close to the record for the presidential election of 2016, which drew 8,969,226 to the polls.

Still others believe that the increase in turnout was due to the personality and policies of Trump, who was approaching the end of his first two years in the White House. As Joshua Blank of the University of Texas at Austin viewed the situation, "A lot of people wrongly characterized the Texas outcome being the result of 'Beto' O'Rourke running against Ted Cruz. That definitely had something to do with it. But, at least among Democrats, the results in Texas, like everywhere else, were a reaction against Donald Trump."[5]

O'Rourke was unsuccessful in his campaign to defeat incumbent senator Cruz, losing by a margin of 223,091 votes, but he gave a strong warning to Texas Republicans that statewide victory was no longer a given. O'Rourke carried all of the Big 6 counties, achieving a vote advantage of 884,737 over Cruz. He carried three of the state's fastest-growing suburbs—Fort Bend, Hays, and Williamson—while cutting the Cruz lead in the other suburban counties to 384,940. The Democratic senate candidate won five of the twenty-one smaller metro counties and kept Cruz's vote advantage from them to 167,117. It was only with the votes in the state's 198 small-town counties, where Cruz ran up a lead of 555,771, that the senator was able to gain re-election.

At first blush it appeared that the votes for governor were more encouraging to Republicans. After all, incumbent governor Greg Abbott improved his overall performance, beating Dallas County sheriff Lupe Valdez by 1,105,124 votes compared to his 960,378 advantage over Wendy Davis four years earlier. Yet it was the overall turnout that affected the vote margin, as Abbott's 55.8 percent of the vote was down from his 60.4 percent obtained in 2014.

With Cruz, Abbott, and all the statewide Republican candidates victorious, it appeared to be a familiar situation. Looking further, however, the losing statewide Democratic candidates had produced a number of close elections. Abbott's 55.8 percent was the highest percentage of the vote any Republican received when running against a Democrat in a statewide race.[6]

While the statewide results were a concern to Republicans, the GOP performance in legislative contests was even more troubling. The party lost two congressional seats from urban and suburban districts around Dallas and Houston as veteran members of Congress Pete Sessions and John Culberson fell to their Democratic opponents. Culberson's reconfigured district had been in GOP hands since George H. W. Bush first won it for the GOP in 1966, and it was held for thirty years by Bill Archer.

In the Texas Senate, Republicans lost two of the sixteen districts up for election in 2018. In Tarrant County, Senator Konni Burton was defeated by

Democrat Beverly Powell, while in Dallas Senator Don Huffines lost his race for re-election in what had been a safe GOP district to Democratic candidate Nathan Johnson. Although they had lost these two seats, Republicans had picked up another one when Pete Flores of Pleasanton won a special election to fill a vacancy in the 19th Senate district. Flores's victory meant that the composition of the Senate was nineteen Republicans to twelve Democrats after the losses of Burton and Huffines.

Of even more concern was the loss of twelve seats in the Texas House, dropping the partisan division to eighty-three Republicans and sixty-seven Democrats. A switch of nine seats in 2020 could produce a Democratic majority in the legislative body that will be responsible for redrawing congressional and state legislative district lines after the 2020 Census report is issued.

THE CHANGING GOP CONSTITUENCY

When Texas Republicans were beginning to become a competitive force in the late twentieth century, the bulk of the party's voter base was in the middle- and upper-middle income areas of Dallas and Houston. As the party began winning more elections, both Dallas and Harris counties were led by Republican county judges. Both Tarrant and Bexar counties also had GOP county judges for several years during the decade of the 1990s. By 2020 only one of the Big 6 counties, Tarrant, had a Republican county judge.

Prior to the 2018 election all twenty-nine suburban counties were headed by GOP county judges. Democrats now count two of the state's fastest-growing and most ethnically diverse counties — Fort Bend and Hays — in their column. Both counties had been reliably Republican in recent years but gave a majority of their votes to O'Rourke as did Williamson County, another fast-growing suburban area. Abbott lost Hays, won Williamson, and barely carried Fort Bend, by 720 votes.

In the twenty-one smaller metro counties, the GOP lost the county judge office in Nueces County, which they had controlled for several years, along with the heavily Democratic counties of Cameron, Hidalgo, and Webb, located in South Texas. Cruz lost all four, along with Jefferson County, in his battle with O'Rourke.

It is now the 198 small-town counties, where declining population and aging residents are facts of life, that have become the bulwark of the Texas GOP in the era of Donald Trump. In 1978, when Bill Clements became the first Republican governor in one hundred years, only 8 percent of the GOP primary vote came from small-town counties. By 2012 that figure had risen to

24.9 percent, and in the 2018 Republican primary these mainly rural counties provided over one-quarter of all votes. Meanwhile, the state's Big 6 counties, from which two-thirds of all GOP primary votes came in 1978, provided less than 30 percent of those who participated in the 2018 primary.

The types of candidates a party nominates and the issues on which the party focuses attention are affected by the composition of the primary electorate. While the state's population is becoming more urban and suburban, rural and small-town Texas voters are having a greater voice in party decisions. As county government in these areas becomes almost totally Republican, contests for local office will take place in the GOP primary, which will be the arena of final decisions. Such a situation will attract even more voters to the Republican primary. In recent years a dozen or more counties have not even held a Democratic primary election, making the GOP primary the only choice for those who wish to nominate candidates.

An additional and related concern for the Republican Party of Texas is the age distribution of those who identify with the party. When the Texas GOP was in its early growth phase, voters age eighteen to twenty-nine represented the highest level of GOP identification. Being a Republican in Texas meant one was unhappy with the establishment Democrats then in control of the state government and most county offices. By 2019 eighteen- to twenty-nine-year-olds had the lowest level of Republican identification. The highest level of GOP support was among those age sixty-two or more, with 61 percent identifying with the party.[7]

This age disparity exists not only with party identification but also with actual voting behavior. In 2018 Cruz was able to garner only 29 percent of the votes from those age eighteen to twenty-nine, and Abbott's share was not that different at 33 percent. Both Cruz and Abbott were relying on strong support from older voters to win. Among those age sixty-five and older Cruz obtained 58 percent of the votes, and Abbott did even better with 62 percent.[8] Unfortunately for Republicans, viewing the areas of GOP strength among today's electorate, it is apparent that rural and small-town areas of Texas are losing population, and older voters are facing the reality of life and death.

A third source of support for the GOP in the twentieth century came from those moving to Texas from other parts of the country, many of whom brought existing Republican loyalties with them. In 1985, 41 percent of recent arrivals identified with the Republican Party compared with 24 percent who viewed themselves as Democrats. By 2019, the partisan division of those who moved to the state was nearly even at 43 percent Democrats and 47 percent Republicans.[9] Texas population growth continues at a rapid pace. Since the 2016 presidential election, "at least 2 million people have moved to Texas, many of them Democrats from places like California, Florida, New York and Illinois. An estimated 800,000 young Latino Americans have turned 18, and a wave of immigrants became naturalized citizens." This growth in the state's population led to more than three million new registered voters between 2016 and 2020.[10]

2020 AND BEYOND

No one could have predicted the events of 2020, which would impact not only the Republican Party in Texas but the entire world. Soon after the year began, the world confronted a health crisis, the COVID-19 pandemic, resulting in millions sick and dying and the economy and social systems of nations worldwide affected. In Texas, this pandemic would affect the ability to hold political meetings and engage in mass campaigning while creating new concerns over voting procedures and policies. The government's response to the coronavirus would cause division and dissent, directed toward officials at all levels. This challenge to the health and safety of Americans and a number of internal party conflicts would make this a presidential campaign year unlike any in recent memory.

The decision by six of the party's twenty-three U.S. representatives to not seek re-election created the challenge of defending open seats. Among the six were the GOP delegation's only Hispanic and African-American members. Texas Republicans confronted another unpleasant reality when, in March 2020—for the first time in twelve years—more Texans chose to participate in the Democratic primary than the Republican primary.[11]

With the coronavirus having an impact on all aspects of public life, both major parties were forced to conduct virtual state conventions. Technical glitches marred the Republican effort and the delegates voted electronically to oust the top two party officials. State chairman James Dickey lost his campaign for re-election to former Florida congressman Allen West, while vice chairman Alma Perez Jackson was defeated by Kat Parks.[12]

Meanwhile, Republican leaders were embarrassed to witness some county chairmen posting conspiratorial items online. After the county chairmen in Bexar and Nueces counties shared a claim that the death of George Floyd, an African-American who died in police custody in Minnesota, was a staged event, Governor Abbott called on them to resign. Harris County chairman-elect Keith Nielsen posted an objectionable email, leading Congressman Dan Crenshaw to say, "Nielsen has no place in our party. Not now. Not Ever." Crenshaw called the post "a sad reminder that such blatant ignorance and bigotry still exists."[13] As the fall campaign began, Nielsen was still GOP chairman of the state's largest county. While the posting of various conspiracy theories was not widespread, at least seven other county chairs were identified as sharing similar posts.[14]

The internal dissension and posting of extreme statements went beyond a subset of county chairmen to include a major party donor and a right-wing political action committee. In response to the demonstrations generated by the death of George Floyd, prominent Houston physician and political activist Steven Hotze left a voice mail for Governor Abbott urging him to respond to any rioters with an order to "shoot to kill the son of a bitches. That's the only way you restore order. Kill 'em. Thank you." In rebuttal, Senator John Cornyn described Hotze's remarks as "absolutely disgusting and reprehensible." Hotze had repeatedly opposed Governor Abbott's actions to deal with the coronavirus pandemic, especially his statewide mask mandate that Hotze said was a "draconian order contrary to the Texas spirit [that] invades the liberties of the people of Texas." According to Hotze, the governor's "mask is starving his brain of oxygen."[15]

Two staff members of Empower Texans, a right-wing group headed by Michael Quinn Sullivan, were heard on a podcast calling Governor Abbott "a revolting piece of shit" and joking about his wheelchair use. The comments met with condemnation from GOP elected officials, and the two employees were suspended from public activities but remained on the organization's staff.[16] George P. Bush, one of the few statewide Republicans not endorsed by Empower Texans, retorted: "Enough is enough. Enough of the lying. Enough of the crude comments made in public and in private about fellow Republicans." Bush said the GOP should "leave the Sullivan era and return to the Reagan era, an era where we focused on shared conservative convictions, united around a common agenda, and didn't intentionally lie about the actions of fellow Republican officeholders."[17]

A number of county GOP organizations went on record as censuring the Republican governor for his measures against the pandemic and especially his statewide mask mandate and closure of bars. Many of the same county organizations had censured Republican House Speaker Joseph Straus two years earlier for not being sufficiently in line with their views on social issues. As state senator Kel Seliger observed, "This has been building for a long, long time. When a party dominates, it also becomes sort of arrogant and exclusive. It used to be, back in the '80s and '90s, let's all get together in this big Republican tent and be a majority. Increasingly, we've been ushering people out of the tent."[18]

The attacks on Abbott continued through the fall as two dozen Republicans filed suit against the governor's extension of early voting by six days and his order allowing individuals to submit absentee ballots in person rather than relying on postal delivery. Among those listed as plaintiffs were the newly elected state GOP chairman, the Republican commissioner of agriculture, and a handful of GOP state legislators.[19] A few days later the Texas Supreme Court denied the motion to hear the case, noting that the election was already under way. As Chief Justice Nathan Hecht noted, "To disrupt the long-planned election procedures as relators would have us do would threaten voter confusion."[20]

Those opposed to Abbott's policies continued their efforts. Just days before the start of early voting, state chairman Allen West was a featured speaker at a protest rally outside the governor's mansion calling on the governor to allow bars and restaurants to open at full capacity and to withdraw his mask mandate. He was joined by Agriculture Commissioner Sid Miller, state senator Bob Hall, a few former legislators, and Michael Quinn Sullivan of Empower Texans. As the protest ended, participants were greeted by conspiracy theorist Alex Jones, who told the protesters he saluted their cause.[21]

While confronting internal division and dissension, Texas Republicans were beginning a fall campaign unlike any they had experienced. Encouraged by their relative success in the elections two years earlier, the sizeable turnout in the 2020 Democratic primary, and the perceived unpopularity of President Trump among suburban voters, Texas Democrats were mounting a serious effort to change the direction of Texas politics. For decades, Texas donors had been a source for funding Democratic campaigns in other states; now the money flow was being reversed as national Democratic political committees and out-of-state liberal donors were sending contributions to Texas candidates.

Many in the Trump campaign were assuming the state would remain in the Republican column, but Texas observers were more concerned. Political consultant Brendan Steinhauser claimed, "Texas is definitely in play this year. We kind of need everybody to not only take it very seriously but to realize we have to play a bit of defense in Texas before we can even think of going on offense in other states."[22] Quickly, it became evident there would not be any "Mighty Texas Strike Force" sending GOP volunteers to other states. This year, all volunteer efforts for the presidential campaign would be needed in Texas. National Democrats were not dismissing their chances in the state either. At the Texas Democratic state convention, former vice president Biden proclaimed, "Texas is an important battleground state for our campaign in 2020. I think we have a real chance to turn the state blue."[23]

As early as July, the Biden campaign began running a Texas-specific television spot, but many GOP operatives dismissed it as not a serious buy. Republican strategist Jessica Colon claimed, "Biden is obligated by his party and the leftist movement to spend money here because they are dying to tell … their narrative that they can turn this place blue if they just drop enough money here. What people forget … is that there is a whole lot of Texas. And dropping into an urban area or two does not a Texas make."[24]

Voter surveys beginning in late spring and continuing through October showed the presidential race to be closely contested, with the difference often within the poll's margin of error. Of six surveys taken in October, three showed a lead for Trump, two a lead for Biden, and one showed them tied, but none had a margin exceeding five points.[25] The seriousness of the Democratic challenge also could be seen in the media buys of the Biden campaign and other entities supportive of the party's candidates. In October, the Biden campaign reserved $6 million for spots to run in the state's major television markets for the final four weeks of the campaign.[26]

One report indicated national Democratic groups were spending in excess of $55 million on the senatorial race, several U.S. House contests, and the attempt to take over the Texas House of Representatives. Meanwhile the spending of out-of-state GOP groups appeared to be no more than $15 million.[27] A national liberal group, Forward Majority, committed $12 million to Democratic candidates for the Texas House, while a coalition of other Democratic groups launched a $1.1 million targeted digital ad campaign in eleven state house districts.[28] Democratic efforts focused on a number of suburban areas where Republicans had been dominant for decades, such as Collin County, north of Dallas.[29]

To meet this coordinated drive, Governor Greg Abbott's campaign committee began spending funds to preserve the GOP state House majority and other down-ballot races in the first election without the "straight ticket" option. The effort included television spots as well as digital ads designed to support twenty-four candidates for the Texas House. Abbott's chief political strategist, Dave Carney, indicated one focus of the effort was "either Abbott supporters or high-likelihood swing voters."[30] Meanwhile, other groups, including the Texans for Lawsuit Reform PAC, the Associated Republicans of Texas, and a new PAC formed by Karl Rove and several GOP incumbents, Leading Texas Forward, together provided over $11.5 million to GOP state legislative candidates in an effort to preserve the party's majority. It was reported that "the eye-popping display of financial power by Republican-leaning groups enabled a dozen GOP candidates to eclipse one million dollars each in contributions."[31]

Maintaining a GOP majority in the Texas House of Representatives, where all 150 districts were up for election in 2020, was important not only to provide support for Governor Abbott's legislative programs but also for the influence the House would have on redistricting after the release of data from the 2020 census. Continued control of both legislative chambers in Austin would ensure the party could have a dominant voice in the creation of new congressional and state legislative districts, which would be in place for the next ten years.[32]

New York billionaire and former presidential candidate Michael Bloomberg spent $15 million on television ads backing Joe Biden that ran in Ohio and Texas. His super PAC, Independence USA, ran commercials backing the Democratic presidential candidate in all Texas television markets. Bloomberg's millions were also going to down-ballot races, as he donated $2.6 million to Chrysta Castaneda, Democratic candidate for the Railroad Commission, in her attempt to become the first Democrat elected to statewide office since 1994.[33] Clearly, Republicans were being challenged by well-financed Democratic opponents at all levels of government.

First as governor and then as president, George W. Bush had built the Republican Party of Texas into a conservative force that represented a broad majority of Texans and dominated politics in the state. Now the Republican Party had become the vehicle for Donald J. Trump, and the 2020 election became a referendum on his leadership abilities, his personal attributes, and his policy preferences. In the midst of a continuing health crisis, voters were deciding whether to continue on the current path or to choose new leadership for the nation. That vote would also influence the future of the Republican Party of Texas and the nature of the state's political competition.

On Election Day 2020, a record turnout of Texas voters provided a clearer picture of the political situation in the state. For years Democrats have claimed that Texas is not a Republican state but rather a nonvoting state, which would turn blue if more people simply voted. With a large swath of newly registered and newly participating voters, the myth of nonvoters being Democrats was torn asunder. As journalist Ross Ramsey noted, "Turnout hasn't been this high, on a percentage basis, since 1992, when two Texans—George H. W. Bush and Ross Perot—topped the ballot in the presidential race."[34]

Likewise, the Democratic hope that an increase in Hispanic turnout would help create a majority vote for their party proved elusive. In twenty-three counties where the population was at least 70 percent Hispanic, both Trump and Cornyn won nearly 40 percent of the vote, with Trump carrying nine and Cornyn eight.[35] In the three most populous counties along the border with

Mexico—Cameron, Hidalgo, and Webb—the Democratic presidential candidate's margin declined from 129,457 in 2016 to 68,286 in 2020.[36]

Despite the many millions spent on behalf of Democratic candidates and the internal disruptions within the GOP, voters reaffirmed Republican domination of Texas politics. The projected "blue wave" never came ashore as GOP candidates carried all ten statewide contests, including the presidential race and the re-election of the state's senior senator to a fourth term. With the elimination of the "straight ticket" option on the ballot, the drop-off in votes for Democratic candidates was substantial, as senatorial candidate M. J. Hegar fell more than 365,000 votes short of the number cast for Joe Biden.[37]

Donald Trump once again carried Texas, and for the eleventh consecutive time the state's electoral college votes would be cast for the Republican presidential candidate. While overall voter turnout was up considerably, Trump's margin over the Democratic candidate fell from 807,179 in 2016 to 648,690. The president's biggest decline in support came in the state's six largest counties, where his vote deficit increased from 655,000 in 2016 to nearly one million in 2020. He made up this shortfall by carrying the twenty-nine suburban counties by 550,000 votes, an advantage slightly down from his 2016 lead of roughly 600,000 votes. The only suburban counties Trump lost were the three with the most rapid population growth and more ethnically diverse populations (Fort Bend, Hays, and Williamson counties). The president outperformed his 2016 totals in other metropolitan counties and in small-town counties, two areas that together provided him with a 1,100,000 advantage over Biden, and helped him establish his statewide victory.[38]

While Trump carried the state as the candidate at the top of the ballot, his was the worst performance among the ten statewide candidates, prevailing by a margin of only 648,690 votes over Biden while John Cornyn was re-elected by a margin of 1,092,123 votes, and the closest that a Democrat was able to come in any of the other statewide races was to lose by a difference of 870,731 votes. Cornyn's victory by more than a million votes was impressive, given that his opponent was well funded, with millions in out-of-state contributions from Democrats seeking to regain a majority in the U.S. Senate.

There was no partisan change in the state's congressional delegation as all incumbents were re-elected, including two Democrats who had captured suburban districts in 2018 and were strongly challenged by well-funded Republican opponents. Republicans were able to retain the seven open districts where Republican incumbents chose not to seek re-election, including the border district stretching from San Antonio to El Paso, where Tony Gonzales kept the seat in Republican hands.

While national Democrats had made a major push to recruit and fund candidates to acquire a majority in the Texas House, their efforts resulted in failure as the partisan division remained at 83 Republicans and 67 Democrats. Only two incumbents in Harris County, one Democrat and one Republican, were defeated. According to political writer Gromer Jeffers, "Gov. Greg Abbott played a critical role in the GOP's rebound. His operatives helped lead a coordinated campaign with candidates and conservative groups looking to protect GOP turf." As Dave Carney, the governor's chief political consultant, concluded, "It is a competitive state. We're not a purple state, we're not a swing state, but we're competitive."[39]

As the year 2021 began, Texas Republicans confronted a number of new challenges. A Democrat now occupied the White House, and Republicans had transitioned from defenders to critics of the president and many of the policies he advocated. In Austin, the Texas House of Representatives selected a new Speaker to lead the chamber and work with Governor Abbott and Lieutenant Governor Patrick. This triumvirate of state leaders attempted to balance the need to reopen the Texas economy with protecting the health of the state's population.

When the legislature convened in January, foremost on the list of priorities was the constitutional obligation to balance the state budget at a time of reduced tax revenues and increased expenditures due to the state's response to the pandemic. Adding to the challenge was the need to draw new state legislative and congressional district lines consistent with constitutional requirements and the data from the 2020 census.

Despite the loss of the White House, Texas Republicans entered the new decade as still the dominant force in state politics. For several election cycles Democrats had preached that they were on the brink of a major breakthrough, but on Election Day they never delivered. After attracting millions of out-of-state campaign contributions and heightening the expectations of local activists, it remains to be seen whether Texas Democrats will be able to retain the financial and voter support to mount a serious challenge to the state's Republican domination in 2022 and beyond.

To continue its dominance of Texas politics, Republicans will need to overcome geographic, demographic, and other difficulties. Texas remains a state that continually attracts new residents and businesses while encouraging homegrown entrepreneurs. To this point, in her book *Big, Hot, Cheap, and Right*, Erica Grieder reminds readers that "the greatest advantage that Texas Republicans currently enjoy ... is that Texans really haven't had a problem with their policies. The evidence is that people keep voting for them."[40]

In July 2017, the Republican Party of Texas commemorated its 150th anniversary. The party and its constituency have changed dramatically since its founding, as has Texas since the time of Reconstruction. A history is not the place for predictions. What is clear, however, is that the Republican Party of Texas is alive and well because it has adapted to changing conditions over the last fifty years, and since the turn of the century it has been the dominant political force in the state.

ACKNOWLEDGMENTS

It would have been impossible develop this manuscript covering more than 150 years of Texas political history without the decision of many participants to preserve records and correspondence and then donate them to one of several educational institutions in the state. This documentary evidence has been essential in researching the history of the Republican Party of Texas. I am grateful to those who provided these materials and to the many archivists and librarians who organized, collated, and catalogued them to allow the use of these materials by researchers. There are too many to cite here but they are referenced in the many endnotes.

Many individuals gave of their time and knowledge in allowing me to interview them or provided insights and materials by mail or email. Their names are cited in the endnotes, but I want to thank them here for their help in constructing this history.

I am appreciative of the assistance of Joshua Blank, manager of polling and research at the Texas Political Project, University of Texas at Austin, who provided contemporary data on demographic support for the Republican Party. Casey Kittrell, acquisitions editor, University of Texas Press, was most helpful once again in ushering this manuscript through the process of creating a final document. His support and the comments and recommendations of the anonymous readers who reviewed the manuscript have improved the original submission. Lynne Ferguson, senior manuscript editor, was most helpful in facilitating the process of moving from manuscript to final product.

Without the support and assistance on this project from my wife, Judith, it would not have been possible. I am blessed to have her as my life partner, computer expert, and proofreader.

NOTES

1. NINETEENTH-CENTURY REPUBLICANISM

1. Regarding the formation of the Republican Party nationally, see George H. Mayer, *The Republican Party, 1854–1966,* 2nd edition (New York: Oxford University Press, 1967), and Eric Foner, *Free Soil, Free Labor, Free Men: The Ideology of the Republican Party before the Civil War* (New York: Oxford University Press, 1970). Unionist support in pre– and post–Civil War Texas is covered in Dale Baum, *The Shattering of Texas Unionism: Politics in the Lone Star State during the Civil War Era* (Baton Rouge: Louisiana State University Press, 1998).

2. Kenneth Wayne Howell, *Texas Confederate, Reconstruction Governor: James Webb Throckmorton* (College Station: Texas A&M University Press, 2008).

3. Carl H. Moneyhon, *Republicanism in Reconstruction Texas* (Austin: University of Texas Press, 1980), 49. During the nineteenth century, the terms *radical, conservative,* and *liberal* took on varying meanings as the issues and times dictated. Thus Elisha Pease is at times described as a radical Unionist and later as a conservative Republican. It would be incorrect to associate such terms with current twenty-first-century usage. Nevertheless, there is no easy way to avoid using them to describe the various factions and elements competing for dominance in the new Republican Party of the time.

4. Randolph B. Campbell, *Grass-Roots Reconstruction in Texas, 1865–1880* (Baton Rouge: Louisiana State University Press, 1997), 10.

5. James A. Baggett, "Birth of the Texas Republican Party," *Southwestern Historical Quarterly* 78, no. 1 (July 1974), 10.

6. Ibid., 13.

7. Moneyhon, *Republicanism,* 57.

8. Paul Casdorph, *A History of the Republican Party in Texas, 1865–1965* (Austin, TX: Pemberton Press, 1965), 4–5. There is uncertainty as to how many participated in this initial convention. According to Paul Casdorph, twenty whites and 150 African-Americans from twenty-seven counties participated in the convention. However, Carl Moneyhon claims that about six hundred people from twenty-one counties attended the convention (Moneyhon, *Republicanism,* 65).

9. Carl H. Moneyhon, "Texas Out-Radicals My Radicalism," in *The Texas Left: The*

Radical Roots of Lone Star Liberalism, ed. David O'Donald Cullen and Kyle G. Wilkison (College Station: Texas A&M University Press, 2010), 25–26.

10. Foner, *Free Soil*.

11. Moneyhon, *Republicanism*, 80.

12. Randolph B. Campbell, *Gone to Texas: A History of the Lone Star State* (New York: Oxford University Press, 2003), 274.

13. Moneyhon, *Republicanism*, 103.

14. Campbell, *Gone*, 241, 271–273. The Democratic candidate was Galveston publisher Hamilton Stuart. Stuart received 380 of the nearly eighty thousand votes cast in the election. Charles W. Ramsdell, *Reconstruction in Texas* (New York: Columbia University, 1910), 286. See also Ben C. Stuart, "Hamilton Stuart: Pioneer Editor," *Southwestern Historical Quarterly* 21, no. 4 (April 1918), 381–388.

15. Carl H. Moneyhon, *Edmund J. Davis of Texas: Civil War General, Republican Leader, Reconstruction Governor* (Fort Worth: TCU Press, 2010).

16. Moneyhon, *Republicanism*, 123. According to Randolph Campbell, whites made up 56 percent of all eligible voters but turned out at a much lower rate than African-Americans in the 1869 election. Campbell, *Gone*, 280.

17. These dates became important when Davis was defeated for re-election in 1873. Davis and his supporters maintained that the four-year term to which he had been elected did not begin until April 1870 when civil government was restored, and therefore his term would not end until April 1874.

18. Campbell, *Gone*, 281. Examples of such violence and Davis's concern are discussed in Moneyhon, *Edmund J. Davis*, 119–121. For violence against African-Americans attempting to vote, see Moneyhon, *Republicanism*, 78–79, 123–124.

19. Moneyhon, *Edmund J. Davis*, 163.

20. Campbell, *Gone*, 282–283.

21. Moneyhon, *Republicanism*, 130.

22. T. R. Fehrenbach, *Lone Star: A History of Texas and the Texans* (New York: Collier, 1968), 417. This period is covered throughout pp. 409–432 in a chapter titled "The Carpetbaggers."

23. Such a position is reflected in Campbell, *Grass-Roots Reconstruction*, and Moneyhon, *Republicanism*.

24. Gregg Cantrell, p. x in Moneyhon, *Edmund J. Davis*.

25. Moneyhon, *Republicanism*, 166–167.

26. Texan participation in the Liberal Republican convention is covered in Casdorph, *History*, 20–23. See also Earle Dudley Ross: *The Liberal Republican Movement* (1923; reprint, Red Lion, PA: Ulan, 2012). The Liberal Republican movement was a one-off effort, and "although they would still oppose Davis, and factions would be formed that would persist in later years, most of the Liberals returned to the ranks of the regular party after 1872" (Moneyhon, *Republicanism*, 177).

27. Casdorph, *History*, 27–28.

28. Casdorph, *History*, 23–27. Speaking of Webster Flanagan, Casdorph maintains that "until his death in 1924, he was a power in the Texas Republican Party" (40). See also

Dale A. Somers, "James P. Newcomb: The Making of a Radical," *The Southwestern Historical Quarterly* 72, no. 4 (April 1969), 449–469. Ruby and Cuney are discussed in Merline Pitre, *Through Many Dangers, Toils, and Snares: Black Leadership in Texas, 1870–1890*, 2nd revised edition (Austin, TX: Eakin, 1997). See also Carl H. Moneyhon, *George T. Ruby: Champion of Equal Rights in Reconstruction Texas* (Fort Worth: TCU Press, 2020).

29. Moneyhon, *Edmund J. Davis*, 215.

30. Moneyhon, *Republicanism*, 181–182.

31. Casdorph, *History*, 28.

32. Campbell, *Gone*, 284.

33. Moneyhon, *Edmund J. Davis*, 216.

34. Moneyhon, *Republicanism*, 185.

35. Casdorph, *History*, 28.

36. Fehrenbach, *Lone Star*, 429.

37. Casdorph, *History*, 29.

38. Moneyhon, *Republicanism*, 189.

39. Campbell, *Gone*, 284.

40. Fehrenbach, *Lone Star*, 429. For a discussion of the Democratic Party's return to power, see Patrick G. Williams: *Beyond Redemption: Texas Democrats after Reconstruction* (College Station: Texas A&M University Press, 2007).

41. There are varying reports on the actual vote count, ranging from 85,549 to 42,663 (Campbell, *Gone*, 284) to 98,906 to 51,049 (*Congressional Quarterly Guide to U.S. Elections* [Washington, DC: Congressional Quarterly, 1975], 431) to 100,415 to 52,151 (Moneyhon, *Republicanism*, 219–223). Moneyhon is the only one to provide county-by-county returns reporting total votes counted for both candidates.

42. Campbell, *Grass-Roots Reconstruction*, 24–25; Casdorph, *History*, 29–31.

43. Moneyhon, *Republicanism*, 192–194.

44. Somers, "James B. Newcomb," 468.

45. Michael Lind, *Made in Texas* (New York: Basic Books, 2003), 5.

46. Fehrenbach, *Lone Star*, 434–437, discusses the 1876 constitutional convention.

47. Campbell, *Grass-Roots Reconstruction*, 26.

48. Moneyhon, *Republicanism*, 194.

49. Republican Party of Texas website, "Overview and History," www.texasgop.org /overview-and-history, accessed on September 23, 2011.

50. Paul D. Casdorph, *Republicans, Negroes, and Progressives in the South, 1912–1916* (University, AL: University of Alabama Press, 1981), 1. Casdorph is quoting here from W. J. Cash, *The Mind of the South* (New York: Alfred A. Knopf, 1944), 129.

51. Roscoe Martin, *The People's Party in Texas* (1933; reprint, Austin: University of Texas Press, 1970), 16.

52. Moneyhon, *Edmund J. Davis*, 233.

53. For a profile of Cuney, his slave-owning father, and his talented daughter, see Douglas Hales, *A Southern Family in White and Black* (College Station: Texas A&M University Press, 2002).

54. Hanes Walton Jr., *Black Republicans: The Politics of the Black and Tans* (Metuchen,

NJ: Scarecrow, 1975), 63–64; Alwyn Barr, "Black Legislators of Reconstruction Texas," *Civil War History* 32, no. 4 (December 1986), 340–352.

55. Moneyhon, *Edmund J. Davis*, 225.

56. Campbell, *Gone*, 316. A valuable profile of Cuney and his leadership is found in William Reynolds Sanford, "History of the Republican Party in the State of Texas," Master's thesis, University of Texas, 1954, 33–34, 37–54; the Lily White movement is discussed on pp. 61–68.

57. For the machinations and intrigue of the various Republican state and national conventions of the nineteenth and early twentieth centuries, see Casdorph, *History*, where this information is spelled out in great detail; "A Hot Fight on in Texas," *New York Times*, September 7, 1892.

58. Fehrenbach, *Lone Star*, 438.

59. Evan Anders, *Boss Rule in South Texas* (Austin: University of Texas Press, 1982), 29. Anders provides an important overview of turn-of-the-century Republican politics in the Rio Grande Valley, especially in Cameron, Duval, and Starr counties, on pp. 26–41.

60. From 1860 to 1912, Republicans controlled the presidency for all but the two nonconsecutive terms of Grover Cleveland (1885–1889; 1893–1897).

61. Paul Douglas Casdorph, "Texas Delegations to Republican National Conventions, 1860–1896," Master's thesis, University of Texas at Austin, 1961), 128.

62. Martin, *People's Party*, 265. As Martin states, "The writer distinctly remembers the day not many years ago when, in a county in East Texas, his grandfather pointed out to him a citizen who looked like other men but who was set apart by virtue of his political beliefs. He was a Republican, the only white one in that part of the county."

63. The 1896 state convention where national convention delegates were selected is discussed in Karl Rove, *The Triumph of William McKinley* (New York: Simon & Schuster, 2015), 168–172.

64. Hales, *Southern Family*, 90.

65. Quoted in Hales, *Southern Family*, 91.

66. Rove, *Triumph*, 169.

67. Casdorph, *History*, 69.

68. Sanford, "History," 70.

2. THE EARLY-TWENTIETH-CENTURY REPUBLICANS

1. Much of the material in this chapter relies on two highly valuable works by Paul D. Casdorph. He is the author of both *A History of The Republican Party in Texas, 1865–1965* (Austin: Pemberton Press, 1965), and *Republicans, Negroes, and Progressives in the South, 1912–1916* (University, AL: University of Alabama Press, 1981). Also helpful for the later period is Roger M. Olien, *From Token to Triumph: The Texas Republicans since 1920* (Dallas: SMU Press, 1982).

2. The ability to deliver the Republican vote in Zapata County was overwhelming and would impress the leaders of the Tammany Hall machine in New York City. Republican

presidential candidates carried Zapata County by margins of 462 to 102 (1900), 369 to 28 (1904), 424 to 0 (1908), 199 to 0 (1912), and 214 to 26 (1916).

3. Evan Anders, *Boss Rule in South Texas* (Austin: University of Texas Press, 1982). In most parts of the state Republican competition had died out before the beginning of the twentieth century. According to Carl Moneyhon, "the collapse of the Republican county officials before violence in Fort Bend County in 1888 marked the fall of one of the last local party strongholds in the state." Moneyhon, *Republicanism in Reconstruction Texas* (Austin: University of Texas Press, 1980), 194.

4. "110 Years (1888–1998) of Mexican-American Republican Politics in Starr County," undated monograph, obtained from Araceli Perez-Hinojosa Davis, great-great-granddaughter of Don Lino Hinojosa. In author's possession.

5. C. P. Alvarez to Clinton S. Bailey, July 8, 1924. Much of the material on early Republican efforts in the Rio Grande Valley was obtained from Araceli Perez-Hinojosa Davis, granddaughter of Casimiro P. Alvarez and an active Republican following in the footsteps of her Hispanic Republican ancestors. Interview with Araceli Davis, San Antonio, February 5, 2015. In author's possession.

6. Chandler Davidson, *Race and Class in Texas Politics* (Princeton, NJ: Princeton University Press, 1990), 21.

7. Moneyhon, *Republicanism*, 194.

8. *Smith v. Allwright*, 321 US 649 (1944).

9. Olien, *From Token to Triumph*, 24. When the party held a strategy meeting in 1926, for example, it was called for two days prior to the convening of the annual state postmasters convention.

10. Casdorph, *History*, 75.

11. Anders, *Boss Rule*, 114.

12. Brian Hart, "Lyon, Cecil Andrew," *Handbook of Texas Online* (tshaonline.org/handbook/online/articles/fly07), accessed April 15, 2013. Published by the Texas State Historical Association.

13. Casdorph, *History*, 80.

14. Casdorph, *Republicans*, 8.

15. Ibid., 2.

16. Recollections of Hobart Huson, July 2, 1962, Jack Cox Papers, 1950–1964, Dolph Briscoe Center for American History, University of Texas at Austin, box 4zd329.

17. Casdorph, *Republicans*, 63.

18. Ibid., 61.

19. Undated news clipping, "MacGregor Claims Texas Will Send Solid Taft Vote," *San Antonio Express*, Eugene Nolte Family Papers, 1886–1964, MS 34, University of Texas at San Antonio Libraries Special Collection.

20. Lewis W. Gould, "Theodore Roosevelt, William Howard Taft, and the Disputed Delegates in 1912: Texas as a Test Case," *Southwestern Historical Quarterly*, 80 (1976), 43.

21. Two recent works discuss the 1912 campaign nationally and are informative regarding the political climate of the time: James Chace, *1912: Wilson, Roosevelt, Taft, and Debs—The Election that Changed the Country* (New York: Simon & Schuster, 2004), and

Lewis W. Gould, *Four Hats in the Ring: The 1912 Election and the Birth of Modern American Politics* (Lawrence: University Press of Kansas, 2008). Debs was the Socialist Party candidate for president from 1900 to 1912 and again in 1920. In the 1912 election, Debs obtained 8.3 percent of the vote in Texas, less than two thousand votes behind Roosevelt and four thousand votes behind Taft.

22. Casdorph, *History*, 100–104.

23. Casdorph, *Republicans*, 143.

24. Casdorph, *History*, 104.

25. Casdorph, *Republicans*, 144–145.

26. Casdorph, *History*, 107.

27. Casdorph, *Republicans*, 170.

28. Casdorph, *History*, 115.

29. William Reynolds Sanford, "History of the Republican Party in the State of Texas" (M. A. thesis, University of Texas, 1954), 97.

30. Anders, *Boss Rule*, 246.

31. Olien, *From Token to Triumph*, 5–7.

32. Sanford, "History," 97–98.

33. Casdorph, *History*, 118.

34. Norman D. Brown, *Hood, Bonnet, and Little Brown Jug: Texas Politics, 1921–1928* (College Station: Texas A&M University Press, 1984), 122.

35. Olien, *From Token to Triumph*, 6–7.

3. CREAGER AND WURZBACH

1. For most of the decade of the 1920s, while Republicans held the White House and control of Congress, Wurzbach was one of only three Republicans in Congress (contrasted with 123 Democrats) from the eleven states formerly part of the Confederacy.

2. Casdorph, *A History of the Republican Party in Texas, 1865–1965* (Austin, TX: Pemberton Press, 1965), 119.

3. Ibid., 123.

4. Sherman C. Kile to Senator Harry New, January 23, 1921, Harry McLeary Wurzbach Papers, 1853–1984, Dolph Briscoe Center for American History, University of Texas at Austin.

5. Paul D. Casdorph, "Creager, Rentfro Banton," *Handbook of Texas Online*, tshaonline.org/handbook/online/articles/fcr15, accessed April 23, 2013; "Harding Arrives at Port Isabel," *New York Times*, November 8, 1920.

6. Norman D. Brown, *Hood, Bonnet, and Little Brown Jug: Texas Politics, 1921–1928* (College Station: Texas A&M University Press, 1984), 122.

7. Harry Wurzbach to W. A. Atwell, October 7, 1921, Wurzbach Papers.

8. Roger M. Olien, *From Token to Triumph: The Texas Republicans since 1920* (Dallas: SMU Press, 1982), 33.

9. Harry Wurzbach to W. M. Hanson, January 10, 1922, Wurzbach Papers.

10. Harry Wurzbach to Captain Sherman C. Kile, March 18, 1922, Wurzbach Papers.

11. Harry Wurzbach to H. E. Dickinson, June 12, 1922, Wurzbach Papers.

12. Olien, *From Token to Triumph*, 33–34.

13. In a letter seeking financial support for Wurzbach's re-election, Captain W. M. Hanson wrote to W. J. Allen of Tyler, asking him to "write McDonald and have him send it to you, for I sent it to him," referring to the original Wurzbach speech before the black audience in Washington. McDonald is a reference to William "Gooseneck Bill" McDonald, a leader of the Black and Tan faction and associate of E. H. R. Green, millionaire former state chairman. The appeal concludes: "Can't you boys get together and get Mr. E. H. R. Green to daddy this fight? If so, we will place him where he belongs in Texas politics." W. M. Hanson to W. J. Allen, May 12, 1922, Wurzbach Papers.

14. Olien, *From Token to Triumph*, 34. Given that his opponent was Jewish, Wurzbach may have been engaging in an appeal to religious prejudice in his response defending his position against the lynching of blacks.

15. Olien discusses the matter in some detail in *From Token to Triumph*, 34–36.

16. Harry Wurzbach to M. R. Hall, December 11, 1925, Wurzbach Papers.

17. Harry Wurzbach to W. A. Fitch, May 5, 1922, Wurzbach Papers.

18. Gary Keith, *Eckhardt: There Once Was a Congressman from Texas* (Austin: University of Texas Press, 2007), 29.

19. Casdorph, *A History*, 133–136. See also Donald J. Lisio, *Hoover, Blacks, and Lily-Whites* (Chapel Hill: University of North Carolina Press, 1985), 60.

20. Rentfro B. Creager to P. G. Lucas, August 16, 1922, Wurzbach Papers.

21. W. M. Hanson telegram to R. B. Creager, October 5, 1922; Harry Wurzbach to H. F. MacGregor, December 14, 1922, Wurzbach Papers.

22. "Little Fight Develops in G.O.P. Ranks," *Dallas Morning News*, undated news clipping, Eugene Nolte Family Papers, 1886–1964, MS34, University of Texas at San Antonio Libraries Special Collection.

23. Olien, *From Token to Triumph*, 36–37. "Texas Land Cases Heard by Senators," *New York Times*, March 25, 1924; "Texas Land Frauds Alleged by Buyers," *New York Times*, April 1, 1924.

24. Concerning the intraparty disputes, Wurzbach was told in 1924, "You have changed Scobey, who now is strong for you." Dr. J. H. Bindley to Harry Wurzbach, February 21, 1924, Wurzbach Papers. Creager's standing with both the Harding and Coolidge administrations was substantial, and he was twice offered the position of ambassador to Mexico. Apparently concluding there was less patronage to be dispensed by an ambassador in Mexico City, Creager turned the appointments down. "Creager Declines Mexican Embassy," *New York Times*, December 16, 1923.

25. Real's senatorial district in 1924 comprised Bexar, Kendall, Kerr, and Bandera counties, with the largest vote coming from San Antonio. He had previously served from 1909 to 1915 as the sole Republican in the Texas Senate, a uniqueness he would have again from 1925 to 1929.

26. Brown, *Hood*, 211–252, covers the 1924 primary and general election for governor in detail.

27. Lee of Houston had originally been nominated by the Republican state convention in August before the Democratic runoff but withdrew a few days later after making remarks supportive of Ma Ferguson and questioning the chances of any Republican candidate to win the election.

28. Casdorph, *History*, 129–130.

29. Brown, *Hood*, 246.

30. William Reynolds Sanford, "History of the Republican Party in the State of Texas," Master's thesis, University of Texas, 1954, 144. C. M. Hughes to Eugene Nolte, December 18, 1924, Nolte Family Papers.

31. Brown, *Hood*, 251.

32. R. B. Creager to Mrs. J. C. Griswold, October 27, 1925, Nolte Family Papers.

33. Kristi Throne Strickland, "The Significance and Impact of Women on the Rise of the Republican Party in Twentieth Century Texas," PhD diss., University of North Texas, August 2000, 95.

34. R. B. Creager to Mrs. J. C. Griswold, October 27, 1925, Nolte Family Papers.

35. Harry Wurzbach to C. H. Donegan, January 30, 1926, Wurzbach Papers.

36. Harry Wurzbach to Alvin J. Wirtz, February 14, 1926, Wurzbach Papers. Wirtz was a partner in the Seguin law firm of Wurzbach, Wirtz, and Weinert and served as a Democrat in the Texas Senate from 1923 to 1931 before moving to Austin. Wirtz was subsequently a close associate of Lyndon Johnson and was involved in Johnson's 1941 and 1948 Senate races. He represented Johnson before the canvassing subcommittee of the Democratic state executive committee, helping to secure Johnson's eighty-seven-vote primary victory. Michael L. Willette, "Wirtz, Alvin Jacob," Handbook of Texas Online, tshaonline.org /handbook/online/articles/fwi70, accessed May 4, 2013.

37. Frank Scobey to Harry Wurzbach, February 27, 1926, Wurzbach Papers.

38. "Speech of Hon. Harry M. Wurzbach of Texas in the House of Representatives, Wednesday, March 3, 1926," *Congressional Record*, 69th Congress, First Session, Wurzbach Papers.

39. "Patronage of GOP in South Is Assailed," *Washington Post*, March 4, 1926; "Assail Republicans on Jobs in South," *New York Times*, March 4, 1926.

40. "Reply to Wurzbach Is Sent to Butler," *San Antonio Express*, March 8, 1926; "Texas Republicans Deny Corruption," *New York Times*, March 8, 1926.

41. "House Republicans Rebuke Texas Party," *New York Times*, March 13, 1926; "Warns Texas Party to Back Wurzbach—Tilden Protests against War on the State's Only Republican Representative," *New York Times*, March 17, 1926.

42. Henry E. Barbour to Leonard Withington, March 15, 1926, Wurzbach Papers.

43. Brown, *Hood*, 336.

44. "Wurzbach Plans State-wide Fight: Complete Turnover of Present Texas G.O.P. Organization Proposed," *San Antonio Express*, March 21, 1926.

45. Brown, *Hood*, 336–337.

46. "Knetsch Out for Wurzbach Seat," *San Antonio Express*, May 2, 1926; "An Opponent for Wurzbach is Announced," *Houston Post-Dispatch*, May 2, 1926. After losing the Republican nomination as Creager's candidate for Congress, Knetsch would be elected to the Texas House of Representatives and serve two terms from 1935 to 1939 as a Democrat.

47. Harry Wurzbach to Frank E. Scobey, May 4, 1926, Wurzbach Papers.

48. Telegram from Robert Coon to J. M. Hoopes, June 18, 1926, Wurzbach Papers.

49. "Angry Delegate Tries to Assassinate Wurzbach," *Dallas Dispatch*, June 22, 1926. The following night Wurzbach's campaign manager, A. A. Luter, was found unconscious and claimed to have been attacked by two masked men. Olien, *From Token to Triumph*, 39. Another fight broke out on primary night when "a free-for-all started in which numerous blows were exchanged and even the ladies got into the fray." Casdorph, *History*, 131.

50. Olien, *From Token to Triumph*, 41.

51. "Knetsch Challenges Wurzbach to Announce How He Will Vote in Fall if He Loses Nomination," *San Antonio Express*, July 21, 1926.

52. Casdorph, *History*, 131–132. Creager was also involved in a dispute closer to home when a number of transplanted farmers in Hidalgo County attempted to overthrow the political machine of Sheriff A. Y. Baker. Baker used political pressure with Creager to have him reject the county convention held by the farmers and recognize one made up of those pledged to inactivity. Sanford, "History," 130–132.

53. "An Historic Example of Devotion to Principle," undated report from Republican State Headquarters, Dallas, Texas, Nolte Family Papers.

54. Frank Scobey to Fred J. Cutting, November 30, 1926, Wurzbach Papers.

55. Harry Wurzbach to Tom J. Darling, December 25, 1926, Wurzbach Papers.

56. Amity Shlaes, *Coolidge* (New York: HarperCollins, 2013), 381–386.

57. Shlaes, *Coolidge*, 397.

58. Brown, *Hood*, 397.

59. News release from R. B. Creager dated December 9, 1927, Nolte Family Papers.

60. "Creager Leadership Threatened," *Houston Post-Dispatch*, undated editorial, Nolte Family Papers.

61. R. B. Creager to Eugene Nolte, January 2, 1928, Nolte Family Papers.

62. "Texas G.O.P. Leaders Out for Hoover," *Dallas Daily Times-Herald*, January 16, 1928.

63. Frank Scobey to Harry Wurzbach, February 8, 1928, Wurzbach Papers.

64. Frank Scobey to Charles Dawes, quoted in Brown, *Hood*, 397–398.

65. "Wurzbach's Trip to Dallas Seen as Presaging Bitter G.O.P. Fight over Kansas City Delegates," *San Antonio Express*, February 10, 1928.

66. "Wurzbach Delegates to Be Unseated, Creager Announces in Telling of Convention Plans," *San Antonio Express*, undated news clipping, Nolte Family Papers.

67. Sanford, "History," 111.

68. Houston Jones to C. P. Alvarez, July 19, 1924: "I will greatly appreciate your naming me as alternate delegate, . . . and I will take pleasure in representing your County in case your delegate should be unable to attend." Jones was a state executive committee member

from Hidalgo County, and Alvarez was Starr County Republican chairman. Copy of letter in author's possession; provided by Araceli Perez-Hinojosa Davis.

69. "Hoover Foes Bolt Texas Convention," *New York Times*, May 23, 1928.

70. Brown, *Hood*, 398.

71. Casdorph, *History*, 133–134.

72. *San Antonio Express*, June 7, 1928. The legal brief submitted by the uninstructed-delegation forces can be found in the Wurzbach Papers; the supporting brief for the Creager delegation is located in the Nolte Family Papers. While both make interesting legal points, their relevance to the committee's final decision is, at best, slight.

73. Richard B. Sherman, *The Republican Party and Black America from McKinley to Hoover, 1896–1933* (Charlottesville: University Press of Virginia, 1973), 229.

74. "Wurzbach Delegates to Be Unseated, Creager Announces in Telling of Convention Plans," *San Antonio Express*, undated news clipping, Nolte Family Papers.

75. Lisio, *Hoover*, 60.

76. "Hoover Men Win Credentials Fights," *New York Times*, June 13, 1928.

77. "Texas Delegates Confederate Sons," *New York Times*, June 10, 1928.

78. Lisio, *Hoover*, 57–60.

79. Casdorph, *History*, 136.

80. "O'Hara Group for Al Smith," *Dallas Morning News*, July 17, 1928.

81. T. R. Fehrenbach, *Lone Star: A History of Texas and the Texans* (New York: Collier, 1968), 649–650.

82. Rentfro B. Creager to Lawrence Richey, Republican National Committee, December 14, 1928. Norman D. Brown Collection, 1921–1933, Dolph Briscoe Center for American History, University of Texas at Austin.

83. Olien, *From Token to Triumph*, 47–48.

84. Ibid., 47.

85. Harry Wurzbach to Franklin W. Fort, September 5, 1928, Wurzbach Papers.

86. Harry Wurzbach to Will R. Wood, September 12, 1928, Wurzbach Papers.

87. Telegram from Harry Wurzbach to James W. Good, Republican National Committee, October 31, 1928, Wurzbach Papers.

88. Sanford, "History," 129; Olien, *From Token to Triumph*, 48–52. The numbers changed frequently after the election. According to Paul Casdorph, "The unofficial tally gave the edge to Wurzbach 29,808 to 29,381. The official returns gave the election to McCloskey 29,762 to 29,085 votes for Wurzbach." Casdorph, *History*, 137.

89. "Jury Indicts Texan Elected to House; McCloskey, Victor over Wurzbach, Charged with Altering Count of Ballots," *New York Times*, December 5, 1928.

90. "McCloskey-Wurzbach Returns Altered, State Witness Says; Adds, 'I Entered False Records,'" *Dallas Morning News*, February 23, 1929.

91. A detailed analysis of the changes in precinct returns in Bexar County can be found in Box 2.325 of the Wurzbach Papers.

92. "McCloskey Gives Up, Election Is Conceded Wurzbach: Democrat Denies Fraud in Surrendering to Foe," *San Antonio Light*, February 3, 1930.

93. "Texas Dry Raid Ban Laid to R. B. Creager," *New York Times*, January 30, 1929.

94. "Says Political Jobs Cost Texans $200,000," *New York Times*, February 17, 1929.

95. "Wurzbach Pins Job Barter on G.O.P. in Texas," *Houston Post-Dispatch*, February 18, 1929.

96. Irvin S. Taubkin, "Texas G.O.P. Unhurt by Senate Inquiry," *New York Times*, February 24, 1929.

97. Mark L. Goodwin, "Wurzbach Took Money from U.S. Employee Is Charge of Creager," *Dallas Morning News*, March 2, 1929.

98. "Links Texas Funds with Patronage—Creager Accuses Representative Wurzbach of Taking Federal Employees' Gifts," *New York Times*, March 2, 1929.

99. "Creager Refuses to Reveal Involvement of Wurzbach Case," *San Antonio Express*, March 4, 1929.

100. "Patronage Gifts Bared in Affidavits," *New York Times*, April 6, 1929.

101. Sanford, "History," 125–126.

102. Telegram from R. B. Creager to Lawrence Richey, April 13, 1929, Brown Collection.

103. *United States v. Wurzbach* 280 US 396 (1930). "Holds Indictment of Wurzbach Valid—Supreme Court Says Corrupt Practices Act Applies to the Primary Campaign Funds," *New York Times*, February 25, 1930.

104. "R. B. Creager Defies Patronage Inquiry," *New York Times*, June 30, 1929.

105. "Patronage Probe at Dallas Ends," *Dallas Morning News*, July 2, 1929.

106. Lisio, *Hoover*, 170–171.

107. Ibid., 177.

108. Sanford, "History," 106.

109. William P. Shepard, "Getting a Job for Jack," *Collier's*, June 15, 1929, 8.

110. Owen P. White, "High Handed and Hell Bent," *Collier's*, June 22, 1929, 14.

111. Casdorph, *History*, 137–138; Sanford, "History," 130–132.

112. "Creager Loses Suit against Collier's, Republican Leader in Texas Sought $500,000 Damages for Story in Magazine," *New York Times*, May 16, 1930.

113. "Federal Job Sales Scored by Senators; Prosecution Asked," *New York Times*, March 16, 1930.

114. Harry Wurzbach to Anderson Jones, February 17, 1930, Wurzbach Papers.

115. Response from Harry Wurzbach to letter from W. M. Corley, February 19, 1930, Wurzbach Papers.

116. "20,000 at Funeral of H. M. Wurzbach—San Antonio Pays Final Tribute to Lone Republican Congressman of Texas," *New York Times*, November 9, 1931.

117. Hobart Huson Recollections, Cox Papers, 1950–1964, Dolph Briscoe Center for American History, University of Texas at Austin.

4. FROM ROOSEVELT TO TRUMAN

1. According to Hanes Walton Jr., "Black and Tan Republicanism came to an end in Texas in 1928" (*Black Republicans: The Politics of the Black and Tans* [Metuchen, NJ: Scarecrow, 1975], 66). See also Richard B. Sherman, *The Republican Party and Black America*

from McKinley to Hoover, 1896–1933 (Charlottesville: University Press of Virginia, 1973). In 1928, for the first time in their history, Texas Republicans sent an all-white delegation headed by Creager to the national convention. "Texas Delegates Confederate Sons," *New York Times*, June 10, 1928.

2. Jan Jarboe, "Lord of the Valley," *Texas Monthly*, January 1986, 232.

3. Paul Casdorph, *A History of the Republican Party in Texas, 1865–1965* (Austin, TX: Pemberton Press, 1965), 144. See also O. Douglas Weeks, "Texas: Land of Conservative Expansiveness," in *The Changing Politics of the South*, ed. William C. Havard (Baton Rouge: Louisiana State University Press, 1972), 209.

4. Roger M. Olien, *From Token to Triumph: The Texas Republicans since 1920* (Dallas: SMU Press, 1982), 64.

5. "R. B. Creager Bankrupt," *New York Times*, May 18, 1935.

6. George H. Mayer, *The Republican Party, 1854–1966*, 2nd edition (New York: Oxford University Press, 1967), 440–441.

7. Casdorph, *History*, 145.

8. V. O. Key Jr., *Southern Politics in State and Nation* (New York: Vintage Books, 1949), 293.

9. Mayer, *Republican Party*, 448.

10. Charles R. Michael, "Hoover Men Press for '38 Convention," *New York Times*, November 7, 1937.

11. Mayer, *Republican Party*, 448–449.

12. "Reported Seeking Hoover Delegates," *New York Times*, April 12, 1939.

13. Casdorph, *History*, 151. The surprising nomination of Willkie is covered in Charles Peters, *Five Days in Philadelphia: The Amazing "We Want Willke!" Convention of 1940 and How It Freed FDR to Save the Western World* (Washington, DC: Public Affairs, 2006).

14. George Norris Green, *The Establishment in Texas Politics: The Primitive Years, 1938–1957* (Westport, CT: Greenwood, 1979), 30. See also James A. Tinsley, "The Progressive Movement in Texas," PhD diss., University of Wisconsin at Madison, 1953. Copy in Ann Fears Crawford Papers, Woodson Research Center, Fondren Library, Rice University, Houston, TX, box 2, folder 1.

15. James H. Madison, *Wendell Willkie: Hoosier Interventionist* (Bloomington: Indiana University Press, 1992). The events of the first month of American involvement are presented chronologically in Craig Shirley, *December 1941: 31 Days That Changed America and Saved the World* (Nashville: Thomas Nelson, 2011).

16. Wendell Willkie, *One World* (New York: Simon & Schuster, 1943).

17. Wendell Willkie to Eugene Nolte Jr., March 2, 1944, Eugene Nolte Family Papers, 1886–1964, MS 34, University of Texas at San Antonio Libraries Special Collection.

18. John W. Bricker to Eugene Nolte Jr., May 29, 1944, Nolte Family Papers.

19. Michael Bowen, *The Roots of Modern Conservatism: Dewey, Taft, and the Battle for the Soul of the Republican Party* (Chapel Hill: University of North Carolina Press, 2011), 64.

20. Casdorph, *History*, 157. For a profile on Dewey, see Richard Norton Smith, *Thomas E. Dewey and His Times* (New York: Simon & Schuster, 1982).

21. "Roosevelt Forces Outvoted in Texas; Bolt Convention," *New York Times*, May 24, 1944.

22. "Texas Furnishes the Fireworks, Some of 'Regulars' Walk Out When 'Rump' Group Is Also Seated and Vote Divided," *New York Times*, July 21, 1944.

23. "'Texas Regulars' File Democratic Electors," *New York Times*, September 26, 1944.

24. Allen Duckworth, "Coalition with Dissatisfied Democrats Sought by Republicans, but Deals Fail," *Dallas Morning News*, September 23, 1944.

25. "Creager Says Coalition May Be Formed," *New York Times*, September 28, 1944.

26. Olien, *From Token to Triumph*, 84–85; Casdorph, *History*, 159–160.

27. William Reynolds Sanford, "History of the Republican Party in the State of Texas," Master's thesis, University of Texas, 1954, 149–162, covers the Texas Regulars–Republican relationship in great detail.

28. Olien, *From Token to Triumph*, 92.

29. "Sells and Mike Nolte Top Texas G.O.P. Candidates," *San Antonio Express*, August 15, 1946.

30. Olien, *From Token to Triumph*, 88–94.

31. "Fight Was 'Rough,' Says San Antonian," *San Antonio Express*, August 15, 1946.

32. "Nolte Promised Creager Aid in State Race; No Bitterness Says GOP Leader after Setback," undated news release, Nolte Family Papers.

33. Statement of November 4, 1946, by Eugene "Mike" Nolte Jr., Nolte Family Papers.

34. Casdorph, *History*, 135; Olien, *From Token to Triumph*, 94–99.

35. "Nolte Assails G.O.P. Clubbers," undated news clipping, Nolte Family Papers.

36. "Sheldon Ousted as G.O.P. Chairman; Hotchkin Elected," *San Antonio Express*, April 10, 1947.

37. "Old Guard Triumphs in State GOP Fight," *Daily Times Herald* (Dallas), July 30, 1947.

38. "'Let Them Come On,' Says GOP Old Guard," *Daily Times Herald* (Dallas), September 9, 1947; Allen Duckworth, "GOP Rebels Pledge War on Old Guard, Ouster of Hopkins and Creager Aim of Insurgents," *Dallas Morning News*, September 9, 1947.

39. "Lane Moves for Showdown in State Republican Dispute," *Dallas Morning News*, September 12, 1947.

40. Everett Collier, "Texas G.O.P. Leader Urges United Front against Democrats," *Houston Chronicle*, September 14, 1947.

41. Jim Carroll, "Creager Spikes GOP Hopes, Infiltration by 'Outsiders' Defied," *Houston Press*, October 11, 1947.

42. Olien, *From Token to Triumph*, 98.

43. Warren Moscow, "Stassen Chances Improve in Texas," *New York Times*, November 18, 1947.

44. Bowen, *Roots*, 65.

45. Olien, *From Token to Triumph*, 99–101.

46. Key, *Southern Politics*, 295.

47. James A. Hagerty, "GOP Lead Disputed as Taft Vote Rises," *New York Times*, May 31, 1948.

48. Michael Bowen, "The First Southern Strategy: The Taft and the Dewey/Eisenhower Factions in the GOP," in *Painting Dixie Red*, ed. Glenn Feldman (Gainesville: University Press of Florida, 2011).

49. Allen Duckworth, "Republicans Meet in Waco," *Dallas Morning News*, August 8, 1948.

50. Texas gave little support to the Thurmond candidacy. The divisions among conservative Democrats are discussed in Kari Frederickson, *The Dixiecrat Revolt and the End of the Solid South, 1932–1968* (Chapel Hill: The University of North Carolina Press, 2001).

51. Allen Duckworth, "Hopkins Comes Up Short at GOP Meet," *Dallas Morning News*, August 9, 1948.

52. Duckworth, "Hopkins."

53. 1948 Republican State Convention, Waco, in Allen Duckworth Papers, 1944–1962, Dolph Briscoe Center for American History, University of Texas at Austin.

54. Bryan Burrough, *The Big Rich: The Rise and Fall of the Greatest Texas Oil Fortunes* (New York: Penguin, 2009), 206.

55. Ibid., 204–208.

56. T. R. Fehrenbach, *Lone Star: A History of Texas and the Texans* (New York: Collier, 1968), 659.

57. According to one writer, Stevenson's loss helped start the movement to the Republican Party among some conservatives. Stevenson subsequently endorsed Eisenhower and Nixon for president. By 1962 Stevenson was voting in the Republican primary. Robert Bryce, *Cronies: Oil, the Bushes, and the Rise of Texas, America's Superstate* (New York: Public Affairs, 2004), 64–65.

58. The 1948 campaign is richly covered in David Pietrusza, *1948: Harry Truman's Improbable Victory and the Year that Transformed America* (New York: Union Square Press, 2011).

59. Wayne Thorburn, *Red State: An Insider's Story of How the GOP Came to Dominate Texas Politics* (Austin: University of Texas Press, 2014), 100-106.

60. Clayton Knowles, "Three Groups Fight for Control of the Party," *New York Times*, July 24, 1949.

61. Olien, *From Token to Triumph*, 109.

62. "Victory in Texas Elates the G.O.P.," *New York Times*, May 8, 1950.

63. Bowen, *Roots*, 63–64.

64. Key, *Southern Politics*, 295.

5. THE EISENHOWER YEARS

1. For a more thorough discussion of the 1952 presidential campaign, see Michael Bowen, *The Roots of Modern Conservatism: Dewey, Taft, and the Battle for the Soul of the Republican Party* (Chapel Hill: University of North Carolina Press, 2011), especially 124–129. Other valuable sources are George H. Mayer, *The Republican Party, 1854–1966*, 2nd edition (New York: Oxford University Press, 1967), 487–491; John Robert Greene, *The Crusade:*

The Presidential Election of 1952 (Lanham, MD: University Press of America, 1985), 91–94, 102–119; and Roger M. Olien, *From Token to Triumph: The Texas Republicans since 1920* (Dallas: SMU Press, 1982), 112–138. The Texas conventions and election are covered thoroughly in O. Douglas Weeks, *Texas Presidential Politics in 1952* (Austin: Institute of Public Affairs, University of Texas, 1953).

2. Bowen, *Roots*, 124; Olien, *From Token to Triumph*, 110–111; Paul Casdorph, *A History of the Republican Party in Texas, 1865–1965* (Austin, Texas: Pemberton Press, 1965), 174–176.

3. Casdorph, *History*, 174.

4. Olien, *From Token to Triumph*, 112–116.

5. Ibid., 113.

6. William Reynolds Sanford, "History of the Republican Party in the State of Texas," Master's thesis, University of Texas, 1954, 174.

7. For a discussion of the Tidelands controversy and the role of Texas oil industry leaders in promoting the Eisenhower candidacy, see George Norris Green, *The Establishment in Texas Politics: The Primitive Years, 1938–1957* (Westport, CT: Greenwood, 1979).

8. Bowen, *Roots*, 127.

9. "Tumult in Texas Leads to a Republican Breach," *Life*, June 9, 1952, 41.

10. H. J. Porter to Dwight D. Eisenhower, December 14, 1951, as quoted in Olien, *From Token to Triumph*, 118.

11. Casdorph, *History*, 179–180.

12. Olien, *From Token to Triumph*, 118–119.

13. Casdorph, *History*, 182.

14. Olien, *From Token to Triumph*, 120.

15. Quoted by Rob Allyn in a draft article attached to a letter from Rob Allyn to Rita Clements, October 22, 1985, Rita Crocker Clements Papers, Cushing Library, Texas A&M University, 4.

16. Sanford, "History," 175.

17. Robert E. Baskin, "Taft Men Prepare Convention Control," *Dallas Morning News*, May 26, 1952.

18. Ibid.

19. Felix R. McKnight, "GOP Action Regarded as Suicide Path," *Dallas Morning News*, May 27, 1952.

20. Robert E. Baskin, "Machine Spurns Ike's Delegates," *Dallas Morning News*, May 27, 1952.

21. Robert E. Baskin, "GOP Ripped Apart by Delegate Battle," *Dallas Morning News*, May 28, 1952.

22. Ibid.

23. Paul Casdorph claims the delegation had thirty Taft, four Eisenhower, and four MacArthur supporters (*History*, 184), while both Roger Olien and Robert Baskin say the split was thirty-five for Taft and three for Eisenhower (*From Token to Triumph*, 125, and "GOP Ripped Apart," respectively). Because the delegation was never seated in Chicago and therefore never cast votes, their intentions cannot be verified.

24. *Dallas Morning News*, May 22, 1952, as quoted in Olien, *From Token to Triumph*, 127.

25. Casdorph, *History*, 190.

26. The "Brief in the Matter of Contest over Seats from Texas," prepared by the Porter supporters, and the "Brief for the Delegates of the Regular Republican Organization of Texas," submitted by legal counsel for Zweifel, can be found in the Allen Duckworth Papers (Dolph Briscoe Center for American History, University of Texas at Austin), along with "The Great Texas Swindle," compiled and distributed by Texas Republicans for Eisenhower. An additional pamphlet, "A Summary Statement on Behalf of the Porter Slate of Delegates, Chicago, July 9, 1952," is available as JK2358 T4 R4685 19852 at the Perry-Castañeda Library, University of Texas at Austin.

27. Olien, *From Token to Triumph*, 130–132.

28. Casdorph, *History*, 193.

29. Robert E. Baskin, "Cross-File Talk Heard in GOP," *Dallas Morning News*, August 25, 1952.

30. Olien, *From Token to Triumph*, 135.

31. Robert E. Baskin, "Fight Kept Up by Old Guard," *Dallas Morning News*, August 26, 1952.

32. Allen Duckworth, "GOP's Old Guard Threatening to Bolt," *Dallas Morning News*, August 26, 1952.

33. "Lane Selected GOP Chairman," *Dallas Morning News*, August 27, 1952.

34. T. B. Brewer interview with Allan Shivers, April 8, 1966, Oral History Collection, University of North Texas, 5.

35. Ibid., 6.

36. Fred Gantt interview with Allan Shivers, October 2, 1967, Oral History Collection, University of North Texas, 7.

37. Weeks, *Texas Presidential Politics*, 88.

38. J. B. Smallwood interview with Harrell Edmund Chiles, January 25, 1980, Oral History Collection, University of North Texas, 10.

39. G. William Domhoff, *Fat Cats and Democrats: The Role of the Big Rich in the Party of the Common Man* (Englewood Cliffs, NJ: Prentice-Hall, 1972), 44, 88.

40. Sandy Sheehy, *Texas Big Rich* (New York: William Morrow, 1990), 77–78.

41. Edward H. Miller, *Nut Country: Right Wing Dallas and the Birth of the Southern Strategy* (Chicago: University of Chicago Press, 2015), 39–44.

42. Donald S. Strong, *The 1952 Presidential Election in the South* (Tuscaloosa: Bureau of Public Administration, University of Alabama, 1955), 371.

43. Casdorph, *History*, 198.

44. Gladwin Hill, "Texas G.O.P. Sees Two-Party State," *New York Times*, November 6, 1952.

45. Strong, *1952 Presidential Election*, 384.

46. T. B. Brewer interview with Allan Shivers, April 6, 1966, Oral History Collection, University of North Texas, 7.

47. Randolph B. Campbell, *Gone to Texas: A History of the Lone Star State* (New York: Oxford University Press, 2003), 417.

48. Meg McKain Grier, *Grassroots Women* (Boerne, TX: Wingscape, 2001), 8.

49. Hill, "Texas G.O.P."

50. Sean P. Cunningham, *Cowboy Conservatism: Texas and the Rise of the Modern Right* (Lexington: University Press of Kentucky, 2010), 31. See also George N. Green, "Establishing the Texas Far Right, 1940–1960," in *The Texas Right: The Radical Roots of Lone Star Conservatism*, ed. David O'Donald Cullen and Kyle G. Wilkison (College Station: Texas A&M University Press, 2014), 96–98.

51. Olien, *From Token to Triumph*, 155.

52. O. Douglas Weeks, "Republicanism and Conservatism in the South," *Southwestern Social Science Quarterly* 36 (December 1955), 252.

53. Olien, *From Token to Triumph*, 142–143.

54. Ibid., 158.

55. Clifton McCleskey, *The Government and Politics of Texas* (Boston: Little, Brown and Company, 1963), 91. This point is also made in Alexander Heard, *A Two-Party South?* (Chapel Hill: University of North Carolina Press, 1952), especially chapter 5.

56. Cunningham, *Cowboy Conservatism*, 31; Thure Barnett Cannon, "The Texas Political System: Shifting Dynamics in Political Party Power," Master's thesis, University of Texas at Austin, 1998, 8. While remaining a Democrat, Shivers continued to endorse Republican candidates during his career, backing Ike again in 1956 and Nixon in 1960, as well as Tower, Clements, and Reagan in subsequent campaigns.

57. Author interview with William Murchison, Dallas, Texas, April 24, 2014. In author's possession.

58. For other views on Shivers and his place in Texas politics, see Sam Kinch and Stuart Long, *Allan Shivers: The Pied Piper of Texas Politics* (Austin: Shoal Creek Publishers, 1974), and Ricky F. Dobbs, *Yellow Dogs and Republicans: Allan Shivers and Texas Two-Party Politics* (College Station: Texas A&M University Press, 2005).

59. Byron Shelton, Mrs. Lillian Collier, and Creekmore Fath to "Dear Democrat," May 29, 1953, Walter G. Hall Papers, Woodson Research Center, Fondren Library, Rice University, box 5, folder 54.

60. "Democrats of Texas" promotional literature, Frankie Randolph Papers, Woodson Research Center, Fondren Library, Rice University, box 3, folder 3.

61. Orville Bullington to Dwight D. Eisenhower, November 3, 1953, referenced in Kristi Throne Strickland, "The Significance and Impact of Women on the Rise of the Republican Party in Twentieth Century Texas," PhD diss., University of North Texas, August 2000, 81.

62. "Texas Faces Test as 2-Party State," *New York Times*, May 2, 1954.

63. Sanford, "History of the Republican Party," 198–201.

64. O. Douglas Weeks, *Texas One-Party Politics in 1956* (Austin: Institute of Public Affairs, University of Texas, 1957), 5.

65. Ibid., 7.

66. "Upset Victory of Texas G.O.P. Congressman Is Laid to Revenge," *St. Louis Post-Dispatch*, November 5, 1954, Bruce Alger Collection, Dallas Public Library, box 1, folder 1.

67. Unnamed leader quoted by Hawkins Henley Menefee Jr., "The Two-Party Democrats: The Study of a Political Faction," Master's thesis, University of Texas at Austin, 1970, 26.

68. John Gizzi, "The First Tea Partier: Remembering Rep. Bruce Alger of Texas," *Newsmax*, April 27, 2015, provided to author by Gizzi.

69. Miller, *Nut Country*, 46, 50.

70. Cyndi Taylor, "Beryl Milburn: The Making of a Conservative," *Austin People Today*, April 1974, Cyndi Taylor Krier Papers, 1963–1972, University of Texas at San Antonio Libraries Special Collections. See also Meg McKain Grier, *Grassroots Women*, 206–238.

71. Walter C. Hornaday, "National Democratic Chief Sounds Warning for Alger," *Dallas Morning News*, April 1, 1955.

72. Olien, *From Token to Triumph*, 143.

73. Grier, *Grassroots Women*, 70.

74. Ruthelle Bacon to Frank Blankenbeckler, October 18, 1955, Eugene Nolte Family Papers, 1886–1964, MS 34, University of Texas at San Antonio Libraries Special Collection.

75. Sanford, "History of the Republican Party," 210.

76. "Texas Republican Sees Parties Split," *Austin American*, undated 1954 article, Nolte Family Papers.

77. Eugene (Mike) Nolte to Don Politico, July 20, 1956, Nolte Family Papers.

78. Speech, Washington, DC, June 16, 1955, box 3, folder 28, "Alger Speech File, 1954–1958," Bruce Alger Collection, Dallas Public Library.

79. Peter O'Donnell to Rita Bass, June 2, 1958, box 2, folder 16, Rita Crocker Clements Papers.

80. Weeks, *Texas One-Party Politics in 1956*, 49.

81. Olien, *From Token to Triumph*, 147.

82. Casdorph, *History*, 212. The final vote for the top three candidates was Yarborough 364,838; Dies 290,869; and Hutcheson 219,591. With no majority required, Yarborough was elected. Mike Kingston, Sam Attlesey, and Mary G. Crawford, *The Texas Almanac's Political History of Texas* (Austin: Eakin, 1992), 150–153.

83. John G. Tower to Thad Hutcheson, May 14, 1957, John G. Tower Papers, Southwestern University Special Collections, Box NA49. Tower played an active role in the party throughout the 1950s.

84. Memo to Party officials from Thad Hutcheson, April 30, 1958, Tower Papers, Box NA49.

85. Sanders had the support of many Dallas business leaders, including Trammell Crow, Angus Wynne Jr., John W. Carpenter, and Raymond Nasher, but Alger held on in a Democratic year, with 52.6 percent of the vote, to win a third term. Sanders was the Democratic nominee against Tower fourteen years later. Casdorph, *History*, 213; Sanders for Congress advertisement, undated, Alger Collection, box 8, folder 12.

86. Blakley had an interesting political career. He had been appointed to serve out Senator Daniel's term with a pledge not to run in the 1957 special election. One year later he ran against Yarborough and lost. In 1961 he was appointed to serve when Lyndon Johnson resigned, and this time he continued as a candidate in the special election, eventually losing the runoff to Tower.

87. "Hutcheson Discussed as GOP Yarborough November Foe," *Houston Post*, August 1, 1958.

88. "Hutcheson for Whittenburg in Senate Race," *Houston Chronicle*, August 1, 1958.

89. John G. Tower to Thad Hutcheson, August 4, 1958, Tower Papers.

90. Olien, *From Token to Triumph*, 151.

91. Confidential memo to special subcommittee of the Republican State Executive Committee from Thad Hutcheson dated August 26, 1958, Tower Papers.

92. Bill Glines, "Hutcheson removes himself as possible Senate Candidate," *Dallas Morning News*, September 8, 1958.

93. Joe S. Sheldon to Thad Hutcheson, September 22, 1958, Tower Papers.

94. Memo from Thad Hutcheson to party leadership, November 26, 1958, Tower Papers.

95. John G. Tower to Thad Hutcheson, December 27, 1958, Tower Papers.

96. Memo from Thad Hutcheson to party leadership, January 9, 1959, Tower Papers.

97. Memo from Thad Hutcheson to party leadership, September 1, 1960, Tower Papers.

98. Olien, *From Token to Triumph*, 152.

99. John Tower quoted in Jimmy Banks, *Money, Marbles, and Chalk* (Austin: Texas Publishing Company, 1971), 183.

100. T. R. Fehrenbach, *Lone Star: A History of Texas and the Texans* (New York: Collier, 1968), 660.

101. "Texas Leader for Eisenhower Quits Post in National G.O.P.," *New York Times*, February 7, 1960.

102. Crystal Rose Dunbar, "The Rise of a Two-Party State: A Case Study of Houston and Harris County, Texas, 1952–1962," Master's thesis, University of North Texas, December 2007, 50.

103. "H. J. Porter, Key Republican in Texas in 50s, Is Dead at 90," *New York Times*, December 10, 1986.

104. James Q. Wilson, *The Amateur Democrat* (Chicago: University of Chicago Press, 1962), 3–4.

105. Don Freeman, "Peter O'Donnell Jr.: Building GOP," *Dallas Morning News*, December 6, 1959. O'Donnell and his wife, Edith, created the O'Donnell Foundation in 1957 and since then have donated hundreds of millions of dollars to various causes and institutions. As of 2012, the O'Donnells had donated $135 million to the University of Texas at Austin. Former UT president Larry Faulkner maintains that "O'Donnell is my candidate for the living Texan with the greatest impact on modern Texas." Ralph K. M. Haurwitz, "UT's 'Mr. Anonymous' a Force behind Research," *Austin American-Statesman*, September 1, 2012.

106. Keith Shelton, "The Party Chairmen," *Dallas Times Herald* magazine, March 10, 1963.

107. Robert Allyn, "How Dallas Switched Parties: Peter O'Donnell and the Dallas Republicans: 1950–1972," Master's thesis, Southern Methodist University, 1983, 7–8. Copy in author's possession.

108. Peter O'Donnell Jr. to Wayne Thorburn, February 26, 2014; Mike Quinn, "Interested Voter at Helm—O'Donnell backs Barry," *Dallas Morning News*, August 4, 1963.

109. Olien, *From Token to Triumph*, 151.

110. Allyn, "How Dallas Switched," 12.

111. Freeman, "Peter O'Donnell Jr."

112. Quoted by Rob Allyn in a draft article attached to his letter to Rita Clements, October 22, 1985, Rita Crocker Clements Papers, 10.

113. Quinn, "Interested Voter."

114. Memo and report on Tag Day 1958, Rita Crocker Clements Papers, Box 27, folder 19.

115. Grier, *Grassroots Women*, 5–6. Grier's book is a valuable source of commentary on the early involvement of women in the growth of the Republican Party from the 1950s forward.

116. Ibid., 102.

117. Ibid., 3.

118. Ibid., xii.

119. Ibid., 48.

120. Kristi Strickland interview with Betty Andujar, September 10, 1993, Oral History Collection, University of North Texas, 6.

121. Grier, *Grassroots Women*, 22, 45–47.

122. Jack Bass and Walter DeVries interview with Nancy Palm, December 16, 1974, Southern Oral History Program Collection, No. 4007, University of North Carolina at Chapel Hill. © This work is the property of the University of North Carolina at Chapel Hill. It may be used freely by individuals for research, teaching, and personal use as long as this statement of availability is included in the text.

123. News release, Republican Party of Texas, September 1960, Tower Papers, Box NA-51.

124. For a fascinating personal memoir of one woman who helped transition the Republican Party into a political force in Texas, see Marjorie Meyer Arsht, *All the Way from Yoakum: The Personal Journey of a Political Insider* (College Station: Texas A&M University Press, 2005).

125. Cyndi Taylor, "Beryl Milburn: The Making of a Conservative," *Austin People Today*, April 1974, 20, 22; copy located in the Krier Papers.

126. Grier, *Grassroots Women*, 211.

127. Rita Crocker Clements Papers, Box 29, folder 4.

128. Rita Crocker Clements Papers, Box 27, folder 19.

129. Jack Monger, "Political Pro On the Go," *Beaumont Enterprise*, May 18, 1980.

130. H. J. Porter to John G. Tower, September 12, 1956, Tower Papers.

131. H. J. Porter to John G. Tower, November 2, 1956, Tower Papers.

132. John G. Tower to Thad Hutcheson, May 14, 1957, Tower Papers.

133. John G. Tower to Meade Alcorn, July 30, 1957, Tower Papers.

134. Thad Hutcheson to John G. Tower, September 16, 1958, Tower Papers.

135. Casdorph, *A History*, 219. According to Casdorph, "The state delegates gave John Tower much credit for keeping the platform committee from writing all of the liberal proposals of Rockefeller into the civil rights plank. Tower was later given a cheering ovation at the caucus of the Texas group after his 'standing up' to the platform committee."

136. Peter Schweizer and Rochelle Schweizer, *The Bushes: Portrait of a Dynasty* (New York: Doubleday, 2004), 113–120. Both Democratic candidates defeated by Prescott Bush would subsequently serve in the US Senate. Ribicoff served from 1963 to 1981, and Dodd was a member of the Senate from 1959 to 1971.

137. Schweizer and Schweizer, *Bushes*, 143; news release, Bush for Senator, September 11, 1963, Alger Collection, box 22, folder 35.

138. Grier, *Grassroots Women*, ix.

139. In a letter from Helen G. Healey, executive secretary, the state party's desires were made known when she added in reference to the state chairman: "Thad also asked me to express again his interest in your possible candidacy—an interest which all of us at State Headquarters share." Helen G. Healey to George H. W. Bush, April 24, 1958, George Bush Collection, Zapata Oil Files, Subseries Political Correspondence Files 1957–1964, George H. W. Bush Presidential Library, College Station.

140. George H. W. Bush to H. J. Porter, February 24, 1959, Bush Collection.

141. Invitation from H. J. Porter, Mrs. John R. Black, Thad Hutcheson, and Mrs. Ike S. Kampmann Jr., December 9, 1959, Bush Collection.

6. THE 1960S BREAKTHROUGH

1. Lee G. Griffin, "2-Party Flop Laid to Porter," *Beaumont Enterprise*, January 20, 1960. Griffin was one of the owners of the Stuart-Griffin-Perlitz Ranch, a nine-thousand-acre property in Zavala County, where white-tailed deer are raised and hunted. Judy Bishop Jurek, "Closing in on a Century: The Evolution of the Stuart Griffin Perlitz Ranch," *Tracks: Official Publication of the Texas Deer Association*, February 2009, 84–86, 90–98.

2. H. J. "Jack" Porter to John G. Tower, February 5, 1960, John G. Tower Papers, Southwestern University Special Collections, box NA-49.

3. Casdorph, *History*, 215–220.

4. Quoted in Grier, *Grassroots Women*, 49–50.

5. John G. Tower, *Consequences: A Personal and Political Memoir* (Boston: Little, Brown and Company, 1991), 13.

6. John R. Knaggs, *Two-Party Texas* (Austin: Aiken, 1986), 3.

7. Peter O'Donnell Jr. to John G. Tower, August 31, 1960, Tower Papers, box NA-52.

8. *Tower Tribune*, published by Democrats for Tower, October 1960, Bruce Alger Collection, Dallas Public Library, box 8, folder 14.

9. "Texas G.O.P. Backs Nixon, Goldwater," *New York Times*, June 15, 1960.

10. Roger M. Olien, *From Token to Triumph: The Texas Republicans since 1920* (Dallas: SMU Press, 1982), 171.

11. William M. Blair, "Firm Rights Plank Offered by Nixon," *New York Times*, July 22, 1960.

12. For a detailed discussion of the platform controversy and the Compact of Fifth Avenue, see Theodore H. White, *The Making of the President 1960* (New York: Atheneum, 1961), 208–227. The summary statement released by Governor Rockefeller on July 23, 1960, can be found on pp. 424–426. See also Rick Perlstein, *Before the Storm* (New York: Hill and Wang, 2001), 78–95.

13. White, *Making of the President 1960*, 224.

14. Delegation statement, July 26, 1960, Tower Papers, box 28. Goldwater had been

invited and addressed the delegates at their caucus. Lee Edwards, *The Conservative Revolution: The Movement That Remade America* (New York: The Free Press, 1999), 92.

15. Stephen Shadegg Barry Goldwater Collection, Briscoe Center for American History, University of Texas at Austin, box 3H506. Goldwater's speech in Chicago and its lasting impact on the development of the conservative movement is discussed in Wayne Thorburn, *A Generation Awakes: Young Americans for Freedom and the Creation of the Conservative Movement* (Ottawa, IL: Jameson Books, 2010), 19–22, and John A. Andrew III, *The Other Side of the Sixties* (New Brunswick, NJ: Rutgers University Press, 1997), 48–55.

16. List of party officials, Tower Papers, box NA-49.

17. Peter O'Donnell Jr. to Tad Smith, August 31, 1960, Tower Papers, box NA-48.

18. News release, September 12, 1960, Tower Papers, box NA-48.

19. The proposal to re-elect Hutcheson and name a new chairman after the election came from Joe Sheldon, Mrs. John H. Wood, and John Goode of San Antonio. Hutcheson was unanimously re-elected in Galveston. Tower Papers, box NA-48.

20. Thad Hutcheson to John G. Tower, December 31, 1960, Tower Papers, box NA-51.

21. Bob Hollingsworth, "P. O'Donnell Eyed for GOP State Chief," *Dallas Morning News*, December 30, 1960.

22. Hilton Hagan, "Nixon Hits Ad Greeting Johnson," *Dallas Morning News*, November 5, 1960.

23. "Many Loudly Protest Being Named in Ad," *Dallas Morning News*, November 5, 1960.

24. *Dallas Morning News*, November 8, 1960.

25. Mary Brinkerhoff, "Lady GOP Taggers Collide with LBJ Welcome," *Dallas Morning News*, November 5, 1960.

26. "Bruce Alger Was There," *Dallas Morning News*, November 5, 1960.

27. Allen Duckworth, "LBJ Calls Pro-Nixon fans at His Rally 'Discourteous,'" *Dallas Morning News*, November 5, 1960.

28. Ibid.

29. "It Was Sad, LBJ Says," *Dallas Morning News*, November 5, 1960.

30. "Urgent Notice to Set the Record Straight," undated flyer, Rita Crocker Clements Papers, Cushing Library, Texas A&M University, box 24.

31. Alger advertisement, *Dallas Times Herald*, November 7, 1960, Alger Collection, box 8, folder 12.

32. A classic example is the recently released work by Bill Minutaglio and Steven L. Davis, *Dallas 1963* (New York: Twelve, 2013), which stresses the anti-Johnson demonstration repeatedly but makes no mention of the fraudulent endorsement advertisement. In a review published by many newspapers, Will Lester wrote for the Associated Press, "Alger whipped his legions of female supporters, many from the most powerful families in Dallas, into a 'mink coat mob,' who descended on the Johnsons at a top Dallas hotel, trapping them briefly." Will Lester, "JFK Brought out Worst in Dallas," *Honolulu Star-Advertiser*, November 17, 2013. See also Don E. Carleton, *Red Scare! Right-Wing Hysteria, Fifties Fanaticism, and Their Legacy in Texas* (Austin: Texas Monthly Press, 1985). When Alger died in 2015, writers of his obituary brought up the demonstration again but failed

to mention the Democratic dirty tricks that preceded the confrontation with Johnson. Matt Schudel, "Bruce Alger, Firebrand Republican Congressman from Texas, Dies at 96," *Washington Post*, April 25, 2015.

33. Thomas B. Brewer, oral history interview with Allan Shivers, August 8, 1966, University of North Texas Digital Library, University of North Texas Oral History Program, 39.

34. "Texas G.O.P. Asks Recount," *New York Times*, November 25, 1960.

35. "Texans Plan Challenge," *New York Times*, November 28, 1960.

36. Price Daniel, quoted in Jimmy Banks, *Money, Marbles, and Chalk* (Austin: Texas Publishing Company, 1971), 152.

37. "Eisenhower Aids Texas Candidate," *New York Times*, May 20, 1961.

38. Sean P. Cunningham, *Cowboy Conservatism: Texas and the Rise of the Modern Right* (Lexington: University Press of Kentucky, 2010), 35–37.

39. Wayne Thorburn, *Red State: An Insider's Story of How the GOP Came to Dominate Texas Politics* (Austin: University of Texas Press, 2014), 73–74.

40. Walter G. Hall keynote address, Democrats of Texas state convention, May 31, 1958, Austin, TX, in Walter G. Hall Papers, Woodson Research Center, Fondren Library, Rice University, box 3, folder 8.

41. Letter from Coke Stevenson dated May 20, 1961, Jack Cox Papers, 1950–1964, Dolph Briscoe Center for American History, University of Texas at Austin, box 4zd322.

42. Kristi Strickand, oral history interview with Betty Andujar, September 10, 1993, University of North Texas Digital Library, University of North Texas Oral History Program, 14.

43. "Remarks by Chase Untermeyer Before the R Club," Houston, November 27, 2007, in author's possession.

44. Knaggs, *Two-Party Texas*, 18.

45. Frank B. Feigert and Nancy L. McWilliams, "Texas: Yeller Dogs and Yuppies," in *Southern State Party Organizations and Activists*, ed. Charles D. Hadley and Nancy L. McWilliams (Westport, CT: Praeger, 1995), 76.

46. Gladwin Hill, "Tower Is Elected Senator in Texas," *New York Times*, May 29, 1961.

47. Kenneth Bridges, *Twilight of the Texas Democrats* (College Station: Texas A&M University Press, 2008), 11.

48. Tower's role in encouraging and developing Republican activists is discussed in Thorburn, *Red State*, 99–110.

49. Author interview with William Murchison, Dallas, April 24, 2014, in author's possession.

50. "Texas: Rallying to Resign," *Time*, October 27, 1961.

51. Dawson Duncan, "GOP Unit Votes Move to Austin," *Dallas Morning News*, June 24, 1961.

52. Knaggs, *Two-Party Texas*, 9.

53. Brian D. Posler and Daniel S. Ward, "Texas," in *State Party Profiles*, ed. Andrew M. Appleton and Daniel S. Ward (Washington: Congressional Quarterly, 1997), 311.

54. Knaggs, *Two-Party Texas*, 19.

55. Cunningham, *Cowboy Conservatism*, 5.

56. Ibid.

57. Quoted in James R. Soukup, Clifton McCleskey, and Harry Holloway, *Party and Factional Division in Texas* (Austin: University of Texas Press, 1964), 262. Robert Wuthnow provides a number of correlation coefficients between the vote for Eisenhower in each county in 1952 and the vote for GOP candidates from 1960 to 1968. He concludes, "County by county, one of the best predictors of how well a Republican candidate would do in the 1960s was how successful Eisenhower had been in 1952." Robert Wuthnow, *Rough Country: How Texas Became America's Most Powerful Bible-Belt State* (Princeton, NJ: Princeton University Press, 2014), 294–297.

58. News release from Marvin Collins, executive director, Republican Party of Texas, April 30, 1964, Cox Papers, box 4zd346.

59. According to *The Republican Bandwagon* (vol. 2, no. 2, February 1962), three candidates filed for governor: Cox, Whittenburg, and Harry R. Diehl of Houston. Diehl was one of the multitude seeking the vacant US senate seat in the 1961 special election, winning only 293 votes. Apparently Diehl dropped out before the ballots were printed as his name did not appear in the subsequent primary.

60. Statement by Jack Cox released on September 10, 1961, Cox Papers, box 4zd329.

61. Robert E. Ford, "The Republican Candidate: Jack Cox Wants to Break 'One-Party Rule' in Texas," *Houston Post*, September 23, 1962.

62. "Tower Backs Cox Shift to Republican," *Houston Post*, undated clipping, Cox Papers, box 4zd322.

63. "Tower Praises Cox Decision to Change Parties," *Dallas Morning News*, September 10, 1961.

64. Jack Cox, *This I Believe … and the Pursuit of Happiness* (San Antonio: Naylor, 1962).

65. Note from U. A. Hyde to Jack Cox, February 28, 1962, reporting on a visit by Frank Driskill with Coke Stevenson, Cox Papers, box 4zd325.

66. Quoted in Max Sherman, ed., *The Future of Texas* (Austin: Lyndon Baines Johnson School of Public Affairs, 1988), 36–37.

67. Letter of Peter O'Donnell Jr. to Judy Breck, March 23, 1962, Cox Papers, box 4z328.

68. Letter of Peter O'Donnell Jr. to Judy Breck, April 16, 1962, Cox Papers, box 4z328.

69. Letter of Peter O'Donnell Jr. to Judy Breck, April 23, 1962, Cox Papers, box 4z328.

70. Request from the campaign office in Austin to Peter O'Donnell Jr., July 23, 1962, Cox Papers, box 4zd328.

71. Primary election returns, Cox Papers, box 4zd328.

72. Olien, *From Token to Triumph*, 180.

73. Knaggs, *Two-Party Texas*, 22.

74. Crystal Rose Dunbar, "The Rise of a Two-Party State: A Case Study of Houston and Harris County, Texas, 1952–1962," Master's thesis, University of North Texas, December 2007, 73.

75. Tad Smith to State Republican Executive Committee, September 6, 1962, Cox Papers, box 4zd321.

76. "O'Donnell Seen in Line for Texas GOP Office," *Dallas Morning News*, August 18, 1962.

77. Campaign letter for State Chairman from Don Napier, September 12, 1962, Cox Papers, box 4zd321.

78. Paul Lenchner, "The Party System in Texas," in *Texas Politics: A Reader*, 2nd edition, ed. Anthony Champagne and Edward J. Harpham (New York: W. W. Norton, 1998), 127–129.

79. James A. Bertron to Tad Smith, June 8, 1962, Cox Papers, box 4zd329.

80. Memo from Tad Smith to Republican candidates, August 1962, Cox Papers, box 4zd321.

81. Charles Holmes, "A Challenger for O'Donnell," *Dallas Times Herald*, September 17, 1962.

82. Charles Holmes, "Dallas' Sims Davidson named by Republicans," *Dallas Times Herald*, September 17, 1962.

83. Campaign brochure, "Peter O'Donnell for State Chairman," Tower Papers, box 24.

84. Mike Quinn, "GOP Job Won by O'Donnell," *Dallas Morning News*, September 19, 1962.

85. "O'Donnell Eyes Texas, U.S. Races," *Dallas Morning News*, September 19, 1962.

86. Wick Fowler, "Let's Win House, Tower Tells 'Em," *Dallas Morning News*, September 19, 1962.

87. "Texas in Political Bondage, Cox Charges at Convention," *Dallas Morning News*, September 19, 1962.

88. Knaggs, *Two-Party Texas*, 24.

89. Hawkins Henley Menefee Jr., "The Two-Party Democrats: The Study of a Political Faction," Master's thesis, University of Texas at Austin, 1970, 53–54.

90. "Jack Cox Liked as Speaker," *Houston Post*, July 18, 1962.

91. Undated statement by Archer Fullingim, Cox Papers, box 4zd342.

92. Campaign letter from George I. Sanchez, September 15, 1962, Cox Papers, box 4zd321. Some of the correspondence between Sanchez and Cox can be found in George I. Sanchez Papers, Benson Latin American Collection, Central Libraries, University of Texas at Austin, box 11, folder 11. Sanchez has been called "the single most important Mexican-American intellectual between the Great Depression and the Great Society." Carlos Kevin Blanton, *George I. Sanchez: The Long Fight for Mexican American Integration* (New Haven, CT: Yale University Press, 2015).

93. Letter from George W. Sandlin, undated, Hall Papers, box 6, folder 89.

94. News release from Tad Smith, October 24, 1962, Cox Papers, box 4zd329.

95. Campaign letter from Volmo Bellinger, undated, Cox Papers, box 4zd321.

96. Knaggs, *Two-Party Texas*, 23–24, 31.

97. Ronald Marcello interview with O. H. "Ike" Harris, November 6, 1969, Oral History Collection, University of North Texas, Denton.

98. "Republicans Elected to Office in Texas in 1962," listing from Republican Party of Texas, Rita Crocker Clements Papers, box 29. Barbara Culver, now Barbara Culver Clack, is quoted in Grier, *Grassroots Women*, 259. The shift in Midland from Democratic to Republican, and the roles played by Ernest Angelo Jr., Tom Craddick, Juandelle Lacy, and Barbara Culver, are discussed in Jimmy Patterson, *A History of Character* (Midland, TX:

The Abell-Hanger Foundation, 2014), 158–172. Both the Young Republicans and the Republican Women's Club were focal points in organizing support for Republican candidates and making the GOP dominant in local politics.

99. Quoted by Rob Allyn in a draft article attached to a letter from Rob Allyn to Rita Clements, October 22, 1985, Rita Crocker Clements Papers, 11.

100. Knaggs, *Two-Party Texas*, 31; Olien, *From Token to Triumph*, 203.

101. Minutes of the State Republican Executive Committee, Austin, January 24, 1963, Alger Collection, box 23, folder 10, 4.

102. Author interview with George W. Strake Jr., Houston, March 25, 2014, in author's possession.

103. F. Clifton White, *Suite 3505: The Story of the Draft Goldwater Movement* (New Rochelle, NY: Arlington House, 1967), 39–40; Theodore H. White, *The Making of the President 1964* (New York: Atheneum, 1965), 114–120. The list of attendees at the initial meetings of this group can be found in J. William Middendorf II, *A Glorious Disaster: Barry Goldwater's Presidential Campaign and the Origins of the Conservative Movement* (New York: Basic Books, 2006), 275–277.

104. Olien, *From Token to Triumph*, 188–189.

105. Knaggs, *Two-Party Texas*, 33.

106. Quoted in Roy L. McGhee, "Peter O'Donnell, a Prime Mover," *Dallas Times Herald*, July 15, 1964.

107. White, *Suite 3505*, 124–129, 131–134, discusses the selection of O'Donnell as chair and the announcement of the committee's formation. See also Bob Hollingsworth, "Texas GOP Chief Launches Drive to Draft Goldwater," *Dallas Times Herald*, April 8, 1963.

108. Ibid., 125.

109. Stephen Shadegg, *What Happened to Goldwater?: The Inside Story of the 1964 Republican Campaign* (New York: Holt, Rinehart and Winston, 1965), 66. Also valuable is box 3H507 of the Shadegg Goldwater Collection.

110. The fascinating story of the effort to recruit, nominate, and elect Barry Goldwater has been told in several works. Among the books by participants in the process are White, *Suite 3505*; Shadegg, *What Happened?*; Karl Hess, *In a Cause that Will Triumph: The Goldwater Campaign and the Future of Conservatism* (Garden City, NY: Doubleday, 1967); and Middendorf, *Glorious Disaster*. Two less supportive narratives that are valuable sources are White, *The Making of the President 1964*, and Perlstein, *Before the Storm*. Some of Goldwater's thoughts on the campaign and its aftermath are recorded in John W. Dean and Barry M. Goldwater Jr., *Pure Goldwater* (New York: Palgrave Macmillan, 2008).

111. Keith Shelton, "Not Rocky for Texas, Says GOP," *Dallas Times Herald*, April 8, 1963.

112. Allen Duckworth, "South Will Help Beat JFK in 1964, O'Donnell Predicts," *Dallas Morning News*, May 12, 1963.

113. Gladwin Hill, "Goldwater Backers Increase in Texas, Along with Republican Strength," *New York Times*, September 17, 1963.

114. Bo Byers, "Goldwater Is Key in Texas Vote," *Houston Chronicle*, September 16, 1963.

115. Stewart Alsop, "Can Goldwater Win in '64?," *Saturday Evening Post*, August 24, 1963.

116. White, *Suite 3505*, 225–226.

117. Ibid., 226. Denison Kitchel was a close associate of Goldwater who had managed his 1952 Senate campaign but had an often-expressed dislike of politics. Goldwater would later choose Kitchel to serve as his campaign manager in both the nomination and general election campaigns. "Denison Kitchel, 94, Chief of Goldwater Campaign," *New York Times*, October 22, 2002.

118. White, *Suite 3505*, 228–229.

119. Middendorf, *Glorious Disaster*, 73, 92.

120. White, *Suite 3505*, 278.

121. Shadegg, *What Happened?*, 90.

122. Walt Mansell, "State GOP Panel Solidly for Goldwater," *Houston Chronicle*, January 19, 1964.

123. Quoted in Ronnie Duggar, "The Lobbyists at Work," *Texas Observer*, May 2, 1963.

124. Knaggs, *Two-Party Texas*, 35.

125. Dunbar, *Rise*, 39.

126. Ibid., 47. A fascinating memoir that speaks to the development of the Harris County party is Marjorie Meyer Arsht, *All the Way from Yoakum: The Personal Journey of a Political Insider* (College Station: Texas A&M University Press, 2006).

127. Braes Republican Women's Club record, 1980–2009, Woodson Research Center, Fondren Library, Rice University, box 1, folder 3.

128. George Bush Collection, Zapata Oil Files, Subseries Political Correspondence Files 1957–1964, George H. W. Bush Presidential Library, College Station.

129. The two major works by Robert Welch, the founder of the John Birch Society, are *The Blue Book of the John Birch Society* (Belmont, MA: Western Islands, 1961), which lays out the reasons for forming the organization presented at its initial meeting in 1958, and *The Politician* (Belmont, MA: Belmont Publishing Company, 1964). By 1962 most nationally known figures, such as Goldwater, Tower, William F. Buckley Jr., and Russell Kirk, had disassociated Welch from the conservatism they advocated.

130. Peter Schweizer and Rochelle Schweizer, *The Bushes: Portrait of a Dynasty* (New York: Doubleday, 2004), 143.

131. George H. W. Bush, *All the Best: My Life in Letters and Other Writings* (New York: Scribner, 1999), 85.

132. "Two County G.O.P. Hopefuls Sound Off," *Houston Chronicle*, February 14, 1963.

133. George W. Strake Jr. to George H. W. Bush, March 15, 1963, Bush Collection.

134. Peter O'Donnell Jr. to George H. W. Bush, February 27, 1963; Jack Cox to Bush, March 11, 1963; James A. Baker to Bush, February 21, 1963, Bush Collection.

135. George H. W. Bush to Lloyd H. Smith, March 18, 1963, Bush Collection.

136. Walter Mansell, "Goldwater Favors Cuban Raids in Houston Speech," *Houston Chronicle*, undated news clipping, Alger Collection, box 23, folder 10.

137. George H. W. Bush to James A. Bertron, April 15, 1963, Bush Collection.

138. George H. W. Bush to William E. Miller, May 7, 1963, Bush Collection.

139. "G.O.P. Official Quits in Goldwater Fuss," *Houston Chronicle*, July 3, 1963.

140. Thomas E. Dixon, John Fonteno, and J. E. Gloster to George H. W. Bush, April 20, 1963, Bush Collection.

141. James Hyatt, "Harris G.O.P. Makes Bid for Negro Votes," *Houston Chronicle*, undated news clipping, Frankie Randolph Papers, Woodson Research Center, Fondren Library, Rice University, box 7, folder 4.

142. Allyn, draft article, Rita Crocker Clements Papers, 17.

143. Ibid.

144. Neil Addington, "GOP's Bush Leads; Runoff Is Probable," *Houston Post*, May 3, 1964.

145. "Cox Says He Could Beat Ralph," *Houston Chronicle*, August 27, 1963.

146. George H. W. Bush to Nancy Ellis, September 6, 1963, in G. H. W. Bush, *All the Best*, 86. The same letter, with the salutation "Dear Milton" and dated September 6, 1963, appears in the Bush Collection. See also Bo Byers, "Opposition to Jack Cox Develops in GOP Ranks," *Houston Chronicle*, September 15, 1963.

147. C. Douglas Forde Jr. to Jack Cox, October 17, 1963, Cox Papers, box 4zd345.

148. "Committee of 64 for Cox in 64," Cox Papers, box 4zd345. Also included in the file are campaign brochures for Milton Davis and Robert Morris.

149. Milton V. Davis to Bruce Alger, October 4, 1963, and Bruce Alger to Milton V. Davis, October 22, 1963, Alger Collection, box 23, folder 10.

150. Lonnie Hudkins, "Robert Morris Likely to Be in GOP Senate Race," *Houston Post*, September 18, 1963. "The Four Republicans," *Texas Observer*, April 17, 1964, discusses the campaigns of the candidates, pointing out that all four were supporters of Senator Goldwater for the presidential nomination.

151. Franklin Jones to Hank Brown and Albert Pena, December 3, 1963, Hall Papers, box 6, folder 110.

152. Quoted in Allyn, draft article, Rita Crocker Clements Papers, 18.

153. Schweizer and Schweizer, *Bushes*, 156.

154. David Hoffman Collection, George Bush H. W. Presidential Library, College Station, box 13.

155. Saul Friedman, "3 Speakers, 3 Approaches, 3 Receptions," *Houston Chronicle*, January 22, 1964.

156. Walter Mansell, "2 Goldwater Men in the Running for County GOP Chairman," *Houston Chronicle*, undated news clipping; "Haden Elected Chairman of County's Republicans," undated news clipping. Randolph Papers, box 7, folder 4.

157. "Rockefeller Stays in Texas Primary," *New York Times*, March 13, 1964.

158. Election returns from "Tabulated Statement Showing Votes Cast in the First Republican Primary Election, May 2, 1964," Lorenzo de Zavala State Archives, Austin. Jack Langguth, "Strength of Lodge's Phantom Candidacy in Texas Vote Assayed," *New York Times*, May 4, 1964.

159. Schweizer and Schweizer, *Bushes*, 161. The coalition's brochure, "Who's Hiding Behind The Bush?" reported that a number of Bush financial supporters were members

of the Council on Foreign Relations, the supposed masterminds behind one-world federalism and disarmament; Alger Collection, box 29, folder 12. The charges of liberalism directed against Bush would continue for some time. In 1967 the Jefferson County GOP chairman wrote to a young Republican leader, advising him, "I hope that you will take my word for it that Javits spelled backwards spells Bush, . . . who is nothing but a wolf in sheep's clothing as far as all conservatives are concerned." Dr. Charles Walker to Richard English, February 1, 1967, James C. Oberwetter Papers, Special Collections, Southwestern University, Georgetown, box 1, folder 4.

160. Bush campaign letter, undated, Rita Crocker Clements Papers, box 30, folder 54.

161. Bob Fenley, "There Was Never a Doubt," *Dallas Times Herald*, June 12, 1964.

162. John E. Grenier to Rita Bass, June 15, 1964, Tower Papers, box 443.

163. Peter O'Donnell Jr. to Mrs. William McKenzie, June 2, 1964, Rita Crocker Clements Papers, box 28, folder 3.

164. "Twin-Star Tower Seconds Nomination," *Houston Chronicle*, July 16, 1964.

165. Keith Shelton, "George Bush's Father Helps Son Polish Southern Image," *Dallas Times Herald*, July 15, 1964.

166. "Memorandum to District and County Chairmen" from Larry R. Faulkner, Chairman, Texas Youth for Goldwater, undated, Rita Crocker Clements Papers, box 29, folder 18. In 1964 Faulkner was a student at Southern Methodist University and would eventually serve as president of the University of Texas at Austin from 1998 to 2006.

167. Author interview with Ronald B. Dear, Houston, May 17, 2012; author interview with Ed Emmett, Houston, March 25, 2014, both in author's possession.

168. Ronnie Dugger column, *Texas Observer*, September 18, 1964, copy in Hoffman Collection, box 13.

169. Schweizer and Schweizer, *Bushes*, 162.

170. George W. Bush, *41: A Portrait of My Father* (New York: Crown, 2014), 77.

171. G. H. W. Bush, *All the Best*, 89–90.

172. Ibid., 192.

173. Banks, *Money, Marbles, and Chalk*, 55.

174. Schweizer and Schweizer, *Bushes*, 163.

7. AFTER GOLDWATER

1. Roger M. Olien, *From Token to Triumph: The Texas Republicans since 1920* (Dallas: SMU Press, 1982), 192.

2. All nine state representatives seeking re-election were defeated. In Midland County, William S. Davis did not run again but was replaced by another Republican, Frank Cahoon, nephew of former state chairman Orville Bullington. When Cahoon did not run again in 1969, he was replaced by Tom Craddick, who continues to represent the district today. E. Dale Odom interview with Frank Cahoon, October 24, 1967, Oral History Collection, University of North Texas.

3. "Republican backs Johnson in Texas," *New York Times*, July 25, 1964. Also endorsing

Johnson was Maurice Carlson, who had preceded Peter O'Donnell as Dallas County GOP chairman. Olien, *From Token to Triumph*, 190.

4. Among those wanting Burch replaced was George H. W. Bush, who, in a letter to Peter O'Donnell and Senator John Tower, urged them to seek a replacement for Burch; he suggested they choose "a man of predominantly conservative persuasion.... I am not for changing the Party's philosophy as outlined in the platform. I am for broadening the base of the Party." Letter from George H. W. Bush to Peter O'Donnell and John Tower, December 16, 1964, as reprinted in George H. W. Bush, *All the Best: My Life in Letters and Other Writings* (New York: Scribner, 1999), 91–92.

5. Earl Mazo, "Burch's Resignation Split the Goldwater Bloc," *New York Times*, January 14, 1965.

6. "Carlson Asks GOP Shakeup," *Dallas Morning News*, November 7, 1964.

7. "O'Donnell Declares He Won't Quit," *Dallas Morning News*, November 7, 1964.

8. Mike Quinn, "Tower Raps Chiefs Who Withheld Support," *Dallas Morning News*, November 7, 1964.

9. Olien, *From Token to Triumph*, 192–194.

10. "Party Purge Sought," *New York Times*, November 21, 1964.

11. Letter from H. Mason Crocker to Keith Shelton, December 1, 1964, Rita Crocker Clements Papers, Cushing Library, Texas A&M University, box 31. Mason Crocker was the father of Rita Crocker Clements.

12. Rob Allyn, draft article, 19, Rita Crocker Clements Papers, box 43.

13. John R. Knaggs, *Two-Party Texas* (Austin: Aiken, 1986), 57.

14. Peter O'Donnell Jr. to John G. Tower, February 22, 1965, John Knaggs Papers, Southwestern University Special Collections, box 15.

15. Peter O'Donnell Jr. to John G. Tower, March 15, 1965, Knaggs Papers, box 15.

16. Peter O'Donnell Jr. to Rita Bass, April 5, 1965, Rita Crocker Clements Papers, box 26.

17. Peter O'Donnell Jr. to John G. Tower, August 14, 1965, John G. Tower Papers, Southwestern University Special Collections, box NA49.

18. Author interview with John Knaggs, Austin, May 13, 2013, in author's possession. See also Knaggs, *Two-Party Texas*, 78–79.

19. "Extremists Lose Texas G.O.P. Test," *New York Times*, July 3, 1965; Stephen Hess and David S. Broder, *The Republican Establishment* (New York: Harper & Row, 1967), 83.

20. Organized right-wing, anticommunist efforts in Harris County did not begin with the Birch Society. In the 1950s, Freedom in Action was a nonpartisan, invitation-only group of whom Cox was the executive director. Among its supporters were conservative Democrats Shivers, William Blakley, Price Daniel, and Abner McCall, as well as GOP leader Jack Porter. Frankie Randolph Papers, Woodson Research Center, Fondren Library, Rice University, box 4, folder 19. See also Don E. Carleton, *Red Scare! Right-Wing Hysteria, Fifties Fanaticism, and Their Legacy in Texas* (Austin: Texas Monthly Press, 1985).

21. Public Opinion Survey Report by John F. Kraft, Inc., January 1966, Knaggs Papers, box 4.

22. Survey by Opinion Research Corporation, Princeton, NJ, April 1966, 88, Tower

Papers, box 882, folder 5. Given that the report indicated that only 6 percent claimed to be Independents and 5 percent to be undecided, it is apparent that survey takers pushed respondents to identify with one or the other major political party.

23. In these counties, neither Cox nor Bush received as much as 35 percent of the vote. Staff report on targeting counties, Republican Party of Texas, January 1966, Tower Papers, box 500, folder 1.

24. Allyn, draft article, 21.

25. Author interview with William Murchison, April 24, 2014, Dallas, in author's possession.

26. List of candidates for 1966 Republican primary elections, Rita Crocker Clements Papers, box 29, folder 19. The party's gubernatorial candidate was attorney T. E. Kennerly of Houston, whose father, Thomas M. Kennerly, had been appointed as a federal district judge by President Herbert Hoover. T. E. Kennerly had previously been a candidate for attorney general in 1962 and for the Texas Supreme Court in 1964.

27. Knaggs, *Two-Party Texas*, 74–75.

28. Peter O'Donnell Jr. to Mrs. George Pearson, June 2, 1966, Rita Crocker Clements Papers, box 27, folder 22.

29. Memo to canvass volunteers from Peter O'Donnell Jr., June 30, 1966, Rita Crocker Clements Papers, box 28, folder 3.

30. Tower campaign newsletters, Rita Crocker Clements Papers, box 28, folder 3.

31. Jimmy Banks, *Money, Marbles, and Chalk* (Austin: Texas Publishing Company, 1971), 182.

32. Louis M. Seagull, *Southern Republicanism* (New York: John Wiley & Sons, 1975), 137.

33. Rita Crocker Clements Papers, box 28, folder 9.

34. Knaggs, *Two-Party Texas*, 87.

35. Ibid., 89.

36. "Texas G.O.P. to Seek Backing by Liberals," *New York Times*, September 22, 1966.

37. Knaggs, *Two-Party Texas*, 87.

38. David Richards, *Once Upon a Time in Texas: A Liberal in the Lone Star State* (Austin: University of Texas Press, 2002), 224.

39. Kemper Diehl, "Sen. Tower Predicts M-A EEOC Appointment," *San Antonio Express-News*, October 26, 1966.

40. Sam Kinch, "Liberals in Bexar Supporting Tower," *Fort Worth Star-Telegram*, October 23, 1966.

41. Edward H. Miller, *Nut Country: Right-Wing Dallas and the Birth of the Southern Strategy* (Chicago: University of Chicago Press, 2015), 139.

42. Olien, *From Token to Triumph*, 207.

43. The experience made a lasting impression on White: "He got the thunder beat out of him. From that point forward, I never thought endorsements were all that important." Interview with Mark White by Chandler Davidson, June 11, 1987, Chandler Davidson Texas Politics Research Collection, Woodson Research Center, Fondren Library, Rice University.

44. Robert Allyn, "How Dallas Switched Parties: Peter O'Donnell and the Dallas Republicans: 1950–1972," Master's thesis, Southern Methodist University, 1983, 35.

45. E. W. Kenworthy, "G.O.P. and Liberal Democrats in Texas Happy," *New York Times*, November 10, 1966.

46. Memo from Marvin Collins to Republican Leadership, February 21, 1967; news release, Republican Party of Texas, February 23, 1967, Knaggs Papers, box 2.

47. Memo from Jerry Stephens to Peter O'Donnell Jr., August 3, 1967, Tower Papers, box 639, folder 3.

48. Memo from Peter O'Donnell Jr. to Republican Party officials, May 10, 1967, Rita Crocker Clements Papers, box 24, folder 18.

49. Knaggs, *Two-Party Texas*, 111–112.

50. J. William Middendorf II, *A Glorious Disaster: Barry Goldwater's Presidential Campaign and the Origins of the Conservative Movement* (New York: Basic Books, 2006), 243.

51. Author interview with William Murchison, April 24, 2014, Dallas, in author's possession.

52. Rick Perlstein, *Nixonland: The Rise of a President and the Fracturing of America* (New York: Scribner, 2008), 175.

53. Ibid., 176.

54. Memo to Fellow Republicans from Peter O'Donnell Jr., April 27, 1967, Tower Papers, box 936, folder 4.

55. Peter O'Donnell Jr. to Peter Malatesta, July 17, 1967, Tower Papers, box 936, folder 4.

56. Thomas C. Reed, *The Reagan Enigma, 1964–1980* (Los Angeles: Figueroa, 2014), 115–117.

57. Minutes of the State Republican Executive Committee meeting, Austin, September 22, 1967, 2, 8–9.

58. Reed, *The Reagan Enigma*, 121–122.

59. Rowland Evans and Robert Novak, "Texas GOP Holds Favorite Son," *Dallas Times Herald*, November 20, 1967.

60. H. J. Porter to John G. Tower, February 15, 1962, Tower Papers, box 936, folder 6. Even earlier O'Donnell had asked Alger's office to write Reagan and request copies of two recent speeches. Carolyn Bacon to Ronald Reagan, December 20, 1961, Bruce Alger Collection, Dallas Public Library, box 4, folder 22.

61. Lewis Chester, Godfrey Hodgson, and Bruce Page, *An American Melodrama* (New York: Dell, 1969), 495.

62. Wayne Thorburn, *Red State: An Insider's Story of How the GOP Came to Dominate Texas Politics* (Austin: University of Texas Press, 2014), 126–129.

63. Jeff Roche, "Cowboy Conservatism," in *The Conservative Sixties*, ed. David Farber and Jeff Roche (New York: Peter Lang Publishing, 2003), 88–89.

64. Robert B. Semple Jr., "Nixon Is Cheered by Texas Crowds," *New York Times*, January 21, 1968.

65. J. R. "Butch" Butler to Mrs. R. D. Bass, March 13, 1968, Rita Crocker Clements Papers, box 28, folder 12.

66. Bill Hunter, "GOP Struggle of O'Donnell, Fay Expected," *Dallas Morning News*, April 5, 1968.

67. Bill Hunter, "Delay by O'Donnell on Ouster Indicated," *Dallas Morning News*, April 19, 1968.

68. Fred Bonavita, "GOP Fight Is Cooled," *Houston Post*, April 19, 1968.

69. Jim Lehrer, "State GOP Fight Only Postponed?," *Dallas Times Herald*, April 27, 1968.

70. Albert B. Fay to John G. Tower, May 15, 1968, Tower Papers, box 639, folder 3.

71. Olien, *From Token to Triumph*, 212–214.

72. Richard M. Morehead, "Reagan Tells Texas GOP He Isn't Running in State," *Dallas Morning News*, April 21, 1968, citing a letter of Reagan to O'Donnell dated April 9, 1968.

73. Texans for Ronald Reagan newsletter, undated, Rita Crocker Clements Papers, box 28, folder 12.

74. Chester, Hodgson, and Page, *American Melodrama*, 229.

75. Texans for Reagan newsletter, undated, Rita Crocker Clements Papers, box 28, folder 12.

76. Chester, Hodgson, and Page, *American Melodrama*, 496. In Miami Beach Nixon ended up with a twenty-five vote majority, testifying to his need for the Texas votes to be cast for him, rather than Tower.

77. "Tower Releases Delegation to Secure Nixon Nomination," *The Texas Republican*, July 1988, Rita Crocker Clements Papers, box 28, folder 12.

78. Carolyn Barta, *Bill Clements: Texian to His Toenails* (Austin: Eakin, 1996), 10.

79. Texans for Reagan newsletter, undated, Rita Crocker Clements Papers, box 28, folder 12.

80. Jim Lehrer, "Fussing Texans Turn to Nixon," *Dallas Times Herald*, August 8, 1968, quoting Jim Campbell of Pampa, Reagan floor leader in the delegation.

81. Jim Lehrer, "Dallasite Maneuvers for Percy," *Dallas Times Herald*, August 5, 1968; Tom Wicker, "Nixon Is Nominated on the First Ballot; Support for Lindsay in 2d Place Growing," *New York Times*, August 9, 1968; Meg McKain Grier, *Grassroots Women* (Boerne, TX: Wingscape, 2001), 168–169.

82. Jim Lehrer, "Dallasite Maneuvers for Percy," *Dallas Times Herald*, August 5, 1968.

83. Jim Lehrer, "Fussing Texans Turn to Nixon," *Dallas Times Herald*, August 8, 1968.

84. Banks, *Money*, 176.

85. Jimmy Banks, "Texas GOP Ho-Hum about Agnew Choice," *Dallas Morning News*, August 9, 1968.

86. Banks, *Money*, 176.

87. Peter O'Donnell Jr. to John G. Tower, October 31, 1967; "Tower Predicts GOP Conservative, undated news clipping, Tower Papers, box 639, folder 3. See also Bill Hunter, "Tower Hits Policy on Enemy Targets," *Dallas Morning News*, October 26, 1967.

88. Banks, *Money*, 180.

89. Quote from Jon Ford, capitol correspondent for the *San Antonio Express-News*, in Knaggs, *Two-Party Texas*, 120–121.

90. Banks, *Money*, 179–180.

91. "Republican Primary Returns of an Election Held May 5, 1968," Lorenzo de Zavala State Archives, Austin. Republican primary election returns prior to 1992 are located in the state archives; since 1992 statewide and county primary returns for state and federal offices are posted on the website of the Elections Division of the office of the Texas Secretary of State: www.sos.state.tx.us/elections/historical/index.shtml, accessed May 30, 2020.

92. Jimmy Banks, "Texas GOP Ho-Hum about Agnew Choice," *Dallas Morning News*, August 9, 1968.

93. Knaggs, *Two-Party Texas*, 125.

94. Quoted in Hawkins Henley Menefee Jr., "The Two-Party Democrats: The Study of a Political Faction," Master's thesis, University of Texas at Austin, 1970, 81.

95. Olien, *From Token to Triumph*, 216.

96. Knaggs, *Two-Party Texas*, 129.

97. Dave Shapiro to Marvin Collins and John Knaggs, June 2, 1968, Knaggs Papers, box 1, folder 7.

98. Peter O'Donnell Jr. to John G. Tower, September 23, 1968, Tower Papers, box 639, folder 3.

99. Knaggs, *Two-Party Texas*, 135–136.

100. The Eggers budget total is in Knaggs, *Two-Party Texas*, 136; the Shivers quote appears in Banks, *Money*, 127.

101. "O'Donnell Did Not Withhold Funds, Eggers' Men Claim," *Houston Post*, November 27, 1968.

102. Jimmy Banks, "Texas GOP Not Doing So Great Despite Claim," *Dallas Morning News*, December 13, 1968; William H. Gardner, "O'Donnell Will Stay as GOP State Leader," undated news clipping, Tower Papers, box 888.

103. Gardner, "O'Donnell Will Stay."

104. "Start '70 Campaign Now, Tower Tells Texas GOP," *Dallas Times Herald*, December 10, 1968.

105. "Republicans Predict Big Gains Ahead in Texas," *Dallas Morning News*, December 10, 1968.

106. Bo Byers, "State GOP Already Looking Ahead to '70 Races," *Houston Chronicle*, December 10, 1968.

107. Rowland Evans and Robert Novak, "Serious Factionalism Strikes Texas GOP, Columnists Say," *Dallas Times Herald*, January 3, 1969.

108. Knaggs, *Two-Party Texas*, 138. Armstrong would soon become national committeewoman, with Milburn replacing her as party vice chairman, while Steger would be selected as state chairman.

109. Oral history interview with Nancy Palm, December 16, 1974, Interview A-0194, Southern Oral History Program Collection (#4007). © This work is the property of the University of North Carolina at Chapel Hill. It may be used freely by individuals for research, teaching, and personal use as long as this statement of availability is included in the text.

110. Knaggs, *Two-Party Texas*, 130.

111. Oral history interview with Nancy Palm, December 16, 1974.

112. Author interview with Chase Untermeyer, Houston, March 24, 2014, in author's possession.

113. Marjorie Meyer Arsht, *All the Way From Yoakum: The Personal Journey of a Political Insider* (College Station: Texas A&M University Press, 2005), 172–173.

114. Ken Sheets, "Mrs. Palm Raps O'Donnell on Nixon Appointments," *Houston Chronicle*, February 5, 1969.

115. News release, Harris County Republican Party, February 4, 1969, Tower Papers.

116. Memo from Mrs. Nancy Palm, Harris County Republican Party, to Republican Party officials and other interested persons, February 7, 1969, Tower Papers.

117. Ken Sheets, "State GOP Chief Hits Attacks by Mrs. Palm," undated news clipping, *Houston Chronicle*, Tower Papers.

118. H. J. Porter to John G. Tower, February 20, 1969, Tower Papers.

119. "Texas GOP Chief Hails Poerner Win," *San Antonio Express News*, March 1, 1969.

120. Knaggs, *Two-Party Texas*, 142.

121. Legislative Reference Library of Texas profile of John H. Poerner: "Party listed as Independent on member card; original listing as Republican marked through, Texas House of Representatives, Chief Clerk's Office." Lrl.state.tx.us/legeLeaders/members, accessed on January 26, 2012.

122. Allyn, "How Dallas Switched," 36. The YR Star, May 1969, James C. Oberwetter Papers, 1963–1972, Special Collections, Southwestern University, Georgetown, box 1.

123. Fred Bonavita, "Fay Resigns GOP Committee Post," *Houston Post*, May 4, 1969.

124. Ernest Stromberger, "GOP Lawmakers Seeking Spotlight," *Dallas Times Herald*, May 18, 1969.

125. Brian D. Posler and Daniel S. Ward, "Texas," in *State Party* Profiles, ed. Andrew M. Appleton and Daniel S. Ward (Washington, DC: Congressional Quarterly, 1997), 311.

126. Banks, *Money*, 16.

127. George Bush to Dr. Walter D. Wilkerson, October 21, 1969, Montgomery County Republican Party Papers, Montgomery County Republican Party, Conroe.

128. George H. W. Bush, *All the Best: My Life in Letters and Other Writings* (New York: Scribner, 1999), 121–122. Peter Schweizer and Rochelle Schweizer, *The Bushes: Portrait of a Dynasty* (New York: Doubleday, 2004), 196–200.

129. "Texas G.O.P. Seeks Two Top Offices," *New York Times*, January 4, 1970.

130. Martin Waldron, "Conservative Beats Yarborough in Democratic Primary in Texas," *New York Times*, May 3, 1970.

131. "Texas GOP Seeks Two Top Offices."

132. "GOP Candidate Fullerton Warns of Power Axis," *Houston Post*, September 1, 1970.

133. Ernest Stromberger, "Eggers Campaign Gains Steam," *Dallas Times Herald*, July 12, 1970. Notes on campaign in Knaggs Papers, box 11, folder 16.

134. Rita Crocker Bass to Bush Belles county chairs, undated, Rita Crocker Clements Papers, box 24, folder 13.

135. Quoted in Olien, *From Token to Triumph*, 222.

136. The endorsements from Galbraith, Gruening, and Northcott are located in David

Hoffman Collection, George H. W. Bush Presidential Library, Texas A&M University, College Station, Early Career Files, box 13.

137. Author interview with James B. Francis Jr., Dallas, April 24, 2014, in author's possession.

138. Bo Byers, "Blow to Nixon's Prestige," *Houston Chronicle*, November 4, 1970.

139. Gayle McNutt, "Rural Vote Decided Race, Bentsen and Bush Agree," *Houston Chronicle*, November 4, 1970.

140. Author interview with Robert Estrada, Dallas, August 11, 2014, in author's possession.

141. Agnich was a geologist who had worked for Geophysical Service, a company that became Texas Instruments, and eventually became president of the reorganized company. He retired in 1961, then served as Dallas County GOP chairman from 1967 to 1969, as a state representative from 1970 to 1986, and as Republican national committeeman from 1972 to 1976. Fred Agnich interviewed by James Riddlesperger, January 6, 1972, OH0152; interviewed by Ronald E. Marcello, December 15, 1974, OH0272, UNT Oral History Program Collection, University of North Texas.

142. Memo from Beryl Milburn to State Republican Executive Committee, December 18, 1970. Tower Papers, box 880, folder 8.

143. Administrative/Biographical History, William M. Steger Papers, University of Texas at Tyler University Archives and Special Collections.

144. Hedrick Smith, "Naming of Bush to UN Reported," *New York Times*, December 11, 1970.

145. Chase Untermeyer Interview, July 27–28, 2000, George H. W. Bush Oral History Project, Miller Center, University of Virginia, Charlottesville.

146. James M. Naughton, "Connally to Get Kennedy's Post at the Treasury," *New York Times*, December 15, 1970.

147. Author telephone interview with Ernest Angelo Jr., August 13, 2014, in author's possession.

148. Quoted in Allyn, "How Dallas Switched," 37.

149. Nicholas C. Chriss, quoted in Banks, *Money*, 248.

8. THE HIGHS AND LOWS OF THE 1970S

1. The Sharpstown scandal is discussed in Charles Deaton, *The Year They Threw the Rascals Out* (Austin: Shoal Creek, 1973), and in Sam Kinch Jr. and Ben Proctor, *Texas under a Cloud* (Austin: Jenkins, 1972).

2. The Dirty Thirty actually comprised thirty-five members, including all Republicans except Tom Christian of Armstrong County. A list of the members can be found in Brian D. Sweany, "Dirty Thirty," *Texas Monthly*, September 2001.

3. It would not be until 1975 that all multimember districts were eliminated.

4. "O'Donnell Resigns GOP Post," *Dallas Morning News*, February 15, 1972; "Texas G.O.P. Leader Resigns," *New York Times*, February 15, 1972.

5. Ron Calhoun, "O'Donnell Talked for National Post," *Dallas Times Herald*, February 15, 1972.

6. Rob Allyn, "How Dallas Switched Parties: Peter O'Donnell and the Dallas Republicans: 1950–1972," Master's thesis, Southern Methodist University, 1983, 38.

7. Tom Johnson, "Tower Backers Seen in O'Donnell's Resignation," *Dallas Morning News*, February 16, 1972.

8. Quoted in Allyn, "How Dallas Switched," 38.

9. "O'Donnell Resigns Post, Gives Personal Reasons," February 15, 1972, no publication indicated. Rita Crocker Clements Papers, Cushing Library, Texas A&M University, box 31, folder 8.

10. Johnson, "Tower Backers."

11. "O'Donnell and the GOP," *Dallas Morning News*, February 16, 1972.

12. Quoted in Allyn, "How Dallas Switched," 39. With his withdrawal from daily involvement in politics, O'Donnell devoted more time and resources to philanthropy. His commitment is outlined in Peter O'Donnell Jr., *Improving Education, Changing Lives* (Austin, TX: Dolph Briscoe Center for American History, 2017).

13. Ron Calhoun, "Agnich Interested in GOP Post?," *Dallas Times Herald*, February 16, 1972.

14. "Texas Democrats to Vote on Busing," *New York Times*, March 14, 1972. Some Republicans had urged Agnich to run for governor in 1972, but he indicated that his preference was to remain a state legislator as well as seek the appointment as national committeeman.

15. Chase Untermeyer, "The Peter Out Principle," *Texas Monthly*, July 1974.

16. Rita Crocker Clements Papers, box 27, folder 3.

17. Rita Crocker Clements Papers, box 26, folder 11.

18. John Knaggs Papers, Southwestern University Special Connections, box 4, folder 1; author telephone interview with Gary Bruner, June 19, 2014, in author's possession.

19. Roger M. Olien, *From Token to Triumph: The Texas Republicans since 1920* (Dallas: SMU Press, 1982), 229.

20. Gayle McNutt, "The Texas GOP: A Rocky Road of Its Own Making in '72," *Houston Chronicle*, February 20, 1972.

21. Art Wiese, "GOP Leaders Throw Down Gauntlet to Grover," *Houston Post*, June 12, 1972.

22. Jane Ely and Art Wiese, "GOP Axes Grover-Led Ouster Bid," *Houston Post*, June 14, 1972.

23. Jane Ely, "GOP Urge Unity," *Houston Post*, June 13, 1972.

24. Billy Hathorn, "Mayor Ernest Angelo, Jr., of Midland and the 96–0 Reagan Sweep of Texas, May 1, 1976," *West Texas Historical Association Yearbook* 86 (2010), 87.

25. John R. Knaggs, *Two-Party Texas* (Austin: Aiken, 1986), 169.

26. Stewart Davis, "Grover Demands GOP Oust Leaders," *Dallas Morning News*, June 14, 1972.

27. Ely and Wiese, "GOP Axes."

28. Ely, "GOP Urge Unity."

29. Ely and Wiese, "GOP Axes."

30. Ibid.

31. Ibid.

32. Mary Rice Brogan, "GOP National Committeewoman Criticizes Grover," *Houston Chronicle*, June 15, 1972. From 1971 to 1973 Armstrong also served as cochairman of the Republican National Committee and became the first woman to give a keynote speech at a national convention when she did so at the 1972 Miami Beach convention. Armstrong was later appointed US ambassador to Great Britain. Judy Harkison, "Two Political Leaders: A Study in Contrasts," *New York Times*, May 23, 1972.

33. "GOP's Milburn Seeks Unity," *Houston Post*, June 15, 1972.

34. "GOP Faction Urges Mrs. Palm to Resign," *Houston Post*, June 15, 1972.

35. Ann Arnold, "Hank Grover: He Plans on Winning," July 24, 1972, unattributed news clipping, John G. Tower Papers, Southwestern University Special Collections, box 639, folder 10.

36. Arnold, "Hank Grover." In the 1968 election gubernatorial candidate Eggers received 1,254,333 votes, while presidential candidate Nixon won 1,227,844.

37. Hathorn, "Mayor Ernest Angelo," 87.

38. Untitled notes, Rita Crocker Clements Papers, box 28, folder 16.

39. Art Wiese, "Nixon Margin Likely to Bring Texas Sweep, GOP Predicts," *Houston Post*, September 19, 1972.

40. Jane Ely, "Unified Optimism Paramount Theme of GOP Meeting," *Houston Post*, September 20, 1972.

41. Art Wiese, "GOP Vote Takes Aim at Unity," *Houston Post*, September 20, 1972.

42. Jane Ely, "Republicans Accept Platform," *Houston Post*, September 20, 1972. More than forty years later this issue was a topic of discussion as the 2014 state convention eliminated a proposed plank supporting research into the potential medical uses of marijuana.

43. Knaggs, *Two-Party Texas*, 172.

44. Olien, *From Token to Triumph*, 231.

45. Martin Waldron, "Sanders Drive Gains in Texas," *New York Times*, October 11, 1972.

46. Carolyn Barta, "Steelman Holds onto Lead to Upset Incumbent Cabell," *Dallas Morning News*, November 8, 1972; Dave Montgomery, "Door-Knocking Drive by Steelman Pays Off," *Dallas Times Herald*, November 8, 1972.

47. Kristi Strickland interview with Betty Andujar, September 10, 1993, Oral History Collection, University of North Texas.

48. Lynwood Abram, "Republican Kay Bailey Analyzes the Voting," *Houston Chronicle*, November 12, 1972. For an interesting overview of this campaign, see Ann Fears Crawford, "A Step in the Right Direction: Kay Bailey Hutchison goes to the Texas Legislature," paper presented at East Texas Historical Association conference, February 21, 1998, Ann Fears Crawford Papers, Woodson Research Center, Fondren Library, Rice University, box 3, folder 5.

49. Miscellaneous notes, Rita Crocker Clements Papers, box 26, folder 1; box 53, folder 22.

50. Carolyn Barta, *Bill Clements: Texian to His Toenails* (Austin: Eakin, 1996), 134–139.

51. Quoted in Michael L. Antle, "The Rise of the Republicans: Party Realignment in Twentieth Century Texas," PhD diss., University of North Texas, December 2012, 223.

52. Knaggs, *Two-Party Texas*, 178–179.

53. Ibid., 179.

54. Rita Crocker Clements Papers, box 30, folder 58.

55. Thure Barnett Cannon, "The Texas Political System: Shifting Dynamics in Political Party Power," Master's thesis, University of Texas at Austin, 1998, 34.

56. Sean P. Cunningham, *Cowboy Conservatism: Texas and the Rise of the Modern Right* (Lexington: University Press of Kentucky, 2010), 149.

57. Untermeyer, "Peter Out Principle."

58. Author interview with Jerry W. Smith, Houston, March 25, 2014, in author's possession.

59. Quoted in Cannon, "Texas Political System," 33–34.

60. Quoted in Knaggs, *Two-Party Texas*, 178–179.

61. Dave Montgomery, "Whither the GOP," *Dallas Times Herald*, November 11, 1973.

62. Randy Fitzgerald, "GOP's Granberry Announces," *Houston Post*, June 22, 1973.

63. John Geddie, "Governor Race Not for Bush," *Dallas Morning News*, March 6, 1973; George H. W. Bush to Verta Hardegree, August 10, 1973, in George H. W. Bush, *All the Best: My Life in Letters and Other Writings* (New York: Scribner, 1999), 169.

64. John Knaggs to John G. Tower, July 31, 1973, Knaggs Papers, box 11, folder 15.

65. George Willeford to Rita Bass, September 18, 1973, Rita Crocker Clements Papers, box 27, folder 4.

66. George H. W. Bush to Rita Bass, undated, Rita Crocker Clements Papers, box 30, folder 54.

67. George H. W. Bush to Neil Calnan, October 2, 1973, Neil Calnan Papers, Southwestern University Special Collections, box 2, folder 2.

68. George H. W. Bush to Thornton Hardie Jr., October 17, 1973, in G. H. W. Bush, *All The Best*, 169.

69. Montgomery, "Whither the GOP."

70. Aris A. "Bob" Mallas Jr. to Rita Bass, October 10, 1973, Rita Crocker Clements Papers, box 30, folder 54.

71. George H. W. Bush to Aris A. Mallas Jr., November 1, 1973, Rita Crocker Clements Papers, box 30, folder 54.

72. Christopher Lydon, "Governor's Race Weighed by Bush," *New York Times*, November 4, 1973.

73. Knaggs, *Two-Party Texas*, 181.

74. "Bush Says 'No' to Texas Race," *New York Times*, November 17, 1973; George H. W. Bush to Rita Bass, November 15, 1973, Rita Crocker Clements Papers, box 30, folder 54.

75. Untermeyer, "Peter Out Principle."

76. Fred Bonavita, "GOP Unenthusiastic to Tower State Race," *Houston Post*, undated news clipping, Tower Papers, box 639, folder 10.

77. "Proposed Candidacy Spawns Charges," *Austin American-Statesman*, December 11, 1973.

78. "Agnich Denial of Hutchison Support Is Challenged," *Houston Chronicle*, December 13, 1973.

79. Richard Morehead, "Hutchison Entry to Race Called Benefit to Grover," *Dallas Morning News*, December 11, 1973.

80. Knaggs, *Two-Party Texas*, 182.

81. "Grover 'Torpedoed,'" *Texas Observer*, March 29, 1974, 7.

82. O'Leary has gone on to be a radio commentator and author of eleven books, including a biting critique of Barack Obama published before his first presidential campaign, *The Audacity of Deceit* (Los Angeles: WND, 2008).

83. Barry Fitzgerald, "Willeford Stepdown Predicted," *Houston Post*, August 24, 1973.

84. George Willeford to Rita Bass, September 4, 1973, Rita Crocker Clements Papers, box 27, folder 4.

85. George Willeford to Rita Bass, October 19, 1973, Rita Crocker Clements Papers, box 27, folder 4; "Willeford Quits GOP Chairmanship," *Dallas Morning News*, October 24, 1973.

86. Montgomery, "Whither the GOP."

87. "Chronology of Events in Agnew Case," *New York Times*, October 11, 1973.

88. Knaggs, *Two-Party Texas*, 181.

89. Montgomery, "Whither the GOP."

90. Untermeyer, "Peter Out Principle."

91. Richard Lyons and William Chapman, "Judiciary Committee Approves Article to Impeach President Nixon, 27 to 11," *Washington Post*, July 28, 1974.

92. Carroll Kilpatrick, "Nixon Resigns," *Washington Post*, August 9, 1974.

93. Peter Schweizer and Rochelle Schweizer, *The Bushes: Portrait of a Dynasty* (New York: Doubleday, 2004), 235–237.

94. Mike Kelly, "Bush Leads Veep Field, Many Feel," *Dallas Times Herald*, August 13, 1974.

95. George H. W. Bush to James A. Baker, August 21, 1974, in G. H. W. Bush, *All The Best*, 194–196. In private, Bush's reaction at not being selected has been described as "mighty angry." According to Eddie Mahe, at the time political director at the RNC, "He was pissed. It was the second time he had been passed over for veep." Craig Shirley, *Reagan's Revolution: The Untold Story of the Campaign that Started It All* (Nashville: Nelson Current, 2005), 28.c.

96. George H. W. Bush to Rita Bass, August 23, 1974, Rita Crocker Clements Papers, box 30, folder 54.

97. Informal notes, Knaggs Papers, box 4, folder 1.

98. "Tower Seeks to Avoid Ford Setback in Texas," *New York Times*, September 16, 1974.

99. Knaggs, *Two-Party Texas*, 185.

100. "Texas G.O.P. Parley Is Critical of Ford," *New York Times*, September 19, 1974.

101. Quoted in Knaggs, *Two-Party Texas*, 185–186.

102. Knaggs, *Two-Party Texas*, 189.

103. "State GOP Urged to Change Tactics," *Dallas Times Herald*, February 16, 1975.

104. Memo from Polly Sowell to Zack Fisher, May 17, 1975, Rita Crocker Clements Papers, box 27, folder 4.

105. Jack Warren to Rita Clements, June 6, 1975, Rita Crocker Clements Papers, box 27, folder 4.

106. Jon Ford, "Hot Two-Way Fight Seen for GOP Chairmanship," *Austin American-Statesman*, June 13, 1975.

107. Ernest Angelo Jr. to "Fellow SREC Members," June 16, 1975, Tower Papers, box 880, folder 9.

108. Jon Ford, "GOP Elects State Chairman," *Austin American-Statesman*, June 30, 1975.

109. Author interview with Chase Untermeyer, Houston, March 24, 2014, in author's possession.

110. John G. Tower to Nancy Palm, June 17, 1975, Tower Papers, box 880, folder 9.

111. Author interview with Mary Jane Smith, Houston, March 25, 2014, in author's possession.

112. Al Reinert, "Big Mamas," *Texas Monthly*, October 1975, 52–57; Taber Ward, "Harris County's Nancy Palm," *Republican Report*, May 1975, Tower Papers, box 880, folder 10; Harla Kaplan, "A Political Maverick Can Make the System Work," *Houston Town and Country*, March 1976, Chandler Davidson Texas Politics Research Collection, Woodson Research Center, Fondren Library, Rice University, box 8, folder 2; Billie Carr Papers, 1956–2003, Woodson Research Center, Fondren Library, Rice University, box 14, folder 6.

113. Chandler Davidson, *Race and Class in Texas Politics* (Princeton, NJ: Princeton University Press, 1990), 182–190.

114. Griffin Smith Jr. and Paul Burka, "The Best, the Worst, and the Fair-to-Middlin'," *Texas Monthly*, May 1976, 111–112.

115. Ron Calhoun, "Steelman Waging Extraordinary Senate Campaign," *Dallas Times Herald*, January 14, 1976.

116. Memorandum for the President from Bo Callaway, October 13, 1975, Richard B. Cheney Files, Gerald R. Ford Presidential Library, Ann Arbor, MI, box 14.

117. Gerald R. Ford to Rita Clements, October 15, 1975, Rita Crocker Clements Papers, box 24, folder 27.

118. Howard "Bo" Callaway to Rita Clements, December 3, 1975, Rita Crocker Clements Papers, box 24, folder 27.

119. Craig Shirley, *Reagan's Revolution*, 44. The preliminary stages of the 1976 campaign are covered on pp. 22–66.

120. Ron Nessen, *It Sure Looks Different from the Inside* (Chicago: Playboy Press, 1978), 195.

121. Shirley, *Reagan's Revolution*, 54–55.

122. As quoted in Jules Witcover, *Marathon: The Pursuit of the Presidency: 1972–1976* (New York: Viking, 1977), 90–91.

123. Author interview with Ray Barnhart, St. Clairsville, OH, June 27, 2012, in author's possession.

124. Gilbert Garcia, *Reagan's Comeback: Four Weeks in Texas that Changed American Politics Forever* (San Antonio: Trinity University Press, 2012), 42.

125. Hathorn, "Mayor Ernest Angelo," 82.

126. News release, Citizens for Reagan for President Committee, November 21, 1975, Tower Papers, box 888, folder 3.

127. The President Ford Committee Texas Campaign, December 29, 1975, Rita Crocker Clements Papers, box 24, folder 27.

128. Greg Jones, "Tower Backing Ford—Reagan No Worry," *El Paso Times*, November 22, 1975.

129. Art Wiese, "Ford, Reagan Battle Lines Already Forming in State," *Houston Post*, January 12, 1976.

130. Memorandum from Mrs. Beryl Buckley Milburn, President Ford Committee, to Texas Republican Leaders, February 20, 1976, Rita Crocker Clements Papers, box 24, folder 28.

131. Shirley, *Reagan's Revolution*, 110.

132. "Republicans: Reagan's Startling Texas Landslide," *Time*, May 10, 1976.

133. Garcia, *Reagan's Comeback*, 70; Jerry Smith interview.

134. Shirley, *Reagan's Revolution*, 192.

135. Garcia, *Reagan's Comeback*, 62–63.

136. Ray A. Barnhart, Barbara Staff, and Ernest Angelo to Reagan Campaign Leaders, March 22, 1976, Rita Crocker Clements Papers, box 24, folder 28.

137. R. W. Apple Jr., "Texas Politicians Give Reagan Edge in May 1 Primary," *New York Times*, April 19, 1976.

138. James P. Sterba, "Ford Believed to Have Cut Reagan's Strength in Texas," *New York Times*, May 1, 1976.

139. James P. Sterba, "Democratic Vote Propels Reagan to Texas Sweep," *New York Times*, May 3, 1976.

140. Knaggs, *Two-Party Texas*, 195.

141. James M. Naughton, "Ford Prepares for a Difficult Fight for Nomination after Texas Defeat," *New York Times*, May 3, 1976.

142. "An Explanation of the Reagan Victories in Texas and the Caucus States," unsigned and undated, Jerry Jones Files, Gerald R. Ford Presidential Library, Ann Arbor, MI, box 25; emphasis in original.

143. Garcia, *Reagan's Comeback*, 147.

144. Interview with Ray Barnhart; Hathorn, "Mayor Ernest Angelo," 86.

145. Richard West, "Texas Monthly Reporter: Together We Could Have," *Texas Monthly*, August 1976.

146. Garcia, *Reagan's Comeback*, 148–149.

147. The Schweiker decision and its aftermath is discussed in Shirley, *Reagan's Revolution*, 272–282.

148. Witcover, *Marathon*, 466.

149. Gerald M. Pomper, "The Nominating Contests and Conventions," in *The Election of 1976: Reports and Interpretations*, Gerald Pomper et al. (New York: David MacKay, 1977), 20–23.

150. Knaggs, *Two-Party Texas*, 196.

151. Garcia, *Reagan's Comeback*, 83.

152. Peter O'Donnell Jr. to Rita Clements, August 25, 1976, Rita Crocker Clements Papers, box 24, folder 27. JBC III is John B. Connally III, the oldest son of former governor Connally.

153. Douglas E. Kneeland, "Dole Avoids Taking Sides in Battle for Control of Texas G.O.P.; Says Republicans 'Must Win' in November," *New York Times*, September 12, 1976.

154. James P. Sterba, "Ford Backers Narrowly Keep Control of Texas Republican Party," *New York Times*, September 13, 1976.

155. Knaggs, *Two-Party Texas*, 199–200.

156. R. W. Apple Jr., "Republicans' Campaign in Texas Handicapped by Financing Curbs," *New York Times*, October 14, 1976.

157. Sean Cunningham, "The Paranoid Style and Its Limits," in *The Texas Right: The Radical Roots of Lone Star Conservatism*, ed. David O'Donald Cullen and Kyle G. Wilkison (College Station: Texas A&M University Press, 2014), 114.

158. Garcia, *Reagan's Comeback*, 171.

159. Richard S. Dunham, "Reagan Revolution Changed the Course of Texas Politics," *Houston Chronicle*, February 6, 2011.

9. BREAKING THE GLASS CEILING

1. Notes, John G. Tower Papers, Southwestern University Special Collections, box 876, folder 2.

2. Douglas S. Harlan, "The Texas GOP, I: What Chance in '78," *Texas Observer*, October 7, 1977, 3.

3. Ray Hutchison to Julian Zimmerman, October 11, 1977, in author's possession.

4. Harlan, "Texas GOP," 5.

5. "Republicans Win Key Special Elections," *Texas Advocate*, March 1978, 1, 3, 7–8.

6. Polly Sowell to Nathan White, October 18, 1977, Tower Papers, box 880, folder 1.

7. Harlan, "Texas GOP," 20.

8. "Grover Weighs Opposing Tower," *Fort Worth Star-Telegram*, May 2, 1977; Tower Papers, box 873, folder 7.

9. Fundraising letter from Nancy Palm, September 1977, Tower Papers, box 880, folder 1.

10. Author interview with John Knaggs, Austin, May 13, 2013, in author's possession.

11. Stewart Davis, "Grover to Challenge Tower in Senate Bid," *Dallas Morning News*, February 7, 1978.

12. Author interview with Robert Estrada, Dallas, August 11, 2014, in author's possession.

13. At this point in the story, the author has become a participant as well as an observer, continuing involvement in Texas Republican politics in various roles over the next several

decades. Since the present work is a history of the Republican Party and not a personal memoir, references to the author will appear in the third person and only when necessary to the overall narrative.

14. "The Ten Best and the Ten Worst," *Texas Monthly*, July 1975, 18–26.

15. "Remarks by Peter O'Donnell Jr. on receiving the Santa Rita Award," December 10, 1986, Rita Crocker Clements Papers, Cushing Library, Texas A&M University, box 8, folder 15.

16. The discussion with Schmitt and the decision to become a candidate is presented in Carolyn Barta, *Bill Clements: Texian to His Toenails* (Austin: Eakin, 1996), 5–9.

17. Ron Calhoun, "Clements: 'Let's Do It,'" *Dallas Times Herald*, November 14, 1977.

18. Barta, *Bill Clements*, 8.

19. Author interview with James B. Francis, Dallas, April 24, 2014, and author interview with Tom Reed, Austin, March 31, 2015, in author's possession.

20. Paul Burka, "The Firing Line," *Texas Monthly*, April 1979, 130–132. According to a memo among the Rita Crocker Clements Papers, the early preprimary advisory committee also included Tom Rhodes, an attorney and executive with Bill Clements's firm SEDCO; Ashley Priddy, former mayor of Highland Park; and Stuart Spencer, a campaign professional from California. George Strake was added to the management committee in March. Rita Crocker Clements Papers, box 21, folder 5.

21. Francis interview.

22. Quoted in Barta, *Bill Clements*, 11.

23. Millard K. Neptune to William P. Clements, December 28, 1977, William Perry Clements Personal Papers, Cushing Memorial Library, Texas A&M University, box 15, folder 30.

24. Memo to Management Committee from T. C. Reed, December 23, 1977, Rita Crocker Clements Papers. Reed's analysis was right in line with the actual 1978 primary turnout, but with the Houston (27 percent) and Dallas–Fort Worth areas (33 percent) providing a slightly higher percentage of the total participation than had been true in 1976. His later estimate of an overall turnout of 150,000 voters was close to the actual total of 158,403. Memo to Management Committee from T. C. Reed, January 6, 1978, Rita Crocker Clements Papers.

25. Quoted in Meg McKain Grier, *Grassroots Women* (Boerne, TX: Wingscape, 2001), 304–305.

26. Reed interview.

27. Quoted in Barta, *Bill Clements*, 195.

28. Ibid., 193–194.

29. Francis interview.

30. Author interview with George W. Strake Jr., Houston, March 25, 2014, in author's possession.

31. Author interview with Chase Untermeyer, Houston, March 24, 2014, in author's possession.

32. Quoted in Adam Clymer, "Party United and Big Campaign Treasuries Raising Hopes of Republicans in Texas," *New York Times*, April 29, 1978.

33. Ibid.

34. "Running All Over the State! GOP Candidates in 68 House Districts," *Texas Advocate*, March 1978, 7.

35. Quoted in George W. Bush, *41: A Portrait of My Father* (New York: Crown, 2014), 126.

36. Adam Clymer, "Texas Republicans Battle in Primary, but Carter Is Their No. 1 Target," *New York Times*, May 4, 1978.

37. Gary Hoitsma, "Carter in Trouble," *Texas Advocate*, March 1978, 4.

38. Quoted in Clymer, "Texas Republicans."

39. Karl Rove, *Courage and Consequence: My Life as a Conservative in the Fight* (New York: Threshold, 2010), 48–51.

40. Sam Kinch Jr., "Connally, Bush Try Different Styles to Reach Same Goal," *Dallas Morning News*, January 12, 1978; "Reagan, Connally, Rhodes Give Early Spark to Six Republican Congressional Races," *Texas Advocate*, April 1978, 1, 6; Harris Worcester, "Travels with Bush and Connally," *Texas Observer*, September 22, 1978, 18–19.

41. Stewart Davis, "Briscoe Wanted Four Years Too Many," *Dallas Morning News*, May 9, 1978.

42. The third candidate in the race, Clarence Thompson of Fort Worth, received only 4,790 votes and was never a campaign factor.

43. "Hill Is in for 'Real Fracas' Clements Warns," *Texas Advocate*, June 1978, 2.

44. Unattributed report on Hill primary campaign, Rita Crocker Clements Papers, box 20, folder 47.

45. Interview with O. H. "Ike" Harris by Ronald Marcello, November 27, 1978, Oral History Collection, University of North Texas, 20.

46. Memo to Republican Leadership from Ray Barnhart, June 6, 1978, in author's possession.

47. "SREC Urges 1980 Presidential Primary," *Texas Advocate*, July 1978, 3.

48. Francis interview.

49. Ibid.

50. Author interview with George Bayoud, Dallas, August 11, 2014, in author's possession.

51. Quoted in Barta, *Bill Clements*, 203.

52. Roger M. Olien, *From Token to Triumph: The Texas Republicans since 1920* (Dallas: SMU Press, 1982), 255–256; Barta, *Bill Clements*, 203.

53. Tarrance poll memos, Rita Crocker Clements Papers, box 21, folder 13.

54. "Clements Building Momentum," *Texas Advocate*, September 1978, 3.

55. Francis interview; "Clements Sees Victory within Grasp," *Texas Advocate*, October 1978, 1.

56. Barta, *Bill Clements*, 210; John R. Knaggs, *Two-Party Texas* (Austin: Aiken, 1986), 230. Knaggs discusses the Tower campaign of 1978 in detail on pp. 201–231.

57. John Dycus, "At the GOP Camp Meeting, the 'Issue' Is 'Unity,'" *Texas Observer*, October 6, 1978; Larry Neal, "Call It the 'Reagan Party,'" *Fort Worth Star Telegram*, September 11, 1978.

58. "Republicans Gather for State Convention," *Texas Advocate*, September 1978, 1; "State Party Pushing Vital Programs," *Texas Advocate*, September 1978, 4.

59. John Dycus, "The 'Issue' Is 'Unity,'" *Texas Observer*, October 8, 1978, 9–11.

60. Bayoud interview.

61. Gary Hoitsma, "GOP Stars Presage Clements Win at Gala Dinner," *Texas Advocate*, November–December 1978, 4.

62. Quoted in Barta, *Bill Clements*, 211.

63. Barta, *Bill Clements*, 212.

64. Francis interview.

65. Estrada interview.

66. Geraldo Cadava, *The Hispanic Republican: The Shaping of an American Political Identity, from Nixon to Trump* (New York: HarperCollins, 2020), 180–181.

67. "Analysis of 1978 Governor's Campaign," Rita Crocker Clements Papers, box 10, folder 2.

68. Sean P. Cunningham, *Cowboy Conservatism: Texas and the Rise of the Modern Right* (Lexington: University Press of Kentucky, 2010), 198, 207.

69. Francis interview.

70. "The Governor-Elect," *Texas Advocate*, November–December 1978, 5.

71. Rita C. Clements interview, *Texas Advocate*, January 1979, 7.

72. Chandler Davidson interview with Mark White, June 11, 1987, Chandler Davidson Texas Politics Research Collection, Woodson Research Center, Fondren Library, Rice University, box 2, folder 3.

73. Author interview with Ed Emmett, Houston, March 25, 2014, in author's possession.

74. Ray Barnhart, "From the Chairman," *Texas Advocate*, November–December 1978, 2.

75. For more on this point, see Wayne Thorburn, *Red State: An Insider's Story of How the GOP Came to Dominate Texas Politics* (Austin: University of Texas Press, 2014), 135–165; William K. Stevens, "Texas Analysts Wonder if Gains by Republicans Will Be Lasting," *New York Times*, November 16, 1978.

76. George Kuempel, "Clements Challenge before Him," *Dallas Morning News*, January 8, 1979.

77. Quoted in Thorburn, *Red State*, 125.

78. Strake interview.

79. Peggy Wilson to Rita Clements, January 10, 1979, in author's possession.

80. Kenneth R. Guest to Rita Clements, January 19, 1979, in author's possession.

81. Francis interview.

82. Bayoud interview.

83. Francis interview.

84. Kenneth R. Guest to Rita Clements, January 19, 1979, in author's possession.

85. Untermeyer interview.

86. Ray Barnhart to Party Officials, April 14, 1979, in author's possession.

87. Ray Barnhart to State Republican Executive Committee, April 26, 1979, in author's possession.

88. Jules Witcover, "Bush Formally Opens '80 Drive," *Washington Star*, May 1, 1979.

89. David Hoffman Collection, George H. W. Bush Presidential Library, College Station, TX, box 1–1980, campaign files.

90. Untermeyer interview.

91. *Texas Advocate*, February–March 1979, 7.

92. Untermeyer interview.

93. Robert Heard, *The Miracle of the Killer Bees* (Austin: Honey Hill, 1981), 3–5.

94. Bill Hobby with Saralee Tiede, *How Things Really Work: Lessons from a Life in Politics* (Austin: Dolph Briscoe Center for American History, 2010), 134.

95. Quoted in Michael L. Antle, "The Rise of the Republicans: Party Realignment in Twentieth Century Texas," PhD diss., University of North Texas, December 2012, 268.

96. Betty J. Andujar, interviewed by Ronald E. Marcello, September 29, 1980, Oral History Collection, University of North Texas, 60.

97. Letter from Wayne Thorburn to Mrs. W. W. Wilson III, November 7, 1979, in author's possession.

98. Ibid.

99. "MART Holds Conference," *Texas Advocate*, March 1980, 5.

100. *Texas Republican Alternative*, Winter 1980, 2.

101. Thomas C. Reed, *The Reagan Enigma, 1964–1980* (Los Angeles: Figueroa, 2014), 122–124.

102. Dave Montgomery, "Clements Secret Trip Part of Ford Decision," *Dallas Times Herald*, March 21, 1980.

103. Hedrick Smith, "Connally Is Said to Have Persuaded 2 Key Governors Not to Back Ford," *New York Times*, March 14, 1980.

104. Hedrick Smith, "With Ford Out, Reagan Is Deemed Overwhelming Favorite for G.O.P.," *New York Times*, March 17, 1980. The names of Baker and Connally would remain on the Texas primary ballot, along with Bush and Reagan, even though they had officially withdrawn from the contest.

105. Author telephone interview with Ernest Angelo, Midland, June 2, 2020, in author's possession; Lou Cannon, "Reagan Gains Connally Endorsement," *Washington Post*, March 26, 1980.

106. Dave Montgomery, "Clements Hosts Reagan in Austin for Political Talks," *Dallas Times Herald*, April 25, 1980.

107. Adam Clymer, "Its Bush vs. Reagan, Reagan vs. Complacency in Texas," *New York Times*, May 2, 1980.

108. Dave Montgomery, "Texas GOP Ready to Join Reagan Camp," *Dallas Times Herald*, May 5, 1980.

109. Felton West, "Clements Endorses Reagan," *Houston Post*, May 6, 1980.

110. Jane Ely, "Goldwater Stresses Republican Unity," *Houston Post*, June 21, 1980.

111. *Texas Advocate*, May 1980, 8.

112. The classic history of the 1980 Republican campaign is Craig Shirley, *Rendezvous with History* (Wilmington, DE: ISI Books, 2009).

113. Quoted in *Republican Party of Texas 1980 Yearbook*, 29, privately printed document in author's possession.

114. Cadava, *Hispanic Republican*, 204–208.

115. *Republican Party of Texas 1980 Yearbook*, 14.

116. Barta, *Bill Clements*, 246; Adam Clymer, "From Lowly Grass Roots, Mighty Votes Are Growing," *New York Times*, October 5, 1980.

117. Jim Davis, "Phone Troopers Shoot for Republican Turnout," *Abilene Reporter-News*, October 5, 1980.

118. Rove, *Courage*, 55.

119. Wayne Thorburn, quoted in the *Texas Advocate*, September 1980, 17. See also Dave McNeely, "Texas Democrats for Reagan-Bush," *Lufkin News*, September 22, 1980.

120. Angelo interview; Hedrick Smith, "Texas Looms as a Close Battle between President and Reagan," *New York Times*, October 9, 1980.

121. *Republican Party of Texas 1980 Yearbook*, 3.

10. THE REAGAN-BUSH YEARS

1. Among Texans joining the new administration were James A. Baker III, Ray Barnhart, and Tom Pauken, along with dozens of others who filled key supportive positions. Chase Untermeyer became executive assistant to the vice president before assuming a number of other federal offices over the twelve years. His recollections of the early years can be found in Chase Untermeyer, *When Things Went Right: The Dawn of the Reagan-Bush Administration* (College Station: Texas A&M University Press, 2013).

2. Steven F. Hayward, *The Age of Reagan: The Conservative Counterrevolution 1980–1989* (New York: Three Rivers Press, 2009); H. W. Brands, *Reagan: The Life* (New York: Doubleday, 2015).

3. John R. Knaggs, *Two-Party Texas* (Austin: Aiken, 1986), 252–253.

4. Author interview with George W. Strake Jr., Houston, March 25, 2014, in author's possession. See also Jo Clifton, "A Strake Check: Looking at the Man Who Wants to Be Your Lt. Governor, " *Texas Observer*, February 12, 1982.

5. Thompson quoted in Knaggs, *Two-Party Texas*, 264.

6. Knaggs, *Two-Party Texas*, 273.

7. Geraldo Cadava, *The Hispanic Republican: The Shaping of an American Political Identity, from Nixon to Trump* (New York: HarperCollins, 2020), 276.

8. "The Election of 1982: What Did Not Happen—Some Post-Election Myths," undated memo from the Republican Party of Texas, in author's possession.

9. Memo from Tom Reed to Bill Clements, July 22, 1982, in author's possession.

10. Knaggs, *Two-Party Texas*, 272.

11. Patricia C. Ashby to William P. Clements Jr., December 19, 1982, Rita Crocker Clements Papers, Cushing Library, Texas A&M University, box 23, folder 12.

12. Ibid.

13. Author interview with James B. Francis Jr., April 24, 2014, Dallas, in author's possession.

14. Carolyn Barta, *Bill Clements: Texian to His Toenails* (Austin: Eakin, 1996), 297.

15. Summary notes on 1982 loss, Rita Crocker Clements Papers, box 23, folder 12.

16. Francis interview.

17. Kyle Thompson, "GOP Must Make Adjustments," *Fort Worth Star-Telegram*, November 21, 1982. Thompson added, "And guess what Gov.-elect White did the minute his election was assured? He admitted that there was little he could do about the fuel adjustments as governor."

18. Karl Rove, *Courage and Consequence: My Life as a Conservative in the Fight* (New York: Threshold, 2010), 57.

19. Memo from Lance Tarrance and Jan Van Lohuizen to Rebuilding Committee re: Post-Election Statewide Survey, 8, in author's possession.

20. Jack Z. Smith, "Turnout Blamed in GOP Loss," *Fort Worth Star-Telegram*, November 12, 1982.

21. Data from Arthur Finkelstein postelection survey conducted for the National Conservative Political Action Committee, quoted in Memo to Officers from Wayne Thorburn, December 27, 1982; document in author's possession.

22. Quoted in Barta, *Bill Clements*, 278.

23. Chandler Davidson interview with White, June 11, 1987, Chandler Davidson Texas Politics Research Collection, 1967–1992, MS 259, Woodson Research Center, Fondren Library, Rice University, box 12, folder 1.

24. Knaggs, *Two-Party Texas*, 273.

25. Rob Allyn, "How Dallas Switched Parties," draft article, October 22, 1985, 30, in author's possession.

26. "Back to Square Two," undated memo from Wayne Thorburn, executive director, Republican Party of Texas; document in author's possession.

27. Author interview with Jerry W. Smith, Houston, March 25, 2014, in author's possession.

28. Tom Pauken, *Bringing America Home: How America Lost Her Way and How We Can Find Our Way Back* (Rockford, IL: Chronicles, 2010).

29. *Texas Advocate*, February 1983, 7; Wesley Pruden, "Bitter Fight over Chairman Divides Texas Republicans," *Washington Times*, February 8, 1983.

30. Quotes from minutes of a January 22, 1983, meeting of seven SREC members in Houston, in author's possession.

31. "Conservatives Threaten to Dump Reagan in '84," *Houston Post*, January 19, 1983.

32. Robert L. Monaghan, memo to county chairs, February 22, 1983, in author's possession.

33. Dave McNeely, "GOP Faction Accused of Try to Block Bush," *Austin American-Statesman*, February 10, 1983.

34. Nene Foxhall, "GOP Rift Goes Much Deeper than Philosophy," *Houston Chronicle*, February 20, 1983.

35. "Adoption of Budget on Hold," *Dallas Times Herald*, February 7, 1983.

36. Quoted in Jim Simmon, "State GOP Chief Resisting Moves to Unseat Him," *Houston Post*, February 7, 1983.

37. Sam Attlesey, "Intraparty Disputes Worry Texas GOP," *Dallas Morning News*, February 20, 1983.

38. *Texas Advocate*, April 1983, 4.

39. Jim Simmon, "Upham Reported Considering Resigning as State GOP Chief," *Houston Post*, March 12, 1983.

40. Nene Foxhall, "State GOP Chief Willing to Resign in Favor of Strake," *Houston Chronicle*, March 12, 1983.

41. Sam Kinch Jr., "Upham Won't Surrender Post as GOP Chief," *Dallas Morning News*, March 18, 1983; Memo to County Chairmen from Chester R. Upham Jr., March 21, 1983, in author's possession.

42. Arnold Hamilton, "Scuffle Mars GOP Debate," *Dallas Times Herald*, April 9, 1983.

43. Jack Z. Smith, "Upham Puts 2 Conditions on Resigning," *Fort Worth Star-Telegram*, April 9, 1983.

44. Arnold Hamilton, "State Republican Chairman Quits," *Dallas Times Herald*, April 10, 1983.

45. *Texas Advocate*, May 1983, 5.

46. Author interview with George Strake Jr., Houston, March 25, 2014, in author's possession.

47. Author telephone interview with Ernest Angelo, Midland, June 2, 2020, in author's possession.

48. Francis interview.

49. *Texas Advocate*, February 1983, 1, 10.

50. Thure Barnett Cannon, "The Texas Political System: Shifting Dynamics in Political Party Power," Master's thesis, University of Texas at Austin, 1998; quotes from pages 34, 38, and 40.

51. Angelo interview.

52. George Strake email to Kevin Moomaw, January 26, 2016, in author's possession.

53. Strake interview.

54. Strake interview.

55. Cragg Hines and William E. Clayton Jr., "Laredo Teacher Appointed to New Civil Rights Panel," *Houston Chronicle*, December 7, 1983; J. J. Velasquez, "Magnificent Teacher: High School Educator Esther Buckley Remembered," *Laredo Morning Times*, February 13, 2013; Personal Papers of Esther Gonzalez-Arroyo Buckley, Texas Women's University, Denton.

56. Mark Nelson, "Tower Backers Nervous; Problems Plague 1984 Campaign," *Dallas Morning News*, June 27, 1983.

57. Knaggs, *Two-Party Texas*, 280–281.

58. Ibid., 288.

59. Author interview with Kent Hance, Austin, August 27, 2014, in author's possession.

60. Sam Attlesey, "Reagan Campaign Greatest Challenge, Key Organizer Says," *Dallas Morning News*, January 30, 1984.

61. "Texas Group Backs Reagan; Independents, Democrats Meet with President," *Dallas Morning News*, July 26, 1984.

62. Michael L. Antle, "The Rise of the Republicans: Party Realignment in Twentieth Century Texas," PhD diss., University of North Texas, December 2012, 299.

63. John G. Tower Papers, Southwestern University Special Collections, box 873, folder 4.

64. Thomas B. Edsall, "Democrats Bet Texas Is in the Cards," *Washington Post*, October 23, 1984.

65. The partisan composition of the 1985 Texas legislature is at lrl.texas.gov/legeLeaders/members/partyList.cfm, accessed May 24, 2020. Immediately after the session ended, Charles Evans of Hurst and Gary Thompson of Abilene switched party affiliation to Republican. Also becoming Republicans subsequently were representatives Billy Clemons of Lufkin, Ric Williamson of Weatherford, and Rick Perry of Paint Creek.

66. Paul Burka, "Why They Won: What the Elections Mean for Texas," *Texas Monthly*, December 1984.

67. Scott Bennett, "Sins of Omission," *Texas Business*, September 1984.

68. Dave McNeely, "State GOP Leadership Expected to Face In-House Critics," *Austin American-Statesman*, November 30, 1984.

69. Young Conservatives of Texas Rates the 69th Texas Legislature, www.yct.org/wp-content/uploads/ratings/YCT_69th_Session_Ratings.pdf, accessed on October 28, 2015.

70. Chandler Davidson, *Race and Class in Texas Politics* (Princeton, NJ: Princeton University Press, 1990), 219.

71. "Hance Says He'll Remain Democrat," *Dallas Times Herald*, April 17, 1985.

72. Hance interview.

73. Wayne King, "In Blow to Texas Democrats, Ex-Rep. Hance Joins Republicans," *New York Times*, May 4, 1985.

74. Jack Germond and Jules Witcover, *Whose Broad Stripes and Bright Stars?* (New York: Warner, 1989), 43.

75. Barta, *Bill Clements*, 315.

76. Ibid., 316.

77. Author interview with George Bayoud, Dallas, August 11, 2014, in author's possession.

78. Hance interview; Francis interview.

79. Letter to Fellow Texans from Bill Archer, Jack Fields, Tom DeLay, July 24, 1985, in author's possession.

80. Barta, *Bill Clements*, 316; Bayoud interview.

81. Francis interview.

82. Hance interview.

83. William P. Clements Jr. to appointees, no date, in author's possession.

84. Memo from Jack Rains to William P. Clements Jr., August 6, 1985, Rita Crocker Clements Papers, box 10, folder 4.

85. Richard Wirthlin, proposed campaign plan, undated, Rita Crocker Clements Papers, box 22, folder 13.

86. Ibid.; "Ex-Rep Hance to Run for Governor of Texas," *New York Times*, October 9, 1985.

87. James Ricketts, "Hance, Loeffler May Quit, Clements Asserts," *Lubbock Avalanche-Journal*, November 7, 1985; Vance Gore, "Hance Says Criticism within GOP Harmful,"

Amarillo Globe-News, November 18, 1985; memo from Karl Rove to Governor Clements, November 29, 1985, in author's possession.

88. Robert Reinhold, "As Texas Republican Party Grows, So Do Rifts," *New York Times*, August 23, 1985.

89. Rob Allyn, "Thou Shalt Speak No Evil of Another Republican," *D Magazine*, April 1986.

90. Peter O'Donnell Jr. to John G. Tower, April 10, 1986, Tower Papers, box 54.

91. Juliana Barbassa, "Fatal Perfection," *Dallas Observer*, March 25, 1999.

92. "Briscoe Banking on Protest Votes," *Victoria Advocate*, April 18, 1986.

93. News release, Bill Clements for Governor, October 14, 1986, Rita Crocker Clements Papers, box 7, folder 27.

94. Sam Attlesey, "Blazing a Political Trail," *Dallas Morning News*, October 14, 1985.

95. George W. Strake Jr., "Leadership Letter," Republican Party of Texas, June 1986, 4.

96. Dave Denison, "Are We There Yet? — Republicans Say Texas Is Finally a Two-Party State," *Texas Observer*, June 13, 1986, 7.

97. Ibid., 8.

98. Paul Burka, "Primary Lesson," *Texas Monthly*, July 1986, 104–105.

99. Strake interview.

100. "Moderate Republicans in Texas Win Party Vote," *New York Times*, June 30, 1986. In reality, none of the candidates for party leadership would describe themselves or can be fairly labeled as "moderate Republicans."

101. Sam Attlesey, "Clements' Investment Aids Terrorists, Democratic Leader Says," *Dallas Morning News*, August 21, 1986.

102. "Cheap Shot," editorial, *Dallas Morning News*, August 22, 1986.

103. Sam Attlesey, "GOP Leaders Rally 'Round Clements," *Dallas Morning News*, August 22, 1986.

104. DMI Surveys, Rita Crocker Clements Papers, box 9, folders 22, 23.

105. Brian McCall, *The Power of the Texas Governor: Connally to Bush* (Austin: University of Texas Press, 2009), 84.

106. Barta, *Bill Clements*, 334–335.

107. Karl Rove, *An Analysis of the 1986 Gubernatorial Election*, December 1986, in author's possession. See also Lawrence Jones, Curtis Hawk, and Delbert A. Taebel, "Political Change and Partisanship in Texas County Government," *Texas Journal of Political Studies* 11, no. 2 (1989), 29–42.

108. Wayne Thorburn, "The Growth of Republican Representation in the Texas Legislature: Coattails, Incumbency, Special Elections, and Urbanization," *Texas Journal of Political Studies* 11, no. 2 (1989), 16–28.

109. Barta, *Bill Clements*, 350–362.

110. Wayne Thorburn, *Red State: An Insider's Story of How the GOP Came to Dominate Texas Politics* (Austin: University of Texas Press, 2014), 159.

111. George Bush for President Campaign Plan, 1988 Texas Republican Primary, July 15, 1987, in author's possession.

112. Sam Attlesey, "Robertson Forces to Seek Top GOP Post," *Dallas Morning News*, March 26, 1988.

113. Sam Attlesey, "Robertson Rally Plan Irks Texas GOP," *Dallas Morning News*, June 8, 1988.

114. *Congressional Quarterly*, August 13, 1988.

115. Sam Attlesey, "State GOP Elects Meyer as Chief," *Dallas Morning News*, June 11, 1988. Penny Butler was married to John Butler Jr., who had lost a race for state chairman at the 1978 state convention.

116. Louis Dubose, "Invisible Army: The Christian Right at the Republican Convention," *Texas Observer*, 10.

117. Maureen Dowd, "Bush Paints Rival as Elitist, with 'Harvard Yard' Views," *New York Times*, June 10, 1988.

118. Anne Marie Kilday, "Bentsen, Other Democrats Pay Close Attention to Debate," *Dallas Morning News*, October 14, 1988.

119. Barbara Linkin, "Poll Reveals Bush Leads on Campus," *Daily Texan*, November 3, 1988.

120. Kenneth F. Bunting, "Bush's Lead Huge in the State, Poll Indicates," *Fort Worth Star-Telegram*, October 30, 1988.

121. Mike Kingston, editor, *Texas Almanac 1990–1991* (Dallas: A. H. Belo, 1989), 372.

122. Hance interview.

123. Roberto Suro, "Texas Tory Democrats Go the Way of the Armadillo," *New York Times*, May 28, 1989.

124. Bayoud interview.

125. Hance interview.

126. Jan Reid, *Let the People In: The Life and Times of Ann Richards* (Austin: University of Texas Press, 2012), 238.

127. Mike Kingston, editor, *Texas Almanac 1992–1993* (Dallas: A. H. Belo, 1991), 423.

128. Mike Shropshire and Frank Schaefer, *The Thorny Rose of Texas: An Intimate Portrait of Governor Ann Richards* (New York: Birch Lane, 1994), 203.

129. Roberto Suro, "Homespun Texan Goes for Republicans' Heart," *New York Times*, March 1, 1990.

130. Francis interview.

131. Hance interview.

132. Dave McNeely, "Politics of Primary Importance," *D Magazine*, March 1990.

133. David Maraniss, "Heading to the Wire, Races for Texas Governor Ridiculed but Watched," *Washington Post*, March 11, 1990.

134. Suro, "Homespun Texan."

135. Roberto Suro, "Race for Governor of Texas Is Surprising in Both Parties," *New York Times*, January 28, 1990.

136. Ann Richards, *Straight from the Heart: My Life in Politics and Other Places* (New York: Simon & Schuster, 1989); Mary Lenz, "Texas Governor's Race Wide Open," *Christian Science Monitor*, March 12, 1990.

137. Rove, *Courage*, 80.

138. Suro, "Race."

139. Ibid.

140. Rove, *Courage*, 58.

141. Mike Shropshire, "Clayton Williams: Texas Crude," *D Magazine*, September 1990.

142. Reid, *Let the People In*, 238.

143. Shropshire and Schaefer, *Thorny Rose*, 204.

144. Max R. Sherman, ed., *The Future of Texas* (Austin: Lyndon Baines Johnson School of Public Affairs, 1988), 36.

145. Sue Tolleson-Rinehart and Jeanie R. Stanley, *Claytie and the Lady: Ann Richards, Gender, and Politics in Texas* (Austin: University of Texas Press, 1994), 59.

146. Shropshire, "Clayton Williams."

147. Sherman, ed., *Future of Texas*, 37.

148. Hance interview.

149. William Maxwell, Ernest Crain, and Adolfo Santos, *Texas Politics Today, 2009–2010* (Boston: Wadsworth Cengage, 2010), 118.

11. GEORGE W. BUSH AND THE REPUBLICAN MAJORITY

1. Ann Fears Crawford, "A Step in the Right Direction: Kay Bailey Hutchison Goes to the Texas Legislature," paper presented at East Texas Historical Association conference, February 21, 1998, Ann Fears Crawford Papers, Woodson Research Center, Fondren Library, Rice University, box 3, folder 5.

2. "Hutchison, Fields Join Race for U. S. Senate," Crawford Papers, box 3, folder 2.

3. Ann Fears Crawford interview with Karl Rove, Austin, September 22, 1995, Crawford Papers, box 2, folder 9.

4. Author interview with James B. Francis, April 24, 2014, Dallas, in author's possession.

5. Laylan Copelin, "GOP Shelves Endorsement in Senate Race," Crawford Papers, box 3, folder 2.

6. Dan Balz, "For Texas Candidate, a Change of Image but Same Goal," *New York Times*, March 6, 1994.

7. Michael Holmes, "Hutchison, Krueger Call on Celebrities for Campaign Help," *Austin American-Statesman*, May 22, 1993.

8. Sam Howe Verhovek, "Woman in the News: From Demure Survivor to G.O.P. Star," *New York Times*, June 7, 1993.

9. Peter Schweizer and Rochelle Schweizer, *The Bushes: Portrait of a Dynasty* (New York: Doubleday, 2004), 421; Christopher Anderson, *George and Laura: Portrait of an American Marriage* (New York: William Morrow, 2002), 122.

10. Sue Tolleson-Rinehart and Jeanie R. Stanley, *Claytie and the Lady: Ann Richards, Gender, and Politics in Texas* (Austin: University of Texas Press, 1994), 141; Jan Reid, *Let the People In: The Life and Times of Ann Richards* (Austin: University of Texas Press, 2012), 387.

11. Karl Rove, *Courage and Consequence: My Life as a Conservative in the Fight* (New York: Threshold, 2010), 82.

12. Quoted in Patricia Kilday Hart, "Little Did We Know …," *Texas Monthly*, November 2004.

13. James A. Dyer, Jan E. Leighley, and Arnold Vedlitz, "Party Identification and Public Opinion in Texas, 1984–1994: Establishing a Competitive Two-Party System," in *Texas Politics: A Reader*, 2nd edition, ed. Anthony Champagne and Edward J. Harpham (New York: W.W. Norton, 1998), 107–122.

14. Data from Wayne Thorburn, *Red State: An Insider's Story of How the GOP Came to Dominate Texas Politics* (Austin: University of Texas Press, 2014), 154–155.

15. Paul Burka, "How the Republicans Beat Ann Richards and Took Over Texas," *Texas Monthly*, December 1994.

16. Quoted in Hart, "Little Did We Know."

17. Molly Ivins and Lou Dubose, *Shrub: The Short but Happy Political Life of George W. Bush* (New York: Random House, 2000), 72.

18. Paul Lenchner, "The Party System in Texas," in *Texas Politics: A Reader*, 2nd edition, ed. Anthony Champagne and Edward J. Harpham (New York: W. W. Norton, 1998), 165–166.

19. Tom Pauken: *Bringing America Home: How America Lost Her Way and How We Can Find Our Way Back* (Rockford, IL: Chronicles, 2010), 22.

20. Thomas W. Pauken: *The Thirty Years War: The Politics of the Sixties Generation* (Ottawa, IL: Jameson, 1995), 192.

21. Novak's comments appear in ibid., xii.

22. Pauken, *Bringing America Home*, 33.

23. Richard L. Berke, "Religious Conservatives Conquer G.O.P in Texas," *New York Times*, June 12, 1994.

24. Sam Attlesey and Lori Stahl, "Pauken to Lead as Social Right Dominates GOP," *Dallas Morning News*, June 9, 1994.

25. Rove, *Courage*, 83.

26. Quoted in Hart, "Little Did We Know."

27. Ibid.

28. Florence Shapiro Papers, Blagg-Huey Library, Texas Women's University, box 11.

29. Mary Beth Rogers, *Turning Texas Blue* (New York: St. Martin's, 2016), 98–99.

30. Reid, *Let The People In*, 403.

31. Sam Howe Verhovek, "Is There Room on a Republican Ticket for Another Bush?," *New York Times Magazine*, September 13, 1998.

32. Paul Burka, "How the Republicans Beat Ann Richards and Took Over Texas," *Texas Monthly*, December 1994.

33. Sam Howe Verhovek, "The 1994 Campaign: Texas; Governor and Her Rival Meet in Debate," *New York Times*, October 22, 1994.

34. Reid, *Let the People In*, 399.

35. Allen R. Myerson, "The 1994 Campaign: Ross Perot; Richards Draws Perot's Backing in Tough Texas Governor's Race," *New York Times*, November 2, 1994.

36. Ibid.

37. Rove, *Courage*, 96.

38. Rogers, *Turning Texas Blue*, 96. It is obvious that the loss made a strong impression on Rogers, who wrote some twenty years later, "Bush won by an astounding million-vote margin" (94), when, in fact, the difference was roughly a third of that.

39. Lou Dubose, *Boy Genius: The Brains behind the Remarkable Political Triumph of George W. Bush* (New York: PublicAffairs, 2003), 75.

40. Reid, *Let The People In*, 405.

41. Stuart Askenazi, "Easygoing George W. Bush," *Houston Press*, October 29, 1998.

42. Paul Burka, "Right, but Wrong," *Texas Monthly*, May 1995.

43. Ibid., 50.

44. Pauken, *Bringing America Home*, 33.

45. Burka, "Right, but Wrong," 55.

46. Paul West, "Texas' New Breed of Bush Politics," *Baltimore Sun*, May 9, 1997.

47. Carl M. Cannon, Louis Dubose, and Jan Reid, *Boy Genius: Karl Rove, the Architect of George W. Bush's Remarkable Political Triumphs* (New York: PublicAffairs, 2009), 105.

48. "GOP Chairman: Would Pauken Really Broaden Party's Base?" *Dallas Morning News*, December 15, 1996.

49. Cannon, Dubose, and Reid, *Boy Genius*, 70.

50. Pauken, *Bringing America Home*, 37.

51. Louis Dubose, "He's Coming Back," *Austin Chronicle*, October 13, 2000.

52. Lisa Tozzi, "Forgiving His Trespasses," *Austin Chronicle*, May 28, 1999.

53. Pauken, *Bringing America Home*, 31, 30.

54. Lloyd Grove, "The Texas Republican Who Hates Bush," *Daily Beast*, July 26, 2010.

55. Jonathan Tilove, "In Texas, Donald Trump Must Rely on Uncertain Allies in State GOP," *Austin American-Statesman*, June 10, 2016.

56. Michael King, "Capitol Chronicle," *Austin Chronicle*, October 1, 2001.

57. Jonathan Tilove, "Longtime GOP Leader Tom Pauken to Run for Governor," *Austin American-Statesman*, March 21, 2013.

58. Christy Hoppe, "Tom Pauken Withdraws from GOP Governor's Race," *Dallas Morning News*, December 5, 2013.

59. Richard L. Berke, "Tough Texan: Phil Gramm," *New York Times*, February 19, 1995.

60. Carolyn Barta, *Bill Clements: Texian to His Toenails* (Austin: Eakin, 1996), 411.

61. Sam Howe Verhovek, "Politics: Bowing Out; Big Budget, Early Start, and the Candidate Are Figured in the Collapse of Gramm's Bid," *New York Times*, February 15, 1996.

62. Ibid.

63. Alyson Ward, "Republicans Aim to Keep 'Revolution' Going," *Baylor Lariat*, February 20, 1996.

64. Mimi Swartz, "Truckin'," *Texas Monthly*, June 1996.

65. Harvey Kronberg, "Texas GOP Voters Bust Right-Wing Paradigm," *Austin American-Statesman*, May 30, 1996.

66. Lenchner, "Party System," 168.

67. Jane Ely, "GOP Gathering Old-Time Revival Service," *Houston Chronicle*, June 23, 1996.

68. Richard L. Berke, "Politics: The Republicans; Chaotic Message to Dole over the Abortion Issue," *New York Times*, June 24, 1996.

69. Ely, "GOP Gathering."

70. Johnson campaign flyer from Rita Davis, SREC Member, SD25, in author's possession.

71. Berke, "Politics: The Republicans."

72. Dave McNeely, "New Guard Shows GOP Who Is Boss," *Austin American-Statesman*, June 25, 1996.

73. Richard L. Berke, "Politics: State Conventions; Dole Forces Lose Texas Delegates over Abortion, but a Senator Wins," *New York Times*, June 23, 1996.

74. Ken Herman, "Dole's Bid Expendable, Says GOP Abortion Foe," *Austin American-Statesman*, June 25, 1996.

75. Lenchner, "Party System," 169–170.

76. Herman, "Dole's Bid."

12. THE YEAR THAT CHANGED TEXAS POLITICS

1. R. W. Apple Jr., "Gradual Shift to the G.O.P. Leaves Texas Least Likely of Big States to Support Clinton," *New York Times*, October 14, 1996.

2. A 1985 survey showed that those who lived in Texas less than ten years were most likely to identify with the Republican Party, while native Texans were most strongly Democratic, and other long-term residents born outside Texas were evenly split in their partisan loyalties. The survey data are presented in Wayne Thorburn, *Red State: An Insider's Story of How the GOP Came to Dominate Texas Politics* (Austin: University of Texas Press, 2014), 152.

3. Ibid., 153–156. In the 1996 election, Senator Gramm's support was weakest among voters over sixty in the All Politics exit poll. http://CNN.com/ELECTION/TXSxp.html.

4. In full disclosure, the author was the director of the Leadership Texas '96 campaign effort.

5. "Where the Money Is," *Texas Observer*, November 22, 1996.

6. Sam Attlesey, "Poll Shows Dole, Clinton Running Even in Texas," *Dallas Morning News*, September 8, 1996.

7. Ibid.

8. Todd S. Purdum, "Clinton Sets His Sights as Wide as Texas," *New York Times*, September 28, 1996.

9. Apple, "Gradual Shift."

10. Sam Attlesey, "Independent Voters Could Hold the Key," *Dallas Morning News*, October 25, 1996.

11. Carolyn Barta, "Dole Slams Clinton, Media on Texas Visit," *Dallas Morning News*, October 26, 1996.

12. Ibid.

13. "Dole Will Appear at Noon Rally, Monday's Event in West Houston," *Houston Chronicle*, November 3, 1996.

14. "Gramm-Morales TV Debate Cancelled," *Dallas Morning News*, September 5, 1996.

15. Richard Murray and Sam Attlesey, "Texas: Republicans Gallop Ahead," in *Southern Politics in the 1990s*, ed. Alexander P. Lamis (Baton Rouge: Louisiana State University Press, 1999), 335.

16. Sam Attlesey, "Poll Shows 50% Support Gramm," *Dallas Morning News*, September 9, 1996.

17. Steven A. Holmes, "The States and the Issues," *New York Times*, October 3, 1996.

18. Sam Attlesey, "Gramm Says Morales Is on Wrong Side of Hispanic Values," *Dallas Morning News*, October 16, 1996.

19. Sam Attlesey, "Morales Has Media's Eye as He Works to Win Texans' Hearts," *Dallas Morning News*, October 20, 1996.

20. Lori Stahl, "Perot's Party Endorses Morales, but Senate Hopeful Guarded on Presidential Race," *Dallas Morning News*, October 18, 1996.

21. Catalina Camia, "Texas Congressional Races Mirror Parties' Struggles Nationwide," *Dallas Morning News*, October 27, 1996.

22. "Dole Win Shows Strength of Texas GOP, Experts Say," *Dallas Morning News*, November 6, 1996.

23. Murray and Attlesey, "Texas: Republicans Gallop Ahead," 306.

24. David Barboza, "Republicans Strike Deep in the Heart of Texas," *New York Times*, November 29, 1996.

25. "Republicans Prevail in All 10 Statewide Races," *Austin American-Statesman*, November 6, 1996.

26. Sue Anne Pressley, "Texas GOP Spotlights Party-Switchers," *Washington Post*, October 14, 1997; Mary Alice Robbins, "Judge, County Politicos Switch Parties," *Amarillo Globe-News*, October 7, 1997; Sam Attlesey, "A Switch in Texas Politics," *Dallas Morning News*, October 20, 1997.

27. Sue Anne Pressley, "Another Bush in Line?," *Washington Post*, May 9, 1997.

28. Ibid.

29. Stuart Eskenazi, "Bush's Free Ride," *Dallas Observer*, October 29, 1998.

30. Memorandum to key leadership from Karl Rove, May 13, 1997, in author's possession.

31. Clay Robison, "Bush Advisor Karl Rove Accuses GOP's Pauken of Attacking Governor," *Houston Chronicle*, May 16, 1997.

32. "A Political Stretch against Pauken?," *Texas Weekly*, June 23, 1997.

33. Frank Luntz, "Attitudes in Texas," July 23, 1997, memorandum to Temerlin McClain, in author's possession.

34. Mary Alice Robbins, "GOP Elects Woman to Lead," *Amarillo Globe-News*, August 3, 1997.

35. "GOP Leader Likes Texas Outlook," *Dallas Morning News*, August 1, 1997.

36. Author interview with Will Lutz, Austin, April 19, 2016, in author's possession.

37. Sam Attlesey, "Bush Aides Say Their Eyes on Re-Election, Not Coattails," *Dallas Morning News*, July 6, 1997.

38. A. Phillips Brooks and Ken Herman, "Bullock Endorses Bush, Not Mauro," *Austin American-Statesman*, November 21, 1997.

39. Carl M. Cannon, Louis Dubose, and Jan Reid, *Boy Genius: Karl Rove, the Architect of George W. Bush's Remarkable Political Triumphs* (New York: PublicAffairs, 2009), 112–113.

40. Dan Balz, "Parties Make a High-Stakes Texas Stand," *Washington Post*, June 30, 1998.

41. Tom Pauken letter, March 20, 1998, in author's possession; Harvey Kronberg, "The Runoff to Watch," *Quorum Report*, March 16, 1998; R. G. Ratcliffe, "Though Neutral, Pauken Asks Voters to Dismiss Williamson," *Houston Chronicle*, March 20, 1998.

42. John W. Gonzalez, "Stockman's Campaign Ad Labeled Racist," *Houston Chronicle*, March 11, 1998.

43. Terrence Stutz and Wayne Slater, "Results Are Mixed for Candidates Backed by Religious Conservatives," *Dallas Morning News*, March 12, 1998.

44. Lutz interview.

45. Rick Lyman, "A Texas Dark Horse Runs at Full Gallup," *New York Times*, August 20, 1998.

46. Sam Howe Verhovek, "Is There Room on the Republican Ticket for Another Bush?," *New York Times Magazine*, September 13, 1998.

47. Rick Lyman, "Again, the Talk around Bush Turns to 2000," *New York Times*, October 18, 1998.

48. Thorburn, *Red State*, 176.

49. Karl Rove, *Courage and Consequence: My Life as a Conservative in the Fight* (New York: Threshold, 2010), 117.

50. B. Drummond Ayres Jr., "Political Briefing; The Eyes of Texas Are on Race for No. 2," *New York Times*, October 26, 1998.

51. Rove, *Courage*, 121.

52. Thorburn, *Red State*, 176–178.

53. See "Studies of Political Statistics: Straight-Ticket Voting in Texas 1998–2016," Center for Public Policy and Political Studies, Austin Community College, December 2016; Thorburn, *Red State*, 207–212; the author's unpublished paper, "Straight Ticket Voting in Texas: Recent Trends," January 2015, in author's possession.

54. One clear-cut impact of eliminating straight-ticket voting will be an increased drop-off in voting, as individuals confront little-known candidates for less familiar elective offices. Whether this decrease in voting for lower-level offices will benefit one or the other political party is unclear, but it will eliminate the GOP straight-ticket advantage. Voter choices will be based more on name familiarity, advertising, and factors such as gender and ethnicity that may be reflected in the candidate names. The need to become known to voters will greatly increase the cost of campaigning for lower-visibility public offices.

13. BUSH 43 AND GOVERNOR PERRY

1. This trend is discussed in more detail in Wayne Thorburn, *Red State: An Insider's Story of How the GOP Came to Dominate Texas Politics* (Austin: University of Texas Press, 2014), 166–212.

2. *The Texas Republican*, 1st quarter 2000, 2–4, newsletter in author's possession; Mary Alice Robbins, "Texas GOP Welcomes Party-Switchers Group," *Lubbock Avalanche-Journal*, September 15, 1999. For other examples of party switching, see Thorburn, *Red State*, 190–195.

3. Jim Yardley, "This Texan, Too, Has a Lot Riding on Bush's Campaign," *New York Times*, October 7, 2000.

4. Adam Nagourney, "Bush Iowa Trip Signals Real Start of 2000 Race for the Presidency," *New York Times*, June 13, 1999.

5. Jim Yardley, "Campaign Tests Bush's Balancing Skills," *New York Times*, April 16, 2000.

6. The quotes from Draughn, Gorman, Lambert, and Weddington appear in Mary Alice Robbins, "Dissension Hits GOP over Endorsements," *Lubbock Avalanche-Journal*, March 5, 2000. All three candidates endorsed by Weddington won their nominations, easily defeating their challengers in the primary.

7. Ibid.

8. Author interview with Will Lutz, Austin, April 19, 2016, in author's possession.

9. Jim Yardley, "For Texas Democrats, It's Much the Worst of Times," *New York Times*, May 9, 2000.

10. Despite the hard-right nature of the platform and the socially conservative backgrounds of state party leaders, some activists on the right, such as David Guenthner, editor of the *Lone Star Report*, remained critical of Weddington and Barton over the next few years. Nate Blakeslee, "Have Republicans Lost the Fire?" *Texas Observer*, March 2, 2001.

11. Bob Herbert, "In America; Keeping His Distance," *New York Times*, June 22, 2000.

12. *36 Days: The Complete Chronicle of the 2000 Presidential Election Crisis* (New York: Times Books, Henry Holt and Company, 2001) contains a collection of news reports by *New York Times* correspondents, as well as coverage of the US Supreme Court's *Bush v. Gore* decision, which concluded the recount of votes in Florida. See also Abner Greene, *Understanding the 2000 Election* (New York: NYU Press, 2001).

13. Thorburn, *Red State*, 192–193. The division of Texas by category of counties is described on pp. 25–41.

14. Earl Black and Merle Black, *The Rise of Southern Republicans* (Cambridge, MA: Belknap, 2002), 344–345.

15. Michael Barone and Grant Ujifusa, *The Almanac of American Politics, 1994* (Washington, DC: National Journal, 1993), 1209. See also Seth C. McKee and Daron R. Shaw, "Redistricting in Texas: Institutionalizing Republican Ascendancy," in *Redistricting in the New Millennium*, ed. Peter F. Galderisi (Lanham, MD: Lexington, 2005).

16. As of 2020 Craddick has served in the Texas House of Representatives continuously for more than fifty years.

17. The redistricting process is discussed in Thorburn, *Red State*, 178–181. For a detailed

but highly critical review of the redistricting process, see Steve Bickerstaff, *Lines in the Sand: Congressional Redistricting in Texas and the Downfall of Tom DeLay* (Austin: University of Texas Press, 2007). As is frequently the case in redistricting matters, those who felt mistreated filed suit in federal court, challenging the plan. Two years after the plan's adoption, a federal court ordered the redrawing of five congressional districts and the holding of special elections in these districts in November 2006, wherein all candidates' names appeared on the ballot and a runoff was held if no one received a majority of the votes. Republican member of Congress Henry Bonilla came 1,725 votes short of a majority and was forced into a runoff with Democrat Ciro Rodriguez. In the December runoff Bonilla was defeated in the redrawn 23rd congressional district, which he had previously represented for fourteen years. A similar court-ordered special election and runoff had led to the defeat of GOP member of Congress Steve Stockman ten years earlier. See also Ralph Blumenthal and Kate Zernike, "Day of Joy Dawns for Republicans, Proud Owners of Texas Districting Map," *New York Times*, June 29, 2006, and Patty Reinert, Bennett Roth, Samantha Levine, and R. G. Ratcliffe, "Most of Texas Map Upheld—Supreme Court Finds Just 1 District, Bonilla's, Violates Voting Rights Act," *Houston Chronicle*, June 29, 2006.

18. B. Drummond Ayres Jr., "Political Briefing; Texas Race to Feature Debate in Spanish," *New York Times*, February 10, 2002; Jim Yardley, "One Texas Candidate Cools on a Debate in Spanish," *New York Times*, March 1, 2002; Andres Martinez, "In Texas, the Republican Party's Sure Thing Faces Un Gran Problema," *New York Times*, March 12, 2002; Jim Yardley, "Democrats Pick Novice in Texas Race for Governor," *New York Times*, March 13, 2002.

19. Sam Attlesey, "Will Morales' Endorsement Pay Off for Perry?" *Dallas Morning News*, October 13, 2002.

20. John W. Gonzalez, "Seadrift Judge Lone Democratic Challenger to Wendy Davis," *San Antonio Express-News*, January 4, 2014.

21. Jim Yardley, "Texas Democrats Pin Hopes on a Big Spender," *New York Times*, October 11, 2002.

22. Wayne Slater and Christopher Lee, "Kirk, Cornyn in Tight Contest—Poll Shows Dead Heat in Race that Could Be Key to Control of Senate," *Dallas Morning News*, May 22, 2002; Wayne Slater, "Poll Has Kirk in the Lead," *Dallas Morning News*, July 3, 2002.

23. Adam Nagourney, "Tough Senate Race in Texas Gets Bush in Gear," *New York Times*, October 6, 2002; Pete Slover, "First Lady Steps Up to Plate for Cornyn," *Dallas Morning News*, August 15, 2002; Todd J. Gillman and Gromer Jeffers Jr., "Another Bush Lends Support to Cornyn," *Dallas Morning News*, October 16, 2002.

24. After the November 2002 election, Republicans held fifty-one seats in the United States Senate, regaining the majority.

25. Wayne Slater, "Perry, Cornyn Triumph in Dream Night for GOP," *Dallas Morning News*, November 6, 2002; Colleen McCain Nelson, "For Sanchez, More Wasn't better—Experts: Cash Wasn't King in 'Memorably Nasty' Governor's Race," *Dallas Morning News*, November 7, 2002.

26. Thorburn, *Red State*, 184; Christy Hoppe, "Craddick Realizes Dream: He'll Be Speaker," *Dallas Morning News*, November 8, 2002.

27. S. C. Gwynne, "Tom Craddick," *Texas Monthly*, February 2005.

28. Lutz interview.

29. Gromer Jeffers Jr., "Skirmishes Add Spice to GOP Convention," *Dallas Morning News*, June 8, 2004.

30. Michael King, "The Elephants at Play," *Austin Chronicle*, June 11, 2004; Matt Stevens, "Politicians Weigh in as Doug Jones Wins Alabama Senate Seat," *New York Times*, December 13, 2017.

31. Christy Hoppe and Gromer Jeffers Jr., "A Shared Stage with Perry but Differing Views — Hutchison, Strayhorn Take Aim at Gambling Plan, Budget Cuts," *Dallas Morning News*, June 6, 2004.

32. Christy Hoppe, "State GOP Delegates Expected to Cheer Perry — Potential Rival Strayhorn Will Also Attend Meeting that Starts Today," *Dallas Morning News*, June 3, 2004.

33. Christy Hoppe, "Strayhorn Rips Perry on Budget," *Dallas Morning News*, August 26, 2004.

34. Christy Hoppe, "Strayhorn Accuses Perry of 'Witch Hunt,'" *Dallas Morning News*, June 25, 2004.

35. Rena Pederson, "She's Not Running for Governor — Yet," *Dallas Morning News*, November 7, 2004.

36. Todd Gillman, "GOP Head Criticizes Hutchison — She Defends Vote against Anti-Abortion Judicial Nominee," *Dallas Morning News*, July 10, 2004.

37. Christy Hoppe, "Hutchison at Top of Ratings Poll," *Dallas Morning News*, September 4, 2004; Christy Hoppe, "Hutchison Weighs Perry Challenge — Senator Contacting Possible Donors about Gubernatorial Race," *Dallas Morning News*, October 30, 2004.

38. "Texas Poll," *Dallas Morning News*, October 30, 2004.

39. Robert T. Garrett, "1 Democrat Survives Redistricting — Edwards' 4 Comrades Targeted by Remap Are Out; 6 Republicans in," *Dallas Morning News*, November 4, 2004.

40. Christy Hoppe, "Sea of Red Leaves Texas Democrats Feeling Blue," *Dallas Morning News*, November 5, 2004.

41. Gromer Jeffers Jr., "Hispanic Support Increases for Bush," *Dallas Morning News*, November 4, 2004; Michael Gonzalez, "Hispanics for Jorge," *Wall Street Journal*, November 8, 2004.

42. Terri Langford and Sherry Jacobson, "Dallas County Gives Democrats a Reason to Smile," *Dallas Morning News*, November 4, 2004.

43. House districts from the small-town counties had shifted to an eleven to nine GOP majority in the 2002 elections after having been overwhelmingly Democratic in all previous years. See Thorburn, *Red State*, 186.

44. Mark Lisheron, "GOP's Unified Front Cracking, Analysts Say," *Austin American-Statesman*, January 9, 2005.

45. Jason Embry and Stephen Scheibel, "Strayhorn Challenges Math Used in Tax Bill — Comptroller's Office Signed Off on School Plan, House Leaders Say," *Austin American-Statesman*, March 23, 2005. Strayhorn's ongoing conflict with Governor Perry and legislative leaders is discussed in Paul Burka, "Carole Keeton Strayhorn Has Guts, Carole Keeton Strayhorn Is Nuts, Discuss," *Texas Monthly*, June 2005.

46. Laylan Copelin, "Comptroller Certifies State Spending Plan," *Austin American-Statesman*, June 4, 2005.

47. Neither Senator Cornyn or Senator Hutchison was asked for an endorsement; nor was Comptroller Strayhorn. Mike Ward, "Perry Trumpets Early Support for '06 Race," *Austin American-Statesman*, January 8, 2005.

48. Chuck Lindell, "Senator Has $6.7 Million to Use in Governor's Race," *Austin American-Statesman*, February 8, 2005.

49. Steve Scheibal, "At the Alamo, Kinky Friedman Draws Gubernatorial Line in Sand," *Austin American-Statesman*, February 4, 2005.

50. W. Gardner Selby, "Hutchison Says She'd Still Love to Be the Gov—But Returning to Washington Is 'Right for Texas,' Lawmaker Says," *Austin American-Statesman*, June 28, 2005.

51. W. Gardner Selby, "The '06 Governor's Race," *Austin American-Statesman*, June 18, 2005.

52. W. Gardner Selby, "Strayhorn Talks Tough in Taking on Perry," *Austin American-Statesman*, June 19, 2005.

53. W. Gardner Selby, "Strayhorn Sees Crossovers as Primary Target," *Austin American-Statesman*, August 14, 2005.

54. Jason Embry, "Will Strayhorn Stay with GOP?," *Austin American-Statesman*, December 31, 2005.

55. W. Gardner Selby, "Strayhorn to Run as Independent," *Austin American-Statesman*, January 3, 2006.

56. W. Gardner Selby, "Teacher Group to Support Strayhorn—Candidate Renounces Vouchers as Association Backs Republican for State Office for First Time," *Austin American-Statesman*, January 11, 2006.

57. Gromer Jeffers Jr., "3 Gubernatorial Candidates Make Pitch for Labor Endorsement," *Dallas Morning News*, May 9, 2006.

58. Jordan Smith, "Here Comes the Gov," *Austin Chronicle*, February 17, 2006.

59. Ralph Blumenthal, "Following a Candidate Named Kinky," *New York Times*, February 17, 2006.

60. The total number of primary voters ineligible to sign independent candidate nominating petitions consisted of those voting in either the primary or subsequent runoff since it is possible to vote in a runoff without previously having voted in the primary.

61. Robert T. Garrett, "2 Major GOP Donors Show Rift in Party—Supporters Back Efforts to Oust Moderate Members of State House," *Dallas Morning News*, February 3, 2006.

62. Terrence Stutz, "Voucher Supporter Has Spent $1.4 million in GOP Primaries," *Dallas Morning News*, February 14, 2006; Robert T. Garrett, "Voucher Advocate Gives Final Push—Almost $600,000 More Goes to Unseat 5 House Moderate Republicans," *Dallas Morning News*, March 4, 2006.

63. Eric Aasen, "Tarrant Representative Blasts GOP Colleagues," *Dallas Morning News*, March 4, 2006.

64. Robert T. Garrett, "PACs Late Aid Altered Races—Group Gave Huge Sums at the Last Minute to Assist Craddick Allies," *Dallas Morning News*, March 10, 2006.

65. Two years later Macias was defeated by former New Braunfels mayor Doug Miller by a margin of seventeen votes. Miller served until 2016, when he was defeated in a primary runoff by Kyle Biedermann.

66. Toya Lynn Stewart, "Patrick 'Had the People' in Primary—Parents, Teachers Gave Professor the Edge over Grusendorf, Experts Say," *Dallas Morning News*, March 9, 2006.

67. Terrence Stutz, "Houston Radio Host Sends Strong Signal in Senate Race," *Dallas Morning News*, March 3, 2006.

68. Wayne Slater, "Independent's Path a Rough Ride in Texas—Kinky, Strayhorn Set Up Petition-Gathering Blitzes to Get on Ballot," *Dallas Morning News*, May 5, 2006.

69. Ibid.; Alexis Grant, "Independents in Race for Signatures—Thousands Work to Get Friedman and Strayhorn on the Ballot," *Houston Chronicle*, May 8, 2006.

70. "Money was Big Difference in Strayhorn, Friedman Petitions," *Lubbock Avalanche-Journal*, May 13, 2006.

71. R. G. Ratcliffe, "Friedman Submits Signatures for Ballot," *Houston Chronicle*, May 12, 2006; W. Gardner Selby, "Strayhorn Submits Names; Bell Gets Labor's Support," *Austin American-Statesman*, May 10, 2006.

72. Clay Robison, "It's a 5-Way Race for Governor—Strayhorn and Friedman Each Get Enough Signatures to Take on Perry, Bell, and Werner," *Houston Chronicle*, June 23, 2006.

73. "A Very Kinky Campaign," *Newsweek*, July 23, 2006.

74. Bob Campbell, "Friedman Calls for Oil Tax, Casinos to Finance Schools," *Midland Reporter-Telegram*, May 10, 2006.

75. Terrence Stutz, "Senate Sends New Business Tax to Governor," *Dallas Morning News*, May 3, 2006; Steve Barnes, "Texas Governor Signs Property Tax Cuts," *New York Times*, June 1, 2006.

76. "Texas GOP Delegates: Bring a Book," *Austin American-Statesman*, June 1, 2006.

77. Ibid.

78. Krista Mack, "County GOP Committee Condemns Perry Tax Bill," *Houston Chronicle*, May 19, 2006.

79. Wayne Slater and Robert T. Garrett, "GOP Convention Opens with Taxing Questions—State Delegates at Odds with Perry's School Fix, Bush Immigration Plan," *Dallas Morning News*, June 2, 2006.

80. Jason Embry, "GOP Tax Foes Stick by Perry," *Austin American-Statesman*, June 2, 2006.

81. John Moritz, "Keeping It Together—As Convention Begins, GOP Upbeat Despite Hints of Dissent," *Fort Worth Star-Telegram*, June 2, 2006.

82. Gary Scharrer, "Perry Hits Illegal Migration, Rouses State GOP Delegates," *San Antonio Express-News*, June 3, 2006.

83. Robert T. Garrett and Wayne Slater, "GOP Delegates Clash on Business Tax—Perry Hopes for Boost from Convention, but Some Predict Backlash," *Dallas Morning News*, June 4, 2006.

84. Gary Scharrer, "Immigration to Take State GOP Spotlight," *San Antonio Express-News*, June 1, 2006.

85. R. G. Ratcliffe, "Perry Attempts to Quell Unease on Tax, Border—He Reminds

GOP Delegates He'll Need Their Support to Face 3 Foes in the Fall," *Houston Chronicle*, June 3, 2006.

86. Moritz, "Keeping It Together."

87. Gromer Jeffers Jr., "GOP Risking Latino Voters—Immigration Proposals Could Reverse Party's Gains with Hispanics," *Dallas Morning News*, May 7, 2006.

88. The June survey is cited in Amy Smith, "She's Her Own Grandma," *Austin Chronicle*, June 28, 2006. A late September and early October poll by Blum & Weprin is in "Poll Watch: Perry Leads, but Most Oppose Him," *Austin American-Statesman*, October 6, 2006.

89. Ralph Blumenthal, "Clear-Cut Race Shifting into Texas-Size Free-For-All, " *New York Times*, September 22, 2006; A. J. Bauer, "Be It Pot or Tuition, Friedman Says What Horns Long to Hear," *Austin American-Statesman*, October 5, 2006. See also Matt Labash, "Kinky Friedman Runs for Governor," *Weekly Standard*, October 23, 2006.

90. W. Gardner Selby, "Bell Asks Friedman to Quit Race," *Austin American-Statesman*, October 11, 2006.

91. Jason Embry, "Kerry Lends Bell Support at Gubernatorial Fundraiser," *Austin American-Statesman*, October 28, 2006.

92. Strayhorn carried Cooke, Falls, Goliad, Nolan, Wharton, and Wilson counties. All six, scattered around the state, had been won by Perry four years earlier.

14. THE BUSH ERA TRANSITIONS

1. Author interview with Will Lutz, Austin, TX, April 19, 2016, in author's possession.

2. Dave Montgomery, "GOP Losses Add to Craddick's Woes," *Dallas Morning News*, November 6, 2008.

3. Ian McCann, "Looking Ahead towards 2010," *Dallas Morning News*, November 6, 2008.

4. Lisa Sandberg and Peggy Fikac, "Craddick Re-elected Speaker after Pitts Bows Out," *Houston Chronicle*, January 10, 2007.

5. R. G. Ratcliffe and Gary Scharrer, "The House Struggles to Move Forward," *Houston Chronicle*, May 27, 2007.

6. Meg McKain Grier, *Grassroots Women* (Boerne, TX: Wingscape, 2001), 353. See also Donnie Radcliffe, "The San Antonio Arm-Twister," *Washington Post*, July 10, 1990.

7. James C. McKinley Jr., "Texas Rebellion Gives a Centrist a Lift," *New York Times*, January 28, 2009.

8. Allie Morris, "Bexar County GOP Censures House Speaker Straus," *San Antonio Express-News*, December 12, 2017.

9. Patrick Svitek, "Texas Republican Executive Committee Censures House Speaker Joe Straus," *Texas Tribune*, January 27, 2018.

10. Lutz interview.

11. Wayne Thorburn, *A Generation Awakes: Young Americans for Freedom and the Creation of the Conservative Movement* (Ottawa, IL: Jameson Books, 2010), 413, 419, 506.

12. Christy Hoppe, "Munisteri wins election as Texas Republican chairman with 59% of the vote," *Dallas Morning News*, June 12, 2010.

13. Lutz interview.

14. Jay Root, "Texas Governor's Race," in *Pendulum Swing*, ed. Larry Sabato (Boston: Longman, 2011), 391.

15. James C. McKinley Jr., "Taking a Texas Primary Ever Further to the Right," *New York Times*, February 14, 2010.

16. James C. McKinley Jr. and Clifford Krauss, "'Yes' for Texas Governor Is 'No' to Washington," *New York Times*, March 2, 2010.

17. Root, "Texas Governor's Race," 392.

18. James C. McKinley Jr., "As Republicans Vote, Texas Primary Seems Close No More," *New York Times*, March 1, 2010.

19. Ross Ramsey, "Perry's Pact with Social Conservatives Vaulted Him Atop His Party," *Texas Tribune*, July 2, 2011.

20. Bernie Becker, "Texas: Changing Her Mind, Senator Says She'll Stay," *New York Times*, April 1, 2010; Anna M. Tinsley, "Tea Party Candidates Vow to Take on Hutchison if She Seeks Another Term," *Fort Worth Star-Telegram*, December 5, 2010.

21. James C. McKinley Jr., "Texas Democrat Is Striving to Make His Name Known," *New York Times*, May 1, 2010.

22. In the 2011 session Hispanic Republican state representatives were Raul Torres, Jose Aliseda, Aaron Peña, Larry Gonzales, Dee Margo, and John Garza. African-Americans in the GOP delegation were James White and Stefani Carter, while Angie Chen Button was the sole Asian-American Republican legislator.

23. Jay Root, "Updated: Perry Opens Campaign with Harsh Attack on Obama," *Texas Tribune*, August 13, 2011.

24. Debi Wilgoren, "Rick Perry Makes Light of Gaffe, Vows Not to Quit," *Washington Post*, November 20, 2011.

25. Richard Whittaker, "Done and Dusted, Rick Perry Suspends Presidential Campaign, Endorses Gingrich," *Austin Chronicle*, January 19, 2012.

26. Adam Batheja, "In Senate Primary, Republican Leaders Take a Back Street," *New York Times*, August 2, 2012.

27. Quote from Jonathan Martin, "Lone Star Rising," *Politico*, February 15, 2013.

28. L. Tucker Gibson Jr. and Clay Robison, *The 2012 Texas Election* (Upper Saddle River, NJ: Pearson Education, 2014), 17.

29. Thomas N. Edsall, "The Republican Autopsy Report," *New York Times*, March 20, 2013. Copies of the Growth and Opportunity Report remain available from the Republican National Committee, 310 1st Street SE, Washington, DC 20003.

30. Martin, "Lone Star Rising."

31. Author interview with Steve Munisteri, Austin, TX, February 13, 2013, in author's possession.

32. Letter from Arcilia Acosta and Victor Leal, July 8, 2013, in author's possession.

33. Gromer Jeffers Jr., "George P. Bush Says Republicans Don't Have to 'Sell Out' to Win Hispanic Votes," *Dallas Morning News*, February 15, 2013.

34. Julian Aguilar, "Early into His Tenure, Villalba Makes His Stands," *Texas Tribune*, February 15, 2013.

35. Robert T. Garrett, "Texas GOP Ramps Up Outreach to Minorities, Young People," *Dallas Morning News*, June 4, 2013.

36. Alexander Burris, "Democrats Lavish Plan to Turn Texas Blue," *Politico*, January 24, 2013.

37. Ross Ramsey, "A Matter of Trust," *Texas Tribune*, May 10, 2010.

38. Jonathan Tilove, "'Blue' Group Turns to Texas," *Austin American-Statesman*, February 23, 2013.

39. Reid Smith, "Battleground Texas," *American Spectator*, July 18, 2013.

40. Steve Munisteri, July 2013 Chairman's Update, Republican Party of Texas, Austin.

41. Wayne Slater, "GOP Stalwart Tom Pauken to Run for Governor, Says Texas Needs 'a Different Style of Leadership,'" *Dallas Morning News*, March 21, 2013.

42. Dave McNeeley, "With or Without Perry, Pauken Announces for Governor's Race," *Abilene Reporter-News*, April 4, 2013.

43. Dan Balz, "Rick Perry's Exit Marks the End of an Era—and a New Frontier for Texas Politics," *Washington Post*, July 8, 2013.

44. Will Weissert, "Perry Reshaped Texas, but Floundered Nationally," *Waco Tribune*, July 8, 2013.

45. Jay Root, "In Launching Bid for Governor, Abbott Says He's Ready to Fight," *Texas Tribune*, July 14, 2013; Alan Greenblatt, "Texas' Next Governor?: Meet Wendy Davis' Opponent, Greg Abbott," *Governing*, February 2014.

46. Jay Root and Alexa Ura, "Easy Primary Victories for Abbott and Davis," *Texas Tribune*, March 4, 2014.

47. Author conversation with Art Martinez de Vara, Mayor of Von Ormy, Austin, June 16, 2014.

48. Root, "In Launching Bid."

49. Christy Hoppe, "Tom Pauken Withdraws from GOP Governor's Race," *Dallas Morning News*, December 5, 2013.

50. Jay Root, "Spotlight on Davis, the Democrats' Big Hope," *Texas Tribune*, September 1, 2013.

51. Helen Davidson, "Texas Abortion Bill Defeated by Wendy Davis Filibuster and Public Protest," *The Guardian*, June 26, 2013.

52. John Schwartz, "Texas Senate Vote Puts Bill Restricting Abortion over Final Hurdle," *New York Times*, July 13, 2013.

53. Peggy Fikac, "Drafting Wendy Davis for Governor," *San Antonio Express-News*, August 13, 2013.

54. James Henson and Joshua Blank, "The Irresistible Plot Arc of a Two-Party Texas," *Texas Monthly*, August 2013.

55. Marice Richter, "Wendy Davis of Filibuster Fame to Run for Texas Governor," *Chicago Tribune*, October 3, 2013.

56. Ross Ramsey, "UT/TT Poll: Abbott's Lead over Davis in Single Digits," *Texas Tribune*, November 4, 2013. Pauken did not officially withdraw from the GOP nominating

contest until December, but as early as October Abbott was assumed by most observers to be the general election candidate.

57. Peggy Fikac and Mike Ward, "Abbott and Davis Battle for Latino Votes," *Houston Chronicle*, September 18, 2014; Wayne Thorburn, "Hispanics Won't Turn Texas Blue," *Politico*, October 5, 2014.

58. Kiah Collier, "Greg Abbott's Mother-in-Law Ad Key to Campaign's Hispanic Success," *Austin American-Statesman*, November 8, 2014.

59. Christy Hoppe and Wayne Slater, "Abbott's Hard Push for Hispanic Votes Has an Eye to the Future," *Dallas Morning News*, September 20, 2014.

60. Corrie MacLaggan, "Texas Hispanics More Republican than Other Hispanics," *Texas Tribune*, February 7, 2014.

61. Richard Parker, "Will Cities Turn Texas Purple?" *New York Times*, October 6, 2014.

62. Bud Kennedy, "For Texas Democrats, the Bad News Gets Worse," *Fort Worth Star-Telegram*, October 24, 2014.

63. Wayne Slater, "Analysis: Texas Democrats Are Running on Empty," *Dallas Morning News*, November 5, 2014; Wayne Thorburn, "How the Democrats Lost Texas," *Politico*, November 17, 2014.

64. NBC News exit poll, www.nbcnews.com/politics/elections/2014/TX/governor/exitpoll, accessed on October 6, 2019.

65. Dave Carney, "How We Won Texas," Politico, February 6, 2015; Slater, "Analysis."

66. www.aaldef.org/press-release/aaldef-2014-exit-poll-shows-asian-american-voters-support-executive-action-on-immigration/, accessed May 27, 2020.

67. Jonathan Tilove, "White Dems Still Lose Ground," *Austin American-Statesman*, December 7, 2014.

15. DONALD TRUMP AND THE REPUBLICAN FUTURE

1. Patrick Svitek, "Texas GOP Chairman Tom Mechler Resigns," *Texas Tribune*, May 20, 2017.

2. Jonathan Tilove, "Dickey Beats Asche, Who Says He Can't Be Trusted, for Texas GOP Chair," *Austin American-Statesman*, June 16, 2018.

3. Patrick Svitek, "Ahead of 2020, Texas GOP Chair Gets a Salary," *Texas Tribune*, December 1, 2018.

4. Three of the four GOP representatives who lost were Hispanic Republicans—Rick Galindo and John Lujan of San Antonio and Gilbert Peña of Pasadena—whose re-election efforts may well have been affected by Trump's various statements on immigration and immigrants. The fourth loss was that of Kenneth Sheets in a predominantly Hispanic Dallas district.

5. Quoted in Ronald Brownstein, "The Biggest Obstacle to Trump's Victory in 2020," *The Atlantic*, June 20, 2019.

6. One candidate for the Court of Criminal Appeals, Michelle Slaughter, had opposi-

tion only from a Libertarian Party candidate and obtained 74.7 percent of all votes cast in her race. The drop-off in voter participation in this contest was nearly two million votes.

7. The author is grateful to Joshua Blank, manager of polling and research at the Texas Politics Project, University of Texas at Austin, for sharing data on age distribution and migration related to partisan identification for 2019 from the February 2019 University of Texas/*Texas Tribune* poll. Data for earlier years appears in Wayne Thorburn, *Red State: An Insider's Story of How the GOP Came to Dominate Texas Politics* (Austin: University of Texas Press, 2014), 153–156.

8. Data from CNN exit polls available at edition.cnn.com/election/2018/exit-polls /texas/senate and https://edition.cnn.com/election/2018/exit-polls/texas/governor, accessed May 27, 2020.

9. Data for 1985 from Thorburn, *Red State*, 152, and 2019 data from the February 2019 University of Texas/*Texas Tribune* poll.

10. Jenna Johnson and Arelis R. Hernandez, "Can Democrats Win Texas? A Surge of New Voters and Trump Antipathy Give Them Reason to Hope," *Washington Post*, October 28, 2020. Ethnic diversity also has impacted the Texas electorate as Hispanics comprise 30 percent of the eligible electorate and Asian Americans nearly 6 percent. Both major parties have devoted followers among the diverse groups. Kelsey Carolan, "In Democrats' Bid to Flip Texas, Maximizing Latino Vote Is Key," *Texas Tribune*, October 26, 2020; Anna Bauman, "Growing Asian American Population Could Help Sway the 2020 Election," *Houston Chronicle*, October 28, 2020.

11. Mark P. Jones, "What's Causing the Congressional 'Texodus'?," *The Hill*, October 3, 2019. An additional open seat developed from the resignation of Republican congressman John Ratcliffe, who became Director of National Intelligence in the Trump administration. On March 3, 2020, 2,094,428 Texas voters chose to participate in the Democratic primary while 2,017,167 voted in the Republican primary.

12. Jeremy Wallace, "Texas Republicans Oust Party Chairman James Dickey in Favor of Former U.S. Rep. Allen West," *Houston Chronicle*, July 20, 2020; Christopher Hooks, "The Texas GOP Held Its Convention on Zoom—and It Was a Comic Disaster," *Texas Monthly*, July 21, 2020, www.Texasmonthly.com/politics/texas-gop-convention-zoom-dis aster/, accessed on October 26, 2020.

13. Patrick Svitek, "Five Texas GOP County Leaders Share Racist Facebook Posts, Including One Juxtaposing an MLK Quote with a Banana," *Texas Tribune*, June 5, 2020. Nielsen had agreed to step aside, but in August he reneged and assumed his position as Harris County GOP chair even though 150 precinct chairmen asked him to vacate it. Congressman Kevin Brady tweeted, "A Bigot whose word is no good. This is not what the party of Lincoln stands for. He needs to be removed now." Patrick Svitek, "Despite Promising to Step Aside after Racist Facebook Post, Keith Nielsen Becomes Harris County GOP Chair," *Texas Tribune*, August 3, 2020.

14. Naomi Andu, Clare Proctor, and Miguel Gutierrez Jr., "Conspiracy Theories and Racist Memes: How a Dozen Texas GOP County Chairs Caused Turmoil within the Party," *Texas Tribune*, June 6, 2020. As of October 23, 2020, the Republican Party of Texas

website indicated that nine of the twelve individuals were still serving as county chairs (www.texasgop.org/county-chairs/, accessed on October 23, 2020).

15. Patrick Svitek, "'Kill 'em': Houston GOP Powerbroker Steve Hotze Left Greg Abbott a Voicemail Requesting That National Guard 'Shoot to Kill' Rioters," *Texas Tribune*, July 3, 2020. Hotze was a plaintiff in a lawsuit attempting to invalidate 127,000 votes cast at drive-through early voting locations in Harris County. Jolie McCullough, "Texas Supreme Court Rejects Republican-led Effort to Throw out Nearly 127,000 Harris County Votes," *Texas Tribune*, November 1, 2020. After losing in state court, the plaintiffs filed in federal court, claiming that drive-through early voting sites violated the U.S. Constitution, and the case was heard by District Judge Andrew Hanen on the Monday prior to Election Day. Hanen rejected the plaintiffs' claim and allowed the votes to be counted. Jolie McCullough, "Nearly 127,000 Harris County Drive-Thru Votes Appear Safe after Federal Judge rejects GOP-led Texas Lawsuit," *Texas Tribune*, November 2, 2020.

16. Todd Davis, "Profane Recording Surfaces of 2 Empower Texans Operatives Joking about Gov. Greg Abbott Being in a Wheelchair," *Dallas Morning News*, June 19, 2020.

17. George P. Bush, "Time to Empower Texas with Real Conservatism," *Austin American-Statesman*, June 24, 2020.

18. Manny Fernandez and J. David Goodman, "Red vs. Red in Texas, with Republicans Battling One Another after Mask Order," *New York Times*, July 23, 2020; Lexington, "It's Messing with Texas," *Economist*, July 4, 2020.

19. Gilbert Garcia, "GOP Lawsuit against Abbott a Pathetic Waste of Everyone's Time," *San Antonio Express-News*, September 25, 2020.

20. Brandon Waltens, "Texas Supreme Court Strikes Down GOP Lawsuit against Abbott's Early Voting Extension," *Texas Scorecard*, October 7, 2020.

21. Patrick Svitek, "State GOP Chair Allen West, Agriculture Commissioner Sid Miller Join Anti–Greg Abbott Protest Outside Governor's Mansion," *Texas Tribune*, October 10, 2020.

22. David Drucker, "GOP Insiders Worry about Trump's Texas Bravado," *Washington Examiner*, July 30, 2020.

23. Jonathan Tilove, "Biden Looks to Texas in Speech before Virtual Democratic Convention," *Austin American-Statesman*, June 6, 2020. While the presidential candidate did not make any campaign appearances in Texas, Jill Biden rallied supporters in El Paso and Dallas on the first day of early voting and vice presidential candidate Kamala Harris held campaign rallies in Fort Worth, McAllen, and Houston on the Friday before Election Day. Gromer Jeffers Jr. and Alfredo Corchado, "'There Are No Do-Overs,' Says Jill Biden as She Rallies Voters in Dallas, El Paso," *Dallas Morning News*, October 13, 2020; Jeremy Wallace, "Kamala Harris to Visit Fort Worth, McAllen, and Houston on Friday," *Houston Chronicle*, October 28, 2020; Gordon Dickson, "VP Hopeful Kamala Harris, in Historic Fort Worth Stop, Calls on Black Texans to Vote," *Fort Worth Star-Telegram*, October 30, 2020; Naxiely Lopez-Puente, "Joined by High-Profile Dems, VP Candidate Rallies Support at UTRGV," *McAllen Monitor*, October 30, 2020.

24. Natasha Korecki and Marc Caputo, "'We See an Opening': Biden Makes a Play for Texas," *Politico*, July 14, 2020; Marty Johnson, "Texas Democrats Plan 7-Figure Buy to

Turn State Blue," *The Hill*, July 27, 2020. See also Will Ford, "Inside the Democrats' New Plan to Flip Texas," *Politico*, October 30, 2020.

25. Benjamin Wermund, "Trump and Biden Tied in Texas, According to New Quinnipiac Poll," *Houston Chronicle*, October 21, 2020; Robert T. Garrett, "Biden Rebounds to Edge over Trump in Texas as Hegar Slightly Narrows Cornyn Lead in Senate Race," *Dallas Morning News*, October 25, 2020; Alex Samuels and Patrick Svitek, "Polls, Late Campaign Activity Suggest Republican Dominance in Texas Could Be at Risk," *Texas Tribune*, October 27, 2020; Alexandra Garrett, "Historically Republican Texas Is Now a Toss-Up State, Says New Poll," *Newsweek*, October 28, 2020.

26. Todd J. Gillman, "Biden Makes $6M Bet on Texas, Ending Drought for Democrats Who've Written off State for Decades," *Dallas Morning News*, October 5, 2020.

27. Benjamin Wermund, "'It's now or Never': Democrats Pour over $55 Million into Newly Competitive Texas," *Houston Chronicle*, October 26, 2020; Robert T. Garrett, "Silicon Valley Billionaires Bankroll $28M Deluge to Help Hegar Oust Cornyn in Texas Senate Contest," *Dallas Morning News*, October 21, 2020.

28. Patrick Svitek, "National Democratic Super PAC Says It Will Double Its Spending to $12 Million in Battle for the Texas House," *Texas Tribune*, October 20, 2020; Patrick Svitek, "Democratic Allies Fighting to Flip Texas House Join Forces for $1.1 Million Digital Ad Campaign," *Texas Tribune*, September 17, 2020.

29. Allie Morris, "In Competitive Collin County, Texas Democrats See a Chance to Flip GOP House Seats," *Dallas Morning News*, October 29, 2020; Patrick Svitek, "Collin County Is the Center of a Political Storm as the Texas Suburbs Become More Competitive for Democrats," *Texas Tribune*, October 30, 2020.

30. Cayla Harris, "Gov. Abbott Gives GOP Candidates over $1.9M in Texas House Races," *Houston Chronicle*, October 27, 2020.

31. Robert T. Garrett, James Barragan, and Allie Morris, "Republicans Roar Back, Defending Texas House Hopefuls with Seven-Figure Wads of Cash," *Dallas Morning News*, October 27, 2020.

32. Ross Ramsey, "Analysis: A Texas Election with a Decade of Politics at Stake," *Texas Tribune*, October 30, 2020; Justin Miller, "If Not Now, When? Dems' Fight for the House Will Shape Texas Politics for Years," *Texas Observer*, October 23, 2020.

33. Jordan Williams, "Bloomberg Spending Millions on Biden Push in Texas, Ohio," *The Hill*, October 27, 2020; Patrick Svitek, "Michael Bloomberg Gives $2.6 Million to Texas Democrat Running for Railroad Commissioner," *Texas Tribune*, October 26, 2020. Despite the influx of campaign funds from New York, Castaneda lost to Republican Jim Wright by a margin of more than one million votes.

34. Ross Ramsey, "Analysis: Texas Voters Elect to Stay the Course," *Texas Tribune*, November 6, 2020; Shannon Najmabadi and Mandi Cai, "Democrats Hoped High Turnout Would Usher in a Blue Wave across Texas. It Didn't," *Texas Tribune*, November 4, 2020.

35. Alex Samuels and Patrick Svitek, "Joe Biden's Struggles along the Texas Border Raise Questions about Democrats' Outreach There," *Texas Tribune*, November 4, 2020. Author's calculations of vote were based on 2010 census data for county population ethnicity.

36. James Dobbins and Manny Fernandez, "In Texas, an Emerging Problem for Democrats on the Border," *New York Times*, November 7, 2020; Jeremy Wallace, "How Texas Republicans Beat Democrats at Their Own Game," *Houston Chronicle*, November 4, 2020.

37. Benjamin Wermund, "Texas Democrats Face 'Fundamental Reckoning' after Another Statewide Sweep," *Houston Chronicle*, November 4, 2020; Maria Recio, "After Sweeping Losses in Congressional Races, Texas Democrats Ask Why," *Austin American-Statesman*, November 7, 2020.

38. Mandi Cai, Matthew Watkins, Anna Novak, and Darla Cameron, "In Texas, Biden's Urban Wins Couldn't Offset Trump's Millions of Votes in Rural, Red Counties," *Texas Tribune*, November 6, 2020; Philip Jankowski, "Suburban Swing: Once Reliably Red, Williamson Voters Back Both Biden, Cornyn," *Austin American-Statesman*, November 7, 2020.

39. Gromer Jeffers Jr., "After 2018 Warning Shot, Texas GOP Outworked State's Democrats to Keep State Red," *Dallas Morning News*, November 5, 2020; Lise Olsen, "As Democrats Divebomb, the Texas Legislature Remains as White and Male as Ever," *Texas Observer*, November 5, 2020.

40. Erica Grieder, *Big, Hot, Cheap, and Right: What America Can Learn from the Strange Genius of Texas* (New York: Public Affairs, 2013), 198.

INDEX